Reval

Baltic Sea

Danzig

I   A

Vistula

Oder

STRO-HUNGARIAN
EMPIRE

Danube

RUSSIAN
EMPIRE

E

S

Moscow •

Kiev •

Dniepr

Danube

Black
Sea

The Three Emperors

The Three Emperors

*Three Cousins, Three Empires and the
Road to World War One*

MIRANDA CARTER

FIG TREE
an imprint of
PENGUIN BOOKS

FIG TREE

Published by the Penguin Group

Penguin Books Ltd, 80 Strand, London WC2R 0RL, England

Penguin Group (USA) Inc., 375 Hudson Street, New York, New York 10014, USA

Penguin Group (Canada), 90 Eglinton Avenue East, Suite 700, Toronto, Ontario, Canada M4P 2Y3
(a division of Pearson Penguin Canada Inc.)

Penguin Ireland, 25 St Stephen's Green, Dublin 2, Ireland
(a division of Penguin Books Ltd)

Penguin Group (Australia), 250 Camberwell Road, Camberwell, Victoria 3124, Australia
(a division of Pearson Australia Group Pty Ltd)

Penguin Books India Pvt Ltd, 11 Community Centre, Panchsheel Park, New Delhi – 110 017, India

Penguin Group (NZ), 67 Apollo Drive, Rosedale, North Shore 0632, New Zealand
(a division of Pearson New Zealand Ltd)

Penguin Books (South Africa) (Pty) Ltd, 24 Sturdee Avenue, Rosebank, Johannesburg 2196, South Africa

Penguin Books Ltd, Registered Offices: 80 Strand, London WC2R 0RL, England

www.penguin.com

First published 2009

2

Copyright © Miranda Carter, 2009

The moral right of the author has been asserted

Set in 12/14.75 pt Monotype Bembo
Typeset by Rowland Phototypesetting Ltd, Bury St Edmunds, Suffolk
Printed in Great Britain by Clays Ltd, St Ives plc

A CIP catalogue record for this book is available from the British Library

ISBN: 978–0–670–91556–9

www.greenpenguin.co.uk

For Finn and Jesse

Contents

The Hohenzollerns
(and how they were related to the Romanovs)

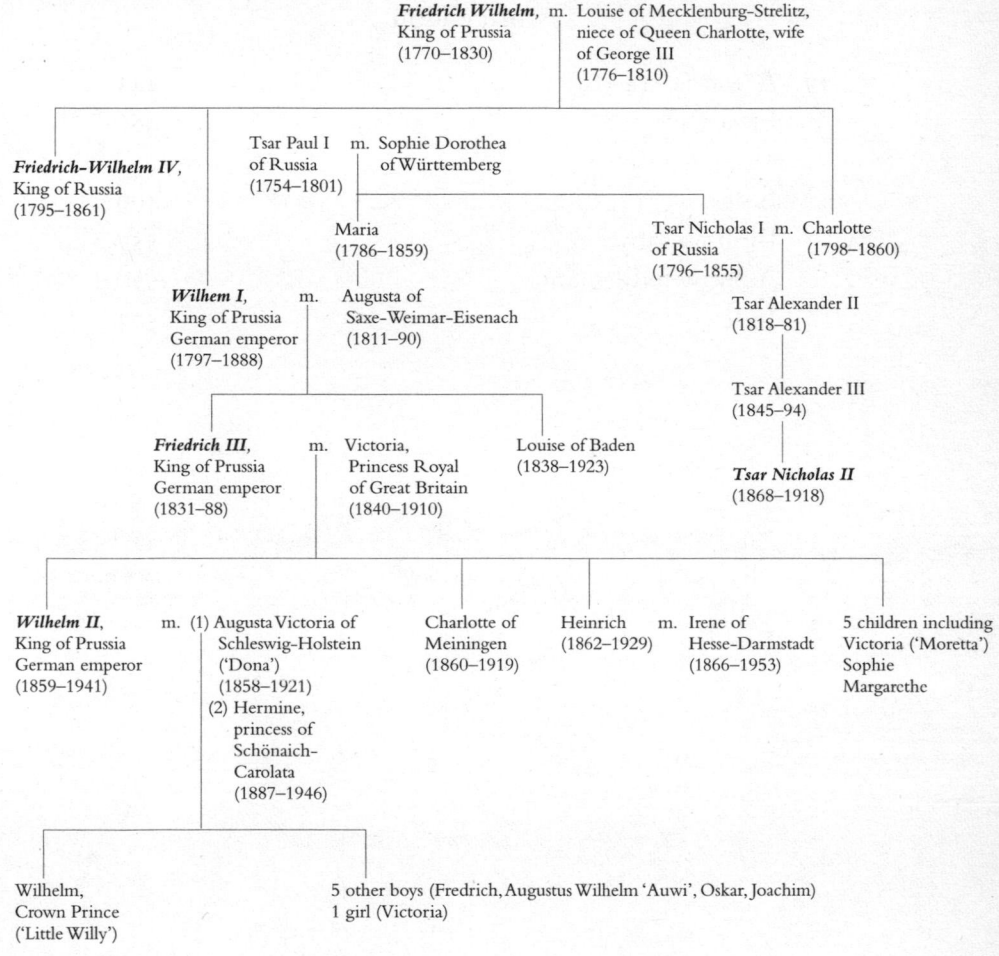

Friedrich Wilhelm, m. Louise of Mecklenburg–Strelitz,
King of Prussia   niece of Queen Charlotte, wife
(1770–1830)   of George III
(1776–1810)

Friedrich–Wilhelm IV,
King of Russia
(1795–1861)

Tsar Paul I   m. Sophie Dorothea
of Russia   of Württemberg
(1754–1801)

Maria
(1786–1859)

Tsar Nicholas I   m. Charlotte
of Russia   (1798–1860)
(1796–1855)

Wilhem I,   m.   Augusta of
King of Prussia   Saxe-Weimar-Eisenach
German emperor   (1811–90)
(1797–1888)

Tsar Alexander II
(1818–81)

Tsar Alexander III
(1845–94)

Friedrich III,   m.   Victoria,   Louise of Baden
King of Prussia   Princess Royal   (1838–1923)
German emperor   of Great Britain
(1831–88)   (1840–1910)

Tsar Nicholas II
(1868–1918)

Wilhelm II,   m. (1) Augusta Victoria of   Charlotte of   Heinrich   m. Irene of   5 children including
King of Prussia   Schleswig-Holstein   Meiningen   (1862–1929)   Hesse-Darmstadt   Victoria ('Moretta')
German emperor   ('Dona')   (1860–1919)   (1866–1953)   Sophie
(1859–1941)   (1858–1921)   Margarethe
(2) Hermine,
princess of
Schönaich-
Carolata
(1887–1946)

Wilhelm,   5 other boys (Fredrich, Augustus Wilhelm 'Auwi', Oskar, Joachim)
Crown Prince   1 girl (Victoria)
('Little Willy')

Queen Victoria and the British Royal Family

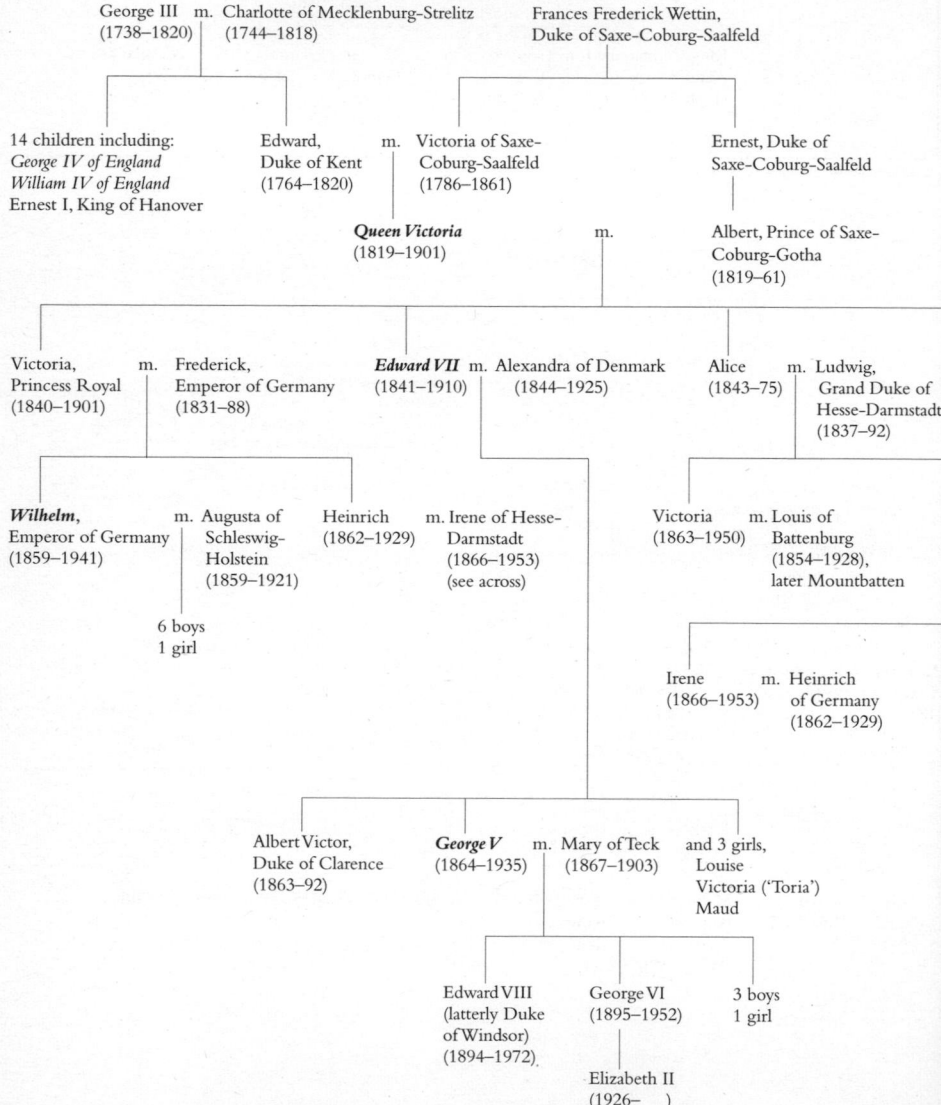

George III m. Charlotte of Mecklenburg-Strelitz
(1738–1820) (1744–1818)

Frances Frederick Wettin,
Duke of Saxe-Coburg-Saalfeld

14 children including:
George IV of England
William IV of England
Ernest I, King of Hanover

Edward, m. Victoria of Saxe-
Duke of Kent Coburg-Saalfeld
(1764–1820) (1786–1861)

Ernest, Duke of
Saxe-Coburg-Saalfeld

Queen Victoria m.
(1819–1901)

Albert, Prince of Saxe-
Coburg-Gotha
(1819–61)

Victoria, m. Frederick,
Princess Royal Emperor of Germany
(1840–1901) (1831–88)

Edward VII m. Alexandra of Denmark
(1841–1910) (1844–1925)

Alice m. Ludwig,
(1843–75) Grand Duke of
Hesse-Darmstadt
(1837–92)

Wilhelm, m. Augusta of
Emperor of Germany Schleswig-
(1859–1941) Holstein
(1859–1921)

Heinrich m. Irene of Hesse-
(1862–1929) Darmstadt
(1866–1953)
(see across)

Victoria m. Louis of
(1863–1950) Battenburg
(1854–1928),
later Mountbatten

6 boys
1 girl

Irene m. Heinrich
(1866–1953) of Germany
(1862–1929)

Albert Victor,
Duke of Clarence
(1863–92)

George V m. Mary of Teck
(1864–1935) (1867–1903)

and 3 girls,
Louise
Victoria ('Toria')
Maud

Edward VIII
(latterly Duke
of Windsor)
(1894–1972)

George VI
(1895–1952)

3 boys
1 girl

Elizabeth II
(1926–   )

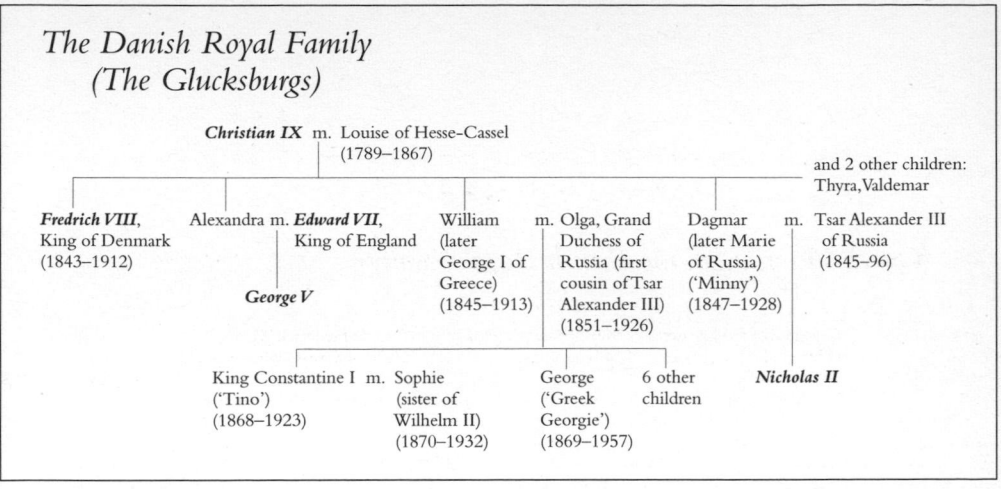

The Danish Royal Family (The Glucksburgs)

Christian IX m. Louise of Hesse-Cassel (1789–1867)

and 2 other children: Thyra, Valdemar

- **Fredrich VIII**, King of Denmark (1843–1912)
- Alexandra m. **Edward VII**, King of England — *George V*
- William (later George I of Greece) (1845–1913) m. Olga, Grand Duchess of Russia (first cousin of Tsar Alexander III) (1851–1926)
- Dagmar (later Marie of Russia) ('Minny') (1847–1928) m. Tsar Alexander III of Russia (1845–96)

- King Constantine I ('Tino') (1868–1923) m. Sophie (sister of Wilhelm II) (1870–1932)
- George ('Greek Georgie') (1869–1957)
- 6 other children
- **Nicholas II**

Tsar Alexander II (1818–81)

Alfred, Duke of Saxe-Coburg-Gotha (1844–1900) m. Marie, Grand Duchess of Russia (1853–1920)

5 children,
Helena m. Christian of Schleswig-Holstein
Louise m. Duke of Argyll
Arthur, Duke of Connaught m. Louise of Prussia
Leopold, Duke of Albany m. Helene of Pyrmont and Waldeck
Beatrice m. Henry of Battenburg

Elizabeth ('Ella') (1864–1918) m. Sergei, Grand Duke of Russia

Alexandra **Alicky** (1872–1918) m. **Nicholas II** of Russia (1868–1918)

Ernst, Grand Duke of Hesse-Darmstadt (1868–1937) m. Victoria Melita (see across)

Alfred (1874–99)

Marie of Roumania ('Missy') (1875–1938) m. Ferdinand of Roumania (1865–1927)

Victoria Melita ('Ducky') (1878–1942) m. (1) Ernst of Hesse-Darmstadt (2) Kirill, Grand Duke of Russia

3 others

The Romanovs

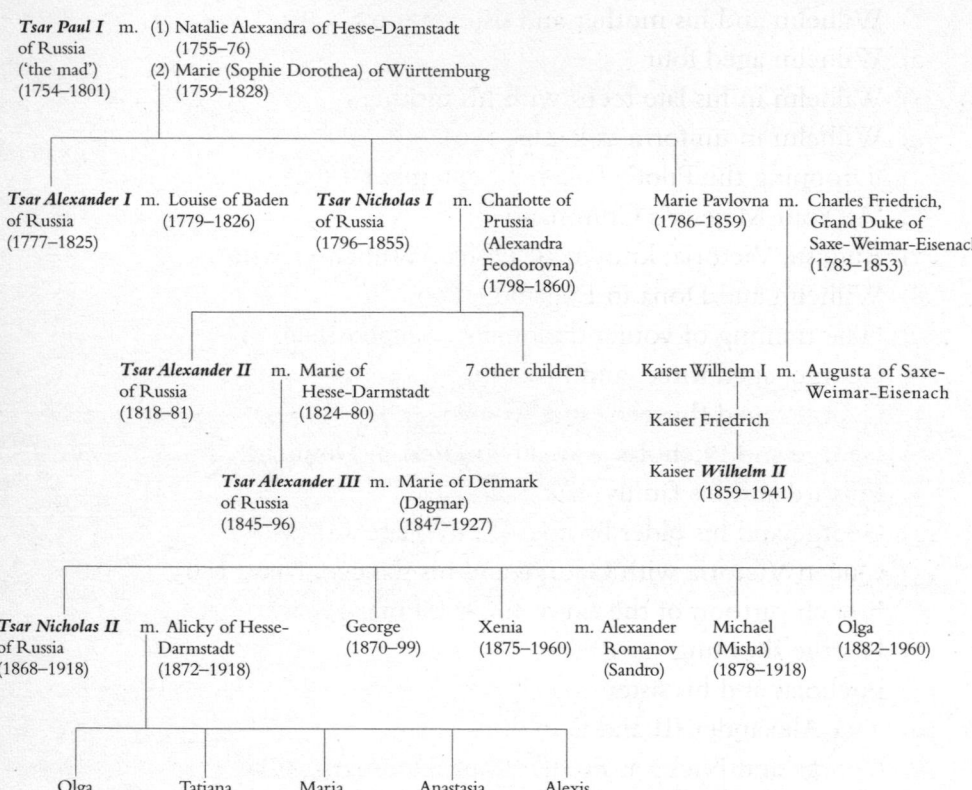

Tsar Paul I m. (1) Natalie Alexandra of Hesse-Darmstadt
of Russia   (1755–76)
('the mad')   (2) Marie (Sophie Dorothea) of Württemburg
(1754–1801)   (1759–1828)

Tsar Alexander I m. Louise of Baden   **Tsar Nicholas I** m. Charlotte of   Marie Pavlovna m. Charles Friedrich,
of Russia   (1779–1826)   of Russia   Prussia   (1786–1859)   Grand Duke of
(1777–1825)   (1796–1855)   (Alexandra   Saxe-Weimar-Eisenach
                                                           Feodorovna)   (1783–1853)
                                                           (1798–1860)

Tsar Alexander II m. Marie of   7 other children   Kaiser Wilhelm I m. Augusta of Saxe-
of Russia   Hesse-Darmstadt   Weimar-Eisenach
(1818–81)   (1824–80)

                Kaiser Friedrich

Tsar Alexander III m. Marie of Denmark   Kaiser **Wilhelm II**
of Russia   (Dagmar)   (1859–1941)
(1845–96)   (1847–1927)

Tsar Nicholas II m. Alicky of Hesse-   George   Xenia   m. Alexander   Michael   Olga
of Russia   Darmstadt   (1870–99)   (1875–1960)   Romanov   (Misha)   (1882–1960)
(1868–1918)   (1872–1918)   (Sandro)   (1878–1918)

Olga   Tatiana   Maria   Anastasia   Alexis
(1895–1918)   (1897–1918)   (1899–1918)   (1901–18)   (1904–18)

List of illustrations

65) George opening parliament, 1923
66) Wilhelm at Haus Doom, 1938

The author and publishers would like to thank the following for permission to reproduce illustrations:

1, 3, 10, 34, 35, 37, 57, copyright Getty Images; 2, 8, 11, 15, 16, 27, 29, 32, 33, 36, 42, 52, 53, 54, 56, 59–66, copyright Corbis; 4, 6, 7, 12, 17, 20, 22, 23, 39, 55, 58, copyright The Royal Collection, 2009, Her Majesty Queen Elizabeth II; 9, copyright Bildarchiv Preussicher Kulturbesitz; 5, copyright Punch archive; 13, 14, 18, 21, 24, 25, 26, 28, 38, 40, 43, 44, 45, 46, 47, 48, copyright the Russian state archive of film and photographic documents, Krasnagorsk.

Introduction

July 1917, as the First World War reached its third exhausting year, was not a good month for monarchs. In London, George V, King of England and Emperor of India, decided to change his name. A month or so before, he had held a dinner party at Buckingham Palace. The occasion would have been slightly grimmer and plainer than usual for a European monarch. In an effort to show their commitment to the war effort, George and his wife, Mary, had instituted a spartan regime at the palace: no heating, dim lighting, 'simple' food – mutton instead of lamb, pink blancmange instead of mousses and sorbets – and no alcohol. The king had taken a pledge of abstinence for the duration as an example to the nation – an example to which it had remained noticeably deaf. Since there was no rationing in England, the aristocratic guests would almost certainly have eaten better at home. Nor, very probably, was the conversation precisely scintillating. The king and queen were known for their dedication to duty and moral uprightness, but not for their social adeptness: 'the King is duller than the Queen', went the refrain of a rather mean little poem by the society wit Max Beerbohm. During the course of the meal, Lady Maud Warrender, occasional lady-in-waiting to Queen Mary and a friend of Edward Elgar and Henry James, happened to let slip that there were rumours going round that because of the king's family name – Saxe-Coburg-Gotha – he was regarded as pro-German. Hearing this, George 'started and grew pale'. He left the table soon afterwards. He'd been shaken by the abdication and arrest in March of his cousin the Russian tsar, Nicholas II; the new rumours made him fear again for his position. He had always been hypersensitive to criticism and was prone to self-pity, though he tended to cover it with barking anger. The war had gnawed at him; it had turned his beard white and given him great bags under his eyes and somehow eroded him: observers said he looked like an old worn-out penny.

Things were worse for George's cousin, Kaiser Wilhelm II, the German emperor. The war had once and for all destroyed the pretence that Wilhelm – supposedly the apex of the German autocracy – was capable of providing any kind of consistent leadership. In early July the kaiser's two most senior generals, Ludendorff and Hindenburg, threatened to resign unless Wilhelm sacked his chancellor. The gesture was a move to demonstrate and secure their hold over the civilian government. Wilhelm ranted and complained, but his beleaguered chancellor resigned anyway. The generals imposed their own replacement. They took away the kaiser's title of 'Supreme Warlord' and awarded it to Hindenburg. 'I may as well abdicate,' Wilhelm grumbled. But he didn't, remaining the increasingly flimsy fig-leaf of a military dictatorship. In Germany, they began to call him 'the Shadow-Emperor'. (In Britain and America mass propaganda portrayed him as a child-eating monster, egging his troops on to ever greater atrocities.) Those closest to him worried about the serious 'declining popularity of the monarchical idea', and sighed over the levels of self-deception – Wilhelm veered between depression and 'his well-known, impossible, Victory mood'. Through the hot July days, a virtual prisoner of the army, he shuffled from front to front, pinning on medals, then dining at some grand aristocrat's large estates: 'Once more a rich dinner and the same bunch of idlers', a particularly disillusioned member of his entourage observed.

Further east, just outside Petrograd in Russia, at Alexander Palace at Tsarskoe selo, 'the Tsar's village', George's other cousin, Nicholas Romanov, the former tsar – to whom the king had always said he was devoted – was in his fourth month of house arrest since his abdication. Throughout July, Nicholas spent his days reading, cutting wood and pottering in the kitchen gardens of the palace. It was a life that in many respects suited him, and he seemed to greet his downfall with a stoic calmness that might even have been relief – but then he'd always been hard to read. On hot days his children swam in the lake, and his son Alexis showed the household his collection of silent films on his cinematograph. Beyond Tsarskoe selo, Russian soldiers at the front were mutinying, and on 3 July angry workers, soldiers and Bolsheviks had taken to the streets of Petrograd. There was fierce fighting as the moderate provisional government struggled to stay in control. The city was full of furious rumours that the hated Romanovs were about to flee the country. A few weeks before, the provisional government's foreign minister had asked the British ambassador for the second time whether Britain could give asylum to the former tsar and his family. The ambassador, deeply embarrassed, said it was impossible. At the end of the month Alexander Kerensky, the new prime minister, told Nicholas that the family would have to get away from Petrograd for their own safety, just for a few months. They must be packed and ready to leave by 31 July. Their destination was Tobolsk in Siberia – which had a certain appropriateness; the old regime had consigned thousands of its enemies to Siberia. Nicholas's wife, Alexandra – perhaps the most hated woman in all Russia – wrote to a friend, 'what suffering our departure is; all packed, empty rooms – it hurts so much'.

Back in England, George came up with a new last name for himself: Windsor – irreproachably English-sounding, and entirely made up. It established the British royal family once and for all as a slightly stolid but utterly reliable product of the English Home Counties. Though, of course, it wasn't. Saxe-Coburg-Gotha – like Windsor, not so much a surname as a statement of provenance – had been given to George's grandmother Queen Victoria (herself half-German) by his grandfather Albert, the Prince Consort, son of the German Duke of Coburg. It was redolent of the close relations and blood ties that linked the whole of European royalty, and which in Britain had been crowned by the fact that Kaiser Wilhelm was Queen Victoria's eldest grandson. George's father was Wilhelm's uncle; his mother was Nicholas's aunt; Wilhelm and Nicholas, meanwhile, were both second and third cousins, through the marriage of a great-aunt, and a shared great-great-grandfather, the mad Tsar Paul of Russia.

When Wilhelm heard that George had changed his name, he made his almost only ever recorded joke: that he was looking

forward to seeing a production of the Merry Wives of Saxe-
Coburg-Gotha.

Fifty-odd years before, these three emperors had been born into a
world where hereditary monarchy seemed immutable, and the
intermarriage between and internationalism of royal dynasties a
guarantee of peace and good international relations. How the
world had changed. This book tells the story of that change,
through the lives of George, Wilhelm, the last kaiser, and Nicholas,
the last tsar, and how they presided over the final years of old
dynastic Europe and the outbreak of the First World War, the
event which set twentieth-century Europe on course to be the
most violent continent in the history of the world.

Throughout their lives, Wilhelm, George and Nicholas wrote
to each other and about each other in letters and diaries. The
history of their relationships – as well as those with George and
Wilhelm's grandmother Queen Victoria and her son Edward VII,
who also ruled during this era and whose relationships with the
three men were crucial (there were moments in this book's writing
when I almost considered calling it 'Four Emperors and an
Empress') – is a saga of an extended and often dysfunctional family,
set in a tiny, glittering, solipsistic, highly codified world. But this
personal, hidden history also shows how Europe moved from an
age of empire to an age of democracy, self-determination and
greater brutality.

Wilhelm and Nicholas wielded real power, more power perhaps
than any individual should have in a complex modern society –
certainly more than any unelected individual. What they said and
did mattered. George did not – though neither he nor his father
nor grandmother liked to acknowledge it – but his role in the
functioning of government was welded into the fabric of British
and empire constitutional politics, and there were moments when
the monarch could make a difference.

And yet, at the same time, they were all three anachronisms,
ill-equipped by education and personality to deal with the modern
world, marooned by history in positions increasingly out of kilter
with their era. The system within which they existed was dying,

and the courts of Europe had turned from energetic centres of patronage into stagnant ponds of tradition and conservatism. The world was leaving them behind. The great technical innovations and breakthroughs, the great scientific theories, the great modern masterpieces of art and letters, were being produced by men – Chekhov, Stravinsky, Einstein, Freud, Planck, Yeats, Wilde, Picasso – who might have been born under monarchies, but for whom the courts meant nothing. As great mass movements took hold of Europe, the courts and their kings cleaved to the past, set up high walls of etiquette to keep the world out and defined themselves through form, dress and precedence. The Berlin court, for example, had sixty-three grades of military officer alone. The Russian court included 287 chamberlains and 309 chief gentlemen in waiting.

Though the world was overtaking them, the three emperors witnessed high politics in the decades before the war from a proximity denied anyone else – even if the conclusions they drew from events were often the wrong ones. Kaiser Wilhelm and Tsar Nicholas led their countries into a conflict that tore their nations apart, destroyed the illusion of their family relationships and resulted in their own abdication, exile and death. George looked on, usually powerless to do anything. Every so often, however, there came an occasion when his decisions did have consequences. By a terrible irony, 1917 – the year he changed his name – would give rise to one of those moments, when he had power over the future of his cousin Nicholas. His decision would vividly demonstrate how Queen Victoria's vision of royal relationships – indeed the whole edifice of European monarchy – was irrefutably broken.

Note

Until 1918 Russian dates followed the Julian or 'Old Style' calendar, rather than the Gregorian one we use today. In the nineteenth century this meant Russian dates were twelve days behind Western dates, and in the twentieth century, thirteen. In my notes I have used the abbreviation 'OS' to mark Julian calendar dates.

I have also taken the decision, where the character or name has a well-established Western or Anglicized alternative, to go with the Anglicization, i.e. Leo instead of Lev (Tolstoy), Nicholas instead of Nikolai, Augusta Victoria instead of Auguste Viktoria.

PART I

Three Childhoods,
Three Countries

1. Wilhelm: an experiment in perfection (1859)

It was a horrible labour. The baby was in the breech position and no one realized until too late. The eighteen-year-old mother had been too embarrassed to allow any of the court physicians to examine or even talk to her about her pregnancy – a prudishness learned from her own mother. The experience of childbirth would cure her of it. To make matters worse, an urgent summons to Berlin's most eminent obstetrician got lost. After ten or eleven hours of excruciating pain – the mother cried for chloroform, she was given a handkerchief to bite on (her screams, her husband later wrote, were 'horrible') – the attending doctors, one German, one English, had pretty much given up on her and the baby. (There were bad precedents for medics who carried out risky interventions on royal patients: when Princess Charlotte, the heir to the British throne, died in childbirth in 1817, the attending physician felt obliged to shoot himself.) The child survived only because the famous obstetrician eventually received the message and arrived at the last minute. With liberal doses of chloroform and some difficulty, the doctor managed to manipulate the baby out. He emerged pale, limp, one arm around his neck, badly bruised and not breathing. The attending nurse had to rub and slap him repeatedly to make him cry. The sound, when it came, the boy's father wrote, 'cut through me like an electric shock'. Everybody wept with relief. It was 27 January 1859.

At the moment of his birth, two, or arguably three, factors immediately had a defining effect on the life and character of Friedrich Victor Wilhelm Albert Hohenzollern – soon known as Willy to distinguish him, his father said, from the 'legion of Fritzes' in the family. Firstly, the baby's left arm was damaged in the delivery – a fact which, in the relief and excitement following his birth, wasn't noticed for three days. It seems likely that in the obstetrician's urgency to get the baby out before he suffocated, he wrenched and irretrievably crushed the network of nerves in Willy's arm, rendering it useless and unable to grow. Secondly, and unprovably, it's possible that those first few minutes without oxygen may have caused brain damage. Willy grew up to be hyperactive and emotionally unstable; brain damage sustained at birth was a possible cause.

Thirdly, an almost impossible burden of conflicting demands and expectations came to rest upon Willy at the moment of his birth. Through his father, Friedrich, one of the ubiquitous Fritzes, he was heir to the throne of Prussia; his mother, Vicky, was the first-born child of Queen Victoria of Great Britain, and he was the British queen's first grandchild. As heir to Prussia, the biggest and most influential power in the loose confederation of thirty-eight duchies, kingdoms and four free cities that called itself Germany, he carried his family's and country's dreams of the future. Those dreams saw Prussia as the dominant power in a unified Germany, taking its place as one of the Great Powers. For Queen Victoria, monarch of the richest and arguably most influential country in the world, Willy was both a doted-on grandchild – 'a fine fat child with a beautiful soft white skin', as she put it when she finally saw him twenty months later – and the symbol and vehicle of a new political and dynastic bond between England and Prussia, a state whose future might take it in several different directions, directions in which Britain's monarch and her husband took an intense interest. Three days after his birth the queen wrote delightedly to her friend and fellow grandmother Augusta of Prussia, 'Our mutual grandson binds us and our two countries even closer together!'

Queen Victoria felt a deep affinity with Germany. Her mother was German and so was her husband, Albert, the younger brother of the ruling duke of the small but influential central German duchy of Coburg. She carried on intense correspondences with several German royals, including Fritz's mother, Augusta, and she would marry six of her nine children to Germans. Although the queen's Germanophilia was sometimes criticized in England, the British were at least less hostile to the Germans than they were to France and Russia, and occasionally even approving. At the battle of Waterloo, Britain and Prussia had fought side by side to defeat Napoleon, and well into the 1850s as a salute to the old alliance there were still German regiments stationed on the South Coast. Thomas Hardy described the German hussars stationed in Dorset in the 1850s as being so deeply embedded in the local culture that their language had over the years woven itself into the local dialect: 'Thou bist' and 'Er war' becoming familiar locutions. Germany – or at least the northern part – was the other Protestant power in Europe. German culture was much admired. In turn, German liberals looked to Britain as the model for a future German constitutional monarchy, its traders admired British practice, and at the other end of the political spectrum, it was to England that some of the more reactionary members of the German ruling elite – including Willy's German grandfather – had fled during the revolutions of 1848. There he and his wife Augusta had become friends – sort of – of the queen and her husband Albert.

Albert, the Prince Consort, an intelligent, energetic and thoughtful man denied a formal public role in England, was even more preoccupied with Germany than his wife, particularly with its future and that of its ruling class. He had seen the German royals rocked by the revolutions of 1848, their very existence called into question by the rise of republicanism and democratic movements. He'd come to believe that Germany's future lay in unification under a modern liberal constitutional monarchy, like that of England. Prussia, as the largest, strongest state in Germany, was the obvious candidate.

Though it was not necessarily the perfect one. Prussia was a peculiar hybrid, rather like Germany itself: it was half dynamic and forward-looking, half autocratic backwater. On the one hand, it was a rich state with an impressive civil service, a fine education system, and a fast-growing industrial heartland in the Western Rhineland. It had been one of the first states in Europe to emancipate Jews, and had a tradition of active citizenship, demonstrated most visibly in 1813, when it had not been the pusillanimous king but a determined citizenry, who had pulled together an army to fight Napoleon. After 1848 a representative assembly, the Landtag, had been forced on the king and liberal politicians and thinkers seemed to be in the ascendant. On the other hand, however, Prussia was stuck in the dark ages: it was a semi-autocracy whose ruling institutions were dominated by a deeply conservative small land-owning class from its traditional heartland on the East Elbian plain, the Junkers. They had a reputation for being tough, austere, incorruptible, fearsomely reactionary, piously Protestant, anti-Semitic, feudal in their attitudes to their workers, their land and their women, and resistant to almost any change – whether demo-cratization, urbanization or industrialization – which might threaten their considerable privileges. These included almost total exemption from taxation. They dominated the Prussian court, the most conservative in Germany. They regarded Prussia's next-door neighbour, Russia – England's great world rival – as their natural ally, sharing with Russia a long frontier, a belief in autocratic government and a pervasive military culture.

Prussia's highly professional army was the reason for its domi-nation of Germany, and in many respects gave Prussia what political coherence and identity it had. It had long been dominated by the Junkers, and was the heart of Prussian conservatism. Almost all European aristocracies identified themselves with the army, but since the seventeenth century the Prussian aristocracy, more than any other, had been encouraged by its rulers to equate its noble status and privileges entirely with senior military rank. It was not unusual for boys of the Prussian ruling classes to wear military uniform from the age of six. History showed that war paid: Prussia had benefited territorially from every central European military conflict since the Thirty Years War in the seventeenth century. In the eighteenth century Frederick the Great had doubled Prussia's size in a series of vicious central European wars. Prussia's inter-vention in the Napoleonic Wars had doubled its size again, making it the dominant power in Germany. But at the same time, Prussia's military culture had arisen not simply from a desire to expand and conquer, but quite as much from the fact that the Prussian ruling class was haunted – obsessed even – by its country's vulner-ability in the middle of Europe, undefended by natural barriers, always a potential victim for some larger power's territorial ambitions. Territorial expansion had constantly alternated with disaster and near annihilation. During the Thirty Years War, Prussia had lost half its population to disease, famine and fighting; the scar remained in folk memory. During the Napoleonic Wars, it had been humiliated, overrun and threatened with dismemberment while the French and Russians squared up to each other. Since then, Prussia had been hostile to France and carefully deferential to the Russian colossus next door. The ruling dynasties of Hohenzollern and Romanov had intermarried and even developed genuine friendships. Willy's Prussian great-aunt Charlotte had married Tsar Nicholas I, and Willy's grandfather, who would become King of Prussia, and then Kaiser Wilhelm I of Germany, enjoyed a long and close friendship with his son, Tsar Alexander II.

The contradictions in Prussia mirrored the extraordinary heterogeneity of Germany and its states as a whole. Within its loose boundaries there existed a plethora of conflicting Germanies: the Germany that led the world in scientific and technological innovation, the Germany that was the most cultured, literate, academically innovative state in Europe – the Germany of Goethe, Leibnitz, the von Humboldt brothers, Bach and Beethoven – stood alongside the Germany of resolutely philistine Junkers. In East Elbia, the heartland of the Junker estates, disenfranchised peasants lived in almost feudal conditions, and yet at the same time Germany was the most industrialized place in Europe with some of the best labour conditions. Germany had some of the most hierarchical, undemocratic states in Europe, ruled by an embarrassment of self-important little princelings, and was also home to the largest and best organized Socialist Party in Europe. Southern, predominantly Catholic, Germany coexisted with northern, Protestant Germany. It seems entirely appropriate that Berlin, Prussia's capital, with its vast avenues, seemed like a parade ground, while also being a centre for political radicalism, for scholarship, for a wealthy Jewish community.

Prince Albert believed there was a battle going on for the soul and political future of Germany. 'The German stands in the centre between England and Russia,' he wrote to his future son-in-law Fritz in 1856. 'His high culture and his philosophic love of truth drive him towards the English conception, his military discipline, his admiration of the asiatic greatness . . . which is achieved by the merging of the individual into the whole, drives him in the other direction.' Albert also felt that in the post-1848 world, monarchy was under threat. He wanted to prove that good relations between monarchies created peace between countries. And he had come to the conclusion that princes must justify their status by their moral and intellectual superiority to everyone else.

One of Albert's projects had been to design a rigorous academic regime for his eight children to turn them into accomplished princes. His eldest daughter, Vicky – his favourite – responded brilliantly to it. She was clever, intellectually curious and passionate – qualities not always associated with royalty. Her younger brother Bertie – the future Edward VII – had suffered miserably under the same regime. Albert thought that, under the right circumstances, a royal marriage between Britain and Prussia might nudge Germany in the right direction, towards unification, towards a constitutional monarchy and a safe future for the German royal families. It might even bring about an alliance with Britain, an alliance which could become the cornerstone of peace in Europe. Albert resolved to send his clever daughter on a mission to fix Germany, by marrying Vicky to Friedrich Wilhelm Hohenzollern, nephew of the childless and increasingly doddery King of Prussia, Friedrich Wilhelm IV, and second in line to the throne after his 62-year-old father, who had already taken over many of his brother's duties.

Fritz, as he was called, was ten years older than Vicky, dashingly handsome, charismatic and an effective officer – so much the Wagnerian hero that in Germany he was actually known as Siegfried. The marriage, which took place in January 1858, looked good on paper – the heir of the rising Protestant German state marrying the daughter of the richest, stablest power in Europe. Unlike most arranged royal marriages, it worked even better in reality. Personally gentle, earnest and prone to depression – somewhat at odds with the emphatically blunt, masculine ideal of the Prussian officer – 27-year-old Fritz adored his clever seventeen-year-old wife, and she adored him. He also showed, Victoria and

Albert noted approvingly, a liking for England and admirable liberal tendencies very much at odds with those of his father and the Prussian court.

At the time, the plan of sending a completely inexperienced seventeen-year-old girl to unify Germany may not have seemed quite so extraordinary as it does now. The external circumstances looked promising. In 1858 the political balance in Prussia seemed to be held by the liberals: they had just won a landslide victory in the Landtag elections. Prussia's king was elderly and had recently suffered a series of incapacitating strokes, and his heir, Fritz's father, was sixty-two years old. Fritz and Vicky shouldn't have to wait too long before they would be in control.

That was the plan. It didn't turn out that way. Firstly, Albert had been away from Germany a long time and didn't understand how suspicious the Prussian ruling class was of Vicky's Englishness, and how touchy about the prospect that larger powers might interfere in its country. 'The "English" in it does not please me,' the future chancellor, Otto von Bismarck, told a friend, 'the "marriage" may be quite good . . . If the Princess can leave the Englishwoman at home.' Secondly, Vicky, though extremely bright, had no talent for politics, was hopelessly tactless and held fast to her Englishness. Thirdly, Fritz's father turned out to be astonishingly long-lived, and appointed Otto von Bismarck, the greatest conservative European statesman of the late nineteenth century, his chief minister.

It went wrong quite quickly. The Prussian court was not welcoming and was critical of Vicky's forthright views and intellectual confidence. Prussian wives were supposed to be silent and submissive; there was none of the leeway allowed in Britain for an intelligent, educated woman to shine. It was said disapprovingly that Vicky dominated Fritz. She met intellectuals and artists, whether or not they were commoners, and this contravened the social strictures of court etiquette: princesses did not host salons or mix with non-royals. Bewildered and isolated, Vicky had no idea what to do. She responded with a social tone-deafness and complete lack of strategic tact which would become characteristic. She complained – imperiously and incessantly – about the philistine, rigid and deadly dull Prussian court; about the threadbare carpets, dirty floors, and lack of baths and lavatories in the Hohenzollerns' ancestral castles;★ about the frequent absences of her soldier husband. Worse, she displayed the insufferable habit of saying that everything was better in England, a habit that became almost compulsive as time went on. This seemed to confirm Prussian suspicions that she intended to bring Prussia under English influence, though it was actually a manifestation of loneliness and homesickness. 'She loved England and everything English with a fervour which at times roused contradictions in her Prussian surroundings,' one of her few allies, her lady-in-waiting Walpurga Hohenthal, later wrote. 'I was perhaps the only one who entirely sympathized . . . but I was too young and inexperienced to reflect that it would not be wise to give them too much scope.'

Back in England her parents didn't understand. The queen tried to micromanage her, sometimes sending her four letters a week and telling her not to get too familiar with her Prussian relatives. Albert limited himself to writing once a week, and was gentler, but in his way just as insistent. He demanded essays on international affairs and told her to study chemistry and geometry – which she duly did. Her in-laws were unsympathetic: Fritz's father, Wilhelm, was a philistine arch-traditionalist whose deepest emotional attachment was to the army. He required only that his son and daughter-in-law attend every court function and be entirely obedient to his will. Fritz's mother, Augusta, who loathed her husband and was hugely disliked at court at least partly for being an educated woman with liberal views, was angry and difficult (the King of Belgium called her 'the Dragon of the Rhine'), and made no attempt to support her daughter-in-law. The Hohenzollerns were a byword for family dysfunction. The father of Frederick the Great (Wilhelm's great-great-great-great-uncle) had locked him up and forced him to watch his best friend's execution. Oedipal conflicts seemed to afflict every generation.

★ 'It is very hard to convey to English readers the medieval conditions in which people in our state of life lived in Germany,' Vicky's niece Mary Louise would write about living in Germany twenty years later.

Within a couple of years of Willy's birth, Vicky's 'mission' was in shreds. 'You cannot think how painful it is, to be continuously surrounded by people who consider your very existence a misfortune,' she wrote to her mother. Then, just before Willy's third birthday in 1861, Albert died and Vicky lost her guide and hero. Later that same year Fritz's 64-year-old father, Wilhelm, came to the throne for what would be a twenty-seven-year reign. He made it clear he wanted to strengthen relations with Russia, and at his coronation he announced that he ruled by divine right – a concept the English crown had abandoned 300 years before. A year later, in the midst of a battle with the Landtag over military reform, which everyone expected to end with the king giving in to more constitutional curtailments of his powers, he appointed Otto von Bismarck as his minister-president. Bismarck closed down the Landtag. Over the next twenty years, he would turn Germany into the political powerhouse of continental Europe, while also eliminating liberals from power and delivering the organs of government into the hands of conservatives and rural property-owners, the Junkers.

Vicky hated Bismarck. 'That wretch Bismarck . . . has done all he could to irritate the King against London and Lord Palmerston and Lord Russell,' she complained in 1862. 'Bismarck is such a wicked man that he does not care how many fibs he tells to serve his own purposes, and this is the man who is to govern this country.' To Bismarck, Vicky and Fritz were a dangerous magnet for liberal sympathies. He set out deliberately to neutralize the couple. He alienated father from son, and used every weapon at his disposal: feeding damaging stories into the Berlin rumour mill and the German press – much of which he secretly funded – to characterize Vicky as a sinister representative of British ambitions in Germany and Fritz as her dupe. Vicky thought she could take Bismarck on. 'I enjoy a pitched battle,' she wrote optimistically. But she was a rank amateur prone to moments of tremendous misjudgement, and he was perhaps the most brilliant political tactician of the late nineteenth century. As if that weren't enough, Vicky's health collapsed: she was plagued for weeks at a time by chronic pains and fevers for which there seemed no cure, symptoms that some historians now think might have been porphyria – the illness which had caused George III's madness.

It wasn't surprising, perhaps, that Vicky's family and children became one of her refuges from the hostility of the court, a place where she could express her frustration with her situation, and where she channelled all the disappointed energy. There were eight children in all: Willy, his sister Charlotte and his brother Heinrich, to whom he was closest; then five subsequent siblings: Sigismund, Victoria (known as Moretta), Waldemar, Sophy and Margaret (or Mossy), of whom the two boys died in childhood. The family dynamic seems to have been in the main warm and loving. When Fritz was in one of his depressions, Vicky believed the company of the children dispelled it. She loved her children, especially her eldest. 'You do not know how dear that child is,' she wrote to her mother when he was a few months old. '. . . I feel so proud of him and it makes me so happy to carry him about.' But her love was complicated, especially for her first three children, and most of all for Wilhelm. She veered between tenderness and love, and brutal criticism, obsessively high ex-pectations and anxiety over their shortcomings. Albert had instilled in her a belief that character could be created and moulded by education, that perfectibility could be achieved by hard work. 'The welfare of the world,' he said, depended on 'the good education of princes'. He'd also – along with the queen, who was a relentless critic of her children – turned his daughter into an anxious per-fectionist compulsively critical of herself, and then of her own children. Vicky was determined that her son would measure up to her father's standards. She scrutinized every bit of the boy – just as her parents had scrutinized her – frequently found him wanting and let him know it. She wrote to her mother when he was nine, 'Still I dote on Willy and think there is a great deal in him. He is by no means a common place child; if one can root out or keep down pride, conceitedness, selfishness and laziness . . . I do not speak as openly of our little ones to anyone but you.' But whatever she said to her mother, she did communicate her dis-satisfactions to her children. She would mark the misspellings in

Wilhelm's letters to her and send them back. She was just as bad with his brother Heinrich, describing 'his poor ugly face', and reporting that he was 'awfully backward' and 'hopelessly lazy'. The question of perfection (or imperfection) was constantly in the air because, of course, Willy's stunted arm meant he was very visibly imperfect.

Within a few months of Willy's birth it was clear that his arm wasn't growing properly. He couldn't lift it and the fingers had curled into a kind of claw. In Prussia, royalty was closely identified with the army and physical prowess. On Willy's birth, in a gesture of typical Hohenzollern tact, Fritz's father had wondered to his face whether it was appropriate to congratulate him on the birth of a 'defective' prince. Vicky worried over it constantly, asking herself whether the nation would tolerate a physically disabled prince. 'I cannot tell you how it worries me, I am ready to cry whenever I think of it,' she wrote to her father when Willy was six months old and had begun to undergo all kinds of peculiar treatments to mend the arm. It was covered in cold compresses, sprayed with sea water, massaged and given a weekly 'animal bath', in which it was placed inside the warm carcass of a freshly killed hare – an experience, his mother noticed, Willy seemed to like very much. Queen Victoria thought the practice medieval, and it was: the idea was that the heat of the dead animal would transmute itself into the arm of the child. At least this was harmless. Less so was the binding of his right arm to his body, when Willy reached toddler-hood, in an attempt to force the other arm to function. It left him with nothing to balance with as he tried to learn to walk. Even nastier were the electric shocks passed regularly through his arm from the age of fourteen months. 'He gets so fretful and cross and violent and passionate that it makes me quite nervous sometimes,' Vicky wrote. By the age of four, Willy had developed torticollis – the right side of his neck had contracted, lifting the shoulder and making him look crooked. (One biographer has suggested that this came about through a desire to turn away from his affliction.) To try to correct this, he was strapped into a body-length machine to stretch the muscles of his right side. Vicky wrote painful, guilty letters to Queen Victoria describing and drawing the contraption, which looked like a medieval instrument of torture. 'He has been a constant source of anxiety ever since he has been in the world. I cannot tell you what I suffered when I saw him in that machine the day before yesterday – it was all I could do to prevent myself from crying. To see one's child treated like one deformed – it is really very hard . . .'

In the end two small operations severed the tendons that were distorting his body and corrected the torticollis. The arm never improved, though there was always another 'specialist' with another crank 'cure'. The electric shocks and stretching machines continued until Willy was ten, when the doctors noted how 'nervously tense' the treatments made him. Wilhelm later claimed they caused 'intolerable pain'. The only thing that made any difference was a course of gymnastics which developed a compensatory great strength in Willy's right arm.

Willy seemed a jolly, boisterous, affectionate small boy. Vicky described him, aged three, patting her face, saying, 'Nice little Mama, you have a nice little face and I want to kiss you.' He slept in her bed when his father was away with the army, and she saw much more of him than most royal parents. 'Willy is a dear, interesting charming boy,' Vicky wrote when he was seven, 'clever, amusing, engaging, it is impossible not to spoil him a little. He is growing so handsome and his large eyes have now and then a pensive, dreamy expression and then again they sparkle with fun and delight.' He could also be aggressive and difficult. He hit his nurses; after a trip to England in 1864, his grandmother complained that he was thumping his aunt Beatrice – who was only two years older and afraid of him. 'We have a gt. deal of trouble to keep him in order – he is so jealous of the Baby,' Vicky wrote after the birth of his sister Charlotte. Aged seven or so, on the beach at the Isle of Wight, he threw a furious tantrum and tried to kick an eminent gentleman and throw his walking stick into the sea. (The eminent gentleman, a former secretary of Prince Albert's, tripped him up and spanked him.) On another occasion, at his Uncle Edward's wedding in England in 1863, aged four, he got bored, scratched the legs of his uncles Leopold and Arthur to get their attention, threw his sporran into the choir, and when scolded, bit one of his uncles in the leg.★ W. P. Frith, celebrated painter of crowd scenes such as *Derby Day*, who had been commissioned to paint the occasion, muttered, 'Of all the little Turks he is the worst.' To modern eyes, this seems like fairly typical obstreperous, spoilt toddler behaviour, but at the time it struck his mother and the British relatives as more than that – though this may have been just as much to do with their impossible expectations of how a young monarch-to-be should behave.

To add to the pressures and confusion there were the competing tugs of his English and German inheritances. The conflict was incarnated in his own name – to his mother and his English relations he was William, to his German relations and his country he was Wilhelm. The more Vicky felt alienated from her German environment, the more she denigrated her son's German heritage. One ten-year-old visitor remembered Vicky reprimanding her children for dunking their cake in their tea: 'None of your nasty German habits at my table!' She was determined to root out any signs of 'that terrible Prussian pride' and she loathed the Prussian obsession with the army. When he was ten, Willy wrote plaintively to his English grandmother, 'There were lately two parades where I marched towards the King. he [*sic*] told me that I marched well, but Mama said I did it very badly.' Vicky told her mother that in his miniature Hohenzollern uniform, he had looked like some 'organ grinder's unfortunate little monkey'.

Everything British, Vicky made it clear, was better. She told her son the Royal Navy was the greatest fighting force in the world and she dressed him up in a sailor outfit, aged two, feeling she'd won a great victory in managing to do it before he'd worn a Prussian army uniform. 'He is so fond of ships,' she told her mother when he was five, 'and I wish that to be encouraged as much as possible – as an antidote to the possibility of a too engrossing military passion.' In his teenage years, she wrote to him extolling England's civilizing imperial mission, contrasting it with Germany's foolish claims to be a player in Europe. She took him as often as possible to visit Queen Victoria at Osborne House, her

★ There seems no consensus on whether this was Leopold or Arthur.

holiday home on the Isle of Wight. Even after the First World War, beaten by the British and in exile, his memories of Osborne were golden. 'How entirely like a second home to me was my grandmother's house, and how England might well have been a second home to me also,' he wrote wistfully. 'We were treated as children of the house.' He recalled a visit in 1871, aged twelve, when his uncle Arthur of Connaught took him round London and how impressed he was by the sharp figure Arthur cut in uniform; he remembered his favourite aunt Louise letting him play in her rooms and giving him sweets: he recalled going to see Nelson's HMS *Victory* at Portsmouth in the queen's paddle steamer and seeing British battleships off Spithead on the way. Osborne, he later claimed, was 'the scene of my earliest recollections'. The family story went that on Willy's first visit in June 1861, aged two-and-a-half, Albert had wrapped him in a towel and dandled him in it.

The Prince Consort died six months later, but the connection remained important to Willy and to his grandmother. 'Albert,' she wrote a month after her husband's death, 'loved that dear child so dearly, felt so anxious about him, was so sure he would be clever – that it only adds to my love for . . . the sweet child . . . You know he is my favourite.' The fact that Willy would be king of the most powerful state in Germany also focused her attention. The queen had never been very keen on babies ('I don't dislike babies,' she wrote, 'though I think very young ones rather disgusting'), and by the time grandchildren came at a rate of three a year, admitted they were 'a cause of mere anxiety for my own children' and 'of no great interest either'. But Willy was the first, and the queen was indulgent with him as she was with few others. He called her 'a duck', and she pronounced him 'full of fun and mischief, and in fact very impertinent, though he is very affectionate with it all'. In turn, Willy was fascinated by the queen. 'She was a proper Grandmother,' he wrote approvingly. The two had a weakness for each other which would endure, despite everything.

It was impossible, of course, for Vicky to keep Prussian influences away from her children. Growing up in Berlin and Potsdam, which was appropriately both the military and leisure capital of Prussia, they were surrounded by the symbols of Prussian military might and ambition – parade grounds and drilling regiments – and they lived in the vast, rather chilly Neues Palais, built by Frederick the Great as an aggressive assertion of Prussian power (having built it, he decided it was a piece of architectural showing off and refused to live in it). A palace of hundreds of huge, echoing rooms, it fronted on to a parade ground. When Willy reached ten, his grandfather, now King Wilhelm of Prussia, began to show an interest in the boy, demanding that Willy turn up at military events and inviting him to dinner in his ostentatiously austere apartments where he slept on his old army camp bed, ate off a card table, and marked the level of the wine on the bottle to make sure the servants didn't steal it. The king, who could be extremely charming when he pleased,★ would talk about his Napoleonic campaigns and the grandson would listen, rapt. The criticism and expectation at home made his grandfather's world very attractive to Willy. The king had a very different view of the obligations of royalty: he was uncomplicatedly absorbed in the army, in being Prussian, and to him royalty didn't need a fancy education to prove itself worthy – it just was.

The king was a hero to his grandson: he had presided – with a little help from Bismarck – over a series of astonishing military successes during the 1860s, Willy's first decade. By 1871, through aggressive campaigns and political manoeuvring, Bismarck had dramatically increased Prussia's size and influence. In 1864 Prussia took Schleswig-Holstein from Denmark. In 1866 it routed Austria out of Germany during the Austro-Prussian War, annexed more German states and turned Willy's father, Fritz, into a bona fide military hero, at the battle of Königgrätz. In 1870 the Franco-Prussian War left France defeated and Prussia with the province of Alsace-Lorraine. It also prompted the unification of Germany

---

★ Wilhelm's English cousin Princess Mary Louise was one of many women to be charmed by his German grandfather, though she was bemused by his attempts to disguise his baldness by securing his comb-over to his left ear with a piece of dirty old cotton.

under Prussia's leadership in 1871 – and made an enduring enemy of France. The tension between the countries would be a dominating fact of European history for the next eighty years; for the moment, though, the Prussians were clearly triumphant. Nine days before Willy's twelfth birthday his grandfather was crowned kaiser of a united Germany in the Hall of Mirrors at Versailles, in a piece of terrifying theatre stage-managed by Bismarck. Naturally, Willy followed the campaign and its aftermath avidly. To his eternal pride, he was allowed to ride behind his father on his triumphal progress through the Brandenburg Gate. It was hardly surprising that, despite her efforts, Vicky found 'a certain receptiveness for the crude, narrow-minded, views of the military' in her son. She worried that her father-in-law and the court were encouraging in Willy a 'mistaken pride, in the idea that it was patriotic'. She worried about her son's admiration for Bismarck. To her English family, however, she hotly defended the Prussian campaigns. As her brother Edward observed, in Germany there was no one more English and in England no one more German.

Vicky was determined her son wouldn't grow up to be a stereotypical Prussian officer type. Following her father's example, she wanted him to be a new kind of prince: educated, self-aware, someone who would confound the forces of republicanism. She found him a group of playmates who came from backgrounds that were not exclusively Prussian aristocrat – ambassadors' and businessmen's children. At seven, when European princes traditionally left the nursery, Willy was handed over to George Hinzpeter, a very serious Calvinist liberal, who planned to implement the most contemporary ideas in education and to show Willy and his brother Heinrich some of the realities of modern life, so they would not 'grow up in ignorance of the wants and interests of the lower classes'. Going to a real school was mooted. It's hard to exaggerate how utterly unlike the average royal education this was: most European princes were handed over to a military governor to whom civilian tutors were subordinate; most were kept completely isolated from the world. It was an admirable plan in many ways, but the combination of Vicky's expectations, her choice of Hinzpeter, and Willy's emerging personality would be a damaging one. Perhaps also the contrast between the expectations of his mother and tutor and the fact that everyone else – the servants, the legendarily deferential Prussian court – treated him as a little god was confusing and unhelpful. Wilhelm would later claim that from the age of seven he had been forced into a regime of 'perpetual renunciation'. In fact, the first few years were rather gentle: there was lots of travel, music and drawing, and unusual excursions to factories and working-class homes. Wilhelm liked to boast later that having seen 'the grim poetry' of working-class life, 'I thus learned to understand the German workman and to feel the warmest sympathy for his lot'.

But when Willy reached eleven, it all began to go wrong. Vicky's criticisms took on an extra intensity. 'He is very arrogant, extremely smug and quite taken with himself,' she wrote to Fritz a month before his twelfth birthday in December 1870, 'is offended at the slightest comment, plays the injured party, and more than occasionally gives an impudent answer; furthermore he is unbeliev-ably lazy and slovenly . . . On the other hand he is more alert and animated than *all* of his playmates, and is more caring and pleasant than all of the rest of them.' He was, she noted – as others would – quick and curious, but had no staying power. Hinzpeter was dissatisfied too. His teaching, he announced, particularly his attempts to mould the 'inner development of mind and heart', had thus far utterly failed. Rather than rethink the plan, they decided to ratchet up the pressure and the discipline. The regime became stricter and harsher. Hinzpeter described fourteen-year-old Willy's 'ill-omened self-adulation' and 'the unpleasant trait of arrogance . . . [which] bolsters the indolence which nature has so generously conferred on him'. He called him lazy and conceited. 'Evidence of positive goodwill towards anyone at all is nevertheless as rare as instances of heartless egoism are frequent . . . his almost crystal-hard egoism . . . forms the innermost core of his being.' It's impossible to say whether Willy's shortcomings were innate or an angry adolescent's response to his mother's and his tutor's impossibly high standards, but these traits would gradually manifest themselves in the adult Wilhelm. Even so, his English uncle Bertie, seeing the nineteen-year-old Willy and his brother for the first time in several years in 1878, recorded, 'It is impossible to find two nicer boys than William and Henry.'

Whatever the truth, the pressure that Hinzpeter and his mother put Willy under horribly backfired, and even Vicky had to admit that Hinzpeter might not have been the best person to have entrusted with the development of a sensitive, tricky teenage boy. A depressive, he seems to have become convinced that he was locked in a manichean battle to mould Willy's character, without being able to see that everything he was doing was making it worse. The plan was, as Wilhelm later wrote, to 'grasp hold of the soul of the pupil . . . to "wrench" it into shape'. Rather than realizing that at least part of Willy's arrogance was an attempt to hold on to some shreds of self-confidence in the face of constant character demolition, Hinzpeter believed that what his charge needed was 'humiliation'. It was decided in 1874 that Willy, aged fifteen, should be sent to a gymnasium – a boys' secondary school. Ostensibly this was an unprecedentedly modern attempt to give the boy a chance to mix with his contemporaries. Its initiators had ulterior motives: Vicky saw it as a way of keeping Willy away from the kaiser's influence; Hinzpeter, as a way of crushing his spirit as much as possible. Being with other boys would squash his 'false estimation of his own ability'. At the same time Hinzpeter played a manipulative game, criticizing Vicky in front of Willy, while telling her and Fritz they were not sufficiently supporting him. Vicky worried, but having taken such a step into the unknown, she was fearful of sacking the navigator.

How Willy felt about all this is evident from his memoirs, written nearly fifty years later, which contain his famous description of being taught to ride – hampered, of course, by having only one usable hand. Hinzpeter put him on a horse and watched him fall off, despite the boy's tears and pleadings, over and over, until he got his balance. 'When nobody looked, I cried,' Wilhelm wrote. It seems likely that this never actually happened,* but clearly the

---

* Wilhelm's painstaking biographer John Röhl has shown that he could ride years before he met Hinzpeter.

emotions it described were real enough. 'The impossible was expected of the pupil in order to force him to the nearest degree of perfection. Naturally the impossible goal could never be achieved; logically, therefore, the praise which registers approval was also excluded.' It could have been a description of his whole childhood. He began to retreat into an alternative reality when real life didn't measure up – a habit that would become pronounced in adult life. And yet, in some respects he had succeeded spectacularly: by the time he reached adolescence, he was so adept with his withered arm that people often ceased to notice it. He could ride and shoot, he was physically robust. He couldn't dress or cut his food without help, but then plenty of European royals were almost ludicrously dependent on their servants. One Russian grand duchess admitted that before the revolution she couldn't button her own boots.

Willy did not enjoy his two and a half years at the Lyceum Fredericianum, the gymnasium in the small, picturesque German town of Cassel which he attended with his brother Heinrich – who, regarded by all as nice but dim, was there mainly for company – supervised by Hinzpeter. The tutor worked him well beyond the normal school day, starting at 5 a.m. and finishing at 8 p.m., six days a week, while simultaneously letting everyone including Willy know that he didn't think he was up to it. In fact, Wilhelm performed quite well in class and he got on with the other boys, but he was discouraged from getting too close to them. Hinzpeter insisted he should be addressed by the formal *Sie*, muttering all the while about the 'poor boy's isolation'. And royal etiquette meant that every time Wilhelm entered a room, one of his tutors noted, everyone was obliged to fall silent and stand still, then follow him around at a respectful distance. Despite the strains, Wilhelm was still most at ease and happy with his family. If anything, he seemed rather fixated on his mother – he sent her intense letters describing dreams in which her hands caressed him, and wrote of 'what we will do in reality when we are alone in your rooms without any witnesses'. The letters were clearly deeply sexual, but they were also pleas for love and support. Vicky, flattered and confused, deflected them with jokes about being his 'poor old Mama', and she never came to rescue him.

Willy graduated from Cassel aged eighteen in 1877 – he came tenth out of sixteen. Released from Hinzpeter and school, he immediately got as far from his mother's influence as he could. Encouraged by his grandfather, he joined the 1st Regiment of Foot Guards, the grandest and most aristocratic regiment in Germany, and moved out of the family home. The officer corps was as much a social club as a training ground: duties were light and amusements were many. Willy found himself surrounded by young men of similar age and class, of right-wing nationalist views and a strong sense of comfortable entitlement, and within a culture in which, as one Berlin observer wrote, 'He was the acknowledged idol of the younger military set, and the easy tool of Bismarck . . . and surrounded by flatterers.' Willy's head was turned. He loved the 1st Foot: the all-embracingness, the male company, the constant activity, the practical jokes, standing at the head of a company feeling splendid – and he especially loved that his peers deferred to and flattered him. Potsdam, he said, was his 'el dorado'. After years of fourteen-hour workdays, he soon lost any interest in applying himself to anything for long, to his parents' disappointment. At Bonn University, where he then spent two years, he dabbled in economics, physics, chemistry, history, philosophy and government, but mainly spent time at the Borussia, the university's grandest duelling and drinking club, peopled by the sons of grand dukes. One of his university tutors commented, 'Like all royalty who had been over-flattered in youth, the prince believed he knew everything without having learnt anything.' Hinzpeter concluded that his entire programme had been a 'complete failure' – though it was often said that it was from him that Willy had acquired a 'coldness' of manner. Fifty years later Wilhelm still couldn't decide whether he was grateful to his tutor, or hated him.

Unsurprisingly, Vicky saw his identification with the army as a pointed rejection, as indeed it was. 'Before I entered the regiment,' he told a friend, 'I had lived through such fearful years of unappreciation of my nature, of ridicule of that which was to me highest and most holy: Prussia, the Army and all of the fulfilling duties that I first encountered in this officer corps and that have provided me with joy and happiness and contentment on earth.'

When his younger brother Waldemar died of diptheria the follow-ing year, 1878, the family were extremely upset that Wilhelm seemed largely unconcerned. Vicky, he told an interviewer decades later, now looked at him with 'bitter disappointment mingled with maternal solicitude'. The irony was that, having avoided – courtesy of his mother – the years of strict military training that a normal Hohenzollern might expect, Wilhelm had none of the disciplined mental habits or experience of a real Prussian officer. Or rather, he looked and played the part – perfectly turned out, moderate if not ascetic in his eating and drinking – but he had no habit of applica-tion. Just as he had been a dilettante student, so he was a dilettante soldier. His military adjutant, Adolf von Bülow, the experienced soldier seconded to see him through his army life, admitted that after five years in the 1st Foot, Wilhelm had completely failed to learn the true values of soldiery.

Vicky's attempt to challenge the stereotypes of royal upbringing and Prussian militarism had produced a strange hybrid. 'A high spirited, sensitive boy who had a ready brain and a quick but not profound intelligence,' the glamorous English aristocrat Daisy Cornwallis, who married into the German aristocracy, wrote of Wilhelm. '. . . He always thought he knew everything and no one dared to tell him he was sometimes wrong. He hated to be told the truth and seldom, perhaps never, forgave those who insisted on telling him.' Obsessive dislike of any criticism would become one of Wilhelm's most marked characteristics. Those who wanted his favour quickly discovered that the way to gain influence with him was to flatter him.

What Wilhelm did have was an identity – or perhaps a disguise. He especially loved the look of the army: the ceremonial, the drilling, the clicking heels, the medals and most of all the uniforms. After the age of twenty he almost never wore anything else. He turned himself into a caricature Prussian officer, with a puffed-up, heel-clicking, hearty manner, an apparent boundless confidence in his own abilities that seemed entirely impervious to doubt or criticism, a new handlebar moustache and views – the opposite of his mother's – to match.

In 1881, at the age of twenty-two, Willy married Augusta Victoria of Schleswig-Holstein-Sonderburg-Glücksburg-Augustenburg, known as Dona, a woman as unthreatening, conventional and obedient as Vicky wasn't, and was granted his own premises, the charmingly intimate – by Prussian standards - Marble Palace in Potsdam. Submissive, devout and fertile, Dona would prove an irreproachably correct daughter of the German empire: she was, and remained, in awe of her husband, agreeing with everything he said, obeying his every stipulation (including taking diet pills to stay thin and wearing outfits he designed for her) and providing constant, unquestioning support. She also, however, shared some of the limitations of the new Germany. She was narrow-minded and xenophobic: she hated Catholics, atheists, liberals and foreigners – the English most of all. Within months of the marriage she was barely speaking to Vicky, who, with her nose for disaster, had picked Dona out as a bride for Wilhelm (even though the Prussian family thought she wasn't well-born enough), in the hope that she might heal the rift between herself and her son.

Within a year Dona had borne an heir, 'Little Willy', and followed this with five more strapping sons, the splendidly named Eitel-Friedrich, Adalbert, Augustus-Wilhelm, Oskar and Joachim, and a daughter, Victoria. Wilhelm, however, spent as little time with his wife as possible because he found her deadly dull and provincial. He was faithful to her, more or less. In the first years of their marriage he kept a couple of mistresses in Vienna and Strasbourg, who had to be bought off by the Bismarcks after he was notably ungenerous over recompensing them for services rendered. It was noticeable, however, that he preferred the company of men, and soldiers most of all, picking himself an entourage of virulently Anglophobic Prussian army officers, and spending as much time as possible at his regiment.

There was more to Wilhelm's keenness on the army than just politics and manliness. As kaiser he would surround himself with tall, handsome, ramrod-backed young ADCs, a predilection which would prompt one member of his entourage to note twenty years later that it was 'nothing short of a religious relationship'. There was definitely an homoerotic edge to Wilhelm's military passion, and it was almost certainly noticed by Bismarck. In 1886 Wilhelm was introduced to Count Philipp zu Eulenburg, a diplomat and amateur composer twelve years his senior. Eulenburg was famously charming, had a gift for informality, and was the leader of a small group of politically reactionary, Anglophobic, 'artistic' and homosexual German aristocrats, called the Liebenburg Circle after the estate where they met. They wrote endlessly to each other about the dreadfulness of modern life, and how it forced them to hide their 'real selves', their *Eigenart*. Bismarck, to whom Eulenburg reported after the meeting, seems to have thought the staunchly conservative Eulenburg would be a useful influence on Wilhelm. In 1888 his son Herbert von Bismarck wrote: 'I have known for a long time that HM loves Phili Eulenburg more than any other living person.'

Eulenburg completely fell for Wilhelm, or at least an idealized version of him, and Wilhelm responded to his palpable affection and admiration. Dona seems to have alternated between viewing Eulenburg as a family friend and feeling deeply jealous. The relationship was carried on through letters and a series of house parties and trips each year, where Eulenburg and his friends laughed approvingly at everything Wilhelm said. They also seem to have been extraordinarily careful never to state their homosexuality explicitly around Wilhelm (whom they privately and devotedly called 'der Liebchen', the 'darling'), though the undercurrents obviously ran not very deeply at all. In twenty years Wilhelm never allowed himself to acknowledge Eulenburg's homosexuality directly.

From 1882 tales began to circulate round the Berlin court that Wilhelm was taking every opportunity to express his aversion to everything English, especially his mother, and that he was politically anti-democratic. 'Prince Wilhelm is, despite his youth, a dyed-in-the-wool Junker and reactionary,' the heir to the Austro-Hungarian empire, Rudolph, reported in 1883. 'He never speaks of the parliament except as "that pig-sty" or of the opposition deputies other than as those "dogs who must be handled with a whip".' One of Wilhelm's new friends, the arch-conservative General Waldersee, wrote, 'The Prince is strongly biased against England, to a great extent this is a wholly natural reaction to his mother's efforts to make anglomaniacs out of the children.' In February 1883 he had himself photographed in Highland costume and sent out the prints to a select group of admirers, with the moustache-twirling phrase, 'I bide my time,' written – sinisterly or hilariously depending on your point of view – along the bottom. The doyen of Berlin gossip, Fritz Holstein, a senior figure at the German Foreign Office, noted that the prince was said to be 'self-willed, devoid of all tenderness; an ardent soldier, anti-democratic, and anti-English. He shared the Kaiser's views on everything and had the greatest admiration for the Chancellor.' Bismarck, who still viewed Vicky and Fritz as a potential threat, was all too happy to exploit the growing rift between Wilhelm and his parents. He offered the prince chairs on government committees and found him a desk in the Foreign Office – all things denied to Fritz. His son Herbert, his closest political operative, ingratiated himself with Wilhelm. 'Willy and Henry are quite devoted to the Bismarck policy and think it sublime. So there we are, alone and sad,' Vicky wrote to her mother.

In a particularly flattering move, Bismarck sent Wilhelm to Russia in 1884, to attend the sixteenth birthday and coming-of-age of Tsarevich Nicholas, his second cousin,★ as the kaiser's representative. Diplomacy was regarded as the highest form of government, the preserve of monarchs and aristocrats. Willy brought a personal letter from Bismarck to Tsar Alexander III, proposing a renewal of the old Triple Alliance of Germany, Austria-Hungary and Russia, the *Dreikaiserbund*, against the rising forces of liberal democracy and anarchy. The visit was an astonishing success. Alexander, legendarily suspicious of foreigners, took to the 25-year-old Willy's upfront manner and frankness. The prince could be very charming. He had a liveliness and energy that cut through the etiquette and form that swaddled most royals and made him impressive and surprising on first meeting. Willy in turn succumbed to hero-

---

★ Wilhelm and the tsarevich were third cousins through their shared great-great-grandfather, Tsar Paul the Mad. Wilhelm's great-aunt Charlotte, sister of his grandfather the kaiser, had married Tsar Nicholas I, Nicholas's great-grandfather, making them also second cousins once removed.

worship – huge, bearded Alexander seemed to him the epitome of monarchical power. Foreign ministers on both sides commented excitedly about the chemistry between the two; the tsar agreed to consider the *Dreikaiserbund*, though nothing actually came of it because Austria-Hungary and Russia had too many unresolved rivalries to be able to work together. Wilhelm returned to Germany bathed in glory, with a high opinion of his own diplomatic skills and a new taste for the pomp, display and fuss of state visits – he'd adored being met at the station by the entire complement of grand dukes in uniform. More dangerously, he had also acquired a completely unrealistic idea of what they could accomplish.

On his return to Berlin, Willy decided to extend his diplomatic success by starting up a correspondence with the tsar. He told no one, not even the Bismarcks. In his first letter, in which he described himself as 'a blunt soldier unversed in the arts of diplomacy', he promised to devote himself to defending Russia against English plots. 'Can I ask you a favour?' he added. 'Don't trust the English Uncle,' meaning his uncle Bertie, the future Edward VII and Alexander's brother-in-law. In the letters he sent over the following year, Wilhelm described a series of English conspiracies against Russia in the Balkans, all headed by Uncle Bertie, 'owing to his false and intriguing nature'. He repeatedly denounced his parents, who were 'directed by the Queen of England'. In 1885, as war between Russia and Britain seemed inevitable, Wilhelm sent the tsar a series of notes he had made on English troop deployments on the Northern Indian frontier – information which he had extracted from the British military attaché in Berlin whom he had flatteringly befriended. Wilhelm still admired the tsar, but he also thought it would be useful for Germany if her two biggest rivals were at each other's throats, and the intended aim of the letters, he eventually confessed to Herbert von Bismarck, was to provoke a war between Russia and Britain: 'It would be such a pity if there was not war.' In fact war was avoided, as the tsar told Wilhelm two weeks later in a letter in which he thanked him for his information, 'as interesting as it was useful', and for the 'lively interest' he took in Russian affairs, adding that he believed that the 'traditional bonds which linked their two countries [Germany and Russia] together would always be the best guarantee of their success and prosperity'. Was there just the hint that Alexander thought the prince was laying it on a bit thick, that the old straightforward relationship was better? If there was, it did nothing to dislodge Wilhelm's growing liking for using personal correspondence to both ingratiate himself with, and manipulate, other monarchs, and his conviction that he had a particular talent for it.

The next time Wilhelm saw the tsar, however, in September 1886 at Russian army manoeuvres, Alexander was just a touch cooler than he had been, and Willy's flattering admiration for him, one of the tsar's ministers observed, seemed a little strained, even obsequious. During their private audience Wilhelm told the tsar several times that Russia had a 'right' to Constantinople and the Straits, and virtually urged him to invade Turkey – a hotspot where Russia and Britain clashed. The tsar told him, a little curtly maybe, that if Russia wanted Constantinople it wouldn't need Germany's permission to take it. Perhaps Wilhelm's clumsy attempts to prod him into military action had begun to arouse Alexander's suspicions.

Back in Germany the family's increasingly bitter split had spilled into the public arena. In 1884 Vicky had become determined to marry one of her younger daughters, Moretta, to Sandro of Battenburg, a minor German royal who had recently been installed as King of Bulgaria by the Russian government. Sandro had promptly bitten the hand that had put him there and positioned himself at the head of the Bulgarian independence movement, and now the Russians hated him, and looked upon all support of him as a deliberate attempt to undermine them in the Balkans, which they regarded as their backyard. The kaiser and Bismarck opposed the match, claiming it would endanger Germany's relations with Russia. In England, Queen Victoria was enthusiastically for it – Sandro's two brothers had married one of her daughters and one of her granddaughters, and she loathed Russia. Publicly, Vicky refused to acknowledge the political aspects of the match; privately, she had grandiose visions of ridding the Balkans of Russian influence. Wilhelm weighed in on Bismarck's side. He convinced himself that his mother and grandmother were masterminding an

English conspiracy to gain influence in the Balkans; he insisted that Sandro was not sufficiently well-born to marry royalty – his great-grandfather had been a valet. He was certainly jealous of his mother's very public approval of the dashingly handsome Sandro.

This enraged his English grandmother. 'That very foolish, undutiful and – I must add – unfeeling boy . . . I wish he could get a good "skelping"* as the Scots say,' Queen Victoria wrote furiously in 1885. She was also angry because Wilhelm had so blithely crossed the line from public to private. The queen believed in the mystique of royalty, she had kept her subjects at arms' length for fifty years. They knew very little about her and that was how she liked it. But Wilhelm had brought a family feud glaringly into the public gaze. This was not done. Even Bertie, whose foibles were periodically, if obliquely, aired in the press, never discussed or acknowledged his behaviour in public. The matter ground on for four years before Vicky finally let it go. (The now-deposed Sandro finally married an actress; Moretta eventually married Adolf of Schaumberg-Lippe). By then, Vicky's insistence on pushing the match through in the teeth of such resistance looked slightly unstable, as did Wilhelm's opposition – he said he would 'club the Battenburger to death' if he married his sister. 'The dream of my life,' Vicky wrote in 1887, just before her mother's Golden Jubilee, 'was to have a son who should be something of what our beloved Papa was – a real grandson of his in soul and intellect, a grandson of yours! . . . But one must guard against the fault of being annoyed with one's children for not being what one wished and hoped, what one wanted them to be!' She couldn't bear, however, to give up on Wilhelm entirely, and persisted in seeing him as a tool of Bismarck. 'He is a <u>card</u> here in the hands of the Chancellor's party . . . he means no harm . . .', Vicky told her mother. 'He hates her [Vicky] dreadfully,' one Berlin insider told another. 'His bitterness knows no bounds. What will become of all this?'

Wilhelm's feelings for Britain seemed no less violent but they were contradictory. He engineered an invitation to Queen

* A flogging.

Victoria's Jubilee celebrations in June 1887 – getting himself made his grandfather's official representative in Vicky and Fritz's place – 'to prove to my mother and all the English relations that I do not need them in order to be popular in England'. When his grandmother implied she would not be pleased to see him, he whipped himself into a fury. 'It was high time that the old woman died . . . One cannot have enough hatred for England,' he told Eulenburg. 'Well, England should look out when I have something to say about things . . .' After the Jubilee he complained bitterly that he had been treated with 'exquisite coldness'. The passion of his complaints caused unease in both British and German diplomatic circles. In November 1887 unease turned to anxiety when it became clear that not only was Willy's ninety-year-old grandfather finally failing, but his father, the crown prince, now diagnosed with throat cancer after months of confusion and misdiagnosis, was dying too. It wouldn't be long before the prince was kaiser.

Rather than bringing the family together, the terrible blow simply exposed the Oedipal struggle to more public scrutiny. Wilhelm more or less accused his mother of conniving to murder his father by delaying the diagnosis of the cancer and persuading him not to have the potentially life-saving – but also very dangerous – operation to remove it. He showed an unseemly keenness to get to the throne himself, arranging for close allies to suggest in public that his sick father renounce his claim so that he could succeed his grandfather directly. Fritz was said to be 'in deep grief that his son could hardly wait for his end'. Vicky, in denial and exasperatingly upbeat, alienated potential sympathizers, and Bismarck used his newspapers to show her in the worst possible light.

Shortly after Fritz's diagnosis, the British prime minister, Lord Salisbury, alarmed by reports of Wilhelm's Anglophobia and admiration for Russia, told the German Foreign Office that he feared that the prince's moods might dictate German foreign policy. Bismarck wrote personally to reassure him of the contrary. What Salisbury didn't realize was that Wilhelm was now as hostile to Russia as he was to England, and that his special relationship with Alexander was in shreds. Over the autumn of 1887 the most astonishing turn-about had taken place between Russia and

Germany – and in Wilhelm's head. By the winter the two countries were in the grip of a war scare. The Russians threatened to march into rebellious Bulgaria, an act which would inevitably draw in Austria-Hungary, its rival in the Balkans and Germany's ally. The circumstances were not dissimilar from those that would lead to the First World War, thirty years later.

Despite years of amicable relations, the Russians had become convinced that Germany was somehow colluding with Bulgaria and Austria-Hungary. This belief was subconsciously an acknowledgement that Germany was now a rival to Russia, no longer a junior ally. Though there was no substantial cause – as the German ambassador to St Petersburg observed, there was not 'the slightest possible reason' for war – Germany, especially Prussia, succumbed to a war scare. With the old emperor dying and his son mortally ill, the country felt vulnerable, and Russia's aggression revived old fears about the country's geographic vulnerability. Hysterical anti-Russian articles appeared in the press. Members of the army began talking about the need for a pre-emptive strike against Russia. Wilhelm agreed with them, convinced by the ambitious General Alfred von Waldersee, his would-be new mentor, who was obsessed with fighting a 'preventive war' against Russia. Bismarck had no desire for a war – though he was as responsible as anyone for the hysterical atmosphere in Germany, having for decades assiduously fanned fears of foreign invasion for his own political ends. To make it hard for the Russians to act, he closed the German stock market to Russian investment (though in such a way that it didn't look as if the initiative had come from him). This was a disaster for the Russian government which relied on the German markets for massive loans, and brought the tsar, along with his son Nicholas, on an emergency visit to Berlin in mid-November 1887. Bismarck said he couldn't reopen the German markets, but the visit cleared the air. The chancellor gave the Reichstag a dressing down, talked tough but accommodatingly to Russia, and the scare subsided. Wilhelm, however, failed to get the *tête à tête* he'd expected with the tsar, and spent two hours on a train platform in full dress uniform, waiting for him. Alexander's coolness rankled with him. 'HM did not speak a word to me about politics, and therefore I remained silent,' he reported huffily to Bismarck.

Within weeks, the gossip in St Petersburg was that Prince Wilhelm wanted 'war with Russia and was generally very anti-Russian'. 'In England,' Bismarck noted wearily, 'the opposite!'

2. George: coming second (1865)

In 1865, when George Frederick Ernest Albert Saxe-Coburg-Gotha was born, Britain was at the top of the pile, the world's financial and economic superpower, the greatest of Great Powers. Britain produced two-thirds of the world's coal, half its iron, well over half its steel, half its cotton and was engaged in 40 per cent of its trade. It was the most urbanized country on earth; London was the world centre of banking, insurance and commodity dealing. Its navy was the most powerful in the world. Its empire of 9.5 million square miles – increasing all the time – was the envy of the rest of Europe, providing lucrative markets and tremendous lustre. Despite areas of miserable poverty such as the East End of London and the newly industrialized towns of the North, Britain had the highest wages and cheapest food in Europe. Not without reason it was pleased with itself. It considered itself the great country of freedom and liberation, the world's civilizer – a claim which infuriated the rest of Europe, which considered Britain's claims to the moral high ground purest hypocrisy.

George's grandmother, Victoria, Queen of the United Kingdom of Great Britain and Ireland, now a reclusive widow, was despite this still perhaps the most vivid incarnation of Britain and its empire and the dominant figure in the family. Britain claimed to be both a monarchy and a democracy (which made no sense to people on the continent, where it was evident to everyone that the two couldn't mix, and democrats invariably lined up with republicans). In reality it was not quite either. The monarchy had, over the previous 200 years, been pretty much stripped of its powers and what it had left was increasingly symbolic; the democracy was more of an oligarchy run by the landed aristocracy which dominated the cabinet, parliament and local government, and populated the two main political parties, the Conservatives and the Liberals, both of which believed in free trade and the avoidance of expensive foreign wars (though they seemed unable to extricate themselves from a steady stream of small colonial ones). Power resided in the prime minister and his cabinet, who were in turn dependent on the confidence of the Houses of Parliament, and the monarch was obliged to follow their advice. Within the system the monarch played a necessary but entirely formal and ceremonial role: bills couldn't become laws, taxes couldn't be levied, ministers, judges, churchmen, ambassadors, army officers couldn't be appointed, peerages handed out or pardons given, without royal assent. The monarch was required to summon and dismiss parliament and appoint prime ministers, declare war or make peace. But there was no question that they could do any of this without having been told to do so by a government minister. What was left were the monarch's rather fuzzily defined 'rights' to be consulted, to encourage and to warn. The true balance of the relationship was decorously camouflaged by the tradition whereby British politicians addressed the sovereign in flatteringly subordinate language and the ceremonial of government which implied that the monarch was more important than she was. In the world of royalty appearances counted for a very great deal, and her subjects and the rest of the world continued to believe that she had power.

Unsurprisingly Queen Victoria didn't much like the idea that she had no function but to look decorative. She resented the description of herself as some kind of disguise, as the constitutional writer Walter Bagehot called her in 1867 – a 'retired widow' behind whose skirts a republic had 'insinuated itself'. Within the confines of her role, she pushed and manoeuvred her royal prerogatives, her 'rights', and exploited any advantage she had to make her convictions noted. These advantages weren't nugatory. Despite her constitutional powerlessness, the queen was en route to becoming the pre-eminent monarch in the whole world, and her dynasty (to some other royals' chagrin) the world's most prestigious royal family. This was primarily, of course, due to the empire and Britain's pre-eminent global position. Before the queen had come to the throne, the British royal family had been mired in rumours of madness, sex scandals, financial profligacy and mismanagement. But twenty-five years of careful investment and exploiting its advantages had somewhat restored the British monarchy itself – under Victoria, the family had become a bastion of irreproachable morality and family values; its jewels were now (with some help from mines in India and South Africa) as good if not better than the Romanovs' famous diamonds; its art treasures as good if not better than the Hapsburgs'; its palaces were perhaps not as numerous and vast but were more comfortable, its estates not as large but well managed, and its private incomes carefully massaged.

The queen's other secret weapon was her relationships with other foreign monarchs, most of whom exercised far more real power than she did. By the traditions of diplomacy they wrote to her as the head of state on matters of foreign affairs. This lent her an influence and weight in British foreign policy that the constitution no longer gave her. The queen worked to extend and tighten those relationships through her children's marriages – eight out of nine of them married into European reigning houses – and subsequently her grandchildren's. It would make her the matriarch of royal Europe. Even the tsarevich of Russia would call her Granny. There was thus some justification that she be kept abreast, as she insisted, of foreign affairs. She demanded, and was given, drafts of treaties, had each line discussed exhaustively. Finally, there was the fact that she was a woman and a widow, which made her seem unthreatening even when she was administering dressing-downs, and gave her considerable leeway in making interventions and giving the kind of 'advice' no prime minister would have taken from a male monarch.

The monarch was supposed to be neutral, detached from and above all political parties. The queen was convinced of her own rightness and was unashamedly partisan. She was also determined and energetic, pouring out letters to her prime ministers, who were obliged to answer her in their own handwriting. She could ignore, or at least strenuously query, the advice of her cabinet. She took an active dislike to some ministers while openly adoring others. Sometimes she wore her governments down. In 1881 she would complain so vociferously about the speech William Gladstone's cabinet had written for her for the opening of parliament that they would agree to amend it. Did she have a tangible effect on policy? She failed to stop her cabinets from doing what they were determined to do, but she could certainly hold things up – as more than one of her prime ministers had noted, handling her was like having a whole separate government department to deal with – and when her ideas chimed with public opinion she could be formidably hard to stop. But history was against her. The Great Reform Act of 1832 and its successor in 1867 expanded the franchise, began to clean up corrupt and archaic electoral practices (whereby, for example, the local aristocrat might effectively choose the local Member of Parliament), and pushed on the gradual but inexorable process of shifting power to the House of Commons. And as far as her ministers were concerned the monarch might give advice, and could sometimes be admirable, but had no real authority in government.

The other side of the British power equation was the aristocracy which dominated the upper echelons of government. The British aristocracy had a serious, deeply entrenched and self-conscious idea of itself as being both entitled to rule and obligated to serve. It was the most unmilitary and the richest aristocracy in Europe; Prussia's militarism was just the most exaggerated form of the continent-wide tendency of aristocrats to present themselves primarily as a soldier class. The British aristocracy's epiphanic moment had been the English Civil War: it had been almost destroyed by the Roundheads' standing army, the New Model Army. This had left it with a profound suspicion of standing armies such as the Germans and Russians had, and had forced it to win its power back by infiltrating parliament and government bureaucracy – institutions with which most European aristocracies scorned to dirty their hands. As a consequence Britain's volunteer army had remained relatively small and under parliamentary control ever since, and the navy had become the vehicle of British expansion. Proof that this worked was the huge empire. But it remained a puzzle to European politicians, German ones especially, who could never quite understand how Britain got along without a decent army.

The British aristocracy regarded serving in government as the highest profession for a gentleman. The power it still wielded made it quite different from the landed aristocracy of, for example, Russia, which had become, under the auspices of a tsarist regime eager to restrict its power, a largely decorative, urban class distanced from the land from which it derived its incomes. The implementation of policies that the more numerous but less well represented sections of society didn't necessarily favour was lubricated by Britain's wealth, and was helped by the roots of deference within the culture. But it also worked because aristocratic government lived in a fine balance with a genuinely functioning, mobilizable and much-vaunted public opinion, fuelled by the country's well-developed infrastructure of good roads, a reliable postal system and railways, alongside high literacy rates and a flourishing newspaper and debating culture. Public opinion – albeit of a relatively limited section of the 'public' – had genuinely existed as a force in Britain for almost a century; in most other European states it was only just starting to mobilize. Its successes were tangible; it had – eventually – forced on a reluctant parliament the abolition of slavery in Britain, and the first Reform Act of 1832. It meant that those without the vote still felt – or sometimes had the illusion – that they had a voice in the democracy. For the moment, however, though the electorate was expanding, the aristocracy showed little sign of being dislodged from its position.

As if to celebrate the success of the British upper classes, in a piece of triumphant cultural imperialism, the image of the English gentleman was becoming the most appealing manifestation of wealth and status across Europe, if not the world. By the 1890s European grandees, Silesian millionaires, Austrian and Russian grand dukes would be taking up tennis, golf, fox-hunting, shooting and ordering their suits from Savile Row and their guns from Purdey. Wealthy Russians would aspire to what Vladimir Nabokov, scion of an aristocratic Russian family, called 'the comfortable products of Anglo-Saxon civilization' – Pears soap, Golden Syrup, fruitcake, Huntley and Palmer's biscuits, toothpaste, playing cards, striped blazers, tennis balls and collapsible rubber baths – purchased from Druce, the English shop on Nevsky Prospekt.

★

The future George V was six years younger than his first cousin Wilhelm and could hardly have been more different. While Willy was idiosyncratic, quick, assertive and determined always to come first, George was resigned to being unremarkable. He was a second son, destined to live in the shadow of his brother, and the family environment seemed to encourage a kind of comfortable mediocrity; neither of his parents was exercised by the idea of having to prove oneself, academically or otherwise. George's father, Albert Edward, the future Edward VII, known in the family as Bertie, had reacted violently against his father's educational expectations, while his beautiful Danish mother, Alexandra, was cheerfully non-intellectual. Bertie admired and loved his older sister Vicky, but the lesson he had drawn from their childhood was the direct opposite of hers. He hated their father's rigorous educational regime.

From the age of three, Bertie's every waking moment had been crammed with improving experiences. 'I had no childhood,' he would say much later, and his early years were, by pretty much everyone's estimation but his parents', wretched. Bertie had fought back with sullen resistance and hysterical tantrums; he was rewarded with more pressure and discipline, sterner punishment, and most miserably the withholding of affection and isolation from other children. His rebellion brought out the absolute worst in both parents: Albert was unimpressed and unrelenting; Victoria endlessly bemoaned her son's 'backwardness', his frivolity and his failure to be just like his father. For his seventeenth birthday she sent him a memo reminding him that 'Life is composed of duties,' and sacked the tutor with whom, despite everything, he'd built a warm relationship. He emerged, aged eighteen, in 1859, a 'disappointment', with an appetite – a large one – for life at its less unserious and most sybaritic: he liked clothes, smoking, shooting, society, gambling, food and girls. Food and girls especially. 'His intellect is of no more use than a pistol packed at the bottom of a trunk if one were attacked in the robber-infested Apennines,' said his mother. At Oxford, despite his parents' best efforts to imprison him among a bunch of elderly celibate dons, he found his way to the richest, louchest, most high-living students. Two years later, on military training in Ireland, he managed to have a fling with a local girl even though he'd been confined to barracks. When the story got back to England, Albert wrote Bertie a hysterical letter painting a future of blackmail and paternity suits, and died a month later in December 1861. Though it was typhoid and sheer exhaustion that killed him, Victoria blamed Bertie. 'Oh! that boy,' she wrote, 'much as I pity him I never can or shall look on him without a shudder.' Within a few years Bertie was famous throughout Europe as the playboy Prince of Wales, celebrated for his immaculate dress, a string of public scandals and his passion for Paris and its *demi-monde*, turning up in Emile Zola's 1879 novel *Nana*, thinly disguised as the 'Prince of Scots', admiring the protagonist's fabulous breasts with 'an air of connoisseurship'.

Victoria determined to marry the 22-year-old Bertie off quickly, and recruited Vicky to find a suitable princess. Having unsuccessfully trawled the German courts, she came up with Princess Alexandra, the beautiful daughter of the soon-to-be Danish king. Her father, Christian, a captain of the Danish Royal Guard, was the godchild of the King of Denmark, who had decided to name him as his heir in 1852. The royals-to-be had lived in genteel poverty in Copenhagen for most of Alexandra's childhood – she had shared a room with her sisters Dagmar and Thyra, and had made her own clothes – and experienced a quite extraordinary change in status. Within two years of Christian's accession in 1863 they had colonized royal Europe. Alexandra married the heir to the British throne; her sister Dagmar married the heir to the Russian empire. Their seventeen-year-old brother William was invited to become King of Greece by the Greek national assembly. The Danish royal family were – perhaps because of their relatively normal upbringing – very much themselves: a bunch of close-knit extroverts, known for being outdoorsy, informal, uncultured and unsophisticated: 'The special joke was to make funny noises and yell if they saw anyone trying to write a letter.' King Christian had no interest in books but pronounced ideas about exercise, and had taught his children gymnastics. Queen Victoria considered the Danes noisy, clannish and frivolous, but envied their closeness: 'They are wonderfully united – and never breathe one word against each other, and the daughters remain as unspoilt and as completely

Children of the Home as when they were unmarried. I do admire this . . .' Alexandra was lively, rode a horse stylishly, had a taste for staying up late, and was beautiful. Bertie met her precisely twice before he proposed. They married in 1863. The queen – still punishing her son – insisted it be a private wedding, wore widow's black and refused to attend the wedding lunch.

Nevertheless, Alexandra was a great hit in Britain, which had been starved of royal spectacle since Victoria had shut herself away after Albert's death. Tennyson christened her 'the Sea king's daughter from across the sea'. As for Bertie, he was bowled over by her beauty and warmth. She was bowled over by her new life. They were both gregarious, spontaneous and irredeemably extravagant – within a few years Bertie was overspending his income by £20,000 a year – and despite Queen Victoria's attempts to prescribe who they saw and what they did – she forbade Alexandra to ride in Hyde Park – they quickly became the centre of the most fashionable clique in London, the Marlborough House set, named after their mansion on Pall Mall. Their doings and those of their friends began to be enthusiastically written about and even occasionally photographed in the British newspapers' embryonic society and gossip columns. Naturally, Victoria disapproved. 'Are you aware that Alix has the smallest brain ever seen? I dread that – with his small, empty brain – very much for future children,' she wrote to Vicky. 'The melancholy thing,' one of Alexandra's ladies-in-waiting wrote of Bertie, 'is that neither he nor the darling princess ever care to open a book.'

In fact, Bertie was by no means stupid. Nor was he only frivolous – though his mother conspired to make him so by refusing him any serious occupation. He was an odd combination: he could be impressively far-seeing, then absurdly trivial-minded. He was selfish, he was generous; he had such a fear of boredom he couldn't bear to be alone or unoccupied for a minute; he was affectionate, courteous and tactful, and despite his mother's endless criticism, extremely patient and polite to her. He was also prone to sudden terrifying rages prompted by the most banal things – a spot of food on his shirt, a child's fidget. These were manifestations of long-suppressed frustrations. He was quick to learn, when he could be bothered, and had an excellent memory. By the time he was six he could speak three languages. But his misery in his father's classroom had turned him off books, education and culture; he felt he didn't need them. Despite his rather unappealing, popping, pale Hanoverian eyes, he had real, bona fide charm. 'He had a capacity for enjoying life, which is always attractive,' one British aristocrat observed, 'but which is specially so when it is combined with a positive and strong desire that everyone else should enjoy life too.' The combination of his crushing childhood and the early realization that charm could be powerful had produced a very unroyal desire to please and make people like him – qualities his parents, famous for their own charmlessness, saw little use for. Royalty should be sufficient unto itself, Queen Victoria believed, and she told her children they should never be seen laughing in public.

Bertie and Alexandra's first child and the heir, Albert Victor, was born in 1864. George – inevitably Georgie, European royalty seemed obsessed with diminutives – arrived eighteen months later, on 3 June 1865 at 1.30 in the morning, a couple of hours after Alexandra had held a dinner party. 'Very small and not very pretty,' was Queen Victoria's comment. She had got over her initial excitement at grandchildren, and now found them 'dismayingly numerous'. Her main preoccupation was ensuring that all her male grandchildren were called Albert. Bertie and Alexandra had developed strategies for obliquely heading off his mother's interference. Albert Victor was known by everyone as 'Eddy'. Bertie insisted on 'George Frederick' for his second son. 'I cannot admire the names you propose,' the queen answered. '. . . Of course you will add <u>Albert</u> at the end.' Four more siblings followed over the next six years: three daughters – Louise, Victoria and Maud – and a son, who died shortly after birth in 1871. Having children inevitably slowed Alexandra down, while Bertie's appetites remained undiminished. Within a year of Georgie's birth there were rumours that he was seeing an actress called Hortense Schneider, and that on a trip to St Petersburg he had 'admired' various women. Then in 1867, in the course of giving birth to her first daughter, Alexandra came down with rheumatic fever. For several hours she was thought to be near death. Bertie, out late at the Windsor races, had to be summoned three times before he finally came to her sickbed. In fear or boredom, he found it hard to stay. Alexandra took months to recover, and one of the after-effects was the onset of deafness that made it difficult for her to function in large groups – or to keep up with Bertie. Elegantly and discreetly she retired into her family. Her dignified silence made it far easier for society to accept Bertie's string of more or less public liaisons; her life as a quiet-living, rural matriarch provided an impeccably respectable counterpoint to his involvement in a series of public scandals. An unspoken dynamic evolved: she punished him in small ways – by always being blithely and chaotically late for everything, while he was obsessively punctual (as his son would later be). He in turn was both gallant and neglectful, never losing his temper with her, loyal except where women or sex was concerned.

This was especially apparent over foreign loyalties – sometimes to dramatically divisive effect. In 1864, barely a year into their marriage, Prussia bullied Denmark into handing over the duchy of Schleswig-Holstein by massing its army on the Danish border. The liberal British press demanded naval intervention on plucky little Denmark's side. Victoria and Vicky's allegiances were with Prussia. Bertie, who found Alexandra weeping each night over her country's humiliation, came out publicly for Denmark. He offered to liaise between his Danish father-in-law and England, and even ill-advisedly contacted the Liberal opposition to show his support, an act that so enraged his mother, who was exercising every ounce of her influence to prevent Britain from intervening, that she used it as an excuse to deprive him of any political experience or influence for the next twenty years. 'Oh! if Bertie's wife was only a good German and not a Dane! . . . It is terrible to have the poor boy on the wrong side,' she wrote to Vicky. Schleswig-Holstein left Alexandra with a lasting animus again Prussia. 'How I hate the hated Germans and most of all the Prussians, who are the most unreliable, false and disgusting people who exist,' she wrote to her sister Dagmar in 1864. She took every opportunity to make her resentment clear: cutting the Prussian ambassador and refusing to speak to her sister-in-law Helena's new German husband in 1865;* refusing to leave her compartment when the Queen of Prussia arrived to meet her train on a stop at Koblenz in 1866; insulting the Prussian king in 1867 when he offered to visit the couple at Wiesbaden. The queen was furious and issued a reprimand. Thereafter Alexandra was more circumspect about expressing her dislike.

Despite his deep fondness for Vicky, Bertie's sympathy for Bismarck's Prussia was increasingly tested. He wanted to support his wife, and the Prussian press regularly criticized him. It was a useful way for Bismarck to smear Vicky and the German liberals who took their inspiration from British democracy, as dangerous and potentially treasonous. The prince was impressively cool about his treatment in public; he recognized that Germany was a traditional ally, and even cultivated Bismarck's ambitious son Herbert. But underneath he smarted, and sometimes he invited criticism. During the Franco-Prussian War, with Alexandra willing the French to win, Bertie unwisely told the Prussian ambassador that he hoped Prussia would be taught a lesson; the ambassador made a formal complaint and Bertie was forced, humiliatingly, to write to the British prime minister, Gladstone, explaining himself.

As a consequence of Alexandra's abiding resentment of Prussia – and the fact that Queen Victoria avoided having more than one set of grandchildren staying at any one time – George and his siblings did not get to know their older Prussian cousins, particularly Willy, as well as they might. By the time Vicky was visiting regularly with her younger children, Willy was off at school and, one suspects, felt himself a little too important for his younger cousins. Marie of Romania, a first cousin to both George and Wilhelm, wrote irritatedly of 'the rough, off-hand manner with which [Wilhelm] liked to treat us, as though we were not really worthy of his attention'.

By contrast, Alexandra vigorously encouraged friendship between her children and their Russian cousins – the children of her sister Dagmar, now renamed Marie, but called Minny in the family, and the heir to the Russian throne, Tsarevich Alexander – even

* Christian of Schleswig-Holstein, whose family had sided with Prussia.

though England and Russia were arch-rivals and absolutely hated each other. Alexandra and Minny remained very close, kept up a regular and intense correspondence, and were determined to bring their families closer together. Both women trod a fine line between being familial and political. Both presented themselves as domestic and uninterested in politics. But in 1873, when Minny, the tsarevich and their five-year-old son, Nicholas, came to London, the sisters made intricate arrangements to wear identical outfits all the way through the visit, a startling image that made front pages everywhere. In 1874 they encouraged and brought about the unlikely marriage between the tsar's only daughter, Grand Duchess Marie, reputed to be the richest woman in the world, and Bertie's boorish younger brother Alfred (known, naturally, as Affie), in the hope that it might improve relations between Britain and Russia. It didn't. They also took every opportunity to meet on visits to the Danish king and queen – known to all their grandchildren as 'Apapa', and 'Amama' – on their estates at Fredensborg and Bernstorff in Denmark. Bertie, who found his Danish in-laws unbearably dull, tried not to look bored. (The English entourage, taking their cue from him, sniggeringly referred to Alexandra's mother as 'droning Louise' – *dronning* is Danish for queen.) He also went out of his way to be accommodating to his Russian brother-in-law, despite the two countries' mutual antipathy and the fact that he had almost nothing in common with the wilfully taciturn and rough-round-the-edges Alexander. He even wrote regular – if rather banally domestic – letters to his sister-in-law Minny. George, meanwhile, became special friends with his eldest cousin, Nicholas, who was three years younger than him.

Despite the huge span of their grandmother's interests and their father's international social life, the childhood of George and his siblings – unlike that of their cousin Wilhelm – was quiet, isolated and unworldly. They were raised on the remote 7,000-acre north Norfolk estate of Sandringham, which Bertie had bought in 1862 and modernized at enormous cost. Sandringham was the height of modern British aristocratic comfort and everything was new: the furniture, the pictures, the books (which, according to his private secretary, were mostly 'trash') and the thirty flushing lavatories ordered from Thomas Crapper and Co. It was there that Alexandra established herself, punctuating her time with long trips with the children to her parents' house parties in Denmark, while Bertie was in Paris or London. The children grew up simply and relatively informally – as Alexandra had herself – under big East Anglian skies, surrounded by nature, lots of servants and a menagerie of dogs, monkeys, parrots, horses, cattle and sheep, but far away from other children, their father's social set and national events. They were unaware of how their grandmother's reclusiveness and their father's rackety lifestyle and large debts had combined to make the monarchy unpopular, sparking a brief flurry of republicanism in the late 1860s and early 1870s (which, however, was largely stilled by Bertie's dramatic bout of near-fatal typhoid in 1871).

The queen, who liked to repeat that her grandchildren should not grow up arrogant or grand – traits she did not check in herself – approved. 'They are dear intelligent and most thoroughly unpretending children, who are never allowed to be "great Princes" than which there is no greater mistake,' she wrote to Vicky. Alexandra was an enthusiastic mother, who unlike most aristocratic parents enjoyed playing boisterously with her children, and like plenty of royals encouraged interminable practical jokes. Practical jokes were a pan-European royal habit, perhaps a consequence of not being allowed to laugh in public, and predicated on the usually unconscious acknowledgement that those below them in rank couldn't complain. There were apple-pie beds and soda-siphon squirting; Alexandra would even allow them on occasion to disappear under the lunch table to pinch the legs of unsuspecting guests – Benjamin Disraeli was one victim. Later, when the children's education began, their parents were only too keen to disrupt lessons with impromptu breakouts from the schoolroom. The result was that as young children the Waleses were known for being rather over-boisterous. Constance de Rothschild, cousin of Bertie's friend Nathan de Rothschild, meeting them at Sandringham one Christmas, recalled their appetite for 'romping' and blind man's buff. 'The Princess said to me: "They are dreadfully wild. But I was just as bad."' In 1872, when George was seven, the queen observed, 'They are such ill-bred, ill-trained children, I can't fancy them at all.' George was by common consent the most physically robust and jolly of the Wales children when they were little: the queen noted when he was three that Bertie's children looked 'most wretched – excepting Georgie who is always merry and rosy'. There was a story that as a small boy, after being reprimanded by the queen for some small piece of naughtiness at lunch and having been sent to sit under the table in punishment, George emerged at her summons, entirely naked. Constance de Rothschild reported that he had 'a jolly little face' and 'looked the cleverest'. By comparison, Eddy, the heir, was fragile: when he was a baby, the queen had described him as 'fairy-like, placid and melancholy'. More worryingly, by the age of six he was generally regarded as languid and listless.

It wasn't all a country idyll. 'The house of Hanover,' a courtier who knew George very well told his biographer Harold Nicolson, 'like ducks, produce bad parents. They trample on their young.' (That remark did not make it into the biography.) Alexandra was a very intense and loving parent but also an erratic and selfish one. For all her graceful acceptance of her husband's systematic unfaithfulness, Bertie's behaviour had actually been a horrible shock. (Years later she admitted to Margot Asquith how totally surprised she had been to be supplanted. 'But I thought I was so-o-o beautiful,' she sighed.) Whether or not she loved Bertie, she was deprived of the exciting life she had enjoyed so much and of Bertie's attention; and her increasing deafness made all social interaction much harder.★ In textbook style, she turned to her children for compensation. Deafness and her retirement into the family seemed to halt her maturity – fixing her for ever at twenty-two, with an ever-youthful face to match. She was a charming, kind, not especially self-aware, slightly superficial girl who never really grew up – another way in which she and Bertie, who slowly

★ The extent of Alexandra's deafness can be gauged by a Russian grand duke's account of a visit in the 1880s. He was taken aback by how everyone had to bellow in her company: 'A stranger walking into the dining room of the palace would have thought he was witnessing a family quarrel.'

did achieve a measure of maturity, grew apart. She and the children became a tight-knit group, a mutual admiration society, resistant to outsiders, the children intensely dependent upon her. Even George's irreproachably correct first biographer concluded that the intensity of Alexandra's demands retarded her boys' development 'to maturity and self confidence'. 'I shall always find my little Georgie quite the same and unchanged in every respect,' she insisted when he was nineteen, and sent him 'a great big kiss for your lovely little face', when he was twenty-five.

George adored her. His letters to her were by far the most expressive and open he ever wrote – not least perhaps because she couldn't hear his words. But Alexandra also conjured anxiety. Passionate avowals of love alternated with periods of neglect, which did little for George's confidence. By the habits of the time and the milieu, her absences – to Egypt when George was three, for example – weren't perhaps that remarkable. But this contrasted with her insistence that her children provide her with love and attention. When George was ten, in 1875, she took her daughters to Denmark for three months, while Bertie went on a six-month trip to India. She failed to write to Eddy and Georgie once, and on the night of her return wrote them a self-serving letter:

> My own Darling little Georgie,
>
> Mother-dear was so delighted to get so many nice dear little letters from her little boys, and I should certainly have answered these long ago but you told me not to do so if I could not find the time – which really was the case; and I was much touched by my little Georgie remembering how busy his Mother-dear very often is . . . I have just received your dear last letter and I too nearly cried that I should not see my darling boys tonight to give them a kiss each before going to bed.

A member of the royal household told George's biographer that Alexandra had 'bullied the whole family'. She certainly ensured that George's sister Toria never married, and became, as her friend and Russian cousin Olga (sister of the future Nicholas II) observed, 'just a glorified maid' to her mother. 'Mama,' George told his wife years later, 'as I have always said, is one of the most selfish people I know.'

As for Bertie, he loved his sons (though he neglected his rather plain daughters), but he was frequently absent, and when he was present, his personality threatened to swamp theirs. George behaved with almost slavish devotion to his father – it was often noted how 'constantly he subordinated not only his inclinations but his whole nature to his father's' – seeking his judgement and opinion on the smallest things. They never argued. George held a special place in his father's affections. Bertie's friend Lord Esher noted how when he spoke of George it was 'with a softening of the voice and a look – half smile and half pathos, which he reserved for those he loved' – though one nephew claimed that his affection derived from George's willingness to 'be his slave'.

George's feelings about his father were not straightforward though, however much he wanted them to be. His letters to Bertie were the diametric opposite of those to his mother – stiff, correct and unrevealing; even his biographer described them as 'stilted and colourless'. As an adult he freely admitted that he had been frightened of his father, adding approvingly that his own sons ought to be scared of him – and they were. According to the Prince of Wales's wry and perceptive private secretary, Frederick Ponsonby, who liked his master – he described him as 'lovable, wayward and human' – everyone was scared of Bertie, except his mother and his wife. George's sister Louise once fainted on the way to Buckingham Palace to see him. Eddy told a friend at university that he was 'rather afraid of his father, and aware that he was not quite up to what his father expected of him'. Bertie didn't see himself as a scary father – he recalled his own miserable childhood and wrote: 'if children are too strictly or perhaps, too severely treated, they get shy and only fear those whom they ought to love'. But he could be insensitive. He would 'chaff' – tease – a little too hard, and then a bit harder still, and his victims felt unable to answer back. His unhappy childhood had left him with a tendency for sudden, unpredictable rages, as well as periods of profound depression and moments of brusqueness, when an almost panicky fear of boredom suddenly surfaced. Overshadowing the

relationship between father and son was Bertie's public and constant betrayal of George's adored mother – a subject that could
never be discussed. Bertie would even write to George about his
women – a letter from 1881 shows him telling his teenage son
about his mistress Lillie Langtry's projected stage debut. His
involvement in various public scandals – usually about women or
gambling – was everything George's moral education condemned.

There were other pressures on Georgie too. From an early age
he knew his prime function was as his brother Eddy's 'stiffener'.
At seven, European princes left the nursery, Eddy acquired a
tutor and Georgie came too. John Neale Dalton was an ambitious
32-year-old curate with an impressively booming voice, chosen
by the queen to take her grandsons in hand. Not long after the
boys had come under his care, Dalton told Bertie and Alexandra
that Eddy had an 'abnormally dormant condition of mind'. He
seemed unable to concentrate, and Dalton suspected he might
even have 'some affliction of the brain'. The solution, Dalton
concluded, was to slow down his teaching, and to use Georgie to
support him. From the age of six or seven it was impressed upon
Georgie, in whom Dalton saw a tendency to 'fretfulness', that his
role was to bolster and protect his older brother.

By the time he was twelve, George was a correct, rather careful
little boy – qualities particularly apparent in his relationship with
the queen. Whereas Willy never felt intimidated by her, once he
was out of the nursery Georgie approached Victoria with fear and
awe. His letters to her were dutiful and impersonal. He hoped that
'Dear Grandmama' was 'quite well' and informed her that he was
'quite well'. (By contrast Willy's letters burst with energy and
idiosyncracy. 'I am so sorry that you are sad,' he wrote, aged ten.
He had planned to come and comfort her 'but I could not because
I had too much to do'. When she invested him with the Order of
the Garter in 1877 when he was eighteen, he thanked her for
'admitting me into that illustrious brotherhood of Knights. I can
assure you, beloved Grandmama that I was quite speechless with
astonishment, when my dear Mama told me that I was going to
be invested with this highest order in Christendom.') To her
younger grandchildren Victoria must have seemed mainly a source

of lectures. At some point she'd send each grandchild a watch and a homily. George got his when he was eight: 'Be very punctual in everything and very exact in all your duties,' she told him, '. . . I hope you will be a good, obedient, truthful boy, kind to all, humble-minded, dutiful and always trying to be of use to others! Above all, God-fearing and striving always to do His Will.' George would try to be all these things, but above all he would be obsessively punctual.

Aged twelve, in 1877, Georgie became the youngest and smallest boy on HMS *Britannia*, a kind of public school for naval cadets, anchored off the town of Dartmouth in Devon. Eddy and Dalton came too. Queen Victoria had suggested that Eddy go to public school – an idea just as revolutionary in England as it had been in Germany, and clearly inspired by Vicky's example. 'Good boys,' she wrote, hopefully, 'of whatever birth, should equally be allowed to associate with them to prevent the early notion of pride and superiority of position which is detrimental to young Princes.' Dalton reported that despite his efforts, Eddy wasn't up to it; both boys were behind their peers and in his opinion Eddy needed Georgie to be his crutch:

Prince Albert Victor requires the stimulus of Prince George's company to induce him to work at all . . . The mutual influence of their characters on one another . . . is very beneficial . . . Difficult as the education of Prince Albert Victor is now, it would be doubly or trebly so if Prince George were to leave him. Prince George's lively presence is his mainstay and chief incentive to exertion; and to Prince George again the presence of his elder brother is most wholesome as a check against that tendency to self conceit which is apt at times to show itself in him. Away from his brother, there would be a great risk of his being made too much of and treated as a general favourite.

Victoria thought the navy 'a very rough sort of life', but reluctantly agreed to Dalton's 'experiment'. How George felt isn't clear. There are several references from this period to his picking fights with Eddy and finding fault with him; on the other hand, neither wanted to leave home and they at least had each other.

The queen was a little preoccupied elsewhere. She was about to become an empress – Empress of India, that is. She had persuaded her favourite prime minister, Benjamin Disraeli, to pass an act through parliament giving her the title in 1876. Bertie thought it 'grandiose'. 'I could never consent to the word "Imperial" being added to my name,' he told Disraeli disapprovingly. It was widely rumoured that the queen had become rather jealous of the proliferation of emperors on the continent – the Russian, Hapsburg and now the new German emperor – and had decided that she, too, ought to be imperial, though she knew the British wouldn't stomach an empress at home. It was also less good-humouredly suggested, and not only by the Liberal opposition, that Disraeli was encouraging in the queen, whom he shamelessly flattered, an unrealistic idea of her own position. 'Is there not just a risk,' one of his cabinet colleagues asked gently, 'of encouraging her in too large an idea of her own personal power, and too great an indifference to what the public expects? I only ask; it is for you to judge.' One reason the measure passed may well have been because the queen was female: it's hard to imagine any British parliament willingly making a male monarch emperor of anything – it would have felt too autocratic. In return for her title, however, Disraeli managed to get through – unhindered by the bullying obdurance that the queen had been known to employ – a series of innovative social bills, including the Trades Union Act and the Public Health Act. It was perhaps no coincidence that the queen seemed to interfere less with domestic legislation after she became empress – though she still had plenty to say on foreign, military and imperial issues.

Like Wilhelm, George did not enjoy school. 'It never did me any good to be a Prince, I can tell you, and many was the time I wished I hadn't been,' he complained years later with what would become a characteristic tinge of self-pity. '. . . So far from making allowances for our disadvantages, the other boys made a point of taking it out on us on the grounds that they'd never be able to do it later on.' He was small for his age and the younger boys would force him to challenge the older boys to fight. 'I'd get a hiding time and again.' Only a particularly bad thump on the nose got him off fighting for good. The bigger boys made him buy sweets for them and bring them aboard illegally. 'I was always found out and got into trouble in addition to having the stuff confiscated. And the worst of it was, it was always *my* money; they never paid me back.' No doubt the bullying was not helped by the fact that George had certain privileges. Instead of sharing with the other boys, he and Eddy had a cabin of their own, servants, and Dalton – under whose supervision George did no better than mediocrely. Perhaps the juxtaposition of his sense of royalty and the democracy of having to compete with other boys, was – as it had been for Willy – uncomfortable. The royal family liked to talk about appearing normal, and being 'humble', but they didn't really believe it. Dalton, who was genuinely fond of George, didn't help by discouraging the boys from mixing with their contemporaries – even though HMS *Britannia* was stuffed with the sons of British grandees. George was taught to keep his distance from other people, Dalton and Eddy remained his world. This would be particularly harsh for him, because while Eddy would turn out to have something of his father's charm and talent for socializing, George was shy, and never mastered the art of making friends easily.

He left *Britannia* aged fourteen, for a three-year round-the-world cruise on a naval training ship, the *Bacchante*. He was still small at four foot ten. 'Victoria [his grandmother] says "So old and so small"!!!' his mother wrote, helpfully. 'Oh my! You will have to make haste to grow or I shall have that sad disgrace of being the mother of a dwarf!!!' (George would never be tall – about five foot six at most – the same height as Willy and Nicholas.) And Eddy was still in tow. Alexandra had been told by a senior commander that his time on board had been a complete failure, but she refused to separate the boys. Dalton came too. He now claimed that Eddy's failings would be even more evident at a public school and anyway, a boat would allow him to keep the boys away from 'evil associations'.

During his three years on the *Bacchante* George saw the Mediterranean, South America, South Africa, Australia, Japan, China, Singapore, Egypt and the Holy Land; shot albatrosses, exchanged photographs with a Zulu chief and his four wives, almost got caught up in the first Boer War, encountered ostriches, saw the twelve stations of the Cross in Jerusalem, had a dragon tattooed on his arm in Tokyo, met the Mikado, was nearly shipwrecked off Southern Australia, experienced the street smells of Peking, travelled in gold barges down the Nile, and adopted a baby kangaroo. But all this failed to imbue him with a sense of curiosity or excitement about the world. A further ten years in the navy, during which he became the best-travelled British prince ever, left him with an active dislike of being abroad. Ships made him seasick and he never stopped missing his family. Setting off on his first two-year cruise, aged fifteen, he had written to his mother, 'As we sang hymns I could not help thinking of you. I think this last parting was horrible and I think what you said was true, that it made it much worse, us having to wait in the hall till dear Papa came, because none of us could speak, we were all crying so much.' At nineteen, he tentatively voiced to his father a desire to give up the navy; the latter made it clear that this was impossible, and George dutifully accepted his fate. But at twenty-one, parting was quite as painful. 'I miss you so very much and felt so sorry when I had to say goodbye,' he wrote after missing a family birthday. 'How much I wish I was going to be there too, it almost makes me cry when I think of it. I wonder who will have that sweet little room of mine; you must go and see it sometimes and imagine that your little Georgie dear is living in it.'

In hindsight it seems obvious that Dalton was a bad teacher whose expectations of his pupils seemed to diminish with the years. George's well-educated wife, Queen Mary, admitted years later that it was slightly shocking that 'the king had not been taught more', and that Dalton had 'never really tried to educate the princes'. Like Willy's tutor Hinzpeter – though less sinisterly – he was extraordinarily successful at laying his own inadequacies at the feet of his pupils. The more he gravely reported the princes' shortcomings, the more the family seemed to admire him. 'What a fearless, honest man he is,' Queen Victoria recorded in her journal in 1877 after another dismal piece of educational news. Others were less charitable. 'What on earth has stupid Dalton been about all these years!' the queen's lady-in-waiting Lady Geraldine Somerset wondered incredulously, and George's Russian aunt Marie was 'withering' about his 'ignorance'. Whether or not Eddy was quite as inadequate as Dalton claimed, after twelve years of his teaching George was said to be 'deficient in even the most elementary subjects', including basic spelling and grammar. Geography, a cousin remarked, 'had not been his strong point', nor could he converse comfortably in French or German, the absolute bottom line of a royal education. Dalton camouflaged his failings by publishing a two-volume, 1,400-page work, *The Cruise of the Bacchante*, implausibly attributed to the two princes but written entirely by him – full of Latin quotations and flamboyant moralistic descriptions. As an adult, George freely acknowledged it to 'be one of the dullest books ever written'.

It's possible that George might have been dyslexic – a condition completely unrecognized in the nineteenth century, and now perhaps an over-fashionable explanation for all manner of learning problems. But his difficulties with spelling, basic grammar and languages, despite years of effort, all fit this diagnosis, as did his problems with writing, which George found torture his whole life. The art historian Sir Kenneth Clark, whom he appointed Surveyor of the King's Pictures in the early 1930s, reckoned he'd never seen anyone find the sheer act of writing so laborious – a classic dyslexic's problem. His cousin Marie of Romania, known as Missy, recalled his 'wrinkled brow' while 'labouring' through letters. Dyslexia would have fed characteristics very evident in George as an adult: anxiety and lack of confidence, a desire for the familiar and fear of the new. And it would have given an extra poignancy and discomfiting complexity to the expression of his feelings. Because of Alexandra's deafness, much of what George wanted to say to her couldn't be expressed verbally. Letters became the most direct way of communicating with her, and the vehicles of George's gentler emotions. They would later become almost the only way he would be able to express love and intimacy to his wife. At the same time, because writing was so hard for him, the expression of feelings – hard enough for many upper-class Englishmen – became associated with difficulty and discomfort.

It was a mark of how deeply George felt wedded to his duty that despite the exhaustion of writing, he began a diary at thirteen and stubbornly forced himself to write it every day until his death in 1936. The volumes are for the most part deadly, the acme of pedestrianism. 'My word they are dull,' his biographer Harold Nicolson wrote privately. They showed the evaporation of his childhood liveliness – and perhaps also a dyslexic's reluctance to move beyond the most basic phrases. Their pages gave almost no sign of interior life, recording day after day the weather, the time he rose, ate and went to bed, and important anniversaries.

The truth was the family colluded in the children's backwardness. Alexandra didn't want them to grow up and leave her, and not even Bertie wanted them to turn out like him. 'Our greatest wish,' he wrote to his mother, 'is to keep them simple pure and childlike as long as it is possible.' Neither could really see the point of academic application. The queen liked the idea of a more vigorous, democratic education in principle, but in practice her sense of caste and tradition (and fear of them turning out like Bertie) was too strong to override her desire for things to remain reliably, even if disappointingly, the same. She believed royalty must be set apart – not least to preserve itself intact – and must never get close to commoners. Even aristocrats were questionable. One could really relax only among other royals. She was far from alone in her beliefs: most royal educations were as limited and lonely as George's; most taught royal and aristocratic children to suppress their own will and not look beyond their circumstances, not be curious or questioning. The Grand Duchess Marie Romanov, a Russian cousin of Tsar Nicholas II, writing about her own education – which was, she said, 'strictly in accord with the standards and rules which prevailed in almost all the courts of Europe in the later part of the nineteenth century' – described how 'every expression of will or independence was at once suppressed'. In hindsight she felt it produced minds conditioned 'towards the banal and the conventional . . . somehow the education that was given us atrophied our powers and limited our horizons'. It's hard not to feel that George's education had just such an effect on him.

In 1883 Eddy was sent to Cambridge – 'How much I miss you in everything *all day long*,' he wrote to his brother – and Georgie, after several months in the North Atlantic, went to Greenwich naval college. Aged nineteen, he continued to be 'protected' from any normal experiences. He wasn't allowed outside the college at all except for sports and then only if accompanied. Balls and dances were forbidden. His letters were read and answered for him. Returning to the college one night with his military governor in a hansom cab, he asked if he might pay the driver – he'd never done it before – then had to borrow the fare. For his twentieth birthday in June 1885, Queen Victoria wrote him a thundering letter, exhorting him to

Avoid the many evil temptations wh. beset all young men especially Princes. Beware of flatterers, too great a love of amusement, of races and betting and playing high. I hear on all sides what a good steady boy you are and how you can be trusted. Still you must always be on the watch and must not fear ridicule if you do what is right . . . no end of young and older men have been ruined, parents hearts broken, and great names and Titles dragged in the dirt.

The following year Alexandra wrote urging him to resist 'temptation'– i.e. sex – and congratulating him on having done so thus far: 'it is the greatest proof you could possibly give me of how much you wish to please me that you should have done it for my sake and the promise you gave me of your own accord a few nights before you left'. Not till he was twenty-three would Georgie record – surprisingly carelessly in his diary – that he had a girl he slept with in Southsea, and had another he 'shared' with Eddy in St John's Wood, who was 'a ripper'.

In 1886, aged twenty-one, he joined the navy proper, and spent the next four years as an officer in the Mediterranean fleet based on Malta. The Royal Navy was the glorious symbol of British power, the glue that held the empire together. By the late nineteenth century, years of peace and inaction (its last major sea battle had been at Navarino in 1827) had made it increasingly conservative, obsessed with tradition and the importance of appearances. 'The success of a commander,' one historian of empire has written, 'was judged chiefly by the appearance of his ship, how white its paintwork, how burnished its brass, how smart its time-honoured drills.' George was pretty much everything his parents and grandmother had hoped he would be: steady, persistent and dutiful. He grew a neat little sailor's beard and ceased to smile in photographs, instead looking into the lens with an intent melancholy stare. Sailors didn't smile on duty, he said.

His leaves, with few exceptions, were spent at Sandringham with his family, shooting – fast becoming his major passion. One exception was the London celebrations in June 1887 for his grand-mother's Golden Jubilee in commemoration of her fifty years on the throne, when he took his position in the procession behind the queen's carriage amidst the fifty royals – thirty-two of them directly related to her – who had come to honour her. The Golden Jubilee was a confident assertion of Britain's Great Power status and ever-growing success. Though Germany and America might be chasing its heels, it was still the world's biggest industrialized nation and its empire now stretched from the South Atlantic, through Africa, across Asia to the Australias. The queen, almost simply by virtue of having been around for so long and despite the fact that – or perhaps because – her subjects knew very little about her, had become a more potent symbol of nation and empire than ever, and enormously popular into the bargain. Though the most recent Reform Act, of 1884, had once again dramatically enlarged the electorate and the queen was finding it harder to get her own way in politics, nearly half a million people turned out to cheer her madly as she processed through London in a plain black dress and a little white bonnet. The procession, wrote George, who, with Eddy, had been made the queen's personal ADC and rode next to her carriage, 'was a most beautiful sight and the cheering was deafening'. To some extent this new burst of royal ceremonial marked a retreat to shiny appearances in compensation for the loss of something substantial.

Abroad, responses to the queen were not quite so enthusiastic. One well-informed member of the German government summed up the Prussian court *on dit*, 'She was an undersized creature, almost as broad as she was long who looked like a cook, had a bluish-red face and was more or less mentally deranged. But she is very rich . . .' In Russia, George's cousin, Tsarevich Nicholas, just embarking on his military training, grumbled that the 'celebrated anniversary of the English Queen' had caused several senior family members to go to London, and thus cut down his time at camp; 'I resent this.'

For the queen, however, the Jubilee had another significance, as a celebration of her dominance of a family that stretched across Europe, and one particular way in which she still had some claim to political influence. The day before the procession Victoria gave a banquet for her fifty 'Royalties' (George's word) – or as she called it, a 'large family dinner'. King Christian of Denmark escorted her in. His son, King George of the Hellenes, sat next to her. Opposite her was her cousin King Leopold II of Belgium, who was in the process of turning the Belgian Congo into a horrible slave colony that would make him unimaginably rich. Wilhelm, grumbling about having been ignored and in bad odour with his grandmother, sat further down the table. George, whose diary was full of lunches with 'Uncle Fritz' and his female 'Prussian cousins' – 'dear little brat' (Charlotte), and 'Vicky, Sophy and Mossy' – made not one single reference to Wilhelm.

Intimacy between monarchies, the queen was certain, created friendliness between nations. It was a theory which neither history nor family relations confirmed.

3. Nicholas: a diamond-studded ivory tower (1868)

All royal childhoods were isolated, but Nicholas Romanov's childhood was isolated even by royal standards. And while his English cousin George's closed childhood was at odds with the increasing openness of English society, Nicholas's was a paradigm of the stagnation and closed nature of Russian society.

Imperial Russia was a colossus anchored to traditions a hundred years out of date. At 8.5 million square miles it covered almost one-sixth of the world's surface, had a population of 120 million (the combined populations of Britain, France and Germany) and a standing army of over 1 million men. Its tsars lived on an unparalleled scale of public splendour; its grand duchesses staggered under the weight of their diamonds, its social season was more spectacular than anything in Europe. At the same time, it was an underdeveloped and miserably poor agrarian society, more sparsely populated than anywhere in Europe, and barely a nation in the accepted sense. Rather, it was an unintegrated collection of eighty-odd nationalities from Poles to Uzbeks who had little in common except varying degrees of allegiance to the tsar. Its institutions were archaic, its communications infrastructure was lamentable, its government administration unable to keep up. Foreign wars had almost brought it to bankruptcy. Five-sixths of its population were peasants – who bore the weight of its taxation. Less than 20 per cent of Russians were literate by the end of the nineteenth century, as compared to around 95 per cent of Britons. Educated Russians, from tsarist bureaucrats to the aristocracy to the small new professional class, knew and hated the fact that their neighbours in Europe routinely regarded the country as backward and 'Asiatic' – a word with connotations of tyranny, decadence, corruption and barbarity. Some, who characterized themselves as social progressives and free-thinkers, longed for Russia to be more Western and 'civilized'. Others, who called themselves Slavophiles, maintained that Russia was different, special, incomprehensible to literal-minded Europeans, and that Russians must stick to their own proud traditions.

Nicholas's family, the Romanovs, had ruled Russia since 1613; but it had been only with the Napoleonic Wars that Russia had become a bona fide Great Power. In 1814. after defeating Napoleon, Tsar Alexander I had ridden down the Champs Élysées as the arbiter of Europe. (It was surely an oblique nod to this epiphanic moment that caused Bismarck to crown his German emperor at Versailles in 1871.) The Russian tsars claimed their imperial status by virtue – somewhat implausibly – of being the heirs of the Byzantine empire. After the fall of Constantinople to Islam in 1453, the self-styled Grand Princes of All Russia had been the most powerful independent rulers left in the Byzantine – or Eastern Orthodox – Church. Prince Ivan the Great married the niece of the last Byzantine emperor, added the Byzantine two-headed eagle to his crest, adopted Byzantine court ritual and started calling himself 'Tsar'. In so doing, he acquired a set of useful messianic myths about Russia's world mission: to recapture Constantinople, or Tsargrad as the Russians called it, for Christianity (and rather more usefully, to gain secure access to Europe and the Mediterranean for its grain and navy), and to 'protect' the Slavic peoples of the Balkans against the Ottoman empire. This dual mission caused his authority to be underwritten by the Russian Orthodox Church. The tsar became the great defender of Orthodoxy; the Church, tied closer to the state than in any country in Europe, declared that the tsar was God's representative on earth and he must be obeyed at all costs.

Theoretically the tsar's power was unlimited – the Romanovs liked to think of Russia and its Empire as one enormous feudal estate in which everything derived from them. They were tenacious in their determination not to let go of a single drop of power. This meant that anyone trying to initiate change found it extraordinarily difficult, as any change could be seen as a challenge to the tsar's prerogatives and summarily repressed. There were no representative assemblies of any kind, and no one, not even ministers and legislators – whom the tsar appointed and sacked as he wished – could be seen to make policy, law or any public initiatives without him. Everything must come from the tsar. Even divorce decrees needed to be personally signed by him. Anton Chekhov remembered a poor wretch from his childhood who languished forgotten for years in the town gaol, having been arrested for collecting money without permission to build a local church. Everyone in Europe who read a newspaper knew how brutally Russia had crushed the Polish separatist movement, how it tacitly encouraged Jewish pogroms, how it persecuted small religious sects, though because of press censorship not everyone in Russia did. The government seemed to go out of its way to persecute its greatest – and often far from radical – writers. Turgenev had been put under house arrest for writing a sympathetic review of Gogol; Dostoevsky was sentenced to death (commuted to four years' hard labour in Siberia) for being a member of an innocuous group of liberal Utopians. European liberals – especially in England – hated tsarism as the symbol of all that was backward-looking and anti-democratic. Monarchists – especially in Germany – saw it as a reassuring bulwark of conservatism.

By the middle of the 1850s, however, Russia's bureaucracy and its ministries were silting up, and the country was falling behind commercially and industrially. The dead hand of the state was the chief reason for this. A good example was the way that Russian society was still locked in the near-feudal hierarchy established by Peter the Great nearly 120 years before. Class segregation was enforced by the government – everyone was registered to a particular social estate, and your estate dictated your dress, the education you were entitled to, the occupations you could follow, where you could travel, how much tax you paid – the more socially lowly paid proportionally more. It was no accident that so many of the great Russian artists and writers of the mid-nineteenth century were aristocrats, and that the country had failed to industrialize. The problem for the government was that if Russia fell too far behind Europe it would lose its status as a Great Power. Being a Great Power, at the top of the international status tree – along with England, France, America, Austria-Hungary and the newcomer Germany – was vital to the tsarist government's sense of itself, and, it believed, the empire's very existence. The question was, could the country modernize and develop, even industrialize, without the tsar sacrificing an iota of his power, or even losing all of it? When Nicholas was born in 1868, it was this conundrum that had caused his grandfather, Tsar Alexander II, to introduce a series of modest reforms that would earn him the title of 'liberator' – abolishing serfdom, liberalizing the press, introducing the beginnings of social mobility, and setting up zemstvos, local rural councils, which had considerable success in building the roads, schools and hospitals the state had signally failed to supply. But at the same time a series of assassination attempts on the tsar convinced conservatives in the government that even a modicum of liberalization was too dangerous for Russia.

Among those conservatives was Nicholas's father, Alexander, the tsarevich. Alexander was a man-mountain of shaggy determination. Like his ancestor Peter the Great, he stood well over six foot and was enormously strong, 'built like a butcher' as one British journalist wrote. His party trick, brought out to intimidate foreign dignitaries and to amuse his children's friends, was to bend pokers and forks in and out of shape. Unlike Peter the Great, he disapproved of Westernization: 'He tried to be Russian down to the smallest details of his personal life, and that was why his bearing seemed less aristocratic than that of his brothers,' one of his courtiers wrote. 'He claimed, perhaps without reasoning it out, that a true Russian should not be too highly polished in his manners, that he should have a touch of something like brutality.' Alexander made a point of being rough and deliberately provincial. He wore a long beard – a mark of deliberate Slavophilism and in stark contrast to his clean-shaven sophisticated brothers – and sack-like Russian peasant shirts, and was famously brusque, taciturn and deeply mistrustful of almost everybody. He was xenophobic, anti-Semitic and deplored his father's reforms. He made a point of disapproving of the extravagance and Europeanized sophistication of St Petersburg, and loathed its winter social season. He had no interest in art or culture, *haute cuisine* or good wine. He did like the country: his children's most vivid memories of him were the walks he took them on, during which he taught them to start a fire, clear a path, follow an animal's tracks. He was not especially bright and, like his nephew George, he was the second son and his education had been neglected – his views had been formed in the army. But he was an impressive figure, not least because he seemed entirely immune to self-doubt.

Alexander's older brother, Nicholas, the heir, had died of TB in 1865. There was a pretty legend that on his deathbed Nicholas had joined the hands of his fiancée, Minny, daughter of the Danish king, Christian, and sister of Alexandra of Wales, and his brother to indicate his wish that they should marry. In reality, Alexander's intended was banished abroad, and he was virtually frogmarched to Copenhagen to propose to his brother's fiancée, who gracefully accepted. They were married in 1866. Minny seemed the opposite of her husband: she was tiny and delicately pretty – though not, everyone said, as pretty as her sister Alexandra – and charming. She was tougher and brighter than her sister; she had actually been known to read books and was an amateur painter. Like Alexandra she was extravagant, loved beautiful clothes, lavish jewels and parties – especially the St Petersburg season. She was popular too – no mean feat as Russian aristocratic society was factional, competitive and gossipy. To everyone's surprise, however, Minny and Sasha, as they were called in the family, were a great success. She charmed St Petersburg so he didn't have to. He turned out, unlike many Romanov men, to be extremely uxorious. They shared a strong, simple religious faith, a love of the outdoors – like her sister, Minny was a fine rider – a devotion to family, and an unsubtle taste for practical jokes. In their case typical 'jokes' involved the throwing of bread pellets at dinner and the turning of water hoses on unsuspecting victims.

Their first son, Nicholas, was born two years later on 6 May 1868, the feast day of Job, whose stoic fatalism would have a certain appropriateness. Minny's sister, Alexandra, wrote to her wishing she could send her own nurse, Mrs Clarke, reminding her what had happened to Vicky's son, 'who came out wrong'. Alexander was present at the birth, showing a tenderness in his diary – 'What joy it was,' he wrote, '. . . I was crying like a baby' – that belied his public image. Five siblings followed: a brother who died in infancy, then two boys and two girls: George and Xenia, and the babies of the family, Michael and Olga.

Nicholas grew up in a series of snow-covered palaces in the northern fastnesses of the Russian empire. Everything about the circumstances of his childhood conspired to make him innocent, naive and young for his years. Alexander loved his children, but his misanthropy, overprotectiveness and insistence on complete obedience were not guaranteed to create big, confident person-alities – and they didn't. The rigid etiquette which surrounded Russian royalty insulated them from modern life and other people even more so than other royals – Alexander's intense distrust of almost everyone beyond the family, his dislike of St Petersburg and his concerns over security, meant that Nicholas was denied even what St Petersburg high society might have offered: a little cosmopolitanism, culture and company. As it was, contact with anyone save his brothers and sisters and servants was difficult and rare. 'Servants, pets and relations, in that order', was how the children prioritized their relationships with the outside world – court and society coming a long way after. Nicholas's most constant playmate was his brother George, younger by three years, whose practical jokes – he was forever tripping up the servants and setting his pet parrot on the tutors – and *bons mots* so delighted Nicky that he would write them down and keep them in a box, bringing them out and shouting with laughter at them years later. He occasionally saw a few grand ducal cousins such as his cousin Alexander Mikhailovich, known as Sandro, and the children of Minny's friend and lady-in-waiting Lili Vorontsova-Dashkova. One of the few children whom Nicky encountered beyond these was his governess's son, Vladimir Ollongren, who joined his classes for three years when Nicholas was seven. For all the warmth within the family it was, inevitably, lonely.

The Romanov children, not unlike their English cousins Eddy and George, were said to be lively and jolly. Sandro, Nicky's cousin, who first met him in 1875 when he was seven, recalled a slightly fragile, sweet-natured, smiling boy, who had a great deal of his mother's charm. Vladimir Ollongren thought him a very happy child, keen on hopscotch and birds, his mother and the long theatrical rituals of the Orthodox Church which he liked to act out. His piety was something his younger sister Olga remembered too. Ollongren couldn't help but compare the boy to his hulking father. Next to him, slight, quiet little Nicky seemed frankly 'girlish'. The tsar Ollongren remembered as 'a quite exceptionally cheerful and simple man'; several people observed that Alexander seemed to prefer children to adults.

Nicholas was utterly in awe of him. He seemed superhuman, so huge and strong, so utterly without doubt. When the imperial family were caught in a train derailment at Borki in 1888 in which twenty people died (whether it was a bomb or badly laid track was never established), Alexander single-handedly lifted the roof of the carriage in which his family was trapped, and saved them. He was extremely loving of his children, but he was ruthless about any sign of weakness, expected absolute obedience and could be extremely frightening. One observer wrote that even when talking normally he sometimes 'gave the impression of being on the point of striking you'. Vladimir Ollongren recalled an occasion when he took the blame for something Nicky had done. 'You are a little girl,' Alexander told his son crushingly. One member of the imperial household felt this created an uncomfortable atmosphere 'of dissimulation and restraint' in the family.

Minny was no less powerful. She could be extremely imperious and took her position in society very seriously. With the exception of her firstborn who adored her, her children found her both demanding and distant. Nicholas deferred to her well into adulthood. 'I hope my Nicky will do everything to be friendly and charming with everybody and will be ready to carry out his personal duties even if they are boring at times,' she wrote to him when he was trekking across Siberia aged twenty-two, as if he were a small boy at someone else's party. Her youngest daughter, Olga, who disliked her, felt that she went out of her way to scupper their sister Xenia's marriage because 'My mother just did not want to lose all control over Xenia.'

It was one of the peculiarities of the age that despite Russia's political Anglophobia there was a strong strain of cultural Anglophilia in

Russian society. Just like his cousins Georgie and Willy, Nicholas and his siblings spent their first years surrounded by English nurses and nannies, and the cold baths, long walks and plain nursery food – porridge and boiled mutton – of an English nursery. Among the Russian nobility, as among many European royalty, English nannies were very much in vogue – one of the consequences being that many Russian aristocrats read and wrote English before Russian. Nicholas and his siblings certainly spoke good English from early on. The xenophobic tsar himself was devoted to his old English nanny, Kitty, who spent forty-six years in imperial service. Behind the walls of his favourite palace, Gatchina, described as an 'English-style' stone palace complete with moat, the royal family lived neither in vast marble splendour as the Prussian did, nor in traditional Muscovite surroundings, but in modestly sized, distinctly English bourgeois-style rooms. Alexander disliked the public, palatial living of his ancestors, and the family inhabited a series of relatively small, stuffy rooms filled with bulky furniture and overstuffed sofas covered with English chintz.

Beyond their domestic arrangements, however, nothing about the Romanovs was small scale; everything was huge. Gatchina Palace outside St Petersburg, where the family moved when Nicholas was twelve, had 900 rooms, most of them except for the royal apartments, empty, dusty and dirty. One estimate put the number of royal servants across the Romanovs' palaces at 15,000. The British royal family never lived on this scale. At George's parents' famously luxurious Christmas at Sandringham ('Dickens in a Cartier setting', was how their grandson, the future Edward VIII, described it), there was one enormous Christmas tree round which presents for the servants were stacked. The Romanovs had six trees just for the family, in a hall many times bigger than any room in Sandringham. The Nicholas ball, the biggest court occasion of the St Petersburg season, had 3,000 guests. Throughout the year there was a constant round of processions, formal receptions, presentations and banquets, all on a vast scale involving thousands of generals, churchmen, chamberlains, gentlemen and ladies of the court. At Anichkov Palace on Nevsky Prospekt, where the family spent the early months of the year, Nicholas would watch his mother dressing each evening, fussed over by five maids and the Mistress of the Wardrobe, stepping into the heavy silver brocade dress prescribed by imperial etiquette, ten rows of pearls around her neck – so covered in jewels she looked like an oriental deity. In spring, the family went to Peterhof, the huge Romanov estate on the Gulf of Finland, and stayed in one of the many family villas that dotted the estate. Summer was spent on the royal yacht, with perhaps a trip to Denmark or to the estates in balmy Livadia in the Crimea. Every move was a logistical nightmare. For a three-week trip to Denmark, the family was routinely accompanied by twenty railway trucks of baggage and an entourage of a hundred, to say nothing of the security around them. Since the first assassination attempt on Alexander II in 1866, the royal family had been surrounded by a wall of security. When they travelled by train from St Petersburg to Moscow, soldiers lined the entire 400-mile track to protect it from sabotage.

The lives of all European royals were circumscribed by ritual and etiquette, but Russian ritual and etiquette was the most interminable. All royalty had to learn to stand for hours, but the Russians stood the longest. At Easter, even the smallest child was stuffed into full court dress and required to stand through a three-hour church service followed by an Easter egg-giving ceremony during which the tsar personally greeted the 5,000 men of the imperial guards regiments, and presented each with a porcelain egg. This could take all day. Once they were out of the nursery, etiquette pursued the children everywhere: at lunch and dinner they often ate with Alexander's entourage. Meals lasted exactly 50 minutes, the youngest were served last, and Nicky's sister Olga recalled that the children often had time for only a few mouthfuls before it was all over. On one occasion Nicky was so hungry that he prised open his gold cross which had in it a fragment of the True Cross embedded in wax, and ate the contents, wood and all. It was, he confided to Olga, 'immorally good'. Henceforth anything really delicious was always 'immorally good'.

There were compensations. At Gatchina, the children had a menagerie including an albino crow, a wolf and a tame hare, and an enormous indoor playground. The palace's Arsenal hall had a billiard table, a fortress full of toy soldiers, a mini mountain to climb and a fully functional model kitchen. Next door was a room of stuffed animals and beyond it hundreds of rooms to explore, including the fairy-tale room, full of frescoes illustrating Pushkin's stories. Outside in the thousands of acres, there was a lake, an echo grotto and secret passages leading back into the palace.

Like Willy and George, Nicky left the nursery when he was seven, with his brother George, to be educated by his governess, Alexandra Ollongren. It was an induction a good deal gentler than that of many of his Russian cousins who were forced immediately into a life of austere military discipline. He saw his parents twice a day, at 11 a.m. to discuss his day, and briefly before bed, and sometimes he would be 'commanded' to accompany his father on an afternoon walk. He was bright, a fast learner with an aptitude for languages, and his English was particularly good. Then, aged ten, in 1879, having easily passed the middle school exam taken by boys of his age, he was handed over in the usual way for a European prince, to a military governor, Grigory Danilovich, who oversaw both his military training and the rest of his education. Even at the conservative Russian court Danilovich was regarded as hopeless. 'That old dotard of a Jesuit', one member of the Romanov household later called him. Nicky referred to him as the 'Cholera', his cousin Sandro thought Danilovich 'simple-minded'. Nicholas's education became skimpy: a smattering of history – which he really enjoyed – a bit of geography and chemistry, and instruction in English, French and German – at which he was very good. He was also taught to dance, as the tsar had to lead the polonaise at every imperial ball. Like Bertie and Alexandra, the tsar and his wife weren't very exercised about education. Alexander felt he'd done perfectly well without it; Minny, like her sister, believed that good manners, religious education and a decent grasp of languages were quite sufficient. Neither they nor Danilovich saw any need for larger thinking about how to prepare the heir for his future rule. Danilovich told Nicky that 'the mysterious forces emanating during the sacrament of taking the oath on the day of the coronation provided all the practical data required'.

Nicky's favourite tutor was his English teacher, Charles Heath. Heath, a popular former master at the Alexander Lycée, St Petersburg's grandest school, didn't just teach English, he taught English public school values: decency, fairness and the virtues of self-control and good manners, the alleged qualities of an English gentleman. 'Aristocrats are born,' he told the boy, 'gentlemen are made.' It was a lesson Nicky absorbed; from his late teens his great courtesy and almost English politeness were frequently commented upon – and not always appreciatively. Such control was 'un-Russian'. As one of the government's most able ministers, Count Witte, would later write with some bitterness, 'I had rarely come across a better-mannered young man than Nicholas II. His good-breeding conceals all shortcomings.' In fact, Heath's concept of gentlemanliness was almost the only novel idea in the whole of Nicky's childhood.

Not surprisingly, Nicky's idea of life outside his tiny world was extraordinarily limited; nor was it helped by his parents' – perhaps understandable – desire to protect their children from the world's harsh realities. The depth of the children's inexperience is encapsulated in the fact that though their mother gave them a relatively spartan upbringing, it had no context: many European aristocrats disdained cash, but the children had no idea of the value of anything. Etiquette forbade any member of the imperial family from setting foot in a shop. As a teenager Xenia gave her mother a sapphire-encrusted silver perfume bottle for Christmas which she'd picked out of a selection that Cartier had sent for her mother to see; Xenia had no idea that it was worth much more than the little presents she stitched herself. The Romanov children knew nothing about their grandfather's reforms. Newspapers were banned from the nursery, as Minny, like Alexandra, insisted that politics be kept out of her children's education. As far as they were concerned, General Cherevin, a senior officer in Okhrana, the brutal secret police, was 'Friendly, generous and humble' and 'very popular in St Petersburg'.

Not that Nicholas wouldn't have liked more experience of the world. When they were in St Petersburg, his and Xenia's favourite pastime was standing for hours behind the high balustrades that surrounded Anichkov Palace, watching ordinary people walking down Nevsky Prospekt.

Overlaying everything was a deeply idealized fantasy about 'Russianness' which Alexander passed on to his children, but which was belied by practically everything about their upbringing. Almost nothing about the Romanovs was 'Russian'. Their lives were those of Westernized aristocrats, their court etiquette was German, their parks and palaces were neoclassical, their home comforts English. Even by blood they were barely Russian at all, the product of endless marriages into German royal families. Nicholas's mother was Danish, his paternal grandmother was German, as his paternal great-grandmother had been. It was perhaps the reason Nicholas became so attached to the rituals of Russian Orthodoxy, the one 'authentic' Russian experience open to him. He and his siblings knew hardly anything about 'the real Russia': they'd never seen the 'black earth' of Russia's central heartland, they barely knew Moscow, its traditional capital. They habitually idealized Russian peasants but never met any. They were told that their father's affectation of peasant clothes was a sign of his deep understanding of the common people. They assumed that the palace servants, who'd often served the family for generations and had as little connection to the peasant communes as they did, represented the average Russian peasant. When they saw the masses beyond the palace, they were invariably soldiers cheering his father at reviews or weddings. 'The look of love and dedication in all those upturned faces was unforgettable,' Nicky's sister Olga insisted decades later. '. . . Between the crown and people was a relationship hardly ever understood in the West. That relationship had nothing to do with government or petty officialdom.'

After the Russian Revolution overturned their lives, several of Nicky's Russian cousins wrote memoirs dwelling on the miserable inadequacy of their childhood, the repression of personality that was demanded, how they were trained to engage with the modern world as little as possible and what a disaster this turned out to be. Sandro recalled the pointless isolation and strictness and how lonely he was. The Grand Duchess Marie, another of Nicky's cousins, bemoaned the closedness and the helplessness it engendered: 'they kept me purposely in ignorance of the situation into which I had been born'.

In March 1881, when Nicky was twelve, his grandfather Alexander II – having just that morning signed a new constitution which set up conditions for a very limited form of representative government – was mortally injured in a terrorist bomb attack. He was carried, bleeding profusely, to his study in the Winter Palace. Nicky was on his way to skate with his mother and his cousin Sandro. Hearing the explosions, the two boys ran to the palace, where they followed the blood on the marble floors to the emperor's study. The tsar's wounds were horrific: his right leg was torn off, his stomach was ripped open, his face covered in blood. 'His face was deadly pale,' Nicholas remembered years later. 'There were small wounds all over it. My father led me up to the bed. "Papa" he said, raising his voice, "your sunshine is here."' In front of his grandson and family, the tsar bled to death.

Alexander II's death meant the end of Russia's experiment with liberalization. His son, now Tsar Alexander III, tore up the new constitution and resolved to restore the autocracy. To ensure that no one misunderstood his intentions his first proclamation announced, 'We shall preside serenely over the destinies of Our Empire, which henceforward will be discussed between God and Ourself alone.' The government bestowed on itself special powers to suspend the rule of law whenever and wherever it felt threatened – a state of affairs that continued until 1917. Alexander brought in a slew of 'counter reforms', including severe press censorship, legislation to ban the employment of those regarded as politically suspect, the abolition of the autonomy of universities, and the harsh exclusion of those from non-noble or non-professional backgrounds from grammar schools and universities – so as to close down the social mobility that Alexander II's reforms had allowed. In the name of quelling 'rural disturbances', the power of the new zemstvos, which had proved such a force for progress, was overridden by new government enforcers, 'Land Captains', who could impose punishments without trial and set aside court decisions at will.

Beyond the Russias, Alexander brutally extended his father's not especially enlightened policy of Russification, from Poland and Finland to Muslim Transcaucasus. Local languages were outlawed; non-Orthodox believers such as Catholics, Muslims and Protestants were discriminated against; Jews, whom Alexander literally regarded as 'Christ-killers', were viciously persecuted: excluded from education, expelled from their homes and subjected to brutal, often police-initiated, pogroms. As a result, the 1880s saw the first wave of Jewish mass emigration from Russia, and created the perfect breeding ground for a generation of furious, disaffected revolutionaries. By the 1890s the disenfranchisement of peasant communities had created intense resentment, and the Russification policies helped a series of equally furious separatist movements to take root across the empire. Nor was Alexander able to put the genie back in the bottle, however much he wanted to: Russia was – slowly and painfully – changing.

At the time, however, Alexander was perceived in Russia as a great success: a big strong man to keep the empire safe. The 1880s were a time of confidence in Russia. It seemed, one of his nephews wrote, as if Russia had recaptured a 'new proud, "imperial spirit"'. The literate classes largely accepted Alexander's new repressive laws as the price of security. His swiftness in hunting down and hanging his father's killers appeared to have utterly crushed the nascent revolutionary movement. Those who worked for him were impressed by his toughness and lack of self-doubt. Even clever, sophisticated men like his minister of finance, Serge Witte, who recognized the tsar was no genius and that his views were simplistic, praised his 'noble outstanding personality'. He even managed at times to look progressive. He supported Witte's plans for Russia's industrialization, though the way capital was raised – through the exportation of grain levied from subsistence peasant farmers who needed it to feed themselves – would contribute to an appalling famine in the early 1890s. And he kept Russia out of expensive foreign wars. Not that Alexander felt any special warmth for anywhere abroad – quite the opposite in fact. 'We have just two allies in this world . . . our armies and our navy. Everybody else will turn on us on a second's notice.' He was inveterately xenophobic – even of the new Germany, led by Russia's traditional ally, Prussia.

The two countries shared not only a long frontier but complex dynastic, cultural and historical links. Like the British royals, the Russian tsars had found the German kingdoms a handy source of wives – so much so that both the British and Russian royal houses were more German than anything else. There had been so much intermarriage with Germans that three of the junior branches of the Romanov family were naturalized German families: the Oldenburgs, the Leuchtenbergs and the Mecklenburg-Strelitzes. And for generations, in the absence of its own indigenous pro-fessional class, the Russian government had welcomed large numbers of clever, ambitious Germans into senior government office, to such an extent that a large proportion of senior Russian statesmen was German by descent. The relationship had always had a delicate balance. Until unification, the German states had always been the junior partner, even if culturally and intellectually they were far ahead. For educated Russians, Germany was the centre of culture: the home of Goethe, Schiller, Kant, Bach, Mozart, 'German symphonism', and more recently Nietzsche and even Marx. Russian audiences had embraced them all. It was Russia's might, however, which had bulldozed Napoleon out of Germany.

Yet there had long been fault-lines in the relationship, and many Russians resented Germany's cultural and intellectual dominance. Many Germans in turn distrusted the colossus which loomed on their eastern frontier. Germany's rise on to the world stage and its implicit assertion that it was Russia's equal, not junior, created a host of new strains and suspicions. In 1878, at the Congress of Berlin, Russia had been deprived of most of the spoils it had just won in the Russo-Turkish War, giving rise to a – not unjustifiable – feeling in St Petersburg that Chancellor Bismarck was not quite the devoted ally he claimed to be. It was true: while Bismarck wanted to keep Russia sweet, he was not prepared to give unquali-fied support to its interests. He had also decided that he needed to be on good terms with Austria-Hungary – for which Russians of all classes felt an almost instinctive hatred born of generations of rivalry in the Balkans. It was becoming increasingly and discomfortingly clear as well that Russia had become vulnerable to German financial muscle. Germany had become the Russian government's main source of borrowed money, and it was the chief market for Russian wheat. If Bismarck closed the money markets or raised grain tariffs – as he would in the late 1880s – Russia was in trouble. It was galling to realize that Russia had nothing like the same purchase on the German economy.

Xenophobia was widespread across Europe, but it was particularly virulent in the Russian educated classes. Instinctive hostility towards other nations was inculcated, according to Nicky's cousin Sandro, by the Orthodox Church 'and the monstrous doctrine of official patriotism': his class hated 'Poles, Swedes, Germans, British and French', while reserving special hatred for Jews, 'the monstrous doctrine'. From the 1880s, moreover, rising nationalism and expansionist ambitions were being channelled into the notion of Pan-Slavism, and pointed at Germany as a dangerous potential rival to their ambitions in central Europe. Pan-Slavism had begun as a romantic, philosophical exceptionalism, a belief that Russian spirituality, the 'all-uniting Russian soul', had a unique ability and a special mission to heal 'the anguish of Europe'. It had quickly turned into a chauvinistic justification of the Russian 'mission' to dominate the Balkans, accompanied by the view that it was inevitable that the Teutons and the Slavs would eventually duke it out.

Nowhere was the complexity of the Russian–German relationship as vividly illustrated as in the new tsar's family. His mother was Willy's great-aunt; his grandmother was a princess from Hesse-Darmstadt. He was well aware how much Russia needed Germany. But his own Slavophilism made him bridle at German influence in Russia, and his wife bore Germany and the 'Prussian barbarians', as she called them, a virulent dislike quite as strong as her sister's. Though she never directly interfered in politics, the German Foreign Office saw her as a worryingly anti-German influence.

Alexander's accession pushed the imperial family further into retreat. The new tsar used his father's assassination to justify his desire to move permanently out of St Petersburg to the country, to Gatchina, 25 miles south-west of the city. Minny hated the palace's vast echoing dreariness. 'Cold, disgusting and full of work- men', she described it to her mother. 'This uninhabited, big empty castle in the middle of winter cost me many tears, hidden tears, for Sasha is happy to leave the city.' A new cordon of soldiers and secret police surrounded it. The children disliked the secret police, who followed them even on their walks in the grounds. Nicky, who would be irked by them his whole life, called them 'naturalists' because they were always jumping out from behind trees. Visits to St Petersburg became rare. The increasing isolation was not necessarily unwelcome, however. The children had become anxious in the aftermath of their grandfather's death. Since then Nicky's cousin Sandro heard 'an explosion in every suspicious sound'.

It was no wonder that even the tsar described the family's almost yearly summer visits to Denmark, to the Danish king and queen's informal royal house parties, as like being freed from 'prison'. In Denmark the imperial family felt 'at glorious liberty' as they never did at home. They spent months there. 'I shall never forget the thrill of walking down a street for the first time . . . It was more than fun! It was an education!' Olga remembered. Nicholas and his siblings found themselves in the unusual situation of being surrounded by other children who were of the same status as they were. The Romanov children regularly met their English cousins in Denmark. There is a group photograph taken at Amalienborg Palace in Copenhagen dated 1869, with George aged four, sitting next to a one-year-old Nicky in a pram. The families met again the following year during the Franco-Prussian War, and again when five-year-old Nicky came to London with his parents in 1873 and stayed at Marlborough House. It was a relationship encouraged by Alexandra and Minny. 'I fear that your sweet little Nicky has forgotten me,' Alexandra wrote when Nicky was eight, 'which would make me sad as I love that angelic child.' There was a gaggle of families: the Danish cousins; the Cumberlands – the heir to the throne of Hanover which had been dissolved by Prussia after the 1866 war, and his wife, Thyra, Minny and Alexandra's younger sister; and the children of their brother George of the Hellenes, recently elected King of Greece, and his Russian wife, Olga, who was the tsar's favourite cousin. The Russian, Greek and British cousins – each of whom had their own Georgie ('Greek Georgie' was particularly boisterous) – formed a club. The *lingua franca* appears to have been English – the British cousins were notably bad at languages and everyone else was fluent. The tsar would take the children off to catch tadpoles or steal apples; he let them ride on his knee and tug his beard; to all the children's delight, he once turned a hose on the King of Sweden, 'whom we all disliked'. George, so intimidated by his own grandmother, referred to the famously terrifying Alexander as 'dear old Fatty', or 'dearest uncle Sasha'.

Nicky and Georgie became, according to Olga, 'close friends'. Georgie teased his girl cousins, reducing Olga to giggles in inappropriate places by quietly invoking an old joke to 'come and roll with me on the Ottoman', and calling Xenia 'Owl'. The boys had much in common: both loved the outdoors; both were shy, young for their age and felt most comfortable at home with their families; both had a predilection for 'romps' and practical jokes; both had possessive mothers (whom they both addressed in English as 'Motherdear') and powerful fathers. They also looked eerily alike: the Danish servants were forever confusing them. In Denmark in 1883, when George was off at sea and he was fifteen, Nicky conceived his first crush on Toria, George's favourite younger sister. 'I am in love with Victoria and she seems to be with me,' he wrote in his diary, '. . . In the evening I tried to be alone with her and kiss her. She is so lovely.'

Despite their similarities the two boys were on opposite sides of a bitter international rivalry. It wasn't too much to say that Russia and Britain were arch-enemies: both ideological opposites and imperial rivals. It was the imperial clashes that gave the ideological conflict bite – otherwise they would simply have been two countries on either side of Europe each minding its own business. But from the late 1870s, Britain and Russia, along with the other Western Great Powers, had launched themselves into a violent phase of territorial acquisition, carving up the globe beyond Europe into colonies and 'spheres of influence'. There are many complex and conflicting arguments as to why the (mostly) Western, (relatively) developed powers all decided they needed an empire: the natural evolution of global power politics made it inevitable that the few rich, militarily superior, technologically developed powers would dominate and exploit the other, more 'backward', weak territories; the need of the industrialized nations for raw materials, and for new places to put their capital; a sense of fierce competition among the Great Powers and a perception that new territories were the way to steal a march on their competitors. All these aspects played their role. The colonizers believed that colonies provided opportunities for wealth and new markets – Britain's empire, the exemplar, had made it the most influential and wealthy country in the world and allowed it to punch way beyond its own weight. As the biggest imperial power indeed, it saw itself as the world's imperial policeman, a disinterested regulator of the world's affairs by virtue of its utilitarian need to maintain the status quo and peace for free trade – a claim which had some truth but which the other Great Powers resented. The frantic new phase of territory-grabbing got into gear after 1882, the year of Britain's quiet takeover of Egypt, which convinced the European powers – including three new would-be colony-hunters, Belgium and the newly unified Italy and Germany – that if they didn't get in first, Britain would grab the whole of Africa. The so-called 'scramble for Africa' revivified the old Anglo–French antipathy, as France tried to prevent Britain from establishing itself too comfortably in Egypt, and gave rise to a new reason for new colonies – that they might not necessarily contribute wealth, but that simply by existing they provided status, and proved the greatness of the Great Powers. For Britain, the arrival of more imperial competitors stimulated a fear that its dominance, its territories and its routes to its furthest-flung colonies might be threatened. The scene was set, as one empire competed with another, for an endless stream of nasty little regional conflicts.

In many respects Russia's empire was different. It was one continuous outstretching land mass which had already in previous decades absorbed the Crimea, much of Poland, Finland, the central

Asian territory bordering Mongolia and all of Siberia to the Pacific. Expansion had never been primarily about trade or markets but more about myths of conquest: that Russia had a God-ordained destiny to take up the legacy of the Byzantine empire and to dominate the Balkans and Asia, even to the Indian Ocean. The new imperial fever, however, gripped just as strongly as anywhere else. For the Russian elite, imperial expansion was an all-too-welcome distraction from Russia's impossible internal problems and the need for domestic reforms. It subscribed to a simplistic equation which papered over a multitude of cracks: since empires kept countries great, why should not Russia keep itself in the first rank through territorial expansion? After all, the one thing it had plenty of was soldiers. The British imperial juggernaut, meanwhile, now had territory and interests in Asia, and the two countries found themselves constantly in conflict. 'It is an axiom of Russian policy,' a seasoned British Russia-watcher wrote, 'that the constant, most persistent and most effective opponent of Russian expansion is England.' One flashpoint was Constantinople and the Bosphorus. The Russians believed they had a God-given mission to take Constantinople for Christendom – and they wanted to secure the narrow channel of the Bosphorus, sometimes called the Turkish Straits, which joined the Black Sea to the Mediterranean. This was the route by which most of Russia's grain travelled out of the country, and the exit for Russia's southern fleet, which by the 1878 Treaty of Berlin was bottled up in the Black Sea.

The British believed Russia couldn't be allowed to take Con-stantinople, firstly because it would threaten the security of their vital overland route to India; secondly, because Russia's presence in Turkey would destabilize the balance of power in Eastern Europe and the Balkans to which the British were wedded; and thirdly because it would give Russia an advantage in next-door Persia. The two countries were competing for control there too: Russia because it was on its border, Britain because the land route to India lay through it, and because of the reserves of oil that were thought to lie hidden beneath it. The clash with Russia had led to Britain's propping up of the crumbling Ottoman empire, and its involvement in the Crimean War during the 1850s, which had sparked frenzied public antipathy between the two countries. In the Russo-Turkish War of the mid-1870s, Britain had not taken part, but British public opinion had angrily demanded intervention and that, as a song of the time went, the Russians 'shall not have Constantinople'. Many Russians in turn believed that Britain had secretly backed and helped the Turks. The other flashpoint was ever-ungovernable Afghanistan, sandwiched between British India's north-west frontier and Russian-controlled Turkestan. The idea that Russia was just waiting to invade India was a great bogey of British foreign affairs, even though the logistics of invading India – simply of getting over the Himalayas – made this virtually impossible. Russia, however, *was* relentlessly pushing forward its frontiers in central Asia, and the British periodically became obsessed with 'securing' Afghanistan, and cast their eyes greedily towards Tibet. Each side was convinced that the other had no business there.

Imperial conflicts gave teeth to ideological divisions: to the British, Russia was the incarnation of tyranny. British opinion regarded itself as especially well informed on this subject, as it was in Britain – with its relaxed censorship laws – that writers such as Alexander Herzen and Tolstoy had published their indictments of the Russian system. The Russian government was infuriated by what it saw as Britain's smug hypocrisy, which allowed it to harbour political enemies of the Russian state in the name of freedom, and to extend itself aggressively across the globe in any way it could, shamelessly exploiting the natives, while claiming it was on a mission to bring the benefits of civilization to the world. It was true that the British imperial justification somehow typically managed to mix two opposite arguments: a belief that the empire had philanthropically taken up the 'white man's burden' to civilize and improve the lot of inferior races (it was a given that subject races were inferior, though it was also understood that it was not done in polite society to talk too explicitly about this); and a conviction that stronger nations would inevitably dominate weaker ones. Though it was also rarely said in public, the British considered that most other empires treated their natives abominably. Sometimes they were right, as Anton Chekhov recognized. Having seen both British-occupied Egypt and Russian exploitation in the Crimea, where the native Tartar population had been systematically impoverished and had their land confiscated, he wrote in 1890, 'Yes, thought I, the Englishman exploits the Chinese, sepoys, Hindus, but then he gives them roads, acqueducts, museums, Christianity; you too exploit, but what do you give?'

Among the two ruling dynasties the conflict had become personal. It was just as well that King Christian banned the discussion of politics at Fredensborg,* as Alexander's Anglophobia was practically written into his DNA. Queen Victoria loathed Russia. 'Those detestable Russians,' she'd complain, 'they will always hate us and we can never trust them.' Over the years she denounced the Russian government as 'wicked, villainous and atrocious', the tsar as 'full of hate . . . and tyranny', and the people as 'horrible, deceitful, cruel'. During the Russo-Turkish War she tried so hard to bully Disraeli into intervening that one politician's wife observed that she had 'lost control of herself, badgers her Ministers and pushes them towards war'. Alexander II detested her right back: 'He said she was a pampered, sentimental, selfish old woman,' as well as 'nasty' and 'interfering'. Visiting German diplomats knew that the best way to put the tsar in a good humour was to tell damaging stories about the British royal family, especially the queen.

Minny and Alexandra, however, were determined that personal relations should be more than civil. To that end, in 1874 they had promoted the marriage of Bertie's younger brother Affie to Alexander's only sister, Marie, a union the queen had yielded to with bad grace.† Their husbands acquiesced, Bertie partly out of

* Bismarck nevertheless liked to claim that it was a hotbed of anti-Prussianism and called it 'The Whispering Gallery'. What was true was that the house parties had their share of the Danish queen's disgruntled German relatives muttering about upstart Prussians.

† The marriage was not a success. Affie was a bully and a drunk who talked incessantly about himself and inflicted appalling violin recitals on everyone, and Marie hated England. The queen, with characteristic perversity, decided she liked her Russian daughter-in-law: 'I have formed a high opinion of her . . . Everyone must like her, but alas! No one likes him! I fear that will never get better!'

loyalty to Alexandra, partly one suspects because it was in his nature to try to get on with people and make them like him; Alexander because the relaxed freedom of Fredensborg was important to him. Both also believed in the idea of the brotherhood of royalty; Bertie called it 'the firm' or his 'profession'; Alexander liked to talk about the 'monarchical principle', the idea that royalty was linked by supra-national bonds – a philosophy contradicted by everything else he believed. According to his daughter, he respected Bertie but didn't really like him. On the other hand, Bertie's much publicized differences with his mother – gleefully covered by the European press – definitely made the Russians warm to him. The Romanovs decided to make a careful distinction between friendliness with the British royals and antipathy to Britain. It must have been a difficult line to hold. 'I loved uncle Bertie and George and so many others,' Olga told an interviewer decades later, 'and they have done so much for me. But, of course, it has never been possible to discuss with them the utterly vile politics of successive British parliaments. They were nearly all anti-Russian – and so often without the least cause. So much of British policy is wholly contrary to their own tradition of fair play.' For Olga, her father's ambivalence was translated into an uncertainty about the British royal family's smell, which for her teetered somewhere between an evocative wintry garden scent and acrid damp mouldiness: 'English royalty smelled of fog and smoke . . . we ourselves smelled of well-polished leather.'

The fragility of the relationship between the two families was exposed whenever international relations became strained. In 1884–5, a crisis in Afghanistan seemed about to erupt into fully-fledged armed conflict. 'I can hardly see how we can avoid going to war with Russia now,' Bertie wrote to the British prime minister, William Gladstone, in the spring of 1885 at the height of the crisis. He told his mother that Russian 'promises and assurances . . . are of no value whatsoever'. In fact, neither side wanted war and Britain and Russia eventually began negotiations that – to everyone's surprise – produced a genuine resolution of boundary disagreements. Bertie met Alexander at Fredensborg that autumn, and reported to George that the visit had been 'very quiet'.

(Nicholas and Toria's romance had cooled into friendship.) There were, however, other, equally bitter, sources of dynastic conflict, namely Bulgaria, which to Alexander's fury had proclaimed independence from Russia, under the leadership of Sandro Battenburg, the German princeling the Russians had themselves installed. The Russians believed the newly independent Balkan states – many of which, like Bulgaria, had been liberated from the Ottoman empire with Russian blood and money – ought happily to acquiesce to Russian dominance. When he heard that Vicky, Wilhelm's mother, wanted to marry her daughter Moretta to Sandro Battenburg, Alexander couldn't quell his suspicions that it was all a plot to build Anglo-German influence in the Balkans. The thought maddened him. In mid-1886 the Russians abducted Battenburg and forced him at gunpoint to abdicate. Bertie and Alexandra did not appear at Fredensborg that year. The couples met up, however, in the summer of 1887, just as Russia and Germany were falling out seriously. Bismarck's son Herbert was convinced Bertie and Alexandra had used the visit to turn the tsar against Wilhelm with stories of his unfilial behaviour. It's possible that the tsar and the Prince of Wales bonded that summer over shared suspicions and stories about the young kaiser-to-be.

In 1885, when Nicky was seventeen, a series of eminent ministers and academics was summoned to Gatchina to lecture the tsarevich on international law, chemistry, military science and finance. It was a two-year mini-apprenticeship in government – a belated acknowledgement that one day he would actually be in charge of the whole Russian empire. How much benefit Nicky really derived from it was questionable. One of his lecturers, Konstantin Pobedonostsev, later said that when he tried to explain the workings of the tsarist state to Nicky, 'I could only observe that he was completely absorbed in picking his nose.' Pobedonostsev was, nevertheless, an important influence in Nicky's life. A senior Russian statesman and chief censor – the intelligentsia, who hated him, called him 'The Grand Inquisitor' – he was fearsomely reactionary and was Nicholas's father's chief political mentor. He had come to believe that only autocracy in its most repressive form could 'save'

Russia and that Alexander II's reforms had been a disaster. The masses, he said, were weak, childish and gullible; everything must be done to prevent the invasion of Western ideas such as freedom of the press and representative government. Russia must effectively stagnate, in order to keep the Romanovs in power. Many people believed Pobedonostsev was the moving force behind the domestic repressions of the 1880s.

His influence over Nicky, however, was predicated on his closeness to Nicky's father's views. The most forceful and pervasive influence in Nicky's life was Alexander III, as one courtier wrote, 'whom he venerated and whose example he followed assiduously even in small details of his everyday life'. But Alexander was six foot one and immune to doubt, and Nicholas, five foot five or six, was a far gentler, probably more intelligent, certainly more accomplished, person. In the claustrophobic, patriarchal atmosphere of his parents' household, however, there had been little space to develop any independence of mind or much confidence in his own judgement. Nicky's future sister-in-law, Victoria of Hesse-Darmstadt, would observe perceptively that Alexander's 'dominating personality had stunted any gifts of initiative in Nicky'.

Pierre Gilliard, who thirty years later would tutor Nicky's son Alexis in similar circumstances, came to believe that raising a child in such an isolated environment was a recipe for disaster. Such a child, he concluded, was

deprived of something which plays a vital part in the formation of judgment. He is deprived of the knowledge which is acquired out of the schoolroom, knowledge such as comes from life itself, unhampered contact with other children, the diverse and sometimes conflicting influences of environment, direct observation and the simple experience of men and affairs – in a word, everything which in the course of years develops the critical faculty and a sense of reality. Under such circumstances an individual must be endowed with exceptional gifts to be able to see things as they are, think clearly, and desire the right things. He is cut off from life. He cannot imagine what is going on behind the wall on which false pictures are painted for his amusement or distraction.

Nicky finally left Gatchina Palace and his family in the summer of 1887, just as he turned nineteen and in London Queen Victoria was celebrating her Golden Jubilee. Like Wilhelm, he joined the army, an elite guards regiment, the legendary Preobrazhensky Guards. 'I miss you <u>terribly</u>, my dear Nicky,' his mother wrote. She also reminded him to be 'polite and courteous', to get along with everyone, but not allow 'too much familiarity or intimacy'. 'One has to be cautious with everybody from the start,' Nicky agreed, but he was very taken with his new life. 'I am now happier than I can say to have joined the army and every day I become more and more used to camp life.' There was drilling and target practice, and then afternoons and evenings of cards, billiards and skittles. What could be nicer?

PART II
Family Ties, Imperial Contests

4. Wilhelm emperor (1888–90)

By the spring of 1888 it was obvious that Wilhelm would soon be Emperor. His grandfather had died in March of old age. By the time Fritz, crowned Kaiser Friedrich, came to the throne, he was dying of throat cancer, had had a tracheotomy, couldn't speak, and no one expected him to live long. His orders, scribbled on little bits of paper, were simply ignored. 'People in general consider us a mere passing shadow soon to be replaced by <u>reality</u> in the shape of William!!' Vicky wrote bitterly to her mother. She poured her displaced distress into her obsessive pursuit of the marriage between her daughter Moretta and Alexander Battenburg, in which the groom had long since lost interest. Wilhelm, meanwhile, told Bismarck that Vicky 'hated him more than anything else on earth', and was killing his father with her hysterical scenes.

Wilhelm was avid to be emperor. He had honed his whole personality to project the heartily masculine, charismatic, can-do soldier-king he wanted to be: the brusquely jocular manner, the staccato vocal delivery, the purposeful physical stance, the deliberately fierce expression he wore in public. He liked to think of himself as another Frederick the Great: politician, soldier, strategist, philosopher, cultural arbiter; someone who, through sheer force of character, would render democracy obsolete. To emphasize his similarity to Frederick, he had even adopted his habit of scribbling marginalia on official memos and documents: 'Lies!', 'Nonsense!', 'Stale fish'.

Some of those who had known him as a prince, however, worried a little about what kind of king he would make. 'Good heavens, whatever will happen if Prince Wilhelm becomes Kaiser as early as this?' one senior general had remarked the year before. 'He thinks he understands <u>everything</u>, even shipbuilding.' Bismarck, meanwhile, muttered about Wilhelm's inflated opinion of his own abilities, the 'aspiring toadies' who surrounded him, and his minuscule attention span: he would 'take a little peek . . . learn nothing thoroughly and end up believing he knew everything'. The British prime minister, Lord Salisbury, thought he'd spotted something dangerously rash in the kaiser-to-be, and worried that he would take Germany into the arms of Russia. Bismarck's most senior adviser at the German Foreign Office, Fritz Holstein, was concerned about Wilhelm's hostility to Britain. Six weeks before Fritz had died the queen had visited Berlin, prepared to have a showdown with her intransigent and disloyal grandson. Salisbury had tried to restrain her. Both he and the German Foreign Office, he told her, were 'afraid that, if any thorny subject came up in conversation, the Prince might say something that would not reflect credit on him; and that, if he acted so as to draw any reproof from Your Majesty, he might take it ill, and a feeling would rankle in his mind which might hinder the good relations between the two nations'. He reminded her that 'All Prince William's impulses, however blamable or unreasonable, will henceforth be political causes of enormous potency; and the two nations are so necessary to each other, that everything that is said to him must be carefully weighed.'

In the event, both Wilhelm and the queen behaved impeccably and anxieties were quietened. Wilhelm told the British ambassador that he'd been 'delighted' by his grandmother. The 69-year-old queen had been, Fritz Holstein observed, 'extraordinarily gracious' to her grandson, 'and vice versa . . . This will somewhat lessen the Prince's foolish hatred of England.' In a private audience with the queen, Bismarck assured her that Germany didn't want a quarrel with England. Vicky reported that he had told her that despite Wilhelm's inexperience ' "If you throw him in the water he'll swim," for he was not devoid of cleverness.' At a state dinner that evening, the chancellor chose a large 'bonbon' decorated with the queen's portrait in icing, and very ostentatiously unbuttoned his frock coat and placed it close to his heart. Privately, Bismarck was confident that he could manage Wilhelm just as he'd managed his grandfather, by shameless manipulation, cajoling and, where necessary, a little light bullying.

Fritz succumbed to his throat cancer on 15 June. He had ruled for three months. Bertie telegraphed George, who wrote in his diary that 'Poor dear Uncle Fritz has died . . . it is too terribly sad.' Wilhelm expressed no such tenderness. Moments after his father died, he ordered that the Neues Palais be cordoned off by soldiers and searched and no one, especially his mother, be allowed to leave. The soldiers were looking for documents – Vicky's letters and Fritz's war diaries – which Wilhelm had been told his mother was trying to smuggle out of the country. He was too late; she'd already got the boxes to England via the British embassy days before.* It was a violent gesture designed to humiliate and distress, 'as though', as Wilhelm's first biographer, Emil Ludwig, later wrote, 'a monarch had been murdered, and his hostile successor, long prepared, had seized upon the newly acquired authority'. It was also an act of Oedipal rage. Fritz was buried three days later, with none of the traditional lying in state. No foreign dignitaries were invited to the funeral and Bismarck stayed away. In contravention of his father's dying wishes Wilhelm ordered an autopsy to confirm he had died of cancer, and forbade the marriage of Moretta and Battenburg. Though the new kaiser would later protest his love and admiration for his dead hero-father and put up innumerable memorials to him, he didn't mention Fritz in his first speech to the Reichstag at all, instead declaiming that he would 'follow the same path by which my deceased grandfather won the confidence of his allies, the love of the German people and the good will of foreign countries'. Few people at court seemed to mind: the Hohenzollerns were famous for their intergenerational hatreds, the Empress Friedrich, as she now was, had been regarded as a dangerous and unpredictable force whose eclipse was long overdue, and the kaiser at least looked forceful. After decades of doddery Wilhelm I and the uncertainties of the previous months, Germany was ready for a charismatic young ruler. Wilhelm seemed just that: modern, energetic, able to connect with his audience.

---

* Her justification of this by no means legal act was that she was saving the documents from Bismarck, who had already conspired to minimize the important role Fritz had played in persuading his initially reluctant father and other German princes to accept unification.

When he rode through the poor areas of Berlin a few weeks after his accession, people cheered, 'Hail to the workers' king!' He seemed present, immediate and quickly showed a passion for making speeches full of resounding phrases, promising a new age of German greatness, expressing his purposefulness and lack of self-doubt.

Edward and Alexandra were two of the few who made it to Fritz's funeral. The Prince of Wales, who had been a regular visitor to his brother-in-law's sickbed, found his sister broken and isolated. She 'cried and sobbed like a child', he reported. Alexandra wrote to George that 'instead of Wilhelm being a comfort and support to her, he has quite gone over to Bismarck and Co, who entirely overlook and crush her. Which is too infamous.' Bismarck's son Herbert, now the German foreign minister, told Edward that Fritz had been 'unfit to reign', and the chancellor told him 'that in fact the Emperor had never been competent, on account of his illness, to reign and that the country had been governed by the Empress but that the Salic law did not exist here'. The couple were angry and offended. At their audience with Bismarck they departed from the usual empty diplomatic pleasantries and started asking awkward questions. What was happening about the kingdom of Hanover, seized and annexed by Prussia during the wars of the 1860s? Its heir, the Duke of Cumberland, was Bertie's cousin and his wife was Alexandra's younger sister, Thyra, and he'd been fruitlessly demanding compensation for years. Was it true that Fritz had been considering handing back Alsace-Lorraine to the French, Edward added – a question which Queen Victoria's secretary later admitted was perhaps 'more . . . than was prudent'.

Bismarck was not accustomed to being interrogated and he didn't like it. The Waleses couldn't have known it, but he was secretly using the Hanover revenues to fund his manipulation of the German press – including the articles that had so traduced Vicky. As for Alsace-Lorraine, it was one of the key triumphs of his political career. But the dictates of diplomatic etiquette forced him to make polite, affirmative noises. The next day Edward sent a written version of Bismarck's answers to his son Herbert, asking that the chancellor sign off on them – just to ensure they were correct. Bismarck was furious – as Edward meant him to be. The German government made a formal complaint to the British government about 'the interview with Their Royal Highnesses when advantage had been taken of a visit of ceremony to put questions to him which it was difficult to answer on the spur of the moment'. Both sides exited angry.

The Germans were determined to get their own back. Berlin gossip soon had it that the Prince of Wales had *demanded* that Alsace-Lorraine be returned to the French – a rumour designed to embarrass Edward and to stir a new wave of antipathy for Vicky. And when Wilhelm, with whom Edward thought he'd parted on good terms, sent his representative to his grandmother to announce his accession, he deliberately chose an officer whose dislike of his mother and father was well known, and who neglected to mention Fritz's name at all. The queen was chilly. Wilhelm complained. 'The Queen is extremely glad to hear that General Winterfeldt says he was received coldly, though civilly; for such was her <u>intention</u>,' she replied.

'I do not like the look of things in Germany,' the British prime minister, Lord Salisbury, sighed barely two weeks after Wilhelm had become kaiser. 'It is evident that the Young Emperor hates us and loves Russia.' In her journal, the queen worried that Wilhelm was 'leaning towards Russia', and bemoaned 'how untrue and heartless' Bismarck had proved to be.

Robert Cecil, Lord Salisbury, nearing sixty, had been prime minister, foreign secretary and leader of the Conservative Party since 1885, with one brief interruption, and was the most important figure in British politics (with the exception of William Gladstone who was coming to the end of his career). The queen trusted and respected him, inviting him to sit in her presence – his knees were starting to go – a privilege she allowed almost no one else. Six foot four, increasingly broad, bald and impressively bearded, he came from a long line of aristocratic statesmen; he was also a misanthropist, a depressive, an intellectual who enjoyed passing himself off as a philistine (he spent his spare time debating theology with his family and working in his laboratory at Hatfield House, where he installed the first electric light system in England) and so famously short-sighted and self-absorbed that he frequently failed to recognize his own family. He was an effective politician with a talent for foreign affairs, combining the prime ministership with the post of foreign secretary, a post invariably held by the grandest aristocrats. Though he presided over the world's self-described great liberal democracy, his political views were not worlds away from those of Bismarck or Nicholas's mentor Pobedonostsev. A conservative in the purest sense, he'd entered politics to defend the ruling propertied classes from the ravages of democracy and an expanding franchise. For him, the upper classes represented the best of human endeavour – birth, intelligence and culture – and they deserved to rule; inherited wealth, he believed, made a man less prone to corruption. It was no small irony – though not to him, he would have seen no contradiction – that Salisbury was shamelessly nepotistic, promoting his sons and nephews so liberally that his last administration was referred to as 'Hotel Cecil'. He regarded the masses with withering scorn, hated socialism, the 'insane passion for equality' and public opinion. He particularly disliked the whole idea of consultative government, claiming that 'Until my own mind is made up, I find the intrusion of other men's thoughts merely worrying,' and could be suffocatingly secretive – especially when it came to foreign affairs. He ran the Foreign Office as if it were his own feudal fiefdom. A natural pessimist, his political creed was: 'Whatever happens will be for the worst and therefore it is in our interests that as little should happen as possible.' His cautious, delicate manoeuvres as the guardian of Britain's world position through keeping the peace in Europe, had been, not entirely accurately, dubbed 'splendid isolation'.

Salisbury's view of the queen seems to have been an ambivalent combination of respect, condescension and occasional exasperation. He came from the tiny group of very grand aristocratic families who, as one of Bertie's cleverer mistresses observed, 'believed they had the prescriptive right to rule England in the same way as they ruled their estates'. There was a hint of condescension in their attitude to the monarchy. But at the same time they gloried in the ritual obeisances they were obliged to make to it. Salisbury said that he respected the queen as a reliable barometer

of public opinion. He coaxed, occasionally indulged and sometimes actively misled her to get his way. But at the same time he
seemed to like talking to her – among the few people he did
regularly discuss and debate with were the women in his close-knit
family; they both shared a very similar political outlook and a
certain world-weary experience. She was a useful ally in the
maelstrom of European politics, with decades of experience behind
her, and was a valuable source of intelligence through her
cousinage. But on the subject of her European relatives (as opposed
to European relations) they disagreed. When he was a journalist in
the 1860s, Salisbury had written an article critical of her German
sympathies, concluding, 'the national will must necessarily be
supreme in the last resort'. Personal relationships between monarchs could be useful, but they mustn't be allowed to compromise
foreign policy. He quietly deplored the fact that his queen was
'very unmanageable about her conduct to her relations; she will
persist in considering William only as her grandson'.

Salisbury urged the queen to try to normalize relations by
writing to her grandson to congratulate him on his accession.
Reluctantly, she agreed. 'Let me also ask you to bear with poor
Mama if she is sometimes irritated and excited,' she wrote. 'She
does not mean it so; think what broken and sleepless nights she
has gone through, and <u>don't mind it</u>.' Willy replied, 'I am doing
my utmost to fulfil [*sic*] her desires.' This wasn't true. In public he
called his mother 'that fat, dumpy little person who seeks influence', he was determined to get her away from Berlin and Potsdam
and eventually settled a measly pension on her. He was far keener
to tell the queen that he was about to go to St Petersburg to meet
the Russian emperor, 'which will', he told her,

be of good effect for the peace of Europe and for the rest and quiet of
my allies. I would have gone later if possible; but State interest goes
before personal feelings, and the fate which sometimes hangs over nations
does not wait till the etiquette of court mournings has been fulfilled. I
hope and trust that much good will come of the proposed meeting, as
I deem it necessary that monarchs should meet often and confer together
to look out for dangers which threaten the monarchical principle from

democratical and republican parties . . . It is far better that we Emperors
keep firm together.

The letter was in English, though the two might just as comfortably
have corresponded in German. But as Wilhelm had been writing
to his grandmother in English since childhood, it seemed natural to
continue and he was proud of his fluency. The contents, however,
seemed to confirm all Salisbury's and the queen's worries about
Wilhelm's enthusiasm for Russia. The swiftness of the visit, barely
a month after Wilhelm's father was in the ground, also offended
Victoria. Mourning the dead was almost a religion with her; forever
in black, she kept the British court in an eternal state of 'light
mourning' for a constant stream of dying relatives, so that the
most exciting colours ladies-in-waiting were allowed to wear were
white, grey, purple and mauve. She wrote a reproving letter. In
his not always reliable memoirs, Wilhelm claimed that Bismarck
'gave way to a violent fit of rage', on reading it. He himself
composed a calm reply which 'laid stress upon the position and
duty of the German Emperor, and that his grandmother must leave
to him the question of deciding in what manner this was to be . . .
From that day onward my relations with the Queen, who was
feared even by her own children, were of the best imaginable.'
This was not how it appeared to the queen. 'How sickening it is
to see Willy, not two months after his beloved and noble father's
death, going to banquets and reviews!' she wrote angrily to
Edward. 'Trust that we shall be very cool, though civil, in our
communications with my grandson and Prince Bismarck, who are
bent on returning to the oldest times of government,' she told
Salisbury.

Nor was Wilhelm feeling amiable. A month later in a speech,
he rebuked 'those people who have the audacity to maintain that
my father was willing to part with what he . . . gained on the
battlefield'. This was a reference to Edward's suggestion at his
father's funeral that Fritz had been considering returning Alsace-
Lorraine to the French. 'We who knew him so well cannot quietly
tolerate, even for a single moment, such an insult to his memory
. . . we would rather sacrifice our 18 battle corps and our 42 millions

of inhabitants on the field of battle than surrender a single stone.'
Wilhelm was becoming famous for his forceful speeches.

From Berlin the British ambassador, Sir Edward Malet, reported
that 'the Emperor', was said to be increasingly 'anti-English' and
leaning 'towards Russia' – though Bismarck was said to be entirely
well disposed towards Britain. 'I am anxious to place on record
that I believe this assertion to be unfounded,' the ambassador
added. He was entirely correct. It had been Bismarck who had
suggested the visit to Russia. Wilhelm's personal quarrels with his
English relations might be the talk of the Berlin and London courts,
but his attitude towards Russia was far more hostile. Barely six
weeks before his accession he had sent the chancellor a memo
proposing a pre-emptive strike on Russia. He had been listening
to his old political ally General Waldersee – the chief proponent
of an attack on Russia, who had been stirring with stories of
Russian troop movements on the border and Russian attacks on
Bulgaria – and had succumbed to the old Prussian fears of invasion.
Bismarck's long, exasperated reply warned Wilhelm that if anyone
found out the soon-to-be kaiser was advocating war against the
advice of his chancellor, international confidence in the German
government would collapse. Somewhat abashed, Wilhelm had
backed down. But when he became kaiser he promoted Waldersee
to chief of the Imperial General Staff, and Bismarck was soon
receiving reports that the Russians considered the new kaiser
worryingly anti-Russian.

Bismarck understood as almost no one else that Germany was
caught in an awkward eternal triangle with Russia and Austria-
Hungary, its other imperial neighbour. Those two empires were
increasingly bitter rivals in Eastern Europe; Bismarck was convinced that Germany needed to be on good terms with both. But
it was like walking a tightrope. Austria-Hungary, ruled over by
the Emperor Franz Joseph von Hapsburg, the latest scion of one
of the longest-reigning royal dynasties in Europe, was territorially
the dominant force in central Europe, a state comprising 50 million
people from about a dozen nations and many different ethnic
groups. But in power terms it was regarded as an empire on
the way down. Within its borders a dozen nascent nationalist

movements were threatening to pull it apart. Respect for the inscrutable, irreproachably correct, dutiful and patient Emperor Franz Joseph, now in the fortieth year of his reign, was increasingly cited as the only thing holding the different groups – among them Croats, Czechs, Poles, Hungarians and Ukrainians – together. Though he presented himself as an autocratic monarch with one of the most stiffly hierarchical courts in Europe, Franz Joseph had kept the empire together through a series of peaceful compromises which had turned him into a constitutional one.

The empire had been further weakened by the loss of Italy after 1848, and Bismarck himself had sent it into eclipse by kicking it out of Germany in the Austro-Prussian War of 1866. But Bismarck – always sensitive to Germany's geographical vulnerability – nevertheless saw Austria as an important bolster and ally against Russia and France, whose politicians made periodic demands for revenge for Alsace-Lorraine. In 1879 Germany and Austria had signed a defensive alliance. At the same time Germany needed to keep Russia friendly because of its proximity, its potential for causing chaos in Eastern Europe, and the absolute need to keep it from going anywhere near France, which Bismarck was determined to keep isolated. The problem was, Austria and Russia had become implacable rivals over who had influence in the Balkans, and dealing with the two – allying with Austria, placating Russia, trying to keep peace in central Europe and not being caught doing either – had become increasingly difficult. Now talk in the German army of attacks on Russia was starting to be backed up by the Pan-German movement, whose traditional arguments for the unification of all germanic peoples were beginning to take on an expansionist, racial dimension, insisting that Germans had a God-given right to dominate central Europe, and that the Slavs – of which Russia was the largest nation by far – were the Germans' natural enemies – and degenerate to boot. In 1887, in an attempt to bring the two countries closer, Bismarck had signed an absolutely secret Reinsurance Treaty with Russia, by which each country promised benevolent neutrality should the other go to war, and Germany additionally pledged to back Russia's claims in Bulgaria and to support it should it 'need' to take Constantinople.

Simultaneously, however, Bismarck had also secretly brokered an agreement between Austria, England and Italy, one of the consequences of which was that – with no visible signs of German encouragement – Britain agreed to bring its naval muscle to bear to prevent Russia from making any gains in the Balkans and the Ottoman empire.

Despite his hostility to Russia, Wilhelm was thrilled by the idea of visiting St Petersburg. It was the site of his great diplomatic triumph four years before – he'd impressed the tsar and almost managed to bring Germany, Russia and Austria-Hungary together. Diplomacy was regarded as the grandest and most senior of the political arts – the field of kings and the highest aristocracy – and carried out behind closed doors. Wilhelm believed that it should be conducted through personal relationships between monarchs. His mother had passed on his grandfather Albert's notion that solidarity between monarchs was the way to preserve strong ties between countries, and he was convinced it would be a triumphant justification of the innate superiority of monarchs and the 'monarchical principle', a repudiation of the claims of democrats and republicans. Wilhelm liked to talk of a 'magic tie uniting him with all other anointed heads. It was a supernatural, a mythic sacrament . . . the mystic fellowship of monarchs was heaven-ordained.' The problem was that more than ever before, monarchs – Wilhelm among them – were increasingly having to weigh the claims of their exclusive supra-national club against the demands of their countries' national interests.

He arrived at St Petersburg in the imperial yacht *Hohenzollern* at the end of July 1888, accompanied by Herbert von Bismarck, with strict instructions to avoid controversy: the visit must be 'friendly, neighbourly, politically disinterested'. He attended a Romanov family dinner at which the tsar and Nicholas threw wet towels at each other; he toasted Alexander in Russian; the two emperors talked privately. The tsar told the German ambassador that Wilhelm's 'frank, guileless character' and 'his mere presence dispelled much of the artificially created mistrust of him'. Even the tsarina, whom the German embassy regarded as indefatigably hostile to Germany, had been 'enchantingly natural'. Herbert von

Bismarck was delighted with his informal audience with the tsar, who wore an old grey jacket. Alexander proposed that the two countries collaborate to combat revolutionary tendencies, and told him how relieved he was that Wilhelm was on the throne rather than Fritz. He also asked how Wilhelm was getting on with his English grandmother – even the Russians knew they hadn't been on good terms. Bismarck had made some pointedly anti-British comments and the tsar had laughed uproariously.

'Rarely before have the hosts and the visitors enjoyed each other's company more,' the German ambassador, von Schweinitz, wrote breathlessly to Bismarck. The emperors' parting had been an 'unforgettably sad moment for everyone'. 'The Russians were never so conciliatory, so humble, so compliant,' another German diplomat wrote to Fritz Holstein, Bismarck's senior adviser at the Foreign Office.

Within a few weeks more sober – and realistic – evaluations emerged. It was quietly acknowledged by both sides' foreign ministers that personally the tsar and the kaiser were 'still not very close', and seemed not to have much to say to each other. But at least peace was in the air.

In early October Edward discovered that he and Wilhelm would be visiting Vienna simultaneously. He wrote to tell Wilhelm and to propose they meet. He received no reply, and when he arrived in Vienna – bringing his spectacularly unflattering German Pomeranian Hussars uniform, in honour of his nephew – it was to be told by an exceptionally embarrassed Austrian foreign minister that he must leave the city, as the kaiser had just informed Emperor Franz Joseph that he would rather there were no other royals present during his visit. It was painfully obvious that the gesture was aimed at Edward – a piece of fantastically calibrated rudeness emphasizing that Wilhelm was now the senior royal, and hitting at Bertie's sense of himself as popular guest and family conciliator. He thought he understood his nephew and had been sending his sister advice on how to handle him. 'Nothing could have been nicer than his manner towards me . . .' he recalled incredulously of seeing Wilhelm at Fritz's funeral in Berlin. 'We parted the best of friends.' Edward was so astonished that he couldn't believe it and wrote to his nephew again, arranging for the British military attaché in Berlin, Colonel Swaine – the man whom two years before Wilhelm had flattered into revealing British military secrets which he had then passed on to the Russians – to deliver it. The kaiser refused to receive Swaine, and when the military attaché came upon Wilhelm the next day by chance, the emperor turned his back on him. Swaine was so upset that he immediately requested a transfer from Berlin. Edward was taken shooting in Romania by Archduke Rudolf, Franz Joseph's son and heir, who detested Wilhelm's brash manner, his autocratic views and his brusque way of expressing them, and was probably jealous of him too. It is his unflattering reports in the Austrian government archives that tell us of Wilhelm's Viennese sexual dalliances in the early 1880s.* The kaiser arrived in Vienna, and was soon – Rudolf was pleased to pass on to Edward – laughingly telling his friends that he much preferred his uncle's rooms (i.e. the city he'd vacated) to his company.

Queen Victoria immediately demanded an explanation from the German government. Bismarck replied with a long point-by-point letter to Salisbury, accusing the Prince of Wales of a series of rudenesses and faux pas: principally that he had claimed that Fritz had planned to return Schleswig-Holstein and Alsace-Lorraine, that he had taken advantage of the chancellor's 'amiability' to 'force' him to agree to recompensing the Duke of Cumberland, and that he treated Wilhelm 'as an uncle treats a nephew, instead of recognizing that he was an Emperor'. He added it had not been appropriate for the two men to meet in Vienna because Germany was in the midst of delicate negotiations with Russia, whose tsar would have been 'irritated'.

Evidently Wilhelm still harboured angry feelings towards the British royal family, and that anger resonated with wider German sensitivities about English superiority and lack of respect: the English family's mistreatment of the kaiser quickly became a

---

* Barely three months later Rudolf would commit suicide with his mistress at Mayerling, the deaths initially presented as an accident.

mantra. 'The Germans all say that the English royal family never treat the Emperor Wilhelm as a sovereign, but like a little boy,' the wife of the British ambassador in Vienna wrote in her diary. Bismarck was happy to air these grievances – they kept Wilhelm's mother Vicky unpopular in Germany and they reminded Wilhelm he needed to be on good terms with Russia.

'As regarding the Prince's not treating his nephew as Emperor,' the queen spluttered, 'this really is too vulgar and too absurd, as well as untrue, <u>almost</u> to be <u>believed</u> . . . To pretend that he is to be treated in private as well as in public as 'His Imperial Majesty'' is perfect <u>madness</u>! . . . If he has <u>such</u> notions, he better <u>never</u> come here. The Queen will not swallow this affront.' She added that her own sources had confirmed that Wilhelm had set out to provoke and humiliate Bertie deliberately, telling Crown Prince Rudolph that if his uncle wrote him a very kind letter '<u>he might perhaps answer it</u>! . . . All this shows a very unhealthy and unnatural state of mind; and he must be made to feel that his grandmother and uncle will not stand such insolence.' Relations between the respective governments should not be affected, she conceded, but 'with such a hot-headed, conceited, and wrong-headed young man, devoid of all feeling, this may at ANY moment become impossible'.

Salisbury was increasingly exasperated by what he saw as a family squabble getting out of hand. He told the German ambassador, Count Hatzfeldt, that Wilhelm would not be welcome in England – though he added emphatically that 'discussions of this kind on personal questions, whatever we might feel upon them, would not affect the general policy of the two nations'. Hatzfeldt, an experienced and respected diplomat – Bismarck called him 'the best horse in the diplomatic stable' – simply did not dare to pass the first part of the message on to his German masters. This was less unusual than it sounds, especially in Germany, where everyone was scared of Bismarck. 'From the hints he let drop,' Lord Salisbury told the queen, with some relish, '. . . the young Emperor was very difficult to manage, that Prince Bismarck was in a great perplexity, and his temper had consequently become more than usually unbearable'. But he also asked the queen to cancel Vicky's upcoming visit to England as a gesture of peace. 'It would be impossible, heartless and cruel to stop my poor broken-hearted daughter from coming to her mother for peace, protection and comfort,' she protested. Politically, it would have been a sensible move; personally, it was unkind. Vicky was desperately unhappy, abandoned by former allies now looking to Wilhelm for favour, and the continuing victim of the Bismarcks' vicious whispering campaign.* The queen, however, couldn't resist turning her daughter's visit into an ostentatious retaliatory snub to the kaiser. She treated her like a visiting head of state: Edward met her in the royal yacht; the English court and the entire German embassy staff, including Hatzfeldt, were summoned and presented to her. The queen let Salisbury know that she wanted no communications on this or any other royal matter to be sent to Wilhelm and the German court.

This was not good news for Salisbury. Politically, Britain needed Germany's goodwill. Germany was a key supporter of Britain's controversial occupation of Egypt – at a time when France was trying to harness international opposition against it. In an attempt to counter the potential political fallout of the family feud, he sent British warships to support a German blockade of the Sultanate of Zanzibar on the East African coast.† The alleged reason for the blockade was to stop an illegal trade of slaves and arms. In reality, it was to pressure the sultan into taking back the German East Africa Company, which had been kicked out of Zanzibar after a local revolt against its heavy-handed treatment of the natives. The German Foreign Office had asked for support, hinting that if it wasn't forthcoming, Germany might rethink its position on Egypt. Salisbury saw it as an inexpensive gesture of friendliness at a moment when it was needed. The reasons he gave to the queen were a little different, though. Britain must send ships, he told her, because of the 'extreme untrustworthiness' of the governments in Berlin and Rome (which also had interests in Zanzibar). He felt

---

* It was claimed that she had passed state secrets to foreign powers, and that she'd had an affair with her court chamberlain while Fritz was alive.
† Present-day Tanzania.

sorry for the sultan, he told her, because German colonialists were famously 'brutal'. As the first year of Wilhelm's reign drew to a close, the hint of a threat and the marked hostility of Wilhelm made Salisbury feel distinctly pessimistic about the future of Anglo-German relations.

It's hard to locate the precise source of Wilhelm's dislike of Edward. He was more than just a proxy for the queen – whom it is true Wilhelm could not have directly insulted. The kaiser's feelings went back at least to 1884, when he had accused his 'false and intriguing' uncle of nefarious plots and double-dealing in his letters to Tsar Alexander III. At the time, Edward had come to Berlin to convince the old kaiser to allow Wilhelm's sister Moretta to marry Sandro Battenburg, the match Wilhelm so angrily opposed. A year later he'd summoned a furious Wilhelm to Hungary to inform him Queen Victoria refused to invite him to England. It may well have dated back further. Edward's slightly louche, relaxed, hedonistic, civilian lifestyle seemed degenerate compared to the austere, puritanical, martial identity Wilhelm wanted to project. And yet he was jealous of his uncle, wanted his approval and resented the fact. He saw Edward, who was so obviously imperfect, effortlessly receiving his mother's approval. He envied – though he would never have admitted it – Edward's great popularity in Europe. It wasn't just in Paris that Edward cut a dash, even in Berlin fashionable young men wanted to copy the Prince of Wales's suits. Wilhelm craved and aspired to the kind of approval that Bertie seemed to attract effortlessly. Although the world talked about his masterfulness, his authority, his promise, he envied Bertie's easiness. It scratched at him. It was all tied up, of course, with Edward being British, which brought out confused feelings of inferiority, desire and anger. He longed for Bertie to show approval of him – years later his best friend Philipp zu Eulenburg would observe crossly that he fluttered 'round fat King Edward like a leaf in the wind round a tower'. All royals minded about their status, but Wilhelm seemed to mind more than most. Slights – real or imagined – touched a nerve that sent him into violent retaliation. He complained that at his father's sickbed his mother had treated him like a dog; that Edward didn't treat him like an emperor; and a few months later he would moan that Bismarck treated him like a schoolboy.

Edward might well have been subtly denigrating of his nephew. He had been disgusted by Wilhelm's unfilial behaviour, and it seems possible he knew about his letters to the Russian tsar. Now his *amour propre* had been dented. Given licence to acknowledge their rift, he was quick to show his hostility, ridiculing Wilhelm's grand new imperial manner. 'My illustrious nephew', and 'William the Great', he called him. He told Vicky, 'his conduct towards you is simply revolting', and that he lacked 'the feelings and usages of a gentleman . . . the time may come quicker than he expects when he will be taught that neither Germany nor Russia will stand an autocrat at the end of the 19th century'. The antipathy was fed by both men's wives. Alexandra regarded Wilhelm as the epitome of a bumptious Prussian. 'Oh he is a mad and conceited ass,' she wrote to George a few days after the Vienna incident, 'who also says that Papa and Grandmama don't treat him with proper respect as the Emperor of old and mighty Germany. But my hope is that pride will have a fall some day and won't we rejoice then.' Dona found Bertie disgusting and immoral. The women didn't like each other either: both their families had claims to the duchy of Schleswig-Holstein but had been on opposite sides during the Prussian-Danish stand-off over it in 1864, and the old rivalry still stirred.

In the New Year of 1889 the Germans were suddenly all friendliness. First Bismarck suggested a formal alliance against France, their mutual enemy. Then a few weeks later the kaiser sent a message that he was very much hoping to visit his dear Grandmama – for whom, as Herbert Bismarck told the British ambassador, he felt such 'great affection and veneration' – later in the year.

There were several reasons for the volte-face. Bismarck was again feeling uncomfortably sandwiched between France and Russia. The Russian press was in the grip of a new wave of anti-Germanism. In France, General Boulanger, the prophet of *revanche* against Germany, seemed about to launch a *coup d'état*. Salisbury refused the alliance – as Bismarck must have expected him to. The prime minister could see little reason for European entanglements. He neither felt particularly threatened by France, nor trusted Germany not to drag him into some European conflict. He was, however, deeply relieved by the overture and emphasized he wanted Britain and Germany to be 'as friendly as possible short of an alliance'. Bismarck might well have suggested it as a way of nudging Russia into a more amenable mood. Wilhelm's dramatic change of heart, however, seemed to be the result of his mother moving away from Berlin. Accepting her political eclipse, she moved to Frankfurt, where she built a house. Wilhelm's Anglophobia seemed to disappear almost overnight. Herbert von Bismarck for one, felt almost betrayed that Wilhelm had cursed 'everything English, simply in order to annoy his mother: there was no other reason for his Anglophobia'.

The queen refused to have him. 'William must not come this year,' she wrote to Bertie. 'You could not meet him, and I could not after all he has said and done.' But the pressure for the British family to take Wilhelm back was insistent from both Berlin and Lord Salisbury, and by the end of February Victoria had reluctantly agreed that Willy might come to stay at Osborne for the week of the Cowes regatta – as long as he made 'some sort of apology' to Bertie for his behaviour in Vienna. Willy refused to apologize. At a dinner at the embassy in March 1889, in the course of a long paean in praise of his grandmother, he looked the British ambassador, Malet, in the eye and said emphatically that like his mother he had 'That good stubborn English blood which will not give way.' More than this, he now denied the Vienna episode had ever happened: 'The assertion that the Emperor had no wish to see the Prince of Wales is an invention. Proposal. To enquire of Sir Augustus Paget [British ambassador in Vienna] where he got his news.'

He claimed he had never received the letter Edward had entrusted to Colonel Swaine and when pressed to write 'a friendly message' expressing regret that Edward had thought he'd been snubbed, he told his uncle-in-law Christian of Schleswig-Holstein, who also happened to be Edward's brother-in-law and who had come to Berlin to try to resolve the quarrel, that 'he could not do anything more, and that as he had never uttered the alleged wish he could not express regret for something that he had never said'. The matter was, as far he was concerned, closed.

It was a flat denial of the truth, and everyone else knew it. The queen, who felt she couldn't withdraw her invitation, made her own attempt to extract an apology. At Salisbury's prompting she offered Wilhelm a carrot if he would write to say how glad he would be to see Bertie, and how sorry he was about the misunderstanding: she would make him an honorary admiral of the Royal Navy, complete with white and gold uniform, on his arrival at Cowes. Privately, the Queen regarded the continental habit of conferring honorary military titles on fellow royals as vulgar. In the past she had prevented Bertie from accepting them.

Wilhelm fell upon his new title as if nothing had ever given him so much pleasure in his whole life. 'Fancy wearing the same uniform as St Vincent and Nelson. It is enough to make me quite giddy,' he wrote to Malet, the British ambassador, who had presented him with the news. 'I feel something like Macbeth must have felt when he was suddenly received by the witches.' Not that, he added, he saw the ambassador as a witch. No, he was more of a good fairy . . . But he completely ignored the queen's quid pro quo. 'Her Majesty wrote to me ten days or so ago that she . . . considered the whole [Vienna affair] as <u>closed</u> and <u>finished</u> to her satisfaction . . . So you see <u>all is right</u>.' Again, this simply wasn't true. But the queen, worn down by Wilhelm's stubbornness and pressed by Salisbury, let the subject drop. Bertie, who felt that the kaiser was implying that he was the rude one and had made it all up, grumpily complained that he had been 'sacrificed by Lord Salisbury to political expediency', but was persuaded to accept the inevitable. The incident was tacitly blamed on the Austrians.

Wilhelm arrived at Cowes on 2 August 1889 in a splendid mood in his new admiral's outfit on the royal yacht *Hohenzollern*, with an escort of twelve German battleships. Arriving on your own large private yacht was the equivalent of arriving in your own Lear jet – most major royal families in Europe had two, though royal yachts weren't quite what most would understand by the word: they were often the size of a warship. The British *Victoria and Albert* had a crew of 120 and could carry fifty guests. Under the gold leaf, *Hohenzollern*, the biggest and most powerful royal vessel afloat, was all too identifiable as the warship it had once been.

The British family was gracious. Bertie met Wilhelm off the boat, accompanied by both his sons: Eddy, who was at Cambridge, and George, who – in stark contrast to his cousin's sudden elevation to the admiralty – had just become a captain after six years in the navy. Neither boy had seen Wilhelm since the Jubilee of 1887 (and before that not since the early 1880s,) when he had held himself aloof from the English relations. Since Wilhelm had become kaiser, George had taken to making little barbed comments about him in letters to his mother, calling him 'William the Fidgety', and affecting to laugh at his endless moving about: 'He must have been to nearly every capital in Europe by this time except London . . . Whatever he may think of himself, he is much too frightened to do that.' The queen was prepared to be chilly. She had assured Vicky that she would not speak to those around Wilhelm who had been deliberately horrible to her – a difficult promise to keep since the kaiser's entire entourage had more or less been hand-picked for their dislike of his mother. But in her grandson's company, she thawed. He 'kissed me affectionately', she noted, and 'made a very pretty speech'. He joined her each day for breakfast, which at Osborne she took outside in a little white tent whatever the weather, and dinner. With Edward he attended a naval review and inspected the warships, making a stream of suggestions about how they might improve their guns. He watched the yacht races at Cowes, instantly conceiving a passion for yacht-racing, and Bertie put him up for membership of the Royal Yacht Squadron. His entourage marched past – demonstrating the goose step, or *Stechschritt*, as it was known in Prussia – the queen wrote, 'beautifully, though in that peculiar Prussian way, throwing up their legs'. He invested his two cousins with the Order of the Black Eagle, told everyone how fond he was of Uncle Bertie, appointed his grandmother colonel-in-chief of his 1st Dragoon Guards, and presented her with a portrait of himself in a pointed Prussian helmet. Encouraged by Salisbury, the queen presented Willy's younger brother Heinrich, a genial plodder whom the English relations liked, with the Order of the Garter, and sent Bismarck her self-portrait.

The family disagreements seemed forgotten. The Bismarcks boasted that 'no Sovereign was ever so fêted'. The queen quietly reassured her daughter, 'It was not in the least for William's sake that he was so well received . . . It was as your and dear Fritz's son, my grandson, and the sovereign of a great country with whom it is ever more important we should be on friendly terms.'

Back home, Wilhelm was seized with a new and voluble Anglophilia. The Bismarcks were in no doubt about its source: the kaiser, the chancellor remarked disgustedly, had been enslaved by a British admiral's uniform. Even Philipp zu Eulenburg noted disappointedly that he was 'like a child' over it. Wilhelm told Herbert von Bismarck that his British naval title meant that 'he would have the right, as Admiral of the Fleet, to have a say in English naval affairs and to give the Queen his expert advice. I looked up in surprise, but HM was perfectly serious in what he said.' This was a little odd, to say the least. Honorary titles were flashy trinkets traded between monarchs as symbols of friendship. It meant your picture went up in the officers' mess and they drank your health and celebrated your birthday. No one took them seriously; but Wilhelm had. 'It really gave me such an immense pleasure that I now am able to feel and take [an] interest in your fleet as if it were my own,' he told the queen after his visit. 'And with keenest sympathy shall I watch every phase of its further development, knowing that the British ironclads, coupled with mine and my army are the strongest guarantees of peace . . .'

In October, arriving on the *Hohenzollern* off the Greek coast for his sister Sophy's wedding to the heir to the Greek throne, Wilhelm put on his admiral's uniform, flew the pennant of a British navy admiral, and invited himself – as a real admiral would – to inspect the British squadron anchored there. The officers were a bit startled, but impressed by his encyclopaedic knowledge of British warships. It was, he told his grandmother, 'a great treat for me and also a source of unqualified satisfaction to me'. In December he sent her a plan for the reorganization of the Royal Navy, along with what he claimed was the *on dit* about the Mediterranean fleet: '"The French look down upon the British Mediterranean Squadron with disdain and are sure of doing away with it in short time after the opening of hostilities!" Fancy! What would Lord Nelson say!' The number of battleships in the Mediterranean must, he insisted, 'be reinforced as soon as is deemed expedient', from five to twelve. In 1891 he would send more 'humble suggestions' – which he claimed other officers of the Royal Navy were too respectful to raise – the chief of which was that if the navy didn't replace its heavy guns now, it would 'seriously jeopardize the "moral" of the men'. The Admiralty's tight-lipped reply was that the guns were already being replaced and the kaiser's other suggestions 'would not be improvements'.

It's hard to know what Wilhelm thought he was doing with these kinds of letters, but they would become a cornerstone of his 'personal diplomacy': letters in which friendliness was combined with unintentional hilarity, presumptuous advice and stories about another country's malignity, which were often clumsy and sometimes even made up. What part was sincere, what part lurking ill-will, he probably couldn't have said himself. He was capable of two precisely opposite wishes at the same time – a desire to be politically close to England combined with a desire to see it at war with France – without feeling there was any contradiction. This may have been a function of his own unresolved personality. It also demonstrated the fundamental conflict between the way all leaders of European nation states saw themselves as in competition with their neighbours, and the notion that friendships between royal dynasties could cross national divides. The culture of German diplomacy, which regarded Bismarck's extremely successful, ruthlessly manipulative diplomacy and the Hobbesian view of the world that informed it as admirable realism, encouraged this. But it also raised the question of whether the young kaiser, who showed not only an ability to flatly deny something that everyone else knew to be true, but a determination to see the world rather too much the way he wanted it to be, might be, perhaps, a bit mad and even dangerous.

Wilhelm manifested many symptoms of 'narcissistic personality disorder': arrogance, grandiose self-importance, a mammoth sense of entitlement, fantasies about unlimited success and power; a belief in his own uniqueness and brilliance; a need for endless admiration and reinforcement and a hatred of criticism; proneness to envy; a tendency to regard other people as purely instrumental – in terms of what they could do for him, along with a dispiriting lack of empathy. On the other hand, plenty of royals shared these attributes. It was hard not to have an inflated sense of uniqueness and self-importance, an expectation of constant deference, a certain blind selfishness and assumption that others were there only to serve if you had been brought up amidst constant deference. Queen Victoria was immensely selfish. Plenty more royals were actively eccentric. The Hapsburg family, for example, had its fair share of odd-balls (though this owed quite a lot to endemic syphilis and in-breeding): one archduke was so obsessively religious that he killed himself by drinking water from the river Jordan; several were enthusiastic cross-dressers. Empress Elizabeth, wife of Franz Joseph, sister of mad King Ludwig of Bavaria, devoted her entire existence to the maintenance of her eighteen-inch waist with a regime of obsessive exercise, leather corsets and a diet of raw steak and milk. She insisted on being sewn into her clothes rather than bear the imperfection of creases. It is hard to say for certain whether Wilhelm's problems stemmed from pathology or the eccentricities of the European royal production line.

If the queen received her grandson's cheerily presumptuous missives with gritted teeth, there was always Lord Salisbury to remind her how much better things now were than they had been. 'The Emperor's attitude towards Your Majesty is now very satisfactory. He is a changed man from what he was twelve months ago,' he reassured her. In some ways she and the navy got off lightly. Wilhelm considered himself an expert on many things and was not shy about saying so. In subsequent years, he would personally inform the Norwegian composer Edvard Grieg that he was conducting *Peer Gynt* all wrong, tell Richard Strauss that modern composition was 'detestable' and he was 'one of the worst'; and, against the wishes of its judges, would withdraw the Schiller prize from the Nobel prize-winning German dramatist Gerhart Hauptmann, whose downbeat Ibsen-esque social realism he didn't like. A hundred years before, when courts had still been centres of cultural patronage, such decisions might have been accepted without comment; now, however, even in Germany the emperor's taste was frequently the subject of hilarity.

Bismarck was not pleased with Wilhelm's new-found passion for England, not least because it was accompanied by a fresh wave of hostility to Russia. Since Wilhelm's trip to St Petersburg in 1888, the tsar had shown no inclination to make a return visit to Berlin. Wilhelm felt spurned, and by early 1889 he was back in General Waldersee's anti-Russian camp, a fact Bismarck also didn't like – he knew that Waldersee had his eye on the chancellorship himself. For his part the tsar had decided he disliked Wilhelm too. In the New Year of 1889, when his ministers pressed him about going to Berlin, he lost his temper and called Wilhelm a German 'pipsqueak' and 'a rascally young fop, who throws his weight around, thinks too much of himself and fancies that others worship him'.

The chancellor and the kaiser were also disagreeing over domestic policy. In the spring of 1889 a miners' strike over reduced wages and twelve-hour days had spread across industrial Germany, had politicized large swathes of the urban working classes, and threatened to become a general strike. It was a manifestation of some of the unresolved contradictions in the new Germany. Bismarck had made no attempt to address the tensions and differences; in fact he'd more often used them to play political factions off against each other, and gradually to close off political power from liberal groups, leaving it in the hands of the old Prussian Junker elite. But Germany also had the largest and best organized Socialist Party in Europe and the disenfranchisement of the emerging lower-middle and working classes only fed it. Bismarck, who regarded the working classes as greedy children who needed to be managed and coerced, wanted to send the army in to smash the strikes and then destroy the Socialist Party with strenuously repressive legislation. The kaiser, however, had different ideas. Encouraged by his old tutor Hinzpeter, he'd decided that the government must try to woo the workers away from socialism by demonstrating the monarchy could be sympathetic to their needs and that he was critical of exploitative and unscrupulous employers. He invited a strikers' deputation to meet him, an unprecedented event in German politics, then a group of mine owners, lecturing them on the welfare of their workers. He proposed legislation to regulate Sunday work and shorten working hours for women and children. Bismarck was utterly horrified – as were the tsar and Queen Victoria.

What was really at stake was who was in charge. Wilhelm had come to the throne determined to rule himself, convinced he could make as good a job of it as Bismarck. The chancellor had been effective master of Germany for nearly thirty years and was not ready to give it up. Wilhelm was not interested in the day-to-day work of government, but he had been far from easy to manage. In May 1889 he had told a group of anti-Russian generals, 'If Bismarck won't go along against Russia, then our ways must part.' He had told Emperor Franz Joseph that should Austria find itself at war with Russia, Germany would come to its aid, whether Bismarck liked it or not. When Bismarck announced his intention of reopening the German markets to Russian securities as a gesture of goodwill, Wilhelm ordered him not to do it. The chancellor went ahead without telling him. When he discovered this Wilhelm was incandescently angry. He complained that the Bismarcks were high-handed and demeaned the throne, but he convinced himself he could deal with them.

Alexander III finally came to Berlin in October 1889. To Bismarck's relief Wilhelm set aside his enmity and with the chancellor reassured the tsar that Germany had no desire for conflict with Russia. In reply, the tsar gave his word of honour that Russia would not attack Germany. As proof of their new intimacy, Wilhelm leapt on to the tsar's train as it departed for 'another short and lively conversation'. He told Waldersee that he had been 'very satisfied with the visit', and when a few weeks later twenty Russian divisions were moved closer to the German border – one more feint in the shadow-boxing that the Eastern European states indulged in – Bismarck was able to persuade him not to be alarmed.

The real story of the visit, however, was the conspicuous attention the tsar showed Bismarck, who had been distrusted in

St Petersburg for years. He was now being hailed as Russia's best friend in Berlin. 'I certainly have full trust in you,' the tsar was reported as saying, 'but unfortunately your Kaiser gives others his ear, especially General Waldersee, who wants war. That we are very certain of.'

With talk of war widespread in Europe, it was an auspicious moment for monarchs to meet and test Albert's theory that close relations between royal dynasties promoted peace. European royalty converged on Athens for the wedding of Wilhelm's sister Sophy to the heir to the Greek throne, the slightly dim Constantine ('A good heart and good character,' Queen Victoria had said of him, '. . . go far beyond great cleverness'), who was first cousin to both George and Nicholas and had spent summers with them in Denmark. It was one of only two occasions in their lives when Wilhelm, George and Nicholas would all be in the same place. George, his brother Eddy and Nicholas spent the time talking and teasing each other in each other's rooms with their boisterous cousin 'Greek Georgie'. Wilhelm had no time for his younger cousins, he and Dona were too busy offending the Greek royal family. (The kaiser, famous for travelling with a vast suite, had 'brought 67 gentlemen with him. A pity he didn't bring a few more,' George observed sarcastically.) They'd publicly expressed their horror that Sophy might convert to the Orthodox Church, and threatened to exile her from Germany if she did. They'd also brought a strict Lutheran pastor to the wedding to perform a Protestant service, without consulting the Greek monarch. King George of the Hellenes was so angry he refused to meet Wilhelm off the boat – a slight for which Wilhelm never forgave him.*

By December 1889 Wilhelm's antipathy to Russia had returned. Waldersee had told him that the Russians regarded his friendliness as a sign of weakness, and that the tsar had said of his Berlin visit,

* When Sophy did convert in April 1891, Wilhelm banned her from Germany for three years. 'Another fine specimen of a domestic tyrant!' Queen Victoria expostulated.

'Everyone laid flat on their bellies before us.' In the first months of 1890 the relationship between Wilhelm and Bismarck disintegrated entirely. In January at a crown council – a meeting of Prussian government ministers – Wilhelm was astounded when Bismarck energetically deprecated his new social legislation in front of the other ministers, who then backed the chancellor. The performance was supposed to show the kaiser who was boss. But Bismarck was not quite as light on his feet and as omniscient as he once had been. He was seventy-five and now spent months on his country estates, eating vast quantities of foie gras for his indigestion.

In his absence, opposition had begun to spring up in the corners of government: courtiers, princes, officials sick of his insistence on dominating everything; disgruntled Foreign Office bureaucrats who opposed his Russian policy; army officers who fancied a war; ambitious politicians; Reichstag members who felt his anti-Socialist legislation went too far; and not least Eulenburg, who had come to disapprove of Bismarck's attempts to dominate Wilhelm. The anti-Socialist laws were defeated in the Reichstag and in February Bismarck's bloc of support, the Kartell, was smashed in the elections, while the Socialists logged their biggest vote ever, nearly 1.5 million. Without a working majority in the Reichstag to pass his policies a chancellor was lost. Wilhelm grabbed his opportunity. Bismarck held on grumpily for a few more weeks, trying to bully Wilhelm into submitting to him, until in mid-March the kaiser came to visit him and demanded his resignation. There was an ugly wrangle in the course of which Bismarck showed the kaiser a letter from the tsar which described him as 'mad, an untrustworthy, badly brought-up boy', an insult that hit its mark. 'Tsar Alexander speaks of me in the most dismissive terms,' Wilhelm told Waldersee. 'He's supposed to have said that I am mad.'

A few days later Bertie and George arrived in Berlin for a state visit. Wilhelm – all smiles and dressed in his British admiral's uniform – had arranged celebrations on a grand scale with gala banquets and military inspections. Bertie couldn't help but enjoy being treated 'like a sovereign', and he listened when Wilhelm talked of his desire to be 'on good terms with this country'. But the air was full of ambivalence. When Wilhelm wanted to make

Bertie an admiral in the German navy, he declined – Alexandra had insisted he turn it down – though George accepted an honorary commission of colonel in a Prussian dragoon regiment. 'So my Georgie boy has become a real live filthy blue-coated Pickelhaube German soldier!!!' Alexandra wrote to her son. 'Well, I never thought to have lived to see that! But never mind; as you say, it could not have been helped – it was your misfortune and not your fault – and anything was better – even my two boys being sacrificed!!! – than Papa being made a German Admiral – that I could not have survived – you would have had to look for your poor old Motherdear at the bottom of the sea.' Father and son watched Bismarck make his final departure from the Berlin Schloss. Edward said of the chancellor who had maligned and offended his family, ' "That's a brave man. I like his spirit. We will call upon him." Which was just what I wanted to say,' George said later. 'I don't think the Emperor ever forgave us.' Wilhelm had told the queen that the chancellor had been having crying fits, and would 'infallibly have died of apoplexy' if he hadn't let him go. They'd parted, he insisted, 'under tears after a warm embrace'. 'We talked to him for sometime,' George wrote in his diary. 'He speaks English perfectly.' Bismarck told them that he had always thought he would only last three years with Wilhelm; he was out by only a year.

The rest of Europe watched Bismarck's fall with fascination. For all his ruthlessness, the chancellor, as Malet reminded Lord Salisbury, had been universally regarded as 'a guarantee of the maintenance of peace in Europe'. The continent was split on whether the impetuous, energetic young kaiser was splendid, ridiculous or frightening. Some months later the British *Daily Chronicle* would hail him as 'the most conspicuous figure in Europe', a man who projected 'indomitable resolution and inexhaustible energy'. But the British satirical magazine *Punch* mocked his grandiose speechifying, and seized on his liking for naval metaphors, running a cartoon of him, 'Dropping the Pilot', in which he stood on deck having sacked Bismarck, declaiming pompously 'the office of watch on the ship of state has fallen to me'. The Russians, extremely alarmed, were suddenly almost fawning. The tsar summoned the German ambassador to explain how much they wanted the Reinsurance Treaty, which was up for renewal, to continue, and how he had 'absolute confidence in our Kaiser, particularly as a representative of the monarchical principle'.

The German Foreign Office allowed the Reinsurance Treaty to lapse in June. Bismarck's subordinates there, to whom he hadn't bothered to explain his policy, had never seen the point of it. As far as they were concerned it had failed to improve relations with Russia and was a betrayal of Germany's treaty with Austria. Wilhelm, gratified by Alexander's apparent desperation to be friends, decided that his own diplomatic advances would be enough to keep the Russians on the boil. No one seemed to understand the huge symbolic significance of the treaty in Russia as a sign of the German government's fundamental goodwill. It was a decision they would come to utterly regret.

Lord Salisbury saw the ironies of Bismarck's fall: 'It is a curious Nemesis on Bismarck. The very qualities which he fostered in order to strengthen himself . . . have been the qualities by which he was overthrown.' Wilhelm, however, worried him. A few months before the kaiser's accession in 1888, the prime minister had been informed by the British Surgeon General, John Erichsen, that some fifteen years before, when Wilhelm was fourteen, a group of German doctors had sent him detailed medical notes about the heir, asking for his opinion of the young man's condition. Erichsen, who admitted he was breaching medical etiquette but felt 'the circumstances were so serious that they justified the breach', had concluded that Wilhelm would never be 'normal'. He would be subject to 'sudden accesses of anger', during which time he would be 'incapable of forming a reasonable or temperate judgement on the subject under consideration', and while 'it was not probable that he would actually become insane, some of his actions would probably be those of a man not wholly sane'.

Salisbury's private secretary would tell George years later that whenever the prime minister encountered some particularly odd piece of behaviour from Wilhelm, he could be heard to mutter 'Erichsen' under his breath.

5. Young men in love (1891–4)

Nicholas loved the army. As in Germany, the officers' messes of the grandest guards regiments were gathering places for the sons of the grandest Russian families – 'a jolly crowd of healthy young men discussing horses, ballerinas and the latest French songs', as Nicholas's cousin Sandro put it. Some of Nicholas's days were full of drill. Plenty more were filled with late-morning lie-ins, skating with fellow guards officers, lunch with grand duke uncles and English afternoon tea with grand duchess aunts. During the season the nights were crowded with receptions, balls and trips to the ballet. Back at barracks, dinner involved getting fabulously drunk on champagne and port, then rushing out into the snow, stripping naked and howling like wolves. In 1891 Nicholas even acquired that obligatory aristocratic accoutrement, a ballerina mistress – with a great deal of prodding from his father, who set him up at the Imperial Ballet School's graduation ball with a young dancer called Mathilde Kschessinska. Until its re-invention fifteen years later by Diaghilev, the ballet was regarded by the rest of St Petersburg as old-fashioned, its main function to please the court and provide grand-ducal mistresses. The girls were both from respectable backgrounds and thrillingly *demi-mondaine*; they were also clean as their health was constantly monitored, which was important in a city where over half the small ads in the newspapers were cures for VD. Giggling and flirtatious, the tiny Kschessinska – at four foot eleven inches nearly six inches smaller than Nicholas – played the charming breathless *ingénue*. She was actually a pragmatic and unsentimental adventuress determined to grab her opportunities. It took her nearly two years of – highly decorous – near-stalking to persuade the extraordinarily diffident Nicholas to install her as his mistress. It was a further six months before the affair was actually consummated.★

Nicholas also had a passion for uniforms and correct dress. He possessed the kit of every regiment in the empire down to the last inch of gold braid, and was starting to collect honorary ranks from foreign regiments. He also had several Russian 'peasant' outfits, which like his father he liked to wear from time to time – trousers and a bright red blouse made out of silk no Russian peasant could have afforded. He thought of himself as frugal – just like his father, he had holes darned, collars and cuffs replaced – but the uniforms and outfits had cost millions of roubles. The appetite for uniforms and their tiniest details had become a mania ubiquitous at all the European courts. Wilhelm's passion was worse than Nicholas's. Even his entourage, the *sine qua non* of court conservatism, regarded him as 'obsessed by this question of clothes and externals', and he was constantly redesigning regimental and court uniforms, the helmets becoming increasingly Wagnerian, the plumes taller, the sashes thicker and shinier. Uniform was a reminder of royalty and the aristocracy's control of the military, but it was also a marker of their superiority to the lower classes – black tail coats, one Russian *grande dame* observed, failed to 'differentiate a gentleman from his lackey'. In Berlin, one writer noted, 'Uniforms, no longer the livery of duty, were worn like feathers, to strut the owner and attract the eligible.'

Though England's upper classes didn't share the continental obsession with uniform, Edward and George were quite as obsessed with clothes as their European relations. Edward had led gentlemen's fashion since the 1860s, despite his increasing girth, and though he looked dreadful in a uniform, he was the epitome of the English gentleman style and even had a tweed check named after him. He harboured what even those who liked him described as a childlike obsession with decorations and 'buttons'. An incorrectly worn medal, an ill-matching pair of trousers and waistcoat,

★ Kschessinska parlayed her way to being one of the stars of the Imperial Ballet and eventually bagged her own grand duke husband.

would send him into paroxysms of irritation, moments when trivia won out over significance. 'It is very interesting Sir Henry,' he once interrupted a minister reporting on the latest exploits of the Amir of Afghanistan, 'but you should never wear a coloured tie with a frock coat.' Lord Salisbury, who was famous for his extreme shabbiness, induced hysterics. Salisbury, who wielded real power and had no interest in clothes, regarded Edward as a fool. George was equally obsessed – the Royal Navy's addiction to appearances merely compounded the tendency. He would never lead fashion, in fact he'd cleave stubbornly to the past. But like his father he was never less than perfectly attired, a white gardenia in his buttonhole. As king, he would send furious little notes to the prime minister of the day whenever a minister wore the wrong frock coat to the House of Commons.

The intricacies of dress were an expression of the pointless arbitrariness and the leisurely emptiness of court life, which had been invented in the eighteenth century by absolutist monarchs to keep control over their most senior subjects. Ironically, it had been embraced by those subjects as a manifestation of their exclusivity and their freedom from having to do anything useful – the more arbitrary and pointless the rules, the more complicated and peacock-like the uniforms, the more differentiated they were from the common herd. Now, by the 1890s, the courts had become disengaged in all senses from the rest of society, and their labyrinthine pointlessness and the elaboration of their uniforms seemed to have grown in inverse proportion. In Russia, as one historian noted, 'The absence of public initiative . . . was attested all too vividly by the prevalence of uniforms.' At the Russian court every official had four uniforms, adorned with peacock and ostrich feathers, gold embroidered oak leaves and eagles, scarlet cuffs and braid – the more gold, measured to an inch, the higher the status.

The obsession with appearances extended further than uniforms into an insistence on certain rules and conformity of behaviour and had more sinister consequences than mere pointlessness and triviality. It almost guaranteed that a kind of hypocrisy became encrusted in the culture of court and the upper classes. In Germany, the dominance of and cultural fascination with the army pressed upon the Berlin court and predominant class a caricature hyper-masculinity. In England the aristocracy's insistence that they lead society by virtue of their virtue meant that they believed they must appear above reproach in everything. Too much was expected, too much forbidden. The conflict could be seen in Wilhelm himself: the imperative to be manly and soldierly all the time had turned him into a caricature and forced him to take refuge in periodic breakdowns. Among Edward's aristocratic set public exposure was the ultimate sanction, but one could do almost anything society in the wider sense condemned – have mistresses, gamble, take an unseemly interest in livestock or small boys – as long as one wasn't discovered or didn't open up that world to scrutiny, for example by leaving one's spouse. It was the price the ruling class found itself increasingly paying for laying claim to social seniority and power on the basis of seemingly pristine morality and perfect appearances. Aristocracies had perhaps always lived by appearances, but with a public increasingly self-aware and demanding, and a press increasingly powerful, when the rest of the world got a handle on scandal behind the court's closed doors, the effects could be devastating; while those who kept irreproachably to the rules would too often be forced to live lives of desiccated self-denial.

Over 1890 and 1891, Nicholas was sent on a ten-month Grand Tour of Asia, from the Near East to the eastern edge of Siberia – the first Romanov heir ever to go so far east. As a child he had received dispatches from the Russian explorer Przhevalsky in Mongolia full of assurances that the people of Central Asia were simply longing to be subjects of the tsar, and he was excited by the idea of Russia's imperial 'mission' to rule Asia. Accompanying him was Prince Ukhtomsky, an Anglophobic Asia expert, who told him that the Eurasian steppe was Russia's historic homeland, and expansion wasn't so much conquering as coming home. But the trip also pointed up the irritating ubiquity of the British empire, taking in Egypt and India, where Nicholas shot tigers and complained sulkily of 'the unbearableness of being surrounded once

again by the English and of seeing their Red Coats everywhere'.
Back in Russia, he began to receive government papers and attend
occasional government council meetings. The experience utterly
bored him. 'I am simply unable to understand how one can possibly
read this mass of papers in one week,' he wrote after he received
the weekly delivery of government files in 1891. 'I always restrict
myself to one or two more interesting files while others go directly
into the fire.' His father did not encourage him to feel otherwise.
'He would not even have Nicky sit in the Council of State until
1893,' Olga recalled '. . . my father disliked the mere idea of state
matters encroaching on our family life.' When Sergei Witte, the
tsar's finance minister, suggested that 23-year-old Nicholas should
be given more responsibility in state affairs, Alexander snapped,
'He's nothing more than a child. His judgment is infantile. How
could he be president of a committee?' In truth, there was something immature and unformed about the young tsarevich. Even in
family photographs his as-yet-unbearded face was hard to pick out;
it seemed yielding and distinctly unassertive.

   It would have been a good time to take an interest in politics.
Beyond Nicholas's little world, a terrible famine was taking hold
in the most fertile regions of European central Russia. By the
end of 1892 it would leave half a million people dead, and many
more helplessly impoverished. Their plight was made worse by the
government's gross incompetence. It initially denied the famine,
forbade private relief efforts, then failed to provide adequate help
itself. When the government finally and unprecedentedly called
on the public, there was a massive wave of voluntary activity which
put it to shame. In its wake came a chorus of criticism, which
grew even louder when the government tried to demonize Leo
Tolstoy, who had spent two years organizing aid for the famine
and volubly criticizing the government. Nicholas, given a seat on
the government's ineffectual Special Committee on Famine Relief,
was all but oblivious to this. Wilhelm, still smarting from the tsar's
rejection, wasn't. He wrote to Queen Victoria with a certain
schadenfreude: 'A great financial catastrophe is looming in the background, and the throng of famished peasants is growing daily . . .
I think this fearful calamity will – with Gods help [*sic*] – for some

time to come keep the Russians from making war upon their unsuspecting neighbours.'

On the other side of the world, George was an officer with the Royal Navy's Mediterranean fleet. In many respects this was the naval equivalent of a European guards regiment: little chance of warfare, lots of parties, lots of sport, in a sequence of Mediterranean cities – Barcelona, Athens, Salonica. His time was constrained only by his parents' constant fussing that he would be corrupted by the dissipations of Malta, where his uncle Affie, an enthusiastic drinker, held court as commander-in-chief of the Mediterranean fleet. Edward asked old naval contacts to keep George busy on exercises, and both parents were very relieved when George was sent to the North Atlantic to be captain of a small gunboat, shuttling up and down the Canadian coast. The extent of his Maltese 'dissipations' had actually been markedly limited. He smoked a bit, drank abstemiously, spent his free time playing cricket and billiards and managed to kiss his cousin Missy – Affie's lively, pretty daughter, ten years his junior, with whom he was at least a little in love – once. Unlike his cousins, he had been properly trained and his promotions were not honorary ones. He still had no love for the navy though, seasickness dogged him, he missed home and found it hard to make friends.

Both young men would be marked by their military experience. Nicholas admired what he saw as the straightforwardness and patriotism of the army, and felt comfortable among the privileged young officers as he would in few places beyond his own immediate family. As emperor he would show a marked preference for the company and – not always appropriate – counsel of aristocratic men from army backgrounds. As for George, in the navy he learned a devotion to strict routine, what his son later called 'an almost fanatical sense of punctuality', an intense suspicion of complication or anything not straightforward, a belief in hierarchy and the need for obedience, and a sense of his own Britishness in contrast to the cosmopolitan roots of the royal family. 'He believed in God, in the invincibility of the Royal Navy, and the essential rightness of whatever was British.' British naval officers, as one historian of the

British empire has observed, 'were often fearfully ignorant of the world and only interested in their beloved navy'. The Royal Navy was not the place for George to have his eyes opened – nor was it meant to be. The forces encircling both young men did not want them to see too far beyond the lives planned for them. The point of Nicholas's Grand Tour of Asia was the opposite of his ancestor Peter the Great's mind-broadening European travels – to emphasize the might and right of Russia's empire, and that its future lay in the domination of Asia.

In June 1891 George came home on leave to shoot, to see his brother Eddy, now a major in the 10th Royal Hussars, a cavalry regiment known traditionally as the Prince of Wales's Own, and to attend his father's fiftieth birthday. Eddy, a rather dilatory officer in Ireland, was a sweet-natured and likeable, if superficial, boy who loved clothes – even his father called him 'collar and cuffs' – and fell in love a little too easily. He'd had crushes on a series of unsuitable princesses and society girls.★ The two returned to Sandringham for their father's birthday in November, an occasion from which their mother was pointedly absent. She was furious at Edward's simultaneous involvement in two high-profile scandals. The so-called 'Baccarat scandal' had put him humiliatingly in the witness box in a public trial for libel, and had led to hysterical denunciations of his gambling habits in the British popular press, especially when it was discovered the prince had his own set of chips with the royal insignia on them. (As the London correspondent of the *New York Herald* commented, you'd have thought the prince had 'broken all the Ten Commandments at once and murdered the Archbishop of Canterbury'.) The other, marginally more private, scandal concerned his former friend Sir Charles Beresford's threat to make public Edward's two-year affair with the beautiful and high-maintenance Frances Brooke, Countess of Warwick – a former mistress of Beresford's. Alexandra, livid at her husband's behaviour, had refused to come home from a holiday in

---

★ Rumours that he might have been caught up in a scandal surrounding the male brothel at Cleveland Street have been convincingly scotched by his biographer Andrew Cook. He had, however, it seems, managed to catch gonorrhoea.

Denmark and had taken their three daughters to stay with the tsar and tsarina in the Crimea.

A couple of days after Edward's celebrations, George contracted typhoid. Alexandra rushed back from the Crimea – the journey took a week – and the family prepared for the worst. The illness had killed Prince Albert, and had nearly done for Edward in 1872. But George survived. By the end of December he was well enough to go to Sandringham for New Year. Then in the second week of January, Eddy, who'd got engaged only seven weeks before, came down with influenza. It turned into pneumonia and he was dead within the week. The children of the rich were almost as vulnerable to the killer diseases of the late nineteenth century as the poor. George had lost a brother at birth; Wilhelm two, both much younger than him: Sigismund, aged two, and Waldemar, aged fifteen. Nicholas had lost a brother in infancy, just the year before his younger brother George had been diagnosed with TB during their Grand Tour. Sent to live in the Caucasus for his health, George would die in 1899 of a coughing fit, while out cycling. Small wonder that educated Victorians, so aware of the advances they had made in taming the world and bending it to their will, were obsessed by the power and pathos of death. 'The only one who can possibly comfort is the Lord who is above us all and whose ways we mortals are sometimes at loss to understand,' Wilhelm wrote to the queen. In his diary Nicky noted, 'The poor boy had just got engaged. I don't know what to think – we are all in the Lord's hands!'

Edward and Alexandra were devastated. They left Sandringham and it was a year before they could bear to go back. Little has been written about the effect of Eddy's death on the Prince of Wales, but it seems that – in an agonizing way – it was the event which launched him into real maturity. Later that year the queen would finally give him access to government papers and he would play a significant role in smoothing over her bad-tempered objections to the Liberal Party's election victory that year, by persuading a politician she liked, Lord Rosebery, to take a position in the government. But George was no less struck. 'No two brothers could have loved each other more than we did,' he wrote to the queen in a moment of unusual emotional openness. 'Alas! It is only now that I have found out how deeply I did before; I remember with pain nearly every hard word and little quarrel I ever had with him.' Eddy was the person, apart from his mother, to whom George was closest, and the one who by his very existence shielded George from a role he had no desire to fill.

While the prince and princess mourned, the queen set her mind to the practical task of turning George into a suitable heir. She quickly made him Duke of York, got him promoted to the respectable rank of post-captain, before he effectively quit the navy (something that didn't in the slightest upset him. 'Hate the whole thing,' he wrote on his last naval exercises off the Irish coast that summer. The rough weather had made him constantly seasick. 'I hope I shall never be in any other manoeuvres.'). And she determined to get him married. While posted in the Mediterranean, George had fallen for his glamorous, outgoing cousin Missy, one of the best-looking and richest princesses in Europe. His parents made the initial overtures, only to have them turned down by Missy's Russian mother. It seems that Marie, who had been unhappy in England, couldn't bear the thought of her daughter coming under the dominating thumb of Queen Victoria. She married Missy off to the dull King Ferdinand of Romania instead. The queen briskly turned to Eddy's fiancée, Princess Victoria Mary of Teck, known as May. She had expended considerable energy in reviewing suitable princesses for Eddy and saw no reason for her efforts to go to waste. There were precedents – the tsar had married his dead brother's bride-to-be. But George, still dazed, didn't want to think about it and found the thought of marrying his brother's fiancée upsetting. The queen, however, was relentless. 'Have you seen May and have you thought more about the <u>possibility</u> or <u>found out</u> what her feelings might be?' she wrote to him two months after Eddy's death.

May was not anyone's first choice as bride for the second-in-line to the throne. She wasn't beautiful, or rich, or, by most European royals' standards, sufficiently royal. Her father was the child of a morganatic marriage, a son of the ruling house of the large German kingdom of Württemberg, but his mother had been 'only' a countess. When the possibility of May marrying the kaiserin's brother had been floated a couple of years before, Vicky had helpfully reported to her mother that Dona had described the idea as a dreadful 'mésalliance!!!' More than this, the Tecks were slightly embarrassing. May's father, Franz, had excellent taste, but also public temper tantrums. Her mother, Mary Adelaide, a grand-daughter of George III, was amiable, selfish, loud and seventeen stone. In the family she was known as 'Fat Mary', and Edward and Alexandra couldn't stand her. Both parents were irredeemably extravagant and had had to flee the country to escape their creditors in May's teens when they had got themselves into terrible debt. As for May's siblings, one brother had kicked the headmaster of Wellington school through a hedge. No doubt as a result of years of being embarrassed by her parents, 24-year-old May, however, was a model of quiet, dignified, slightly remote self-control, quali-ties which, as her biographer wrote, maybe a little ungenerously, 'made it unlikely that Princess May would ever inspire a violent emotion'. But the queen, who didn't care about morganism, and had dismissed a slew of other European princesses for being vari-ously Catholic, 'ugly, unhealthy and idiotic', decided she was perfect for Eddy, whom she judged needed a firm, moral hand. May had other qualities too; she was far better educated than either Eddy or George, and, perhaps in the manner of a poor relation who had always felt herself slightly outside the magic glow of royalty, she was utterly fascinated by and was delighted to be part of, the British monarchy.

No one had predicted emotional fireworks but during the seven weeks of May's engagement to Eddy, they had got on far better than anyone would have expected. But George and May, both extremely shy, did not immediately get on and remained awkward with each other. George was not so diffident with other women. There had been no awkwardness with Missy, who called him her 'Beloved Chum', and in his teens he'd fallen in love with Julie Stonor, the Catholic orphaned daughter of one of his mother's ladies-in-waiting. His mother had allowed the friendship to develop, while rather cruelly making it clear it had no future. His three German cousins – Wilhelm's younger sisters Sophy, Margaret (Mossy) and Moretta, who had stayed close to their mother and seen more of their English cousins – knew him as good-humoured, jolly and energetic. 'George is such a dear & so awfully amusing,' wrote Sophy (but then she was married to the very dim Constantine). 'Dear George! pretty red lips and white teeth that are always my delight,' wrote Moretta. As for Mossy, Vicky had rather hoped he might marry her.

It must have been almost a relief for George to escape to Europe. His mother and he went to Copenhagen in May, where they met up with Nicholas and the Russian family – a meeting which seems to have renewed the young men's friendship. They spent hours talking in each other's rooms. In the autumn George was sent to Heidelberg, a last-ditch attempt to improve his German and to do the rounds of the German relatives. After two months he had made no discernible progress, 'It certainly is beastly dull,' he confided to a friend, longing to return to Sandringham for the shooting, but he visited Wilhelm in Potsdam, where the kaiser – no doubt because he was now a direct heir – paid him more attention than he ever had before: 'William was most kind and civil to me. I have never known him so nice.'

Back in England it was clear that resistance was futile. By the spring of 1893, with everyone – apart from Alexandra – urging him to marry May, George went on a last holiday with his mother. In Athens, he had a long chat with Queen Olga of Greece, who during his years in the Mediterranean had kept a motherly eye on him and called him 'Tootsums'. She told him that May would make a good wife. At home, bundled into the Richmond garden of his aunt Louise, a near-neighbour of the Tecks, where May just happened to be sitting, he proposed.

The whole affair had a pragmatic, anticlimactic air. The queen's acerbic lady-in waiting Lady Geraldine Somerset described the bride-to-be as 'abundantly satisfied, but placid and cold as always', and George as 'apparently nonchalant and indifferent'. 'Quite pleased and contented', was the queen's laconic description of George. The poet and anti-imperialist Wilfrid Scawen Blunt, observing them at a party a month later, noted, 'He is a nice-looking young man, but she one of the least attractive of girls, coarse-featured, with an ill-tempered mouth and a certain German vulgarity, which will be terrible at 35.' The couple were not in love and they had almost nothing in common. May was as close as the royal family got to an intellectual, with a genuine appetite for art and books. George was indifferent to both and obsessed with shooting and stamp-collecting. His mother was still the most powerful force in his life and was determined to remain so. 'It is sad to think that we shall never be able to be together and travel in the same way,' Alexandra wrote after their Mediterranean trip. 'Yet there is a bond of love between us, that of mother and child, which nothing can ever diminish or render less binding – and nobody can, or shall ever, come between me and my darling Georgie boy.' But they were both well trained in doing their duty, and for May the marriage meant deliverance from a life of probable spinsterhood and financial security for her parents.

Time would not relax their mutual and sometimes excruciating shyness. For months after the engagement they remained incapable of talking to each other with any ease, instead sending each other painfully diffident letters. 'I am very sorry that I am so shy with you,' she wrote. 'I tried not to be so the other day, but alas failed . . . It is so stupid to be so stiff together and really there is nothing I would not tell you, except that I <u>love</u> you more than anybody in the world, and this I cannot tell you myself so I write it to relieve my feelings.'

He replied, 'Thank God we both understand each other, and I think it really unnecessary for me to tell you how deep my love for you my darling is and I feel it growing stronger and stronger every time I see you; although I may appear shy and cold.'

In Russia, Nicholas was still a young man in need of a wife, and so far his marital hopes had been frustrated. For years his heart had been set on Alexandra of Hesse-Darmstadt, another of Queen Victoria's numerous grandchildren. They'd first met in 1884 at her older sister Ella's wedding to his uncle Grand Duke Sergei.* She

---

* This was another unhappy royal marriage: Sergei was a chilly, authoritarian homosexual, who had no idea how to communicate with his wife. Ella, however, became very popular with the rest of the Romanov family.

was twelve, pretty and tragic – her mother had died when she was six; he was a young sixteen. After several days of 'romps', he wrote in his diary that they were in love. Four years later in 1889, Ella brought her sister to St Petersburg for the season with the conscious intention of snaring the tsarevich for her. By the end of the trip Nicky was well and truly caught. 'My dream –' he wrote in his diary two years later, in 1891, 'one day to marry Alix H. I have loved her a long time, but more deeply and strongly since 1889, when she spent six weeks in Petersburg.'

Alix was the sixth child of Queen Victoria's daughter Alice, who'd married Louis of Hesse-Darmstadt. Darmstadt was a small, picturesque German duchy, best known as a centre of the arts, and for its well-connected, if impecunious, ruling family. Alix's great-aunt had married Tsar Alexander II – a relationship that had helped keep the duchy from being absorbed by Prussia after it backed the losing side in the Austro-Prussian War of 1866. Alix's mother had died in 1878, while nursing the family through diphtheria. Though she could be somewhat cavalier about her proliferating grandchildren, the queen had taken an intense interest in her six motherless Hessian grandchildren. She found them English governesses and tutors from whom she demanded monthly reports. Each autumn they came to stay at Windsor and Osborne – 'the best part of the year', according to Alix. She described the queen as 'a combination of a very grand person and Santa Claus' – rather different from the near-divinity who intimidated her English grandchildren. The queen allowed the Hesse children a levity she didn't permit many of the other grandchildren. (She patronized their father dreadfully, and when he secretly married his Russian mistress a year after Alice's death, she browbeat him into having the marriage annulled.) Alix was noticeably her favourite. She was blonde and good-looking – at least after the fashion of the time – and Queen Victoria, who was very susceptible to beauty, described her as 'the handsomest child I ever saw'.

Perhaps as a way of feeling closer to the mother she had lost so young and to the grandmother who favoured her, Alix insistently described herself as English rather than German, speaking and writing by preference in English. It also expressed a sense of intense alienation from her circumstances. This was in part a not unusual aristocratic resentment at the Prussian domination of Germany – Alix claimed that Hesse-Darmstadt was separated 'completely from the rest of Germany, which she looked on as Prussia and as a different country'. But it was personal too. Without a mother, a father, an army aristocrat who was often away, and with siblings considerably older than her, she had had a solitary childhood and had grown up self-absorbed, prone to pessimism and deeply religious. She was also mistrustful of, and extremely uneasy with, anyone beyond her immediate circle. She described an occasion on which she had to play the piano in front of her grandmother and guests as 'one of the worst ordeals of her life'. Even her close family found her self-dramatizingly melancholic. 'There was a curious atmosphere of fatality about her,' her English cousin Mary Louise wrote. 'I once said, "Alix, you always play at being sorrowful; one day the Almighty will send you some real crushing sorrows and then what are you going to do?"' Her aunt Vicky couldn't resist observing that the lack of a mother had made her 'a little vain and conceited and affected at times'. But with shy, gentle Nicholas she had let her guard down. He was fascinated by her intensity and wanted to take care of her; she responded to his gentleness, vulnerability and warmth, and also perhaps to his slight air of submissiveness.

There were, however, obstacles. Queen Victoria was implacably against her granddaughter marrying a Russian, and she was also 'bent on securing Alicky [the British family's name for her] for either Eddy or George'. Alix had scotched that plan by making it abundantly clear, when she was summoned for appraisal to Balmoral in the summer of 1889, that she wasn't interested. Eddy, her older sister Ella (who was determined that Alix would marry Nicholas) said dismissively, 'doesn't look overstrong and is too stupid'. Eddy, for his part, developed a massive crush on her. It was a measure of how much the queen liked her that, though stung by her rejection, she decided it showed strength of character.

The second problem was that Nicholas's parents didn't like Alix – perhaps recognizing her tricky personality would not be an asset in a tsarina. They had refused to give him permission to propose.

Ella, who was popular with her in-laws, worked hard to bring them round. The third obstacle was altogether more difficult to overcome. When Nicholas finally gained his parents' approval in January 1893 and went to Berlin to propose to Alix at another royal wedding – that of Wilhelm's youngest sister Mossy to 'Fischy' (Frederick Charles) of Hesse-Cassel – she turned him down. She couldn't, she said, give up her Lutheran faith and convert to Russian Orthodoxy.

Reeling from her rejection, Nicholas was cornered by Wilhelm. Since the Reinsurance Treaty had lapsed in 1890, relations between Russia and Germany had been markedly chilly. A war on import duties between the two nations had intensified to the point that German industrial heavy goods had been all but excluded from Russian markets, and Russian grain from Germany, its one-time largest market. Relations between the emperors were no better. 'My father thought him an exhibitionist and a nuisance,' the tsar's daughter recalled. Wilhelm complained bitterly to Queen Victoria that Alexander had snubbed and avoided him, and that he was massing troops on the German border. The two things – the snub and the threatening army – seemed equally offensive. In retaliation Wilhelm had told the German army to contact the Russian Polish separatist movement, with the apparent aim of encouraging an uprising – though nothing came of it. Most worryingly, however, a few months before, Russia had done the unthinkable and made a defensive alliance with republican France, sandwiching Germany between two potential enemies – a disastrous situation for Germany, one that Bismarck had spent decades working to stave off.

Nicky's arrival in Berlin revived Wilhelm's appetite for 'personal diplomacy'. He decided to arrange a one-to-one with the tsarevich as a first step to improving Russo-German relations. He gave Nicholas a paper in which he argued that Russia should join the Triple Alliance of Germany, Austria and Italy. The tsarevich smiled and nodded and Wilhelm was convinced he detected a pronounced aversion towards France – an indication that the French alliance might perhaps not be long-lived. 'Niki [*sic*] made an excellent impression on all of us, and proved himself in every respect a charming, agreeable and dear boy,' he wrote to Queen Victoria.

'. . . he showed sound judgment [*sic*] and a quiet clear mind, which understands European questions much better than most of his countrymen and family' – a little parry at the tsar. In truth, however, Nicholas was just being amenable. Politics was the last thing on his mind. Crushed by Alix's rejection, he confided in his diary that he wanted only to go home.

Germany and Russia did end up round the negotiating table later that year, but it owed nothing to Wilhelm or Nicholas. The German chancellor, Leo Caprivi, feeling the need for a dramatic gesture to counteract the new French alliance, offered the Russian government a new trade treaty on extremely good terms. Its passage, however, enraged the government's Junker supporters who counted on high tariffs to keep Russian imports from competing against their own more expensive grain. The treaty would play a significant role in Caprivi's later downfall, and expose, not for the first time, the great divisions in German society.

Back in St Petersburg, Nicholas sought comfort from Mathilde Kschessinska and finally consummated the relationship. 'I am still under her spell – the pen keeps trembling in my hand!' he wrote in his journal.

George's wedding was set for early July 1893. It was the biggest royal event in Britain since the 1887 Jubilee, and the first public royal wedding in decades. 'I should so much like Nicky to come, and he has never been in England. I do hope it can be arranged,' George asked his grandmother. (In fact, Nicky had come in 1873 aged five, but all he could remember was that the Shah of Persia who had been there too had shocked everyone with his 'barbaric habits'.*) The Romanovs accepted the invitation and Edward, who loved organizing such things, set about arranging the tsarevich's visit. It was a mark of the young men's closeness (and perhaps also of how few close friends George had) that Nicholas stayed at Marlborough House, where they spent George's final bachelor

---

* This was true. The shah had shouted at his servants, spat out his food, belched in public, groped women and advised Bertie (who was highly amused) to execute the Duke of Sutherland because he was too rich.

evenings chatting until late in their rooms. Lest anyone thought that such informality implied casualness, Edward had crammed every moment of Nicky's visit with incident – starting with a visit from his tailor, a bootmaker and a hatter. 'Uncle Bertie is in very good spirits and very friendly, almost too much so,' Nicky, who found his uncle overwhelming, told his mother. '. . . felt rather dizzy at first.' He was made an honorary member of the Marlborough Club; taken to watch polo; shown George's new rooms in St James's Palace, which he thought 'looks like a jail from the outside'; and taken to dinner with London's grandest society hostess, Lady Londonderry ('Our hostess was delightful but a terrible flirt'). He went to 'Captain Boynton's World's Watershow' twice. He gasped at the heat and marvelled at the 1,500 wedding presents – including a cow – the couple had been sent from across the empire. Watching the riders on Rotten Row, he commented, 'what a pity we have nothing of the kind!' He even went to the Houses of the Parliament to hear the now elderly Gladstone speak. Though he was anathema to the European Right, Gladstone was world-famous as a great orator.* 'I am delighted with London, I never thought I should like it so much,' Nicky wrote.

What Nicholas didn't love was that 'Everyone finds a great resemblance between George and me, I am tired of hearing this again and again.' He may well have found the round of events – garden parties, dinners, luncheons – at which the British royal family had to show themselves off to the people and be gracious to them, an exhausting contrast to Russian court life, which actively discouraged too much interaction. The likeness, however, was powerful and it was now emphasized by Nicholas's cultivation of a carefully trimmed Van Dyck beard just like George's. It led, the queen wrote, 'to no end of funny mistakes, the one being taken for the other'. At one garden party George was asked what

---

* According to the British ambassador in St Petersburg, Gladstone had apparently become bizarrely popular in Russia because he'd said that the Russian government's treatment of prisoners in Siberia was no worse than the British shooting of three Irish tenant farmers at the so-called 'Michelstown massacre' in 1887.

he thought about London and Nicky was congratulated on his forthcoming wedding.

The most surprising outcome of the visit was the effect that Nicky had on Queen Victoria. Age had not dimmed her intense dislike of Russia, and the two nations were bitterly arguing over Russia's attempts to take over the Pamirs – the mountains bordering Afghanistan and Northern India. The British foreign secretary, Lord Rosebery, had recently threatened to send troops to root out Russian soldiers there. The queen received Nicholas at Windsor, arranging that she should be at 'the top of the staircase' for his arrival and then process down slowly, presumably to demonstrate that she could keep anyone waiting if she pleased. She remembered the tsarevich's great-grandfather Nicholas I for his 'undiplomatic bellowing', and said publicly that she did not regard the current tsar as quite a gentleman. But Nicholas wasn't at all what she had expected. He was so polite, so unassertive, such a gentleman (keen, naturally, to win the approval of his love object's grandmother). '"Nicky" as he is always called' – you can virtually hear her melting – '. . . is charming and wonderfully like Georgie.' Even better, 'he always speaks English & almost without a fault', and he was – and this she really approved of – 'very simple and unaffected'. Nicholas described Victoria as 'a big round ball on wobbly legs', who was 'remarkably kind to me . . . She then awarded me with the Order of the Garter which was completely unexpected.'

The wedding took place on 6 July. Nicholas wrote that May was 'radiant' and 'much better looking than her photograph'. She wore white satin embroidered with silver roses, shamrocks and thistles. A number of courtiers complained rather meanly among themselves about the stiff little bows she gave her acquaintances. Alexandra, Nicky noted however, 'looked rather sad in church . . . George and his sisters also'. George had written solemnly a few days before of going to church with Motherdear for 'the last time alone with her'. While Nicholas stayed on in London, George and May went to Sandringham to spend their honeymoon in their new home, York Cottage, a few hundred yards from his parents' mansion, answering mountains of correspondence. Three weeks later they came to Osborne for Cowes Week, and were greeted with arches garlanded with flowers, flags and 900 schoolchildren cheering from carts draped with green branches. That night May sat next to the kaiser at dinner. 'Fancy me, little me, sitting next to William, the place of honour!!! It seemed so strange,' she wrote to her mother. Wilhelm – another family outsider – brought all his charm to bear upon her, though he had been as dismissive of her morganatic antecedents as his wife.

Now it was Nicholas's turn to win a bride. In March the following year he found himself reluctantly in the duchy of Coburg for the wedding of Alix's brother Ernie of Hesse-Darmstadt, to 'Ducky', younger daughter of Affie, the queen's second son, who had recently inherited the duchy from a childless uncle, and Princess Marie of Russia. Victoria herself and the kaiser and his mother were also guests. No one was very happy about the marriage except Queen Victoria, who had bullied the couple into it – Alix least of all. Ernie was homosexual but, as his grandmother endlessly reminded him, needed an heir, Ducky was very young and rich, and they were first cousins.* Alix's father had died two years before, she was very close to Ernie and now she was about to lose her status as the head of his household. She forlornly planned a three-month trip to England 'as I would only be in their way here'.

The drama of the tsarevich and the bridegroom's sister up-staged the wedding. Everyone knew that Alix had rejected Nicky, everyone speculated what would happen when they met. 'Even my dear Mama thought she would not accept him, she was so pointed about it,' Vicky wrote. 'I was in a state of painful anxiety,' Nicholas wrote to his mother, who had insisted he be present. 'All the relatives one after another asked me about her.' Everybody – except possibly Queen Victoria – wanted Alix to say yes. Her family felt she was throwing away a glorious opportunity. The English hoped she might improve Anglo-Russian relations.

---

* The two would split several years later when Ducky ran off with Nicholas's cousin Grand Duke Kirill, for which Nicholas exiled him from Russia.

Wilhelm hoped she would improve Russo-German ones. Over several days the couple were locked in rooms together. 'She cried the whole time and only whispered now and then, "No, I cannot!"' Nicholas wrote to his mother. 'The Emperor did what he could. He even had a talk with Alix.' Willy, ever keen to place himself at the centre of things, would later take full credit for playing 'the part of cupid' with the lovers – though no one else did. In his memoirs he described himself dragging the bashful suitor up to his room, giving him a sabre, putting his fur cap on his head, and thrusting a bunch of roses into his hands. 'Now,' he said, 'go and ask for Alix.'

On the last day of the wedding party, with Nicky's uncles Grand Dukes Vladimir and Sergei sitting next door with Wilhelm, the couple was closeted one more time. 'We were left alone,' Nicholas told his mother, 'and with her very first words she consented . . . I cried like a child and she did too; but her expression had changed; her face was lit by a quiet content . . . She is changed. She is gay and amusing and talkative and <u>tender</u> . . . William was next door waiting for the end of our conversation with the uncles and aunts. I took Alix to see the Queen and then to Aunt Marie, where there were great embraces from the whole family.'

The queen was 'quite thunderstruck, as though I knew Nicky much wished it, I thought Alicky was not sure of her mind. Saw them both. Alicky had tears in her eyes, but looked very bright, and I kissed them both . . . People generally seemed pleased at the engagement, which has the drawback that Russia is so far away . . . But as her mind is made up, and they are really attached to one another, it is perhaps better so.' She wrote of Nicholas: 'He is so sensible and nice, & expressed the hope to come quietly to England to see Alicky at the end of June.' She insisted that Nicholas call her 'Granny', and for the rest of the visit she summoned them for morning coffee in her rooms and made them pose for photographs – photographs in which Alix remained resolutely unsmiling.

Victoria was deeply proprietorial of Alix. 'As she has no Parents, I feel I am the only person who can really be answerable for her,' she told Nicky. 'All her dear Sisters . . . looked to me as their second Mother.' She worried about her too, bombarding Nicholas with letters through the spring and summer of 1894 about Alix's health and her 'nerves'. Since her father's death Alix had begun to complain regularly of exhaustion and pains in her legs. She seems to have had a period of depression, possibly even a breakdown. Did the queen acknowledge to herself the obvious truth that Alix's 'nerves' and her almost pathological discomfort in the company of people she didn't know made her entirely unsuited for the public role of tsarina? Alix put the queen's anxiety down to possessiveness. 'Please do not think that my marrying will make a difference to my love for You,' she reassured her. 'Certainly it will not, and when I am far away, I shall long to think that there is One, the dearest and kindest Woman alive, who loves me a little bit.' There weren't many people who dared to call the queen a 'Woman'.

'I am quite certain that she will make you an excellent wife and she is charming, lovely and accomplished,' George wrote to Nicholas – in English naturally – in what seems to have been his first letter to his cousin, signing himself, 'Ever your most loving cousin Georgie'.

'My dearest old Georgie . . .', Nicholas replied, writing as he would to all the British royal family, in his own impeccable English, 'you can judge of my joy & of the state of happiness I am in now. I am delighted to be here at Coburg & find this place beautiful. Only the time is so taken up by the family (as in Denmark) that I find it even cruel to be torn away from my beloved Alix for a few hours, as I would prefer spending them with my own little bride!' An affectionate, if uninspired and somewhat desultory – once or twice a year at most – correspondence was born.

Nicholas decided to visit Alix while she was on her three-month trip to England, arriving on board his father's new white yacht, *Polar Star*, nearly a year after his previous visit, in mid-June 1894. The month he stayed there, he wrote, was 'paradisiacal happiness'. He and Alix spent several days at Henley with Alix's sister Victoria, who was married to Louis of Battenburg (brother of the ill-fated Sandro and a rising man in the Royal Navy), then went on to Windsor (where Nicholas managed to lock himself 'in a certain place' – i.e. a lavatory – and only got out half an hour later with

Alix's help) and Osborne. They went boating on the Thames, picnicking at Windsor, and at Osborne they put on new-fangled swimming costumes and 'walked in bare feet like a child by water'. When he confessed his affair to Alix she wrote in his diary, 'I love you even more since you told me that little story, your confidence in me touched me, oh, so deeply . . .' She had taken to leaving little notes and quotes in English in his diary. 'Sweety dear, have confidence and faith in your girly dear, who loves you more deeply . . . than she can ever say.' When George and Mary's first child, a boy called David, was born during the visit, Nicholas travelled with the family to Richmond to see him and stand godparent. He worked hard to win the queen's approval. Nicky 'is most affectionate and attentive to me', she observed. 'She is very fond of you,' Alix had reassured him. Underneath, he bridled at 'good Granny's' supervision, her reluctance to let them out without a chaperone and her attempts to shoehorn him into court occasions: 'I have to appear in a tail coat with red collar and cuffs and breeches and pumps – how ghastly!'

Beyond the family, Nicholas cut a less impressive figure – he was such a 'delicate-looking stripling' compared to his father, one courtier noticed; very young, 'very bashful', a German diplomat at the London embassy observed, lapsing into an 'almost childish silliness, which, however, was rather likeable than otherwise'.

What must have struck Nicholas forcibly, as on his previous trip, was the way that the English family – or at least Edward – made themselves so much more available than his own Russian family. Towards the end of the visit, he went to spend a few days with George and his father at Sandringham. The deceptively modest but (on the way to being) modern stately home was very different from the immense, draughty, malachite halls of St Petersburg or Berlin's vast chilly schlosses, a monument to leisurely wealth in which a royal family chose not to be on duty. Edward took Nicholas to a horse sale in nearby King's Lynn, where they ate lunch in a huge tent along with all the other diners, separated only by the dais on which their table was perched, everyone 'gaping more at us, than the horses'. In Russia a Romanov would never have eaten among, and in full view of, the lower orders, but Edward positively enjoyed being on show. Even more unusual were Edward's house guests. 'Most of them were horse-dealers, among others a Baron Hirsch. The Cousins rather enjoyed the situation and kept teasing me about it; but I tried to keep away as much as I could, and not to talk.'

Baron Maurice de Hirsch was a Jew, probably the first Nicholas had ever met. Though in Europe Jews had had, more or less, the same rights as anyone else since the 1840s, in Russia anti-Semitism was still energetically inculcated by the Church, and they remained the poorest and most persecuted of minorities, victims of pogroms (the word comes from the Russian 'to wreak havoc'), and a whole raft of persecutory and restrictive laws. Hirsch was a millionaire entrepreneur and philanthropist of German extraction who was known in Russia – though Nicky had clearly never heard of him – for his attempts to improve the lives of Russian Jews and for the millions he was spending on resettling Russian Jewish emigrants in America and Argentina.

Whilst nowhere was as anti-Semitic as Russia, Edward's friend-ship with Hirsch was a mark of his worldliness and openness. He had made a point of admitting to his social circle a number of rich Jews and self-made millionaires, including the Rothschild brothers – Alfred, Nathan and Leopold – whom he had met at university, along with the Glasgow-tenement boy turned tea millionaire Thomas Lipton and the furniture manufacturer Sir Blundell Maple. By contrast, the Romanovs spoke of 'trade', i.e. the new Russian industrial rich, with only slightly less disgust than they did of rich Jews, and many of the British upper classes exercised a 'salon' anti-Semitism, welcoming in new money but sneering at it behind their backs. Edward's friendliness was certainly due in part to his rich Jewish friends' willingness to pay off his debts – it seems Hirsch had. But he was also fascinated by the energy and power of people who made and manipulated money, and he understood the importance of the new rich far better than the rest of his contemporaries among European royalty and the *haute* aristocracy. The Rothschilds, for example, were not just rich – their bank was the biggest financial institution in the world, and, as the British empire's bankers, they had lent Disraeli the capital to buy shares in the Suez Canal and Cecil Rhodes the money to launch De Beers. Edward took a simple view of class and caste: there was royalty, and there was everyone else. This could manifest itself both as a pleasing lack of snobbery and colour-blindness, and as blunt racism. 'Because a man has a black face and a different religion from our own there is no reason why he should be treated as a brute,' he commented on the way the colonial authorities treated Indians. 'Either the brute is a King, or else he is an ordinary black nigger, and if he is not a King why is he here?' he reasoned when he placed the King of Hawaii ahead of the German crown prince, at the 1887 Golden Jubilee.

In late August Wilhelm told the queen that the tsar was said to be mortally ill.

Alexander was dying of kidney failure. He had been moved to the imperial family's estates at Livadia by the Black Sea, in the hope that the Crimea's famous 'velvet' climate would revive him. The best German doctors had been summoned, but nothing could be done. By mid-October, when Alix arrived at Nicholas's request, Alexander was almost blind and so weak he could hardly rise to kiss her, though he insisted on doing so in full dress uniform. Minny sent a telegram pleading for Edward and Alexandra to come. Perhaps mindful of the comfort she had given Alexandra after Eddy's death, the Prince and Princess of Wales, plus an equerry, a lady-in-waiting and the prince's friend Lord Carrington, the Lord Chamberlain, immediately set off across Europe. Alexander died painfully two days before they arrived on 2 November. He was forty-nine. 'Lord, Lord, what a day,' Nicholas wrote in his diary. 'God has called to him our adored, our dear, our tender Papa. My head spins, I can't believe it . . . it was the death of a saint!' The afternoon of his father's death, he took the oath of allegiance in the gardens of the palace, surrounded by dozens of courtiers, family and servants all dressed in gold. The next day everything was draped in black.

Edward and Alexandra arrived to find the family in a kind of seizure. Minny had locked herself in her rooms. Nicky seemed cowed by his tall, confident uncles, Grand Dukes Vladimir and

Sergei, and 'harassed' by his ministers. The prospect of becoming tsar horrified him. In private with his family he tearfully confessed his terror. 'What am I to do?' he asked Sandro. 'What is going to happen to me, to you, to Xenia, to Alix, to mother, to all of Russia. I am not prepared to be Czar [*sic*]. I never wanted to become Czar. I know nothing of the business of ruling.' Olga remembered, 'He was in despair. He kept saying that he did not know what would become of us all. That he was wholly unfit to reign. Even at that time I felt instinctively that sensitivity and kindness on their own were not enough for a sovereign.' It was Bertie, according to Olga, who 'quietly began calming down the tumult that met them on their arrival . . . The last days at Livadia would have been beyond anyone's endurance were it not for the presence of the Prince of Wales.' Alexandra took care of her sister; for the next month she accompanied her everywhere, even sleeping in her room. Bertie took over the funeral arrangements, tirelessly questioning their organizer, the minister of the imperial court (perhaps slightly to the minister's exasperation), and set himself to befriend and encourage Nicky. 'I cannot tell you what awful and trying days we are living through,' Nicky wrote to 'Granny'. '. . . Dear aunt Alix and uncle Bertie being here – help also dearest Mama in her pain.' 'I wonder what his tiresome old mother would have said had she seen everybody accept uncle Bertie's authority in Russia of all places,' Olga observed.

It was Edward's fourth visit to Russia. Since his marriage he had put himself out to be on good terms with his Russian in-laws, and in the last few years he had bestirred himself to meet them in Denmark – even if only briefly – almost every year. Though suspicious of Russia, he liked the idea of being an agent for the improvement of relations between the two countries, and no doubt Alexandra's enthusiasm played its part. He had first gone to St Petersburg in 1866, when Minny had asked him to swell her family's numbers at her wedding. Almost bankrupted by a 60,000 crown dowry, the Danish family could afford to send only the crown prince, Freddi. The queen disapproved of his inveterate gadding about and thought he ought to stay at home more. But the British government had encouraged the trip, seeing it as an opportunity to clear some of the bad blood left since the Crimean War. Edward had leapt at the opportunity: 'It would interest me beyond anything to see Russia . . . I should be only too happy to be the means in any way of promoting the <u>entente cordiale</u> between Russia and our own country . . . I am a very good traveller so that I should not at all mind the length of the journey.' He had made a good impression and returned in 1881 for Alexander II's funeral and later for Alexander III's coronation – but repeated imperial clashes had meant that diplomatic relations had never warmed up in the eighteen years since that first visit. A British official at the embassy in St Petersburg had reported in June 1894 – as Nicholas floated down the Thames – that 'Popular opinion in Russia is strongly adverse to England.'

The British were just as unfriendly. In May the British foreign secretary, Lord Rosebery, had issued warnings that the Royal Navy would counter with force any attempt by the Russian Black Sea fleet to venture into the Mediterranean, and the year's runaway bestseller was *The Great War in England* by the popular spy-writer William Tufnell Le Queux, a fantasy about a Russian invasion ('Throughout the land the grey-coated horde of the White Tsar spread like locusts') which bespoke an almost hysterical fear and dislike of the enemy. Within the government, however, there was beginning to be a feeling that the traditional enmity with Russia was expensive and impractical. British naval strategists had started to admit that the Royal Navy would not necessarily be able to hold back the Black Sea fleet if it chose to enter the Mediterranean. British ministers had begun to agree that the chances of Russia invading India were extremely remote – though the Indian government disagreed with them. And now that Britain occupied Egypt and controlled the Suez Canal, the overland route to India didn't matter so much. Edward – briefed by Lord Rosebery, who had recently taken over the prime ministership from the retiring Gladstone – planned to make a lastingly strong impression on the new tsar, in the hope that it might mark the beginning of a thaw.

When the tsar's body made its seventeen-day journey to Kazan Cathedral in St Petersburg, Edward and his entourage followed. They sent their observations back to Queen Victoria, who demanded descriptions. ('That old, tiresome woman at Windsor Castle telegraphs . . . for more letters,' grumbled the prince's equerry, Sir Arthur Ellis.) They were overwhelmed by Russia. Everything seemed extreme: the tens of thousands of soldiers who lined the railway tracks from the Crimea to Moscow and St Petersburg, the crowds of sobbing peasants, the vast suffocatingly overheated palaces and the gorgeous, interminable, agonizingly slow ritual. On each of the seventeen days, the tsar's family, its attendants and Edward – determined to show his support – and his entourage, attended two services in dress uniform, kneeling for hours, then kissing the icon now held rigidly between the corpse's fingers. It was exceptionally uncomfortable, boring and soon revolting, as 'dear Papa' was 'unfortunately starting to decompose very quickly'. Embalming didn't solve the problem and by the time Alexander was buried his face had begun to rot. Ritual decreed it could not be covered, and the English visitors came to dread the 'barbarous and unseemly custom'.

The funeral was on a vast scale and relentless. Sixty-one European royals arrived in St Petersburg for it, making it the largest royal event the Russians had ever hosted. George – summoned by his father because the 'opportunity to see the great capital of Russia is not one to be missed'– was a pallbearer.* It took four hours for the funeral cortège to reach Kazan Cathedral, 'most fatiguing for those who walked in the procession'. George watched ice form on the Neva. Inside the church, 'the crowd was so great that the master of the ceremonies could hardly get a passage for the Empress to enter, and 3 ladies fainted'. In the Russian Orthodox Church there were no pews so everyone stood. Throughout it all, Bertie was next to Nicky, and along with the Romanovs he kissed the lips of the dead monarch though 'the smell was awful'.

A week after the funeral Nicholas married his fiancée. In Windsor, the queen wrote ominously, 'Tomorrow morning poor dear Alicky's fate will be sealed. No two people were ever more

---

* He had come by train with Heinrich, Wilhelm's brother, bringing the latest British bestseller, *The Prisoner of Zenda*, an adventure novel about romantic but untrustworthy Eastern Europeans.

devoted as she and he are and that is one consolation I have, for otherwise the dangers and responsibilities fill me with anxiety.' Nicky spent the night before the wedding quietly with George, Greek Georgie and a Danish cousin, Waldemar. George told his grandmother,

Dear Alicky looked quite lovely at the Wedding . . . she went through it all with so much modesty but was so graceful and dignified at the same time, she certainly made a most excellent impression . . . I do think Nicky is a very lucky man to have got such a lovely and charming wife . . . I must say I never [saw] two people more in love with each other or happier than they are. When they drove from the Winter Palace after the wedding they got a tremendous reception and ovation from the large crowds in the streets, the cheering was most hearty and reminded me of England.

But no one else was quite so sanguine, not even the bride and groom. Nicholas looked 'dreadfully pale and worn', and confessed that it felt like 'somebody else's wedding and not mine'. Alix was pinned to the floor by the weight of the traditional silver brocade and cloth of gold, diamond-encrusted, ermine-lined, Romanov wedding dress that encased her, and it required eight pages simply to lift the train. She later said gloomily, 'Our marriage seemed to me a mere continuation of the masses for the dead with this difference, that now I wore a white dress instead of a black one.' In her wedding photos, she looked thin-lipped and frowning. Her unease and discomfort when confronted by the vast company was palpable. 'Even at this supreme moment no joy seemed to uplift her, not even pride,' wrote her cousin Marie of Romania, who didn't like her. 'Aloof, enigmatic, she was all dignity but she had about her no warmth.' Arthur Ellis, Edward's equerry, noted, 'Everything had the appearance of a forced air of mock festivity. All mourning put aside and an effort to appear cheerful – which was manifestly put on . . . a shadow of sadness seem [*sic*] to hang over the whole ceremony.' In the streets of St Petersburg, 40,000 soldiers all took their hats off simultaneously. As they drove off in their carriage to Nicholas's old childhood quarters in Anichkov

Palace, Olga thought, 'They looked so lonely, like two birds in a golden cage.'

'This is the first time I have been to Russia, I certainly have got a most excellent impression of the people and the country,' George told the queen. '. . . Nicky has been kindness itself to me, he is the same dear boy he has always been to me, and talks to me quite openly on every subject . . . and he does everything so quietly and nicely and naturally; everyone is struck by it and he is very popular already.' Actually George was not comfortable in St Petersburg. He felt hemmed in and would go walking off into the city, which 'greatly embarrassed the police who had charge of his safety', and astonished the court. The Prince of Wales's equerry observed, 'The Duke of York is rather bored here and pining to get back to shoot.' In the two weeks he was away, he wrote twenty letters to May, all of them asking what was happening at home.

Despite the gloom, the wedding marked a revival of excitement in the rest of the British contingent. The new reign looked promising, and the Russian press was suddenly full of praise for the Prince of Wales. 'It is impossible not to be struck with the gratitude evinced by all to the expression of English sympathy,' Arthur Ellis wrote. 'We *were* not popular and suddenly we are almost *beloved*. This is mainly owing to two things – the manner in which the P. and Princess of Wales have thrown themselves into earnest sympathy with their relatives and the accepted fact that the new and beautiful Empress is almost an Englishwoman (we don't say this to the Hessians).' They began to wonder over-excitedly whether the nice young tsar might turn out to be much more liberal than his father. A story did the rounds that after the wedding service Nicholas had gone into the street and told his troops to fall back so he could walk among the crowd without the usual wall of security. The London *Daily Telegraph* described it as 'a liberality unheard of in Russia'. It seemed impossible not to make comparisons with 'another young Emperor to his mother – under late similar circumstances – greatly to the Czar's [*sic*] advantage.' Even Edward himself felt 'The character and personality of the new Tsar give assurance of the benefits which would come of an alliance between England and Russia.'

Edward returned to England to a sea of praise. The prime minister told him, 'Our relations with Russia are, I honestly believe, more cordial than at any period since the German war.' The British press – more accustomed to reviling the prince's indiscretions – crooned over his 'unsurpassed tact, dignity and good feeling. He has practically been the special ambassador of this country entrusted with a mission which only one standing very near to the throne could carry out,' *The Times* enthused. 'It is scarcely an exaggeration to say,' the London *Standard* exaggerated, 'that his personal intercourse with the new Czar has effected more in a few weeks than the most painstaking and sagacious Diplomacy would have brought about in a decade . . . the influence of the Throne in determining the relations between European Powers has never been disputed by those at all familiar with modern politics, it is sometimes lost sight of or ignored by the more flippant order of Democrats'.

'I can't tell you, my dear Nicky,' George wrote from Sandringham, 'how pleased I was to see you these few days in Petersburg, although it was all so terribly sad . . . you have always been so kind and dear to me; ever since we have known each other, I look upon you, if I may do so, as one of my oldest and best friends.'

6. Wilhelm Anglophile (1891–5)

In the months after Bismarck's dismissal it became clear that Wilhelm was not about to launch any cataclysmic wars and that he wanted England as an ally. Instead of appointing the alarmingly hawkish General Waldersee as his new chancellor, he chose a liberal army general. Leo von Caprivi was a surprisingly radical, well-regarded, if politically inexperienced, soldier who had done a good job of running the German Admiralty. The new regime, which was called 'the New Course', seemed to promise a more inclusive government, less reliant on Bismarck's right-wing Junker elite, and a raft of social and education reforms based on Wilhelm's ideas, alongside anti-protectionist measures to improve Germany's fractious relations with its near neighbours. Hand in hand with this liberal turn was a new foreign policy orientation towards England. Wilhelm, it was said in the embassies of Berlin and Vienna, intended to be 'his own Minister for Foreign Affairs', though he'd appointed an Anglophile foreign minister, Adolf Baron Marschall von Bieberstein, who was also from Catholic Baden rather than Prussia, as 'a sort of undersecretary to carry out the orders'.

Within three months of Bismarck's departure Britain and Germany had signed an agreement, the Heligoland Treaty, whereby Britain handed over the tiny rocky island of Heligoland in the North Sea and recognized German dominance in South-West Africa, while Germany recognized Zanzibar in East Africa as a British protectorate and renounced claims to other African territories that German and British would-be colonists had been arguing over, including Uganda. Wilhelm was delighted. He had decided that Heligoland was the perfect sea anchorage for a future German navy. He hoped that the new treaty would be the first step in a closer relationship between the two countries by which Britain would support Germany's quest for colonies abroad and would eventually join the Triple Alliance with Germany, Italy and

Austria. The treaty was far from popular in Germany, however. The increasingly voluble German colonial movement regarded any renunciation of claims to parts of Africa as a bad thing, and even neutral onlookers saw it as an indication of how far the new German regime was willing to go to buy British friendship. Within the Berlin court, moreover, and among the traditional ruling elite and the army, there were many who deplored Wilhelm's liberal turn.

Still, the young kaiser was certainly a vibrant public force, and popular. He moved across the public stage in a blur of activity, constantly travelling, constantly seen – because constantly photographed. There he was at the head of a column of immaculate German soldiers, ever the army officer; or visiting a factory – daringly modern and energetic; or devotedly surrounded by his six tall, healthy sons – the father of the fatherland. Even his moustache – teased into the shape of a wide up-thrusting 'w' – was so famous it acquired a name: *Er ist erreicht*! 'It is achieved!' Manipulated through the miracle of pomade – its key ingredient the remarkable new product, petroleum jelly – it was the very model of a modern moustache, a controlled riposte to the great bushy, biblical patriarch beards and side-whiskers of the previous generation.*

The kaiser addressed the publics of Germany and beyond, constantly. The speeches, hundreds of them, were reported exhaustively in the press, reaching a larger audience than any monarch had before. Sometimes they were alarmingly bellicose, sometimes they claimed a divine mission, always they were full of confidence, revealing a man equally at home with tradition and the pulse of the new age. He was, he told an audience in Düsseldorf in May 1891, 'an instrument of the Lord without regard for views and opinions of the day'; but, he told a teachers' conference in 1890, 'I believe I have rightly understood the aims of the new spirit and of the century which is now nearing to a close.' There was no other monarch in Europe with such an instinct for publicity, image

---

* It was so famous that a species of South American monkey with luxuriant whiskers was named 'Emperor Tamarin' after him, although confusingly its whiskers curl – impressively – downwards.

and presentation. And the image promised much: that he might reinvent monarchy for the twentieth century; that, as one British magazine had it, he was 'at least . . . a man of strong character, possibly with a touch of true genius'; that he would unite a country that had not resolved its many internal differences; that he would lead Germany to the very top of the world powers.

Prussia had a tradition of austerity and simplicity. Wilhelm wanted an end to all that. His monarchy would be lavish, large, extravagant and public. He, Dona and their children moved into the vast baroque Neues Palais in Potsdam and the 650-room Berlin Schloss. Millions of marks were spent on renovations and extensions; heating, electric lights and bathrooms were installed. More huge sums were spent on the new imperial train – eleven gilded carriages, one big enough to contain a table seating twenty-four; and a new royal yacht *Hohenzollern* in cream and gold. It was the biggest private royal vessel afloat, large enough to sleep eighty guests and staff. Then there were the no-expense spared racing yachts, all called *Meteor*, designed to beat Bertie's racers. Living on such a grand scale had drawbacks: at the Berlin Schloss the kitchens were so far from the dining rooms (a mile) that food was invariably cold before it got to the table, though Wilhelm didn't really care about what he ate. The royal apartments, by contrast with the private rooms of the Russian and British royal families, were large, grand and full of gilt – as if Wilhelm had no interest in private life or family intimacy, as indeed, he did not really.

He didn't spend much time with his family. Soon after his accession he established a habit of travelling almost incessantly, mostly without Dona. Even when he was at home, she often – to her own disappointment – saw him only for breakfast and perhaps a ride after lunch. Forced to stay in Berlin with her and his entourage, he would complain about the unutterable boredom, while she longed for his company. Nor did he have close relationships with his sons. They seemed to feature more as a photo opportunity than as part of a close family. Only his daughter Victoria, the youngest, as 'Little Willy', the crown prince, later wrote, 'succeeded from childhood onwards to win a warm place in his heart'. From the boys he expected total obedience; in order to speak to him they had to apply first for permission from their tutors or military governors. Aged ten they entered either the army or the navy and were packed off to cadet school in Plön near the Danish border – there were none of the civilian influences his mother had visited upon him. The crown prince in particular resented his father's distance and strictness. From his early twenties he would do his best to rebel against his father. It was Dona who provided the boys with their emotional nourishment – she was loving and devoted, but stultifyingly traditional – and their outlook. Deploring Wilhelm's moments of Anglophilism, she had taken care, she told one of Wilhelm's ministers years later, 'that her sons would think differently'. Dona's relationship with Vicky eased after Wilhelm became kaiser but she was careful never to leave her children on their own with her mother-in-law for fear they might absorb her dangerous liberal impulses. Three out of six would later flirt – or more – with Nazism.

The young 'Siegfried' came to England for his first proper state visit in July 1891. The streets of London were decked out with garlands and banners carrying the words 'England and Germany; the peace of Europe'. Crowds gathered outside Buckingham Palace to get a glimpse of the glamorous young emperor and his world-famous moustache. The British press were almost unanimously enthusiastic about the visit. 'The importance of the Emperor's visit to England . . . is at once a solace in the present and a hope for the future,' noted the London *Standard*. 'He will be able to judge for himself . . . how keen and strong is the sympathy that unites the two great European branches of the Teutonic race, and how little either branch can afford to part company with the other,' intoned *The Times*. (Only the left-wing paper *Justice*, which saw in Wilhelm's assertive pronouncements 'the old jackboot junkerism' and a dangerous appetite for autocracy, and satirical magazines such as *Punch*, which had from early on found the kaiser's Wagnerian grandiosity too tempting not to ridicule, dissented.) He almost brought the house down at a huge banquet at the Guildhall when he told a cheering audience of the great and good, 'I have always felt at home in this lovely country, being the grandson of a Queen whose name will ever be remembered as the most noble character

. . . and whose reign has conferred lasting blessings on England. Moreover, the same blood runs in English and German veins . . . I shall always, as far as it is in my power, maintain the historical friendship between our two nations . . . My aim is above all the maintenance of peace.'

Unsurprisingly the British were extremely curious about this paragon. At a soirée given by the society hostess Lady Londonderry, the Liberal politician and intellectual John Morley observed him closely:

He is rather short; pale, but sunburnt; carries himself well; walks into a room with the stiff stride of the Prussian soldier; speaks with a good deal of intense energetic gesture, not like a Frenchman, but staccato: his voice strong but pleasant, his eyes bright, clear, and full; mouth resolute, the cast of face grave or almost stern in repose, but as he sat between those two pretty women . . . he lighted up with gaiety, and a genial laugh. Energy, rapidity, restlessness in every movement from his short, quick inclinations of the head to the planting of the foot.

Everything bespoke purpose, but the perceptive Morley also mused, 'I should be disposed strongly to doubt whether it is all sound, steady and the result of a . . . right coordinated organiz-ation.' Lord Salisbury's clever, elegant nephew, Arthur Balfour, was impressed by Wilhelm's 'extraordinary energy, self-confidence and interest in detail', and his conviction that 'he has a mission from Heaven'. This, Balfour mused, might send him and his country 'ultimately to Hell', but also, 'may in the meanwhile make him do considerable deeds on the way there'.

Wilhelm's visit was not so joyously anticipated at court. 'They are all very much bored at the Emperor of Germany's visit and are dreading what he will say and do,' the queen's new lady-in-waiting, Marie Mallet, wrote in her diary. 'The more I hear of him the more I dislike him, he must be such a despot and so terribly vain. However, poor man, he has a most insipid and boring wife who he does not care for and from whom he escapes by prancing to the four corners of the world.' The queen had been inflamed by regular letters from Vicky complaining about

Wilhelm's latest exploit, banning his sister Sophy from Germany because she had converted to the Greek Orthodox Church. She was also irritated that he had ignored her request to delay his visit by several weeks, while she hosted the wedding (which she'd masterminded) of another grandchild, Mary Louise,* to Prince Aribert of the small German duchy of Anhalt. She'd told him his presence would upstage the bridegroom's parents, but he'd insisted on coming anyway. Edward was disgruntled because barely a month before the kaiser had sent him a scolding letter about his involvement in the Tranby Croft affair, the gambling scandal in which Edward had been caught up and which had exposed him to sheaves of criticism in the British press. Wilhelm told Edward he was unsure whether he could continue to associate with him. The letter was really an aggressively timed reminder that the kaiser could pull rank whenever he wanted.

But, as Victoria's Russian daughter-in-law Marie observed to Wilhelm's sister Charlotte, however much in his absence the queen might denounce 'that dreadful tyrant Wilhelm who always takes things so badly and makes rows about anything', when he arrived it would 'all disappear'. He seemed able to charm her every time – but then his admiration for her was always palpable: he told his friend Phlipp zu Eulenburg, 'How I love my Grandmother, I cannot describe for you. She is the sum total of all that is noble, good and intelligent. With her and my feelings for her, England is inextricably connected.' Sure enough, when the kaiser arrived, the queen relented – at least a little. He was on his best behaviour and took such pleasure in being in England. She was, she wrote in her journal, pleased at his enthusiastic welcome in London, but she found his visits wearing, not least because he always brought such an enormous entourage – 100 this time – who were squeezed into the inns and hotels of Windsor. (Everyone found Wilhelm exhausting, even Eulenburg who spent most of the time away from Berlin on diplomatic postings.)

---

* Daughter of Victoria's youngest daughter, Helena, and Christian of Schleswig-Holstein. The marriage was a disaster: Aribert treated her appallingly and was almost certainly homosexual. They separated in 1900.

Rather, it was Dona who made a bad impression. Unable to hide her Anglophobia, or indeed her suspicion of all foreigners, she had what George's cousin Missy called a 'stereotyped graciousness which too much resembled condescension to be quite pleasant'. She behaved with what one German diplomat described as 'stiffness, rudeness and arrogance'. Wilhelm may have chided her privately. He often spoke slightingly in public about what he called her provinciality, and said that you could always tell 'she was not brought up at Windsor but rather in Primkenau'. She would take care afterwards to be courteous on foreign trips, though occasionally her hostility would seep out.

From Windsor Wilhelm went on to the Isle of Wight. The kaiser made a great thing of loving Osborne, his grandmother's home there. 'I shall count [the hours] until the moment when I can again sight dear Osborne rising out of the blue waters of the Solent,' he told his grandmother in January 1893. His childhood memories of it, and the two large portraits of himself which hung in the house, gave him a reassuring sense of inclusion in the English family, a feeling he sometimes had to struggle to keep hold of. But his very enthusiasm for it was a reminder of how unlike the rest of the family he was. Osborne might once have been fun for children, but by the 1890s no one but the queen liked it. It had become a mausoleum to the dead, from Albert to the queen's latest dog, and Victoria presided over it with an increasingly selfish hand. 'Even as a child I was struck by the ugliness,' George's eldest son would later recall. An odd combination of Italianate palazzo and English stately home on the outside, lined inside with Stuart tartan and filled with antler-horn furniture, it was cold, oppressive and deathly silent because the queen insisted on absolute quiet. She would also spend days in her rooms, the royal servants hanging around whispering in corridors, not allowed to go out until she did. When she did leave the building, the entire household rushed out too, but would flee in all directions because 'it was a great crime to meet her in the grounds'. When this happened, one private secretary recalled, 'we hid behind bushes'. These rules, of course, did not apply to the kaiser.

To Wilhelm, Osborne was especially alluring in July because of

Cowes Week, the most glamorous international social and sporting event of the year, when the super-rich and English high society – not always the same thing – gathered on their yachts and raced each other. It was an event which confirmed England's place as glamour and lifestyle capital of the world. So fashionable was it that the Russians liked to call Yalta, the resort on the Black Sea, the 'Cowes of the Crimea'. After Wilhelm's first visit in 1889, to the horror of austere Prussian traditionalists such as Waldersee, he had spent 4.5 million marks on buying and refitting his racing yacht, *Meteor*. In 1895 he even created his own version of Cowes, Kiel regatta, complete with its Imperial Yacht Club. Cowes brought together all the things that Wilhelm admired about England: not the cultural and democratic traditions his mother had pressed on him, but the luxury, the sense of a country on top and at ease with itself, its upper echelons confident and cosmopolitan. He was fascinated by the English upper classes, and he especially liked, one of his naval entourage observed, 'unrestrained conversation with distinguished English society which he finds he values most and searches for in Germany in vain, because the great majority here bend before the Kaiser like a grainfield before the approaching storm; he finds at Cowes an unselfish exchange of opinion with independent, strongly formed characters and personalities'. At home, 'unrestrained conversation' wasn't much to the kaiser's taste; he didn't expect contradiction, and Prussian aristocracy was accustomed to solemn deference. But for a few days the insouciance of British society was rather thrilling, though this wasn't quite how the kaiser put it himself. 'The old and strong monarchical principle showed itself in all its vigour in the bearing of the people whenever one met them,' he told the queen afterwards. 'It showed the . . . wish to make me feel quite at home among them, as I am a good deal of an Englishman myself.'

The visit seemed to go so well that it was widely assumed England must be considering joining the Triple Alliance. The thought did not reassure either the French or the Russians. Barely a week after Wilhelm returned from England in August 1891, the French navy visited the Russian naval base at Kronstadt, just outside St Petersburg, and the great autocrat Alexander III stood bareheaded for the republican anthem, the 'Marseillaise' – a song which had previously been banned in Russia. Europe was amazed. The republic and the autocracy were clearly preparing to draw closer.

Though tirelessly polite to the Germans and keen to seem friendly, Lord Salisbury could see no reason to make a formal alliance and forfeit Britain's long-maintained detachment from Europe, a detachment which he believed gave it important room for manoeuvre. Nor could Germany help Britain where it was vulnerable, in Asia; and he saw no reason to make any concessions to the Germans in the colonies – he thought they made brutal colonists. In any case, he distrusted Wilhelm. Neither Wilhelm nor his Foreign Office took the hint. The kaiser, who constantly failed to differentiate between the queen and the British government, contined to write flattering letters to his grandmother, telling her she was the 'Nestor' and the 'Sybilla' of Europe – 'revered by all; feared only by the bad'. He tried to please her by returning to the dukes of Cumberland –the claimants to the kingdom of Hanover – money sequestered by Bismarck. He even kept his temper when she unveiled a statue to his father and failed to ask him to the ceremony. In March 1892 he asked 'to visit you quite privately at Osborne this summer', a request to which she reluctantly agreed even though the timing was bad – Eddy had just died. It may well have been because she'd heard that Wilhelm had been unwell. The official version was that he'd had an ear infection. In London there were rumours that he'd suffered some kind of 'nervous breakdown'. At the German court there were more alarming rumours that members of the medical profession had suggested that Wilhelm might be mad.

The kaiser had taken to his bed for two weeks. He told his grandmother he'd been 'too much overworked', a description which would have raised a snigger among his ministers. The truth was that, having laid claim to being Germany's saviour and the most brilliant man in Europe, Wilhelm had proved quite unable to live up to his promise, and Bismarck's retirement had left him exposed. Although he'd told Caprivi that the chancellor's job was just a temporary role until he himself was ready to take the reins of government, he had no staying power at all. 'Distractions,' Waldersee had observed increasingly bitterly, '– whether they are little games with his army or navy, travelling or hunting – are everything to him . . . He reads very little apart from newspaper cuttings, hardly writes anything himself apart from marginalia on reports and considers those talks best which are quickly over and done with.' Wilhelm was all front. He'd filled his first years as kaiser with a round of pageants, processions, parades and elaborate memorials celebrating long-forgotten Hohenzollerns and historical events. He showed himself off to his people constantly and travelled incessantly – indeed he was so seldom in Berlin that he'd been nickamed *der Reisekaiser*, 'the travelling kaiser'. After four years, he was still rushing around, the pageants were quite as frequent but there seemed precious little otherwise to show for it all. Wilhelm appeared unable to distinguish the trivial from the important – he'd spend hours looking at photographs of warships or moving the position of the smoke stacks on a new cruiser, rather than read government reports. He had no idea how he was going to accomplish all the great things he had promised. For him kingship had been a rather vague notion of having power, being great and beloved. Worse, he was an appalling vaccillator, changing his mind – he was too often influenced by the last person he'd talked to, and constantly in quest of popularity – with such frequency that it drove his ministers mad and made the government look irresolute and confused. Chancellor Caprivi praised Wilhelm's habit of 'continually talking to all kinds of people', but observed wearily that 'he often contradicted his official announcements and misunderstandings arose in consequence'. His colleague Marschall, the foreign minister, was more forthright: 'It is unendurable. Today one thing and tomorrow the next and after a few days something completely different.'

Although the government passed its social legislation, Wilhelm's liberal leanings and appetite for being the 'King of the Workers' hadn't lasted long, just as long, in fact, as it took him to realize that the German workers were not going to forsake the Socialist Party for him. He took the working classes' 'betrayal' personally, and denounced their 'ingratitude'. He longed to gather the nation around him, and at the same time worried about incurring the displeasure of his traditional constituency, the court, his military entourage, the right-wing parties in the Reichstag on whom the government relied to pass their bills. Then there was his habit of making sudden rogue interventions, going off-piste in a speech and announcing a new law that completely contradicted agreed government policy, or writing to foreign monarchs without telling the Foreign Office, or appointing someone completely inappropriate to a government position – he particularly prized his power to choose and dismiss ministers. (Caprivi once received a Captain Natzmer who said that the kaiser had made him governor of the Cameroons the previous night, having met him at an imperial reception.) He was also quick to resent anyone he felt wasn't sufficiently supportive. He was soon complaining of Caprivi, he 'never thinks of doing something <u>simply</u> because I ask him to . . . I cannot call such behaviour <u>having confidence in me</u>.'

Around Wilhelm there was a force field of approval. Few members of his entourage – his civil and military cabinets, his ministers, his friends even – could bring themselves to contradict him. People around him found themselves agreeing with his version of reality rather than the one that actually existed outside his head, partly out of a traditional deference to the dynasty, obsequiousness and to stay in favour, but also because it was so exhausting not to. Anne Topham, an English governess who later taught the kaiser's daughter, described how his entourage lived

in a state of constant self-suppression, for the one thing their master could not bear was for anyone to disagree with him, to have an opinion apart from his own. What he seemed to seek in his surroundings was a chorus of approval from persons who had sunk their own personalities, submerged them for the time, while they themselves played the role of listeners. At first I rather despised this complaisant [*sic*] courtier-like attitude, yet insensibly I too fell into it, found myself searching for points of agreement with the Emperor, rather than risk displeasing him by any form of polite argument.

Even Philipp zu Eulenburg, who repeatedly tried to make him understand his mistakes, wrapped his criticisms up in elaborate flattery. 'Wilhelm II wants to shine . . . to decide everything himself,' he would tell a rising politician. 'But what he wants to do often goes wrong. He loves glory; he is ambitious and jealous. In order to get him to accept an idea, you must act as if the idea were his.' When dealing with the kaiser, he advised above all, 'Don't forget the sugar.' The professional costs of failing to do this were obvious. In 1890 General Waldersee – unable, after nearly a decade of toadying, to bite his tongue any longer – had told the kaiser that his participation in military manoeuvres and insistence on winning, despite making hopeless mistakes, was wrecking the entire point of the exercise. Wilhelm demoted him.

This might not have mattered so much if Wilhelm hadn't believed his own publicity, and been so possessive of his personal power, refusing to turn the government over to professionals. As it was, it put him right in the firing line when things went wrong. In early 1892 there was a hysterical Protestant backlash within the government and the liberal and conservative press to a bill to liberalize religious teaching and specifically to allow Catholics to set up and administer their own schools. Catholics were a large minority in Germany, especially in the South, and they were represented politically by the Centre Party, a liberalish party on whom Caprivi had had to call to pass much of his social legislation. Suspicion of Catholicism, and Catholic allegiance to Rome, however, was still a deep-seated prejudice among the traditional Prussian elite who ran the government and headed the right-wing Conservative and (confusingly named) Liberal (who weren't actually liberal at all) parties. Wilhelm, who regarded himself as enlightened about Catholicism, panicked, first publicly supporting the bill, next seeming to denounce it, then condemning 'grumblers', and finally killing it with the insistence that it be amended to meet Protestant criticism. Caprivi, a decent man who was struggling to juggle all the different interest groups and felt publicly abandoned by Wilhelm, tendered his resignation. It would not be the last time: he would resign ten times in four years, usually because it was the only way to bring Wilhelm into line. The crisis was a stark illustration of just how politically cracked, even broken, Germany was, and how hard it was for anybody to make a popular appeal across partisan loyalties. It also demonstrated that to make the kind of popular appeal to the nation that Wilhelm wanted, he would have to be seen to extricate himself from politics as Emperor Franz Joseph had done in Austria. But that would involve renouncing the exercise of personal power, and this was something he refused to do.

Criticism of Wilhelm and his regime was coming from all sides. From retirement Bismarck had begun to take revenge by orchestrating a cleverly pitched press campaign consistently attacking the government's policies. One of its effects had been to encourage criticism from other parts of the Right, for example from the newly formed Pan-German League, which – inspired by anger over the Heligoland Treaty, by which 'The hope of a great German colonial Empire was ruined!' – had been set up to campaign against government policy which 'weakened' Germany. Wilhelm himself had begun to attract a torrent of personal criticism for a series of public gaffes. In 1891, on a visit to Munich, he'd offended the whole of South Germany by inscribing *Suprema lex regis voluntas*, 'The will of the King is the supreme law', in the town hall 'golden' book. It might have been a joke, but it was interpreted as a crass assertion of Prussian might. He'd shocked the nation in a speech to a group of new army recruits in which he said that, should he order it, they would have to 'shoot down' their own families 'without a murmur'. On another occasion, he'd denounced the German Socialist Party as the 'enemy of the Fatherland' and said he intended to 'crush' it. While this might play well in the Prussian heartland of rural Brandenburg, it was not acceptable in Germany's sophisticated urban centres. August Bebel, the Socialist Party leader, said that every time the kaiser made a speech the party gained another 100,000 votes. A speech to the provincial Landtag in Brandenburg, in February 1892, had had a particularly bruising reception, and prompted suggestions that the kaiser was suffering from megalomania – or 'Caesaromania' as contemporaries liked to call it. He'd spoken a little too emphatically about how he had 'been appointed by an authority on high, to whom I shall later have to account for my actions', and told his audience, 'I shall lead you on to ever more splendid days. I am taking the right course and I shall continue full steam ahead.'

Four years before such words would have been greeted more sympathetically, now the honeymoon period was over. 'The World,' the now-demoted Waldersee commented with more than a little *Schadenfreude* in March 1892, 'which was initially enthusiastic about him, is now completely disillusioned.' Couldn't someone, his English grandmother wondered, 'Altogether beg him not to make so many speeches'? The irony was, Wilhelm's aggressive absolutist rhetoric was almost never matched by action. But as he knew all too well, in public affairs appearances counted.

The combination of the criticism and Caprivi's resignation pushed Wilhelm over the edge. In March 1892 he took to his bed for two weeks in 'nervous collapse'. It would not be the last time that he would have to acknowledge the gaping difference between how he wanted to see the world and how it actually was, and that he was not quite Siegfried and Bismarck rolled into one. Collapse was his response and his coping mechanism. It was his way of processing failure and disappointment without actually having to do anything about it. Behind his bedroom doors he recalibrated reality with his view of himself. Then he would bounce up, ready to conquer the world again.

The crisis was weathered. As would be future crises. Even though large sections of the country would continue to feel disconnected from the court and the government – industrial workers, the Left, progressive liberals, large swathes of the South, Catholics – and there would be periodic waves of criticism of government policy from across the political spectrum, the fact was Germany was rich, and wealth was a great political emollient. The boom that had started in the post-unification years continued and continued; money poured into the country. There was also a large mass from the rising lower-middle classes – in England their equivalent would have been the 'clerks' who read the *Daily Mail* and embraced its patriotic imperialism – for whom Wilhelm would continue to be the heroic leader, despite his idiosyncrasies and gaffes. Extreme Pan-Germans might oppose government policy, but they still felt loyal to the kaiser. In some strange way, moreover, Wilhelm truly did embody Germany, a fact that even his decriers allowed. It was almost as if his personality – his touchiness, his unpredictability, his restlessness, his lack of resolve – resonated with the young country which, only seventeen years old when he had acceded, was in its own adolescent spasm: quick to detect a slight, overexcited by the idea of flexing its muscles, prey to sudden switches in mood, desperate not to appear weak, insistent on being acknowledged. This struck contemporaries. Wilhelm, the Jewish intellectual Egon Friedell would conclude in 1926, 'almost always was the expression of the overwhelming majority of his subjects, the champion and executor of their ideas, the representative of their outlook on life. Most Germans were nothing more than pocket editions, smaller versions or miniature copies of Kaiser Wilhelm.' Heinrich Mann would write a novel, *Der Untertan, The Man of Straw*, about just such a figure, a slavish admirer of the kaiser.

So in April 1892, a month after his nervous breakdown, Wilhelm Tiggerishly waylaid the queen on her return journey from a visit to Italy, and tried to persuade her to come to Berlin. Lord Salisbury, who regarded the queen as one of the few people who could manage the kaiser, suggested 'it would be a very good thing if your Majesty would see him and calm him'. The queen couldn't face the idea: 'No no I really cannot go about keeping everyone in order,' she protested, and took the opportunity to complain to her private secretary about his forthcoming summer visit. 'The Queen never invited the Emperor . . . she wd. be very thankful if he did not come.' She asked that Sir Edward Malet, the English ambassador in Berlin, might 'hint that these regular annual visits are not quite desirable', a message that Malet – like so many of those who had dealings with Wilhelm – never quite got round to delivering.

When Wilhelm did come, however, he was on his best behaviour, respectful of the family's terrible recent loss of Eddy. 'Not in the least grand, and very quiet, and most amiable in every respect,' Edward wrote to George. The queen had stipulated that he must lodge on his own boat, and refused his enthusiastically proffered brass bands. Nevertheless Wilhelm enjoyed himself 'immensely,' Bertie's private secretary, Sir Edward Knollys, wrote.

'So much indeed, that I am afraid it will tempt him to repeat his visit very frequently.'

There was no movement, however, on the diplomatic front. By 1893 there was palpable disappointment in the German Foreign Office that there seemed to be nothing to show for three years of explicit friendliness to Britain – no alliance, no colonies. A Liberal victory in the British general elections of 1892 brought no change of attitude. Though the two countries were supposed to be on excellent terms, the German Foreign Office began to feel intense irritation towards what it felt was British condescension and obstructionism. It was aggrieved and upset by the British reluctance to talk about an alliance, because Russia – spurned by Germany – and France had now done the unthinkable and made a secret defensive alliance (of which every politician in Europe was aware), sandwiching Germany between two potential enemies – Bismarck's worst nightmare. At the same time, Britain and Germany found themselves in disputes over colonial claims in Fiji, New Guinea, Congo, South-West Africa and Samoa.

The crucial change was that the German government had begun eagerly to pursue a colonial empire. Bismarck had regarded colonies as an expensive distraction. Realizing that Germany's wealth came largely from its manufactured goods sold to other developed countries, he'd only occasionally encouraged would-be German colonizers as a sop to the German Right, and otherwise viewed the imperial scramble as a way to sow dissension between France and Britain. This he'd done very successfully, particularly with the Berlin Conference of 1884, which ordained that Africa should be carved up into the spheres of influence, the divisions decided by who occupied a piece of territory more convincingly, or aggressively, than anyone else – a recipe for constant clashes. After Bismarck's departure, however, Wilhelm had seized on the notion of creating a great colonial empire as the achievement that would demonstrate how he had surpassed the chancellor, and unite Germany around him. After all, throughout his childhood his mother had drilled into him the greatness of the British empire as a uniting, civilizing force that had brought the country lasting riches and status.

An empire seemed to offer many attractions: wealth, trade and, perhaps more importantly, status. Increasingly it seemed incomprehensible to many educated Germans that a country as dynamic and powerful as their own should have only a few colonies. Moreover, there were many like Philipp zu Eulenburg, who believed that imperial expansion might be a good way of displacing domestic discontent among the masses, getting them to identify with the state in an exciting imperial project abroad. Having lost his enthusiasm for social reform, Wilhelm seemed to regard this as a particularly attractive proposition. The German political Right – a group the government felt increasingly keen to please – moreover, had within it a well-organized and assertive colonial lobby. The problem was that the Germans were late to the imperial scramble. Wherever they went, they found Britain there first. The British opposed every German incursion. This looked particularly ungenerous to the Germans since the British empire was now heading in size for one quarter of the world's land mass. What were a few thousand African square miles or a small archipelago in the Pacific to it? There was angry criticism of Britain in the German press and from the German government's traditional supporters in the National Liberal Party, where colonial enthusiasm was strongest. Fritz Holstein, a senior adviser in the German Foreign Office, who had enthusiastically advocated the German pursuit of England, commented resentfully, 'We assist England every day – even by sitting still – simply by being there. England assists us damned little up to now . . . it is always non possumus.'

Fritz Holstein was the most influential political operator in the German Foreign Office, despite the fact that in his whole time there – he would retire in 1906 – it was said he met Wilhelm only once. Whether or not this was literally true, it was certainly the case that he had an instinctive dislike of the limelight, and was already wryly unimpressed by Wilhelm, deliberately keeping out of the kaiser's way, and relying on others, notably Philipp zu Eulenburg, to sell his policies. This skulking in the shadows, combined with a lack of interest in the diplomatic social whirl, and his unkemptness – in Berlin he was famous for his shabby hat, threadbare coat, shaggy beard and bent, short-sighted, purposeful gait – helped to fuel a myth of sinister and aggressive ubiquity, secrecy and conspiracy. In reality, Holstein was an able, acerbic, workaholic bureaucrat, committed to his work in the Foreign Office, with a dry sense of humour and an omnivorous appetite for gossip and foreign affairs, fuelled by an obsessive letter-writing habit. Little else occupied him – except perhaps the schnitzel with a fried egg on top to which he gave his name. He also had, however, a dangerous weakness for taking offence too quickly and political setbacks too personally. And with Eulenburg he had become involved in backroom manipulations to, as they regarded it, keep the kaiser on track, and to maintain some consistency in German policy. The alliance, such as it was, was a marriage of convenience. Holstein knew Eulenburg had the emperor's ear; Eulenburg disliked the pro-British policy. While Holstein was beginning to think that Wilhelm needed to be reined in, Eulenburg persisted in believing the opposite – but he valued Holstein's grasp of politics and foreign affairs and his influence, so tailored his words to him accordingly.

Holstein still wanted an alliance, but he concluded that Britain needed to be taught a lesson about German support and that Germany should be more robust in pursuing its own interests. So in early 1893 the German Foreign Office told the British government that it must step aside to give Germany a railway concession the two countries had been competing for in Turkey. If it failed to, Germany would withdraw its – vital – support for the British occupation of Egypt. The British were startled by the brusqueness of the demand, but acquiesced. At that precise moment they found themselves in need of German support – more than they had done in decades. The expanding borders of the empire had finally brought them into conflict with every other imperial power at the same moment: the US in Venezuela, the French in Africa, the Russians in Asia. The new Liberal foreign secretary, Lord Rosebery, began to wonder whether Britain might need a genuine ally.

In July 1893, when the kaiser came to Cowes, Rosebery went out of his way to demonstrate that Britain was interested in getting much closer to Germany. On the kaiser's first evening on the Isle of Wight, an overnight crisis arose between Britain and France over a long-running rivalry for dominance in the kingdom of Siam. For a few hours war seemed possible. Rosebery telegraphed the queen requesting that the kaiser be informed and sounded out about whether he would be willing to support Britain if war broke out. Wilhelm was at that moment dressed in his British admiral's uniform, giving a dinner for Edward and his younger brother, Arthur of Connaught, on his yacht. He 'expressed satisfaction' at the turn of events, announced himself delighted to help, and spent the rest of the evening aggressively teasing his uncle Bertie that he might soon see active service in India – a sore point as the prince had always felt embarrassed by his mother's refusal to let him serve in the British army.

After the guests left, however, Wilhelm's blustery confidence collapsed. Alone – apart from a few of his entourage and Eulenburg – he became panicky and tearful, talking himself into a state about Germany's (or perhaps his own) inability to prosecute a war. If there was a war, he said, Germany would have to be part of it in order to show its status as a world power; but what if Russia came in with France? The Royal Navy couldn't beat the combined navies of France and Russia, and Germany would lose a war on two fronts. 'If one is not a world power, one is nothing,' he said. 'I really have never seen him so overcome,' Eulenburg wrote, 'and I had to bring the whole force of my mind to bear upon finding reasonable arguments which would soothe him.' Under Wilhelm's hearty Prussian warlord lurked a deeply vulnerable, fearful man, whose fragility was another reason why his entourage and coterie were so unwilling to trouble him with awkward news. The Jewish industrialist and intellectual Walter Rathenau, who met the kaiser perhaps once a year, remarked how visible the contrast was up close between the man Wilhelm wanted to be and the man he was – with his little white hands, his soft hair, his small white teeth. Rathenau found himself rather moved by a man 'continuously fighting with himself, overcoming his nature in order to wrest from his bearing energy, mastery . . . a nature directed against itself, unsuspecting'. Wilhelm's fragility lay at the heart of his friendship with Eulenburg, perhaps his only real friend.

In many respects Eulenburg was the anxious, indulgent un-

critical parent the kaiser had never had. He was also a hypochon-
driac, volubly emotional and 'artistic', and around him Wilhelm
was able to be both masterful and in charge, but also to shrug off
the exhausting hyper-macho persona he felt obliged to adopt
so much of the time. Because of this, Eulenburg was one of the
few people to whom Wilhelm would listen; he in turn had set
himself to smooth over the many problems the emperor encountered. Inevitably, he had become enmeshed in the incessant
intriguing endemic in the German government, his extreme
monarchism causing him to encourage Wilhelm to ignore or dismiss ministers, and his influence gaining other members of the
so-called Liebenburg Circle influential posts which made them
deeply unpopular. But he was also a pragmatist and virtually the
only person who could moderate Wilhelm's more extreme and
unreasonable behaviour.

By the next morning the crisis had blown over. Britain and
France reached agreement, Wilhelm recovered his sang-froid and
went out yachting, leaving Eulenburg with 'the fat unwieldy'
Edward, whom he watched disgustedly, 'breakfasting steadily from
ten till four'. Like most of Wilhelm's entourage, the majority of
them Prussian soldiers with an instinctive suspicion of the British,
Eulenburg had no great liking for England (he complained that
the beer tasted like 'rubber Mackintoshes') and he dreaded its
effect on the kaiser. He was highly suspicious of Edward, whom
he regarded as 'a capable, amiable, but very crafty man, with a
remarkably sinister look in his eye – <u>not</u> our friend'. Bertie, he
later wrote, passed amused, hostile comments about Wilhelm,
professing confusion at his 'colonial game', and concern at his
one-armed nephew's interest in boats: 'one can't help being a little
afraid he may do himself some damage'.

Two days later there was a major family falling-out when
Wilhelm refused to cut short a race between his yacht *Meteor* and
Bertie's *Britannia*, when it became clear that the race wouldn't
finish in time for a gala dinner which the queen had organized in
his honour. Bertie, clearly irritated, felt he couldn't refuse Wilhelm
though he was fully aware of how angry the queen would be.
'Much startled and put out at hearing only after 8 that William and

Bertie could not be here for dinner,' she wrote irritatedly in her journal. 'Georgie [who had just returned from his honeymoon] was in a great state and everything had to be rearranged. It was extremely vexatious.' Perhaps Edward secretly wanted to finish the race – he beat the kaiser, who had spent a fortune trying to get himself a yacht faster than his uncle's. The two men didn't arrive at Osborne until 10.30 p.m., just as the queen was sweeping furiously out of the dining room. One – not always entirely reliable – German onlooker described the scene: as Wilhelm apologized, Bertie stepped behind a pillar for a moment to compose himself and mop his brow, then came out to apologize to his hatchet-faced mother, retiring immediately afterwards behind his pillar.

The trip was generally agreed to have been a great success.

Over the autumn and winter of 1893 Lord Rosebery made ever warmer overtures to Germany. In the New Year of 1894 he made it clear that he was willing to enter into real negotiations with the Triple Alliance. Wilhelm congratulated himself on Rosebery's 'new about-turn', claiming that it stemmed 'from my initiative'– he had, he claimed, sent the British foreign secretary a blunt message stating that only 'complete honesty' would do.

But instead of meeting Britain half-way, the German government rejected the offer, even though it was exactly what they had been working for since 1890. Their frostiness was, as one historian has written, 'almost incomprehensible'. It seems the Germans got themselves tied up in knots, caught between suspicion that the British were planning to ensnare them in some trick they hadn't anticipated, and a belief that if the British needed them it was a good time to extract concessions. They took an aggressive line on a number of simmering colonial disputes. In April 1894, as Wilhelm and Queen Victoria celebrated Nicky and Alix's engagement in Coburg, the German Foreign Office demanded sole possession of the Samoan islands, over which the countries had been arguing since 1889. The British, highly irritated, baulked. The German ambassador, Hatzfeldt, was urged by his masters to break the stalemate. Hatzfeldt was a conscientious servant of the state who had long seen his role as trying to coax Britain into the Triple Alliance. At the same time he had noticed that since 1890 his government had become more and more obsessed with the desire for colonies. He wrote a long memo to the chancellor in which he observed that if Germany applied pressure on Britain's colonial empire it might both 'demonstrate the disadvantages of our hostility' and force the British to be more amenable over the question of Samoa. The irony was, Hatzfeldt himself didn't believe in pressure politics, he regarded them as counterproductive. He told a colleague wistfully that if the Germans could only be patient, 'turtle doves would fly into their mouths, but their vacillations meant they defeated themselves all the time'.

The kaiser was extremely enthusiastic about the new idea. 'Splendid, corresponds entirely with my views and our policy is to be conducted as recommended here.' He would tell one of his English cousins a few years later, 'We must have an alliance with England and if she won't agree we shall have to frighten her into it.' Hatzfeldt's plan was almost eerily similar to his own semi-bullying attempts to force his English relatives to give him attention. Even though the relationship was supposed to be thriving, Wilhelm had pointedly failed to attend a memorial service for Eddy in Berlin, and had refused to let his brother Heinrich go to England for the funeral. When the queen had told him he wouldn't be invited to George's wedding, he had refused to let Heinrich, who was invited, go. Edward suspected ill-feeling. He asked the queen to demand an explanation, whereupon Wilhelm pretended that he had always meant to let his brother attend. The kaiser suspected, and it pained him, that the British preferred Heinrich to him. He wasn't entirely wrong. Heinrich was much more easygoing and friendly than he. Since marrying Irene of Hesse, one of Alix's older sisters, he had become an enthusiastic and frequent visitor to England. He'd got to know George, to whom he sent occasional inconsequential letters notable for their kindly warmth, very different from Wilhelm's own productions: his mother, he passed on to George in one letter, had praised George so highly that he was almost jealous. 'Never you mind, Georgie,' he added. 'I think you are fully entitled to a good name and character!'

The policy was soon put into action. In the spring of 1894 the

British were trying to negotiate agreements with various imperial parties over the Congo, as part of a long-running rivalry with France in North Africa. The German government refused to come to an agreement. The refusal backfired because the British negotiated a treaty with the more obliging Belgians. The German Foreign Office, working itself up into a great rage, denounced the treaty as 'shameless', because it ignored German claims in the area. Then, when the British offered to amend the treaty, the Germans insisted it be abandoned.

Wilhelm was in an awkward position. In Germany he professed himself furious at the Congo Treaty and British trickery. Almost simultaneously, however, the queen had just made him colonel-in-chief of the 1st Royal Dragoons. It was quite a gesture: the first time a foreign monarch had appeared on the British army list. Wilhelm had been begging for a rank in the British army – preferably with a Scottish regiment, he liked the kilts – for months, and had cunningly got Edward campaigning on his behalf by offering him in return an honorary title *à la suite* in the queen's German regiment. Victoria disapproved: 'This fishing for uniforms on both sides is regrettable,' and besides, 'The Queen thinks he is far too much spoilt already.' What if he started to interfere with army policy? Rosebery had initially agreed with her. He was beginning to find the Germans' abrupt tone 'thoroughly insufferable', and he thought the title would seem like an endorsement of their rudeness. Lord Salisbury, from whom Rosebery occasionally took advice, pointed out, however, that it was a cheap way to keep the kaiser sweet. The queen gave way and Wilhelm was characteristically fulsome: 'overwhelmed', and 'moved, deeply moved, at the idea that I now too can wear beside the Naval uniform the traditional British "redcoat"'. He told the British ambassador that he utterly deplored the German Foreign Office's regrettable attitude in the Congo and implied that he had nothing to do with it. At Cowes that summer he was all smiles, wearing his new Royal Dragoons uniform, as he 'graciously acknowledged the hearty cheers'. What a shame it was that the usually impeccably organized British somehow forgot to remind his new regiment to send a detachment to greet him.

Germany's threats so alarmed its Austrian and Italian allies, who felt their security depended on the Royal Navy's commitment to defend the eastern Mediterranean from Russia, that they quietly insisted the German government accept the amended Congo Treaty. The damage was done though, and to no one's advantage. And over the autumn and winter of 1894 there were more imperial clashes between the two nations in Morocco, the Sudan, the Transvaal and, once again, Samoa, where by the end of the year the two countries so distrusted each other that they had stationed warships there despite the onset of the hurricane season. The Prince of Wales's success in St Petersburg occasioned angry complaints in the German press and even the usually phlegmatic ambassador Hatzfeldt complained that after years of being rebuffed by England, his government viewed Britain's cosying up to Russia with extreme disappointment. The next time England wanted anything from Germany, it would have to pay a very high price for it.

The plan to bully the British into closer friendship often looked indistinguishable from plain hostility. 'The abrupt and rough peremptoriness of the German action,' wrote one British junior foreign minister, '. . . gave me an unpleasant impression . . . the method adopted by Germany in this instance was not that of a friend.' Thirteen years later this man, Sir Edward Grey, would be foreign secretary himself, one with a deep-rooted mistrust of German power politics. As for Rosebery, the one British statesman who might have considered an alliance, he was an enthusiastic imperialist, very sensitive to accusations that the Liberal Party was not as committed to the empire and its defence as the Conservatives. The harder the Germans pushed on colonial issues, the more obstructive he became. By the end of 1894 he had concluded that an alliance was impossible. What the British Foreign Office couldn't make out was why the Germans were being so gratuitously aggressive. 'It is difficult to understand what advantage they expect to gain by such a policy,' the new foreign secretary, Lord Kimberley (Rosebery having become prime minister), wrote, '. . . I can't pretend to read the riddle.'

The fact was, the German government wasn't quite sure what

its goals were either; or at least different people had different ideas. Marschall, the foreign minister, had become convinced that Samoa was the key issue and that Germany must take control of it by any means in order to demonstrate to a critical domestic audience that the government's foreign policy was effective. Holstein, angry with the British uncooperative attitude, continued to be committed to bullying England into an alliance. 'England would only be a reliable ally for us,' he told a friend in 1896, '. . . if we left her in no doubt that we would simply abandon her to her fate unless she concluded a formal alliance with us.' Eulenburg, who represented the feelings of many of the Prussian elite, had always felt Germany's pursuit of Britain was a mistake. 'I cannot deny that this new turn against Albion warms my heart. The centre of our future lies in world trade, and our deadly enemy in this field is England.' As for Wilhelm, he contained all the contradictions: he wanted an alliance, he wanted to trounce Britain, he wanted an empire, he wanted to be popular at home.

One thing that seemed to appeal to almost everyone in the German Foreign Ministry, however, was the notion of plain-speaking, of cutting through the flowery nonsense of international diplomatic language, of pursuing an explicitly self-interested aggressive foreign policy, and being entirely honest about it – unlike the British, who dressed their acquisitiveness up in myths about the white man's burden. It seemed in the blunt, realpolitik tradition of Bismarck, for whom, after four years, the German Foreign Office was starting to feel a little nostalgia. Salisbury told the incoming British ambassador to Berlin in 1895 that 'The rudeness of German communications [had] much increased since Bismarck's time,' and attributed it 'to the wish for smaller men to keep up the traditions of the Great Chancellor'. Perhaps it was also a subconscious attempt to mimic the admired military values of the German army, aggressively pursuing one's goals with no distraction or mitigation. In fact the policy was clumsy and muddle-headed and more to do with relieving feelings and striking poses than getting results. The British were far from the only ones to observe this. A British diplomat in Vienna reported in November 1894 that the Austrians were complaining that German foreign

1. Wilhelm with his mother
Vicky and sister Charlotte, 1860

2. Wilhelm in Highland gear at his uncle
Edward's wedding, aged four

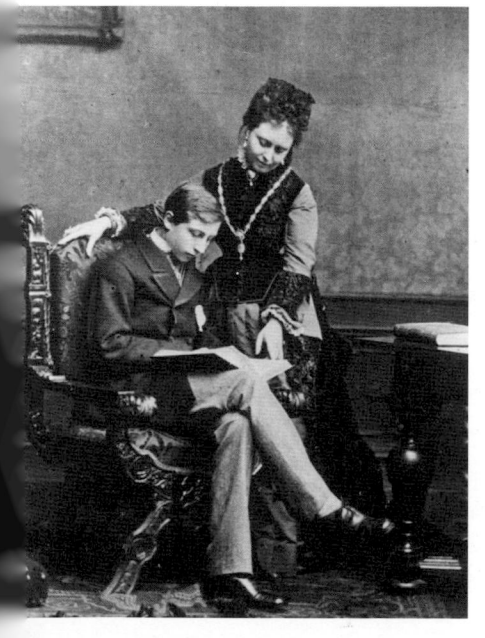

3. Wilhelm in his late teens
with Vicky before the split

4. Wilhelm complete with his now famous moustache and in uniform, to which he was addicted. Even his entourage considered him 'obsessed by the question of clothes and externals', 1891

5. 'Dropping the Pilot', *Punch* magazine's response to Wilhelm's sacking of Bismarck, 1890

Zu Befehl, Majestät!

6. At Your Majesty's Command! The kaiser as paterfamilias and military chief: from early in Wilhelm's reign, his sons were employed to bolster his public image

7. Wilhelm's wife Augusta Victoria, known as 'Dona'. She provided unquestioning devotion and support, and he found her terribly dull

8. Wilhelm and Dona in England durin the Boer War in 1899. In honour of hi grandmother, the kaiser was unusually in *mufti*

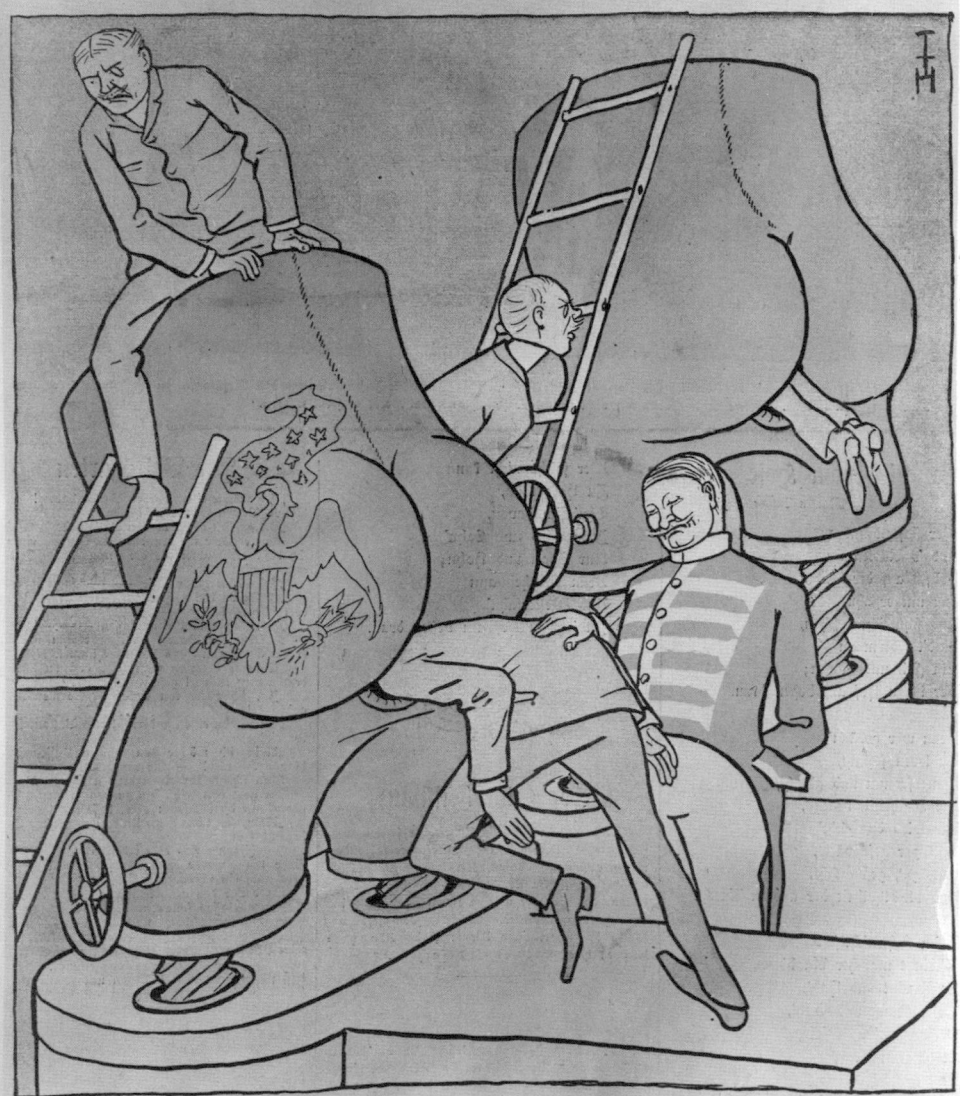

(Zeichnung von Th. Th. Heine)

Es dürfte nicht allgemein bekannt sein, daß in Berlin ein Institut besteht, das sich ausschließlich mit der Heranbildung junger Diplomaten befaßt. Nur wer diese Schule mit Erfolg absolviert hat, besitzt die Fähigkeiten, die zur Bekleidung eines auswärtigen Gesandtschaftspostens unbedingt nötig sind. Durch systematische Schulung ist es gelungen, die letzten Spuren Bismarckischen Dilettantentums aus unserer auswärtigen Politik zu tilgen.

9. By 1903–4, German diplomacy had gained such a reputation for clumsy flattery and bullying that the German satirical magazine *Simplicissimus* ran this cartoon showing the training of young diplomats

10. Alexandra and Bertie with Eddy (*standing*), George (*front*) and baby Louise, indulging in the royal passion for pretending to be Scottish, *c.* 1868. George was about three

11. Alexandra and George, aged thirteen, the youngest and smallest naval cadet at Dartmouth Naval College. 'Nobody can, or shall ever, come between me and my darling Georgie boy,' she wrote

12. A summer house party at Amalienborg, the Copenhagen residence of King Christian and Queen Louise of Denmark. The Waleses, the Romanovs and the Danish royals are all present. George (*standing*) and Nicholas, in his pram (*both far left*)

13. Bertie and his family, late 1870s, on board the yacht *Victoria and Albert*. Eddy, at the back, George, to the right, and the three daughters, Louise, Toria and Maud

14. Albert Victor, 'Eddy', and Georgie, pre-beard, late 1880s

15. George and May after their engagement, with Queen Victoria, 1893. The queen, then seventy-four, made a point of never looking into the camera lens

16. After the China land grabs of 1898, a French cartoon shows Wilhelm and Queen Victoria squabbling over a pie representing China, while Nicholas eyes it up and a Chinese government official raises his arms in horror

17. George's two passions were shooting and stamp collecting

18. Nicholas and his sisters Xenia (*centre*) and Olga (*right*)

19. Tsar Alexander III and his family: *clockwise from top left*: Minny, Nicholas, Xenia, Georgy, Olga and Misha

20. George and Nicholas with George's siblings Eddy and Louise at Fredensborg, the summer residence of the Danish royal family, 1889

21. Nicholas (*centre*, in grey suit and white pith helmet) and his entourage on his grand tour in Jobindram, India, 1891. Nicholas complained of 'the unbearableness of being surrounded . . . by the English and of seeing their Red Coats everywhere'

22. Nicholas and George in London, July 1893. The two were constantly mistaken for each other

23. Alexandra, or 'Alicky', aged eleven. Queen Victoria said she was the handsomest child she ever saw

24. Nicholas and Alexandra at Coburg, just after she had agreed to marry him, 1894

25. Family photograph at Coburg in 1894, after the wedding of 'Ducky' to Alexandra's brother Ernest, and Nicky and Alicky's engagement. Wilhelm is bottom left; Nicholas and Alicky next to him; Queen Victoria is seated in the middle, next to Wilhelm's mother Vicky

26. Balmoral, 1896: Queen Victoria in the pony carriage, with Nicholas behind and Alix, as he called her, to the right

27. Nicky and Alix with their first child, Olga, at Balmoral with Queen Victoria and Bertie, 1896. Nicky described Queen Victoria as 'a big round ball on wobbly legs'

28. Nicky and Alix as medieval Russian Tsar and Tsarina, c. 1903

29. Wilhelm pulling the 'fierce' expression he deliberately adopted for photographs, his famous moustache now fully realized, in the uniform of the 'death's head hussars', the Prussian regiment famous for striking fear into the enemy

30. The salon in Wilhelm's new imperial train, one of eleven gilded carriages, 1891

31. Philipp zu Eulenburg

32. Lord Salisbury

33. Otto von Bismarck

34. Bernhard von Bülow

policy was ruled by 'the sudden impulse'. There was 'an absolute want of a guiding hand in Berlin in Foreign Affairs', and 'thorough confusion in the Ministry'.

This lack of focus, even chaos, was becoming characteristic of German politics. Even those embedded in the system could see it. Holstein privately complained that sometimes he seemed to be working in an 'operetta-style government'.

The problem was that when he had drawn up the German constitution in 1871, Bismarck had left great holes and contradictions, deliberately failing to define the precise powers of and relationships between the offices and institutions at the top of government. This allowed him to exercise unprecedented control over every part of it. For example, the precise balance of power between the emperor, chancellor and council of princes had never been defined; and there were effectively two central governments – the German, with its unbiddable representative assembly, the Reichstag, and the Prussian, dominated by a conservative Junker clique, with its own assembly, the Landtag, whose franchise was weighted dramatically towards the Junkers themselves. What was missing was a systematized, overarching, professional body or process at the top to coordinate policy and decision-making, such as existed in Britain. Bismarck had done this job himself, and Wilhelm was simply not competent to fill his shoes. 'In view of the absence of an overwhelming personality under whom the department heads . . . might be absolutely subordinated, the most contradictory opinions are now urged at high and all-highest level,' one German diplomat observed a year after Bismarck had gone. Probably no one could have done the job – each year government business increased and became more complicated – but Wilhelm, with his insistence that he was in charge, his erraticness, his susceptibility to flattery and dislike of criticism, made it worse. With Bismarck's departure, a 'Hobbesian war of all agents within government against all other agents' was taking hold.

The problem was not just confined to the government, it was also an issue in the army. Virtually Wilhelm's first act as kaiser had been to address his army. 'The army and I were born for one another,' he announced in his first proclamation, 'and will stick together forever, be it, by God's will, through peace or war.' He constantly expressed his passion and admiration for the armed forces, and had identified himself closely with them, spending a good part of every week in Potsdam inspecting his regiments, redesigning their uniforms, taking part in war games – which he was invariably allowed to win. By the terms of the German constitution he was the army's supreme warlord, and it reported exclusively to him – not to the nation or the government. It was a power Wilhelm hugged to himself. When he was angry, he would mutter about using the army to launch a *coup d'état* to get rid of the Reichstag. When he was feeling martial, he would describe how he would lead it into battle. Behind their hands, the chiefs of staff expressed their exasperation and laughed at his postures. No one in the officer corps was under any illusions that Wilhelm could 'lead three soldiers over a gutter', as his disgruntled former mentor General Waldersee liked to say. And just as with the government, he was incapable of providing a consistent focus and overview of military planning and policy, and wouldn't allow anyone else to do it either, deflecting any attempts – Caprivi, himself a general, made several – to bring the army under government control and scrutiny. No one outside the army, not even the chancellor, had the authority to be informed of the chiefs of staff's plans and intentions. Rather than sapping its effectiveness – as it had the government – the effect was to make the German military more independent and more assertive. It also encouraged an inward-looking, solipsistic culture not sufficiently mediated by contact with civilian Germany, along with a set of assumptions not outlandishly different from other armies', but more extreme. Within the German officer corps war would be increasingly regarded as inevitable and necessary, and plans would be made without any consideration for political or diplomatic realities. The threads of these tendencies had existed long before Wilhelm. The army was one of the most visible and impressive symbols of the new Germany and the central part it had played in its creation had spawned an uncritical cult of admiration for its manners and methods in all regions and classes that would have its own damaging effects. But Wilhelm's public identification with it, his encouragement of its independence, his refusal to allow that this might be unwise, would exacerbate these tendencies.

The end of 1894 marked the end of Wilhelm's liberal phase, and of Germany's explicit pursuit of Britain as an ally. Caprivi resigned for the last time in October 1894, exhausted. The government lurched back to the Right. Wilhelm ordered legislation for the suppression of the Social Democratic Party – just as Bismarck had done four years before – as well as demanding big increases in military spending and military service. Caprivi's replacement, found by Eulenburg, was the 75-year-old Prince Chlodwig Hohenlohe von Schillingfurst, a grand former diplomat and distant relative of Wilhelm's with Russian estates and sympathies, chosen because Eulenburg reckoned he was old, tired and would do as he was told. The Reichstag, however, remained as unbiddable as ever. The centre and Left parties, with whom Wilhelm (and his advisers) refused to treat, voted against the government. The main parties of the Right, the Conservatives and National Liberals, whom Wilhelm had hoped to rally with his moves against the Left, demanded concessions for their own agendas, particularly the privileges and protectionism that kept the Junker class so influential. The government was now often forced to go further than it actually wanted – its ministers making aggressive speeches against whichever country the parties currently hated most, and keeping tariffs high on imported grain, which made food expensive for the poor, to keep them on-side. And all the time, support for the Socialist Party had been growing. In the 1893 Reichstag elections it had won 25 per cent of the vote. The old divisions seemed more entrenched than ever, and Wilhelm's government both unable and unwilling to try to resolve them.

At Wilhelm's Cowes visit of 1895 it was all too evident that Anglo-German relations had passed their honeymoon phase. Edward grumbled that Wilhelm now sashayed around as if he was 'the Boss of Cowes', and when Wilhelm's *Meteor* finally beat *Britannia* the following year, he sold his yacht. Wilhelm, meanwhile, was smarting because the English family had been unenthusiastic about his first regatta week at Kiel. Eventually George had reluctantly attended the madly lavish celebrations (a whole island was built in the middle of a lake outside Hamburg, for a week only, for Wilhelm's gala dinner for 600), but bluntly announced that he couldn't accept any honorary titles. Wilhelm had taken this as a slight and blamed it on Alexandra's plotting.

At Cowes his entourage saw British insults everywhere. 'Fat old Wales has again been inconceivably rude to HM,' one member wrote to Holstein. Wilhelm himself was far from a model of tact. At a drinks party on board the *Hohenzollern*, crammed with grand English guests, he allegedly called Bertie 'the Old Peacock'. He brought a thirty-strong brass band which performed, without invitation, at every possible opportunity, and two new flashy German gunships, which blocked the yacht's course and fired a 21-gun-salute – giving the visit an official status it was not supposed to have. On the anniversary of the Prussian victory over the French in 1870 he gave a speech praising the supremacy of the German army. The British press were scaldingly critical. The hitherto pro-German *Standard* suggested the kaiser go home before he insulted anyone else, a comment Wilhelm still recalled five months later when he told the queen that the newspaper had been 'very unkind' to him.

To make matters worse Lord Salisbury, lately re-elected prime minister, failed to take his own advice that the kaiser should be treated 'like a jealous woman who insists on the undivided devotion of all her admirers'. He was two hours late for a meeting with him. The audience had been arranged to discuss the Eastern Question – the apparent imminent collapse of the Ottoman empire and how to stop it causing chaos in Eastern Europe. Salisbury had a plan to partition its territories. Wilhelm – between furious little jokes about the prime minister's tardiness – was dismissive. Salisbury was taciturn and impenetrable. The next day the kaiser decided he wanted to talk it over once more. Salisbury failed to show. He claimed afterwards with profuse apologies that he had had a simultaneous meeting with the queen, had not received the message, and had been caught in the rain. Wilhelm summoned him again. This time he didn't turn up because he said he had to be in London early. No one entirely believed him, especially the kaiser. One of the less devoted members of Wilhelm's entourage told Holstein that he thought the prime minister simply couldn't bear to see the kaiser again.

Even so, Wilhelm's entourage and ministers continued to worry about their master's susceptibility to England. 'I very much hope that his Majesty will soon return . . . because I very much fear the English influence,' one member wrote to Holstein.

7. Perfidious Muscovy (1895–7)

Everyone was excited by the accession of Nicholas II. Educated Russians longed for liberalization. The government's attempts to prevent social change and its supine failure to manage the terrible famine of the early 1890s had hugely discredited it, and Alexander's Russification policies had spawned the beginnings of angry separatist movements in the further reaches of the empire. Beyond Russia, however, expectations were even higher. Both Queen Victoria and the kaiser hoped that the young tsar would lean towards them, and were convinced that the key would be royal relationships. The British – inspired by Edward's triumphant Russian visit – even thought they could see the seeds of a genuine liberalization. 'The first acts of the new reign point to liberal measures,' the Prince of Wales's equerry Arthur Ellis had reported to the queen, '– press censure of telegrams removed . . . to the dismay and astonishment of the ultra-Conservatives.' The tsar had told a deputation from much-persecuted Poland that 'all his subjects were equal and alike in his own eyes'. 'How not to admire him,' his second cousin Konstantin Romanov wrote in his diary, 'such simplicity, such calm, the modesty in which there is so much majesty, and particularly that clear, deep expressive look, cannot fail but charm and enchant.' The truth was, Nicholas was such a blank canvas, so unknown, except for his much-admired personal charm and gentleness, that it was easy to project all kinds of wishful thinking on to him.

Within Russia, the illusion didn't last long. In February 1895 a polite zemstvo delegation from the province of Tver petitioned the tsar that 'the expression of the needs and thought not only of the administration but of the Russian people may reach to the height of the throne'. The British ambassador in St Petersburg noted that their words had been 'couched in the most loyal language and merely expressed the hope that the zemstvo might prove the means of direct communication between His Majesty and the People'. But the minister of the interior had told the tsar that it was an infringement of his prerogatives and an implied criticism of his father's policies. Nicholas decided it represented a dangerous precedent, an attempt to take part in government. Replying to the zemstvo's petition he dismissed it as 'senseless dreams'. 'I shall maintain the principle of autocracy just as firmly and unflinchingly as it was preserved by my unforgettable dead father,' he added. In government circles it was understood that the speech had been written by Alexander III's most reactionary adviser, Pobedonostsev. 'The speech had created a most unfavourable impression,' the British ambassador wrote; 'the most distressing impression', echoed a senior Russian diplomat. The fact was, all the way through the century, the arrival of a new tsar had always set off fantasies of liberalization and reform; they had always been disappointed.

Still, the tsar continued to express his fondness for his 'English relations' and told the British ambassador how much he wanted 'cordial relations with England', and that since there was no longer any difference of opinion between the two countries, they should act 'in perfect harmony' to solve the world's problems. He wrote enthusiastically to Edward in the New Year of 1895 about the delegation from the Scots Greys Guards regiment who brought him his new uniform: 'I find them such nice fellows . . . I cannot say how proud and pleased I was.' Not long afterwards Russia and Britain began negotiations to resolve the arguments over the boundaries of the Pamirs in the Himalayas. To demonstrate the new closeness, a portrait of the queen hung over the mantelpiece in the tsarina's private sitting room. Alix and the queen corresponded regularly,* and the queen took to writing regularly to 'Dearest Nicky', signing herself 'Grandmama', enquiring after 'poor dear Alicky's' health and offering up tidbits of family gossip. When their first child, Olga, was born in November 1895, the imperial couple asked the queen to be godmother. The *Daily Telegraph* wrote that the birth 'would be received with much friendly interest in this

---

* Alix destroyed the correspondence after the queen's death.

country, where all that concerns the present and future of Russia is the subject of intelligent and sympathetic appreciation'. It seemed natural that the warmth would lead to a new attitude in Anglo-Russian relations.

In the spirit of hopeful cooperation, the British government began to invite the Russians to work with it. It asked them to apply pressure to the Ottoman government, which had colluded in a series of massacres of Armenians, a Christian ethnic group within the Turkish empire campaigning for self-determination, in 1894 and '95. The Russians declined. In early 1895 it asked the Russians to back a call for an armistice in the Far East, where the Chinese, having provoked a war with Japan, had been thoroughly beaten and were begging the Great Powers for help. The Russians were evasive; in fact, it was impossible to get an answer at all. The requests were not outlandish: Russia had long claimed to be the defender of Christians within the Ottoman empire. As for the Far East, it was in no Western power's interest to let Japan establish a foothold in China, the last great unplucked colonial plum, which also happened to be on Russia's doorstep. The British were disappointed. Then the two countries argued in April 1895, when the Russians – suddenly realizing the Japanese were planning to annex the northern Chinese province of Manchuria on which they had their own designs – demanded that the British back their campaign to evict them. This time the British refused. They saw no reason to alienate the new *de facto* rising power in the Far East, and they felt British interests weren't directly threatened. Lord Rosebery took care, however, to say no with 'great delicacy', not wanting to 'shut the door with a bang'. The Russians were unimpressed. The ambassador in London, Baron Georges de Staal, a comfortable fixture on the capital's society scene who played cards with the Prince of Wales, complained crossly that Rosebery was just fuelling the Russian anti-British party which would 'now exclaim, "Just what we always told you, that England would leave us in the lurch whenever a pinch came"'. The Russian press denounced Britain and its refusal to help evict the Japanese – characteristic double-dealing, they said.

Queen Victoria wrote to Nicholas assuring him 'how deeply

I & my Government deplored not to be able to join in the
Representations of Russia and the 2 other Powers to Japan but
the feeling was so strong in this Country that it was impossible'.
She couldn't resist, however, complaining about

Some most violent and offensive articles against England in the Russian
Newspapers signed by . . . the Gentleman (whose name I can't recall at
this moment [the Russian expansionist Prince Alexander Utkhomsky])
but who helped you in writing the account of your journey to India.
These [articles] have been translated in to the English papers and I need
not say have caused an angry feeling. But the worst of all is, that they
say he is your friend and possesses your confidence, and what I am so
anxious for, is that it should be known that you know nothing of these
articles and disapprove of them and I am sure you will not mind my
writing to you so openly.

'I must say that I cannot prevent people from putting their opinions
openly in the newspapers,' Nicholas wrote back. Actually the
Russian press was the most state-controlled and strictly censored
in the world. 'How often have I not been worried to read in
English gazettes rather unjust statements in connexion with my
country! Even books are being constantly sent to me from London,
misinterpreting our actions in Asia, our interior politics, etc. I am
sure,' he finished rather sharply, 'there is as little hostility intended
in these writings, as there is in the above mentioned ones.' It was
true that sections of the British press regularly attacked the Russian
regime. In October 1895 *The Times* ran Leo Tolstoy's account of
the brutal persecution of the pacifist Dukhobor sect, members of
which had been beaten and starved for refusing to do military
service. Like many people in autocratic states Nicholas was convinced that despite British insistence to the contrary, the British
government controlled the press and that the queen's complaints
were disingenuous. Russian press hostility towards Britain continued unabated. In November, the same month the queen became
godmother to the tsar's daughter, the outgoing British ambassador,
Sir Francis Lascelles, told the tsar in his final audience how 'discouraging' the British found this, adding delicately that such articles

'would not be written were it not that they were agreeable to the majority of the people' – by which he meant those who controlled the press, i.e. the government. All the emperor would say was 'the press had very little importance in Russia'.

In the autumn, only months after the two countries signed an agreement on the Pamirs, the British Foreign Office received reports that Russian troops had been sighted on the borders of Tibet. Then came rumours – constantly denied by the Russian foreign minister, Prince Lobanov-Rostovsky, a very grand, clever, rather haughty aristocrat from a rich old St Petersburg family, but confirmed by Chinese sources – that they had made a secret 'loan' of £8 million to the cash-strapped Chinese, who, having lost the war with Japan, had been left with a huge war indemnity. In return the Russians demanded trading concessions and the right to extend the Trans-Siberian railway through Manchuria, the large northern Chinese province that pushed deep into Siberia. The British hated the thought of Russia sniffing around in China, where they had made a great deal of money by propping up the imperial govern- ment with their own loans, selling the Chinese British goods (opium in particular), and in return for their loans taking control of Chinese customs taxes. They feared a partition or African-like scramble would disrupt their position there. The suave and irritat- ingly evasive Prince Lobanov, they decided, was 'at heart un- friendly'. After a year of negotiations, the British ambassador described him as having 'almost a diseased mistrust of England and of British machinations'. In 1896 the British discovered that Russia was, as the queen put it, 'encouraging France against us with regard to Egypt'. It seemed that however warm the Russian avowals of friendship, nothing had really changed at all. When the queen met Nicholas's mother, Minny, on her annual trip to the South of France in April, she told her how 'very unhappy' she was that things seemed worse now than in Alexander's time, and 'begged her to mention this to Nicky'.

To be honest it was hard to know what was going on in the Russian government. One reason was that the whole functioning of the administration was chaotic. Not unlike Germany, no one organ coordinated policy; ministers reported singly to the tsar, acted unilaterally, and frequently in contradiction with each other. Intrigue was rife. Another reason was that, like most autocracies, the regime felt little need to explain itself to its subjects – or anyone else. The press, tightly controlled by the government, was either official propaganda or unreliable. It had none of the authority of the British press, which covered and discussed government business, debate and policy. Communicating with foreign powers, the Russian government never disclosed internal disagreements or the reasons for delay, and seemed to feel no obligation to be straight-forward. The American president, Theodore Roosevelt, would wearily describe it as 'a government with whom mendacity is a science'. When the German ambassador in St Petersburg complained a Russian minister had never been honest with him, Wilhelm scribbled on the report, 'No impossible demands! No Russian has ever done that!'

Another reason for Russian opacity was that Nicholas himself was extraordinarily hard to get access to – unlike Wilhelm, whose endless opinions were printed in the press, and who dropped into the British embassy to let off steam whenever he felt like it. From the start the new tsar shied away from public scrutiny. How active he was in government – whether he was making the decisions or was leaving ruling to a cabal of ministers – and what his position was on a whole range of political issues, were extremely hard to gauge. What he was actually like was just as moot. A rumour that 'the Tsar drinks', the German ambassador informed Holstein in November 1895, was 'a false scent. It transpired he had been confused with his brother, who drank a great deal . . .' In fact Nicholas was inscrutable even to his own ministers. He rarely lost his temper, he spoke calmly, he deflected confrontation and difficult subjects, he almost never directly disagreed with or contra-dicted the person he was talking to – though he might in reality completely disagree with them. He was, his finance minister Sergei Witte later wrote, 'exasperatingly polite'. He 'possessed in a supreme degree', a Russian diplomat observed, 'the art of agreeing with his interlocutor in such a way as to make him believe that he had been much impressed and quite convinced by what he had been told – a most delicate kind of flattery.' Often the opposite was true. Nicholas's sister Olga felt this inscrutable courtesy had become a shield to hide the constant 'nervous strain' and anxiety he felt about his inadequacy for the job. 'The Grand-Duchess held that the Emperor's impassivity was a mask he wore to hide his feelings; [she said] ". . . none of them [his people] knew that their Tsar felt everything so deeply that he was afraid he might break down in public . . . perhaps only Alicky and I knew how deeply he suffered and worried."' It also, of course, cut him off even more from the people he dealt with, as if he had personally ingested the physical barriers to the world set up during his childhood, and erected more of his own. It was hardly surprising that diplomats resorted to collecting gossip, tapping foreign correspondents, and weighing the murmurings of ministers with their own agendas. 'Nothing remains secret here long,' a senior British diplomat wrote, 'the difficulty here is to sift the truth from the lies.'

The truth was Lobanov *did* harbour a very traditional Russian hostility to the British and the Russians *were* trying to insinuate themselves into China. Lobanov had refused to cooperate with the British over the Armenian massacres because he was convinced that the British wanted to stir up tension in Eastern Europe and hoped to grab a sizeable piece of Turkey if the Ottoman empire came tumbling down by itself. The British had a bad habit of moving in their troops on high moral grounds and then accidentally taking over – as they had done in Egypt in 1882. It was also the case that the Russians had an Armenian community of their own and had no desire to stir up demands for self-determination at home by encouraging the Turkish Armenians. Moreover, despite Nicholas's words about the two countries having no real areas of conflict, the Russian government was raring to pursue an expansionist policy in Asia and the Far East – where Britain was Russia's chief imperial rival. Only lack of funds had held it back. The Russian finance minister, Sergei Witte, perhaps the smartest official in Nicholas's government, however, had studied the way the British had acquired their colonies and markets without armies and on the cheap – through 'peaceful penetration' – and was following their model, with loans and railways. He regarded himself as a new economic imperialist – unlike most of the Russian ruling elite, who saw the empire primarily in terms of armies, status and land. There was a certain irony in the fact that in order to make loans to the Chinese, he in turn was having to take out huge loans with the French.

Just like the British, Wilhelm nursed hopes of breaking the chill between Russia and Germany. In mid-1894 Germany had signed a trade treaty with Russia which had reduced German tariffs on Russian grain. (One of its consequences had been to enrage the Junker parties but that, for the moment, was another story.) Wilhelm planned to continue the thaw with a new friendship with 'charming, agreeable and dear' Nicholas. 'I can only repeat the expression of absolute trust in you and the assurance that I shall always cultivate the old relations of mutual friendship with your House, in which I was reared by my Grandfather,' he'd written to the young tsar a week after the death of the (to him) unlamented Alexander. Wilhelm was convinced that if he could appeal to Nicky's monarchical instincts, dazzle him with his personality and his winning way with an argument, the tsar's natural German sympathies would rise to the surface. He would throw over the French alliance, stop flirting with the British and jump into the German fold. Wilhelm decided that the vehicle for his new diplomacy would be a secret correspondence – emperor to emperor – not unlike the early letters he had sent to Alexander III. Not even Eulenburg was to know. (The kaiser's friend, however, soon realized that something was up. 'Our relations with the new Tsar do not please me a bit, and I am watching HM's family politics with real anxiety,' he wrote.) Though he'd written to Alexander in French, the traditional language of Russian diplomacy (Russian ambassadors still made their reports in French) and a legacy of the tsarist admiration for pre-revolutionary France, Wilhelm wrote to Nicholas in English. Why isn't immediately clear. Nicholas was certainly proficient in German. Perhaps Wilhelm spurned French because he was keen to demonstrate his scorn for all things Gallic, and chose English because it was neutral territory for both.

Just as he'd tried to turn Alexander against the British, Wilhelm's first letter in February 1895 denounced the latest French administration for 'opening the doors to all the worst malefactors the former people with difficulty had managed to imprison'. He congratulated Nicholas on his hard line to the Tver zemstvo, 'I am so glad at the capital speech you made the other day to the deputation in response to some addresses for Reform!' He complained that his own Reichstag was behaving 'as badly as it can, swinging backwards and forwards between the socialists egged on by the Jews, and the ultramontane Catholics [sic]; both parties being soon fit to be hung all of them as far as I can see'. He described the British Liberal government collapsing 'amidst universal derision! In short everywhere the "principe de la Monarchie" is called upon to show itself strong.'

The kaiser was far from the only German who believed that Germany could and should detach Russia from France. 'I have great hopes, incidentally, that the German sympathies of the Tsar will come to the surface . . . ,' the German ambassador in Paris wrote to Holstein. 'The quite unnatural love affair between the Republic [France] and the absolute Tsar is like the bastard of a lioness and a tiger, not the product of love but of evil.'

While the British refused to join Russia's campaign to get the Japanese out of Manchuria, Germany pointedly supported it. More than that, Wilhelm urged Nicholas to make a bigger effort in the Far East – to take on 'the great task' – 'to cultivate the Asian Continent and to defend Europe from the inroads of the Great Yellow race'. The second goal of his diplomatic correspondence was, he told his Foreign Office, 'to tie Russia down in East Asia so that she pays less attention to Europe and the near East'. He told Nicholas he would 'do all in my power to keep Europe quiet, and also guard the rear of Russia so that nobody shall hamper your action'. He proposed they meet that summer on their yachts to 'have a quiet little chat between ourselves . . . It would be so nice.' He repeated his offer to guard Russia's western front if there was a war in the East to various visiting Russian grandees, while failing to inform any of his own ministers that he'd done so. This promise was an extraordinarily serious one, since it presumably included countering Austria if necessary. When Eulenburg eventually found out about it, he was horrified. 'His Majesty has thus <u>committed himself – without Hohenlohe</u>. This gives me yet more problems to solve, which fill me with with <u>dread</u>! . . . If Hohenlohe hears of the letter from someone <u>other than me</u>, he will go [i.e. resign] at once. And yet he <u>must</u> know about it!'

Wilhelm's promises and professions of intimacy, however, brought nothing concrete from the Russians, just Nicholas's relentless politeness. He charmed every German, including the chancellor, whom Wilhelm sent to pay their respects, and complained, gratifyingly, about the perfidiousness of the English. But there was no distancing from France. In fact, Lobanov made a much publicized visit to Paris in September 1895 which Wilhelm complained about at length to – among others – the foreign minister himself, and repeatedly to the tsar. Lobanov's visit had encouraged those 'damned rascals' the French to start moving troops around on the border, one letter complained. 'One day my dearest Nicky, you will find yourself <u>nolens volens</u> suddenly embroiled in the most horrible of wars Europe ever saw! Which will by the masses and by history be fixed on you as the cause of it,' he wrote a few days later. '. . . Think of the awful responsibility for the shocking bloodshed!' The letter was accompanied by an allegorical drawing, 'Against the Yellow Peril', Wilhelm had drawn (it had, in fact, been 'sketched' by him and 'finished' by the artist Hermann Knackfuss), in which Germany, shield and sword in hand, stood ready to defend Russia – a beautiful woman leaning on Germany's arm – while England and France hung back, dazed by smoke and flames from a vast plain below in which faceless masses held aloft a buddha and a Chinese dragon. Only weeks later he sent an aide-de-camp to St Petersburg to repeat his warning, along with yet another letter lecturing Nicholas on 'the danger which is brought to our Principle of Monarchism through lifting up the Republic on a pedestal by the form under which the friendship is shown . . . Nicky take my word on it the curse of God has stricken that People for ever!'★

★ Queen Victoria felt quite as anti-republican. When the French president, Felix Faure, came to pay his respects to her in 1898 in the South of France, she told Edward he was a commoner and could not be treated as an equal. Edward must remain on the stairs when he arrived, forcing the president to climb up to meet him. Faure, perfectly aware of the intended snub, was very insulted.

Nicholas continued to smile. By November Wilhelm was losing patience. 'HM is beginning to be quite angry with the Tsar,' Holstein wrote to the new German ambassador in St Petersburg, Prince Radolin, 'because of the repeated cool rebuffs . . .'

The truth was the Russian government didn't want to alienate the Germans, but it had no wish to abandon the French alliance. The French had proved useful. They might be ghastly republicans (which was how the Russian regime regarded them) but this was outweighed by their keenness to provide the huge loans on which the Russian state depended – stepping in when Bismarck had refused to. They shared Russia's suspicion of Britain, and most of all their antipathy to Germany meant that Russia had a reliable ally to counterbalance Germany in Europe. Slavophilism was gaining ground in government and at court, where influential conservative figures such as Nicholas's uncle and brother-in-law Grand Duke Sergei, who once would have seen Germany as an ideological ally, now regarded it as a political, territorial and ideological rival.

As for Wilhelm's personal charms, Nicholas was thoroughly familiar with his parents' distrust of the kaiser. Minny's dislike had certainly played its role, but Nicky was himself irked by the kaiser's pushy, often brutally obvious, attempts at manipulation. He found him patronizing. 'I received Moltke, the aide de camp who brought me a letter and drawing from the irritating Monsieur Wilhelm,' he wrote in his diary after yet another of Wilhelm's urgent missives in September 1895. He would tell Lord Salisbury that he found Wilhelm nervous and excitable, and as 'a quiet man . . . he could not stand nervous men. He could not endure a long conversation with the Emperor William, as he never knew what he would do or say. I understood him to say that the Emperor William's manners were bad; that he would poke him in the ribs, and slap him on the back like a schoolboy.' Alix had nothing good to say about Wilhelm either. Though Wilhelm liked to take the credit for bringing her and Nicholas together, she remembered his childhood visits to Hesse-Darmstadt: he'd been boorish and bossy. He'd been rude to her father, who had been one of the few public figures who had stood by Vicky after his father's death, and to her brother Ernie; and she couldn't forgive him and Dona for publicly branding her sister Ella (on whom Wilhelm had once had a childhood crush) as a 'traitor to her faith and her Fatherland' for converting to Russian Orthodoxy.

There was a part of Nicky, however, that was susceptible to Wilhelm. Wilhelm was one of the few people who understood what it felt like to be emperor, and he had an odd ability to home in on people's preoccupations and vulnerabilities. The 'monarchical principle' was one of the few supra-national ideas that appealed to Nicky. Like many upper-class Russians, he found the alliance with republican France made him uneasy, and he instinctively distrusted the British. There were moments when Wilhelm's probings hit a nerve and when Nicholas was persuaded to confide in the German emperor. 'I quite agree with what You say in the end of Your letter about the Britishers,' Wilhelm replied to a complaint from Nicky. 'Their fanfarronades against us make them supremely ridiculous.' Nor was a move towards Germany unthinkable. Amid the many factions in the Russian government was a pro-German one which included men such as Nicky's Germanophile uncle, Grand Duke Vladimir, as well as the tsar's minister of court, Count Fredericks, who considered Germany 'the last stronghold of the monarchical idea; we need her just as she needed us'. The finance minister, Sergei Witte, believed that Russia needed to be on good terms with her neighbour, if only to decrease the vast sums spent on arming the frontier with Germany since the lapse of the Reinsurance Treaty in 1890.

By 1896 both the Germans and the British were frustrated by their failure to make any headway with the Russians. Instead of blaming the tsar, both pinned the responsibility on his ministers – specifically Lobanov, the foreign minister. Wilhelm and Holstein concluded the tsar was 'uninterested' in politics and Lobanov was running foreign policy; they saw him as a protégé of the dowager empress, whom they regarded as notoriously anti-German. But the truth was that Nicholas's views were indivisible from his foreign minister's, and he liked Lobanov, who was famously witty and amusing. They shared the casual xenophobia which seemed to characterize the Russian court and the Foreign Ministry. The tsar called the Japanese yellow monkeys, and managed comfortably to separate his feelings for his English cousins from his instinctive suspicion of England – and Germany. When the Russian loan to the Chinese government went through in 1895, Nicholas was delighted, pausing only to grumble in his diary that it had been delayed by 'the intriguing of the British and Germans at Peking'.

The British and Germans, however, chose to see the tsar as they wanted him to be: a good man, at base well disposed to them. Even Britain's foremost Russian expert, Donald Mackenzie-Wallace, described Nicholas as a man of 'strong humanitarian sympathies', and warm feelings for Britain, who disliked Lobanov but had yielded reluctantly to his 'great diplomatic experience and his worldwide reputation'. Wilhelm, meanwhile, regarded Nicholas as an innocent who needed to be freed from the manipulations of his ministers and family.

The problem with coming late to the colonial feast, the Germans kept finding, was that everyone else had already staked their claims, especially in Africa. To draw back would be to resign themselves to a few minor colonies, to press on meant conflict with other empire-builders; colonial conflict had become the subject of virtually all arguments with Britain. In November 1895, at a farewell shooting party, the outgoing British ambassador to Berlin, Sir Edward Malet, told the German foreign minister, Marschall von Bieberstein, that he was happy with the general drift of Anglo-German relations (leaving aside, of course, the unmentionable subject of Wilhelm's disastrous Cowes visit of that summer). But there was, he ventured, just one 'dark spot': their two countries' rivalry in Southern Africa, specifically in the Transvaal, the enclave in the middle of Southern Africa run by the Boers, the descendants of white Dutch settlers. The British empire, through Cecil Rhodes's British South Africa Company, controlled the rest of South Africa. The Boer republic looked like an irritating anomaly to empire-builders like Rhodes. The fact that gold had been discovered there also made it eminently covetable. The Germans, however, had interests too. They were some of the tiny state's biggest investors, and were known to sympathize with the Boers; they had given them diplomatic and economic support; Krupp was also selling guns to them. Their most substantial colony, South-West Africa, was not far away. Encouraged by the Boers them-selves, who reckoned that German muscle could help them against the increasingly bullying British colonial government, there had been talk of making the Transvaal a German protectorate. The thought of a rich foothold in Southern Africa excited Wilhelm and the German colonial lobby. The British, needless to say, hated the idea. Malet told Marschall he felt bound to point out that there might be 'serious consequences' if Germany's aid continued. Marschall replied that the Germans couldn't help it if the Boers hated the British.

The conversation appears to have gone no further, but when Wilhelm received a report of it he was furious. He told Nicholas that the ambassador had issued Germany with an ultimatum and been 'even so undiplomatic as to utter the word "war"'. It was a moment when nothing seemed to be going right and Wilhelm was especially touchy. The Reichstag had rejected legislation to which he'd publicly attached himself; his ministers – sick of his erratic interventions – had for once resolved to act collectively and were threatening to resign in order to get their way; it seemed possible they might force some kind of constitutional limits on him. His frequent spitting rages had left Eulenburg fearing for his sanity and at least one minister wondering if he was 'entirely normal'. Summoning Colonel Swaine, the British military attaché,★ Wilhelm complained bitterly that, having rejected his friendship, Britain was now threatening him. Malet's 'astonishing accusations,' he said, were the last straw. 'For the sake of a few square miles full of negroes and palm trees England threatened to declare war on its one real friend, the German Emperor,' he later reported himself as saying. Swaine, completely taken aback, assured him that there must be a misunderstanding. No, said Wilhelm, it was all of a piece with the way Britain's 'government press' had

---

★ Swaine was the man from whom Wilhelm had extracted military information which he had then passed to Tsar Alexander III. The military attaché had remained a consistent and sympathetic advocate for what he believed was Wilhelm's underlying sympathy for his mother's country.

'behaved in a most unwarranted way towards me. Germany and the Triple Alliance had been perpetually calumnied and teased.' But it was England who was making the mistake. England had brought total isolation on herself by her 'selfishness and bullying'. Sooner or later Britain would have to make a choice – Germany and the Triple Alliance, or the other side. 'The Colonel seemed profoundly shaken and affected,' Wilhelm ended his account of the conversation.

Salisbury, alerted to Wilhelm's snit, sent a message that Malet's words, whatever they had been, had no official force. The kaiser, calmed, decided that his diplomatic skills and eloquence had extracted an apology. This was a conclusion belied by Salisbury's briefing of the new British ambassador to Berlin, Sir Francis Lascelles, who had just come from St Petersburg. 'The conduct of the German Emperor is very mysterious and difficult to explain,' it ran. 'There is a danger of him going completely off his head . . . In commercial and colonial matters Germany was most disagreeable, her demand for the left bank of the Volta was outrageous, so much so that Lord Salisbury thought it must have been an idea of the Emperor himself as no responsible statesman could have put it forward.'

As if to confirm Salisbury's prognostications, Wilhelm was in the process of making a series of dangerously inconsistent interventions in foreign affairs, which – had they known of them – would have confirmed to his ministers that his intrusions in politics could be laughably inept, if not actively dangerous. Since early in 1895 it had been widely predicted that the Ottoman empire was about to fall apart. Its government in Constantinople seemed to exist in a state of constant and advancing chaos, and its collapse threatened a dangerous free-for-all in Eastern Europe and the Levant.* The question of what would happen to Constantinople and the Straits to the Black Sea – or the Eastern Question, as it was called – preoccupied the British, the Russians and Austria, which particularly dreaded the possibility of Russian warships in

---

* In fact rumours of the Ottoman empire's collapse would turn out to be premature; it would lumber along into the First World War.

the Mediterranean. 'I declare quite plainly that I shall stand at Austria-Hungary's side with all the forces at my disposal,' Wilhelm told the Austrian ambassador, about three days after having made exactly the same offer to Nicholas. The Austrian foreign minister said it was the warmest manifestation of German friendship in all the years of the Austro-German alliance. Towards Christmas Wilhelm said the same thing to the hapless Colonel Swaine, whom he had summoned to hear another speech in which he accused the British of deliberately stirring up a crisis over the future of the Ottoman empire – then suggested they take the Turkish capital. The revelation of the kaiser's offers threw the usually calmly cynical Fritz Holstein into a panic. 'What happens now if Salisbury, whom HM has deeply offended, communicated the contents of that conversation to St Petersburg?' he demanded of Eulenburg. As it was, none of the Powers chose to move on Constantinople, and Wilhelm's offers stayed secret.

Paradoxically, while this dangerously rogue intervention remained undisclosed, Wilhelm found himself at the start of 1896 in the midst of an international furore over something relatively banal and not entirely his fault. On the last day of 1895, 600 armed men – some of them said to be officers of the British army, all of them British – led by Dr Leander Jameson, a close associate of Cecil Rhodes, the most powerful man in South Africa, creator of De Beers and self-confessed British empire-builder, crossed the border into the Transvaal in an attempt to overthrow the Boer government.

When Wilhelm heard the news he was reported to be 'rabid' with anger. 'The Transvaal republic has been attacked in a most foul way,' he wrote to Nicholas on 2 January 1896, 'as it seems not without England's knowledge. I have used very severe language in London, and have opened communication with Paris for common defence of our endangered interests . . . I never shall allow the British to stamp out the Transvaal!' He wasn't alone; the whole of Europe loudly condemned the Jameson raid, which was widely suspected of having been backed, or even launched, by the British, though the colonial minister, Joseph Chamberlain, swiftly condemned it and denied the government had been in any way involved. (In fact, the British government was up to its eyes in the Jameson raid. It had been planned with the explicit encouragement of Chamberlain, whose involvement was now being vigorously covered up.) Condemnation was especially loud in Germany. Later that day the news came that the Boers had completely routed the raiders. Nevertheless, on 3 January Wilhelm strode into a meeting with his ministers demanding invasion forces and warships. Europe should teach England a lesson. His ministers talked him out of using force, but they were quite as angry as he. (Marschall had already sent Salisbury a threatening formal note – an acknowledged first step along the route to war – protesting at the 'invasion'. In a moment of almost theatrical farce, Hatzfeldt, hearing of Jameson's failure, only just managed to snatch it off Salisbury's desk before he saw it.) It was finally agreed that Wilhelm should send a personal telegram of support to the Boer leader, Paul Kruger.

Today the text seems distinctly banal: 'I express my sincere congratulations that you and your people have succeeded, by your own energetic actions and without appealing for help to friendly powers, in restoring order against the armed hordes that invaded your country as disturbers of the peace, and in safeguarding the independence of your country from external attack.'

In Britain the 'Kruger telegram' brought forth a violent and sudden outpouring of hysterical anger, a confused combination of defensiveness, entitlement and aggression. 'The Nation will never forget this telegram, and it will always bear it in mind in the future orientation of its policy,' the *Morning Post* snarled. The kaiser was denounced not only in the press, but in gentlemen's clubs; society ladies sent him poison-pen letters. German shopkeepers had their windows smashed. In hindsight the level of the public response seems quite out of proportion with the act itself. The telegram didn't even mention Britain, the rest of Europe was equally condemnatory, and the British government had denounced the raid and denied involvement. The reaction stemmed from a con-fusion of half-realized assumptions: that the personal should trump the political, the kaiser, as half-English, ought not to question British actions. One expected such things from the French, but Germany was supposed to be Britain's friend. There was also, however, a new sense of direct hostility towards Germany, that it might be a serious colonial rival that needed to be kept at bay. Overarching all this was a furious sense of entitlement and defensiveness, a manifestation of an aggressive new imperialist spirit that asserted that, because Britain was special, because it was the greatest promoter of civilization that the world had ever seen, it not only had the right to impose its own rules on others, but the normal rules didn't really apply. No one had the right to criticize its actions.

Wilhelm's English relatives were quite as angry as everyone else. The queen described the telegram as 'outrageous, and very unfriendly towards us'. Edward called it 'a most gratuitous act of unfriendliness', and giving full rein to his dislike of his nephew continued, 'he has shown in addition the worst possible taste and good feeling in congratulating the Boers on their victory over a body . . . composed exclusively of the Queen's subjects. But independently of this, the Prince of Wales would like to know what business the Emperor has to send any message at all.' For years afterwards he referred to the Kruger telegram as the event which revealed Wilhelm's 'true feelings' about England. Even George 'spoke loud and abused the German Emperor, not caring what he said', one of the queen's ladies-in-waiting observed.

The queen administered a lofty grandmotherly reprimand to her German grandson:

As your grandmother . . . I feel I cannot refrain from expressing deep regret at the telegram you sent President Kruger . . . It is considered very unfriendly towards this country which I feel sure it is not intended to be, and has, I have to say, made a very painful impression . . . The action of Dr Jameson was, of course, very wrong and totally unwarranted; but considering the very peculiar position in which the Transvaal stands towards Great Britain, I think it would have been far better to have said nothing . . . Our great wish has always been to keep on the best of terms with Germany, trying to act together, but I fear Your Agents in the Colonies do the very reverse, [which was rich] which deeply grieves us.

Wilhelm, who was completely amazed by the unanimous chorus of excoriation he received, crumpled immediately. He wrote a grovelling reply: 'I was so incensed at the idea of your orders having been disobeyed, and thereby Peace . . . endangered, that I thought it necessary to show that publicly . . . I was standing up for law, order and obedience to a Sovereign whom I rever [*sic*] and adore.' Subsequently he would blame the telegram entirely on his ministers. Victoria called the letter lame and illogical, but Salisbury advised her 'fully to accept all his explanations without inquiring too narrowly into the truth of them'.

In Pretoria President Kruger told the German consul, 'the old woman just sneezed and you ran away'.

Wilhelm, backed by Fritz Holstein in the German Foreign Office, who was so concerned by the British response he thought England might fall into the arms of France, immediately embarked on a charm offensive to re-endear himself to the British. Before the end of January Hatzfeldt had offered Salisbury a formal alliance, which the prime minister as usual politely turned down. In February, when the queen's son-in-law Henry of Battenburg died of malaria in the Ashanti wars, the kaiser sent a huge deputation to the funeral. When Colonel Swaine, the British military attaché, retired that month, Wilhelm loaded him with lavish decorations and pronounced him a personal friend. In March, unable to restrain the familiar impulse to make anxious those whose intimacy he wanted, he told Sir Francis Lascelles, the new British ambassador, that despite his appalling treatment by the British press, he had to let England know that the Russians wanted 'to destroy England', and annex the Balkans, while France was planning to sabotage the Suez Canal route to India. (As it happened, the Russians had been encouraging the French to cause trouble for the British in Africa, and had invited the Germans to support them.) These plans, he insisted, had been sanctioned by Nicholas himself. The intervention backfired. Hatzfeldt reported dejectedly that Lord Salisbury had been 'literally horrified' by the kaiser's warning, having only just begun to relax again in their meetings.

Nor were the English relatives placated. In April, at a family wedding in Coburg,★ George informed Wilhelm that he would not be welcome at Cowes that year. Wilhelm, he reported to Nicholas, 'seemed more excitable than ever, he hardly spoke to me at all which was a good thing'. As for the British public, Hatzfeldt advised the kaiser that if he came to England that year he'd certainly be booed. The rebuffs only caused Wilhelm to redouble his efforts. In August he invited the entire British embassy staff to dinner, receiving them in his Royal Dragoons outfit. In the autumn he made the extraordinary suggestion to Lascelles that he might hand over Germany's African colonies to Britain in return for compensation – an idea that, had it known about it, would have had the German Right baying for his blood.

The bizarre thing was that in Germany – and indeed across Europe – the Kruger telegram had brought Wilhelm the thing he wanted most: wild approval. The raid had prompted a wave of intense anti-British feeling in Germany, much of it focused on Queen Victoria, the symbol of the British empire. One British journalist reported an elderly German lady telling him what a shame it was that the queen 'should be so unworthy a sovereign'. She was well known to be 'perpetually tipsy and to drink whisky out of a teapot'. Among themselves senior Prussian diplomats referred to her as the kaiser's 'tippling grandmother' and 'the hucksteress'. Wilhelm was seen as having stood up to bullying, hypocritical Britain and supported the plucky Boers. Yet he barely seemed to notice. A couple of years before, Waldersee had observed crossly that the British had worked out exactly how to manipulate the kaiser – they had only to treat him badly.

Despite no tangible signs of a change of Russian policy towards Britain, Queen Victoria persisted in believing that she could win over the tsar. Like Wilhelm, who had learned the lesson from Vicky, she was committed to the idea that personal relationships could supersede or guide foreign affairs. Her favourite

★ Between Wilhelm and George's cousin Alexandra (youngest daughter of Affie, now Duke of Coburg, and Marie of Russia) and the German diplomat Prince Ernst zu Hohenlohe-Langenburg.

granddaughter was tsarina, and she'd decided that gentle, charming Nicholas was part of the family – even though in April 1896 she discovered that Russia had been doing its own intriguing against Britain in Africa, egging on the French to cause trouble over Egypt.

As if to punch home the message that nothing had changed in Russia, Nicholas's coronation in May 1896 was overshadowed by the kind of awful human disaster that seemed to dog Russian affairs. George had expected to attend the ceremony, but the queen sent his uncle Arthur instead. 'I must say I was furious,' he told Nicky, 'but there was nothing to be done.' It was just as well. On the day after the coronation the tsar traditionally gave the people of Moscow an open-air feast at Khodynka field north of the city. In the midst of the festivities there was a rumour that the food was running out, the crowd of half a million people stampeded and thousands were crushed to death. The tsar's uncle and brother-in-law, Grand Duke Sergei, was largely responsible for the disaster. He'd neglected the preparations, more interested in pursuing a feud with another court official whose authority over the event clashed with his. Basic work to fill in deep wells in the ground was not completed, there was a derisory police presence and chaos ensued. The severity of the disaster seemed initially to have been hidden from Nicholas – at Windsor it was said that bodies had been shovelled under the grandstand on which he stood, so he could not see them. But even afterwards he never quite seemed to grasp its significance. On the night of the disaster he went to a ball at the French embassy, rather than staying home as a mark of respect to the dead. The picture of the tsar drinking champagne while his subjects mourned was a lasting stain on his personal image. By contrast, Queen Victoria received seventeen on-the-spot reports from Khodynka field, describing in detail the circum-stances of the stampede, the thousands of mangled bodies laid out across the other side of the vast field, and the anger and demands for retribution it had inspired. Worse, Nicholas failed to punish anyone. It was widely agreed within the imperial court that Grand Duke Sergei, who towered over his small quiet nephew, had bullied him into closing down an inquiry into the disaster by threatening to boycott the court. He was rewarded by being promoted to commander-in-chief of Moscow. Even within the Romanov family there were mutterings. 'How outrageous can you get!' Konstantin Romanov, Nicholas's second cousin, wrote of Sergei in his diary. '. . . If only the Emperor was sterner and stronger!' The government looked supine and corrupt, and Nicholas appeared weak. Khodynka field cast a long, inauspicious shadow over the new reign.

In Windsor, the queen's sympathies were clannishly with her new in-laws and fellow royals. Her first thought had been that 'poor Serge', who was married to Alix's older sister Ella, 'may be blamed'. Her next was concern for the imperial couple, whom the British ambassador assured her had done 'violence to their feelings' in attending the French ball while their subjects lay dead and injured. The queen would never have expressed such sympathy for Nicholas's father – she would have complained about Russian barbarity. While Wilhelm tried in vain to get himself invited to Cowes, Nicholas and Alexandra were asked to Balmoral for the end of September.

Balmoral was the large, remote estate in the Scottish Highlands where the queen passed the months from August to November. She loved it and felt free there. She loved it so much in fact, that she had decided that she *was* Scottish. As she crossed the border her voice would take on a peculiar approximation of a Scottish accent, and she'd talk about handing over 'woon poond' to some deserving crofter. Everyone else found Balmoral dispiritingly remote, incredibly dull, freezing cold – the queen never felt the cold and forbade fires – and full of tartan. Lord Rosebery said he thought the drawing room at Osborne was the ugliest room in the world – until he saw the drawing room at Balmoral. Salisbury referred to it as 'Siberia', and came as rarely as possible.

On 22 September 1896 the imperial couple and their baby, Olga – along with an entourage of several hundred, including their plainclothes secret servicemen, plus twenty-four constables and four sergeants from the Metropolitan Police – arrived sodden, having driven through Edinburgh in an open carriage in the pouring rain, and nauseous from having been violently rocked about in the royal train. They were greeted with bonfires and torches. The queen was enthusiastic, Edward wore a Russian uniform – astrakhan hat, knickerbockers, Norfolk jacket, red greatcoat. He never looked his best in uniform as it was invariably too tight. George wore a kilt. 'She is marvellously kind and amiable to us, and so delighted to see our little daughter!' Nicky told his mother. 'Dear Nicky and Alicky are quite unspoilt and unchanged and as dear and simple and as kind as ever. He is looking rather thin and pale and careworn, but sweet Alicky is in great beauty and very blooming,' the queen wrote to Vicky.

The queen's household called the visit 'the Russian occupation', because the tsar's retinue was so enormous; the Balmoral maids had to sleep four to a bed. George and May were boarded out up the road. Nicholas, the household observed, looked absurdly young, but Alicky was 'unmistakably lovely . . . one is always in rapture with her'. Both seemed initially a little aloof. Edward had made zealous preparations to entertain his nephew, and was relentlessly 'jolly'. Nicholas, as he had before, found Edward rather exhausting. 'From the very first day my Uncles took charge of me. They seem to think it necessary to take me out shooting all day long with the gentlemen. The weather is awful, rain and wind every day and on top of it no luck at all – I haven't killed a stag yet. I see even less of Alix here than at home.' The tsarina was swept off by the queen's ladies-in-waiting and given the kind of unadulteratedly enthusiastic welcome she rarely got in Russia. Nicholas was relieved when Bertie went to Newmarket to see a horse race. 'I could at least do what I wanted to, and was <u>not</u> obliged to go out shooting every day in the cold and rain.' 'I'm glad Georgie comes out to shoot too – we can at least talk over the good times we've just had in Denmark.'*

'Had a talk with dear Nicky,' was as expansive as George got. 'He is just the same dear boy as he always was.' In his way George was right, Nicky wanted to be the same dear boy and with George

---

* Nicholas and George had just spent a few days with their grandparents in Denmark.

he could be. George had no interest in talking politics and required nothing of him except that he was familiar.

The queen saw things differently. Family bonds should be put to practical use. She went to work on the tsar the day after he arrived. Something must be done about the disintegration of Turkey and the Armenian massacres, she announced. 'I remarked that, if England and Russia went together, there must be peace, and something ought to be done to bring this about.' Nicky nodded, as he did when cornered, but said it would be difficult. 'The Emperor is extremely well-disposed and is anxious to put a stop to the Sultan's iniquities,' she told Lord Salisbury, who arrived the next day.

After years of backing Turkey, which he now considered to have been 'the wrong horse', Salisbury had come to the conclusion, just like Rosebery before him, that an accommodation with Russia had much to recommend it – though almost all his fellow ministers thought the likelihood of Russia agreeing vanishingly remote, and the country still hated Russia. But with the Suez Canal under its control, Britain no longer had a pressing need to keep Russia out of Turkey. In fact, the Royal Navy had recently concluded it no longer had the capacity to defend Constantinople from Russia, a prospect Salisbury seems to have accepted but didn't relish. He also believed the Russians might be persuaded to work with Britain to force a settlement or resolution on the Ottoman empire, perhaps even a change of regime, before its much prophesied collapse caused further international instability. The prime minister was sufficiently keen on the idea to make one of his rare visits to Balmoral in order to see the tsar personally – though he also instructed his private secretary to inform the queen's private secretary that it would be actively dangerous for him to come, unless his room was heated to a minimum of 60 degrees Fahrenheit. An added bonus was the fact that Nicholas's tricky foreign minister, Lobanov, had suddenly died of apoplexy in August, as the imperial cortège had set out on a visit to Austria – so the tsar would be all on his own.

'I had two very serious talks with [Lord Salisbury],' Nicholas reported to his mother. 'It's good at least for him to learn from the source what the opinions and views of Russia are.' The source, however, didn't always seem entirely clear on those opinions. The first meeting went well enough. The tsar assured the PM that Russia had no designs on India – his own visit in 1891 had convinced him of 'the absurdity of Russia ever trying to obtain it . . . no sane Russian Emperor could ever dream of it'. Salisbury suggested that Russia and Britain should act together to stabilize the Ottoman empire. There had been another massacre in Armenia several weeks before, and Salisbury told the tsar that petitions and letters demanding some form of action had been pouring into the British Foreign Office. There was a certain irony in the prime minister referring to public opinion since he despised it, though the demands coincided with his own pragmatic belief that Turkey needed to be brought under control. There was another irony in his appealing to Russia on moral and humanitarian grounds – a country which had authorized its own pogroms and ruthlessly suppressed basic democratic rights. Nicholas didn't seem at all averse to putting pressure on the sultan, and he became positively animated when Salisbury suggested that Britain would no longer object to Russia taking control of Constantinople and the Bos-phorus, though he didn't like the idea of opening it to all ships, as this created the possibility of foreign warships getting into the Black Sea, not just the Russian fleet getting out. The Straits to the Black Sea, he told the prime minister, were 'the door to the room in which he lived', and he needed the key – a phrase that had become a cliché in Russia when discussing Constantinople. When Salisbury pointed out that Austria and the Balkan states might feel rather differently about this, and would have to be compensated, Nicholas seemed surprised. The prime minister must have been taken aback by his naivety.

The tsar, Salisbury observed, also 'expressed himself in terms by no means friendly to the Emperor of Germany'. Two weeks before, Nicholas had made an overnight stop with Wilhelm at Breslau. 'I am extremely satisfied with my interview with Emperor Nicholas,' Wilhelm had purred after the meeting. 'He was natural, open, communicative and heartfelt as he has always been with me.

We completely agreed on all issues.' Nicholas told Salisbury that he couldn't bear Wilhelm's company for long and added that the kaiser had told him that England was trying to set up a 'rival Sultanate' in Arabia – i.e. trying to stir up trouble in the Ottoman empire for its own advantage. The prime minister told the tsar, 'this was a rather perfidious proceeding, as he was at the same time telling us that Russia was preparing an attack upon us about Egypt'. Salisbury was pleased with the meeting, and told the queen that he'd been 'much struck by [the tsar's] great candour and desire to be on the best terms with us'. He was also overheard observing to the Prince of Wales that the tsar was 'very different from the other Emperor!'

When they met again two days later, however, Nicholas had changed his tune. It was obvious that someone, almost certainly the Russian ambassador, de Staal, had got to him. He was now 'distinctly averse, at this stage, to any effort to dethrone the Sultan', and worried about the dangers of 'interfering in other people's concerns'. When the subject moved on to Egypt, he seemed to be about to say he had no objection to the British occupation, 'But he stopped suddenly and turned the conversation, as though he felt he was committing an imprudence.'

The queen refused to be put off by Nicholas's opacity. On his last night she summoned him to her room before dinner and asked him bluntly what he thought about deposing the sultan. Nicky said 'he thought it would be a great risk, and might lead to dangerous complications'. She went further and asked him about the 'friendship' between Russia and France, and his visit to Paris, where he would be travelling the next day. Nicky explained that 'It was a purely military agreement,' which had come about because both countries had been excluded by the Triple Alliance. 'Nicky did not seem at all to relish the French, and regretted the visit to Paris, which was unavoidable,' she reported optimistically. 'I said it was so important that Russia and England should go well together, as they were the most powerful Empires, for then the world must be at peace.'

The Russian party departed the next day for France. The emperor left a breathtaking tip of £1,000 for the staff, the empress a trail of diamond and pearl brooches among the ladies-in-waiting. The queen pursued Nicholas to Paris with a letter, asking him – with a persistence that Salisbury could not have employed, and an expectation of the power of the family relationship which Salisbury did not share – to 'kindly use your influence and let the French understand that you do not intend to support them in their constant inimicality towards England, which is the cause of much annoyance and difficulty to us, in Egypt amongst other subjects'. She added, in an attempt to mollify, 'I would not have written this had you not told me that the agreement, or alliance, or whatever it is called, was only of a military nature.'

From Paris – where to their great surprise and eventual pleasure, the imperial couple were mobbed and cheered everywhere – Nicholas was more forthright. He told Victoria he had not discussed hostility to England with the French, and 'As to Egypt, I must own, dearest Grandmama, the question is of a very serious character.' The Russians felt the same as the French on the subject; they wanted Britain out of Egypt because her control of the Suez Canal was a 'threat to our maritime route to the Far East . . . Politics alas! are not the same as private or domestic affairs and they are not guided by personal or relationship feelings. History is one's real positive teacher in these matters and for me personally, except that, I have always got the sacred example of my beloved father and also the result and proof of all His deeds!' Among competing nation states, Nicholas let Grandmama know as gently as he could, family was worth little or nothing – a more realistic acknowledgement of the state of international affairs than the queen's.

The answer must have been a blow to the queen. It can be no accident that the flow of chatty family letters from her to Nicholas now shrank to a dribble. Salisbury, however, persisted. He made more overtures to the Russians in the autumn of 1896, but their response was unenthusiastic. Just to illustrate the Russian detachedness, in late December Nicholas – contrary to everything he had said to Salisbury at Balmoral – was persuaded to green-light an extraordinarily rash secret plan to solve the Eastern Question with a Russian-backed *coup d'état* in Constantinople to depose the sultan.

The Nelidov Plan, named after the Russian ambassador who proposed it, would have alienated all the Great Powers and quite
possibly have started a war in the region. As a senior Russian
diplomat later wrote in his memoirs, it 'would unquestionably
have spelt disaster for Russia'. It was quashed by Sergei Witte and
the horrified French. But it showed that Nicholas was worryingly
susceptible to risky imperialist adventures.

Wilhelm's pursuit of Nicholas also came to nothing. Watching
the tsar's progress around Europe, he felt less and less confident
that his meeting with him at Breslau had made the lasting impression he'd hoped. The German Foreign Office reported that
between Breslau and Balmoral Nicholas had met his mother in
Copenhagen and that she had talked him out of his good impression with Wilhelm; then there had been all the cheers in Paris. In
a panic, the kaiser invited himself to Hesse-Darmstadt, where the
tsar was staying with his brother-in-law Ernie before returning
home. It was a great blunder. Nicholas regarded his stays at Hesse-
Darmstadt as his private holiday when he could unwind from the
demands of formal travel. He and Alix relaxed there as they did
nowhere else. Wilhelm's arrival was unwelcome. Moreover, the
French visit had coloured Nicholas's view of Germany. Crossing
the border into Germany, he observed that everything suddenly
seemed 'black, dark and boring!' Confronted by a blankly
unfriendly Nicholas, Wilhelm decided to blame his failure on
Grand Duke Sergei, the tsar's bullying anti-German uncle. 'In his
presence the Emperor is remarkably awkward and reserved . . .
Sergei is the Emperor's evil demon and our most energetic enemy.'
It was hard to blame it all on Sergei, though. When Nicholas got
back to St Petersburg, he asked Wilhelm to stop writing personally
to him, giving as the reason his concern that Chancellor Hohenlohe was not aware of the letters. Wilhelm ignored this. The new
Russian foreign minister – appointed an indecisive five months
after Lobanov's death in Vienna – was another disappointment.
Count Mikhail Muraviev was smooth and courtly, an enthusiastic
Russian imperialist with a taste for champagne, and regarded as
inveterately hostile to Germany – not least because a couple of
years before Wilhelm had personally blocked his appointment to

a post in Berlin. Fritz Holstein's informant in Moscow called him a 'swine' and bootlicker. On the plus side Holstein's contact observed, he wasn't 'a friend of France . . . he thinks the English are disgusting and he has a fanatical hatred of the Poles'. Holstein concluded that Wilhelm's personal interventions had backfired. 'Without Breslau and without Darmstadt things might perhaps be better. There is no question that the Tsar had no desire whatever to meet our Kaiser again, and it is really deplorable that the latter absolutely runs after him.'

Messages from Russia, however, were contradictory. Just at the moment when Nicholas appointed Muraviev, whom the British considered 'conceited and vain as a woman', Nicholas's finance minister, Sergei Witte, now widely regarded as his most impressive and influential adviser, hinted to the latest British ambassador, Sir Nicholas O'Conor, that the Russian government might after all be interested in a resolution with Britain. In the New Year of 1897 Witte told the ambassador, 'Russia doesn't want a foot more of territory, she has more than she can develop in the next 200 years. She wants peace; to foster trade, commerce and industry and to improve the condition of the people. The old school who wanted to extend Russia to the Bosphorus is dead.' As the Nelidov plan showed, this might have been how Witte felt, but there were plenty of 'old school' politicians and army chiefs who felt quite the opposite. Nevertheless, somewhat desultory talks were begun between England and Russia to discuss their mutual policies in China, and behind the scenes and despite public sympathy in Britain for Russian dissidents, Special Branch began to cooperate with Okhrana, the Russian secret police, on the surveillance of Russian anarchist and terrorist groups based in London.

In early January 1897, almost a year to the day that he'd sent the Kruger telegram, Wilhelm wrote hopefully to his grandmother, 'Have you any plans or wishes about our coming or not coming for Your Jubilee, and whether some of our children are to come with or not?' The queen's Diamond Jubilee, celebrating her sixty years on the throne, was planned for June. Her answer was to the point: he couldn't come; as the Jubilee was to be a celebration of empire, no foreign crowned heads were to be invited. Instead, the queen told him, his brother Heinrich would come 'as one of her grandchildren'. 'And I am her eldest grandchild,' Wilhelm scribbled forlornly on the letter. Determined to change her mind, he wrote her a splendid letter in April, likening himself to a horse:

> I feel like a charger chained in the stables who hears the bugle sounding, and stamps and champs his bit, because he cannot follow his regiment. I had hoped to lead the Royals as their Colonel past their Sovereign, if not as her Escort, and to join their cheers when they salute their Queen in the exuberance of their loyal pride . . . in the great final charge I would have borne my sword proudly before the saluting point at the head of that magnificent regiment . . . But it was all idle dreams! But such dreams are hard to give up for a passionate soldier!

The queen would not relent, and whatever the justification given, it was hard not to see it as a punishment for Wilhelm's position over the Boers. She became angry with him again when a small war broke out between Greece and Turkey a month later. Wilhelm favoured the Turks, while she felt obliged to back the Greek royal family. She blamed his position on his 'personal hatred of Greece and enmity to the King and the whole royal family'. She wasn't entirely wrong, there had been bad feeling between Wilhelm and the Greek royal family since his sister had married the Greek heir; but he also had political reasons for siding with the Turks, whom he'd been pursuing as potential allies since the British had withdrawn from being their supporters in Europe. It was the queen's position that was informed by personal feelings – the Greeks had brought the war on themselves by landing an army on Turkish-run Crete. That made no odds at the British court. 'The German Emperor is in bad odour everywhere,' wrote the queen's lady-in-waiting Marie Mallet, 'and the final coup is his acceptance of six Greek guns presented by the Sultan. He ought to be kicked; my only joy is that he is simply frantic at not coming for the Jubilee and would like to kill his poor brother for daring to accept the Queen's invitation.'

The Jubilee was a statement of Britain's moral right to dominate and expand across the globe, an assertion of its status as top dog in the dog-eat-dog world of international politics, and a declaration of Britain and the empire's sufficiency unto themselves, their need for no one else. It demonstrated that the British empire was, as the *Kreuzzeitung*, the leading German newspaper of the Prussian establishment, noted both admiringly and enviously, 'completely unassailable'. It now occupied 25 per cent of the world's landmass, not including the informal influence it exercised over the economies of several South American countries such as Argentina and Brazil, and encompassed 444 million people.

In spectacle the Jubilee was quite as splendid as its predecessor. More so. On the day itself, 21 June, the long glittering parade of soldiers from all parts of the empire followed the queen's carriage through London to St Paul's, where she attended a service of thanksgiving. George described it as 'the most wonderful crowd I ever saw, perfect order and no accidents, 8 miles of streets we passed through, never heard anything like the cheering, decorations beautiful, fine and hot'. The presentations, garden parties, march pasts and street parties went on well into July. At Spithead the Prince of Wales reviewed the largest assembly of shining warships ever gathered in one place: 173 battleships in a line seven miles long. The navy claimed that no ship had been withdrawn from foreign stations to make it. It was, as everyone knew, the navy that had turned 'a loose aggregate of States', as *The Times* put it, into an empire.

And yet a note of diminuendo and superstitious uncertainty seemed to hang around the celebration's penumbra. *The Times* published Rudyard Kipling's new poem 'Recessional', an oddly downbeat commentary on the empire's triumph, a kind of *memento mori* warning of complacency and hubris, 'frantic boast and foolish word', reminding his readers that empires fell as well as rose:

> all our pomp of yesterday
> Is one with Nineveh and Tyre!

A commentary next to the poem ran, 'The most dangerous and demoralizing temper into which a state can fall is one of boastful pride.' The flipside of the Jubilee's proud and confident assertion of power, wealth and self-sufficiency was the fear that the empire might have peaked, that there was nowhere to go but down, and the worry that Britain might *have* to be sufficient unto itself because it was surrounded by countries who hated it. The Kruger telegram had forced on the British the realization that the rest of Europe resented their influence and power. At the end of 1896 Salisbury, whose attempts to coordinate the Great Powers over Turkey, China and the Greek War had been consistently rejected, had observed that the only Great Power 'which does not hate us' was Austria (which was also the only power with no interest in a colonial empire). The queen, meanwhile, was 'very much depressed by the knowledge that we are so actively hated by other countries. She frequently refers to the subject and says she cannot see why it should be so.'

Even as the Jubilee celebrations broke out, the uglier side of empire was making itself internationally visible. India was in the grip of a horrifying famine exacerbated, if not caused, by an obsessively free-market colonial government which continued to export grain surpluses to England while India starved. Photographs of the hideously starved victims – courtesy of the new light handheld Kodak cameras – were seen around the world, though they were markedly absent from the British papers, which operated conscious self-censorship on the matter. Away from public gaze, the colonial government in South Africa was quietly importing Chinese indentured labour – effectively slaves – to work in the mines, in order to undercut local wages.

When Wilhelm made a state visit to St Petersburg after the Queen's Diamond Jubilee, in August, his new foreign minister, Bernhard von Bülow, took great delight in reporting that 'Emperor Nicholas, Count Murawiew★ [*sic*] and Mr Witte expressed mistrust and tension with England at every opportunity.' Nicholas said he believed that the English were trying to provoke a European war. Actually the tsar was about as personally enthusiastic about the

★ The new Russian foreign minister, usually rendered as Muraviev.

kaiser as he was politically about the British. 'Thank God the German visit is over,' he wrote to his mother afterwards. '. . . On the whole Wilhelm was very cheerful, calm and courteous, while she [Dona] tried to be charming, and looked very ugly in rich clothes without taste; the hats she wore in the evenings . . . were particularly impossible.' (It was an open secret that Wilhelm designed Dona's clothes and forced her to diet to stay slim.) Nicholas added that he had had to make Wilhelm an honorary Russian admiral because he'd accepted a similar rank in the German navy the year before, and the thought – 'C'est à vomir!' – made him sick.

Only a few months later, in mid–November 1897, another German colonial intervention provoked paroxysms of rage in Russia quite as strong as and distinctly similar to the British reaction to the Kruger telegram. Wilhelm sent a naval squadron to occupy the northeastern Chinese port of Kiaochow. The reason – the pretext – was the murder of two German missionaries. 'We have . . . to show them with the most brutal ruthlessness that the German Kaiser is not one to fool about with,' he told the German Foreign Ministry. The truth was, with Africa looking distinctly crowded with would-be colonial empires, Germany had begun to cast its eye – just like Russia – over China. It fancied acquiring a province and a port in which to refuel its ships in the Pacific, from which it might claim some Pacific islands. Kiaochow was as yet not dominated by other foreign influences, it was easily accessible, with a good protected harbour. Having seized it, in the New Year of 1898 the German government took a lease on it and the surrounding region from the Chinese government.

The Russians were furious. They believed the Germans had grabbed the port from under their noses. They'd long fancied Kiaochow, which was in Manchuria, the Chinese province that bordered Siberia, as a warm-water port for their own navy. They issued a formal demand that Germany vacate it, going so far as to threaten war. In response, Wilhelm claimed that the tsar knew all about it. He had mentioned his interest in Kiaochow during their meeting that summer, he said, and Nicholas had raised no objections. This was true. During his summer visit the kaiser had asked Nicholas whether he had any intentions towards Kiaochow. Nicholas had replied vaguely that he wasn't opposed to the German fleet making use of it as long as they asked permission first. Wilhelm decided this amounted to a formal 'agreement with the Emperor in person', and another victory for his personal diplomacy. Nicholas, who had clearly never expected the Germans to mount a land grab in China, felt misled and cheated.

Military action against Germany, the Russian government admitted to itself, was not really an option. The new foreign minister, Muraviev, proposed that instead Russia send warships to take over the nearby Chinese port of Port Arthur. Witte opposed the idea; sending ships and troops ran absolutely counter to his plans to create a sphere of influence in Manchuria by promising friendly diplomatic support and loans. It made his previous inroads look dishonest, it would be expensive, and it would instantly alert the British to Russia's intentions. Initially Nicholas listened to Witte. But Muraviev went behind Witte's back, asked for a private audience and convinced the emperor to send the ships because the 'yellow races' understood only force. The Russians sailed into Port Arthur weeks later. 'Thank God we managed to occupy Port Arthur . . . without blood, quietly and almost amicably!' Nicholas wrote to his brother George. 'Of course, it was quite risky, but had we missed those docks now, it would be impossible later to kick out the English or the Japanese without a war. Yes, one has to look sharp, there on the Pacific ocean lies the whole future of the development of Russia and at last we have a fully open warm water port . . . What did you think of the articles in the English papers? Greedy scoundrels! – they are never satisfied! The devil take them!'

Now it was the turn of the British to be furious. The last thing they wanted was a scramble for China. Moreover, the Russians consistently lied about their intentions. They had initially turfed British ships out of Port Arthur, insisting their warships needed to winter there; then they assured the British that the occupation was temporary, while taking out a lease on Port Arthur in return for paying off China's indemnity to Japan. Finally, they promised that Port Arthur would be open to foreign ships, but, when asked to put his assurances in writing, Muraviev admitted the Russians had no intention of making it an open port. All the while, he had sweetened his denials with occasional mentions of an Anglo-Russian agreement. He'd even got the tsar to charm the British ambassador, O'Conor, at the Winter Palace ball, and murmur encouragingly about Anglo-Russian relations.

In Africa it had become accepted that if one Great Power acquired a large amount of territory, other powers with rival interests could expect some form of compensation. So the British, half-reluctantly since they'd preferred the old less formal arrangement, demanded their own port in China, and got nearby Weihaiwei, in compensation.

Now Germany was disgruntled. The country had been almost hysterically delighted at the acquisition of Kiaochow, but almost immediately it was eclipsed by the Russians and the British. And when Wilhelm wrote to Nicky in the New Year of 1898 boasting of the German success – 'We follow in the fulfilment of the task, which has been set us by the Lord of all Lords . . . in promoting civilization, ie Christianity in the Far East!' – the tsar's reply was 'cold and reserved'. He would pointedly avoid Berlin and the kaiser for the next three years. In 1899 a German diplomat would report that Nicholas's hostility towards Wilhelm was so strong that it was now an obstacle to good relations, and the kaiser's own indiscretion was making it worse. On the report Wilhelm scribbled, 'I never say anything about him in front of strangers.' He was actually only too quick to describe Nicky as a 'ninny' and a 'whimperer', and barely a year later would tell the British foreign secretary that the tsar was 'only fit to live in a country house and grow turnips'. Though the Russians had made it clear that warm personal relationships wouldn't be allowed to affect politics, it was obvious that bad relationships could.

8. Behind the wall (1893–1904)

Even people who disapproved of Nicholas talked about his 'kind eyes'. The British journalist W. T. Stead, given several very rare audiences with him in 1898, reported breathlessly to his readers that the tsar was 'charming, sympathetic, alert, lucid, modest'. As a man Nicholas took an appealingly modern view of marriage: he was a far more devoted, faithful and supportive husband than most men – or monarchs – of his generation. Entry after entry in his diary complained about the amount of time he had to spend away from his wife and children. 'After tea,' he wrote a few days before the birth of his first child, Olga, in late October 1895, 'I read, and set myself to composing a reply to Wilhelm. A thoroughly irritating thing to be doing when one has so many things to do, and so much more important!' His daily routine was arranged so he could take his daughters – there were three by 1899 – and his dogs – English collies – out for a daily walk, or in winter a sledge at 11 a.m., and have his meals with his family. In the evenings, unless he had to go to the opera or ballet, he liked to retire to his wife's boudoir. Alix created a cosy, *gemütlich* nest within the echoing imperial grandeur of the Romanov palaces. The world, including the royal household, was shut out. 'Never did I believe there could be such utter happiness in this world,' she had written in Nicholas's diary after their wedding night. 'I am indescribably happy,' he added a few weeks later. They called each other 'hubby' and 'wifey' (using the English words). 'My sweet old darling, many kisses, wifey loves you so deeply and strongly! You are my one and all,' she wrote in his diary. They would chat together in English, or German or French; he would read Pushkin, Tolstoy or the latest fashionable English or French novel to her; they might paste photographs of themselves into an album – albums which still today conjure a vivid portrait of idyllic turn-of-the century family life.

The only blight was Alix's chronic ill health and their failure to have a son. From the beginning of their marriage she lived in a permanent state of exhausted semi-invalidity. It's possible the symptoms were psychosomatic; the court doctor, Eugene Botkin, seems to have thought so. It's also possible, however, that along with the carrier gene for haemophilia which would manifest itself in their son, Alexei, Queen Victoria had passed on to Alix porphyria, the illness that sent George III mad, but which also had a range of more common chronic physical symptoms.★ As the evening closed they went to sleep in the same bed – unlike most of their royal contemporaries.

The problem was that Nicholas wasn't a simple family man who could shut himself away from the world. From the start of his reign, it was clear that domestic life was more vividly important to him than anything to do with his public office. Even the most reactionary members of the court recognized that this was a problem and the tsar was isolated. The head of his Chancellery, A. A. Mossolov, actually gave it a name; he called it 'sredostenie', 'the wall', that surrounded Nicholas, preventing him from getting 'fresh ideas' and 'sound information'. Mossolov, like other court conservatives, believed the wall was made up of the bureaucracy and its ministers, the intelligentsia and the press. Ministers deliberately obscured the information the tsar received and perpetrated all sorts of unknown evils in his name; the intelligentsia agitated against the regime; the press 'misrepresented' the tsar and his relationship with the people. In truth, the wall was made up of tradition, etiquette and Nicholas's own withdrawal and refusal to accept the need for change. Russia was in the grip of great social and economic change, and the government was increasingly inadequate to confront it, and he himself believed utterly that he was the only man who could rule it. But he closed himself away. 'I only hear good reports about No 1,' the German diplomat Prince

---

★ For more about this genetic disease see John Röhl et al., *Purple Secret*. Röhl and his fellow authors make a good case for Wilhelm's sister Charlotte having porphyria and suggest that more of Queen Victoria's descendants, including Vicky and Alix, were sufferers.

Radolin told his friend Fritz Holstein in late 1895. 'The only thing I regret is that he cuts himself off and sees only Lobanov and Witte, who don't like each other. People think that this shutting himself off will cease after the coronation.'

In the winter of 1895, however, the couple moved out of St Petersburg altogether, fifteen miles east, to Alexander Palace in Tsarskoe selo, 'the Tsar's village', fifteen miles east of St Petersburg. Tsarskoe selo was an elegant provincial town, though in Russia there weren't any other towns like it. Built originally by Catherine the Great, it was a weird, idealized miniature royal theme park – two royal palaces and the holiday homes of the highest aristocracy, set in 800 acres of perfectly manicured gardens and hedges, sur-rounded by a high fence and cossack guards, maintained by thou-sands of servants and a permanent garrison of 5,000. Within its borders were the only town-wide electrical system in the country, the first railway, a telegraph and radio station, and the most advanced water and sewage system in the whole of Russia. Most Russian villages had no running water or drains.

There, in the midst of vast neoclassical splendour and circum-scribed by imperial etiquette, they lived a life of almost self-conscious bourgeois moderation. Nicholas wore his clothes until they wore out. They ate simply – Alix wasn't interested and his digestion couldn't take it. The family apartments were comfortable rather than grand. Alix, her lady-in-waiting Sophy Buxhoeveden observed, 'loved a homely home, with children and dogs about it'. The rooms had been made more intimate and 'cosy' with dark polished wood galleries and panels in the Jugendstil (German art nouveau) style patronized by Alix's brother Ernst of Hesse-Darmstadt. They were decorated in English chintzes – 'just like those in a comfortable English house' – and packed with small framed photographs, knick-knacks, bookshelves and icons. The knicks-knacks, however, came from Fabergé and the icons were priceless. The food arrived on silver platters, the palace chef was one of the greatest of his generation, and Alexandra came to the family dinner table wreathed in diamonds.

The imperial household and the imperial court consisted of 16,500 persons, mostly servants. Among them were four large black men, known in the palace as 'Ethiopians' (though at least one was American), dressed in a kind of northern *fantaisie* of Turkish harem dress – white turbans, gold-embroidered jackets, slippers curved at the toe – whose sole function was to stand outside the tsar's study ready to open the doors silently. There were hundreds of court officials: 287 chamberlains, 309 chief gentlemen-in-waiting, 103 stewards, 40 gentlemen of the bed-chamber, 22 churchmen, and in the imperial suite, hundreds of officers from major-generals to adjutants. So numerous was the court that the office which ran it itself required a staff of 1,300.

Then there were the palaces: in addition to the hundred-room Alexander Palace at Tsarskoe selo, there was the larger Catherine Palace, the Winter Palace in St Petersburg, the many summer villas at Peterhof, the various hunting lodges – including three in Poland – the estates at Livadia in the Crimea, a bunch of other royal palaces occupied by various relatives such as the Anichkov and Pavlovsk. And there were the yachts – the grandest of which, *Standart*, elegantly black with a gold stripe down the sides and a gold double eagle on the stern, was the size of a warship and weighed 4,500 tons, sat eighty for dinner and housed a full balalaika orchestra. Everything was paid for by a one-off payment which Nicholas received each year on 1 January, and which also covered, among other things, his Romanov relatives' lavish lifestyles, the court personnel's pensions, and all the various theatres and ballets and initiatives of which the tsar was patron. It was a much repeated truism among the Romanovs that poor Nicholas was often 'broke' by the autumn, which rendered the thriftiness all the more Marie Antoinettish and out of kilter with reality.

The move to Tsarskoe selo represented more than just geographical distance from the aristocratic and governing elite of St Petersburg. In his father's time, the tsar's antipathy to St Petersburg had been mitigated by his mother, who had been a bridge between the emperor, court and society. Nicholas had inherited his father's suspicion of the city and desire to be in the country, and preferred the intimacies of home to wider society. Alix had quickly developed an intense dislike of St Petersburg and was almost hysterically shy and uncomfortable in public – 'She longed to disappear under the ground,' she told her friend Sophy Buxhoeveden, 'her French evaporated, and her conversation languished; she blushed and looked ill at ease.' Rushed into the role of empress, she had had no time to acclimatize to the strangeness of Russia, and her shyness tended to manifest itself as buttoned-up unfriendliness, quickness to take offence, and as an instinctive suspicion of strangers. Even her greatest defenders admitted she was 'over sensitive and in a way haunted by the notion that she was unpopular and unloved'. Like many self-conscious enclosed elites, gossipy, frivolous St Petersburg was not especially welcoming or generous. 'If Alicky smiled they called it mockery. If she looked grave they said she was angry,' her sister-in-law Olga recalled. Those who did make the effort frequently felt their good intentions were met with 'stinging answers'. She showed her disapproval of society's frivolity by publicly reprimanding ladies whose dresses she thought were too revealing at imperial balls, and even on occasion sending them home. The ladies of St Petersburg riposted by wearing overlong feathers in their headdresses, which swept across her face when they curtseyed to her, and made her sneeze. She got no points for the philanthropic and charitable projects, hospitals and sewing circles in which she involved herself; nor for her chronic ill health – 'It was contrary to Russian Court etiquette even to mention the health of the sovereign or his wife.' Her illnesses, however, provided another excuse for her, and her husband's, less frequent appearances outside Tsarskoe selo.

Within Tsarskoe selo, and despite having a personal suite of 600, including 200 ladies-in-waiting to call on, Alix confined herself to her family and a small, tight coterie of women. She viewed the rest of the world with intense mistrust and, Mossolov recalled, 'showed jealousy of everything that deprived her of the company of her husband' – including affairs of state. When she once complained that she and the tsar saw very few people, a courtier suggested that perhaps they should see more. 'Why? So as to hear still more lies?' she answered. Nicholas, who as a bachelor had enjoyed parties and dancing, found it only too easy to follow her. 'Neither the Tsar nor the Empress had any desire to enlarge the circle of the persons admitted to their presence,' Mossolov wrote.

By mid-1897 a Russian-based German diplomat expressed concern to the German chancellor that the tsar was 'so reserved and closed-off that one fears he might lose touch with the living element of his people'.

Like so much about Nicholas's life, the seeds of this withdrawal from the aristocracy predated him. There had always been a gap between the emperor and the aristocracy, which was by the laws of the autocracy as subject to the whims of the tsar as anyone else. Previous emperors had been suspicious of St Petersburg's frivolity and tendency to intrigue, but while the tsar had a foot in the city and in the world, this mattered less. Nicholas and Alexandra's willed and intense isolation and evident wariness of their natural constituency would create a wedge that would alienate even members of the elite.

Nicholas and Alix claimed to be bored by court etiquette, but were utterly in thrall to the processes which kept them separated from the world. 'The sovereigns themselves always insisted that they valued in people nothing so much as simplicity and sincerity . . . they actually appraised people almost solely according to the amount of attention these people gave to quite outward and often nonsensical etiquette,' wrote Gleb Botkin, son of the imperial family's doctor, who grew up in the imperial family's orbit. On their travels in 1896 the household at Balmoral had found them at first a little stand-offish and 'on their magisterial dignity'; and in France it had been noted that the imperial couple spoke only to the most senior government figures and generals. Beyond the court and government Nicholas met virtually no one and he took no interest in the Russian new elites: Jewish society and the new industrial millionaires of Moscow – in constrast to his uncle Bertie in England. 'Neither [group] touched us,' one of Alix's ladies wrote. Nicholas's distance from these and the St Petersburg elite meant that, even though he and Alix were more literate than their English and German cousins and he knew about the great Russian portraitist Ilya Repin because he painted the court, and he'd seen some plays by Chekhov, who was now world famous, he had little sense of the extraordinary artistic flowering taking place in his country. Nicholas's ancestors had been the great builders and collectors of Russia, but though he paid for some of the theatres and concert halls where music, opera and ballet were performed, Nicholas had very little direct involvement in patronage.

Once the exclusiveness of the Russian court had been a way to keep the monarch in control and the aristocracy under control; now it simply kept the court from the rest of the world. This was the pattern throughout all the European courts, all desperately trying to keep out new forces – trade, the bourgeoisie, industry, democracy – which they saw as threats to their status and influence, but their only weapon besides barricades was a desperate holding on to the past. They had ceased to be places where one went to seek one's fortune, where art was created or political debate took place, as they had been in the eighteenth century, instead becoming strangled by hierarchy and a million tiny rules, the more arbitrary the better. But most of all they were crushingly boring – even the tsar admitted this – and most of what took place kept everyone busy but was pointless. In Russia, Nicholas's preoccupation with his own family and the fact that it was not done to receive anyone who wasn't noble, meant his court had become little more than a huge extended domestic household full of people obsessively measuring their gold braid. The famous court balls of the winter season, said to be the most glittering and lavish in the world, had their own interminable formal demands. Most people's experience of them involved standing in a room allotted by class (no chance for the beautiful daughter of minor gentry to be swept off her feet by the handsome prince), and waiting for hours for the emperor to arrive so one could bow to him. Even the head of Nicholas's own Chancellery admitted to being 'royally bored'.

It was the same in England. The British court had long since given up any claim to being a nexus of power and influence, and now consisted of the queen's household and a series of annual social engagements. Victoria's retirement had turned it into a quiet pool of tedium where the outside world rarely intruded, dictated by her whims. The queen would disappear into her apartments for days at a time, leaving her courtiers to hang about bored in corridors, unable to leave the building until she did, or smoke, or warm themselves, as she believed fires were unwholesome.

It was worse in Berlin. Dona's puritanism – she'd banned modern dances like the polka and the two-step – and Wilhelm's bossiness made the court so dull that many aristocrats had absented themselves altogether. The main preoccupations of the court had become precedence, rigid ceremonial, the maintenance of endless petty, arbitrary rules and, of course, complete obedience to the sovereign. 'It almost seemed like living in a prison,' wrote Ethel Howard, an English governess to Wilhelm's children. The court's humourlessness and protocol were legendary. Wilhelm liked to say that he did not give balls as amusements but as lessons in deport-ment. 'Anything stiffer and more wearisome . . . is difficult to imagine,' one British attaché observed. Members of the court were not allowed to use public transport, or wear spectacles because no one was permitted to look at the monarchs through glass,* and everywhere members were reminded of their position in the hier-archy. They were graded and classified by colour-coded passes; these decided, among other things, which room they stood in at balls and how large a Christmas present they received from the imperial couple. Even the size of Christmas trees set up for members of the imperial family at the Berlin Schloss each year was determined by how high up the scale they were.

Being part of the kaiser's entourage seems to have been in large part simply an exercise in fortitude and standing up: no one was allowed to sit in his presence or allowed to go to bed until he did. In the evenings he would insist on reading – with expostulations – or lecturing them for hours as they tried to stay awake. 'The elderly generals of the Kaiser's suite were much to be pitied,' one English governess noted. 'They wore a smile of patient suffering most of the time, for William showed little consideration for their age and infirmities . . . As a rule he exacted every ounce of service that a man could give – in a pleasant affable way, it is true – still he exacted it. They looked tired to death sometimes, these gentlemen, bored with the incessant trivialities of their office, bored with William's flow of conversation which gave them little

---

* And perhaps also because glasses showed physical weakness in men – monocles were the accepted alternative among German army officers.

opportunity to express their own thoughts.' So awful was spending time in the kaiser's entourage that one adjutant, Gustav von Neumann-Cosel, particularly renowned for his obsequiousness and his enthusiasm for kissing the kaiser's hand, would return home after his statutory time at court, lock himself in his room, swear loudly, then sleep for twenty-four hours.

Because Nicholas and Alexandra were closed off within the court, their experience of other classes remained minimal. While they might imitate the modest values and habits of the middle classes, they actually viewed them as potentially troublesome opponents whose aspirations were a direct challenge to the structures of Russian hierarchy and the tsar's authority. The educated middle class in particular, which made up the questioning liberal opposition, the 'intelligentsia' – a Russian coinage – Nicholas hated. Sergei Witte recalled that 'one day at table someone had used the words "intellectual",' to which the tsar replied, 'How I detest that word.' He added that he 'should order the Academy of Sciences to suppress it in the Russian dictionary'. As for the poorest and the workers, Nicholas saw them from his carriage, cheering him, or encountered the odd peasant on rides he made out of Tsarskoe selo (surrounded naturally by secret police) and would ask how the harvest had gone, unaware of the wretched situation in which they lived. His attitude to them was like the sentimental British colonialists' attitude to the savages they were 'civilizing'. He was their little father, they were honest, innocent children, susceptible to evil influences from which he must protect them. After the Winter Palace massacre of 1905, when government troops shot into a peaceful crowd, Alix wrote, 'The poor workmen who had been utterly misled, had to suffer, and the organizers have hidden as usual behind them . . . I love my new country. It's so young, powerful, and has much good in it, only utterly unbalanced and childlike.'

In this the Russian royal family were more cut off than any of their contemporaries. Even in Germany Wilhelm had broken through some of Prussia's tight etiquette to meet Jewish banking and shipping magnates, to visit the yachts of American millionaires, to become friendly with the heir to the Krupp empire, the largest company in Europe. More significantly, through his speeches and use of the press, Wilhelm had made himself available to the non-aristocratic literate population of Germany, the German equivalent of the new *Daily Mail* readers of England – nationalistic, patriotic, aspirational, urban – as no monarch had done before. While he encountered opposition in government or the Reichstag, these new classes increasingly formed the bedrock of his national support. But whereas Wilhelm felt truly alive and in tune only when he was exposing himself to the world, public events still made Nicholas sick with anxiety. 'I felt green and trembled all over,' he told his mother, after addressing the Viennese court in 1896. The British royal family, meanwhile, were forced to meet influential commoners – even upstart radical politicians such as Joseph Chamberlain and David Lloyd George – by virtue of their constitutional position.

The truth was Nicholas had no idea – and didn't want to know – how Russia was changing; how the state was no longer the only organizing force, how the zemstvos were increasingly the most effective providers of services in the country; how his grandfather's reforms had, despite his father's best efforts, begun to break down the old rigid class determinants – serfs were becoming merchants, tradesmen's children were becoming teachers, engineers and doctors; how peasant life was impoverished and in crisis and the urban working class was living in misery. And how could you process the changes the modern world was bringing, if, like Nicholas and Alexandra, you had convinced yourselves that protocol and etiquette were so ubiquitous that you were, as Alix's closest friend Anna Vyrubova said, 'unable to change a single deadly detail of the routine of the Russian court', and that even afternoon tea was immutable. 'The same plates for hot bread and butter on the same tea table were traditions going back to Catherine the Great.' Nicholas could see no reason why this should change – the country must remain as it always had been. It was as if he had made it structurally impossible for himself to learn from experience – just like Wilhelm, who for different reasons was quite unable to learn from his mistakes – as if he was systematically disqualifying himself from taking part in the modern world.

As the son of Dr Botkin, the imperial doctor, wrote, 'The enchanted little fairyland of Tsarskoe selo slumbered peacefully on the brink of an abyss, lulled by the sweet songs of bewhiskered sirens who gently hummed "God Save the Tsar".'

Driving Nicholas ever more intensely into the arms of his family was his fear, discomfort and dislike of his new role as emperor. He took his inheritance exceptionally seriously, but he had no ideas save holding on to his father's truisms: only autocracy could save Russia; liberal reform and a free press were recipes for disaster; close family were the only people you could trust; Russia must be preserved in aspic. He quickly acquired a reputation as a good man, but neither as firm nor consistent as could be wished. He was too susceptible to his bullying uncles and the last person who'd spoken to him. 'Our young monarch changes his mind with terrifying speed,' sighed one senior Foreign Office bureaucrat in 1896. 'He remains too often under the impression, and consequently under the influence of the last words spoken to him,' his cousins Sandro and Konstantin agreed in 1897. 'The Emperor is influenced by the arguments of his last adviser,' one British ambassador reported. 'The reputation of the monarchy has suffered . . .' the German ambassador told the chancellor in 1898. 'Like a reed in the wind, Tsar Nicholas is wavering between the Ministers and Grand Dukes and last but not least his own mother.'

Wilhelm, of course, had been accused of the same thing. 'It is unendurable. Today one thing and tomorrow the next and a few days after that something completely different,' one minister had written wearily. The personal roots of their inconsistency were different – Wilhelm's manic restlessness, Nicholas's insecurity – but in both cases it reflected an underlying inability to grapple with the ever-expanding demands of modern government, and a deep desire not to rely on any one person who might undermine their power.

Nicholas compensated for his anxious feelings of inadequacy and lack of preparedness by holding tenaciously to his belief in divine right. The moment the crown had touched his head, he had become a vehicle for God's purpose and had magically absorbed a kind of spiritual superiority which made him, whatever his inadequacies, better equipped than any minister to know what Russia needed. It was a mystical idea far more literal even than the pronouncements about his relationship with God which had brought Wilhelm such derision in Europe, and in Nicholas it encouraged a kind of fatalism which would make him oddly passive in a crisis. It also made him extremely possessive of his authority, and sensitive to anything that could be interpreted as interference. While Nicholas the family man was gentle and charming, Nicholas the emperor was often touchy, mistrustful and stubborn.

As the years passed, this sense of entitlement and magical ability provided an uneasy counterbalance to his lack of confidence. While on individual issues he remained susceptible to one or another minister's, or even his family's, opinions, Nicholas was increasingly resentful of what he regarded as trespasses on his wider authority, or contradiction, especially from the imperial household, who could be dismissed for mentioning politics or the wider world – especially if they implied criticism of the system. Among Nicholas's entourage, according to A. A. Mossolov, the emphasis was on scrupulous politeness and obedience, 'the motto was "lie low" and "do nothing on your own responsibility"'. Despite mountains of paperwork Nicholas refused to have even one secretary, or to let anyone else seal his letters or lick his stamps – 'It would have been necessary to take a third party into his confidence, and the Tsar hated to confide his ideas to anybody.' He persisted in seeing Russia as a large private estate which he could run like a paternalistic landowner. Without a secretariat, mountains of trivia fell across his desk. The tsar was the only person in the empire who could grant a divorce or sanction a name change; ministers were obliged to consult him over the smallest changes of personnel. Concentrating on the trivial allowed him to think he was actually running the country.

As for the government, Nicholas seemed intrinsically to distrust and dislike his ministers, even though they were virtually his sole source of information about the world outside. This was partly to do with class and codes. In Russia the landed aristocracy – in contrast to Britain – looked down on the not so elevated 'bureaucratic' nobility, who dirtied their hands in government. Nicholas, like George, had absorbed an aristocratic military code which perceived the world in black and white, and found the complexities, ambiguities and grey areas of politics distasteful. As the court saw it, the bureaucratic class – themselves nobles, of course, but of a lower sort – were self-interested careerists, who intrigued and deliberately misled the tsar for their own ends. 'The bureaucracy is interested . . . in keeping the Tsar in ignorance of what is going on; it is in this way that it makes itself more and more indispensable,' wrote Nicholas's deputy minister of the court. The tsar also showed a tendency to look to, and rely on, his largely useless, self-serving cousins and uncles in the Romanov clan, and to have his head turned by wild schemes brought to him by totally inexperienced aristocratic former guards officers, whose company and outlook he found more congenial. It was just such a plan that eventually drew Russia into its disastrous war with Japan.

And it was true that the Russian government *was* full of back-stabbing, intrigue and muddle, a state of affairs which had arisen because, in the absence of anything providing policy coordination, each minister and department ended up fighting its corner against the rest. Nicholas was supposed to be the figure who controlled and coordinated policy, who took the overview. But like Wilhelm, he was entirely incapable of doing so and the country was so large, and the government so primitive and chaotic, that probably no one could have run Russia on their own. In the absence of established policy priorities, ministers and departments slugged it out for dominance. Ministers had one-to-one interviews with the tsar which weren't minuted. Decisions made in one meeting were often swept away by the next. Contradictory orders were not resolved. Long, carefully researched reports went unread – for lack of time and the tsar's patience. Like his cousins, Nicholas was irritated by too much complexity. Annotated reports disappeared. His habit of changing his mind complicated everything, and led ministers to ever more byzantine and manipulative efforts to keep him on track, which in turn alienated him still further. In the 1900s a couple of attempts were made to get all the ministers round one table for a weekly meeting with the emperor. Nicholas refused to see the point of it. He was, besides, extremely bad at running a meeting, and got bored and irritated quickly. Perhaps it was his loathing of any form of confrontation, perhaps it was his increasing dislike of being contradicted. Certainly he was reluctant to accept that discussion and debate could lead anywhere useful. 'The very idea of discussion was wholly alien to the nature of Nicholas II,' wrote Mossolov, head of the tsar's Chancellery – the office which organized government matters which needed the tsar's personal attention, but which had become overwhelmed by paper and trivia. He seemed unable to see policy in any larger context. 'He only grasps the significance of a fact in isolation without its relationship to other facts,' his old tutor Pobedonostsev wrote dismissively in 1900. 'Events, currents . . . wide general ideas worked out by an exchange of views, arguments or discussion are lacking.'

Nicholas's most able minister, Sergei Witte, particularly offended him. Witte was the man who had supervised and shepherded Russia's industrialization – to such an extent that the Russian economy was now growing almost as fast as the German one. Iron, steel and coal production tripled between 1890 and 1900, though the human costs of this had been devastating in some places. The famine of the early 1890s had been exacerbated, if not caused, by Witte's insistence on exporting wheat in exchange for foreign capital. Witte was as tall – six foot six, it was said – as Nicholas was small, as aggressively uninterested in the niceties of etiquette and courtesy as Nicholas was preoccupied with them. He emanated a kind of brute force, was openly ambitious and ruthless in pursuit of his ends and convinced of the correctness of his policies. He believed that to better Russia's position in the world its government had to improve the economy, through industrial development, railways and new markets. There was nothing suave or courtly about him, he was cynical, manipulative and often rude. He once shouted so angrily at another minister in front of the emperor that Nicholas left the room. Nicholas hated this. He recognized that Witte was able but he didn't trust him, and consciously or not, he felt threatened by Witte's confidence and ability. He preferred the acknowledgedly mediocre and supine

Goremykin, who behaved 'like a butler, taking instruction to the other servants'. Nicholas and Alexandra nursed a fantasy that beyond the ministries there were good honest advisers with whose counsel he would be able to solve everything. 'He has nobody on whom he can thoroughly rely and who can be a real help to him,' Alix wrote at the height of the revolutionary crisis of 1905. '. . . He tries so hard, works with such great perseverance, but the lack of what I call "real" men is great . . . The bad are always close at hand, the others through false humility keep in the background.'

Not that the tsar expressed his feelings openly. Just as in his foreign dealings, he was always calm, never lost his temper and frequently seemed entirely amenable to whatever was being said to him. He would smile, nod, and do something else entirely, erecting his own wall around his emotions and reactions. In his memoirs Witte described being sacked by Nicholas: 'We talked for two solid hours. He shook my hand. He embraced me. He wished me all the luck in the world. I returned home beside myself with happiness and found a written order for my dismissal lying on my desk.' Such sackings were not isolated incidents. Nicholas told Wilhelm he never appointed anyone without having a replacement should he decide to sack them.

At the same time, Nicholas was entirely implicated in the regime's most ill-advised excesses. He knew there was a growing agricultural crisis and was aware of Russia's increasingly parlous financial situation. He knew of the brutal measures that his government took in the name of national security, he encouraged extravagant spending on the Russian fleet, and the huge sums spent on taking parts of China. He supported the aggressively ham-fisted Russification of the peaceful and independent duchy of Finland, which began in 1898 with the appointment of brutal General Bobrikov as governor-general. By 1904 Finland was on the edge of revolt, and Bobrikov had been assassinated. In 1902 Nicholas's mother, in an unprecedentedly critical letter, wrote to him: 'It is a complete puzzle to me how you, my dear, good Nicky, whose sense of fairness has always been so strong, now choose to be guided and deceived by a liar like Bobrikoff! . . . the people were perfectly happy and contented, now everything is broken up, everything changed, disorder and hatred sown . . . All that has been and is being done in Finland is based on <u>lies</u> and <u>deceit</u> and leads straight to <u>revolution</u>.' Nicky disagreed. Tough choices were necessary, he said. His father had russified the Baltic states: 'a strong and steady hand brought complete appeasement, and now all those troubles are quite forgotten'. (In fact, émigré German Balts had become some of the most vociferous anti-Russian propagandists in Germany, at the forefront of anti-Slavic Pan-Germanism.) The tsar added that he had just suffered 'a very heavy personal grief': his favourite dog had died and he had cried all day. Perhaps the juxtaposition is unfair – but it was Nicholas who made it.

Like Nicholas, George was only too happy to keep himself as much as possible away from public scrutiny and to withdraw into a quiet, rural domestic life. After he and May married in 1894, they moved into York Cottage, a 'glum little villa' on the Sandring-ham estate, a few hundred yards from his father and mother's grand home. He loved it because Sandringham was the place he felt most comfortable in all the world, because there were 30,000 acres to shoot on, and because it was too small to have to entertain in – it was his own barrier to the outside world. It was, by everyone's estimation – apart from George's – gloomy, dark and cramped: 'a poky and inconvenient place, architecturally repulsive and always full of the smell of cooking', his cousin Princess Alice wrote. 'George adored it, but then he had the only comfortable room in the house, which was called the "library," though it contained very few books . . . the drawing-room was small enough when only two adults occupied it – but after tea, when five children were crammed into it as well, it became a veritable bedlam.' It was covered in rough cast, set with fake Tudor beams, sat in the eternal shadow of high trees, looking on to a dark pond on which 'a leaden pelican gazed in dejection upon the water lilies and bamboo'. Inside, the red cloth from which the French army made its trousers, 'saddened', one observer reported, the walls. During the daytime York Cottage accommodated ladies-in-waiting, the equerries and private secretaries, assorted nurses, nursemaids, housemaids, ten footmen, three wine butlers, a valet and a chef –

a small suite by royal standards, though the house was bursting. George remained there, despite all attempts to dislodge him, until 1910 – and even after, as king, he refused to move into the big house at Sandringham until his mother died.

There he lived the life of a Norfolk country gentleman, an extremely rich one, with an income that after 1901 was worth £100,000 a year (£40,000 from parliament, £60,000 from the duchy of Cornwall). His tastes were simple but expensive. His suits were from Savile Row and his guns were from Purdey, the cartridges engraved with little red crowns. Having all but left the navy, he had virtually no obligations apart from the very occasional public engagement. (His engagements for 1895 were receiving the Freedom of the City of London and making a speech in thanks; sailing to Germany for the opening of the Kiel Canal, where he had dinner with Wilhelm on the *Hohenzollern*; watching Lord Rosebery's horse win the Derby; going to Goodwood for more horse-racing and Cowes for the yachting; shooting on the grouse moors of various friends; visiting Balmoral, then returning to Sandringham.) His father's staff ran the estate. 'For seventeen years,' his biographer Harold Nicolson wrote exasperatedly, 'he did nothing at all but kill animals and stick in stamps.'

Shooting and stamp-collecting were George's passions. The stamps had begun with a present of his uncle Affie's collection, bought for him by his father in the early 1890s. Attracted by the pastime's solitary, methodical orderliness, he would spend several afternoons a week arranging and rearranging his stamps, poring over catalogues, occasionally bidding vast sums for rare issues. By the end of his life he had amassed the largest collection in the world – 325 albums full. After 1910, when he became king, he collected only stamps with his own face on them. As for shooting, it was the one thing George did exceptionally well. By the late 1890s he was generally acknowledged to be one of the two or three best shots in the country. Shooting was one of the great signifiers of leisurely aristocratic life. The aristocratic shooting party – complete with thousands of available animals hiding in the brush, plus beaters, someone to carry the guns and lunch – could be staged only on vast, uncultivated estates. Like so many of the leisure habits of

British aristocratic life, it had become madly popular abroad among the European super-rich. Nicholas and Wilhelm were both obsessive about hunting and shooting. As tsarevich Nicholas had spent five or six hours a day shooting in mid-winter: '667 dead creatures for 1596 shots fired', he recorded for one day in 1893. Wilhelm, who shot leaning on the shoulders of a nearby servant, kept a list of everything he'd ever killed: by 1897 it totalled 33,967 animals, beginning with 'two aurochs, 7 elks', and ending with '694 herons and cormorants and 581 unspecified beasts'. George could bring down 1,000 pheasants in one day. At Sandringham the quantities of game shot were positively obscene. By the time George was king, the politician Lord Crewe couldn't help but remark, 'it is a misfortune for a public personage to have any taste so simply developed as the craze for shooting is in our beloved monarch . . . His perspective of what is proper seems almost destroyed.'

George didn't want to engage with the wider world. He couldn't, as his uncle the Duke of Cambridge remarked, 'bear London and going out, and hates Society'. Despite his devotion to his father, he was not part of fashionable society. As one observer noted delicately, George's set were chosen 'not for their social brilliance, for the wit or sparkle or novelty which their hospitality offered, but for more solid qualities based on old traditions'. He belonged to what the radical Liberal Arthur Ponsonby – royal secretary Fritz Ponsonby's rebellious and radical brother and author of *The Decline of the Aristocracy* – described as the 'reactionary', 'dull' part of the upper class, which deplored the modern world while enjoying its conveniences, yearned for the past, and expected 'unlimited deference' from its social inferiors. He hated going abroad, even though, through his grandmother's efforts, he was now related by blood or marriage to all twenty of the reigning monarchs in Western Europe. Travel made him homesick and seasick and exposed his inability to speak any foreign language. He dreaded making speeches in public, and in general being pushed beyond his comfort zone. He didn't even know about the Sandringham estate on which he lived. When he inherited it in 1910, he had no idea that his labourers were among the worst paid in Norfolk.

His marriage had been hailed as a great success. May produced an heir within a year – David, the future Edward VIII. The couple quickly became a beacon of respectable and contented domesticity. 'Every time I see them I love and like them more and respect them greatly,' Queen Victoria wrote in 1897. 'Thank God! Georgie has got such an excellent, useful, and good wife.' May was regarded at court as having bolstered George's shyness, lending the partnership a ramrod-backed, rather severely splendid public poise. She showed a particular propensity for draping herself in diamonds and expensive jewellery. Although no extrovert, she enjoyed the public obligations of royalty.

George loved May, as much as he was able. 'You know by this time,' he wrote to her several months after their wedding,

that I never do anything by halves, when I asked you to marry me I was very fond of you, but not very much in love with you, but I saw in you the person I was capable of loving most deeply, if you only returned that love . . . I have tried to understand you and to know you, and with the happy result that I know now that I do love you darling girl with all my heart, and am simply devoted to you . . . I adore you sweet May. My love grows stronger for you every day, mixed with admiration and I thank God every day that he has given me such a darling devoted wife as you are. God bless you my sweet Angel May, who I know will always stick to me as I need our love and help more than ever now.

On paper, George brimmed with the tenderest feelings towards his wife, and told her he couldn't do without her. In St Petersburg, for Nicholas's wedding in 1894, he wrote her twenty letters in two weeks. Face to face, however, he continued to be quite unable to express his feelings. 'I know that you understood what I felt & what agony it was having to take leave,' he wrote after he left for Russia in 1894; and after their tour of the Commonwealth in 1901, 'Somehow I can't tell you, so I take the first opportunity of writing to say how deeply I am indebted to you darling for the splendid way in which you supported and helped me on our long Tour. It was you who made it a success.'

The relationship was complicated. George remained very close to his sisters and mother, who lived only minutes away. They were extremely possessive of him and often insensitive and hostile to her. George's closest sister, Toria, who had remained unmarried because Alexandra wanted a companion, and who regarded May as an interloper, made little effort to hide her antipathy. 'Do try to talk to May at dinner,' she told a guest shortly after the marriage, 'though one knows she is deadly dull.' Alexandra never openly clashed with her daughter-in-law, and treated her with her characteristic breezy friendliness. But there was no mistaking 'her jealousy of her daughter-in-law', according to May's oldest friend, Mabell, Countess of Airlie. Alexandra made a point of demonstrating her power over her son, turning up at the house whenever she felt like it; moving the furniture around when her daughter-in-law was away, 'which certainly gives ever so much more room, and I think looks much prettier', George wrote tactlessly to May. 'Of course, if you don't like it . . . we can move it all back again in a minute.' Alexandra was quick to point out anything that May did which might be construed as the tiniest neglect of her husband: 'So my poor Georgie has lost his May who has fled to London to look at her glass.' As for her father-in-law, May found Edward's chaffing discomfiting and disapproved of his lifestyle. Her family, who were enthusiastically pro-German, also disliked what they saw as his 'dreadful Russian proclivities'. But George still lived in his father's shadow, consulting the king about everything, even what colour livery his footmen should wear.

George seemed oblivious of his family's treatment of his wife, just as he was of how dull and monotonous Sandringham and his sporting life must have been to her. Shooting and horse-racing bored her, sailing made her sick. Upper-class wives, however, were expected to fall in line with their husbands' pursuits, and so she followed the shooters, day after day, smiling enthusiastically. He had no time for her interests – literature and art – and possessed an upper-class philistine contempt for people he thought too clever, referring to them as 'eyebrows'. 'Sometimes,' George's earliest authorized biographer admitted, 'the Duchess's intellectual life there may have been starved and her energies atrophied in those early years.' Nor would he consider moving to somewhere larger and further away from his family. When in 1901 she proposed they move to Houghton Hall, a nearby Norfolk estate, he vetoed it, egged on by his mother.

May never complained. She had committed herself utterly to accommodating her husband and future king, to boosting his confidence and to demonstrating her devotion to the monarchy. This was, more or less, what was expected. As one biographer of a more recent English princess – Diana – has written, upper-class women of her caste were trained for 'a life of low emotional expectations and husbands who were not focused on being attentive'. May 'sacrificed everything to his needs and to the preservation of his peace of mind, thinking of him before she thought of anyone else, her children, and, of course, herself, included', wrote her biographer James Pope-Hennessy. '. . . She believed that all should defer to the King's slightest wish, and she made herself into a living example of her creed . . . Inwardly it required a constant and dramatic exercise of imagination, foresight and self-control.' Her devotion and abasement and her insistence that everyone else in the household act the same way, did indeed build George's confidence.

It also encouraged an already well-established royal habit of behaving like an autocrat within one's own household. At York Cottage the clocks were all set half an hour fast, because of George's obsession with punctuality. The head of the household was never contradicted, questioned or criticized. 'King George V hated all insincerity and flattery, but after a time he got so accustomed to people agreeing with him that he resented the candid friend business,' recalled Fritz Ponsonby, one of the royal family's longest-serving private secretaries, whose plain-speaking was accepted – though not without irritation – both by the queen and Edward. 'No one ever contradicts him; no subjects are aired but those which they [royals] choose for themselves, and the merest commonplaces from royal lips are listened to as if they were oracles,' the writer Augustus Hare observed when he met George in the mid-1890s. He wondered how George could bear the dullness of the conversation. George took to expressing his opinions and political views – the views of a high Tory Norfolk squire – loudly and at length to anyone who would listen. 'Just a little bit too outspoken,' the secretary of the Viceroy of India noted when he met George in 1905. George had taken an intense dislike to the previous incumbent, Lord Curzon, and couldn't stop himself from letting everyone know.

May's submissiveness encouraged George to treat her badly too. 'Off the record,' the Duke of Windsor told his mother's biographer, 'my father had a most horrible temper. He was foully rude to my mother. Why, I've seen her leave the table because he was so rude to her, and we children would follow her out.' Within his own castle, George was quick to anger. A barking temper and often expressed exasperation became two of his most marked characteristics. The anger may have derived from his difficulty in expressing his tenderer feelings; and perhaps because his whole existence was overshadowed by a constant low-level anxiety, uncertainty and dread of the future – that one day he would have to be king. This fed a latent sense of self-pity. Did it also, perhaps, express a tiny, unsayable twinge of disappointment in George about his marriage? A feeling that his irreproachably correct, utterly self-controlled, admirably devoted wife was a little unreachable, even cold; that her deepest attachment was to the monarchy itself, rather than to him? Consciously, George believed utterly in his own uxoriousness. In December 1901 the shocking news came that George's cousin Victoria Melita, or 'Ducky', had left Alix's brother Ernst – a union the late queen had bullied them into – for Nicholas's cousin Kirill. George wrote to Nicholas, 'I did not think they were at all happy together, but I never thought it would come to this; I am very sorry as I like them both. You and I, thank God, are both so happy with our wives and children, that we can't understand this sort of thing.'

On May, the marriage had a constraining effect. Three years after the wedding, Marie Mallet, the queen's lady-in-waiting, wrote in her diary that she hoped 'Princess May will not be too shy to speak to me. She looks pale and thin as if she longed for sympathy but was too shy to seek it.' A year later she observed, 'Princess May is very stiff. I am sure she means to be kind but in her case it is often necessary to take the will for the deed.' May's old friend Mabell,

Countess of Airlie felt that a 'hard crust of inhibition . . .' had 'gradually closed over her, hiding the warmth and tenderness of her own personality'. Away from George, David felt 'She was a different person.'

George's autocracy also extended to the treatment of his six children: five boys – the youngest, John, an epileptic who died at thirteen – and one girl, Mary, all born between 1894 and 1905. The eldest, David, the future Edward VIII, was born during Nicholas's visit to England in 1894, and the tsar became his god-father. The second, Albert, the future George VI, came a year later. Having been damaged by his own parents' indulgent neglectfulness, George duly damaged his own children. He was strict, bullying and impatient. He found it as hard to show tenderness to them as he did to his wife. 'He retained a gruff blue-water approach to all human situations,' his eldest son, David, wrote. 'I have often felt that despite his undoubted affection for all of us, my father preferred children in the abstract.' He expected them to behave like adults – or rather, well-trained sailors: punctual, clean and always obedient – while giving them a second-rate education almost identical to his own. And like his father, he frightened them; a summons to the library for lateness, dirty hands, making a noise or wriggling in church, was terrifying. 'No words that I was ever to hear could be so disconcerting to the spirit,' David recalled. Albert developed a stammer which was not improved by his father's habit of shouting 'Get it out,' at him as he struggled to speak. There is something genuinely sad in George's claim that his favour-ite book was *Wrong on Both Sides*, described by his biographer Harold Nicolson as a 'revolting' Lord-Fauntleroy-esque story about a strict aristocratic father and his son, who love each other but can't express it because of pride. 'Such a lovely book, I always cry over it,' George wrote.

May also found it difficult to connect with her children, at least when they were small. After David was born, she seemed disinclined to hold him and left for St Moritz not long after, while George went to Cowes. It might have been her natural reserve, or post-natal depression, or her insistence that George always come first, or the aristocratic habits of the time, whereby children were bundled off to nursemaids and nannies and barely ever encountered on their own, but she found it hard to get close to her children and hated being pregnant. It took her three years to realize that one nanny was routinely abusing her two eldest boys. 'The tragedy was that neither had any understanding of a child's mind,' May's friend Mabell, Countess of Airlie admitted. 'They had not succeeded in making their children happy.' It was no wonder that for the children, trips to their grandparents, Edward and Alexandra – who seemed 'bathed in perpetual sunlight', and spoilt and indulged them in the big house – were like 'being given an open-sesame to a totally different world'.

John, the youngest, epileptic and probably autistic, was eventually sent to live separately with his own staff in a cottage on the Sandringham estate called Wood Farm. Children like him were often regarded as an embarrassment to their families, though his life may well have been much freer than his siblings'. The queen ensured that her last-born was looked after by a devoted nurse; he had space, wonderful toys and local children to play with. Her diary suggests she felt tenderness for her child, but, apart from her, the family seems to have cut themselves off from him. George never referred to him, though he was president of the National Society for the Promoting of the Employment of Epileptics. For a long time John didn't appear on Windsor family trees, and when he died in 1919, aged thirteen, David told his then mistress Frida Dudley Ward that he greatly resented having to go into mourning: 'He was more of an animal than anything else.'

There were more similarities between George and Nicholas than their looks. They were both shy men who loved the life of the country gentleman, and were happiest when massacring a few thousand birds a week on enormous estates. Both felt most comfortable with the simple patriotic codes of the military; like Nicholas, George would display an instinctive dislike for the ambiguities and grey areas of realpolitik. Both preferred their families and domestic life to court society. Both were aesthetically blind, though nothing in Nicholas's homes quite ranked with the sheer ugliness of York Cottage. Both were addicted to routine: Nicholas would arrive for tea at precisely the same moment every day;

George liked to know exactly what he was doing at every moment in the day, and hated any disruption to his timetable. Both felt an intense uneasiness at change of almost any sort. Even their politics weren't far from each other: George had a noisy line after 1900 in violent denunciations of Socialists, the Liberal Party, and in particular the radical Liberal David Lloyd George, whose political platform was founded on improving the lives of the poorest and taking pot shots at inherited, unthinking privilege. Inasmuch as George thought about the tsarist system, he seemed to feel sympathy for his cousin, who he told the German ambassador in 1900, 'was reliable, but his power was constantly being undermined by subversive powers'. Both felt deeply anxious about their role in the world and tried to dull their worries with familiarities and routines. Both were in many respects lamentably out of touch with the world around them. And both found it impossible to see beyond public shows of loyalty and flattering words.

When, in September 1897, George made a rare public visit on behalf of his grandmother to Ireland – the first by a member of the royal family in over eighty years – he was met by cheering orderly crowds, even in the Catholic parts of Londonderry. The whole event had been carefully choreographed. George never saw, for example, the poorest parts of Dublin, which had some of the worst slums in Britain. He was told repeatedly that the visit had been a 'remarkable success'. 'The devotion to your person you have inspired is not only a result gratifying to yourself,' Lord Salisbury, whose party was determined not to grant Ireland Home Rule, told him, '. . . but it will have a most valuable effect upon public feeling in Ireland and may do much to restore the loyalty which during the last half century has been so much shaken in many districts.' The visit made absolutely no difference to Irish politics. It left George, however, with a false impression of the state of Ireland, and a mistaken faith in the significance of cheering crowds, the power of royal pageantry, and the magic of his own presence. Likewise, Nicholas could persuade himself that a few minutes of experiencing the hysterical cheering of his subjects told him more about their loyalty and the state of the nation than any ministerial report. And for Wilhelm the addictive reassurance of a cheering

crowd would still his unquenchable thirst for affirmation and popularity – and lull him into saying anything that came into his head.

The modern world, however, was encroaching on the walls the
monarchs had built around themselves in insistent and increasingly
direct ways, most particularly in the form of the press and public
opinion. By the mid-1890s newspapers all over Europe suddenly
seemed more politicized, more engaged by international affairs,
more aware of themselves as organs of public opinion, and much
more aggressive. The shift was partly predicated on cheaper production processes, which meant cheaper papers; partly on governments' acknowledgement of how powerful the press and public
opinion could be; and partly on rising literacy rates. Even Queen
Victoria was paying attention. The British newspapers had long
salivated over her eldest son's involvement in a series of scandals
(though they were careful never to mention his mistresses
explicitly). In 1895 the queen had been upset by the hostility of
the Russian press; in 1896 she wrote of the Kruger telegram, 'I
wish that the newspapers in both countries could be restrained
from writing with such bitterness and violence.' Reading the
world's press now led her to wonder why 'we are so actively hated
by other countries'.

Nicholas and Wilhelm both tried to dismiss the increasing power
of public opinion and the press, but were increasingly obliged to
acknowledge it. Wilhelm liked to claim that he was immune to
public opinion; in fact he was obsessed by and utterly susceptible
to it. A critical news story could send him into paroxysms of fury
or dejection. A flattering article about him in the English papers
would inspire a burst of love for 'dear old' England, demands for
alliances, and enthusiastic midnight visits to the British ambassador.
Wilhelm's entourage and his chancellors exploited his susceptibility
to the press – and his habit of never reading all the way through a
paper. Both kept discomforting things from him and presented
him with a cocktail of selected press cuttings from home and abroad
to keep him on-message. Nicholas, whose father had referred to
newspaper editors as 'swine' and 'half-wits', insisted the Russian
press had no consequence; references to Russian public opinion

made him angry. He admitted, however, to reading a German, French, English and Russian newspaper each day – even though he said he didn't believe what he read because he knew 'how they are made. Some Jew or other sits there making it his business to stir up the passions of different peoples against each other and the people, who mostly have no political opinion of their own, are guided by what they read.'

What all three monarchs were convinced of was that what foreign newspapers said about one was an accurate measure of how one was regarded abroad. Rising nationalism and chauvinism across Europe meant that coverage was more often unfriendly than not. Just who the press spoke for, however, was another matter. For Wilhelm and Nicholas it was obvious that the press was the mouthpiece of its government. That was, after all, how the press functioned in their countries. The Russian press – such as it was (Sergei Witte told a British diplomat in 1897 that 'he doubted if 100,000 people in all Russia read the newspapers or cared what they wrote') – was the most heavily controlled and censored in the world. Nicholas told a German visitor in 1895 that he would 'never set the Russian press free as long as I live. The Russian press shall write only what I want . . . and my will alone shall prevail throughout the country.' The German government's control of its press was a byword. In 1899 Joseph Chamberlain told the German chancellor, Bernhard von Bülow, 'that in Germany there is no such thing as public opinion. The German people had only the emotions which its Government required it to have.' Large parts of the press were either controlled or subsidized by the government. The *Kölnische Zeitung* reflected the views of the German Foreign Office; the *Norddeutsche Allgemeine Zeitung* was the creature of the government and the kaiser. Many other papers took subsidies and ran articles fed to them by the government, and would even print the bowdlerized versions of the kaiser's speeches that the government sent them, or excise the embarrassing bits themselves. (Though, even more embarrassingly, their omissions were often printed in the Austrian papers.) The effect could be considerable. Two weeks before a visit from Edward in 1902, Wilhelm demanded that the German press put out only pro-English articles, and it was pretty much so.

In Britain it was different. The independent press had a much longer history, and literacy rates were high. By the 1890s successful British papers had circulations much larger than their European counterparts, large enough not to need or want government subsidies, and possessed an intense self-consciousness about their importance as the cornerstones of liberal democracy. No matter how often British statesmen assured foreigners that they did not control the press, when British papers attacked Germany or Russia, they were regarded as carrying the force of the government's antipathy. *The Times*, which was almost universally seen abroad as the semi-official organ of the government, often diverged embarrassingly from the official line. The British Foreign Office cringed at its accounts of Russian brutality in Manchuria, and frequently asked the paper to tone down its coverage. It almost invariably refused, or swapped direct first-hand reportage for an equally critical editorial. Wilhelm took British press criticism of Germany personally, and couldn't resist seeing his English relatives' – especially his uncle's – hands in it, consistently overinflating the British royal family's influence. It was a sign of how successfully the queen had come to be seen as a disinterested force in British politics that in 1898 she managed to persuade the editors of the major papers to tone down their anti-German coverage. Even so, her intervention lasted only a few months. By 1900, the new tabloid newspaper, the *Daily Mail*, with the unheard-of circulation of 1 million copies a day, would be putting out a message that was unashamedly populist, emotive, aggressively imperialist, even xenophobic – and quite beyond the control of any government. It would identify Germany as Britain's key enemy well before the British government did. Salisbury, who loathed it, despite its Conservative affiliations – he called it the paper 'for those who could read but could not think'– could see it spoke powerfully to and for a new strident and sometimes ugly strand of public opinion.

In Germany, and even in Russia after 1905, the press and public opinion were developing a voice, or voices, forcefully separate from government. The German government's relationship with its press was, without the former quite realizing it, becoming increasingly symbiotic. The German papers represented a whole range of interests: powerful new groups such as the Pan-German League and the agricultural and industrialists' lobbies highly critical of government pussy-footing, as well as the often forgotten left-wing press, which preached a completely different message of internationalism and cooperation. Wilhelm might tell Edward, 'I am the sole master of German policy, and my country must follow me wherever I go.' But his chancellor, Bernhard von Bülow, wrote, 'public opinion even in Germany had to be reckoned with by every Government, and by the Kaiser too, if he did not want to suffer unpleasantness'. Both Wilhelm and Bülow felt increasingly moved to play to public opinion – at least the views of the Right – and increasingly nervous of its power and potential to undermine them. Both, indeed, felt they lived and died by press approval, Bülow was quite as susceptible and vain about his press coverage as the kaiser. He used the German Foreign Office press bureau to feed *Hello!*-style stories to the papers about where he took his holidays and how close he was to the kaiser. In his desire to sell himself to the country, he even wrote his own PR: 'Probably in no other question could I have shown more judgement, composure and caution,' went one self-penned encomium. He would try to curry favour abroad by sending stories he'd planted in the German press sympathetic to a particular country, to its embassy. In Russia, even before the October manifesto granted press freedom in 1905, some in Nicholas's government identified a kind of public opinion emerging from the educated class, the press and the bureaucracy, which held strong and sometimes diverse views on foreign policy in particular – whether its future lay in the Balkans or the East, whether Germany was friend or foe. For the moment, however, 'All parties were agreed in believing Great Britain to be the arch-enemy . . . blocking the way of our forward policy.'

For the moment governments could exert influence over their respective national presses, but with the power of public opinion growing, how long a monarch could absolutely resist its demands was questionable.

9. Imperial imperatives (1898–1901)

'The bad feeling between England and Germany is indeed a great distress and anguish to me – as to you and to many,' the queen wrote to Vicky in the summer of 1897. It never occurred to her that the situation wasn't fixable if Wilhelm would just keep quiet. 'I trust this will pass away gradually if William will not keep it up by speeches and colonial follies. The peace is again rendered difficult by him which is incredible. These railings you have so often spoken of have something to do with it doubtless.' Within the British government too, most people assumed the situation with Germany was reversible. Sir Thomas Sanderson, Salisbury's senior civil servant at the Foreign Office, for example, thought that while German brusqueness and hostility might be irritating, Britain should make a few allowances for the adolescent state's understandable if clumsily asserted desire for world recognition, and things would return to normal.

But they were wrong. There had been a tangible shift towards hostility to Britain in the highest quarters of the German government – a hostility once discernible only in certain parts of Germany – and it was to some extent, but by no means entirely, due to Wilhelm. The architects of this new position were two men whom Wilhelm appointed in the summer of 1897, having purged the latest band of ministers to have displeased him: his new favourite, Bernhard von Bülow, the new secretary of state for foreign affairs, whom Wilhelm planned eventually to make chancellor, and Admiral Alfred von Tirpitz, the new head of the Naval Ministry.

Bülow was a pure and fascinating manifestation of how Wilhelm's whims and near-pathological reluctance to hear criticism had affected government. A former diplomat, he was a clever opportunist and a great conversationalist (his not altogether reliable four-volume memoirs are still a hoot), with an astonishingly obvious but successful line in extravagant ingratiation. Among those he had cultivated on the way up was Fritz Holstein who – years later when everyone had comprehensively stabbed everyone else in the back – said that Bülow had 'read more Machiavelli than he could digest', and Eulenburg, whom he had assiduously flattered since the 1880s. But most of all he flattered Wilhelm. 'He is so impressive!' he told Eulenburg. 'He is, along with the Great King and the Great Elector, the most impressive Hohenzollern who has ever lived. In a manner which I have never seen before, he combines genius – the most genuine and original genius – with the clearest good sense. He possesses the kind of fantasy that lifts me on eagles' pinions above all triviality . . . And with it, what energy! What swiftness and sureness of conception.' He persuaded Eulenburg that he was the man to turn the kaiser's ideas and intentions – thus far so imperfectly interpreted – into reality, and reveal the kaiser as the great monarch he promised to be. With him as chancellor, he told Eulenburg 'personal rule – in the good sense' would begin. It was nonsense but Eulenburg and Wilhelm wanted to hear it. Bülow's big idea was 'Weltpolitik' – a clever piece of naming to bring to mind Bismarck's 'Realpolitik' – the aggressive pursuit of what Bülow described as Germany's 'place in the sun', in other words the colonial empire it so obviously deserved. This would be done by operating a ruthless opportunist policy of exploiting other country's weaknesses, while remaining untied by any more formal alliances, so that Germany would be the country which held the balance in Europe. It was actually a rather vague idea, and not that different from what the German Foreign Office had been doing for some years, but it sounded marvellous and the German public loved it.

Bülow's fellow appointee, Alfred Tirpitz (he was given a 'von' in 1900), was a naval officer with a plan to turn the German navy into the second largest in the world. Building a real navy was a dream Wilhelm had nursed for years, since his mother had regaled him with the wonders of the Royal Navy, when he was a child. It had been confirmed by his reading of *The Influence of Sea Power upon History*, by the American naval historian Alfred Mahan, a book which claimed that naval power was the key to national prestige, power and wealth – and the colonies which were now regarded as the index of status in the world. Wilhelm had signally failed to persuade the Reichstag of this – it couldn't see the point of a big navy when Germany had the most powerful land army in Europe and only a tiny coastline. Tirpitz, however, promised to deliver a navy, and he did, launching a successful propaganda crusade to persuade the country that it was absolutely necessary if Germany was to get its colonial empire. He was extraordinarily successful at extracting money from the Reichstag, and he managed and manipulated Wilhelm, whom he realized at his very first meeting did 'not live in the real world', more successfully than almost anyone else. Tirpitz was utterly single-minded and determined, and this fascinated Wilhelm. More dangerously, he was imbued with the German military world view which saw military strategy as almost an end in itself, and was unable, or unwilling, to take as consequential other policy considerations, such as the need to make compromises with one's near neighbours in the interests of peace.

The appointment of the two men marked a shift: Wilhelm and Bülow liked to call it the start of Wilhelm's 'personal rule'. It was a move to the Right, and with it came a lurch towards institutionalized hostility to Britain. Paradoxically, both men, like their emperor, were fascinated by Britain. Tirpitz ordered his suits from Savile Row, spoke English at home, and sent his daughter to Cheltenham Ladies' College; Bülow adored the British upper classes and modelled his style in the Reichstag on the aristocratic insouciance of the Tory politician and parliamentary star Arthur Balfour – practising Balfour's mannerism of holding his coat lapels and looking personable, in front of the bathroom mirror. England, Bülow liked to say half-ironically, was 'the most wisely and successfully governed country' in the world.

They also, however, both regarded Britain as the chief obstacle to Germany's imperial destiny. At the end of 1897 Bülow told the kaiser it was no longer possible to consider a 'really honest, trustworthy Anglo-German alliance'. He had the Prussian aristocrat's traditional suspicion of Britain combined with a new sense of direct rivalry. He claimed that the British looked down on Germany 'with indifference or even now and again with contempt and sometimes intolerable arrogance,' and were jealous of its economic success. Instinctively he leaned towards Russia; counting himself a Bismarckian, he felt it had all gone wrong with the lapse of the Russian Reinsurance Treaty in 1890. It wasn't sensible, besides, to be on bad terms with a next-door neighbour with a million-man army. He believed that if Germany pulled too close to Britain, 'we would definitely lose Russia's friendship and Russia is worth more to us than England'. Hostility to England and imperial rhetoric, moreover, won him cheers from the right-wing parties he needed to cultivate in the Reichstag in order to get legislation through. As for Tirpitz, in his first memo to Wilhelm in June 1897, he told him, 'For Germany, the most dangerous enemy at the present time is England. It is also the enemy against which we most urgently require a certain measure of naval force as a political power factor.'

The notion that countries must inevitably clash and fight for dominance had become a truism of the 1890s, given a spurious pseudo-scientific credibility by theories of Social Darwinism which interpreted Darwin's phrase 'the survival of the fittest' as the survival of the most aggressive, rather than the most well-adapted. By extension it had become an established cliché that an empire that didn't expand would find itself being torn apart by other circling imperial predators. As Germany began to catch up in industrial output and trade with England, the idea was gaining ground in Germany that the latter had reached its peak and that, as the German nationalist historian Heinrich von Treitschke put it, the sceptre was inevitably falling from British hands into German ones. Tirpitz believed that the German navy was the vehicle which would replace Pax Britannica with Pax Germanica. If Germany could build the second largest navy in the world, so powerful that in a conflict its ships could inflict enough damage to threaten the Royal Navy's dominance, Britain would choose to back down in order to keep its naval superiority, and allow Germany to become the world power it ought to be.

The new line was not made explicit, however. The reason for the navy's expansion was kept deliberately vague so as not to alert the British or to attract opposition within Germany. Abroad,

Bülow's justification was that it was to protect Germany's growing merchant marine and colonies; playing to his audience in the Reichstag, he presented it as anti-British. Even the government's own senior officials, such as Holstein, were not clear as to precisely what Germany's position was. And then there was Wilhelm, charging in and changing his mind all the time. The kaiser might have appointed Bülow and Tirpitz, and he certainly had moments when he was furious with England and fantasized about punishing it, or suddenly convinced himself that Britain was planning to attack Germany. But there were other moments when he loved and longed for England; or saw his navy as something to impress Britain with; or as an engine of tough love, the thing that would force it to take him seriously and join with him.

Indeed, his tendency to succumb to moments of fondness for Britain led other anti-British members of his retinue to extreme measures to keep him hostile. In February 1898 the chief of his naval cabinet, Admiral Senden-Bibran, an Anglophobe and hawk, returned from London claiming that Edward had deliberately cut him when he visited Marlborough House. The complaint brought Wilhelm storming to the British embassy, declaring that Edward's behaviour would have serious international consequences. Edward denied the charge: 'Nobody is more anxious for friendly relations with the Emperor than I am – though on more than one occasion I have been "highly tried" . . . I think I have the character of being civil to everybody.' He pointed out that he had personally arranged for Senden-Bibran to join the Royal Yacht Squadron. When the British ambassador read the letter out to Wilhelm, he muttered that Edward had always regarded him as a 'silly boy'. British diplomats were convinced that Senden-Bibran had cooked the whole thing up to drive a wedge between Wilhelm and the English family.

It was perhaps, then, a slightly inopportune moment for Joseph Chamberlain, the British colonial secretary – taking advantage of Salisbury succumbing to a bout of flu – to arrange a private meeting with the German ambassador at the end of March 1898, Hatzfeldt, in which, without consulting the prime minister, he seems to have proposed a fully fledged defensive alliance between the two countries. The German response was somewhat confused.

Chamberlain was a unique and unignorable figure in British politics. A self-made Birmingham industrialist from a lower-middle-class home – which in itself made him different – he had spent the first half of his political career as a popular hero in the Liberal Party, championing a revolution in workers' conditions. After leaving the Liberals over Irish Home Rule, he had joined the Conservative Party, and now occupied himself with imperialism, British greatness, and ways to unify and extend the empire. He was the most popular politician in the country, someone the Conservatives needed in the new democratic age, though Salisbury and the other Tory grandees did not rejoice to admit it. (When Chamberlain was invited to stay with the then Duchess of Devonshire at Chatsworth for the weekend, she claimed to be anxious that 'he would eat peas with his knife'.) While Salisbury looked increasingly tired and distant, Chamberlain was charismatic, dynamic and indisputably modern. He tapped into a new strain in British politics with which Salisbury had no connection – populist and demotic, but also jingoistic, aggressive, touchy and anxious. He had been furious about Russia's grabbing of Port Arthur and had been all for declaring war – a move Salisbury had wearily dissuaded him from. He worried about Britain's isolation, and had impressed on Arthur Balfour, Salisbury's nephew and deputy, along with other ministers, his view that Britain should befriend Germany, using fashionable phrases about race and destiny – he talked about the natural links between the British Anglo-Saxons and the German Teutons. But his buccaneering passion, his quickness to antagonism and his unsure grasp of foreign affairs (not helped by Salisbury's habit of keeping secret so much of what the Foreign Office did), made him a loose cannon in international relations. Salisbury complained Chamberlain wanted 'to go to war with any Power in the world and has no thought but Imperialism'.

Once Salisbury returned to office, Chamberlain became rather sheepish about his overtures and claimed they had all come from the German side – though he supported them. The confusion didn't help the negotiations, which Salisbury and Bülow, for different reasons, worked to close down. Bülow – publicly stating how extremely anxious he was for an understanding with Britain – seems to have encouraged the German Foreign Ministry to make excessive demands that he knew the British would reject. Under the impression that the British were desperate for German friendship – it presented a bullish list of colonial demands as a prerequisite for negotiations, which Salisbury refused. He saw no reason to hand over colonies for no obvious advantage and had no desire for an alliance with Germany. Talks limped along into May. Neither side wanted to be seen as the supplicant. As Salisbury's clever nephew Balfour observed, both countries wanted to be 'the one that leant the cheek, not that imprinted the kiss'.

In the meantime a mangled version of Chamberlain's original proposal and Salisbury's subsequent negotiations found their way to the British royal family. At the end of May Vicky – recently diagnosed with cancer and convinced it was her last chance to bring about the alliance she had so long dreamed of – wrote an emotional letter to Wilhelm, urging him to grab this 'world-saving idea'. Germany, she added, 'need never fear the Russians and French again . . . It seems to me that you can have this ripe fruit of inestimable value in the hollow of your hand if you will and can but seize it!' Unfortunately, with her characteristic tactlessness, Vicky also let slip that Salisbury himself was probably the greatest stumbling block to an alliance. The news confirmed Wilhelm's suspicions that Salisbury had taken against him. He sent his mother a long complaint against the prime minister and Britain. 'I for the last three years have been abused, ill-treated and a butt to any bad joke any musikhall [*sic*] singer or fishmonger or pressman thought to let fly at me!' Now the British dangled the possibility of an alliance, but expected him to come in by the back door, 'like a thief in the night whom one does not like to own before one's richer friends'. The tsar by contrast, had happily given him a coaling station in China. (In fact, he and Nicholas were still barely on speaking terms.)

Nevertheless Vicky's letter convinced Wilhelm that, apart from Salisbury, the rest of the British government wanted an alliance. Though Bülow tried to remind him that 'We must hold our selves independent between the two [Russia and Britain] and be the tongue on the balance, not the pendulum oscillating to and fro,' he and the German Foreign Office drew up another, even longer, list of colonies they wanted from Britain. Once again Salisbury refused. At the end of July the prime minister told Hatzfeldt there could be no agreement because Germany asked for too much. 'Shameless scoundrel!' Wilhelm scribbled on the report of Salisbury's words. 'Positively jesuitical, monstrous and insolent!' Bülow, meanwhile, worked Wilhelm up with stories that 'Princess Beatrice', his least favourite aunt, along with 'the entire English-Battenburgian-Hessian-Danish etc cousinage is quietly plotting against His Majesty'. Furious, Wilhelm fired off a telegram to his mother, who was now staying at Windsor with the queen, complaining that his offers of alliance had been received with 'something between a joke and a snub'. As he hoped she would, Vicky passed on his complaints. The queen asked her prime minister for an explanation. Salisbury swore he had no idea what 'snub' Wilhelm was talking about. He told the queen the disagreement was purely over colonies which public opinion made it impossible to hand over to Germany.

In hopes of resuscitating the idea of an alliance, Vicky asked the kaiser to meet the British ambassador, Sir Frank Lascelles, at her home, Schloss Friedrichshof, near Frankfurt, in mid-August. Lascelles was, in many respects, Wilhelm's perfect ambassador. An old-school diplomat who had previously served in St Petersburg, he was scrupulously polite and congenial, and regarded his prime function as to establish the best relations he could with the kaiser. He noted that the kaiser really took notice of only four ambassadors: the Italian, the Austrian, the Russian and himself. He had also come to believe that beneath all the sound and fury, Wilhelm sincerely loved England, and as a result the ambassador made himself an ever-available ear and tactful filter between the kaiser and the British government. Years later, he told Philipp zu Eulenburg that if he'd reported everything Wilhelm had said to him in the twelve years he spent in Berlin, England and Germany would have been at war twenty times over. The kaiser regularly subjected Lascelles to earfuls of enthusiasm, or fury, at all times of the day or night. Other embassy staff were less enthused. Shortly after the

Kruger telegram in early 1906, Wilhelm turned up at 10 p.m. and stayed until 1.30, helping himself to whisky and cigars and talking for hours 'about Grand Mamma and Cowes and Lord Dunraven and his journey in Cumberland', while the embassy staff stood and listened and longed for him to leave.

Though Bülow had tried to remind him to be calm and collected, within minutes Wilhelm launched into a tirade about Britain's 'scant consideration', and the 'curt refusal which His demands usually met with'. Lascelles tried to explain that the British had found the German demands for African territory 'exorbitant'. But he added cautiously that there *might* be those in England who would support a strictly defensive alliance which would come into force *only* if one side were attacked by two other powers simultaneously. The problem with saying things like this to Wilhelm was that he heard what he wanted to hear. The next day he sent Lascelles a telegram thanking him for his 'energetic intercession' and looking forward to a 'favourable conclusion'. The day after, there was another enthusiastic telegram telling a bemused Lascelles that he'd given 'instructions' to London and Berlin. With that, Wilhelm set off on a tour of the Holy Land, which climaxed in his grand entry into Jerusalem.

He returned to Europe in autumn to find Britain on the point of war with France over a dusty little fort in the middle of nowhere in Eastern Sudan called Fashoda. Fashoda was the point where French plans to dominate Africa east to west, from Dakar to Djibouti, intersected with British plans to connect South Africa to Cairo. A French army occupied the fort, a British one besieged it – very politely.★ Back in Europe, however, French and British public opinion was hysterical about the threat from the other – demonstrating the pitch to which imperial competition had come. Then, in early November, the French government became engulfed in the latest fall-out from the Dreyfus case and reluctantly withdrew. Though the crisis had passed, Wilhelm wrote to his mother – expecting her to send the letter on to the queen, as she did – encouraging the British to go to war with France. 'The

★ The two commanders, Marchand and Kitchener, took tea together.

moment – militarily spoken – is well chosen as nobody will dream of helping France . . . I of course in private as Grandmama's grandson will pray for the success of her arms with all my heart . . . Officially as the head of the German Empire I would uphold a strict and benevolent neutrality. Should a second Power think fit to attack England from the rear, whilst it is fighting, I would act according to our arrangements made with Sir Frank Lascelles.'

Poor Sir Frank. What 'arrangements', the queen and Salisbury wanted to know? Lascelles tried to resolve the misunderstanding, not entirely successfully. At dinner in mid-December, Wilhelm firstly told him that Britain was about to go to war with France, a pronouncement 'I attempted, though I am afraid in vain, to combat'. Then, when Lascelles suggested that perhaps Wilhelm might have 'attributed too great importance to what I then said' at their August meeting, the kaiser explained that the agreement was that 'if either of our two countries were to be attacked by two powers at the same time the other would come to its assistance, and that he would be prepared to act accordingly'. Trying not to look completely dazed, Lascelles said carefully that while this might be a *possible* starting point for negotiation, he of course had no authority to make such an agreement. Wilhelm said he understood, but naturally if England was ever in danger, he 'would certainly come to her assistance'. Lascelles reminded Wilhelm that the German ambassador had recently said that the Germans believed that 'no formal agreement was necessary between England and Germany' because if it came to a war, such arrangements could be made 'in 24 hours'. 'Half an hour', Wilhelm said. A few days later he wrote to his mother that as a result of his 'understanding' with Lascelles, he had been able to inform the Russian ambassador that England was about to attack France but that Germany and Russia could remain uninvolved because it would take place on water.

Lascelles wasn't the only one who found the kaiser exhausting to deal with. Bülow found managing him far more difficult and time-consuming than he had expected – especially over Britain. 'You cannot have the faintest idea what I have prevented,' he grumbled to Eulenburg, 'and how much of my time I must devote to restoring order where our All Highest master has created chaos.'

At the same time, the endemic intrigue in the German court meant Bülow felt obliged to devote a great deal of time to staying in his master's favour. 'No one,' one member of Wilhelm's entourage observed, 'could fail to admire – though it shook one's confidence – the inconceivable skill with which he would almost imperceptibly shift his ground whenever he had inadvertently expressed an opinion which did not quite find favour with the Emperor, and veer to his side.' He would even change his trousers if Wilhelm happened to express a dislike for their particular shade of grey. It was by no means always clear who was the manipulator and who the manipulated.

Months after the war with France failed to materialize, Wilhelm was still telling anyone who would listen that Britain had missed a perfect opportunity to annihilate France. The reason, he claimed, was that Grandmama refused to forgo her annual holiday in the South of France.

At the end of August 1898 Nicholas astonished the world by proposing an international conference to discuss disarmament and 'universal peace'. His open letter described nations 'building terrible engines of destruction', which were 'transforming the armed peace into a crushing burden that weighs on all nations and if prolonged will lead inevitably to the very catastrophe which it is desired to avert'. To publicize his initiative, Nicholas took the unprecedented step of giving no fewer than three audiences to the most famous journalist in the English-speaking world, W. T. Stead, the man who had campaigned against slavery in the Congo, exposed child prostitution in London, and turned Gordon of Khartoum into a saint. The excitable Stead was completely starstruck. He gushed about Nicholas's perceptiveness, his modesty, his disarmament ideas, his desire to be on good terms with England, his conviction that Queen Victoria was 'the greatest living statesman', and pronounced himself 'grateful to God that such a man sits upon the Russian throne'.

Nicholas had been inspired by the writings of a Polish banker and railway entrepreneur called Ivan Bloch, whose six-volume tome *La Guerre Future* – published in English as *Is War Now*

Impossible? – painted a grim picture of the consequences of a full-scale European conflict, pointed out how crushing the costs of defence spending were becoming to all European states, and argued that war must become impossible. Bloch managed to get an audience with the tsar – despite being Jewish – and Nicholas had been horrified, not so much by the projected casualties, as by Bloch's all-too-convincing predictions of social collapse and revolution. The Russian government knew only too well how defence spending could impact on an economy. Its vast expenditure on its western frontier with Germany, for example, was directly reducing the money available for internal development.

Across Europe there was an enormously positive response from the public and press. What Bloch and Nicholas described seemed frighteningly true: nations were at each other's throats; the largest, richest manufacturers in Europe were now armaments companies: German Krupp, British Vickers Maxim and French Schneider-Creusot. It was no accident that 1898 was the year H. G. Wells published the mother of all invasion-scare novels, *The War of the Worlds*, with its devastating death rays and mass destruction. In certain lights the future looked pretty scary. The political elite, however, was more cynical and resistant. Vicky, who saw some merit in the idea, pointed out to her mother, 'Nicky is quite against constitutions and liberty for Russia . . . peace seems hardly in accordance with the oppression and suffering of a race still governed by despotism.' Edward was convinced it was a 'dodge' cooked up by the unscrupulous foreign minister, Muraviev: 'It is the greatest rubbish and nonsense I ever heard of . . . the thing is simply impossible . . . France could never consent to it – nor we.' When Nicholas met George at their Danish grandmother Amama's funeral in September, and tried to persuade him to head the British campaign (somewhat paradoxically, since what Nicholas had always liked about George was that he made no political demands upon him), Edward flatly refused. As for Wilhelm, he was disgusted. 'Imagine!' he scolded Nicholas. 'A monarch dissolving his regiments sacred with a hundred years of history and handing them over to Anarchists and Democracy!'

Cynicism was not entirely misplaced. The Russian government's chief reason for taking up the idea was its discovery that the Austrian army was about to adopt a new generation of rapid-fire field guns, which Russia, currently rearming its infantry, simply couldn't afford. And when, a couple of months before the Hague peace conference took place in May 1899, the British ambassador in St Petersburg raised the issue of the four new battleships Russia had commissioned, Nicholas replied that it wasn't the right moment for 'exchanging views about a mutual curtailment of naval programmes'. By then, the tsar's enthusiasm had waned when, according to the British Russia expert Donald Mackenzie Wallace, it had been pointed out to him that the proposed alternative to war – an arbitration court – would undermine the intrinsic superiority of the Great Powers, since small countries would have just as much muscle as big ones; and that there were thirty outstanding small disputes with other Asian powers which Russia would almost certainly lose in arbitration. Nor did he like being hailed as a hero by European socialists.

All the major European nations and America felt obliged to send delegations to the Hague conference, but most of the government delegates were pro-war and the proposals were endlessly watered down. Disarmament disappeared from the agenda, and the modest suggestion to freeze arms levels was almost universally opposed. The German delegation was particularly obstructive, utterly opposed even to the idea of arbitration, which Wilhelm claimed was an infringement of his divine right.* Within six months of the conference, Russia would be sending large numbers of troops into Manchuria, and Britain would be at war in Southern Africa – both would prove horribly expensive mistakes in all senses. Despite the grim credibility of Bloch's arguments, no European government would accept the idea of arms reduction. Writing in the *Contemporary Review* in 1901, he put his failure down to the fact that his ideas ran too much counter to 'the vested interests of the most powerful class of the community', and 'the steadfastness

---

* The conference did, however, against all the odds, agree a series of rules of warfare and set up a permanent court of arbitration.

with which the military caste clings to the memory of a state of things which has already passed away'.

The truth was there were highly influential voices within the international political elite proclaiming the inevitability and even the morality of war. It wasn't just the chauvinistic German historian Treitschke – required reading for all German army officers and government officials – who insisted that states existed in a constant state of Hobbesian conflict and that war purified and united, ennobled and invigorated, and that too much peace led to decadence. In all the colonial and would-be colonial states, war had become legitimized as a test of national racial fitness, and pronounced inevitable as a vital mode of natural selection by the idea of Social Darwinism – which also, by no coincidence, legitimized the domination of 'backward' and 'inferior' races by 'advanced', 'superior' ones. Theodore Roosevelt had told the American Naval War College in 1897, 'No triumph of peace is quite so great as the supreme triumphs of war . . . the minute that a race loses the hard fighting virtues, then . . . it has lost its proud right to stand as the equal of the best,'and the rest of the country had applauded. And in an article implicitly critical of the peace conference, the admired naval historian Alfred Mahan, whose single vote at the Hague conference was said to have prevented the banning of 'asphyxiating gas', described war as an 'honest collision' between nations, a 'heroic idea' and a 'law of progress'.

That's not to say that everyone who believed in the inevitability of war wanted it right now. It was dawning on Queen Victoria, for example, that her German grandson showed a worrying propensity to create conflict where it wasn't wanted. In March 1899 she wrote to Nicholas warning him that Wilhelm took

every opportunity of impressing upon Sir F. Lascelles that Russia is doing all in her power to work against us; that she offers alliances to other Powers and has made one with the Ameer of Afghanistan against us. I need not say that I do not believe a word of this, neither do Lord Salisbury nor Sir F. Lascelles. But I am afraid William may go and tell things against us to you, just as he does about you to us. If so, pray tell

me openly and confidentially. It is so important that we should understand each other, and that such mischievousness and unstraightforward
proceedings should be put a stop to. You are so true yourself, that I am
sure you will be shocked at this.

It was an extraordinary thing to do in view of the queen's lifelong antipathy to Russia and her sense of kinship with Germany.
But Wilhelm had worn her down. He had recently been sending
her messages that Russia was about to attack Northern India.
Neither Salisbury nor she believed him, it was just, she wrote,
another attempt 'to set [Russia] against us'.

Nicholas's reply confirmed the queen's suspicions:

I am so happy you told me in that open way about Wilhelm. Now I
fully understand what he is up to – it is a dangerous double game he is
playing at. I heard very much the same from Count Osten-Sacken from
Berlin about the English policy, as what you and Lord Salisbury must
have learnt from Sir F Lascelles about us. I am very glad you did not
believe the story of the alleged alliance between us and the Amire [*sic*]
of Afghanistan, for there is not a syllable of truth in it. As you know,
dearest Grandmama, all I am striving at now is for the longest possible
prolongation of peace in this world.

Anglo-Russian relations had not themselves been in an especially
happy place. The British Foreign Office knew the Russians had
offered to help the French military during Fashoda, and the two
sides were still locked in furious rivalry over China, but they had
agreed to try to negotiate a settlement, to split China into a Russian
sphere of influence north of the Great Wall and a British one south
of it. The British hadn't really wanted it, but at least it promised
to put a curb on Russian expansion. 'All that Russia wants,'
Nicholas told the queen, 'is to be left quiet and to develop her
position in the sphere of interest which concerns her being so close
to Siberia.' The negotiations had been tortuous. 'Mouravieff [*sic*]
is a terrible trickster, and always contrives on some plea or other
to put off the final meeting,' one British minister commented. At
least part of the delay was due to an internal power struggle

between Muraviev, who believed Russia needed a hiatus to establish itself in Manchuria without constant international hostility, and Witte, who was utterly against limiting Russia's railway and financial expansion in China. The agreement, a historic one between England and Russia, was signed – after the Foreign Office delivered a blunt, irritated ultimatum – in April 1899.

Wilhelm, meanwhile, remained in the queen's bad books. It was not just the going behind her back and the lame attempts to set her against Russia. They had also argued when Affie's only son had killed himself in the early New Year of 1899,★ leaving the duchy of Coburg without a direct male heir. The queen was exasperated by Wilhelm's lack of sympathy and they clashed over who should inherit. She wanted the duchy to go to one of her other sons, Arthur of Connaught or Leopold, or their sons. Wilhelm threatened to pass a law to make it impossible for a foreigner to inherit. The queen retaliated by not inviting him to her eightieth birthday celebrations in May. Wilhelm saw this as a personal rejection, and it set off another geyser of resentment, antipathy and suspicion. He summoned the British military attaché, Colonel Sir James Grierson, and calmly told him that it would be impossible for him to come to his grandmother's birthday party, or to visit England at all, while Salisbury, 'his consistent enemy', with his 'disgraceful' foreign policy, remained prime minister. He had, he continued, been England's 'one true friend' for years, but had 'received nothing in return but ingratitude'. One day, he told Grierson, England would be sorry. Then he began to talk about Joseph Chamberlain and the City, saying they wanted to go to war with Germany because it had fewer ships than France. The kaiser, Grierson reported, was perfectly friendly, but 'from the above, Your Excellency will not fail to see that his Majesty was talking somewhat at random'. Privately, Grierson told his friend Arthur Bigge, the queen's deputy private secretary, that he had not

★ Prince Alfred shot himself on the day of his parents' twenty-fifth wedding anniversary celebrations in January 1899 and died two weeks later. Various rumours suggested that he was in the last stage of tertiary syphilis, and that he had been ordered to separate from his mistress.

reported everything that Wilhelm had said, and that he seriously wondered if the emperor might be slightly mad.

The Queen remarked drily that if Wilhelm refused to come until Salisbury left office he'd have to wait a long time. She nevertheless wrote reminding him that she had invited him to Osborne in August. Salisbury told her, 'I cannot help fearing that it indicates a consciousness on the part of His Majesty that he cherishes some design which is bound to make me his enemy . . . It is a great nuisance that one of the main factors in the European calculation should be so ultra human. He is as jealous as a woman because he does not think the Queen pays him enough attention.'

Wilhelm's rage about Salisbury and the lost birthday could not be assuaged. Two weeks later he wrote the queen a furious nine-page letter, accusing Salisbury of deliberately stalling negotiations with Germany, most recently over disagreements over the Samoan islands.

This way of treating Germany's feelings and interests has come upon the people like an electric shock and has evoked the impression that Lord Salisbury cares for us no more than for Portugal . . . if this sort of highhanded treatment of German affairs by Lord Salisbury's Government is suffered to continue, I am afraid that there will be a permanent source of misunderstandings and recriminations between the two Nations, which may in the end lead to bad blood. I of course have been silent as to what I have <u>personally</u> gone through these last six months, the shame and pain I have suffered and how my heart has bled when to my despair I had to watch how the arduous work of years was destroyed – to make the two Nations understand each other and respect their aspirations and wishes . . . Lord Salisbury's Government must learn to respect and treat us as equals, as long as he cannot be brought to do that, People over here will remain distrustful and a sort of coolness will be the unavoidable result . . . Now you will understand dear Grandmama why I so ardently hoped to be able to go over for your birthday. That visit would have been perfectly understood over here, as the duty of the grandson to his grandmother.

He added that until now he had maintained a dignified silence hoping that Salisbury might mend his ways, 'and therefore gulped everything down and held my tongue'.

It was unprecedented for a monarch to attack another monarch's chief minister in a private letter, a contravention of what Wilhelm himself described as 'the European rules of civility'. The queen rallied herself to administer a reproof. She was feeling her age. Almost blind, completely lame, increasingly tired, she had been gradually withdrawing from public affairs, avoiding her ministers and even her private secretaries, because she said she couldn't bear to argue with them any more. (She insisted, instead, that her daughter Beatrice read her official missives. This had given rise to some awkward misunderstandings when, for example, Beatrice was called upon to explain major foreign policy issues, or vaccination, to the queen.)

'I doubt,' she wrote, frostily, 'whether any Sovereign ever wrote in such terms to another Sovereign and that Sovereign his own Grand Mother, about their Prime Minister. I never should do such a thing, and I never personally attacked or complained of Prince Bismarck, though I knew well what a bitter enemy he was to England and all the harm he did.' The truth was, however, that Salisbury was once again stalling on negotiations, this time over who should run Samoa, where Germany and Britain had taken opposite sides in a civil war. And his distant attitude during the negotiations had not just maddened the kaiser, it also had a lastingly disenchanting effect on one of the influential pro-British voices in the German Foreign Office, Fritz Holstein.

'Old Victoria's rude letter has hurt Him unutterably deeply!' Eulenburg wrote to Bülow from Wilhelm's annual Scandinavian yachting trip in July. He was once again worried about Wilhelm, who seemed constantly on the edge of hysteria. Eulenburg watched him bully his entourage, fly into rages and launch into flights of terrifyingly violent rhetoric, demanding the gunning down of the Socialists who had once again done well in the German elections. Wilhelm had indulged in this kind of bloody rhetoric for years; he rarely, if ever, acted on it. What upset Eulenburg was the realization that the kaiser would never grow up. 'Psychologically speaking, there is not the slightest change,' he wrote miserably to Bülow. 'He is the same explosive being, if not even more violent and unaccountable . . . When so markedly eccentric a nature dominates a realm there cannot but be convulsions.' Like an indulgent parent Eulenburg had tolerated the spoilt child in Wilhelm, while nursing the conviction that if all the obstacles were removed from the kaiser's way, he would somehow become the monarch and the man Eulenburg sincerely wanted him to be. He wrote sad, disillusioned, disappointed letters to Bülow, describing Wilhelm's erratic behaviour and his own failed attempts to modify it. No friend to Britain, nor especially to Russia, he worried particularly over Wilhelm's anger towards the two countries. It was still, he thought, better 'to <u>run after</u> Russia <u>and</u> England than to <u>anger</u> them both'.

In the late summer of 1899 the British performed a remarkable volte-face which melted Wilhelm's anger overnight. Salisbury suddenly agreed to give up British claims to Samoa in return for Germany renouncing claims to a few Pacific islands and parts of Western Africa and agreeing to be neutral, should anything blow up in the Transvaal. The kaiser was delighted. Having sulkily refused to come to England in August, he asked to visit Windsor in November. The likeliest reason for the British change of heart became apparent six weeks after the Samoan agreement, when the Anglo-Boer War broke out on 11 October.

The alleged British *casus belli* was the Boers' refusal to grant basic rights to British immigrants who had come to the Transvaal to mine gold. The Boers had refused to do this as they would have instantly been vastly outnumbered. The real motivation for Britain's entry into the Boer War is still disputed – to absorb the Orange Free State and Transvaal into South Africa, to get at the Boers' gold, to teach them a lesson. Whatever the reason, it was an ugly, expensive little conflict encouraged by Cecil Rhodes and Joseph Chamberlain, and one which Salisbury in earlier days might have headed off. Unlike Chamberlain, who was excited by imperialism, he'd always considered war a manifestation of failure: 'I am an utter unbeliever that anything that is violent will have permanent results.' An economic imperialist, he nevertheless deplored the rising tide of jingoism and strident nationalism which Chamberlain articulated. He said it was like having 'a huge lunatic asylum at one's back'. But the times were increasingly against him, his age was beginning to tell, and his wife was ill – she would die six weeks after the war began. Salisbury's zest for politics was dribbling away, and he had allowed the government to drift into a conflict which he himself called 'Joe's war'.

The campaign quickly inflicted on Britain a series of nasty, intense shocks. Firstly, there was a succession of humiliating defeats: the Boers were the first properly armed force the British had faced in decades, and their effectiveness exposed gaping weaknesses and bungling at the highest levels. Second, there was the horror at the state of the British volunteers: between 40 and 60 per cent of them were too malnourished and unfit to join up, exposing levels of abject poverty and ill-health in a country which considered itself the best governed and, if you subscribed to those views, the most advanced of all races. These facts had an absolutely devastating effect on Britain's myth of its own imperial invincibility. After the first burst of enthusiasm for the war, there was the hypocrisy of the Conservative government, which championed the basic rights of British immigrants in the Transvaal, while withholding them from its own subjects in Ireland. (No one, of course, took much interest in the far more numerous and far more ill-treated – by the Boers as much as by the British – indigenous black population, who in the racial assumptions of Europe hardly counted as people.)

Abroad, the war unleashed what Edward called an 'incessant storm of obloquy and misrepresentation . . . from every part of the Continent' – part resentment of Britain's super-power status, part dislike of its bullying. The Boers were hailed as underdog heroes. In France a cartoonist from *Le Rire* was decorated by the Ministère des Beaux Arts for his obscene caricatures of British leaders. In Germany, colonial groups demanded that aid and arms be sent to the Boers, and the mainstream press, which had spent the summer complaining about British behaviour in Samoa, became feverishly denunciatory. Several German officers went to fight with the Boers – a fact which Wilhelm repeatedly denied to his grandmother. In Russia senior members of the government demanded that Russia should exploit Britain's vulnerability and cause trouble in Afghanistan and on the Indian border. Though Nicholas, like the rest of the Russian elite, thought it an 'unequal and unjust war', he repeatedly assured the queen that he would not allow his government to take advantage of Britain's situation, and had no desire to involve Russia in African affairs. The assurances seemed to owe more to pragmatism and Russia's overstretchedness in China than any family ties, for he toyed with the thought. 'My dear,' he wrote to his sister Xenia, who was vigorously pro-Boer, 'you know I am not proud, but I do like knowing that it lies solely with me in the last resort to change the course of the war in Africa. The means is very simple – telegraph an order for the whole of the Turkestan army to mobilize and march to the Indian frontier. That's all.' At Windsor, the queen took to 'declaring the devotion of the Czar [sic] to her and England as genuine only'.

While Salisbury seemed to fade, the war revived the queen. She summoned up for it a last burst of splendid certainty. She was in no doubt that it was just, having been assured by the Governor-General of South Africa, Viscount Milner, that the English 'Uitlanders' were just like the 'downtrodden serfs of ancient Sparta'. (This was an extraordinary analogy by Milner – one of the instigators of the war – given that he was at that moment encouraging the use of real serfs, indentured Chinese labourers, in the South African mines.) She furthermore claimed that it was good for all those 'idle young men to miss a Season and rough it with the troops'. When, in mid-December, the British suffered three defeats in 'Black week', she told a minister who dared to offer his commiseration, 'Please understand there is no one depressed in this house.'

In Germany, the kaiser's first visit to Britain for five years was deeply unpopular. Dona – usually the acme of submissive obedience – was so against it she claimed she was too ill to travel and it would have to be cancelled. She told Bülow that British 'mammonism' was strangling 'the brave and godly Boers'. Deciding it was too late to cancel the visit, Bülow accompanied Wilhelm to keep an eye on him, and Holstein was drafted in to persuade the kaiser to keep his Anglophilic tendencies under control. He wrote a flattering memo assuring Wilhelm that he was 'more gifted' than his relations, but too honest and open with them. It suggested that he play hard to get, and urged him to 'avoid all political conversations', especially with Salisbury. 'The impression made on him [Salisbury] will be all the greater if Your Majesty does not express a desire to receive him . . . but . . . merely disposes of him fairly quickly and with immaculate politeness.' As it turned out, Salisbury's wife died the day Wilhelm arrived in England, so he was absent, a cause of relief on both sides.

Wilhelm viewed the visit in a haze of conflicting daydreams. He fancied himself as Britain's lone white knight in Europe. He simultaneously decided to exploit hostility to Britain in the Reichstag, ordering Tirpitz to bring forward the next stage of naval expansion by a year – though this was not to be announced until *after* the visit. He also insisted on bringing with him two members of his entourage whom Edward loathed: Kessel, a con-firmed Anglophobe, who had persecuted Vicky after Fritz's death, and Senden Bibran, who had the previous year accused the prince of deliberately slighting him.

He arrived in England on 20 November 1899, along with his reluctant wife and two of his sons. England began to work its magic at once. There were troops of strapping horse guards, cheer-ing crowds. There was no hint of condescension. A pleasing cluster of cousins and uncles all professed their gratitude that he had come at such a time. Edward made gracious speeches. The papers, which had always been susceptible to the kaiser's talent for public show, and were only too aware of the rest of Europe's condemnation of the Boer War, showered him with an embarrassment of praise – the Kruger telegram seemed entirely forgotten. 'His tenacity of will, his power of political adaptation, his genuine gift of elo-quence, his extraordinary versatility, his clear insight into some of the tendencies of the time, cannot fail to impress,' gushed the *Daily News*. 'A man whose remarkable personal qualities are hardly less fully appreciated in England than in Germany itself,' enthused *The Times*. The only shadow for Wilhelm was discovering the counsellor of the German legation, a small, short-sighted man called Count Karl Puckler, wearing blue evening dress with gold buttons, a painful *faux pas* for someone who, as Bülow noted, 'In England . . . felt himself, at all events in externals, entirely an Englishman.' The kaiser winced. Bülow quietly advised Puckler to cover himself with a coat. But Puckler, who was also very nervous, had lost his overcoat on the journey, and managed to startle the kaiser twice more before he arrived at Windsor.

At a grand banquet in St George's Hall – to which the queen was brought on a litter carried by four bejewelled 'Hindus' – they dined off gold. (Bülow beadily remarked that the queen looked like a 'mushroom' – presumably pale and bulging – and that the way she prodded her potatoes to see if they were soft reminded him of 'some good old soul' in Hanover.) 'This is the finest reception and the most inspiring impression of my life,' Wilhelm told Bülow. 'Here, where as a child I went along holding my mother's hand and marvelling, modestly and timidly at the splendour, I am now staying as Emperor-King.' His suite felt differently. 'Every morning,' Bülow wrote, 'Wilhelm II annoyed the gentlemen of his military entourage by pointing to Windsor Tower and saying to them, "From this tower the world is ruled."' His mood was jolted by the sight of the unfortunate Puckler, still in his blue tail coat with gold buttons, 'trying to worm his way through the riders, disturbing some of the horses'. The counsellor, definitively damned in Wilhelm's eyes, was quietly transferred to the Vienna embassy.

The war was hardly mentioned, though everyone, from the queen down, buttonholed Wilhelm and Bülow about the 'spiteful utterances' and 'shocking tone' of the German press. Wilhelm said it was all the doing of Bismarck, who in retirement still ran a series of papers. Bülow noted that the British were much less anti-German than the Germans were anti-British.

Among the retinue at Windsor was Joseph Chamberlain, who was impressed, as people often were on their first meeting, by Wilhelm's directness and ability to range knowledgeably across a huge variety of subjects. Chamberlain had been directly attacked by the German press, but despite this he was more certain than ever that Britain needed Germany as an ally, and he had the support of most of the cabinet. With Salisbury absent, he told Wilhelm how much he wanted a 'comprehensive understanding' between Germany and Britain. The kaiser had been warned by Holstein to avoid the seductions of Chamberlain, who was fantastically unpopular in Germany because of the Boer War. To Bülow's relief, the kaiser observed that Britain didn't traditionally conclude formal alliances, and that Germany was too close to Russia to consider such a move (which wasn't true). But he allowed that they perhaps might agree on various outstanding matters case-by-case. The British, he added, must bear in mind that 'the German' was touchy, must avoid 'trying his patience' and must 'show him goodwill even in small things'. The next day Chamberlain met Bülow and proposed a union of the US, Germany and Britain against France and Russia. Bülow suggested Chamberlain might speak positively of Anglo-German relations in public to create a favourable atmosphere in which talks might begin.

The visit concluded with three days of pampering and shooting at Sandringham. It was Wilhelm's first visit to his uncle's home since 1880. Edward was faultlessly solicitous. For some time he had let it be known at the German embassy that he was prepared to 'do everything that lay in his powers to remove all misunderstandings, both of a personal and political nature'. Like his mother, he very much wanted to see an improvement in Anglo-German relations. He and Bülow, however, did not take to each other. Edward called Bülow a 'humbug' – a trickster and deceiver. Bülow described watching Edward with Wilhelm as like 'a fat malicious tom-cat playing with a shrewmouse'. George, drafted in to take Wilhelm shooting, wrote approvingly that he 'shot remarkably well considering he has only got one arm'. The following year he and May invited Wilhelm to be godfather to their third son, Henry, and attended the coming-of-age of the kaiser's eldest son 'Little Willy'.

On the day of Wilhelm's departure, Joseph Chamberlain made a grand public overture to Germany in a speech at Leicester, in which he said that no 'far-seeing English statesman could be content with England's permanent isolation on the continent of Europe . . . The natural alliance is between ourselves and the great

German Empire.' Barely two weeks later, introducing the new navy bill in the Reichstag, which in one go doubled the size of the German navy, Bülow described, to cheers, Britain's arrogant jealousy and growing hatred of Germany and its shameful conduct in the Boer War. Not unsurprisingly, Chamberlain felt profoundly insulted.

But Wilhelm, who had personally arranged for the navy bill to be brought forward, was now in the grip of another Anglo-passion, informed as ever by the familiar combination of enthusiasm, tactlessness and ill-will which his exasperated entourage struggled to hide. When the British defeats reached their climax in 'Black week', two weeks after his departure, he wrote cheerfully to his uncle, 'Instead of the Angel's song "Peace on Earth and Goodwill amongst men," the new century will be greeted by the shrieks of dying men killed and maimed by sydditte [*sic*] shells and balls from Quickfirers!' Never mind, he concluded, at least the 'British aristocracy' were showing 'the world that they know how to die doing their duty'. And he enclosed a series of what he called 'aphorisms', advising Bertie on how Britain could do better. He sent another set two months later, in February 1900, and with it a letter likening the latest British humiliation to a defeat by Australia at cricket. Bertie and the queen were privately infuriated by his presumption, but Bertie took care to thank the kaiser, though he complained about his nephew's inappropriate sporting metaphor. A possibly apocryphal story claims that at this time the kaiser bounced into Sir Francis Lascelles's bedroom one morning while he was still in bed, to present him with his strategy for beating the Boers. The ambassador, horribly embarrassed, tried to get up: 'he pushed me back on the pillows and advanced nearer, unfurling and placing before me a roll of documents and maps'. Lascelles struggled to recover his dignity and his dressing-gown as the kaiser demanded his plan be sent to London. In his next letter to Edward, he told him how pleased he was that Lord Roberts, the new commander in South Africa, had followed his advice: 'This clearly shows the correctness in my calculations in my last Gedankensplitter [aphorisms].'

★

Meanwhile, Russia, France and Germany secretly discussed how they might intervene to impose a Great Power settlement on Britain, or even exploit its vulnerability. In the New Year of 1900 Muraviev suggested that Russia should get a foothold in Persia while Britain was indisposed with a big loan and some well-applied pressure, and start making trouble on the North-West Frontier. Nicholas approved the plan. The Russians, however, accepted they had to be careful. The costs of running Manchuria had become crippling. The new 'border' between Russian-occupied China and the rest and the railway lines required lots of soldiers to patrol them, and the single track of the great Trans-Siberian railway meant that moving men and goods to China was slow and expensive. The Chinese remained deeply unimpressed by dear and poorly made Russian goods, so money wasn't coming in. The whole colonial project was becoming horribly expensive. Angering the British too much might be an even more costly mistake in the long run. The Russians restricted themselves to a large loan to the Persian government, and moved their troops up and down the Afghan border, which always alarmed the British. Wilhelm, meanwhile, offered to guard the frontier, should the Russians wish to attack Northern India. The Russians greeted the offer without enthusiasm; they regarded it as a provocation. Russo-German relations had not recovered since Germany had taken Kiaochow in late 1897, and had lurched uneasily along since, punctuated by the kaiser's clumsy demands for attention from Nicholas and suggestions that they act together either against France or Britain. Bernhard von Bülow claimed to want to improve relations with Russia, but he had not been very effective in bringing the two emperors together. In 1899 he'd allowed a visit by the tsar to Potsdam – which Bülow had pestered the Russians for for months – to be entirely upstaged by the signing of the deal with Britain over Samoa. And Dona had deliberately insulted Alix by refusing to escort her to the railway station on the imperial couple's departure.

Then in February 1900 Muraviev suggested that Russia, Germany and France combine to impose a diplomatic solution on the Boer War. Wilhelm now said that he must sound out London first – which persuaded the Russians even more emphatically that he was up to something. A few days later the kaiser wrote to Edward warning that 'Sundry Peoples are quietly preparing to take liberties and foster intrigues and surprises in other parts of the world . . . Be on the look out! . . . Humbugs! Ware wolf!! We must both keep our weather eye open!'

Two weeks later he wrote, 'My warnings have not been too soon. Yesterday evening I received a note from St Petersburg in which Count Mouraview [*sic*] formally invites me to take part in a collective action with France and Russia against England for the enforcing of peace and the help of the Boers! I have declined . . . Sir Frank has been informed by me of this preposterous step in a <u>very confidential</u> manner.' The kaiser told Lascelles that Russia had made a large loan to Persia with an eye to getting an advantage over Britain there, and that if England went to war with France, 'he would keep his bayonets fixed on the land side'.

At the end of March Wilhelm assured his grandmother that he'd saved England 'from a most dangerous situation'. 'There lingers,' the prime minister told the queen, 'in Lord Salisbury's mind a doubt, whether a proposal for a combination against England was ever really made by France and Russia to Germany; but still, it is very satisfactory to receive from the German Emperor such clear expressions of good will'. When Edward was shot at in Belgium by a teenage would-be anarchist in April, Wilhelm rushed to see him – national interest might divide royal families, but everyone in the ruling class hated an anarchist. In Copenhagen, where he went afterwards, however, Edward appears to have been shown papers which suggested that it was Germany which had made the preliminary overtures to France and Russia to join a coalition, and that it had encouraged Russia to invade India.

Wilhelm's account of how he saved England from a Russian plot would become more elaborate with the years. In 1908 he told a British newspaper that he'd prevented a Russian attempt to 'humiliate England to the dust'. By the time he came to write his memoirs, he had fought off a Franco-Russian conspiracy to attack Britain by threatening to make war on them in return. When he telegraphed the queen with the news, he claimed, she had said she would never forget his help.

In the months towards the end of 1900, the 82-year-old queen-empress began to fail. Almost simultaneously, just after the general election of October, which the Conservatives, with a campaign orchestrated by Chamberlain, won, Salisbury gave up the post of foreign secretary, an inescapable sign of his waning energy. The burst of righteous fervour that had got the queen through the first months of the Boer War had gradually evaporated. Then Affie died of throat cancer early in 1900, and the news came that Vicky's cancer was also entering its final virulent phase. The queen had insisted on keeping up a positive front through the war, but as the months passed, she became, her household observed, 'lachrymose about the senseless waste of human lives'. She started an album for the dead, but abandoned it because she found it too sad. Her ladies-in-waiting would find her crying over the casualty lists. By December, ensconced at Osborne, the mausoleum, she was almost completely blind and increasingly feeble. By the New Year of 1901 she was dying.

In Berlin, Wilhelm was in the midst of celebrating the 200th anniversary of the Prussian crown. When he heard, he dropped everything and rushed to his grandmother's deathbed. No one wanted him to go: Bülow and Eulenburg dreaded both the effect of his departure on German public opinion – with news of British successes in South Africa, the German press had become hostile again, running cartoons of the queen decorating a British soldier for raping Boer girls, referring to Chamberlain as the devil and Kitchener, now running the war, as a butcher – and worried that Wilhelm would succumb to the temptations of England. Just the week before, Joseph Chamberlain had made another request for an Anglo-German alliance. 'I think of all the things he will say!' Eulenburg wrote worriedly. 'He will be like a child amidst all these people.' Bülow sent a diplomatic minder to keep an eye on him.

The kaiser's imminent arrival upset everybody in the English family too. Victoria's daughters, Helena and Louise, who had been supervising her care, sent frantic telegrams trying to fend him off.

Wilhelm merely laughed that 'the petticoats' were 'fencing off poor grandmama from the world'. He arrived at Victoria station, where Edward and George met him. In his memoirs, Wilhelm wrote that as he emerged from the train an 'ordinary man' said 'Thank you Kaiser!' Bertie nodded, '"That's what they all think, every one of them, and they will never forget this coming of yours." Nevertheless, they did forget it,' Wilhelm wrote bitterly years later, 'and quickly.'

They set off for Osborne the next day. To everyone's surprise, Wilhelm played it exactly right. 'He behaved in a most dignified and admirable manner. He said to the Princesses, "My first wish is not to be in the light, and I will return to London if you wish. I should like to see Grandmama before she died, but if that is impossible I shall quite understand."' Edward wrote to Vicky, who was now too ill to come herself, 'William was kindness itself and touching in his devotion.'

As the queen's condition worsened, each member of the family had a few minutes with her. 'She looked just the same, not a bit changed,' George wrote in his diary, 'she was almost asleep and had her eyes shut . . . I kissed her hand, Motherdear was with me.' On the afternoon of 22 January the whole family gathered around her bed. 'She was conscious up til 5.0 and called each of us by name and we took leave of her. I shall never forget that scene in her room with all of us sobbing and heartbroken round her bed. It was terribly distressing.' As Wilhelm very much liked to say later, the queen 'softly passed away in my arms' (or arm). In a feat of physical stamina much remarked on by the household, he knelt by her bedside and held her for two and a half hours without moving. He had the queen laid out on the dining table and at his request the Union Jack was laid across her coffin. He would have put her in the coffin all by himself if Edward and his brothers hadn't jumped in to claim it as their right.

Messages of condolence and grief poured in from across the globe. In St Petersburg, Alix broke down at her grandmother's memorial service – a rare public display of emotion that brought her no credit in Russia. She hadn't seen the queen for four years, but her grandmother's letters had been a solid connection to

Europe and her old life. The rest of the Russian family's reaction to the queen's death was a paradigm of their confused attitudes to Britain. The fervently pro-Boer Xenia wrote, 'The Queen was everything that was best about England; she was so much loved, and exuded such enormous calm!' Nicky wrote to Edward, 'She was so remarkably kind and touching towards me since the first time I ever saw her . . . I shall forever cherish her memory. I am quite sure that with your help dear Bertie, the friendly relations between our two countries shall become still closer . . . notwithstanding the occasional slight frictions in the Far East.' In Manchuria, Russia was using its 170,000-man army to blackmail the Chinese government and gain advantage at Britain's expense. Witte had demanded that it formally acknowledge Russia's annexation of the province and make the Russo-Chinese bank the only foreign bank from which it would take loans. He also demanded exclusive rights to railway concessions and raw materials in neighbouring provinces such as Mongolia, and a concession to build a branch line from the north to Peking.* Naturally, when asked by the British, the Russians denied making any such demands. 'The lying is unprecedented even in the annals of Russian diplomacy,' sniffed the British secretary of state for India.

The British papers lavished Wilhelm with praise. 'We may be pardoned if we cannot help regarding him a half Englishman,' the *Telegraph* wrote. '. . . we have never lost our secret pride in the fact that the most striking and gifted personality born to any European throne since Frederick the Great was largely of our own blood.' Even the *Daily Mail*, the country's most nationalistic paper, called him 'a friend in need'. (The left-wing press was less impressed: *Justice* railed at the way the mainstream papers worshipped 'This presumptuous and half-mad Emperor . . . because he has shown respect and handsome behaviour.') It was very tempting to stay. Days turned into a week, one week into two. At

---

* In fact, the Russian plan to annex Manchuria would simply crumble the following spring, defeated by the collective opposition of Britain, Japan, France and Germany, and – rather more pressingly – Russia's own massive economic problems and the expense of the project.

the funeral he rode a great white horse next to Edward at the head of the funeral cortège. George, who had come down with measles, was absent. Henry James, watching the final journey of his adoptive homeland's queen, picked out the kaiser, in his shiny Wagnerian helmet, as its most inspiring figure: 'We seem to have suddenly acquired a sort of unsuspected cousin in the person of mustachioed <u>William</u>, who looked wonderful and sturdy in the cortege and who has done himself no end of good here by his long visit and visible filiality to the old Queen . . . May it make for peace!'

Edward indulged his nephew. He arranged for him to drive around London in an open carriage so the public could cheer him – which they obligingly did. He presented him with the Order of the Garter inlaid with diamonds, he made him a field marshal in the British army. Then he introduced him to the new foreign secretary, the irreproachably aristocratic Lord Lansdowne. Wilhelm followed Bülow's instructions and avoided the implied invitation to closer relations, instead he lectured Lansdowne: 'The old English strategy of keeping Europe in balance, of trying to play one nation off against the other for the benefit of England, was "exploded". No one on the continent would fall for that anymore.' He himself, Wilhelm explained, was now 'the balance of power in Europe'. He also, however, awarded Lord Roberts, the commander who had led the British army in the Transvaal, the Order of the Black Eagle.

In Germany, there were howls of fury – Bülow described it as 'a slap in the face' for German public opinion. The press groused about his absence – 'Oh! If only the Kaiser realized what a wealth of love and trust he loses with his own people by so openly manifesting his affection for a <u>foreign</u> people.' Several key government bills were voted down in the Reichstag as the right-wing Anglophobic agrarian vote, which the chancellor had strenuously cultivated, melted away in anger. No one quite understood the significance of the visit for Wilhelm. His grandmother had been acknowledged as the most senior monarch in Europe. The kaiser believed that just as Germany was the natural heir to Britain's position, so he – rather than 'Fat Edward' – should be his grandmother's natural successor among the kings and emperors of

Europe. He went to England not merely to say goodbye to his grandmother, but also to receive what he saw as the anointing kiss of the dying monarch.

At a special lunch at Marlborough House the day before he left, however, he couldn't resist making an impassioned speech calling for a union between 'the two Teutonic nations' (he had recently met Houston Stewart Chamberlain, English author of *The Foundations of the 19th Century*, a synthesis of nineteenth-century thinking about race, which heavily advanced the primacy of the 'Teuton race'). Standing shoulder-to-shoulder, they would help keep 'the peace of the world. We ought to form an Anglo-Germanic alliance, you to keep the seas, while we would be responsible for the land; with such an alliance, not a mouse could stir in Europe without our permission.' That it had no effect, he blamed on the fact that the British failed to make it public.

Victoria's death left Britain feeling intensely vulnerable. 'Who can think of the nation and the race without her?' the *Daily Mail* asked. The nation, Henry James wrote, had felt 'safe and mothered' by the 'old middle-class queen who held the nation warm under the fold of her big, hideous, Scotch-plaid shawl'. 'Her death in short, will let loose incalculable forces for possible ill. I'm very pessimistic.' In Europe there was no such sympathy; ugly and even obscene caricatures of her continued to appear. In Germany, the satirical magazine *Simplicissimus* published a cartoon of the dead queen struggling through a sea of blood to reach the shore where St Peter and the Boer president, Kruger, stood by the gates of heaven.

PART III
A Bright New Century

10. The fourth emperor (1901–4)

No one seemed especially pleased that Edward, 'the arch-vulgarian', as Henry James called him, was finally king. The country had lost its all-powerful grandmother; a 59-year-old play-boy did not seem like much of a substitute. It would be fair to say that almost everyone expected him to be a flop as king. Even Edward was ambivalent about his new role. When his mother died he was in the throes of depression – a legacy, like his tempers, of his miserable childhood. His health was bad, he was recovering from pleurisy, his bronchitis was becoming chronic, a broken knee-cap made it hard to walk. Along with his mother's death, there had been that of his brother Affie the year before, and now Vicky was in a last, dark, painful descent into cancer. The Boer War was an ongoing mess, morale in the country was fragile at best, and the rest of the world seemed uniformly hostile.

The reservations were not unjustified. Not only had the queen denied Edward any formal experience of government, but even at fifty-nine, he was still spoilt, self-indulgent, obsessed with clothes and tetchy when he didn't get his own way. He liked, for example, to travel incognito, but not *too* incognito – he hated being kept waiting in a restaurant or hotel. He was still terrified of boredom, and needed constant external stimulation to keep it at bay. While he had more or less settled down to a kind of monogamy with his mistress Alice Keppel – thirty years his junior and thankfully dis-creet – he was accustomed to the life of a super-rich aristocratic hedonist, 'a world where pleasure felt like a ripened peach for the outstretching of a hand', where anything was allowed – apart from the sin of exposing one's circle and class to the scrutiny and opprobrium of the rest of the world. A world that was, in the words of Vita Sackville-West, 'immoral, lavish and feudal'. There are less than appealing glimpses of the king – or 'Kinki' as he was known by some – making horrible single entendres, 'insinuendoes', to his mistress's stoically grinning husband, George; and at dinners at Marlborough House, laughing at the obsequious clowning of the resident fool, Christopher Sykes, who would crawl drunkenly about under the dinner table, splashed with brandy, snuffling 'as your Royal Highness pleases'. In some respects he wasn't entirely unlike his nephew Wilhelm – the amusement at someone else's expense, the impatience, the restlessness, the susceptibility to the rich and the flattering – though it was a comparison he would have hated. Then there was his gargantuan appetite. The new king smoked twenty cigarettes and twelve cigars a day, two of the former and one of the latter before breakfast, and ate five mountainous meals. Dinner might typically be twelve courses, and include oysters, caviar, plovers' eggs, ortolan, sole poached in cream, pheasant stuffed with truffles, quails stuffed with foie gras, frogs' legs in jelly. He was said to take a whole roast chicken to bed. Small wonder he could now barely climb a flight of stairs.

But, as the king's ex-mistress Frances Warwick observed, during his years of enforced idleness Edward had longed 'for some intimate contact with the affairs of the greater world outside'. He was fascinated by international politics and, though his mother had tried to restrict his access to the government, a number of Liberal politicians had been sending him cabinet papers for years. Now he revelled in his new role, and longed to show he could make a difference. His first forays into government, however, were none too impressive. He quickly found himself at odds with the Conservative government. As far as it was concerned, the monarchy had lost all real constitutional power and there was no winning it back. Besides, in the previous ten years, government business had grown so extraordinarily in complexity and volume that it was impossible for the monarch – especially one who spent three months a year on holiday – to be consulted or even informed about everything. Edward, however, believed that crucial royal prerogatives – the right to be briefed about cabinet discussions before decisions were made, the right to steer official appointments and the right to dissolve or call parliament – must be reasserted after falling into disuse in his mother's last years.

Lord Salisbury had little respect for Edward, perhaps because over the years he had been obliged to extricate him from some extremely embarrassing and grubby situations. Salisbury's successor and nephew, the clever, insouciant Arthur Balfour, who took over from him just after the end of the Boer War in July 1902 in what was effectively an astonishingly undemocratic little coup,★ treated the king with barely hidden condescension, which Edward hated. The differences were also tribal: Edward belonged to the ostentatious, wilfully philistine, fashionable aristocratic set. Salisbury (though he liked to pretend otherwise) and Balfour were essentially aristocratic intellectuals who looked down on everybody else.

The conflict came to a head in August 1902 just after Balfour became prime minister. In an effort to counteract Russian influence in Persia – where Britain had its eye on oil reserves – the Foreign Office had lured the shah to England with promises of glamorous court balls, gala dinners and the Order of the Garter. Edward, however, had not been consulted about the Garter, which he alone could present. He retaliated bad-temperedly by saying he couldn't give a Christian order to an 'infidel' (though his mother had given one to the shah's father and as a rule he was notably religion-blind). The foreign secretary, Lord Lansdowne, sent him drawings for a Garter divested of its Christian motifs. Edward, who was on his yacht at Cowes, hurled them into the sea. He told Lansdowne that he should sort out Persia by coming to an agreement with Russia. The shah, who hadn't enjoyed the trip nearly as much as he'd expected – the weather was awful, he hated the opera, the trains made him sick – went home in a sulk. Lansdowne threatened to resign. Balfour put his foot down. He wrote to Edward, politely informing him that if Lansdowne went, the entire cabinet would resign too, creating a constitutional crisis. The king grumpily backed down. It's worth noting that such jostling for influence was not unlike – in a much paler shade – the conflicts his nephews were engaged in with *their* ministers.

His powerlessness made Edward lose his temper frequently. It was hard for the British royals to reconcile themselves to this. The

★ Salisbury was in failing health and depressed by the death of his wife and would die just over a year later.

habit of deference and courtesy around them meant that the reality
of their lack of power was not reflected by the way people felt
obliged to treat them. It was most confusing. Edward's capable
private secretary, Sir Francis Knollys, who'd been with him since
1870, along with Fritz Ponsonby, quietly redrafted the brusque if
not rude memos he'd dictate when angry. Nor – just like his
imperial nephews – did he seem able to differentiate between
the important and the trivial. When the famously badly dressed
Salisbury turned up to a court event in a pair of old trousers
that didn't match his tail coat, Edward wailed in front of twenty
ambassadors, 'What will they, what can they, think of a premier
who can't put on his clothes?' Salisbury replied, 'I am afraid that
my mind must have been occupied by something less important.'
As so often with Edward, the less appealing side and the attractive
quality were peculiarly proximate to each other. 'He had the most
curious brain,' Fritz Ponsonby wrote, 'and at one time one would
find him a big, strong far-seeing man, grasping the situation at a
glance and taking a broad-minded view of it; at another one would
be almost surprised at the smallness of his mind. He would be
almost childish in his views, and would obstinately refuse to understand the question at issue.' That said, Ponsonby, whose plain-
speaking did not always endear him to Queen Victoria or George,
liked the king. He was 'very businesslike but exacting', but 'far
more considerate and human than the Queen . . . always thinking
of small acts of kindness', whereas she had 'rarely considered the
feelings of her Household' or wondered whether her needs 'might
cause inconvenience'.

Edward had no desire to wrest policy-making from the government – in most respects his views reflected those of the Conservative government. But he wanted respect. His preoccupations were
the traditional ones of European monarchy: the army, the navy,
foreign affairs. He took his role seriously – as seriously as a man
could who took a quarter of the year off and was essentially part
of an eighteenth-century amateur tradition of government. He
believed that Britain needed to raise its profile in Europe, and
needed to be at peace. His instincts were towards agreement and
compromise; he liked to think of himself as a smoother-over

and he believed that the crown should be a popular symbol of unity, even – especially – in a society which was undergoing extraordinary social change and profound political reformation. After an encounter with Kier Hardie, the Socialist MP who was an outspoken critic of social privilege, to whom the king was carefully solicitous, his friend Admiral Jackie Fisher was both taken aback and impressed when, in response to his own sniping comment about Hardie, Edward snapped, 'You don't understand me! I am King of ALL the people!' The nitty-gritty of domestic politics, however, didn't interest him much, and he took no role in addressing the condition of the poor and the fact that the Boer War had exposed appalling levels of poverty and deprivation in the richest country in the world. Among the bottom third of the population life expectancy was forty-five – thirty-five for dockers, which explained why their union was one of the most militant. One in three died in infancy; another third of those who lived to over seventy-five ended up in the poorhouse; and in the slums of major cities even the air made you sick. As Kier Hardie himself had pointed out in parliament, the prince owned 'some of the vilest slums' in the country, and made £60,000 a year from them. But then sympathy for the poor – particularly the politically active poor – was not widespread in the Conservative government and its adherents, which still regarded strikers as lazy troublemakers. In 1901 it upheld the Taff Vale judgment, a law case which made trade unions liable for employers' strike damages – and in one blow made strikes impossible.*

The lesson was clear: if Edward wanted to exercise influence he would have to find other, more informal, ways of doing it – and he did find them. He'd always been good at being charming, he was a great networker and had an eye for cultivating the right people. As Prince of Wales he had gathered a loose coterie of rising men who kept him abreast of government and foreign policy, while he praised them in the salons of aristocratic England – their talents and his talking up blurred whose reputation was benefiting whom, and suggested that royal patronage still had some pull in

---

* Taff Vale would be reversed in 1906 by the incoming Liberal government.

British politics. Among these men were Admiral Jackie Fisher, the eccentric but persuasive architect of the reform of the Royal Navy; the fiercely anti-German diplomat Sir Francis Bertie; the future war minister Sir Richard Haldane; and the creepily obsequious, self-styled royal *éminence grise*, Reginald Brett, Viscount Esher, who had the ear of three prime ministers, but was fascinated by royalty and encouraged Edward to demand his prerogatives.

He also had great confidence and possessed a rare – especially in the British royal family – talent for public performance. The high aristocracy of the late nineteenth century have been dubbed 'the great ornamentals' – as their actual power declined, they became ermine-draped symbols of civic pride. Edward was the greatest ornamental of them all. He created for himself a larger-than-life public persona of bonhomie and good humour which would eventually prove, at home and abroad, to be a more than adequate substitute for his mother's po-faced longevity, creating a glamorous public image for the monarchy. He took pleasure in show, prided himself on always being affable and courteous in public (when he didn't always feel it) and was determined to be visible – as his mother had rarely been. Perhaps because he had been one of the first public figures to weather the force of press scrutiny and salaciousness, he had an understanding of what the press could do and – unlike both his nephews – some idea of how to work it. He played to the nascent stirrings of celebrity culture. The public might claim to be shocked by his scandalous past, but a lot of them loved the racing, the yachts, the theatregoing, even the stylish women – the papers never quite stated the nature of his relationships with them. He allowed the *Daily Mail* to take and publish photographs of himself with his grand-children. To bolster his claims to be a man of substance he culti-vated a reputation for speaking off the cuff in public in three languages. Less generous historians have suggested that the speeches were written by others and committed to memory – but witnesses at the time denied this. And in Europe, where monarchs with real power demonstrated it through show and ceremonial, Edward's talent for publicity and public demonstrations would give his actions a whole different dimension.

★

For George, the new century had brought a few, though hardly momentous, changes. He'd taken up golf, cycling, bridge and the new *sine qua non* of royal luxury life, cars – Edward had a fleet of them by 1903 – all fashionable new pastimes. As the Prince of Wales, he acquired two further homes – Abergeldie, near Balmoral, and Frogmore, half a mile from Windsor Castle; he was made a trustee of the British Museum, in which he took no interest; and was found a place on the Committee for Food in Wartime. Edward placed a desk next to his to ensure that his son had the experience of government that his mother had denied him. He was given a private secretary, Arthur Bigge, who had worked briefly for the queen, an effective, literate, organized, Conservative-voting ex-soldier, who told George not to look cross or bored in public. George quickly became as dependent on him as he was on May, and equally rude on occasion too. 'I fear sometimes I have lost my temper with you and often been very rude, but I am sure you know me well enough by now to know that I did not mean it . . . I am a bad hand at saying what I feel, but I thank God that I have a friend like you, in whom I have the fullest confidence.'

What George's new position did open him up to was the empire. After the queen's death in 1901, he and May were sent to Australia to be present at the inauguration of the country's first parliament and its transformation from six colonies into one 'Common-wealth'. Edward had wanted to cancel the trip, but Balfour argued that he should go. The Boer War, which had exposed such hostility in Europe, had paradoxically turned Britain in on its empire, and made the government all the keener to emphasize the colonies' bonds with the 'Mother Country'. Balfour had come up with a new, more visible role for the monarchy in the empire. 'The King is no longer merely King of Great Britain and Ireland and of a few dependencies whose whole value consisted in ministering to the wealth and security of Great Britain and Ireland,' he told Edward. 'He is now the great constitutional bond uniting together in a single Empire communities of free men separated by half the circumference of the Globe.' Australia's citizens knew 'little and care little for British Ministries . . . But they know, and care for, the Empire . . . and for the Sovereign who rules it'. George's visit,

Balfour argued, was a great opportunity to make that connection real. But the war, together with the issue of Home Rule in Ireland and the growing independence movement in India, had also raised questions about whether the colonies actually wanted to be part of the empire. And grand though Balfour's conception sounded, it was really another ornamental role, a job that required being rather than doing. George and May set off for eight months in March 1901 – George was so upset at parting from his parents that he could barely speak and had to take refuge in his cabin – with an entourage of twenty-two. They went via Singapore and New Zealand, with stop-offs in South Africa and Canada. In their absence, Edward and Alexandra spoiled their children egregiously. George described the experience purely in terms of numbers in his diary: 45,000 miles travelled, 21 foundation stones laid, 544 addresses received, 4,329 medals presented, 24,855 hands shaken at official receptions. Being on show endlessly he found a trial. He complained to Nicholas in one of the very occasional letters they continued to exchange (in 1902 George managed a record of three to his cousin), about the 'tiresome functions' he had to attend, but he was also, almost despite himself, excited by the empire. Its breadth, its cheering crowds were suddenly real, and he returned convinced that there was 'a strong feeling of loyalty to the Crown and deep attachment to the Mother Country in Australia'.

Abroad, Edward's ageing playboy reputation meant that his accession had been greeted with little more excitement than it had been at home. And feelings in Europe about the Boer War and Britain's prosecution of it ran so high that when the king went abroad he was more likely to be booed than anything else. Anti-British cartoons, especially in Germany and France, showed British soldiers bayoneting Boer babies; Edward himself was drawn standing on the mutilated bodies of Boer women and children. As the war entered its second year, the British army, under the leadership of Lord Kitchener, had become utterly ruthless in an attempt to flush out the last Boer guerrilla fighters. It burned farms, shot prisoners, and interned women and children, Boer and black, in concentration camps, an efficient new invention pioneered a few years before by the Spanish during the Spanish-American War. There the internees died in shaming numbers of famine, thirst, cholera and mistreatment. The conditions were so appalling that criticism was beginning to leak into mainstream British politics. The leader of the Liberal Party, Henry Campbell-Bannerman, described the British army's methods as 'barbaric . . . The vulgar and bastard imperialism of irritation and provocation and aggression . . . of grabbing everything even if we have no use for it ourselves.'

In Russia – where Edward had hoped his bonhomie might make a difference – Britain was resented not just because of the war, but because it had led a coalition of Japan, France and Germany in the spring of 1901 which successfully pressured Russia into halting its attempt to annex Manchuria and bully the Chinese government – though the project's crippling costs had also played a crucial role. 'I fear,' Edward wrote to Lord Lansdowne at the end of 1901, 'that there is hardly a country that exists concerning which England and Russia hold similar views, and both distrust the other.' When Wilhelm's brother Heinrich came to St Petersburg in December that year, Nicholas told him that he mistrusted British policies, 'despised' the British army and political system. He liked his uncle personally, he said, but had little respect for him as a monarch: 'He has got nothing to say in his own country.' Heinrich, patriotic but also Anglophilic and genuinely fond of his English relatives, was virtually the only person who couldn't see why the three countries couldn't simply get on. He was, Bülow observed, 'very pro-England, and thus regrets Nicholas' anti-English attitudes'. Heinrich was regarded as very naive in Berlin. Edward, meanwhile, privately thought Nicholas well disposed to Britain, but as 'weak as water' and entirely at the mercy of his ministers. 'The Russians have got quite out of hand in China,' he observed when the British and other European powers sent the Russians an ultimatum to get their soldiers out of Manchuria. '. . . The Emperor seems to have no power whatever, as I am sure the idea of war between our two countries would fill him with horror.'

Such attitudes made British politicians feel increasingly isolated and vulnerable. Lord Lansdowne, the new foreign secretary, was seriously considering the need for an alliance with a foreign power. One place where there seemed to be possibilities was Germany. Even though public opinion was virulently anti-British, Wilhelm was still glowing from the success of his deathbed visit, and just a week before the queen had died Joseph Chamberlain had once again proposed an alliance to the German government. Talks had begun in the spring of 1901.

Edward did his best to capitalize on the relationship. After Wilhelm returned to Germany, he wrote thanking him for his support and suggested they set up a direct channel of communication to 'smooth matters down'. He visited Germany twice in that first year – more than once encountering boos and hisses in the streets. Firstly, to see his gravely sick sister, when he tried to persuade her doctors to give her more pain relief (the Germans seemed more puritanical about this than the British, who were enthusiastic tipplers of laudanum), and then again after she died in August 1901. But mastering his irritation with the kaiser was always an effort. Each time he met Wilhelm, he endeavoured not to show he was cross when the kaiser did what he always did and ignored Edward's requests that the visits be private and informal, turning out instead in full dress uniform, forcing the king to inspect 15,000 soldiers, and delaying lunch by hours.

When Edward was given an opportunity to behave like a real international statesman, he flunked it. The occasion was a lunch with Wilhelm several weeks after Vicky's death in August 1901. The foreign secretary, Lord Lansdowne, had taken the unusual step of preparing a memo for him outlining British foreign policy, rehearsing the areas of conflict, and suggesting what he might say about various issues. It was a flattering acknowledgement of Edward's potential role in foreign affairs. But as lunch ended, instead of using Lansdowne's paper as an aide-mémoire for a serious talk on foreign policy, Edward fished it out of his pocket and handed the whole thing to Wilhelm. It was a *faux pas* which would have got any senior diplomat fired. Lansdowne was not amused. For a king who claimed to want a role in government, it demonstrated a lack of staying power, though Edward's blushes were saved. The German Foreign Office took the paper as a policy document and prepared a formal answer to it.

It may have been that Edward was too lazy, or too upset after his sister's death, to bother. It seems likely that he simply couldn't bear the thought of spending a couple of hours arguing the finer points of British foreign policy with his nephew. Through lunch Wilhelm had complained constantly that the British were obstructing the latest round of negotiations with Germany on a potential alliance. He also seemed to know all about things on which Edward hadn't been briefed – British plans to give Malta self-government, British overtures to Japan. It's also likely Edward had heard about Wilhelm's final aggressions against his dead mother. The moment Vicky died he had Friedrichshof surrounded and searched (nothing was found – with the unofficial help of Fritz Ponsonby Vicky had already secretly evacuated her papers during Edward's previous visit). Then he spread a rumour that she had at the last revealed her true loyalties by demanding that her naked body be wrapped in the Union Jack and sent to England for burial. Not only was the story a lie – she'd asked to be buried at Potsdam by her husband – but the detail of the nakedness was cruelly over-intimate. It was, however, eagerly repeated at the German court – the kaiser's last, damaging blow against his mother.

The two men's complicated relationship was evident to everyone around them. 'King Edward never liked him,' Fritz Ponsonby wrote, 'and therefore, while conversations in public were ostensibly very amicable, one always felt that it was an effort on both sides to keep them so.' An English cousin observed, 'Uncle Bertie thought William was bumptious and tiresome and William thought Bertie patronized him.' Bülow said that at moments Wilhelm literally hated his uncle. Edward was, however, far from being the only monarch who found Wilhelm difficult. Apart from Nicky, the kaiser had alienated many of Europe's crowned heads with his over-familiarity and rudeness. He slapped Ferdinand of Bulgaria on the bottom during a state visit, behind his back called him 'Fernando naso', because of his large beaky nose, and claimed he was a hermaphrodite. He called the admittedly teeny Italian king, Umberto I, 'the dwarf' in the hearing of Umberto's entourage.

The Greek royal family quietly loathed him, and his cousin Marie of Romania found him unbearably condescending. The paradox was, of course, that being so bad at personal relationships, Wilhelm should believe so deeply in conducting international relations through personal relationships.

Edward's efforts, however, had no effect on the latest round of Anglo-German negotiations. Bülow had told Wilhelm that if he seemed slightly cool about Joseph Chamberlain's proposals, Germany would extract better terms, and in due course the talks had collapsed just like the ones before. The Germans demanded more than the British were willing to give: a long list of colonies in Southern Africa and China, plus an insistence that rather than making a one-to-one defensive treaty, Britain must join the Triple Alliance – Germany's bloc – and commit itself to the defence of Italy and Austria-Hungary as well as Germany. The conditions seemed designed to put the British off, which Bülow may well have hoped they would. Gradually the foreign secretary, Lord Landowne, backed away. Fritz Holstein blamed Bülow for clinging 'to all the obstacles which stood in the way of the alliance', but he too was abrupt and hostile with the British. By nature someone who couldn't help but see ulterior motives and conspiracies, he'd come to mistrust the British and believed that Salisbury had deliberately misled him during previous negotiations and had behaved dishonourably over Samoa. As for Wilhelm, he was told by Bülow that the obstruction was all on the part of the British. The kaiser complained noisily about British delays and called the British cabinet 'a pack of unmitigated noodles' – a phrase he liked so much he used it several times. The British cabinet ignored his words, but Edward minded, and couldn't stop himself grumbling to Hatzfeldt's deputy at the German embassy, Hermann von Eckhardstein, that he had 'already had to put up with many of these jokes of the Kaiser's and even worse than this one too, and I suppose I shall have to put up with many more'. Even without Bülow's intriguing, there was, as in the past, a fundamental gap between the two sides' expectations which made any accommodation very hard. The Germans were sure that the Boer War had forced Britain on to the ropes, that it signalled a genuine decline, and they expected its desperation to allow them to drive a hard bargain for their friendship. The British, still the richest nation in the world, were not that desperate. They were, however, taken aback by the abruptness of the Germans.

In October 1901 Joseph Chamberlain, who – to his chagrin – had become the particular butt of German attacks on the war, made a speech in defence of the government's policy and the British army's conduct in South Africa, claiming it was certainly no worse than anything other Great Powers had done, and included among his examples Prussian soldiers in the Franco-Prussian War. Though Chamberlain had equally impugned the Russians and Austrians, it was the German press that went berserk. It's important to understand that in Germany the army had become almost sacred and inviolate. It was intensely respected, it was seen as the vehicle of German unification, and in the absence of many other national institutions with which the whole country could identify, it seemed to incarnate the nation's dignity and identity. Bülow demanded an apology. Chamberlain, in no mood to back down – which he in any case never liked to do – said he'd meant no harm and therefore there was no need to apologize. In Germany his effigy was burned in the streets, and in Berlin there was a brisk trade in spitoons with his face on them. In London *The Times* ran a report on German Anglophobia, illustrating it with some of the more shocking cartoons.

Despite the personal friction between them, Edward and Wilhelm consciously made an effort to remain on good terms. The king sent the kaiser a Christmas message stressing how much he wanted an 'entente cordiale' with Germany, and how, despite the Anglophobia of the German press, England wished to be on good terms with Germany, 'and walk hand in hand together harmoniously for the sake of peace and the welfare of mankind'. Wilhelm's answer was grandiose but friendly: 'The press is awful on both sides, but here it has nothing to say, for I am the sole arbiter and master of German Foreign Policy and the Government and Country <u>must</u> follow me, even if I have to face the musik [*sic*]!

May Your Government never forget this, and never place me in the jeopardy to have to choose a course which could be a misfortune to both them and us.'

But in the New Year of 1902, Bülow – contrary to the advice of the German Foreign Office – couldn't resist making a public riposte to Chamberlain. He said the German army was blameless and Chamberlain's words were an outrageous attack on Germany's heroic struggle for independence. It illustrated why Germany must be strong, so 'no one can be indifferent to our enmity'. Chamberlain's reply, in a speech in Birmingham, was similarly grand-standing: 'I withdraw nothing, I qualify nothing, I defend nothing.' The two governments' foremost imperialists faced off. It was a sign of an underlying and growing resentment of Germany in Britain, that Chamberlain instantly became – just as Bülow did – the most popular man in his country, and vilified in the other.

The monarchs' assurances of goodwill faltered. The kaiser denounced Chamberlain's speech as a 'conglomeration of bluff and overbearing and secret insult', and said the colonial minister should be shot. But he told Ambassador Lascelles that despite British obstruction and calumnies <u>he</u> was still full of goodwill – though London must remember he was not a '<u>quantité négligeable</u>'. In London, Salisbury counselled that Bülow's speech should be ignored and they should register their disapproval by cancelling George's upcoming trip to Wilhelm's birthday party in Berlin at the end of January – a visit arranged months before to demonstrate the new closeness of the two families. 'I think that under the circumstances it would be better for him not to go where he is liable to be insulted, or be treated by the Public in a manner which I feel sure no one would regret more than yourself,' Edward wrote to Wilhelm. The kaiser did not reply. 'This is most disagreeable for me especially if I have to go in the end,' George complained to his secretary Arthur Bigge. 'I hate the very idea of going.' When Lascelles gingerly broached the situation to Wilhelm days before George was due, the kaiser claimed he'd never received Edward's missive, and threatened a dire diplomatic crisis – 'another Fashoda' – if the visit were cancelled. Fourteen years before, in equally sticky circumstances, Wilhelm had claimed that a crucial letter had gone missing. No one, especially Edward and Lascelles, believed him. The king relented but demanded a polite telegram from Wilhelm guaranteeing that George would be treated with respect. It never arrived.

George went off to Berlin in January 1902 with understandable trepidation, but he reported that everyone, from princes to the officers in the barracks of the 8th Cuirassiers, of whom Wilhelm made him a colonel, was 'most civil', and his cousin, with whom he dined and breakfasted, was 'kindness itself'. In his not always reliable memoirs, Bülow claimed that a 'frank talk' with the 'clear-headed, sensible and manly' (and almost unrecognizably articulate) George smoothed over the disagreements and bitterness of the previous months. 'We must forget the past and strive only to be friends in the future,' the prince was quoted as saying, and assured Bülow that his father regarded him as a friend – which wasn't true. George's letters home were Eeyore-ishly self-pitying. 'The amount one is expected and has to do is simply awful,' he grumbled. His Cuirassier helmet 'looked somewhat like an extinguisher on a candle', his uniform didn't fit, and he had 'absolutely walked miles in the Schloss as W's rooms are at the other end of the Castle and every minute I have to come back and put on another uniform'. Worst of all his new boots 'hurt abominably'.

It was in Bülow's interest for the visit to go well. Tirpitz and he believed that it was vital to remain on decent terms with Britain while the German navy was in its current critical phase – big enough to attract curiosity from England, but small enough to be easily dispatched. Under the courtesy and smiling, ill-will towards Britain lurked everywhere at the German court, according to Anne Topham, the British governess who went to work for Wilhelm in 1902. While the English still thought they were 'admired and beloved' in Berlin, they were, she wrote, 'nothing of the kind. They were looked upon with suspicion and hatred as possible rivals, often with contempt as belonging to a nation whose glory was in decline, whose day was past.' In Germany, George seems to have been regarded as a rather blinkered nationalist – 'nothing but an English Jingo', as a German diplomat described him later that year, against which Wilhelm scribbled, 'Exactly.' He was known to have made tactless comments about the kaiser in the past, but it was obvious he felt none of his parents' heat about him, and May – half-German and anti-Russian – liked Wilhelm and the attention he showed her, though she also acknowledged that he sometimes made 'royalty ridiculous'. Wilhelm seems to have looked down slightly on his cousin – but then he looked down on many of his cousins. On the other hand, he didn't see him as a personal threat, and found it easy to be polite to him. 'Georgy', [sic] he wrote to Edward, left 'all safe and sound and we were very sorry to have to part so soon from such a merry and genial guest'.

Only a few days after George's visit however, on 30 January 1902, the British dropped a bombshell on the international community and revealed that they were signing a defensive alliance with Japan. The world – especially Russia and Germany – was extremely surprised. For decades Britain had kept aloof from such deals and its new ally Japan was regarded as a second-rung power, one of the 'yellow races' whom Wilhelm, with classic racist logic, claimed to despise while at the same time regarding the 'Yellow Peril' – it is to him that the phrase, so redolent of the turn-of-the-century fear and fascination of the East, is attributed – 'as the greatest danger threatening the white race'. Not that the British were immune to such views: the languidly sophisticated British prime minister, Arthur Balfour, did not consider the Japanese quite as 'civilized' as the British – though he would never have said so in public. However, they had a not inconsiderable navy and their proximity to China made the alliance a cheap way of defending British interests in the Far East against Russia, with whom the Japanese had repeatedly clashed over Manchuria and Korea. They were also sufficiently far away to make this first toe-in-the-water of alignment seem not too dramatic. The effects were gratifying. The Russians were both angry and rattled. Almost immediately Lamsdorff, the Russian foreign minister, promised the British that all Russian troops would be evacuated from Manchuria by 1903, and agreed to an open-door trading policy in China and Korea, which they had blocked for years. The Germans were taken aback that their negotiations with Britain had not been quite as centre stage, nor Britain quite as desperate or without friends, as they had imagined. Edward, as courteously as he could, had made sure that Wilhelm was the first foreign head of state to be informed about the defence treaty with Japan. Willy replied gracefully that his government regarded the new alliance as a 'guarantee of peace in the East' – though it was almost certainly not what they really thought.

As if to confirm that the British were indeed putting their house in order, in May the Boer War finally ground to its grim close. 'Thank God it is over at last,' George wrote in his diary. Almost immediately the British government handed over £3 million for reparations and the reconstruction of the two Boer states and promised their incumbents self-government within the British empire – a gesture which kick-started the country's international rehabilitation, but also signalled the pointlessness of the struggle, and prompted questions for the first time about whether the empire was costing Britain rather than enriching it. The cost had been monstrous. A fortune spent, the goodwill of Europe forfeited, the idea of Britain as both invulnerable and as a force for good blown out of the water, an estimated 75,000 dead – between 22,000 and 28,000 British soldiers, 7,000 Boer soldiers, 20,000 to 28,000 Boer civilians (of which the majority had been children under sixteen), somewhere between 14,000 and 20,000 non-combatant black Africans.

With the end of the war, it was assumed that the reasons for the hostility between Germany and Britain would diminish and calm down. After all the two nations still had close trading ties, many Germans and British attended the other country's universities, the British Left had closer relations with the German Social Democrats than any other European left-wing party, and of course there were the blood ties of the royal family. But in one section of the British press the antipathy did not go away. In the right-wing papers a new kind of story about Germany began to appear, suggesting that it had long-term hostile intentions against Britain, and noting with some anxiety that Germany was overtaking Britain: its population was bigger, its shipbuilding outstripping the British for the first time. The stories were true: by 1913, Germany would have a population of 65 million to Britain's 46 million; and while in 1870

Britain's GDP had been 40 per cent bigger than Germany's in 1870, by 1913 it would be 6 per cent smaller. More seriously, *The Times*'s Berlin correspondent, George Saunders, who had lived in Germany for years, was convinced that there was institutionalized ill-will towards Britain in the German government. Germany, Saunders told his editor, was 'a <u>new</u>, crude, ambitious, radically <u>unsound</u> Power', insidious in its methods: 'It is <u>not business</u>, it is <u>dining, shooting, toasts, finance, honours, marriages, dynastic friendships</u>. It is not hard Steel, like Joe Chamberlain . . . It is not <u>English</u>.' Saunders's coverage so alarmed Bülow that in mid-1902 the German government tried and failed to get the journalist recalled. The new German ambassador, Count Paul von Wolff Metternich zur Gracht, a rare Anglophile in the German diplomatic service, went to see Edward about it. The king, by way of response, waved a viciously anti-British German article which *The Times* had reprinted. In truth, he had been dismayed by *The Times*'s reporting, and had personally approached its editor to ask that coverage of Germany be modified, just as his mother had done five years before. To his quiet humiliation, the editor, Charles Moberly Bell, refused.

Seeds of concern about Germany had also begun to germinate in several government departments. The Admiralty called a conference in 1902 about Germany's suddenly expanding navy and what it was for. In the Home Office, Special Branch, the Metropolitan Police's intelligence unit, reported that German army intelligence had recently started to gather information on British coastal defences, when previously the Germans had freely swapped information on the Russians and the French. In the Foreign Office, Salisbury's former right-hand man, Thomas Sanderson, who had always felt Germany's posturing was more irritating than effective, observed glumly to his friend Francis Lascelles that he was starting to feel a 'settled dislike' and mistrust of Germany taking hold among the younger generation.

Wilhelm and Edward, meanwhile, went on demonstrating their amicability in public. In the autumn of 1902, against the advice of his entourage, Wilhelm invited the British 'hero' of the Boer War, Lord Roberts, to army manoeuvres, and declined to meet three

Boer War generals who toured the European capitals, an unpopular decision in Germany which irritated Bülow. Edward, whom Saunders considered too pro-German, invited Wilhelm to Sandringham for his birthday in November, and arranged for the kaiser's British regiment to be briefly stationed near Dover so he could inspect it.

The kaiser was shocked by the new strain of hostility he discovered in the British papers – though they gratifyingly still made a distinction between himself and the German government. His own welcome, as he told Bülow, had been 'as hearty and affectionate as ever', it was the chancellor and the government 'they would like to send to the devil'. He and George went out and shot 2,201 pheasants in one day. 'He made himself most agreable when he came here,' George told Nicholas. The interaction between the monarchs was as prickly as ever, though. When the king proudly showed off his new motor car, Wilhelm was keen to show off his own expertise. What did it run on? Edward – hating being made to feel ignorant by his nephew – had to admit he had no idea. Ah, potato spirit was the thing, Wilhelm announced. Far better than petrol. He promised – despite Edward's protestations – to have his experts whip up a sample by the end of the week. As Wilhelm departed, one German diplomat claimed to have heard Edward grunt, 'Thank God he's left.'

The strength of new anti-Germanism was made alarmingly evident at the end of 1902. The British and German governments sent a flotilla of warships to blockade the coast of Venezuela which – as South American states were wont to do – was threatening to renege on large debts it owed both countries. When members of the British government – Chamberlain, now rabidly anti-German – and the Conservative press led by *The Times*, kicked up a fuss, the British ships were almost immediately withdrawn. In fact the situation was more complicated than it looked: the Conservative administration was also bowing to American pressure to withdraw, and because it was very unpopular in the country, it felt more obliged than it otherwise might have to listen to its more right-wing elements; most Liberals were not opposed to working with the Germans. Then the same thing happened a few months later. The government organized a conference with the German government to arrange for British financiers to invest in the German-backed Baghdad railway, the right-wing press hissed again, and the government withdrew. The new British hostility wasn't helped when in February 1903 the *National Review*, the country's most passionately anti-German publication, published an article claiming that the previous summer, on board a yacht belonging to some rich Americans, the kaiser had launched into a stream of invective against Britain and his uncle, voicing his dislike 'with such brutal frankness' that his audience was shocked. The kaiser denied it, but even Lascelles, who vainly tried to minimize the damage – 'We should remember that he always exaggerates and that people who do not know him well are apt to misunderstand him' – believed it was true. There was another splurge of anti-German rhetoric in the British press, and this time the finger pointed at the kaiser and his new navy. 'There is a menace growing up in the east which cannot be ignored and which means that an adequate squadron must be at some strategical point in home waters,' reported the right-wing *Morning Post*, a paper which in the past had glowingly praised Wilhelm.

When relations with Britain were going badly it had now become almost a cliché that Germany would find itself getting on better with Russia, and so it proved. In September 1901, after nearly four years of frostiness on Russia's part, Wilhelm and Nicholas, with Bülow and Lamsdorff, had met in the North German town of Danzig. The Germans knew by now that the tsar found the kaiser difficult, and so Wilhelm's uncle, the Duke of Baden – to whom he was said occasionally to listen – had sat him down beforehand and carefully suggested that he must simply be friendly and make no obvious demands. It seemed to work. Nicholas wrote with some relief to his mother that Wilhelm was 'in good spirits, calm and very amiable'. He told Bülow he hoped the two countries would 'always fight shoulder to shoulder', and showed some keenness when the Germans proposed a continental league with France. Even better, the Russian press reported favourably on the meeting.

In fact, the original impetus for the Russian thaw had come not from Anglophobia but from a pragmatic financial calculation made by the new foreign minister, Count Vladimir Lamsdorff, who had taken over in June 1900, when Muraviev, aged fifty-five, had dropped dead. (Some said it was too much champagne, though it might as easily have been exhaustion; both his predecessors had keeled over in the job.) Lamsdorff, a short, shy man (he wore stacked heels), famous for his beautiful manners – one British diplomat called him 'the politest man in the world' – had spent his career as a backroom boy among the files of the Russian Foreign Ministry and had been deputy to the more showy but less knowledgeable Muraviev. He was also regarded within the Russian government as Sergei Witte's man. Like Witte, he believed that good relations with Germany were common sense, since Russia's defence of their mutual border now took a big bite out of its defence budget. In 1900 Russia had spent ten times more on the army than on education, and more on the navy than on the ministries of agriculture and justice put together. Before the lapse of the Russo-German Reinsurance Treaty in 1890 those sums had been almost negligible. It was obvious that better relations ought to have a tangible effect on Russia's defence budget.

Bülow was delighted. He'd been angling for the tsar and the kaiser to make up for years, though having shut Russian grain out of Germany with exceptionally high tariffs in order to please the Junker land-owning lobby in the Reichstag, he was as responsible as anyone for the deeper reasons for the rift between Russia and Germany.* As Russia's biggest-selling newspaper, *Novoe vremia*, observed, closer relations could hardly come about 'between peoples with tense economic relations'.

Wilhelm instantly took against Lamsdorff – as he had every Russian foreign minister since Lobanov – and made him the butt of his 'jokes' all through the meeting. It seemed the kaiser had envisaged himself and Nicholas putting the world to rights all by themselves, and resented the foreign minister's presence. Lamsdorff's discomfort – and it was considerable – was shared by

---

* While keeping the Reichstag Right happy, this policy, incidentally, had simultaneously alienated the German urban poor, who were voting in ever bigger numbers for the Socialists.

the entire imperial entourage who found meetings with the kaiser 'a thorough martyrdom'. He would lecture them on Russian ballet, ask them abrupt personal questions, or deliberately get their names wrong and laugh uproariously. Worse, he would play humiliating practical jokes on his own entourage in front of them – smacking his chief-of-staff on the bottom, or snipping someone's braces – so the Russians didn't know where to look. The minister of the court, Fredericks, said that every encounter with the kaiser left him 'a complete wreck'.

A few weeks later, to demonstrate his goodwill, Wilhelm rode across the Russian border to a small village called Wyshctyen, which had recently experienced a devastating fire. There, in the town square, he distributed several purses of money to the mostly Jewish inhabitants, and made a speech in German which none of the villagers understood. It was meant as a kindly gesture – though it's hard not to see it as an unconscious attempt to invade and usurp his fellow monarch's space – and Nicholas took it as such, though he apparently thought it rather odd.

From then on the relationship seemed to improve by leaps. In the spring of 1902, when the argument between Bülow and Chamberlain had caused such bitterness between Britain and Germany, Bülow sweetened the latest harsh rise in German tariffs on Russian grain with a large state loan to Russia of 2 million roubles. In August, when the Germans complained about the hostility of the British press, the two emperors again met on their yachts at the Estonian port city of Reval (present-day Tallinn) in the Russian Baltic states. Privately, it was not an encounter Nicholas was looking forward to. 'Be friendly and severe so that he realizes he dare not joke with you,' Alix told him before the meeting, 'and that he learns to respect you and be afraid of you – that is the Chief thing. How I wish I were with you.' On the day, Wilhelm referred to himself constantly as 'the Admiral of the Atlantic', and to Nicholas as 'the Admiral of the Pacific', which intensely irritated the tsar. As he departed on his yacht, Wilhelm signalled, 'The Admiral of the Atlantic bids farewell to the Admiral of the Pacific.' Nicholas muttered to his entourage, 'He's raving mad!' Once again the kaiser didn't help things by insulting

Lamsdorff, refusing to award him a decoration, the German Order of the Black Eagle, that he'd been promised. He claimed that Lamsdorff was intriguing against Germany,★ which made no sense as he had initiated the thaw between the two countries, and told Bülow that Nicholas disliked his foreign minister and he'd soon be sacked. 'I will arrange everything directly with the Tsar.'

This was familiar wishful thinking from Wilhelm, but he had touched on something true about Nicholas. After eight years as tsar, he was beginning to feel more confident, and since the beginning of 1902 had shown a marked disinclination to listen to his senior ministers. Having agreed to evacuate troops from Manchuria, and despite the increasingly perilous state of Russian finances, he stopped the evacuation, closed Russian-controlled ports to foreign trade, and took the control of Manchuria's civil and diplomatic administration out of the hands of Witte and Lamsdorff, giving it to a general, the ambitious but remarkably incompetent General Alekseev. This was an extraordinarily bad idea: the entire Manchurian plan had become an imperial vanity project which ate money. Between 1897 and 1903 Russia spent 1,141 million roubles on China – only slightly less than the entire state budget for 1903. It would make only one-tenth of that back in Chinese customs tariffs, and only a little more in selling Russian goods. It seems unlikely Nicholas had any notion of what a financial catastrophe Manchuria was, however. He had a very sketchy grasp of economics. He told Mossolov, who ran the tsar's chancellery, that he had no idea which was worth more, 25 roubles or a gold watch. (The watch was worth hundreds of roubles.) 'It is one of the big gaps in my education,' he said blithely, '. . . I don't know the price of things; I have never had reason to pay for anything myself.'

The Manchurian plan made Nicholas and his cohorts feel that Russia was still a Great Power – and made the British and every other Power with interests in China furious. The timing, however,

---

★ An ambitious Russian military attaché had been whispering against Lamsdorff to the Germans – but there was endemic intriguing at both the Russian and German courts, and Bülow considered the stories nonsense.

could hardly have been worse. There had been peasant risings and general strikes across Russia since the spring. Even the most fertile regions were in the grip of an agricultural crisis the government had no idea how to handle. In the towns, food prices were rising and living conditions were among the worst in the world. Assassinations of government officials had become endemic, the universities were in uproar. ('I am so sorry to see the Students have again been kicking up a row in the different universities,' George wrote to Nicholas in early 1902, 'as I know it must be a great worry to you.') At Easter a police-condoned pogrom in Kishinev in Bessarabia, in which a large number of Jews (estimates range from between forty-seven and 120) were murdered, caused such an international uproar that the Russian government felt obliged to publish an official condemnation. There were whispers – unfounded – that the tsar had been personally involved. Things had got so bad that Russia's great secular saint, Leo Tolstoy, wrote an open letter to the tsar, begging him to hear the suffering of his people and reconsider the whole basis of autocracy. Unsurprisingly, the missive merely irritated Nicholas; Tolstoy found himself excommunicated – which in turn made the government look vindictive and on the wrong side. In September Nicholas effectively sacked Sergei Witte, sidelining him to a powerless position on the Council of Ministers. Witte opposed the Far Eastern policy, and his economic policy had by no means been an unadulterated success, but he was also the only minister with any ideas on how to deal with the agricultural crisis. Witte's demotion left his rival Vyacheslav Plehve, the deeply repressive minister of the interior, as Nicholas's most senior and influential minister. The tsar was not just being inconsistent, he was actively playing one minister off against another in order to keep the upper hand.

Donald Mackenzie Wallace, the Russian-speaking former foreign editor of *The Times*, who had begun to send regular reports to Edward via his private secretary, Sir Francis Knollys, felt the Russian government was becoming 'more and more conservative', and lurching towards an atavistic anti-Westernism. The new line at the Russian court was, 'Russia ought not to adopt certain peculiarities of European Civilization which are generally supposed in Western Europe to be a symptom of national progress.' He thought the government was in 'chaos' however, and reported that his Russian friends predicted 'a great political change'.

By early 1903 Edward's public bonhomie had begun to win over the British public, and in the spring he finally made his great splash on the European stage. In March he set off on a five-week cruise to the Mediterranean, making stop-offs in Lisbon, Gibraltar, Malta, Sicily, Naples and Rome and, at his own instigation, a last-minute state visit to Paris. He refused to take a government minister with him, as was the custom, instead picking Sir Edward Hardinge, an ambitious young diplomat with good connections at court through his wife. In European terms it was as if Edward had got himself a diplomatic aide-de camp such as the kaiser might have, an act of self-assertion which the foreign secretary, Lansdowne, didn't much like. Hardinge was clever, confident, had a talent for pleasing the right people and, some said, 'an unbecoming degree of self regard'. He was part of a new generation in the Foreign Office which argued that Britain needed to rebuild its bridges with France and Russia, and ought to be wary of Germany. Edward's patronage would have a profound effect on his career: within three years, he would become successively ambassador to Russia and the senior civil servant at the Foreign Office.

The King set out on the *Victoria and Albert* with a small all-male party that included Fritz Ponsonby. The yacht was accompanied by eight battleships, four cruisers, four destroyers and a dispatch vessel, which slightly spoilt the effect when he insisted on drawing into Naples 'incognito'. Right from the start, however, it was clear that Edward had a flair and enthusiasm for this kind of project. Fritz Ponsonby was surprised to discover that he had 'made all the arrangements and supervised every detail'. In public Edward showed endless good humour, stood for hours, remembered names. He walked into the crowds and refused police protection. Everywhere he went, the public went wild, the press enthused. The Italians loved it – it was the first time a British monarch had visited since the Middle Ages. Little gestures brought the house down: in Rome, he stopped and bared his head as he went through the Porta Pia, and met the Pope – despite Balfour's suggestion that it would play badly back home.

Paris was the greatest success of all. It was actually the French foreign minister, Théophile Delcassé, who had proposed it. For two or three years he had been of the opinion that it was time to resolve the two countries' wearyingly long-standing quarrels. Germany was France's most dangerous European enemy, and antagonism with Britain, which had reached such a hysterical pitch over Fashoda, was a distraction France could do without. Lord Lansdowne, the British foreign secretary, could see the advantages of an accord with France. It would save Britain a great deal of money and end the quarrels about Egypt, but he was cautious. Public opinion in both countries was still very hostile to the other, to such an extent that the French approaches had been top secret, and the British cabinet needed to be won over. Delcassé believed a visit from Edward, Britain's most famous Francophile, might help the mood. Lansdowne was reluctant. He worried that Edward would be booed (he had no desire to travel himself); Balfour thought state visits accomplished nothing. The king, however, seems to have supported the idea of *rapprochement* from the first, and in March 1903 he decided he wanted to go to Paris. Bypassing both Lansdowne and the British ambassador in Paris – which neither man liked – Edward made the arrangements direct with the French president, Emile Loubet, via the British military attaché. The visit was kept secret until the last minute. 'Most of the suite,' Fritz Ponsonby recalled, 'had no idea where they were going.'

It was like a fairytale. The king arrived to boos and jeers. Crowds in the Champs Élysées shouted, 'Vive Fashoda' and even 'Vive Joan of Arc', which as Ponsonby nervously noted, 'seemed to be going back a long way in history'. The nationalist paper *L'Autorité* ran an open letter which began: 'Your presence in Paris shocks, offends and revolts us patriots . . .'; *La Patrie* enumerated every Anglo-French quarrel since the Middle Ages. By the time Edward left, three days later, the Paris crowds were cheering him frenziedly. He turned in a pitch-perfect performance – aided by the fact that the French government had made the second day of his visit a public holiday. The whole city turned out to see him, and the

Paris papers covered his every move in minute, breathless detail. In a perfect volte-face, they seemed simply to forget Fashoda and the Boers. Edward walked into the crowds, spoke in fluent French about how much he loved the city and how at home he felt there, looked constantly delighted. Parisians, who like so many in Europe felt a curious combination of fascination and dislike for Britain, had long harboured a soft spot for an English 'milord', and though he hadn't been back since the mid-1890s, Edward had had the equivalent of film-star glamour ever since he had pursued actresses there in the 1860s.

After Paris, Edward went to Dublin and then to Vienna, to meet Emperor Franz Joseph. Though they had almost nothing in common – Franz Joseph was well-known for rising at 4 a.m., eating his lunch at twelve, his dinner at five and being in bed by seven; Edward had barely drunk his first cup of coffee by ten – Edward admired the Hapsburg emperor. He had chosen to place himself above the general mêlée of politics, embracing the role of a ceremonial and dutiful leader, and was almost universally respected. His famous inscrutability probably made Edward want to charm him all the more.

From Vienna, the king progressed to Marienbad, the most fashionable spa in Europe, a diplomatic bazaar of princes, aristocrats, statesmen and dieters, made more so by Edward's subsequent annual visits. There he networked, cut a figure and was followed everywhere by thrilled crowds. Few other royals had Edward's appetite for being in public – Wilhelm was almost the only one. 'I can still remember Uncle Bertie sitting unperturbed in front of his hotel,' Nicholas's sister Olga later wrote, 'puffing a cigar while hordes of Germans stood staring at him with awe and curiosity. "How can you stand it, Uncle Bertie?" I asked him one day. "Why, it's as much entertainment for me to stare at them as it is for them to stare at me," the King replied.'

Wilhelm watched Edward's success with growing jealousy and irritation. Within days of the king's departure from Rome in April 1903, he arrived, announcing that *he* too had come to see the Pope – Bülow putting it about, a little too insistently perhaps, that the trip had been planned for months. When Edward left Vienna,

there once again was Wilhelm on his way to see his old friend
Franz Joseph. The one place Edward failed to visit was Berlin – he
said he was too busy. The truth was that when it came to Wilhelm,
his bonhomie failed him. Wilhelm made a scene to the latest British
military attaché, who gloried in the name of Colonel Wallscourt
Hely-Hutchinson Waters, listing his myriad acts of sacrifice for
Britain, and said how wounded he was that Germany had been
excluded from the king's favour.

In October, seething with resentment of Edward, Wilhelm
waylaid Nicholas on his annual visit to Hesse. Revealing a pleasing
anxiety about the direction of Anglo-French relations, Nicholas
told Wilhelm that 'he had to keep up relations with France and
prevent them from joining the English'. Afterwards, Wilhelm
wrote to Nicholas. The world was polarizing, he said, the 'democratic countries governed by Parliamentary majorities, against the
Imperial monarchies'. In April the following year, when Britain
and France signed the Entente Cordiale, his words rang only too
true.

Although it was essentially an agreement about colonial disputes,
particularly in Egypt, where France acknowledged Britain's dominant influence, and in Morocco, where Britain reciprocated, the
Entente Cordiale couldn't but seem a great sea change in Anglo-
French relations. It promised a new era of cooperation between
the two major democratic powers in Europe, it appeared to set
aside a thousand years of hostility, and it was hard not to feel that
it owed more than a little to each country's suspicions of Germany.
Though he had taken no role at all in the negotiations nor had
invented the policy, Edward was given much of the credit for the
Entente, and he showed no inclination to disabuse anyone of the
notion. The miraculous turnaround his visit to Paris had caused
was certainly an amazing public relations coup and a catalyst for
serious negotiations. It helped to convince the doubters in the
British cabinet. But if Delcassé and Lansdowne hadn't been ready
to get down to serious talks, the effect of the visit, like so many
royal visits such as the king's subsequent trip to Dublin that year,
would have been negligible. To illustrate Edward's new status,
Count Osten Sacken, the Russian ambassador in Berlin, sent to

the Russian Foreign Office a summary of an article in the German magazine *Der Tag* published just after the Entente was made public in April 1904. It said that Edward, once 'regarded with scepticism', was now held up 'as one of the wisest state figures of our time. Having made a clever use of circumstances, King Edward has managed to restore England's prestige as the master of Europe's fate.' It was painful irony, the piece added, that Bülow's failed attempts to promote German interests 'had greatly contributed' to this. 'Germany has failed to secure its interests in either the Persian Gulf, the Far East, or the Northern Coast of Africa.'

In little over a year Edward established himself as the face of British foreign policy, as well as the most glamorous monarch in Europe. He at last looked effective and successful. He enjoyed his newfound reputation, and it had its uses for Britain. The country needed a front man in Europe, and Edward fitted the role perfectly. With the exception of Chamberlain – who would resign from the government in 1903 to campaign and waste the rest of his career on the excitingly named tariff reform – the British government was notably lacking in charismatic public figures or statesmen who took talking to the public seriously. Lansdowne didn't travel and his only foreign language was French. His successor, Sir Edward Grey, was even less inclined to travel. Both would be increasingly swamped with the sheer volume of Foreign Office paperwork. Frederick Ponsonby believed that the foreign secretary resented the credit the king was given for work that Lansdowne had actually done; on the other hand, he was happy to exploit the access and influence the king's new reputation offered. When, in late 1903, Lansdowne decided that there was nothing to be lost by suggesting a similar Entente to Russia, Edward was brought in to make sure the proposals got through to Nicholas personally. Everyone knew the tsar was hard to get at. The king also charmed the new Russian ambassador, Count Alexander Benckendorff, whom he invited to Windsor, spoke to of his enthusiasm for the proposal, and asked back to play bridge. After the Entente Cordiale was announced, it was Edward who went round Europe reassuring the various monarchs and presidents that it had only peaceful implications.

Historians still argue over Edward's contributions to foreign

policy. Sentimental monarchists invariably overestimate his importance. Brisk political historians dismiss him as a genial sybarite who
was surrounded by an efficient circle of aides, such as Knollys and
Hardinge, who managed him. Arthur Balfour's words to Lord
Lansdowne after Edward died are often quoted, 'So far as I can
remember, during the years which you and I were Ministers, he
never made an important suggestion of any sort on large questions
of policy.' Policy was never what Edward was about. Sir Edward
Grey was nearer to the mark when he wrote that while Edward
was not one for 'long sustained discussion about large aspects of
policy', he had a remarkable abilty for 'projecting his personality
over a crowd', and a real talent for personal relationships. His effect
was almost Reaganite. There is also a whiff of jealousy about
Balfour's words – his time as prime minister, as it happened, had
had less-than-glowing reviews. The truth was that Edward could
be selfish, lazy, indulgent, trivial. He was a conventional thinker
and an amateur. But within his own limitations and because of
the needs of the time, he made a significant contribution to the
furtherance of British foreign policy, the consequences of which
would be by no means all benevolent.

11. Unintended consequences (1904–5)

For Russia, even more than for most countries, war had often proved disastrous. The Crimean War and the Russo-Turkish War of the 1870s had been disasters. Both had left Russia in debt and near-bankrupt, had crippled development, created internal disaffection and lasting hostility with foreign powers. The government and its institutions were in no state to bear the strains of war, and unlike, say, Britain, the country couldn't bear the expense. It was a lesson the Russian government would have done well to remember before it found itself at war with Japan in February 1904.

The two countries had clashed over rival claims to Korea – the country, connected like a small appendix to the edge of Northern China, which lay between Siberia and Japan – and Manchuria. In fact most Russian government ministers opposed the war, while the court hailed it. Nicholas was in constant denial about the ricketiness of Russia's institutions. The tsar had told his war minister the year before that he dreamed of extending the Russian empire to China, Tibet, Afghanistan and Persia – and his actions had directly contributed to the hostilities. He had taken the running of the Far East out of the hands of his ministers and put it under the command of the hawkish and incompetent General Alekseev – who was said to owe his senior position in the army to having rescued Nicholas's favourite uncle, Grand Duke Alexis, from a French brothel. He had given policy-making to a 'special committee', a group of inexperienced, over-excited court aristocrats who included his own cousin Sandro, who wanted to annex Korea. And whether deliberately or through sheer incompetence, he'd allowed pre-war negotiations with the Japanese to descend into insults. According to Edward VII, whose country had an alliance with Japan, the tsar had rejected his personal attempts to bring about a diplomatic resolution.

The truth was the Russians expected to beat the Japanese. No Great Power had ever been defeated by a minor one, certainly not one with an army as huge as Russia, and most Russians regarded the Japanese as an 'inferior race': Nicholas referred to them as 'little short-tailed monkeys'. The head of the army in Manchuria, General Alekseev, claimed that he needed only two Russian soldiers for every three Japanese. In the world of the Great Powers, making an aggressive demonstration seemed a sure way – and perhaps an overly easy one – of reminding everyone of, or even restoring, one's status, especially when one felt insufficiently respected.

When the Japanese sent torpedo boats into Port Arthur, Russian military headquarters in China, in February 1904, and sank the two most modern ships in the whole Russian navy, then declared war, the entire government and military seemed completely surprised and unprepared. The government found out only when Sergei Witte was informed by a telephone call from a Russian trader in Port Arthur. The Russian war effort went downhill from there. Defeat followed defeat. At every turn the conflict exposed the staggering incompetence of overstretched Russian institutions – the army in particular. War planning had been virtually non-existent. Russian generals, whose average age was sixty-nine, spent more time infighting than actually fighting. The conflict would cost 2 billion roubles – all the money Witte had saved up to stabilize the Russian economy. Even then, there wasn't enough to give the soldiers hot breakfasts, or supply them with powder for their guns. Despite an early surge of patriotic enthusiasm, support for the war soon began to haemorrhage. By May 1904 the new British ambassador in St Petersburg, Sir Charles Hardinge, Edward's former protégé, reported that 75 per cent of the population were 'absolutely indifferent' to the war, and most of the educated classes were furious at the incompetence and expense; rising opposition was making itself felt in a series of assassinations of hated senior officials.

One predictable consequence of the war was an outbreak of virulent Anglophobia in Russia. It was almost too easy to blame Russia's disasters on Britain's secret support of its ally. At court,

Nicholas and the pro-war clique around him fulminated against Britain. The tsar took to referring to the English as 'zhids' – Jews. Sandro, the tsar's cousin, muttered darkly about the 'British-built battleships of the Mikado', and in St Petersburg the British ambassador was boycotted by society. Wilhelm, so good at spotting his fellow monarch's vulnerabilities, had been writing to Nicholas since 1903 informing him that the British were helping with 'the Japanese mobilization'. He sent copies of British newspaper articles demanding the government help plucky Japan against the beastly Russian leviathan. 'To us . . . this hypocrisy and hatred is utterly odious and incomprehensible,' he wrote. 'Everybody here understands perfectly that Russia is following the laws of expansion.'

The war demonstrated the ambivalence of British feelings towards Russia too. The British government initially worried that the war would destroy the Entente by forcing France and Britain to back their allies, but at the same time toyed with helping the Japanese. It had hoped the Entente Cordiale would bring Britain closer to Russia, but now also hoped the war would disrupt Russia in Asia. In the end Britain, like France, had agreed on friendly neutrality. As Balfour said, even if Japan was beaten – as the British at first assumed it would be – 'nothing could be better for us than that Russia should involve herself in the expense and trouble of a Corean [sic] adventure'. But to cover their bets, Edward, at Lansdowne's suggestion, sent a personal message to Nicholas guaranteeing British goodwill and non-intervention. The British version of 'friendly neutrality' didn't seem particularly friendly. Russian ships were refused access to British ports around the world to refuel. The Entente Cordiale, announced in April 1904, looked to the now-harassed and vulnerable Russians like an attempt to snatch France away from them. And just as Russia had exploited British vulnerability during the Boer War, now the Viceroy of India, Lord Curzon, sent a military force to Tibet, led by the British soldier and explorer Sir Francis Younghusband, in March 1904.

Wilhelm, by contrast, was only too eager to help his Russian cousin. He offered Nicholas the use of German coaling stations, while telling him repeatedly that the British were pressuring him not to. He promised to 'guarantee' the Russian Western Front from attack. German support came at a price, however: Bülow demanded an enormous hike in the German tariffs on Russian imports.

Lord Lansdowne, the British foreign secretary, who after his agreements with Japan and France had gained a reputation as an adept international player, still saw an Entente-like agreement on colonial issues with Russia as an appealing prospect. A bad war might produce a Russia so chastened that it would at last succumb to British overtures. He recruited Edward to massage his Russian relatives. Through the spring and summer of 1904 the king ener-getically – as energetically as a very large 62-year-old man could manage – demonstrated his goodwill. He wrote to Nicholas to reassure him about the Entente, and offered himself as a mediator with Japan – an offer Nicholas unsurprisingly turned down. In Copenhagen with Alexandra, Edward spotted Count Alexander Izvolsky, Russian minister to Denmark,★ a coming man in Russian politics, not least because he was known to enjoy the patronage of Minny – she may possibly have tipped the king off about him. Izvolsky, like most of Nicholas's leading government ministers, opposed the war with Japan; he also saw an agreement with Britain as a future necessity for peace. And he was *very* ambitious. The king expressed his desire for an agreement, and Izvolsky showed him a copy of the extravagantly flattering letter he planned to send to Lamsdorff about their meeting: that Edward's views on a deal with Russia were so important 'that I ought to transmit them to Your Excellency as verbatim as possible', and attributing the Entente Cordiale 'above all to the great personal influence of his Majesty'. When Hardinge took over as ambassador in St Petersburg in May, the king gave him a letter for Nicholas which personally recommended Izvolsky as 'a man of remarkable intelligence and . . . I am sure, one of your ablest and most devoted Servants'. He added that it was his 'earnest desire . . . that at the conclusion of the war our two countries may come to a satisfactory settlement

★ Only the Great Powers were regarded as important enough to deserve 'ambassadors', smaller countries made do with 'ministers'.

regarding many difficult matters'. And when on 30 July, at the imperial couple's summer residence of Peterhof, just after the soup, 32-year-old Alix finally gave birth to a baby boy, Alexis, Edward proposed himself as godfather.

While war continued there could be no real resolution. Edward's patronage might give Hardinge entrées to the highest Russian social circles, including to the imperial couple themselves. '. . . I am looked upon as the bearer of an olive branch,' he told the king. But when Russian warships from the Black Sea sailed into the Suez Canal and began to seize British cargo ships, claiming they were carrying contraband bound for Japan, the British press howled, and Lansdowne threatened reprisals if the ships weren't released.* And in September 1904, late at night, Hardinge discovered an intruder hiding under a sofa in the embassy drawing room, and almost killed him with a curtain pole. It transpired it was one of the footmen trying to break into the embassy safe in order to find evidence that England was helping the Japanese. The tsar, moreover, Hardinge observed, was utterly committed to the war with Japan, and surrounded himself with Anglophobes. The same month, having killed a couple of thousand Tibetans, the Younghusband expedition signed a deal with the rulers of Tibet guaranteeing trading concessions and the exclusion of other powers – Russia specifically. The Russian press breathed fire. In Britain the expedition had been extremely controversial. Since the Boer War the country's 'right' to murder a few natives in the prosecution of its business was no longer felt to be a given – but Edward, the alleged champion of a Russian *rapprochement*, met Younghusband and told him, 'I approve of all you did.'

For the Germans, news from St Petersburg of Edward's overtures to the Russians suddenly cast the Entente Cordiale in a rather different light. Though some German observers had seen it as a

---

* The situation was resolved only when the Americans and Germans began to complain that the Russian definition of contraband – which turned out to be just about anything that could be put on a boat – was too elastic and they wanted their ships back too.

dangerous shift, Bülow had initially decided to be unconcerned by it — it was, after all, a purely colonial agreement — and he told the kaiser that it couldn't last. He may also have thought that anything which might alienate Russia from France was to the good. Now British diplomacy — and Edward's efforts — didn't look so innocuous. Wilhelm began to complain that Edward seemed to want alliances with everyone except him.

To mitigate his nephew's frequently expressed feelings of rejection, Edward agreed to attend the Kiel regatta in June 1904. Regarded by both sides as a chance to relieve some of the friction between the king and the kaiser, and between England and Germany, the visit would have one big unintended consequence.

Preparations for the visit were epic. It was apparent to Wilhelm's entourage that, however much he might dislike his uncle, the kaiser was painfully desperate to impress him. An observant new comptroller of the imperial household, Robert zu Zedlitz-Trützschler, kept a diary in which he confided his daily amazement at the excesses of the large child whose household he managed. 'The importance the Emperor attached to this visit was extraordinary,' he wrote. 'He interfered with the smallest details of decoration.' The *Hohenzollern* was decked out with great canopies and spouting water features. Every cabinet minister was present, every secretary of state, and 'a whole troop of Excellencies, magnificent in Orders and gold braid, were arranged in a dignified row along the shore. All the Royal Princes had been ordered to swell the Guard of Honour.' Wilhelm grew so overexcited that he put on his parade uniform hours in advance and paced the deck 'hardly able to wait for the appointed time'. When Edward did arrive, Bülow later cruelly remembered, Wilhelm looked agitated, while Edward appeared positively serene. He was at his zenith: even to Wilhelm's people his glamour seemed palpable. He was a 'man of the world, ten times tried in the furnace, who had every move of the game at his finger tips', Zedlitz-Trützschler wrote. Wilhelm by contrast was an 'idealistic big child, who had grown up with none but flatterers about him in ignorance of the world'. The king's private life might be open to criticism, 'but to-day he has all the glamour of a personality that has gained the high esteem of his country. I believe that he has acquired in his life an experience of the world such as seldom falls to the lot of a royal personage. He has a keen knowledge of men, the value of which for a prince cannot be overestimated.'

Edward talked about peace – 'a universal necessity', he said, 'since all countries groan alike under the burden of their armaments taxations' – and the peaceful aims of the Entente. His 'one desire', he added, was 'to reduce all points of frictions between the Great Powers'. Wilhelm wrote, 'Bertie's visit is going, of course, off well,' experiencing that surge of desire to have a real relationship with his uncle that often occurred when they first met. 'He is very lively and active and most kind. His wish for peace is quite pronounced as is his motive for his liking to offer his services wherever he sees collisions in the world.'

But everyone knew the amicability was phoney. 'Everyone is pretending that we are on the best possible terms with England. As a matter of fact, however, all the differences between the English and the German people remain as they were,' Zedlitz-Trützschler wrote. The smiling veneer between the two monarchs cracked just once. They disagreed volubly on the Russian-Japanese War. Wilhelm talked about the 'Yellow Peril' and how it must be crushed. Edward said there was no such thing. The Japanese were morally in the right, Nicholas had rejected their diplomatic approaches, and they had done brilliantly. They were 'a brave, chivalrous and intelligent people – every bit as civilized as Europeans from whom nothing except the colour of their skins distinguishes them'. Bülow observed that Edward spoke of the tsar 'with all the affection of a kinsman', and noted how much he enjoyed giving his German nephew a 'rap on the knuckles'.

Wilhelm, meanwhile, simply couldn't resist the urge to impress Edward. Tirpitz and Bülow would have preferred the visit to take place almost anywhere in the world rather than at Kiel, which was where the German navy was being built. They had tried to extract a promise from the kaiser that he would curb his wish to show off how it had grown, and that its expansion would be played down as much as possible. But the night before the naval review, he personally instructed his naval cabinet to send 'everything, down to the smallest boat' to Kiel. At a gala dinner for 180 the next day, he drew attention to how large the navy had grown, observing to his audience that King Edward had 'been greeted by the thunder of guns of the German fleet'. And with tears in his eyes he described how his desire to build a navy had been born when he had visited Portsmouth as a child: 'There awoke in me the wish to build ships of my own like these some day.'

The new German navy certainly impressed the British spectators – but not in a good way. In his memoirs Bülow wrote that the king warned him there was a growing 'conviction in England that the Germans are only building their navy with the intention of falling on England as soon as they have made it strong enough, of ruining her for ever, either by breaking her commerce or even by an invasion'. Naturally, *he* didn't think this but, since England's safety depended on her fleet, the British Admiralty would always build two new English ships for every new German one. It was advice which Bülow and Tirpitz might have done well to take. Among Edward's party was Lord Selbourne, First Lord of the Admiralty – who in 1902 had written a cabinet paper arguing that the German navy was being expanded to target the Royal Navy – and Louis of Battenburg who ran British naval intelligence. A month after the visit, Selbourne gave his formal support to radical plans to update and expand the Royal Navy, drawn up by the energetic, eccentric and increasingly anti-German Admiral Jackie Fisher. The plans included the commissioning of the Dreadnought, a new species of enormous battleship which would render all other warships obsolete, and which in turn would spawn a new, paranoid and vastly expensive wave of rivalrous ship building in Britain and Germany.

The bad feeling between Britain and Russia reached a crisis on 21 October 1904 after the Russian fleet fired on a small flotilla of fishing boats from Hull, sinking two boats and killing two fishermen. Nicholas had ordered the Russian Baltic fleet to travel round the world to the Pacific to replace the Russian Pacific fleet, which had been destroyed by the Japanese. The Russian admiral in charge panicked and failed to stop to pick up survivors, or to inform his own government. Edward, who heard the news as he was watching his horses at Newmarket racecourse, fired off splutteringly angry letters to Lansdowne demanding satisfaction: 'Mere apologies to us will not suffice. Some punishment must be meted out to the Russian officers,' he wrote. He sent a telegram to Nicholas telling him what a 'painful impression' the squadron's failure to stop had caused. The Russians were irritatingly impenitent. The British refusal to allow Russian ships into their ports was making the fleet's journey much harder, and St Petersburg was in the grip of a Japanese spy scare. There had been rumours that Japanese torpedo boats were shadowing the Baltic fleet – which was why the warships had been so trigger-happy. 'These suspicions,' one Russian minister wrote years later, 'of course, existed only in imagination,' but the government couldn't shake off the thought that the British were somehow colluding with the Japanese. Nicky insisted to Edward that the Japanese had been 'luring' the fishing boats to camouflage their torpedo boats. Even the usually pragmatic Lamsdorff charged round to the British embassy and accused Hardinge of 'English perfidy'. 'The politest man in the world was nearly rude to me,' Hardinge wrote. 'If they imagined they were Japanese destroyers,' George told his father, 'all I can say is they must have been drunk or else they must have been in such a state that they are not fit to go to sea in Men of War.'

For five days the atmosphere between the two countries was extremely tense. 'The English are very angry and nearly at boiling point,' Nicky told his mother. 'They are even said to be getting their fleet ready for action. Yesterday, I sent a telegram to Uncle Bertie expressing my regret, but I did not apologize – I do not think the English will have the cheek to go further than to indulge in threats.' Lamsdorff, however, apologized to Hardinge for having lost his temper. Angry as they were, the Russians could not afford another enemy. In the meantime, Edward, taken aback by a violent British press reaction, calmed down. 'Strongly deprecate pressuring for punishment of Admiral. Russia could not accept such a humiliation,' he telegraphed Lansdowne, and Nicky had 'a violent military party to contend with'. In a face-saving move, the Russians suggested the matter be taken to arbitration at The Hague, and eventually paid £65,000 in damages.

Escalation had been avoided, but Nicholas was still furious. 'I have no words to express my indignation with England's conduct,' he wrote to Wilhelm, who had been terribly sympathetic. British public opinion seemed to overwhelm the 'more reasonable attitude of her government', Nicholas wrote. British attempts to stop Germany from coaling Russian ships were indefensible. 'It is certainly high time to put a stop to this. The only way as You say would be that Germany, Russia and France should at once unite upon an agreement to abolish Anglo-Japanese arrogance and insolence. Would you like to lay down and frame the outlines of such a treaty and let me know it?'

Wilhelm didn't need telling twice. Two days later he sent Nicholas a draft treaty, assuring him that it was entirely secret – though in fact Bülow had written it. He added that a 'private source' had assured him that the Hull fishing fleet *had* seen foreign vessels – 'So there has been foul play.' The alliance, he told Nicholas, would be 'purely defensive, exclusively directed against a European aggressor or aggressors . . . a mutual fire insurance company against incendiaries'. The gist of it was that if either country was attacked by a third European power, the other would come to the aid of their ally with all their forces, though they both knew it was really directed against Britain.

The treaty, however, left many questions unanswered. What if France attacked Germany or Austria Russia? Within a couple of weeks both sides were hesitating. Nicholas wanted to show it to the French before he signed it. Wilhelm said no, the French president and foreign minister 'not being Princes or Emperors I am unable to place them . . . on the same footing as you my equal'. Then he told Nicholas he was worried the British might see the treaty as 'direct provocation'. The two monarchs exchanged urgent assurances of their absolute loyalty to each other, and the whole idea was dead before Christmas.

One reason was that Wilhelm had fallen into the grip of a paranoid conviction that Britain was about to attack Germany.

Since Edward's 1904 visit to Kiel, the British had been increasingly sensitive to the growth of the new German navy. In fact, the new First Sea Lord, the excitable Admiral Jackie Fisher, who had taken up his post in October on the day of the Dogger Bank incident, had made a speech advocating 'Copenhagening', i.e. making a pre-emptive strike on, the German fleet. Fisher was known to be capable but eccentric, and though the government clearly didn't approve, the right-wing press did. Then after the Russians agreed to arbitration, the British papers suddenly turned on Germany, accusing its government of inciting the Russians against Britain. Incitement was precisely what Wilhelm had been engaging in. He seems to have worried that his letters to Nicholas had leaked out. In November he told his entourage that he was 'convinced that it is England's aim to bring a serious conflict about'. It was certainly now accepted by Wilhelm's officials that, as Bülow said, the British were 'absolutely apprised of his habit of stirring behind their back'.

'The Emperor has often . . . expressed himself without restraint, not to say vulgarly, about their Majesties,' Zedlitz-Trützschler wrote, 'and this naturally has come to their ears.' As if to confirm this, Edward told the French ambassador in mid-November that he knew all about his nephew's intriguing, especially with Russia, and had been writing to the tsar to counteract it. The kaiser's anxiety may also have derived from his own guilty, vivid, destructive fantasies about England. In early December he told his entourage he had dreamed of the Russian Baltic fleet arriving in Asia and descending on British India.

The other reason the German-Russian treaty idea lapsed was that by Christmas Russia was in absolute crisis. Nicky's cousin Grand Duke Konstantin wrote in his diary that the country was like a piece of cloth 'that is beginning to rip up and tear along the seams'. The war was an ongoing disaster. Port Arthur surrendered to the Japanese after a 156-day siege on 21 December 1904 (2 January 1905 in the Russian calendar). 'A terrible and painful event,' Nicky wrote. '. . . It is the will of God!' Two weeks later, the imperial guard shot into a large, peaceful demonstration of workers and their families gathered in front of the Winter Palace to deliver a petition begging the tsar to help them and support their pleas for workers' rights. They killed about 1,000 people. 'A terrible day', Nicholas, who had absented himself and given permission for the troops to shoot, wrote in his diary, but '. . . the troops had to shoot'. Even the ever-tactful Hardinge couldn't disguise his disgust for the Winter Palace massacre. It was, he wrote, 'indisputable' that the crowd was 'both peaceful and harmless'. He recalled the 'tragic' men who had stood for hours in the freezing cold bare-headed, 'for fear that the "little Father" might look from the window and see them standing in the street with their hats on'. He thought the emperor had 'missed the chance of his lifetime . . . if he had received at the Winter Palace a small deputation and promised to give them what has sincerely been promised to them in his name, he would have obtained the undying loyalty and admiration of the lower classes'. The Winter Palace massacre was the moment in Russia when the loyalty of even those with a stake in the system broke irretrievably. It was an occasion when Edward did not send messages of support. Wilhelm, however, did. 'I am glad your soldiers showed themselves reliable and true to their service to their sermon [*sic*]* to the Emperor.' But later he too suggested that Nicholas might have done things differently: he should have showed himself to the crowd – as Wilhelm himself loved to do – 'such an appearance would have calmed the masses'.

After the Winter Palace massacre Nicholas met a small, carefully chosen delegation of workers and told them they had been 'duped' by 'the traitors and enemies of the country', and that they must have 'patience and consideration for their employers'. By the end of January 1905, 400,000 workers were on strike in the environs of St Petersburg. In February Nicholas's Uncle Sergei, the now utterly loathed governor-general of Moscow, was blown up in his coach. His boots, apparently, were the only bits that remained intact. The country was in revolution, but 'the Tsar viewed the internal tumult rather indifferently; he . . . kept repeating that it had spread over only a very small part of the country and could not be very significant'. Nothing, indeed, seemed to penetrate the

---

* He probably meant *serment*, which is French for 'oath'.

carapace of the emperor's inscrutability and received ideas. 'He lets everything unpleasant run off him,' the latest interior minister sighed exasperatedly. Hardinge was amazed at how even the terrible defeat at Mukden in February 1905 – 90,000 casualties – seemed to have no effect on him. The rest of the world, meanwhile, adjusted itself to the fact that a Great Power was on the way to being beaten by a second-rank one.

The British ambassador told Edward that the tsar was almost preposterously out of touch. 'I feel very sorry for the Emperor and Empress,' he wrote to Knollys, the king's secretary. 'They live at Tsarskoe Selo in a world apart, and are almost like prisoners since it is not considered safe to come even to St Petersburg.' The fences around Tsarskoe selo had risen higher and higher, until by July 1905 the barbed wire was ten foot high and accompanied by spiked railings. It looked 'like some zoo enclosure for wild beasts'. 'I often wonder,' he added, 'whether the Emperor realizes upon what a volcano he is living – I am told he never speaks of either the war or the internal state of the country if he can help doing so, but that he seems perfectly happy, interesting himself in all sorts of trivial affairs and that the Empress is beaming with happiness.' It had also been remarked that the empress was exercising increasing influence on the emperor, urging him – with all the zeal of a convert – never to give way, and fixing him with 'her fierce stare' if she felt he might be weakening. When asked by English visitors, as she often was, about the state of Russia, the empress, who had been raised in one of the most liberal states in Germany, would say that the 'illiterate Russian' was simply not ready for 'freedom of thought'.

Behind his habitual inscrutability, Nicholas felt utterly confused and powerless. He seethed and blamed his ministers. 'It makes me sick to read the news,' he wrote to his mother. 'Strikes in school and factories, murdered policemen, Cossacks, riots. But the Ministers instead of acting with quick decision, only assemble in council like a lot of frightened hens and cackle.' But there were other reasons why he seemed so oddly detached from events outside Tsarskoe selo. The excitement of his son Alexis's birth had given way to anxiety when it was discovered six weeks later that the child was haemophiliac – his blood wouldn't clot, or at least could take days to do so. Small knocks and tumbles produced ugly dark blue swellings on the boy's body, and terrible pain. The gene came from Queen Victoria and within the extended royal family of Europe the subject seems to have been unmentionable, even though the queen's youngest son, Leopold, had died of it, as had one of Alix's brothers and a nephew. As a father and husband, Nicholas was tirelessly supportive, giving, warm and loving. The contrast between his sensitive responses within his little domestic world and his blinkered insensitivity beyond it is almost painful to observe. Fatefully, the couple decided to keep the illness a secret. Doctors were sworn to silence; palace servants weren't told what was wrong with Alexis, they had to work it out for themselves. The imperial couple's instinctive tendency to keep the world at arm's length, together with court etiquette which forbade the discussion of the health of the royal family, convinced them not to reveal the problem. They may also have worried that if Alexis's situation was known, it would call into question his suitability as heir. George and May took a similar decision some years later when they discovered their youngest son, John, a year younger than Alexis, was epileptic, and probably also what we would now call autistic. George knew that Alexis was prone to illness, but he appears never to have mentioned John to Nicholas at all; the child seems not to have been present when the Romanovs came to visit the Isle of Wight in 1909. Either way, the decision to keep up appearances, somehow so characteristic of *fin de siècle* royalty, might have denied the imperial family much sympathy and support they might otherwise have enjoyed.

It was only after the Baltic fleet, having steamed around the world, was annihilated by the Japanese at Tsushima, the largest sea battle since Trafalgar, at the end of May 1905, that Nicholas reluctantly agreed to a peace conference. Acknowledging defeat was a prospect he could hardly bear. 'All reports seem to agree that he is for continuing the war at all costs,' Hardinge wrote. 'The Government and the great majority of the people are strictly in favour of peace.' Several weeks later Hardinge reported that the governing classes had been thrown into utter panic by the Potemkin mutiny. They had assumed that as long as the army and navy could be relied on, 'the agitation and disturbance throughout the country presented no real danger to the dynasty'. Sedition, he added, was rife. A Russian officer friend told him that 'they would have got rid of the Emperor long ago if there had only been a capable Grand Duke to take his place'. Even as he agreed to the peace conference, Nicholas was talking of sending another 200,000 men to Manchuria, and in August told his ministers that St Seraphim had appeared to him in a dream to let him know that Russia would defeat Japan and Britain and emerge stronger than ever. 'Such nonsense is incredible,' Hardinge commented drily, 'but the Emperor is known to be mystic and all things are consequently possible.'

Nicholas stalled, but in the autumn sent Sergei Witte to the peace conference at Portsmouth, New Hampshire, brokered by President Roosevelt, who complained all the way through of Russia's chaotic behaviour and 'literally fathomless mendacity'. Russia continued in free fall. What had gone wrong was not all Nicholas's fault – the military had been degraded over decades, the hunger for imperial success as a salve for internal failure was deep-rooted across the whole governing and educated class, the institutions of government had long been incapable of running the country, repression had long been a substitute for real governance, and such a large and complex state simply couldn't run properly with one man making all the decisions. But Nicholas, the wrong man at the wrong time, by taking his country into a war it couldn't afford and could have avoided, by encouraging the system's repressions, by allowing his personal revulsion to reform to trump reality, had certainly helped to bring his country to crisis.

It was something Wilhelm never really wanted to do that brought his relationship with Edward to its absolute nadir. On 31 March 1905, in the midst of a Mediterranean cruise, the kaiser made an unscheduled visit to Tangier, on the northernmost tip of Morocco, which France was trying secretly to turn into a French protectorate. The plan, hatched by Bülow and Holstein, was to make a demonstration of German force to frighten France while its ally Russia was busy, humiliate France and perhaps elicit a concession or two, and create division in the Entente – the British, they believed, would not sweep to France's defence, because its underhand attempts to gain control broke international agreements and because Germany would look as if it meant business. The idea was that if Germany appeared dangerous and threatening enough – willing to risk even war – everyone else would back down. It seemed a perfect example of what Bülow had intended 'Weltpolitik' to be. As an attempt to gain face and status, it was not unlike Russia's initial almost enthusiastic dive into the Japanese War; like that conflict, it would have devastating unintended long-term consequences for Germany.

But the kaiser initially refused to go. He wasn't interested in Morocco and had been toying with the idea of making up with France in order to gather together a European alliance against Britain. Besides, the thought of landing in a strange place, dealing with a strange horse, frightened him. Bülow, however, was determined and bombarded him with telegrams telling him that if he didn't go to Morocco he'd be seen as a victim of French pressure, whereas if he did he would be a hero to the German people. Wilhelm relented. At the port of Tangier, before a crowd, and sweating profusely, he struggled down the ship's ladder in full dress uniform and sword, clutching on with his one usable hand. By the time he reached the bottom he had to be virtually carried on to the quayside, visibly pale and shaking. With the German consul he rode nervously on a large unfamiliar white horse to the Sultan's palace, where he made a speech promising to defend Moroccan independence with German might. When a bunch of flowers hit him in the face, the horse – made jumpy by rounds of ammunition let off by enthusiastic locals – nearly threw him: 'the horse was within an inch of costing me my life', he told Bülow later. Within a few hours he was on Gibraltar, the Royal Navy's Mediterranean headquarters, boasting about the incident to Louis of Battenburg and happily taking responsibility for it.

The visit provoked an international crisis. Everyone saw it as dangerously provocative. Lamsdorff thought it gratuitous. Lord Lansdowne called it 'clumsy'. Edward said it was 'The most mischievous and uncalled for event which the German Emperor has ever engaged in since he came to the throne . . . one can have no faith in any of his assurances.' He didn't stop there; he told Louis of Battenburg it was 'A gratuitous insult, and the clumsy theatrical part of it would make one laugh were the matter not a serious one . . . I have tried to get on with him and shall nominally do my best to the end, but trust – never. He is utterly false and the <u>bitterest foe</u> that England possesses.' An attack on the Entente, Edward felt, was an attack on him. It didn't help that he'd just discovered that Wilhelm had been badmouthing him to President Roosevelt – to whom the two men had simultaneously been writing.★

The personal and the political were now quite as confusingly and unhelpfully intertwined for Edward as they were for Wilhelm. He probably could not have said whether he was angry because Wilhelm had attacked the Entente or himself. He believed that fellow monarchs could have relationships across national boundaries, but any sense of family kinship with Wilhelm, a relationship which had once been a strong link between Germany and Britain, was now broken. As a riposte to Wilhelm he made his own provocative, partisan gesture. He went to Paris and sent Delcassé – now under pressure from the French Left to resign for inflaming relations with Germany – a personal telegram encouraging him to stay in office. As soon as Edward left Paris, however, the German government demanded Delcassé resign and the French government accept an international conference to decide Morocco's status, or it would find itself at war with Germany in Africa *and* Europe. Delcassé resigned on 6 June, and the French government agreed to a conference on Morocco. The British government was dismayed by what it saw as French weakness. The Germans' intervention had worked splendidly. The kaiser made Bülow a prince. He rather spoilt the effect, however, by subsequently telling a French general that he had no intention of going to war over Morocco – a crack in Germany's threatening stance which had

---

★ Roosevelt, who though he'd never met him got the point about Wilhelm, told his friend the British diplomat Cecil Spring-Rice, 'It is a wild nightmare to suppose that he can use me to the detriment of any other nation.'

Bülow biting his tongue. In fact, Delcassé's departure was the catalyst which stiffened French resolve. In July the French asked Lord Lansdowne if the British would be prepared to discuss secretly a cooperative military strategy in the event of a war. He agreed. Wilhelm's day in Tangier had released ugly and dangerous tensions in Europe. The Entente, which Edward had seen as a means to peace in Europe, had done nothing to head them off. The kaiser's gesture had made the Entente look like a treaty based on European priorities rather than colonial ones. The focus of international politics seemed suddenly to have shifted from imperial conflict back to the crowded continent of Europe.

As a result of Tangier the king and the kaiser's relationship lapsed into arm's length tit for tat. George had intended to attend the German crown prince's wedding, but Edward cancelled, claiming his son had a prior engagement. The kaiser refused to let *his* son the crown prince go to England for the king's birthday. He accused his uncle of trying to 'divide father and son', and of corrupting his son's morals – the last time 'Little Willy' had stayed with Edward there had been 'unseemly romping in unlighted corridors' and a lady had 'removed her slipper'. Willy, aged twenty-three, disappointed by his father's strictness and distant lack of interest, was in the grip of a familiar Hohenzollern filial rebellion. He had both identified himself with the extreme far Right who criticized the kaiser for being insufficiently nationalist and aggressive, and upset his father even more by deliberately modelling himself on Edward and his English playboy style. At Willy's wedding Wilhelm snubbed Sir Frank Lascelles, who was so upset he immediately tendered his resignation. Bülow talked him out of it. Then at the Kiel regatta in June, the kaiser made off-colour remarks about Edward's relationship with Alice Keppel, all of which got back to Edward. In mid-1905 the French chargé d'affaires in London reported to Paris that there was no trace left of the German sympathy that had existed at the English court in Queen Victoria's day. What worried the older generation of diplomats like Lascelles, who was looking increasingly out of place at the Foreign Office, however, was not the family feud, but that it mirrored a wider loss of confidence in Germany among British politicians and diplomats.

It could be seen in George, who had exchanged a dislike of Wilhelm for a dislike of Germany. 'Although I like Lascelles very much,' he wrote, 'I fear he has become too German in his ideas for my taste.'

There were older diplomats and officials in Germany who felt quite as anxious as Lascelles about the shift in feeling. In August 1905 Count Gotz von Seckendorff, a former and loyal member of Vicky's household, was so worried at the bad turn in royal relations that he wrote personally to Edward begging him to meet Wilhelm on his way back from his annual spa trip to Marienbad. A meeting, he suggested, 'might create wonders'. Edward treated the letter as an impertinence. His reply, written by Knollys, was crushingly haughty. He insisted he had no quarrel with Wilhelm, but refused to 'run after [him] . . . it would be undignified for him [Edward] to play such a part, and it would not meet with the approval either of the British Government or the British Nation'. He added that he no longer knew whether Wilhelm had 'any affection for him, but from one or two things which he had heard recently, he should say not'. There was no doubt that both men were not far off hating each other. Lord Lansdowne wrote of Edward, 'he talks and writes about his royal brother in terms which make one's flesh creep'. As for Wilhelm, his descriptions of Edward were said to be unrepeatable.

On 24 July 1905 Wilhelm and Nicholas met secretly off the coast of the northern Swedish town of Björkö. Wilhelm had brought the draft treaty Nicholas and he had discussed the year before, without telling Bülow. Nicholas had stolen away on his yacht from his summer residence at Peterhof on the Gulf of Finland, without telling his own ministers. They had planned it like two naughty children playing truant. 'At home nobody informed,' Nicholas wrote. 'Am so delighted to be able to see You.' Both were fleeing from intractable problems: Nicholas facing the collapse of the Russian state and putting off ending a war that had brought the country to its knees, and Wilhelm in flight from all the disappointments and frustrations, along with the worst strikes since 1888, demonstrations in Berlin demanding the reform of the Prussian

Landtag,★ and the imminent prospect of the Social Democrats, the Socialist Party, becoming the largest party in the Reichstag.

The two men met for dinner on the *Hohenzollern*. They both agreed, Wilhelm wrote in his account of the meeting to Bülow, that Edward was 'the greatest mischief-maker and the most danger-ous intriguer in the world'. The tsar, he said, fumed over the Dogger Bank incident – and said that France's failure to support Germany over it was proof that the British were using the Entente to draw France away from him. He complained bitterly that the king had made the Entente without telling him. Bertie, Wilhelm opined, had an 'absolute passion for making a "little agreement" with every country, everywhere'. At this, according to Wilhelm, Nicholas banged the table with his fist and said, 'Well, I can only say, he shall not get one from me, and never in my life against Germany – my word of honour on it.' Wilhelm proposed that they make 'a little agreement' of their own. 'That's quite splendid,' Nicholas said, 'I entirely agree.' Wilhelm drew the treaty from his pocket. 'Would you like to sign it?' he asked coyly. 'Yes, I will!' Nicholas said. 'You are Russia's only friend in the world.' Their signatures were witnessed by Wilhelm's latest foreign minister, Heinrich von Tschirrsky, and one of Nicholas's men, Birulov, who was not permitted to see what he was signing. As he laid down his pen, Wilhelm told Bülow, 'a ray of sunlight gleamed through the cabin window onto the table . . . it was as though his Grandfather William I and Tsar Nicholas I had clasped hands in Heaven, and were looking down with satisfaction upon their grandsons'.

The agreement stated that if one country was attacked by another European power, the other would come to its aid with all its forces within Europe. There was an extra clause that the Russian government would show the treaty to the French and that the French could join the agreement. France, Wilhelm wrote to Nicky three days later, 'must remember she is wedded to you and that she is obliged to lie in bed with you, and eventually to give a hug

★ The Prussian representative chamber which still had a limited franchise and gave an equal number of seats to the Junker aristocracy as to the lower estates.

or a kiss now and then to me, but not to sneak into the bedroom of the ever-intriguing touche-a-tout [all-groping] – on the Island' – i.e. Edward.

Björkö was a fantasy of autocratic effectiveness. The two men were drawn together by a sense of lost control, by personal frustration and failure, by a desire to feel effective. 'The 24th of July 1905 is a cornerstone in European politics and turns over a new leaf in the history of the world,' Wilhelm wrote grandly to Nicholas. He returned to Germany certain that he had won a great victory, restoring Russo-German relations, dealing a deathblow to the Franco-Russian alliance and delivering Germany 'from the hideous pincers of Gallo-Russia'. Not that he was quite sure whether he wanted to administer another crushing blow to France or ally with her, for he was still fantasizing about forming an international union against England. In time, he mused, 'even Japan may fell [*sic*] inclined to join it . . . This would cool down English self assertion and impertinence.' As for Nicholas, plagued by the endless evidence of his own ineffectuality, it's not hard to see why the treaty appealed. It allowed him to feel he was acting independently of his ministers, countering bureaucracy with imperial decisiveness, doing something that might have some effect. Moreover, life as an autocrat was lonely. Wilhelm was one of the very few who understood. 'You were like a dear brother to me,' Wilhelm told him afterwards. 'I shall always respond to your feeling with the same warmth and with the same intensity as you and you can count on me as a firm friend.' There must, however, have been a part of Nicholas that knew it couldn't work. In his diary, he made no mention of having signed the treaty, and back in St Petersburg, when he showed it to Lamsdorff he seemed 'very much worried and even embarrassed'.

Lamsdorff was horrified by Björkö; he regarded it as a crude attempt by Wilhelm to cut Russia off from France, just when France was most vulnerable. Like Sergei Witte, he was in favour of an agreement with Germany, but it was obvious that France – forced by German threats to participate in a conference on Morocco and with a German gun still at its head – would never sign. Nicholas made murmuring protestations that he'd signed the thing and therefore it must stand, but with the country in the throes of revolution he did not press the point.

When the kaiser proudly showed the treaty to Bülow, the chancellor threatened to resign. He said that Wilhelm had made emendations to the original draft of the treaty which rendered it unusable. The kaiser had limited Germany's obligations to defending Russia just to Europe rather than Asia too. As Bülow had made better relations with Russia one of the cornerstones of his policy, his reaction was unexpected. It seems most likely he did it to punish Wilhelm for once again acting without him. He had become heartily sick of managing the kaiser, complaining to Tirpitz about his 'boundless vanity', his 'abnormal lack of logic' and his 'incessant boasting'. Moreover, Eulenburg was back in favour after several years in retirement, and Bülow was furious at the thought that his former patron might become a rival. Wilhelm was astonished by Bulow's reaction and became hysterical. 'To be treated in this way by the best and closest friend I have . . . has been such a terrible blow to me I have quite broken down!' He wrote to him, and begged Bülow not to leave him in the lurch. 'Such a thing I could not survive . . . The morning after the arrival of your resignation would not find the Kaiser alive . . . Think of my poor wife and children.' Bülow relented and agreed the treaty could be ratified. But when the Russians said the treaty couldn't be ratified, the German Foreign Office did not pursue the matter, and when Wilhelm insisted to Nicholas, almost plaintively, that the treaty must stand – 'We joined hands and signed before God, who heard our vows!' – Nicholas replied that it could not come into force unless France signed it. Within a few months Nicholas's answers to Wilhelm's letters were coming later and later, and Wilhelm was freely insulting his cousin.

By October 1905 there was no question but that the Japanese War had been an unrivalled disaster for Russia. It had brought defeat, debt, humiliation and now all-out revolution. The trains stopped, the factories ceased production, riots broke out. Ugly pogroms took place in the Ukraine and White Russia. 'In England, of course,' Nicholas wrote resentfully, 'the press says that those disorders were organized by the police; they still go on repeating this worn-out fable.' The government was losing control. It was Sergei Witte, triumphantly returned from the Portsmouth peace conference having extracted extraordinarily good terms for Russia, who drew up the October manifesto. It promised civil liberties – freedom of religion, of speech, of assembly, of association – as well as an elected assembly, whose consent would be required for laws to come into force, and universal male suffrage, though all this was subject to the tsar's right of veto. Nicky hesitated to sign it; he wanted his cousin, Grand Duke Nicholas, head of the army, to quell the rebellion by force, but he refused. 'Either you sign it, or I shoot myself,' the grand duke allegedly said. 'There were only two ways open,' the tsar wrote in justification to his mother.

To find an energetic soldier and crush the rebellion by sheer force . . . that would mean rivers of blood and in the end we should be where we started . . . The other way out would be to give the people their civil rights, freedom of speech and press, also to have all laws confirmed by State Duma – that of course would be a constitution. Witte defends this very energetically.

From all over Russia they cried for it, they begged for it, and around me many – very many – held the same views . . . There was no other way out than to cross oneself and give what everyone was asking for. My only consolation is that such is the will of God, and this grave decision will lead my dear Russia out of the intolerable chaos she has been in for nearly a year.

For Nicholas the manifesto, which he signed on 30 October (17 October in the Julian calendar), signified absolute failure, and the abandonment of a 600-year-old sacred birthright.

12. Continental shifts (1906–8)

The problem with aggressive programmes of imperial expansion in distant places is that, when they go wrong, the consequences are felt much closer to home. Russia had already experienced the bitter results of an imperial misadventure; now it was Germany's turn. In early 1906 the Great Powers met at the Spanish town of Algeciras for a conference to resolve the status of Morocco and France's attempts to surreptitiously turn it into a French protectorate. The conference happened because Wilhelm's visit to Tangier and Germany's subsequent threats had blackmailed France into agreeing to it – not an auspicious genesis for such an event. And so it would play out: for Germany what had felt like a master stroke, exposing French imperial ambitions, defeating them and flexing its own military muscle all at the same time, would end in the biggest diplomatic reversal since unification. By the time the conference was in its second week Germany had alienated almost all the other delegates by giving the impression that it was happy to hold Europe hostage with war threats, by seeming openly opportunistic, being abrupt, inconsistent and refusing everyone else's proposals. 'Germany's conduct', the chief American delegate wrote to President Roosevelt, was 'paltry and unworthy of a great power'. The British, whom the Germans had hoped to split from France, had thrown themselves in with France from the start, convinced from the first that the whole thing was a ploy to destroy the Entente Cordiale.

The German delegation's line – or lack of it – at Algeciras was an example of the muddle that seemed to reign at the top of the German government. Is wasn't clear what they wanted: a war? To humiliate France? Free trade? Or a role in running the Moroccan government? The Foreign Office was in confusion. The foreign minister, Oswald von Richthofen, had died of overwork the previous year. His replacement, Tschirrsky, a favourite of Wilhelm's, was out of his depth and Bülow hated him. Holstein was tired, frustrated and sick of Wilhelm and Bülow's vanity – the chancellor appeared to base his day-to-day instructions on how the European press covered him personally. No one was pleased to see Eulenburg back and apparently advising Wilhelm again. The only consensus was that mediatory behaviour would be a sign of weakness. Germany's position pushed the new British Liberal government, which had won a landslide at elections in January, straight into the arms of France. In fact, the new foreign secretary, Sir Edward Grey, immediately summoned Metternich, the German ambassador, and told him that should – perish the thought – Germany go to war with France, Britain would find it very hard to stand by and do nothing. German aggression delivered the Italians, Germany's Triple Alliance allies, to the other side. It eventually forced the Russians into the French camp too. The Russians had been desperate not to have to take sides at Algeciras, as Russia was still fighting its revolution and needed to be on good terms with everyone. But it also needed a loan, which the French cleverly refused to finalize until the conference was over. When, in February 1906, the Russians asked the Germans to consider giving way a little so the proceedings might come to an end, Bülow reacted furiously, and told the Russian ambassador that, having forced France to the table, there could be no compromise. It was 'a question of honour for us and especially for the Kaiser'; the Russians ought to put pressure on the French instead. Yet he might have bought the support Germany so needed with a little more tact and an offer of a German loan. When the conference dribbled into April, Sergei Witte and Vladimir Lamsdorff decided they had to back France simply to bring it to an end. Isolated save for Austria and Morocco, Germany finally had to agree a face-saving solution which gave the French a protectorate in all but name, but guaranteed free trade and German investments.

Algeciras was an absolute disaster for the Germans: it was a public humiliation and it immeasurably tightened the Entente. Tschirrsky moaned that the whole of Europe had turned against them. The country was furious and disappointed. The press blamed Bülow and Wilhelm. Significant parts of the German General Staff felt that an opportunity to have a war with France and 'settle' it once and for all, or at least to not lose face – had been squandered, because Wilhelm and Bülow had shrunk from the logical consequences of their actions. Eulenburg told Wilhelm he should sack Bülow for mishandling the affair, and suggested Bülow had done so to force Wilhelm into line. Rather conveniently, Bülow collapsed dramatically at the Reichstag in the middle of a speech claiming that Germany was as satisfied with the outcome as France – his words were greeted by jeers. He remained out of politics until October, though not before he'd made Holstein – who by the end of the conference had been demanding they send troops into France – the official scapegoat and forced him to resign. Holstein, unaware of the author of his demise, blamed Eulenburg.

Exhibiting his usual perspective, Wilhelm said the whole of Europe had betrayed him – especially the monarchs, despite 'all his attempts to curry favour with them', and it was 'unpardonable' that Russia had ranged itself 'recklessly on the side of the powers hostile to Germany'. But most of all he was convinced that the outcome demonstrated his uncle's 'machinations' against him.

During the conference Edward had written to Wilhelm to congratulate him on his forty-second birthday. 'We are – my dear William – such old friends and near relations that I feel sure that the affectionate feelings which have always existed may invariably continue, be assured that this country has never had any aggressive feelings toward yours, and that the idle gossip and silly tittle tattle on the subject emanates from mischief-makers and ought never to be listened to.' Wilhelm replied, 'The whole letter breathed such an atmosphere of kindness and warm, sympathetic friendship that it constitutes the most cherished gift among my presents . . . it is my most earnest endeavour and wish to remain in peace with all Countries, especially my neighbours!' Both letters, paradigms of insincerity, demonstrated only how much the two men disliked each other and how little they had to say to each other.

When Alfonso XIII, King of Spain, announced he was marrying a British princess in March, Wilhelm decided that Edward had manipulated the Spanish into backing the French at the conference (he himself had been trying to persuade Alfonso to marry a German princess for similar reasons). 'All the wretched degenerate Latin peoples have become instruments in England's hands in order to combat German trade in the Mediterranean.' When Edward went to Rome on his annual Mediterranean cruise, Wilhelm, in a spiralling state of near hysteria, told his suite that his uncle was 'carrying on against him . . . The whole press of the world, including that of America, had already been mobilized against him by English money, and it was extraordinary how much personal animosity his uncle's attitude revealed.' He told them, 'He is a Satan; you can hardly believe what a Satan he is.' There was one genuine reason, however, to feel anxious about British plans: in February they had launched the Dreadnought, a new generation of warship – vast, armoured and carrying big guns – which immediately threatened to make obsolete everything that had come before.

Even Wilhelm's own staff considered Algeciras a victory for Edward – even though he'd played no role in it at all. The king had 'a clear, practical knowledge of men and facts', the comptroller of Wilhelm's household, Robert zu Zedlitz-Trützschler wrote in his diary. 'The Emperor on the other hand, has remained a complete stranger to the realities of life, and the value of the purity and virtue of his private life is really discounted by his hypocrisy and pharisaical unctuousness.'

After Algeciras, the German government seemed to be pulled in two directions: on the one hand, there were those who accepted that sabre-rattling hadn't worked, and that something needed to be done to defuse the tensions the conference had produced; and on the other, there was a feeling that Germany hadn't played hard enough, that the government had pusillanimously shied away from the logical consequence of its policy – war with France. Tschirrsky, Metternich, the eminently sensible, plain-speaking ambassador in London, and Eulenburg were in the first camp; many of the German officer class were in the second. After fifteen years under the command of General Alfred von Schlieffen, the senior army staff constituted of a small Junker elite obsessed with its own privileges and superiority, fearing and fending off dilution by the middle classes, utterly opposed to socialism which it regarded as degenerate, saturated in the ideas of the nationalist historian

Treitschke – who saw Europe as a Hobbesian battlefield where might was everything and the Slav the enemy – actively welcoming war as a force that would cleanse Germany inside and out. Wilhelm had just replaced the retiring Schlieffen – the appointment was entirely in his gift – with Helmuth von Moltke, who was the nephew of the elder Moltke who had delivered the Prussian victories of the 1860s. Within the army Moltke was regarded as a controversial choice: not quite tough enough, and a little too arty – he played the cello, liked to paint and read Goethe. In other respects he was absolutely a product of the solipsistic world of the German General Staff; different only in that he didn't welcome the European war that he thought was inevitable. He had told Wilhelm it would be apocalyptically awful, and even the victor would emerge exhausted. But he considered that the sooner it came the better, and that Germany would probably have to attack first. The kaiser had told him that he absolutely agreed. It's hard not to feel that he found Moltke's gloomy fatalism rather bracing; it made him feel serious and fatalistic too.

But though Wilhelm indulged in violent rhetoric, like most of the country including the government and press, he was in reality caught in a muddle between the would-be negotiators and the warmongers: furiously disappointed, teetering between a desire for better relations with the rest of Europe and a lurking sense that if they'd risked a little more they'd have got what they wanted. 'In his heart of hearts it is true the Emperor does not want to go to war,' Zedlitz-Trützschler wrote, almost regretfully, 'because he knows perfectly well how stupendous the crisis would be, but he always wants to achieve great objects with the smallest trouble, and win laurels without danger . . . he never learns; he deceives himself and is deceived by others.'

Through the summer of 1906 the language of moderation gradually returned to foreign relations. The new British foreign secretary, Sir Edward Grey, assured Metternich that he didn't want conflict with Germany, and an attempt was made to repair Edward and Wilhelm's relationship, which was publicly acknowledged to have become so bad that a cartoon appeared in a German magazine, *Lustige Blätter*, in August 1906, showing Edward poring over a map of Europe, trying to find a route that would get him to Marienbad without seeing Wilhelm, and hitting on Berlin. 'I'm sure not to find him there.' It was arranged that they would meet briefly in mid-August, at the German spa town of Homburg, when Edward was en route to Marienbad.

Neither looked forward to the event. 'Meetings with Edward have no lasting value, because he is envious,' Wilhelm scribbled. Edward grumbled that Wilhelm would inevitably spring some awful surprise on him. The kaiser spent most of the occasion teasing Lascelles and laughing about the latest Hague peace conference. He said he had 'not the slightest intention of diminishing the armaments of Germany in any way or sort, and that he was quite convinced that if he did it would mean war with some European power'. After lunch he drove Edward off to show him his latest passion, a Roman fort he'd 'excavated' and rebuilt at Saalberg. Possibly because Edward could now not bring himself to raise 'difficult subjects' like politics with Wilhelm, the visit was said to have gone well. But Fritz Ponsonby felt 'There was thunder in the air.' (The following summer of 1907 the kaiser laid on 50,000 soldiers and a three-hour march past, which left Edward grumpily longing for his lunch. Once again, the two men studiously avoided all references to political questions.) A brief visit could not dislodge a growing conviction in Germany that Edward was the sharp end of British foreign policy, committed to encircling Germany – a revival of the old fear of being vulnerably in the middle of the Central European plain. Now Edward's every visit to the continent sparked reports in the German press that he was negotiating a new secret deal. When he met the Italian king in Rome in the spring of 1907, the *Neue Freie Presse* wrote:

Who can fail to receive the impression that a diplomatic duel is being fought out between England and Germany under the eyes of the world? The King of England, however, is in serious earnest over the duel, and is no longer afraid of appearing to throw the whole influence of his personality into the scales whenever it is a question of thwarting the aims of German policy . . . already people are anxiously asking themselves everywhere: What is the meaning of this continual political labour, carried on with open recklessness, whose object is to put a close ring round Germany?

Another German paper called Edward a 'twentieth-century Napoleon', using diplomacy rather than arms to subjugate Germany. When he went on to see Franz Joseph after the German visit of 1907, the Berlin court was full of rumours that he was now trying to detach Austria from Germany.

Most of the time Edward wasn't politicking at all, but there were occasions when he encouraged the confusion. Immediately after meeting Wilhelm in 1907, he was seen in Marienbad with the French prime minister, Georges Clemenceau, and then the Russian foreign minister. The king, moreover, had publicly associated himself with outspokenly anti-German British public figures such as Admiral Jackie Fisher, who had a bad habit of calling for pre-emptive strikes on the Germany navy; Sir Charles Hardinge; and Lord Esher, who served on the Committee of Imperial Defence, the institution charged with defining military strategy. After Algeciras, Esher had written in his diary, 'L'Allemagne, c'est l'Ennemie, and there is no doubt on that subject. They mean to have a powerful fleet and commercially to beat us out of the field before ten years are over our heads.' These men didn't view war with the enthusiasm of some of the German General Staff, but they did see Germany as a threat to be energetically countered.

Sir Edward Grey did nothing to counter the impression of Edward's influence or that Britain was increasingly suspicious of Germany. A shy, ascetic, hard-working 44-year-old aristocrat from Northumberland whose main passions were bird-watching and fishing, he hated foreign travel even more than Lansdowne had and spoke no foreign languages. He was happy for the king to do the visiting while he laboured over the mountainous piles of Foreign Office paperwork, because ultimately he didn't think the visits mattered. 'Germany,' he wrote after Algeciras, 'is our worst enemy and our greatest danger . . . The majority [of Germans] dislike us so intensely that the friendship of their Emperor or the Court cannot really be useful to us.' In some respects he was right – Edward didn't make policy and German antipathy towards

Britain had spread well beyond the court – but the king's trips did help to focus and concentrate German anxiety about Britain. Grey, meanwhile, had regarded Algeciras as a deliberate attempt by the Germans to sabotage the Entente, and distrusted Germany. As a young minister in the early 1890s, he had experienced at first hand the German Foreign Office's attempts to extract advantage by threat. His staff agreed with him. In 1907 the Foreign Office expert on Germany, Eyre Crowe, wrote a report on Germany concluding that it was 'consciously aiming at the establishment of a German hegemony at first in Europe, and eventually in the World'. During Algeciras Grey had taken the momentous decision of agreeing to secret talks between the French and British military about how the British army might help if France was attacked by Germany. Only the Liberal prime minister, Henry Campbell-Bannerman, one other minister and the king were informed. Grey made it a condition that Britain would not automatically intervene if Germany attacked France, because he thought this might encourage the French to instigate conflict themselves. Edward disliked the secrecy; Campbell-Bannerman worried that simply having the conversations would create a sense of obligation to France – as indeed it would prove. It was a question Grey would wrestle with for the rest of his life. 'With more experience,' he admitted years later, 'I might have shared that apprehension.'

Well into 1906 the Russian government was still fighting to quell the revolution. It did so, the British diplomat Cecil Spring-Rice told King Edward, by employing 'the most violent and unscrupulous methods', including encouraging extreme-right groups to attack leftist revolutionaries, and exploiting anti-Semitism as a way of rallying 'patriotic Russians' – there were 690 pogroms in the two weeks after the October manifesto was announced. The worst, in Odessa, was encouraged by pamphlets paid for by the government and printed by the local police. Nicholas, rationalizing the pogroms with a mixture of wilful blindness and naivety, told his mother they were the result of 'a whole mass of loyal people suddenly making their presence felt . . . nine-tenths of the trouble-makers are Jews, the people's whole anger turned against them.

That's how the pogroms happened. It's amazing how they took place simultaneously in all the towns of Russia and Siberia.'

As the government regained control, Nicholas expected Russia to return to how it had been before. He utterly misunderstood what had happened. The revolution had let loose a hunger for democracy and representation that couldn't be denied. But there was no way for the tsar to see the political yearning and excitement of his newly enfranchised subjects. He had so thoroughly cocooned himself at Tsarskoe selo that he now had even less idea of what was going on than he had had before the revolution. The house-hold and entourage – the most conservative enclave in the land – were entirely unable to represent to him the extraordinarily widespread hostility to the regime which had built up across every class and region. And his isolation only intensified his tendency to reject anyone who delivered news he didn't want to hear, or tried to pressure him to do things he didn't want to do. He told his mother that he and Alix were 'virtual prisoners' there, but as Cecil Spring-Rice, chargé d'affaires at the British embassy, and one of the most perceptive of British observers, wrote in April 1906, 'The Emperor is perfectly happy at Tsarskoe, where he leads the life which suits him best, playing with his children and only seeing the people he wishes to see.' As the new British ambassador noted in early 1907, 'Personal contact with the Court is exceedingly rare, far more infrequent probably than in any other country.' After a year and a half in the job he had met the tsar only three times. While the newly liberated Russian press was full of stories of naval mutinies, running battles between police and mobs, mass executions and huge demonstrations, the tsar's diary dwelt on the weather, his walks, troop inspections and dinner with the family.

In the weeks after the October manifesto, when the risings failed to stop, the lesson Nicholas drew was that it had made no difference; he suspected the autocracy had never really been under threat and he should never have signed it away. He began to resent Sergei Witte for having forced the constitution upon him. The old jealousy of his own powers and prerogatives reasserted itself. It wasn't hard to criticize Witte: he was difficult, abrupt, made enemies easily and was by no means always successful. 'I have never seen such a chameleon of a man,' Nicholas wrote in January 1906. 'That naturally, is the reason why no one believes in him any more. He is absolutely discredited with everybody, except perhaps the Jews abroad.' When Witte returned to Russia in triumph after Algeciras in April 1906, having negotiated a vast French loan – the largest in Russian history – to keep the government afloat, Nicholas sacked him. Lamsdorff resigned days later, exhausted and dreading the new constitution. He would die the following year.

Alix missed little about the world outside too. She constructed the walls of the family's cocoon, spending her days in her mauve parlour, its walls crammed with icons and family photographs, surrounded by her children and those few people whom she regarded as allies. Alexis's birth had aged her, and her health seemed ever more fragile. She was permanently exhausted, complained of shortness of breath, and her lips went blue with alarming speed, but no one could diagnose what was wrong. The imperial family's doctor, Botkin, seems to have regarded the symptoms as psychosomatic – he called them 'progressive hysteria'. The empress's participation in public life declined to almost nothing, and when she did appear, it was always obvious that she was in extreme discomfort, both physical and mental. By 1906 the formal connections with St Petersburg and society had dwindled and dwindled. The winter season with its imperial balls and levees had been cancelled in 1904 because of the war, and the royal couple saw no reason to reinstate it. Nicholas's sister Olga worried about the ill-feeling their withdrawal was producing in the capital. But Nicky and Alix seemed equally determined to push the family away too. Minny complained that Alix made less and less effort to see her, and Nicholas barely listened to her any more. Nicholas's sister Xenia, who considered herself a loyal supporter of Alix, was extraordinarily upset when the empress implied that she and Sandro had fled the country during the revolution – they'd been in France. 'Only those who were there, really know what it was,' the empress said pointedly. 'I was silent and my head started to ache,' Xenia wrote. When Misha, Nicholas's brother fell in love with a commoner, the tsar had the girl arrested as she attempted to leave the country, so as to prevent them getting married. And he exiled two of his first cousins for making what he regarded as unsuitable marriages.

The family was alienated by Alix's predilection for taking up with faith healers and self-proclaimed miracle workers. St Petersburg society, like many of Europe's fashionable centres, was in the grip of a fad for charismatics, mysticism and the occult. Increasingly and passionately immersed in the mysticism of the Russian Church, Alix was all too susceptible. In 1900, desperate for a son, she had been introduced to a self-proclaimed faith healer called M. Philippe, who promised her an heir. For a while, much to Minny's disapproval, he had been constantly in attendance, until Alix failed to produce a son in 1902, and then he had fallen from grace. 'It is more Alicky who is under this horrid man's influence than Nicky,' May had reported to George. 'Aunt Minny is in despair.' More worryingly he was replaced in 1905 with Grigori Rasputin.

Rasputin was a self-styled 'starets' (a holy man and faith healer), a peasant from Siberia, who had made a splash in St Petersburg. Famous for his allegedly hypnotic pale blue eyes, he claimed to be a reformed sinner – the name 'Rasputin' means 'debauched' – who had been touched by God and could effect miracles. The key to Rasputin's intimate relationship with the imperial family was that he seemed to alleviate Alexis's haemophilia. It is likely that through some kind of light hypnosis he calmed and reassured the tsarevich. Whatever he did, on several occasions his proximity to Alexis seemed to bring about miraculous recoveries – the agonizing swellings subsided, the internal bleeding stopped. He further won the imperial couple's trust by presenting himself as their idea of a simple, effusive, pious, salt-of-the-earth peasant. Nicholas said that Rasputin made him feel at peace. Alix called him 'Our Friend' and decided he had been sent by God to help them. Both, however, refused to explain to anyone outside a very small circle why Rasputin was important to them – doing so would have revealed the truth about Alexis's haemophilia.

Away from the imperial family Rasputin was a different person: manipulative, coarse, bullying, surrounded by a motley assortment of clients and hangers-on. Descriptions of encounters with him conjure up an aggressively insinuating man, snowing his victims under with a barrage of over-intimate questions. His standing with the imperial couple meant that everyone felt obliged to listen. But for the moment his reputation was limited to the royal family and its retainers.

When Nicholas and his court first encountered the members of Russia's first elected assembly, the Duma, on 27 April by the Russian calendar, in the St George Room at the Winter Palace, they saw it as a terrible defeat, an opposition that must be countered. To Nicholas its members represented his own abject failure to defend 300 years of the sacred tradition. The head of the imperial household, Count Fredericks, said, 'They gave one the impression of a gang of criminals who are only waiting for the signal to throw themselves upon the Ministers and cut their throats. What wicked faces! I will never again set foot among those people.' Xenia wrote of their 'repulsive faces and insolent expressions'. In truth, though there were some angry radicals, plenty of the new elected members were part of the traditional establishment with no desire to bring down the monarchy. Vladimir Nabokov's father, for example, was a landowner whose family had been in service to the tsars for centuries.* He had come to believe the government had cynically abdicated its responsibilities. What shocked the royal contingent most was the Duma's lack of forelock-tugging deference. 'They looked at us,' Nicholas's mother said, 'as upon their enemies, and I could not make myself stop looking at certain faces, so much did they seem to reflect an incomprehensible hatred for all of us.' Several months later Xenia's husband, Sandro, had the same uncomprehending reaction when he was briefly taken hostage by 'his own' sailors during a mutiny. He'd thought they loved him. 'I felt so proud of being considered their friend and confidant. A hostage! I feared I was going to collapse!'

This puncturing of expectations of deference, loyalty and love

---

* Nabokov's great-uncle avoided being blown up with his friend Grand Duke Sergei only because he declined the offer of a carriage ride home. (He also refused a ticket for the *Titanic*.)

from the lower classes was by no means limited to Russia. Democracy had taken a big step all over Europe, and aristocratic elites were reluctantly realizing both the loss of their authority and that they had not been regarded with unqualified admiration by the lower orders. There was the same mystified surprise (not to say irritating naivety) in the reaction of George Wyndham, chief secretary of Ireland in the British Conservative government of 1902–6, and member of the intellectual aristocratic and political coterie called 'the Souls', when he lost his seat in the Conservative wipeout in the election of January 1906. He'd thought he'd won before 'because the working men love me, simply because we liked each other and love the traditions of the past and the glory of the future'.

In Britain the 1906 general election delivered a death blow to such assumptions. Wyndham's fellow Soul Arthur Balfour described the election, somewhat melodramatically though not without truth, as part of the same convulsion that had brought about 'the massacres in St Petersburg, riots in Vienna and socialist processions in Berlin'. After twelve years in government the Conservatives were an exhausted force. It was surprising perhaps that a party so predicated on privilege had lasted so long, though as governments have learned since, you can get voters to vote against their own economic interests if you can find something sufficiently powerful to counter them with – religion, a powerful hate, a collective (even if unrealistic) aspiration. The Tories had remained in power with a little judicious aristocratic paternalism, because the country had become richer and because they had kept it excited about the empire. Now, however, they had alienated the electorate with a bad war, a series of colonial scandals and anti-labour laws, and had little to offer but the unthinking support of privilege for its own sake. The Liberals won a landslide victory and the aristocratic oligarchy lost control of the British government.

The new Liberal government still had its aristocrats – Sir Edward Grey, Winston Churchill and the new prime minister, Sir Henry Campbell-Bannerman, who took his holidays in Marienbad with the king – but after twelve years in the wilderness it was a different animal from the aristocratic party of the early 1890s. Its new MPs came predominantly from the professional middle class and its acknowledged rising stars were the solidly middle-class Herbert Asquith and the dazzlingly charismatic, witty, brilliant and occasionally unscrupulous David Lloyd George, who had grown up in poverty in Wales. Moreover, it had radical plans to transform the lives of working people with health insurance and pensions. With it came twenty-nine new MPs from the Independent Labour Party. 'The old idea that the House of Commons was an assemblage of gentlemen has quite passed away,' Lord Esher wrote mournfully. When Asquith became prime minister in 1908, he took it as given that all ministers of senior government departments should sit in the Commons not the Lords because the cabinet was responsible to the electorate, not the aristocracy.* Under the previous administration, many of the cabinet had never stood for election at all.

The Conservative political aristocracy, like its German and Russian counterparts, was not ready to admit its day was past. 'The great Unionist party,'† Arthur Balfour announced after the defeat, 'should still control whether in power or opposition the destinies of this Great Empire.' In the House of Lords, where they had a majority, the Conservatives deliberately began blocking Liberal legislation. It wasn't long before Lloyd George, who with Herbert Asquith was shaping the new plans for health insurance and pensions which would lay the foundations of the Welfare State, was asking 'whether the country was to be governed by the King and His Peers or by the King and his people'. An unabashed class warrior, Lloyd George didn't mince his words: 'All down history nine tenths of mankind have been grinding corn for the remaining tenth and have been paid with husks and bidden to thank god they had the husks.' Edward, who in his younger days liked to claim that the French statesman Léon Gambetta had almost converted him to republicanism, hated Lloyd George's rhetoric, which he considered dangerously divisive. Knollys, the king's private

---

* By the time the Conservatives were back in power in 1918, their social make-up was also different and their leader a brusque Scottish businessman.
† The Conservatives and the Liberal Unionists – that is, Liberals who opposed Irish Home Rule, like Chamberlain – began to work together in 1895.

secretary, was soon complaining about Lloyd George's breaches of 'good taste and propriety', and demanding that he keep the monarch's name out of his 'violent tirades'.

Outwardly, Edward's relationship with the new government was in some respects better than the one he had had with the Conservatives. There were areas of agreement: reforms of the army and the navy, the aims of foreign policy, and Knollys, a long-time Liberal supporter, had good contacts in the party. But he deplored their frequent crimes against fashion, their newfangled ideas about women's suffrage, the new culture of outspokenness and their plebeian habits. Winston Churchill, Edward confided quietly to his son, was 'almost more of a cad in office than he was in opposition'. Herbert Asquith was 'deplorably common not to say vulgar!' George, who had a growing reputation for tactlessness, told Churchill that Asquith was 'not quite a gentleman' – a comment Churchill thoughtfully passed on. Asquith regarded the king's demands to be consulted over cabinet decisions with barely suppressed condescension. 'These people have no right to interfere in any way with our deliberations,' he said – though he claimed to consider the king shrewd.

From Burma, where he was shooting tigers, George, a traditional Tory, wrote after the 1906 election, 'I see a great number of Labour members have been returned, which is rather a dangerous sign, but I hope they are not all Socialists.' He soon conceived a genuine loathing for Lloyd George, which he freely expressed. After witnessing one of the prince's tirades against the Welshman, the writer Edmund Gosse described him as 'an overgrown schoolboy, loud and stupid, losing no opportunity of abusing the government'. On becoming king, George told Lloyd George's own permanent secretary that he couldn't imagine 'how you can go on serving that damned fellow Lloyd George'.

The difference between Britain and Russia was that political institutions obliged George to meet Lloyd George and be courteous. In Russia, Nicholas, now equipped with a large French loan, could refuse to work with the Duma, and veto its decisions. He dismissed its requests for amnesties and for land reallocation, ignored its reform programme and dissolved it, in July 1906. He imprisoned those members who protested and changed the suffrage qualifications, so subsequent Dumas would be more conservative and deferential. But, however conservative they became, the Dumas would not stop insisting they had a stake in governing the country. Nicholas went on resenting them and dissolving them. 'One must let them do something manifestly stupid or mean,' he told his mother, 'and then – slap! and they are gone!'

For Russia, the disastrous consequences of its attempt to prove its manifest destiny in the East were not just a barely contained revolution, but also the humiliating necessity of going cap-in-hand to Britain, and agreeing to an Anglo-Russian Convention, a move which reversed fifty years of foreign policy and imperial dreams. The British government had been proposing an Entente since the end of the Japanese War in 1905. The Russians had mimed agreement, but the pill was almost too bitter to swallow. There was still tremendous anger over Britain's role in the war. The Russian army in particular hated the idea of any reconciliation with Britain or any curtailment of territorial expansion in Asia. The Russian court still tended instinctively to Germany. The agreement finally came about because the Russians needed it, the French – who held their purse-strings – wanted it, and the new Russian foreign minister, Count Alexander Izvolsky, the diplomat who had caught Edward's eye in Copenhagen, and who replaced Lamsdorff in 1906, pushed for it. He argued that Russia was so vulnerable that all reasons for external conflict must be eliminated. There would be no more Asian adventures for the foreseeable future, so it was vital that Russia's influence and position in Asia be secured against future incursions, including British ones.

Even so, the secret negotiations were tortuous, and several times the sheer weight of ideological difference seemed on the point of derailing the talks. In July 1906 a delegation of Duma members travelled to London for the interparliamentary conference, and were welcomed with a special message from King Edward. On the eve of the conference, however, the news came that Nicholas had dissolved the Duma. The prime minister, Henry Campbell-Bannerman, was due to make the opening speech at the

conference. He said, not unreasonably, that he couldn't address a
conference on parliamentary democracy and ignore the tsar's
action. At the end of his speech he said, 'La Douma est morte!
Vive la Douma!' The Duma is dead! Long live the Duma! The
words drew a chorus of conference cheers and a formal complaint
from the Russian ambassador, Count Benckendorff. Grey refused
to apologize and the negotiations stalled. Then in September 1906
some backbench Liberals decided to visit Russia in support of
the dissolved Duma. Nicholas was deeply offended. 'A grotesque
deputation is coming from England . . . Uncle Bertie informed us
that they were very sorry, but were unable to take action to stop
their coming. Their famous "liberty" of course! How angry they
would be if a deputation went from us to the Irish to wish them
success in their struggle against their government!' Grey managed
to dissuade the group from going. Izvolsky sent his thanks and said
it had saved much embarrassment as the visitors would certainly
have been prevented from travelling. Then, only two months
before the Convention was signed, the British ambassador was
summoned to London amid rumours that the Russians were calling
the whole thing to a halt.

The Anglo-Russian Convention was finally signed in August
1907 and published in September, to less than ecstatic acclaim.
From retirement, Sergei Witte sourly called it 'a triumph of British
diplomacy'. Grey, meanwhile, found himself forced into the role
of apologist for the Russian government, having to play down
unpalatable news. 'Russian despotism was repugnant to British
ideals,' he wrote, 'and something was constantly happening in
Russia that alienated British sympathy or stirred indignation.' The
Convention established frontiers and spheres of influence in
Afghanistan, Tibet and China, and Persia was split into three: the
Russians taking the northern third, the British the southern third,
and the shah and the Majlis, the democratic assembly squeezed in
the middle. The British informally conceded that they no longer
felt obliged to block Russia influence in the Balkans and agreed to
consider seriously the possibility of supporting the opening of the
Bosphorus to Russian ships. There were still plenty of people in
Russia who enormously resented the thought that any restraints

should be placed on Russian expansion in Asia. In England, there was great anger from the Liberal backbenches and the Labour Party that Britain should have made a treaty with a regime such as Russia's. Between the negotiators there was a carefully disguised mismatch of intentions: the Russians believed the Convention was mainly about securing its Asian frontiers, whereas Grey and the British Foreign Office saw it in terms of European politics. 'It will complete and strengthen the Entente with France,' Grey wrote, 'and add very much to the comfort and strength of our position.' This was not at all how the Russians wanted to see it. They had no desire to alienate anyone, especially the Germans. But when Izvolsky started negotiating a deal with the Germans in the autumn of 1907 over control of the Baltic and Sir Edward Grey found out, he was furious; Izvolsky was given a stark lesson in just how difficult it would be to steer a balanced course in an increasingly polarized Europe.

Predictably, the Germans attributed the Convention to Edward's politicking. A German acquaintance of the English-born aristocrat Daisy, Princess of Pless told her that he'd asked his Russian acquaintances if they were now praying to little Edward icons. One of Wilhelm's longest-serving ministers wrote on the day of its publication that the Convention was clearly the product of both countries' fear of 'the German army, the German navy, our business sense and the potential of the German people as a whole'. Next to this the kaiser scribbled that Izvolsky had 'always been an Anglomaniac and is now more so than ever', and that both countries were clearly 'against our nation as a whole'. In Britain, some people, such as the journalist W. T. Stead and David Lloyd George, were beginning to wonder whether the king and the 'Hardinge gang,' far from securing peace in Europe, were actually damaging relations with Germany.

In fact, Edward's role in the Convention was very limited. He and George continued to write occasional letters to Nicholas. ('What a long time it is since we met,' George wrote to his cousin at the end of 1907, 'you are often in my thoughts, dear Nicky – I am sure you know that I never change and always remain the same in my old friends. I trust that your Duma will work better than the last two and that the country will gradually quieten down and give you less trouble and anxiety than it has during these last few years!') The king charmed Nicholas's sisters and Sandro, whom he met in Biarritz in the spring of 1907, which may have helped warm Nicholas up to the idea – though the tsar was no longer as close to them as he'd previously been. Bertie's personality, Sandro – hitherto a confirmed Anglophobe – now claimed, 'made everything look different'. 'None could surpass him in clearness of thought or in quality of statesmanship. I am not surprised that Kaiser Wilhelm hated him. It could not have been otherwise because with all his insane conceit the jumping Billy must have felt a miserable dwarf next to that natural-born ruler of overwhelming greatness.' Arguably Minny worked as hard as Edward to make the family links bear fruit. She came to England for the first time in thirty-four years in February 1907, and the two sisters, as they had in 1873, went out in public and the papers ran excited stories about the queen's closeness to the Russian dowager empress. 'Everything is so tastefully and artistically arranged,' she wrote breathlessly from London, '. . . it makes one's mouth water to see all the magnificence! . . . Everyone is so very kind and friendly to me . . . I do wish you too could come over here a little to breathe the air and live for a while in different surroundings. How good for you that would be!'

How to calm the inevitable accusations from Germany that the Convention was aimed at them? For lack of any other ideas, the British government went for the tried, trusted and utterly unsatisfactory method of a state visit. Hardinge pressed Edward to invite Wilhelm for November just after the Convention was published. Enthusiasm was muted on all sides. The Foreign Office had suggested the visit as much to counter criticisms from the left wing of the Liberal and Labour parties, as anything else.

Nor, for once, was Wilhelm keen to come. He had been engulfed in a desperately embarrassing sex scandal, the ramifications of which showed no signs of abating. In April *Die Zukunft*, a newspaper highly critical of the kaiser's 'personal rule' and his anti-democratic habit of listening to favourites and unofficial advisers such as Eulenburg, had launched a campaign against Eulenburg and his circle – several of whom had been aides in Wilhelm's entourage – and accused Eulenburg of being the real power behind Wilhelm's rule, exercising his influence through patronage, 'little threads that are strangling the Reich'. More shockingly it directly accused Eulenburg and his circle of homosexuality, 'moral degeneracy', and even of passing secrets to the French. The kaiser was not mentioned, but his name inevitably hovered over the scandal, though the revelations seem to have come as a genuine shock to him. 'Little Willy', the crown prince, described in his memoirs having to tell his father about the accusations against Eulenburg – he never forgot the 'despairing, horrified' look on his face. Wilhelm had wilfully ignored Eulenburg's homosexuality for twenty years; it was never referred to in his presence though it had been a more or less open secret in diplomatic circles. Denial allowed him to exhibit his own feelings for Eulenburg without embarrassment. In his memoirs (written seven years afterwards), Sergei Witte rather wickedly recalled meeting Wilhelm and Eulenburg on his way back to Russia from negotiating a French loan in 1906. 'He [Wilhelm] sat on the arm of the Prince's chair, his right hand on Eulenburg's shoulder, almost as if he was putting his arm round him.' Very quickly, homosexuality became the story rather than Eulenburg's influence, which had peaked in the late 1890s. More than anywhere else in Europe, homosexuality was taboo in Germany, where – perhaps because of the obsessive admiration for military virtues – there was an intense emphasis on masculinity and masculine behaviour within the establishment. One historian has written: 'the repression of the feminine was pushed to an extreme unknown anywhere else in Europe'.* Exposure was unthinkable: when Wilhelm's friend Fritz Krupp, heir to the armaments fortune, was accused of homosexuality in 1902, he committed suicide; Emperor Franz Joseph's brother Ludwig Victor

---

* It is no small irony that at the same time, in the other Germany, of innovation, creative thought and intellectual investigation, Magnus Hirschfeld and Krafft-Ebing were undertaking the most advanced, explicit, serious and sympathetic research into sexual orientation in the world.

(known, improbably, as 'Luzi-Wuzi') was sent into exile after having an affair with a male masseur. Eulenburg's own brother had been accused of homosexuality in 1898. Wilhelm had forbidden his friend ever to see him again – an order which began the process of Eulenburg's disillusionment with the kaiser. After Wilhelm learned about Eulenburg, he cast him out instantly, depriving himself of one of the few people who genuinely cared about him and who had managed occasionally to restrain him.

Wilhelm made it all the worse by forcing the accused men to sue for libel – for the 'honour' of the government. Then, subsequently – heavily pressed by his military entourage who had long hated Eulenburg because his influence over the kaiser rivalled their own – he allowed his friend to be pursued through the courts for perjury. The cases went on and on. Perhaps the ugliest aspect of the whole affair – and a natural corollary of the way that Wilhelm had allowed his government to become a place dominated by intrigue and competition for favour – was the fact that the information about Eulenburg had come from the government itself: from Wilhelm's entourage, from Holstein, who blamed Eulenburg for his dismissal, and from Bülow, who had begun to fear the re-emergence of Eulenburg as a rival.

Naturally such juicy pickings ended up in every paper in Europe. The pervasiveness of the story can be seen in the way that the German word '*Homosexualität*' became the popular noun for same-sex sex in Europe, taking over from Proust's preferred 'inversion', the old British favourite 'sodomy', and even the delightful German synonym '*warm*' – as in, 'he's quite warm'. Only a week before the kaiser was due in England, *The Times* ran an article about Eulenburg and the 'disgusting orgies' he was supposed to have taken part in, together with another attacking Bülow for associating with extreme Anglophobic German nationalists.

Embarrassed and concerned that his reception in Britain might for the first time actually be hostile, Wilhelm tried to cancel. 'Am suffering since a week from Bronchitis and acute cough, effect of a very virulent attack of influenza, which have quite upset my constitution,' he informed Edward. As Lascelles had just seen the kaiser galloping through the Tiergarten 'in very good spirits',

Edward was not inclined to let him off. 'Your telegram has greatly upset me – as your not coming to England would be a terrible disappointment to us all – my family – and the British nation. Beg of you to reconsider your decision.'

There was no booing. The English crowds loved a show and they still harboured a soft spot for the showy kaiser, who smiled with such pleasure when in public. George, who met Willy and Dona★ in his Prussian field marshal's uniform at Victoria station, wrote, 'There were great crowds in the street and they got a splendid reception.' At Windsor, the town corporation put on a medieval pageant for Wilhelm, who told the gathered crowd that they had made him feel as if he were 'coming home again'. Edward played the solicitous host, avoided politics, but observed in what 'good health' Their Majesties were suddenly looking. Members of the new Liberal government who hadn't met the kaiser before were impressed. 'Even those who were the most sceptical about any good coming of it now admit that the visit has been in every way advantageous,' wrote John Morley, one of the party's most respected figures. Sir Richard Haldane, who was both war minister and a genuine Germanophile, was charmed when Kaiser Wilhelm invited him to join a late-night discussion on Britain's long-standing opposition to the Berlin to Baghdad railway going through Persia. 'Be a member of my Cabinet for tonight,' the kaiser said. Haldane believed that by the end of the evening they had come up with the germ of a solution. Not everyone was impressed. Lord Esher wrote, 'Our King makes a better show than William II. He has more graciousness and dignity. William is ungraceful, nervous and plain. There is no "atmosphere" about him. He has not impressed Grey.'

★ One can only speculate what Dona felt about the Eulenburg scandal. She conducted herself publicly with the irreproachable dignity which had made her very popular in Germany – rather in the same way that Alexandra's forbearance had brought her admiration in Britain – but it must have pierced her. The couple were locked in a painfully imbalanced relationship. Wilhelm, Zedlitz-Trützschler observed, found her company oppressive, while she clung to him and longed for him to pay her attention. 'He is always anxious to get away, but his wife's one desire is to keep him in sight as much as possible.'

Only three days after Wilhelm arrived back in Germany, the proposals for the German Navy Bill of 1908 were published. They called for the commission of four more battleships per year for the next three years and guaranteed that ships would be replaced every twenty rather than twenty-five years. It was a very dramatic increase – a direct response to the new British Dreadnought ships. In Britain, anger at the increases led to the founding of a naval lobby group, the Imperial Maritime League. No more was heard of Haldane's late-night solution to the Baghdad railway impasse. It transpired that the kaiser had deliberately delayed publication of the new bill until his return from England. Holstein wrote that no one 'except perhaps the Kaiser himself' could deny that this had made 'all his kindnesses useless and meaningless, and even given them the air of fraud'. John Morley was genuinely puzzled: he'd been convinced that the kaiser intended 'peace'. 'You may laugh at this in view of the fine brand-new naval programme which the Germans have launched,' he wrote in his diary.

In February 1908 Viscount Esher allowed a letter he'd written to the new Imperial Maritime League to be published in *The Times*. It was very clear from it that Esher believed the German navy had malign intentions towards Britain, and he added, 'there is not a man in Germany from the Emperor downward who would not welcome the fall of Sir John Fisher'. Wilhelm – not for the first time paying more attention to the British press than to the one at home – decided the letter must be protested against. But he didn't write, as etiquette demanded, to the king, but instead to the naval minister, the First Lord of the Admiralty, Lord Tweedmouth. In his most excitable, high-blown prose he denounced Esher's letter as 'unmitigated balderdash' and said it was 'preposterous to infer' that the German government would connive against Fisher. 'It is as ridiculous as it is untrue and I hereby repudiate such a calumny.' In his 'humble' opinion, the British obsession with the 'German danger' was 'nearly ludicrous . . . Once more the German Naval Bill is not aimed at England and is not a challenge to British supremacy of the sea.'

Like so many of Wilhelm's foreign initiatives, the letter spectacularly backfired – and not just because he failed to send his complaints through the sovereign, though Edward completely lost his temper over that. Lord Tweedmouth was suffering from an undiagnosed brain tumour from which he would die the following year; his behaviour had become erratic. He sent the kaiser all the latest estimates for British naval spending which had not yet been presented to parliament, and showed the letter to almost everyone he met. The story ended up in *The Times*; the paper's military correspondent described it as an outrageous attempt to influence British policy. The kaiser's letter put the German navy on the front of every British newspaper for months – Esher couldn't have hoped for a better outcome. By mid-March 1908 Arthur Balfour had extracted from the prime minister, Herbert Asquith, who had recently replaced the seriously ill Campbell-Bannerman, a promise that Britain would build enough new battleships to maintain its naval superiority over Germany – the one thing Tirpitz had wanted to avoid.

Wilhelm decided the whole furore had been engineered by Edward, though Metternich assured him that the king had reprimanded Esher for starting the affair. 'Only now! After five weeks!' Wilhelm scribbled on Metternich's report. 'He never did the slightest thing four or five weeks ago, when the attack of his friend and official on me took place, to make known his displeasure and regret!' On the bottom of the memo he wrote, 'it is not our fleet that is responsible, but the absolutely crazy "Dreadnought" policy of Sir John Fisher and His Majesty'.

The British press – the Left especially – was also angry with the king at the news that Edward was to make a state visit to Russia in June 1908, or rather, meet Nicholas off the coast of Russia. The British government kept the Russian trip a secret until the last minute, precisely in order to head off domestic criticism. It was right to be apprehensive. The Labour MP Ramsay MacDonald published an article called 'An Insult to our Country', in which he scolded the king for 'hobnobbing with a bloodstained creature' – the tsar – and a group of Labour and Liberal MPs signed a Commons motion deploring the visit. The reaction in parliament was so negative that Grey had to deny publicly that the government had any plans to make any further formal arrangements with

Russia, and agree to a Commons debate on the visit. Several MPs
were highly critical of Edward, and Kier Hardie, the leader of the
Labour Party, made a speech describing the tsarist government's
treatment and execution of political prisoners, implying that the
king was condoning atrocities. The government won the debate,
but Edward was affronted at being criticized. He took the position
that it was not for him to judge other monarchs (at least not in
public); the loyalty of one monarch to another, he said, 'couldn't
be destroyed by the faults of a regime'.* He responded by disinvit-
ing the offending MPs – among them Hardie and Fritz Ponsonby's
brother, Arthur, a radical Liberal MP highly critical of Grey's
anti-German foreign policy – from a garden party at Buckingham
Palace. Hardie said the crown had been outside politics since
Charles I and ought to stay there. The whole of the parliamentary
Labour Party signed a resolution condemning Edward's behaviour
and sent their invitations back. Dynastic relationships and domestic
politics directly collided, and parliament, unsurprisingly, won. The
king was forced to reinvite those whose invitations he'd withdrawn, attempting, unsuccessfully, to hold out against Ponsonby,
whom he said 'should have known better'.

  Edward, Alexandra and their suite arrived on the *Victoria and
Albert* on 9 June 1908 at Reval (now Tallinn), in the Gulf of
Finland to meet Nicholas, Alix, his sister Olga and the children on
Standart and *Polar Star*. The weather was calm, and the sun didn't
set until 11.30. In his Kiev Dragoons uniform, Edward told
Nicholas how splendid he looked in his Scots Grey uniform. On
the spur of the moment he made the tsar an admiral of the British
navy (for which, having failed to consult his government in
advance, he was told off by Asquith). Though he might consider
Nicky 'deplorably unsophisticated, immature, and reactionary',
Edward had learned the value of tact. He knew not to offer
unsolicited advice, and said he had 'no desire to play the part

---

* When earlier that year the Portuguese king had installed in government a
hugely unpopular extreme right-wing dictator, however, Edward told his
doctor, 'A constitutional monarch must not do such things.' The Portuguese
king and queen were later assassinated in a horrific bomb attack.

of the German Emperor, who always meddles in other people's business'. Nicky was visibly grateful – and his palpable ease was perhaps the most important outcome of the whole event. Nicholas's latest chief minister, Peter Stolypin, observed to Hardinge the 'marked difference' between the tsar's 'spirits and attitude during the King's visit to Reval compared with what they were at the Emperor's recent visit to the German Emperor at Swinemünde, where he felt anxiety all the time as to what might be unexpectedly swung at him'. (Less tactfully, at his friends the Rothschilds' request, the king raised the subject of Jewish persecution to Stolypin, who was politely noncommittal. He also rather tackily asked the tsar to meet his friend Ernest Cassel, who wanted to get into the Russian money markets, and he told Alix that the children spoke English with a *déclassé* accent. She was so mortified she hired an English tutor almost at once.)

The Russians were struck by what seemed to them the incredible informality of the British. On the *Victoria and Albert*, Mossolov observed how the king sat in an armchair, with an empty chair next to him, on which one might be beckoned to sit. 'Except when on duty, no account was taken of rank. What a contrast there was between the visits of Wilhelm II and the reception of the King and Queen of England at Reval! How entirely at ease everybody was in their company!' Edward flattered Stolypin (whose luxuriant beard the British particularly admired), casually dropped into the conversation the Russian facts he had extracted from ambassador Nicolson on the trip over, and greeted the *Standart*'s sailors in Russian. Olga laughed so raucously at Admiral Fisher's jokes that she felt obliged to apologize to her uncle.

Late on the first night, after dinner on board the *Standart*, Sir Charles Hardinge came upon Alix, sobbing alone on deck. She declined his offers of help.

What struck the British were the mountains of caviar sandwiches and the Russian obsession with security. In preparation for the imperial family's arrival at Reval every house and boat had been searched, and during the course of the visit no one, including the British, was allowed ashore. When a local choral society, invited to 'sing weird Russian songs', couldn't be heard from the boat on

which they were performing, the Russian chief of security cheerfully told the head of Edward's police detail that there was no
danger in bringing aboard the choir — mostly local ladies — as he
had arranged for them all to be strip-searched. Envisaging the headlines in Britain, Ponsonby managed to have him talked out of it.

In Russia the meeting was an enormous hit. It was called the
'feast of peace'. Aside from a small court rump, Russian public
opinion, such as it was, had become very keen indeed on the
Convention in the nine months since it had been published. Even
the most conservative constitutionalists regarded the agreement
with Britain as a sign that the tsarist regime was gradually moving
in the right direction, and that Britain had renounced its historic
opposition to Russia's influence in the Balkans — in contrast to
Germany. The truth was that the starkest reason for the new
popularity of the Entente was a rising hostility towards Germany.
Since 1906, the new independent Russian press had become
noticeably anti-German. It expressed resentment of Germany's
success, its wealth, its economic dominance and its aggressively
high tariffs, and a fear of being overwhelmed by Germany, being
sucked dry and being turned into a dependent vassal. The coverage
bespoke a sense of terrible vulnerability, hair-trigger xenophobia,
which seemed now to be common to every country in Europe,
and a revived sense of territoriality about the Balkans. Now that
Russia's plans to expand into Asia had been so summarily curtailed,
nationalists, imperialists and patriots were turning their attention
back to Russia's traditional preoccupations with Slavdom. And
there Germany and Austria were, more powerful than ever, with
their own doctrines of Pan-Germanism and their own anti-Slavic
doctrines. When the German ambassador complained about the
coverage, Izvolsky had been forced to 'confess his impotence under
the present system of liberty'.

With Edward's now annual summer visit to Wilhelm coming up
in August, Sir Edward Grey thought that if the king spoke to the
kaiser direct, he might perhaps convince him that a slow-down in
naval construction would be good for everyone. How much he
really knew about the state of Edward's relationship with the kaiser

isn't entirely clear. What the British also underestimated was how riled Wilhelm had been by Edward's Russian trip. He had decided it was final proof that the Russian deal was about a military alliance against Germany. That Admiral Jackie Fisher, who had become rather fond of suggesting that the British burn the German fleet, had been taken along too simply confirmed it. Metternich was sent to tell Sir Edward Grey that Germany had regarded the visit 'very searchingly, since several international agreements have already been linked with his [Edward's] travels'. In June Wilhelm told a cavalry review that France, Russia and England were conniving to encircle Germany. After the visit, by way of a riposte, he ordered that no British officer be allowed to join the German army in the future. Nevertheless Grey was sufficiently hopeful to prepare two different memos for Edward on the subject of naval construction, so he could choose which one to use, a move which just irritated the king.

The two monarchs spent the morning together at Kronberg, Vicky's former home. They agreed on a replacement for Sir Francis Lascelles, who was retiring – Sir Edward Goschen, the ambassador in Vienna. His selection was largely due to Edward's influence, who knew him much better than Grey did. Goschen regarded the post as 'the blackest and most nauseous of pills'; in his diary he called the kaiser 'German Bill', and he agreed to take the job only because he was a fervent monarchist and Edward had personally asked him to. 'I cannot resist the King,' he told a British journalist. 'But . . . I am certain my mission to Berlin will end in failure, for there will be no means of avoiding catastrophe.' He would prove a dismal manifestation of new British attitudes to Germany.

Edward raised the navy once, saying he had a memo on the matter. Wilhelm immediately changed the subject, and Edward couldn't bring himself to raise it again. After lunch, as he went to have his post-prandial cigar in the summerhouse, he told Sir Charles Hardinge that it was up to him to discuss the navy with the kaiser.

Wilhelm invited Hardinge to speak to him. Hardinge started in on British worries about the German fleet. It was hard, he said, to reconcile the kaiser's reassurances with the constant increases in the German naval programme, and if Germany continued to build at her current rate, Britain would feel obliged to keep up with it, which would lead to bad feeling. Britain, he emphasized, had no argument with the size of Germany's land armies, but as an island it believed it needed a larger navy to defend itself. He wanted Wilhelm to agree to a ratio of British naval superiority to German: say five British ships to every three German. Almost immediately Wilhelm lost his temper. He refused to accept Hardinge's figures on German shipbuilding. 'That's complete nonsense. Who has been telling you such ridiculous tales? . . . Your documents are wrong. I am an Admiral of the British Navy, which I know all about and understand better than you, who are a civilian with no idea of these matters.' He said there was no reason for the British to fear a German attack, nor to increase its fleet, and that invasion talk was 'sheer nonsense and no serious person in Germany had ever contemplated such an idea'. Anyway, England had started it all by building the Dreadnoughts, and Fisher had initiated the war talk with his threats to burn the German navy. He ended grandly, by stating he would rather go to war than consider slowing down.

At dinner, the kaiser, all smiles, invited Hardinge to sit next to him. Wilhelm talked, Hardinge wrote, 'a lot of nonsense as to his own friendly feelings towards England . . . "The future of the world," he said, "was in the hands of the Anglo–Teuton race, and that England without a powerful army could not stand alone in Europe but must lean on a Continental Power and that Power should be Germany!"' Later Wilhelm told Bülow that the 'frank conversation with me, in which I had shown him my teeth, had not failed to have its effect. That is always the way to treat Englishmen.'

But it was not only the English who wanted the kaiser to cut back on his naval programme. 'The only result of our naval armaments at the present moment is that we have succeeded in arousing the envy and suspicion of the whole world,' Robert zu Zedlitz-Trützschler had written in his diary in 1907. 'England, not without reason, sees in our navy a threat . . . What is the use of all this enormous expenditure, and of arousing mistrust and jealousy?'

There were plenty of ministers and men of influence who felt that, just as Tangier had demonstrated that German aggression tended to backfire, so the naval race had gone too far. Tschirrsky, the former foreign minister, had recommended an agreement on naval quotas after Algeciras. In London, Metternich was convinced that the sole reason for the deterioration of Anglo-German relations was naval rivalry – and was brave enough to say so, which earned him Wilhelm's respect but also impatience. Albert Ballin, the Jewish millionaire director of the Hamburg-America shipping line, whom Wilhelm liked to describe as a friend, had recently recommended that the crisis in Anglo-German relations should be solved by an agreement on building warships. He'd also said that while Edward might be rude about Wilhelm, there was no doubting that he wanted peace.

For a man who changed his mind almost as often as he changed his clothes, Wilhelm was extraordinarily stubborn about his navy. He refused to acknowledge what it cost – when Tirpitz asked for four more ships than had been budgeted for in 1907, he'd told him it was 'a mere bagatelle'. And he refused to countenance any slowdown.

Why is hard to answer. The navy was very popular in certain sections of German society, but it was also known to be very expensive and by 1908 its cost had brought about a financial crisis and the prospect of huge tax increases. Somehow the ships had become tightly attached to Wilhelm's sense of himself: to his deep-seated longing to be connected with Britain, to strike at it, to force it to take notice and to his desire to show that he wasn't hopelessly irresolute. Tirpitz's uncompromising refusal to acknowledge any diplomatic or financial limits to the naval pro-gramme stiffened Wilhelm's resolve and seemed to re-arouse his ever-present desire to show that he was the perfect, implacable German soldier. And he seemed genuinely to adore his ships. Tirpitz spoke, witheringly, about the kaiser's love for his 'mechanical toy'. Perhaps most of all the humiliation of Algeciras made him feel he couldn't be seen to react to British pressure – a feeling shared by many Germans.

Edward was genuinely taken aback by Wilhelm's absolute refusal to discuss the naval programme. When he saw the eighty-year-old Franz Joseph a few days later, he asked him straight out to raise the subject of the ships with the kaiser, a request Franz Joseph, who had learned long ago to keep clear of the grimy details of politics, politely declined. In Marienbad, the king met the French prime minister, Georges Clemenceau, and told him how disappointed he was that Wilhelm had refused to discuss a naval agreement, and that, while European peace might hold for the next five or six years, a certain 'impulsive sovereign' would almost certainly eventually do something that would lead to war. Britain, he assured Clemenceau, would keep building ships so as to outstrip Germany. Back in London, he told Lord Esher that Wilhelm had been '"impossible . . . Two keels to one, is the only right and safe thing," said the King!' In Berlin, Wilhelm scrawled that 'Stop the King!' should be the goal of German policy.

13. A Balkan crisis (1908–9)

Part of the logic and tragedy of empires is that they are always looking to expand, they can never stand still. The European empires had mostly pursued their conquests in far-flung places. But a great opportunity for expansion closer to home promised itself in the break-up of the Ottoman empire, which still ran large swathes of the Balkans. The Ottoman empire's government – corrupt, chaotic and apparently unreformable – had been in a state of near-collapse for decades. The pickings attracted lots of would-be empire-builders, however, which meant that land-grabbing in the Balkans always produced conflict. Sometimes, though, an opportunity seemed too good to pass up. In mid-1908 a revolt by the liberal opposition in Constantinople, the 'Young Turks', turned the Ottoman government upside down. Several European countries took their chance. On 6 October 1908 Austria-Hungary announced to the world that it was formally annexing the small Ottoman-owned Balkan state of Bosnia-Herzegovina. Bulgaria declared its independence from the Ottoman empire (and its ruler Ferdinand proclaimed himself 'tsar'), and Greece claimed the island of Crete. Of these, the one most potentially explosive and likely to trigger wider conflict was Austria's grab of Bosnia because – though Austria had been administering the state for thirty years – it was bound to enrage Russia, which regarded itself as the protector of the independent Balkan states (whether they wanted protecting or not), and Serbia, the most ambitious and aggressive of them, which aspired to absorb Bosnia into its own Slavic empire, and was Russia's closest Balkan ally.

The Russians immediately expressed their utter outrage at Austria's evil Germanic appropriation of poor Slavic Bosnia. At which point the Austrians announced that Alexander Izvolsky, the Russian foreign minister, had given his unconditional approval to the annexation. It was embarrassing but true. In September the

Austrians had summoned Izvolsky to a secret meeting and told him they were going to annex Bosnia with or without Russian approval. Knowing this would enrage Russian opinion, Izvolsky had tried to extract some benefit for Russia by offering formal approval of the annexation in return for Austria agreeing to the opening of the Bosphorus to Russian ships. He thought he had a deal, but the Austrians announced the annexation and Russia's approval without mentioning the Bosphorus at all. Izvolsky was utterly humiliated, the Russian government was angry and wrong-footed, the Russian press was furious that its government had been involved in grimy backroom politics and failed in its duty to protect a Slav state. Serbia, meanwhile, declared that if Austria didn't withdraw it would mobilize its army. The two states had a history. After a bloody coup in 1903, Serbia had morphed from an obedient Austrian satellite into a territorially hungry independent state, the self-styled leader of all Southern Slavs not only outside, but more dangerously inside, Austria-Hungary. The Austrians regarded Serbia as a cancer undermining their multi-ethnic empire. If matters escalated, it seemed certain that Austria would ask for German support, while the Russians would back Serbia.

Desperate to stave off a possible war – and to save his career – Izvolsky begged the British government to support a conference on the annexation and the opening of the Turkish Straits. The British were less than enthusiastic. The Russians had recently breezily been breaking the terms of the Convention, moving troops into Persia to put down a democratically inspired rebellion against the shah, and planting soldiers on the Afghan border. Grey agreed to support a conference, but the Austrians and Germans refused. Only the king, Izvolsky's long-time patron, was all for backing him up. 'Unless some hope is given to Russia . . . ,' he wrote anxiously to Prime Minister Asquith, 'Isvolski will return to his country a discredited [man] . . . and it is impossible to say who his successor might be.' With Grey's support, however, he did write to the tsar telling him how vital the British regarded Izvolsky to Anglo-Russian relations.

To everyone's amazement Izvolsky held on to his job, though the Russian chief minister, Stolypin, would keep him on a tight leash: there was no more secret negotiating. That he survived was due to Stolypin's conclusion, as the threat of war showed no sign of abating, that Russia needed Britain. The tsar suddenly gave the British ambassador, Sir Arthur Nicolson, a rare audience and told him, smilingly, that he hoped the two countries would get much closer. Nicolson, deeply flattered, reported what a 'very straight-forward and honourable man' the tsar was. (Actually Nicholas had known all about the annexation from the start and had encouraged Izvolsky to pursue a deal on the Straits. Now, however, he denied all knowledge and said he was disgusted that his foreign minister had shamed him.) Almost simultaneously, Izvolsky asked Nicolson, and Benckendorff, the Russian ambassador in London, asked Grey, what Britain would do if there was a war in the Balkans and Germany supported Austria. Grey, who was becoming practised at answering such questions, never committed himself to going to war. He answered that Britain would not automatically fight with either France or Russia, but would naturally place itself against the 'aggressor'.

As the international situation continued to look gloomy, Wilhelm managed to introduce a little light relief – at least for everyone apart from the Germans. On 28 October the *Daily Telegraph* published an interview with the kaiser written by Colonel Edward Montagu-Stuart-Wortley, a none-too-bright senior army figure and champion of Anglo-German relations, who had amalgamated a series of conversations he had had with Wilhelm when the kaiser had come to stay at his home, Highcliffe Castle near Bournemouth, the previous winter.* The interview was a sincere attempt to show the British public what a keen Anglophile the German emperor was. The authentic Wilhelm was unmistakable: pompous, unerr-ingly tactless, more than a little deluded and unintentionally funny. 'You English are mad, mad as March hares,' he said. 'What on earth has come over you that you should harbour such suspicions against us.' British suspicions were a 'personal insult', bolstered by the British press's repeated 'distortions' of his 'repeated offers of

---

* Wilhelm had proposed to rent the castle for several weeks for the hunting; Stuart-Wortley had insisted he come as his guest.

friendship'. Out came the litany of selfless acts he had performed for Britain – now so often repeated that he had come to believe them himself: how he personally had prevented France and Russia from combining to attack England during the Boer War, how he had thought up the strategy with which Lord Roberts had won the Boer War. He finished by assuring his readers that the German navy existed only to defend German trade from the likes of the Japanese. In so doing, he calumnied, among others, the Russians and the Japanese – both took umbrage – and implied that apart from himself the rest of Germany hated Britain.

In England, the piece caused amusement. The kaiser genuinely seemed to want to be Britain's friend, but he sounded so ridiculous, an observation even the kindest reactions in the British press couldn't resist: the *Nation* called the interview 'sincere and impulsive'; the *Westminster Gazette*, 'well meant' but 'embarrassing'. Lord Esher described it as 'amazing', and added, 'he thinks himself immortal and omnipotent'.

In Germany, however, the article prompted a frenzy of anger and resentment against the kaiser, both at the revelation that he had supported Britain during the Boer War, and – almost more painful to the prickly adolescent nation – that he had made himself and the country a laughing stock. In his memoirs, Bülow described the interview as a 'dynamite bomb . . . sad effusions, which could scarcely have been surpassed in tactless stupidity'. The *Telegraph* interview seemed the last straw, after the rumours of Wilhelm's insanity, the intemperate speeches and the Eulenburg scandal. The case had ended only in July, with Eulenburg fainting while standing trial for perjury, amid a welter of pitiful and half-substantiated stories about sex with fishermen and milkmen, which dated from the 1880s.★ 'Of all the political gaffes which HIM has made, this is the greatest,' Edward told Hardinge.

Within days of the interview, the press, the Reichstag, even the

---

★ Eulenburg would pass the next twelve years of his life in depressed, hypochondriacal seclusion. He wrote, 'The Emperor is the greatest disappointment of my life, I hoped everything of him, and he has not fulfilled one of my hopes.' As for Wilhelm, from time to time he could be heard to mutter pitifully to himself, 'Poor Phili'.

princes of the German empire in the Bundesrat and ministers in the Prussian government were queuing up to express their seething anger. There were calls for Wilhelm's abdication, or at the very least for some constitutional curtailment of his power. Bülow told the kaiser he needed a free hand to deal with the crisis and offered his resignation just to make it clear, bundling him off to Austria to see his new friend Archduke Franz Ferdinand, heir to the Austro-Hungarian empire. He then issued a statement in the *Nordeutsche Allgemeine Zeitung*, claiming he'd had nothing to do with the article, that he'd been too burdened with other state matters to look at it, and that all the fault lay with the Foreign Office. In fact, he was thoroughly implicated in it. The kaiser had personally asked him to read the draft, after Tirpitz among others had advised that it shouldn't be published. Bülow had read it, suggested some cuts and had then gone on holiday – passing it on to the Foreign Office. The article was handed from minion to minion and the various cuts and editorial suggestions seem not to have been incorporated, before it was sent back to its English author. It's impossible to say for sure whether this was Bülow's carelessness, a deliberate decision to allow Wilhelm to embarrass himself or institutional disorganization. It was probably all three. The new British ambassador, Sir Edward Goschen, reported that he'd seen 'more muddle – more confusion – [in the German government] than I have found in any country during my 35 years experience. Chaos is the only word for it.' He wondered what, if anything, was getting through to Wilhelm.

At a Reichstag debate on 10 November, member after member rose to criticize the emperor with a directness that was completely unprecedented. Bülow spoke just once. He seemed ostensibly to be taking responsibility for the gaffe, but it was clear to his audience that he was actually saying his sympathies were wholly with the kaiser's critics. He made Wilhelm sound like a childish fantasist, when he explained that what the kaiser had described as the winning strategy of the Boer War was in fact a series of clichéd 'aphorisms'. He promised that in future Wilhelm would act 'with restraint', and as a guarantee of this, he said that if the kaiser overstepped his position, he would feel obliged to resign. When

Bülow's speech was reported to him, Wilhelm burst into tears and denounced it as all-out betrayal.

In an effort to distract him, the kaiser's entourage decided to put on an entertainment, the kind that amused him: a ballet spectacular performed by the middle-aged members of his various cabinets. The climax was a performance by Field Marshal Count Dietrich von Hülsen-Haeseler, the hefty, 56-year-old chief of Wilhelm's military cabinet. Described in some sources as wearing a pink tutu ('not for the first time', Zedlitz-Trützschler wrote), in others a pink ball gown – what was undisputed was that he was in drag – with a large feather in his hair, he performed a series of energetic pirouettes, jumps and capers, flirtatiously blew kisses to his audience, stumbled off the stage and suffered a massive heart attack that killed him instantly. It was reported that by the time the doctors arrived, rigor mortis was so far advanced that it was extremely difficult to get Hülsen out of his tutu and into his military uniform. The story made Wilhelm look even more irresponsible and odd; in the French, Italian and British papers there were gleeful screeds about German moral degeneracy.

Back in Berlin on 17 November, four days after Hülsen's death, an uncharacteristically silent and shocked Wilhelm was persuaded, after hours of haranguing by Bülow, to issue what amounted to an apology for his behaviour, an admission that he had breached his constitutional responsibility, that he had confidence in his chancellor, and that he wouldn't do it again. He regretted it almost immediately.

It must have seemed as if things couldn't get any worse. But then, on 22 November, the *Observer* newspaper in London printed an account of an unpublished interview Wilhelm had given the previous July to an American journalist, which seemed to contradict everything he'd said in the *Telegraph*: America and Germany, he said, were the two Great Powers of the future. England was 'rotten and marching to her ruin, and ought to be wiped out'. Germany was 'ready for war at any moment with her and the sooner it came the better'. He also expressed 'the greatest contempt' for Edward. Bülow immediately repudiated the article as a fake, but the whole British Foreign Office and the king had seen the original. Edward told Knollys, 'I know the E[mperor] <u>hates</u> <u>me</u> and never loses an opportunity of saying so . . . whilst I have always been civil and nice to him.'

The day the *Observer* story appeared, Wilhelm anounced that he could no longer cope, he would have to abdicate, and collapsed in a heap. The entourage gathered him up off the floor and put him to bed. He spent the next two weeks, his daughter's English governess, Anne Topham, later wrote, in 'a kind of stormy stupor . . . crushed under the weight of the universal displeasure'. For a few weeks the crown prince, Willy, took over his official functions – reviewing soldiers, leading parades, meeting Bülow, though he took no significant decisions – while the kaiser paced up and down for hours, quiet, for the first time in decades, but giving way occasionally to tears. 'One felt pity for the tortured man suffering so acutely under the blow to his self-esteem, his infallibility.' In her memoirs Topham remembered 'the ghastliness of the dreadful luncheons of the next few days . . . the silence that prevailed was terrifying'. Periodically Wilhelm would complain about Bülow's betrayal.

He seemed exhausted. Fritz Ponsonby saw the extent to which Wilhelm's martial identity was a disguise, and the tired, confused little man beneath it. 'He was the creation of the Germans them-selves,' he wrote. 'They wanted a sabre-rattling autocrat with theatrical ways, attempting to dominate Europe, sending telegrams and making bombastic speeches, and he did his best to supply them with the superman they required.'

Masochistically, Wilhelm bared himself to the family members who liked him least, and for whose approval and sympathy he perhaps most longed. He sent a telegram to Alexandra and Edward early in December, asking after Edward who had had a bad cold. When Alexandra responded, enquiring tactfully after Wilhelm's own 'cold', he replied – *en clair* so everyone could read it – 'I am not suffering from cold but from complete collapse.' Edward commented, 'We do live in marvellous times.'

Sir Edward Grey wrote to an old friend after the *Daily Telegraph* interview.

The German Emperor is ageing me; he is like a battleship with steam up and screws going, but with no rudder, and he will run into something some day and cause a catastrophe. He has the strongest army in the world and the Germans don't like being laughed at and are looking for somebody on whom to vent their temper and use their strength. After a big war a nation doesn't want another for a generation or more. Now it is 38 years since Germany had her last war, and she is very strong and very restless, like a person whose boots are too small for him. I don't think there will be war at present, but it will be difficult to keep the peace of Europe for another five years.

Serbia and Austria continued to swap threats. With the kaiser in the equivalent of quarantine, Bülow had decided that Austria had to be supported because it was now Germany's only reliable ally and couldn't be seen to be weak – a reaction on which the Austrian foreign minister, Aloys von Aehrenthal, had counted – though at the same time he said that Germany must take care not to be dragged into a war over Bosnia. Wilhelm, however, had initially been angry about the annexation – he had called it 'a piece of brigandage' – and said he was 'wounded in my deepest feelings' that Franz Joseph had failed even to give him a hint about it. Nor was he entirely certain that Austria deserved German support. Bülow, however, told him that Germany should encourage Austria not to back down. If there were to be a future 'European conflagration', he told Wilhelm, the two would fight together, and Austria would 'concentrate all her powers against Russia'. It was a sign of how easy it had become in Germany's governing circles to talk about war. Helmuth von Moltke, the chief of the German General Staff, went further. He told his opposite number in the Austrian army that Germany would protect Austria even if it invaded Serbia and provoked a war. Moltke actively welcomed a war with Russia; he felt the timing and circumstances, with Austria ready to take part, were 'propitious'. His views were shared by many senior German officers – such as the head of Wilhelm's military cabinet, Moritz von Lyncker, who talked freely about war as a solution to Germany's 'internal and external difficulties'.

In Russia, meanwhile, the press was demanding action against

Austria more and more insistently. The government, painfully aware of Russia's post-war weakness, knew it simply couldn't offer Serbia military support. In late December Nicholas wrote directly to Wilhelm asking him to use his influence with Austria to resolve the crisis once and for all. Wilhelm refused, but he insisted that the annexation had been a genuine surprise to him – as indeed it had – and added, in a tone that combined an unconvincing airiness and aggrievedness, that, while he quite understood why Russia had to cosy up to Britain, he was disappointed that since 1906 it had pulled away from Germany 'more and more'. He asked Nicky how he could support Serbia, a nation which had assassinated its monarch.★ If only, he said, the tsar had approached him sooner, he might have been able to help.

A few weeks later, in February 1909, Edward and Alexandra arrived in Berlin for their long-delayed state visit. The king had made strenuous efforts not to come but Grey said that the times required that 'informal relations' be as friendly as possible. 'The FO to gain their own object, would not care a pin what humiliation I should put up with,' the king grumbled.

Edward was not in good shape. 'The King of England is so stout that he completely loses his breath when he has to climb upstairs,' Zedlitz-Trützschler wrote in his diary. 'The Emperor told us that at the first family dinner he fell asleep . . . he eats, drinks and smokes enormously.' Edward was now sixty-eight and his chronic bronchitis and great weight were wearing him down. The striking energy of a few years before was on the wane. The only accommodation he would make for his worsening health was to promise his doctor – who, with a nurse, numbered among the thirteen members of his suite – he would smoke only two cigars before breakfast. He asked, uncharacteristically, that speeches might be read rather than made impromptu – dreading that Wilhelm might slip in some unexpected horror to which he would have to respond. But Edward's demeanour was not merely the result of illness. He had been terribly upset by what he saw as Franz Joseph's

---

★ The Serbian king had been assassinated in 1903.

dishonesty. In August 1908, just before Bosnia, the Hapsburg emperor and his foreign minister, Aehrenthal, had gone out of their way to assure him of their desire for 'the closest cooperation between the two countries especially in the Balkans', and insisted they were committed to stability. Afterwards, Edward had persuaded the emperor to take his first trip in a motor car. They'd reached the princely speed of thirty miles an hour. The king had been proud of his relationship with Franz Joseph, 'the dearest and most courteous old gentleman that lives', as Hardinge called him. He'd regarded it as a prime example of his diplomacy, a genuine friendship which mitigated some of the hostility with which he was regarded in German-speaking Europe. Now it seemed to have been worth nothing. His dreams of peace appeared to be ebbing away, and at home he had seen a government schism blow up over the extent of the German threat.

Wilhelm, by contrast, seemed to have bounced back remarkably from his collapse. Despite everything, he persisted in feeling excited. He told the tsar that he expected the visit to have 'useful results for the Peace of the World'. While he was still bruised by the *Daily Telegraph* affair, the new year had brought a resurgence of sympathy for him in parts of the press, where it was being suggested that the chancellor had not been altogether supportive of his emperor. He was very solicitous of his uncle and aunt, though Fritz Ponsonby found him brittle and full of 'forced jokes'.

Truth be told the whole visit had a slight air of farce and disaster about it. When the train rolled up at the Berlin station, the king was in the queen's carriage, and the emperor, empress and their entourage had to scuttle undignifiedly down the platform to greet them. Then the horses drawing Alexandra and Dona's carriage in the procession to the Berlin Schloss stopped and refused to move, two cavalrymen were thrown off their horses, and the whole procession had to be re-ordered. Wilhelm and Edward arrived at the Berlin Schloss to find no one behind them. On the second day, after a long lunch at the British embassy, Edward sat down on a sofa with a cigar next to the glamorous English aristocrat Daisy Pless, began to cough horribly, and passed out, the cigar popping out of his fingers. Daisy and Alexandra scrabbled to loosen his – even tighter than usual – clothing, and Edward's doctor rushed into the room and ordered everyone out. The king reappeared fifteen minutes later, insisting that everything was fine. But his projected trip to Potsdam was downgraded to a day in Berlin, visiting Wilhelm's stables, Wilhelm's motor cars, Wilhelm's ballet (one he had 'devised') and the Hohenzollern museum, most noted – apart from its collection of Frederick the Great's snuffboxes – for memorabilia about Wilhelm. Edward recovered his old easy charm only once: when he addressed a large crowd of Berliners at the town hall with an off-the-cuff speech in fluent German, which was greeted – to everyone's relief – by enthusiastic applause. The kaiser, meanwhile, was piqued by the snootiness of some of the British entourage. He complained that they had behaved as if Germany was in the Stone Age; one lady 'openly expressed her astonishment' that there were 'bathrooms, soap and handtowels'. Another was amazed that Berlin 'actually had streets on which one could find handsome hotels and big stores'.

The king and queen departed on 14 February, escorted by the kaiser to the Berlin station. The two men embraced. Edward boarded his train. They never saw each other again.

Both men colluded in the fiction that the meeting had achieved something. Edward told the banker Ernst Cassel it was 'in every respect a success'; Wilhelm told his new friend and correspondent Franz Ferdinand that it had 'had a very relieving and satisfactory effect'. Fritz Ponsonby, however, was sure that 'The effect of this visit was nil. One felt that a few charming men really liked us, but with the majority one derived the impression that they hated us.'

By early March 1909 the Austrian army was mobilizing to attack Serbia. In response Russia – its press already in a lather about its failure to defend the Slavs of Bosnia-Herzegovina from the Hapsburg empire – began to mass soldiers on the Austrian border. The Russian government knew it could not afford to go to war, but it was desperate to glean a shred of dignity from the crisis. It appealed to the German government to intervene on its behalf – effectively to broker some face-saving device with the Austrians.

Bülow and Moltke decided that the request must be refused.

That Germany might negotiate a deal between the two countries and emerge the power broker of middle Europe was nowhere in German Foreign Office calculations. Instead on 22 March Germany sent the Russian government a brusque ultimatum that left Russia with no graceful way out, insisting that it back down and unconditionally accept the annexation or it would find itself at war with Germany. 'We expect a precise answer, Yes or No, any vague, complicated or ambiguous reply will be treated as a refusal.' Bülow approved the tone of the message, presumably feeling that a show of toughness would lend the government an air of brute effectiveness that it was sorely lacking.

'Once the matter had been put as definitely and unequivocally as that, there was nothing for it but to swallow one's pride, give in and agree,' Nicholas wrote bitterly to his mother, who was staying with her sister in London. The Russian government's capitulation brought an end to the crisis, but Russian public opinion was furious, unable to understand why the government had backed down. It seemed one more blow to the country's status. 'Shame! Shame! It would be better to die! . . .' Russia's leading Pan-Slavist, General Kireev, wept into his diary. 'We have become a second rate power.' In the Duma the largest party, the Octobrists, accused the government of having betrayed Russia's historic mission in the Balkans. *Novoe vremia* described the decision not to fight as a diplomatic Tsushima,★ and began to call for stronger ties with France and in particular with England: 'the enemies of enemies are friends to each other'. In the aftermath of Bosnia, Slavic societies would spring up all over Western Russia, demanding formal government support for the Slavs against the German powers, the imposition of Russia's imperial influence in the Balkans, and the acquisition of the Turkish Straits. 'It was considered not only in the Press,' the British ambassador in St Petersburg wrote to Sir Edward Grey, 'but also, so far as I have been able to observe and ascertain, in all classes of society that . . . there has never previously been a moment when the country had undergone such a humiliation.'

★ After the devastating defeat inflicted by the Japanese on the Russian navy in 1905.

For once Nicholas was in tune with Russian public opinion – such as it was – though he could do nothing about it. 'The form and the method of Germany's action – I mean towards us – has simply been brutal and we won't forget it. I think they were again trying to separate us from France and England – but once again they have undoubtedly failed. Such methods tend to bring about the opposite result.' Wilhelm sent Nicholas an Easter egg – 'a token of undiminished love and friendship' – and thanked him 'sincerely for the loyal and noble way in which you kinly [*sic*] led the way to help to preserve peace. It is thanks to your high-minded and unselfish initiative that Europe has been spared the horrors of universal war.' By way of an answer, Nicholas summoned the British ambassador and told him that he wanted to see Russia's relationship with England strengthened, and that the Entente must stand up to Germany. This time ambassador Nicolson felt there was no mistaking that the tsar was asking for the Convention to be turned into a military alliance. The kaiser and the tsar met for a day at Björkö in June, but by the end of the year the German ambassador in St Petersburg was reporting that there was no point in the kaiser continuing to write to the tsar, as his expressions of sympathy towards Russia were considered worthless.

For Wilhelm the ultimatum – in which he played no part – had been deeply discomfiting. As the threat of war loomed, Lyncker, the chief of his military cabinet, had disappointedly noted that the kaiser lacked all appetite for it – in contrast to his military entourage and generals. Afterwards, however, when it was hailed at the German court as a 'great diplomatic triumph', he felt obliged to prove that he had led Germany's aggressively pro-Austrian course all along. In Vienna, the following year, he announced that he was Austria's knight in shining armour. He told an Austrian diplomat that they should have gone ahead and invaded Serbia. 'I hate the Slavs, I know it is a sin but I cannot help myself.' 'When Germany made up its mind to go in a given direction,' Theodore Roosevelt would say of the kaiser, 'he could only stay at the head of affairs by scampering to take the lead.'

The British were bemused and worried by the way the Germans had behaved over Bosnia. The former prime minister Arthur

Balfour noted that Herbert Asquith had said to him after Bosnia that 'incredible as it might seem, the Government could form no theory of German policy which fitted all the known facts, except that they wanted war'. He added that the internal conditions of Germany were so unsatisfactory that it might be 'driven to the wildest adventures in order to divert national sentiment into a new channel'. When Edward went to Marienbad that summer, he refused invitations from both Franz Joseph and the new German chancellor.

Back in London after his Berlin visit, Edward put his weight behind the campaign, led by the Admiralty and the Conservative Party, to increase British shipbuilding in order to stay ahead of the German navy. The issue was splitting the government. Jackie Fisher was convinced that Germany was building more ships than it was admitting to – he had Edward informed that Germany was buying more building materials than its published plans required. The Admiralty demanded six, better still eight, new Dreadnoughts to stay ahead. Many members of the Liberal Party regarded this as paranoid profligacy which would eat into the money set aside for the new pensions and national insurance plans drawn up by David Lloyd George and Winston Churchill. The arguments became bitter. Jackie Fisher and the naval minister, Mckenna, threatened to resign. Edward's secretary, Knollys, wrote that Churchill could not possibly be acting from 'conviction or principle. The very idea of his having either is enough to make anyone laugh.' Grey, meanwhile, had come round to the Admiralty's view: he had repeatedly asked Metternich for the correct naval figures, while reassuring him that Britain would slow down its shipbuilding if Germany would too. The ambassador wanted to oblige but couldn't. The kaiser had told him to stonewall any attempts to find out the true figures. In his reports home, Metternich said that the British reaction was understandable given that Germany looked as if it had something to hide, and as far as he could see did seem to be clandestinely building more ships. Wilhelm scribbled 'Nonsense!' . . . 'This is absolutely not so!'

The situation was resolved only when Asquith came up with a

compromise to commission four ships in 1909 and another four in 1910. The irony was, however, that though it was true that Tirpitz had started building more ships than the Reichstag – or even the kaiser – had given him permission for, German government finances couldn't support the weight of defence spending which now took up nearly 90 per cent of the Reich's budget. Despite a further naval bill to try to catch up with the British increases in 1912, Tirpitz would never realize his goal.★ Such is the way of arms races. The British naval bill, meanwhile, managed to frighten and alarm the Germans just as the German bill had alarmed the British. In 1909 on a visit to London, Wilhelm's notably Anglophile brother Heinrich told Fritz Ponsonby that in Germany people were convinced 'that England would on the slightest excuse come and smash the German fleet, and at the present they were at our mercy'. And Heinrich added – an unconscious admission of the underlying tension and aggression between the two countries – that the Germans 'had studied European history and they knew that whenever any European power rose to any predominance, we [the British] smashed them. He instanced, the Dutch, the Spanish, and later the French. They did not in Germany mean to follow the example of the others. They had no wish for war, but they did not mean to remain defenceless and at our mercy.'

In Britain, the cost of the additional ships, added to the new pensions and national insurance, forced David Lloyd George to look for a new source of taxation. He found it in the rich and aristocratic, which gave him an opportunity to bring about a confrontation with the Conservative-dominated House of Lords. In Germany, in a strange parallel, Bülow found himself in a similar – even more pressing – situation, with a fiscal crisis brought on by the vast expenditure on defence. Germany had a fantastically inequitable and outmoded tax system which left the Junkers largely untaxed. Echoing Lloyd George, Bülow's solution was to try to impose death duties and new land taxes that impinged on the aristocracy as never before.

By the spring of 1909 Bülow was fighting for his political life.

★ By 1912 Germany had thirteen Dreadnoughts to Britain's twenty-two.

The kaiser was raring to sack him. The *Daily Telegraph* affair had destroyed Wilhelm's trust in him, and the kaiser had resolved to keep him only until he had steered the necessary financial reforms through the Reichstag. Bülow had been casting around for a way of securing his position without the kaiser. He seems to have seriously considered trying to institute some kind of constitutional government, with himself as chancellor. He wrote to Fritz Holstein, 'If I am supported by the Reichstag, there is a possibility that from now on there will be a different kind of rule.' Bülow appealed to the German conservative parties to agree to make a fair contribution to the country's finances in return for real power in government: he seems to have hoped that, with their help, he might wrest the constitutional initiative from Wilhelm and establish a parliamentary system where he, Bülow, would govern at the head of a coalition of Reichstag parties, a plan that would effectively turn them from lobby groups into real parties with responsibility for government and to their electorate.

Lloyd George's 1909 Budget, by contrast, was an attack on aristocratic privilege and the unelected Conservative bigwigs in the House of Lords, rather than an invitation to power. In the end it was forced on the unelected peers, and their resistance resulted in the loss of the Lords' veto on legislation, the last hurrah of aristocratic power in Britain. The British aristocracy would be left intact as a class, and in 1918 it would still be in existence. In Germany, Bülow failed to persuade the Junker parties to part with their privileges and exemptions, his financial reforms were defeated in the Reichstag in June 1909, his coalition fell apart and Wilhelm sacked him two days later. The system remained inequitable, Junkers held on to their privileges and the government's finances continued to limp along, a situation which would contribute to Germany's revolution in 1918.

To display the warmth of their relations with Britain, and no doubt to make a show of it to the Germans, in August 1909 the Russian imperial family, along with Stolypin and Izvolsky, came to Britain. Or rather – perhaps as a riposte to Edward's reluctance to set foot on Russian soil – the royal yachts *Standart* and *Polar Star* anchored off the Isle of Wight. In London, seventy MPs and two bishops made formal complaints the day the Russians arrived despite the fact that to sweeten the pill Sir Charles Hardinge had produced a series of reports listing a number of entirely fictitious improvements in Russia's civil liberties record. Confidentially, the British ambassador had recently noted that the regime had executed 2,835 people in the three years up to October 1908.

'Dear Nicky looking so well and Alicky too,' George wrote. There are no hints in his diary as to the flow of feelings or the strangeness – it was eleven years since he had last seen them. George took the imperial family to inspect twenty-four battleships and sixteen heavy cruisers gathered at Spithead; they steamed through three rows of ships in the *Victoria and Albert*. Guns saluted and each crew cheered on cue, a demonstration of force and coordination as much for the sake of the Germans as the Russians. Apart from a few trips to Hesse and Kiel, it was the first time any of the Romanov children had been anywhere outside Russia. Not that they can have seen much. They were allowed to set foot on dry land precisely once, when they were conducted around Osborne House, now a rest home for naval officers. The tsar and the Prince of Wales still looked extraordinarily alike. As they posed in their white British admiral's uniforms, with their sad eyes and their Vandyke beards, one might almost have mistaken them for twins. David, George's thirteen-year-old son, who was the tsar's godson, however, could later remember almost nothing about him, though he vividly recalled his 'elaborate police guard'.

Alix went to visit the 82-year-old former French empress Eugénie, who was in her thirty-eighth year of British exile in the Hampshire town of Farnborough. She seemed particularly fascinated by deposed queens and owned various pieces of Marie Antoinette memorabilia, including a series of four tapestries that had belonged to her. Nicholas was, as ever, polite and inscrutable. At the Russian court, the last stronghold of Russian Germanophilia, it was said that Izvolsky had had to force him to make the trip and that the tsar still harboured reservations about a closer relationship with Britain. The tsar's favourite court official, old Count Fredericks, warned that the Cowes visit would irretrievably embroil the imperial couple in the British democracy's feud with the kaiser. 'Britain would never be a loyal ally,' Fredericks was reported as saying, 'and he predicted the worst perils for our country.'

14. Edward's mantle (1910–11)

Edward died on 6 May 1910. He'd just returned from his annual spring visit to Biarritz with Alice Keppel, where his coughing and wheezing had been so bad he'd barely left the hotel in six weeks. Back in England he seemed to rally, playing bridge until midnight, managing five hours of Wagner at the opera, meeting various ministers. But on Sunday 1 May he went for a walk at Sandringham, stayed out in a cold wind and caught a chill. The following Friday, after a series of minor heart attacks, he lapsed into unconsciousness. It was somehow appropriate that the last thing George was able to tell him was that his horse, Witch of the Air, had won at Kempton Park.

In Britain Edward had made royalty visible, glamorous and enormously popular. The same papers that had covered his vices in salacious detail when he was Prince of Wales now extravagantly praised him. Hundreds of thousands of mourners filed past his coffin in Westminster Hall. From Europe came grandiloquent tributes. In Russia *Novoe vremia* wrote that Edward had 'moulded the destinies of his realm'. A Viennese paper called him 'The most influential man of the present day. His own foreign minister.' In Germany the *Rheinisch-Westfälische Zeitung* described him as 'the great opponent . . . We stand at his bier as at that of a mighty and victorious antagonist.' 'He might have been a Solon and Francis of Assisi combined if characters drawn of him were true,' the anti-imperialist poet and diplomat Wilfrid Scawen Blunt noted drily.

In some respects, however, Edward had failed to be what he had set out to be – a peacemaker. He had helped to put Britain back in Europe, he had encouraged the deals with France and Russia, but he had become the incarnation of Germany's old fears of being trapped and surrounded by hostile forces – and though the accusation was ridiculous, he was unable to summon the energy or inclination to counter it. His association with the anti-German hawkish party in Britain and the very public failure of his relationship with Wilhelm had compounded this. A few months before he died he had confidentially told a British journalist that in a European war Britain would be obliged by 'honour and interest', to come to France's aid against Germany.

Before he set out for the funeral, Wilhelm passed judgement on his uncle. 'The scheming and intrigues . . . which for so long have caused unrest abroad and made Europe hold its breath, will hopefully come to a stop,' he told his new chancellor, Theodore von Bethmann-Hollweg. 'All the Cabinet alliances and private coalitions will fall apart without a man at the top to bind them together.' Edward, he claimed, would be missed only by 'the French and the Jews'. Europe would be 'much calmer'. As for George, Wilhelm described him, unusually perceptively, as 'An English country gentleman without political interests . . . whose sketchy linguistic abilities will incline him towards staying at home.' Finally, Wilhelm felt, he was the pre-eminent monarch in Europe. And relations with the British royal family would be more temperate since George was perfectly friendly. It was unlikely, however, that this would make any difference to the impacted nature of Anglo-German relations.

George was devastated by his father's death – though the sheer dread of becoming king was inextricably enmeshed in his feelings of loss. 'I have lost my best friend, and the best of fathers,' he wrote in his diary. 'I never had a word with him in my life. I am heartbroken and overwhelmed with grief. I am quite stunned by this awful blow.' Nicholas wrote to him, 'How <u>deeply</u> I feel for you; the terrible loss you and England have sustained. I know alas! By experience what it costs one. There you are with your heart bleeding and aching, but at the same time duty imposes itself and people and affairs come up and tear you away from your sorrow . . . How I would have liked to have come now and be near you!'

Even without Nicholas an embarrassment of European royalty turned up at the funeral: seven kings (of Belgium, Greece, Norway, Spain, Bulgaria, Denmark and Portugal), one emperor (Wilhelm), and thirty European princes and heirs, including Franz Ferdinand of Austria, Alix's brother Ernst of Hesse, Nicholas's younger brother Misha and their mother, Minny. The United States was represented by Theodore Roosevelt, who had recently, and rather reluctantly, stepped down from the presidency. The bill for feeding the kings alone was said to have come to £4,644 (around £325,000 in today's money). Nothing politically significant was said or suggested. The kings changed into their uniforms, waxed their impressive beards and moustaches, ate their dinners, posed for photographs. British guards regiments marched perfectly through the streets; the funeral was, as Minny wrote back to Nicholas, 'beautifully arranged, all in perfect order, very touching and solemn. Poor Aunt Alix bore up wonderfully to the last. Georgie, too, behaved so well and with such calm.'

Only five months later the first of the royal guests would lose his throne: Manuel of Portugal, deposed by a country tired of his attachment to the extreme Right. He escaped to Gibraltar and was brought to exile in England on George's yacht the *Victoria and Albert*. In 1912 the Italian king Vittorio Emmanuele, whose father had been assassinated, would narrowly avoid the same fate. George's uncle George of Greece would fall victim to an attack at Salonika in 1913. Franz Ferdinand would die in Sarajevo in 1914. Misha would be murdered the day after his brother in 1918. Kings were parting company with history.

Once again the London crowds cheered Wilhelm – but then the London crowds cheered almost anyone; pageantry was entertainment. In Germany, the endless displays, the reviews, the monuments unveiled, the processions and the speeches that had become so much a feature of the Wilhelmine era, had gradually bored the public into apathy or derision, but in Britain Wilhelm was still good value. Alongside the antagonism so vividly expressed in the press, his appearances in England triggered a yearning that the tensions in Europe would simply go away. He looked so forceful and effective in his spiked helmet, so pleased to see his English relatives, surely it all must count for something? The *Telegraph* piously expressed the wish that Wilhelm, 'the great arbiter of peace and war', would take up Edward's mantle as international peacemaker: 'if the German Emperor takes up decisively the moral role in international affairs', he might be 'the world's new hope'. He accompanied George to Westminster Hall, 'where we put wreaths on dear Papa's coffin, most touching to see the thousands of people passing in absolute silence'. The kaiser had always had an instinct for a public gesture – though never for its consequences. He clasped the king's hand across the coffin. The press seized on it as 'a symbol', as the *Daily Chronicle* said, 'of the friendship that should ever unite the two great Empires they represent in the bonds of peace'. 'None who saw it was unaffected by this display of simple affection between the cousins,' gushed the *Daily Mail*, the gesture would 'never be forgotten'.

Wilhelm wrote home to his chancellor that being at Windsor again revived all his happy childhood memories, and even though the intervening years had been 'particularly hard to take', he was 'proud to call this place my second homeland and to be a member of its royal family'. Within days he was very much at home. When Alexandra, a widow of two weeks, showed no sign of wanting to move out of Buckingham Palace or of relinquishing the trappings of her position, and George seemed reluctant to raise the matter, the kaiser decided to tackle it himself. 'Willie dear,' Alexandra said to the nephew she had disliked for thirty years, 'you know that you always speak rather indistinctly, I am afraid that I have not heard a single word that you were saying.'

It was all rather different from Germany, where half the country now despised Wilhelm's gaffes, his unsteadiness, his triviality, his slavish identification with the army and the Prussian Junker class, and at least half the press treated him as a bad joke. The notion of 'personal rule', moreover, had evaporated with Bülow's retirement. Wilhelm's relationship with his new chancellor, Bethmann-Hollweg, was quite different. He had not been Wilhelm's first or even second choice and regarded himself as a professional administrator and servant of the state, not a courtier. He was thoroughly 'Prussian' in his outlook – anti-democratic, anti-Socialist, pro-agrarian, nationalistic – but he did not flatter or kowtow, and the kaiser now more or less allowed him to pursue his policies and appoint ministers as he thought best. Archaeology was the kaiser's new passion. Each spring he would disappear off to Corfu, where the disgruntled entourage were forced to dig for hours. 'Let him get on with it,' Bethmann-Hollweg told a colleague, 'for as long as he is digging, he does not send telegrams and interfere with politics.' Not that Wilhelm had stopped making speeches or trying to keep up the public fiction that he was still in control. Nor would he – despite all the fond memories – allow Bethmann-Hollweg to meddle at all with the naval programme. On becoming chancellor in 1909 the latter had tried to tackle what he saw as Germany's worrying international isolation. He had proposed Anglo-German talks on the navy, but had immediately come up against Wilhelm and Tirpitz's stubbornness. Bethmann-Hollweg regarded Tirpitz's naval policy as the 'unending screw' preventing a *rapprochement* with Britain. But he could offer only a slowdown in construction, not an acknowledgement of the Royal Navy's numerical superiority, and in return he wanted a diplomatic treaty by which Britain promised not to interfere in Europe in the event of a European war, a gesture he insisted was vital in order to secure the approval of the kaiser and German public opinion. Unsurprisingly, the British response had been tepid and the talks had lapsed.

Though his father had tried to prepare him for kingship, George felt utterly unready. At Sandringham and among the shooting aristocracy he had kept himself insulated from the twentieth century, public attention and the messy world of politics. Becoming king thrust him into a scary and foreign world. He confided to Esher that he found himself at five in the morning scribbling anxious notes to himself. He described meeting his father's privy councillors the day after his father's death, as 'the most trying ordeal I ever had to go through'. Appearing in public was excruciating. Reading his speech to open Parliament – 'a terrible ordeal' – made his hands shake so hard the text had to be set in extra large type. His coronation in June 1911 was quite as bad. His anxiety was obvious. The society wit and satirist Max Beerbohm, watching him at the opening of Parliament, felt a stab of pity for him, 'The little King, with the great diamonded crown that covered his eyebrows, and with the eyes that showed so tragically much of effort, of the will to please . . . the will to be all that he isn't and that his Papa <u>was</u> . . . Oh such a piteous, good, feeble, heroic little figure.'

For all his anxieties about becoming king, and his innocence when it came to politics, George possessed – not unlike his cousins – very conservative views and a fierce sense of entitlement. The narrowness of his naval education and his almost pathological aversion to change put him on the side of reaction. The new Edwardian world left him bewildered and alarmed. If he'd had the chance, he would have capsized all the policy decisions the ruling Liberal Party made in his first years as king: he would have kept the House of Lords just as it was, prevented Irish Home Rule and sponsored anti-trade union legislation – though he would have agonized over each decision. He viewed socialists and the radical wing of the Liberal Party as the enemy, and construed everything they did as an assault on him and his world. He found strikes and trade unions incomprehensible. In 1912 he asked Asquith to come up with a law to stop peaceful picketing, which he considered disgraceful; during the 1926 General Strike he would suggest that the government arrest union leaders. He even disapproved of the Royal Navy reforms which his father had backed, particularly the redeploying of the Mediterranean fleet to the North Sea; he especially disliked Admiral Fisher, whom he regarded as devious.

Where George did have control – over the court and his household – he was an autocrat. What he wanted he got. With her husband's accession, May resolved that she must be even more deferential and acquiescent to him; she never contradicted him over anything now, even within the family. The cost, her old friends noticed, was high. Her friend Mabell, Countess of Airlie wrote that 'Her devotion to the Monarchy demanded the sacrifice of much of her personal happiness.' She encouraged everyone else to defer too. Fritz Ponsonby, whom George took against for a while because he disagreed with him too often and too directly, felt that George's household indulged him appallingly. He described once beating the king at tennis. George sulked and refused 'to try'. He was used to being allowed to win. 'He told us we didn't understand the game and we ought to send easy ones. I was furious as pat ball is such rot.' It was a small example, but the lack of challenge meant that there was nothing to check his bad temper and resistance to new ideas.

George's dislike of what his wife's biographer has described as 'everything complex', led him to insist that May must choose only one of her two given names, Victoria Mary, as queen. She chose Mary. He dressed insistently in the style of the late 1890s and demanded that Mary, who secretly would have liked to wear more fashionable clothes, do so too, so she would remain for ever in the constricting toques and bustles and corsets of a late-Victorian lady. Longing for the certainties of his grandmother's world, he returned the court to the staidnesses of the 1890s. 'We are back in Victorian times,' Viscount Esher wrote in his diary. The more open, less orthodox style of Edward's court and social life disappeared almost overnight. The new king's court was cloistered and irreproachably correct. ('We have seen enough of the intrigue and meddling of certain ladies, I'm not interested in any wife but my own,' George said. It was the closest he ever came to criticism of his father.) It was also crashingly dull. Even Lord Esher, lover of all things royal, began to bemoan the loss of 'that curious electric current which pervaded the surroundings of King Edward'.

Like many anxious men, George felt put upon, the more so because 'duty' was his guiding mantra. The result was a tendency to – often inappropriate – self-pity, indulged by the culture of deference of his wife and household. 'Is it not hard on me?' he complained when mistakes were found in the ceremonial orders written up for Edward's funeral – though there was a courtier and four clerks ready to spend the day fixing them. In 1914, when the conference on Home Rule, convened at Buckingham Palace to resolve the conflict between the Irish nationalists and the Ulster loyalists, failed, he wrote, 'I want sympathy in these days and I can't help thinking I am being badly treated.'

From the start it was clear George wasn't going to engineer an active role for himself in the way that his father and grandmother had. He had neither the drive, imagination or charm to do so. Nor was he a very effective intervener because – just like his cousins – he could not distinguish between the trivial and the important. Like his father he was obsessed with correct dress, and would fire off pages of complaints – or rather his private secretary, Bigge, would – about an MP's failure to appear in parliament in the right frock coat or the correct hat, or about some minister's phrase that had offended him. When Winston Churchill wrote a report for him about a day's debate in the House of Commons and added, apropos a piece of employment legislation, that there were as many 'idlers and wastrels' at the top of the social ladder as at the bottom, George complained furiously to Asquith, and anyone else who would listen, that Churchill's phrase had been 'very socialistic and utterly uncalled for'. No one corrected his own moments of tactlessness. He excoriated Lloyd George in front of the chancellor's own staff and colleagues: on one occasion because he'd made another speech attacking big landowners who kept vast uncultivated estates. What had really angered George was that Lloyd George had claimed that pheasants ate whole fields of 'mangold-wurzels', and pheasants couldn't eat mangold-wurzels.

He didn't like it when it was too clearly spelled out that his role was purely symbolic. In 1914 Viscount Esher described his outrage at 'the extraordinary assumption of his ministers that he would agree with any proposal they might make'. He felt both intimidated by his ministers and entitled to lecture them – which he did, often at length. During audiences, ministers would find themselves barely able to get a word in, while George gave them his opinions. They in turn found him a bit of a joke. 'The King is a very jolly chap,' Lloyd George wrote after meeting George and Mary for the first time in the autumn of 1910, 'but thank God there's not much in his head. They are simple, very, very ordinary people, and perhaps on the whole that's how it should be.' 'I understand that it is your turn to go to Balmoral next week,' the prime minister, Asquith, wrote to Winston Churchill. 'So I send you a word of friendly warning. You will find the Royal mind obsessed and the Royal tongue exceptionally fluid and voluble.' 'He is a nice little man with a good heart and tries hard to be just and open-minded. It is a pity he were not better educated,' Asquith told his confidante Venetia Stanley. 'The King talked more stupidly about the Navy than I have ever heard him before,' Churchill wrote in 1912.

'Really it is disheartening to hear this cheap and silly drivel with which he lets himself be filled up.'

As for foreign affairs, it never occurred to Grey that the new king would try to play the role his father had. George hated going abroad; he spoke no languages; he had no real interest in foreign affairs and sometimes expressed nostalgia for 'splendid isolation'. Moreover, the international situation had changed so much since 1901; it seemed impossible that the relationship between two people could have an effect on the relationship between two countries. The situation with Germany was impacted by vivid, deep-seated nationwide hostilities and the navy impasse. George regarded the French as effeminate, and deliberately pronounced French words incorrectly. He disapproved of republicanism and claimed to dislike Paris – which might have been because it had been the location for some of his father's most famous misdemeanours. As for Russia, George's relationship with Nicholas seemed one of the most warm and uncomplicated among the extended European royal families, but it had always been strictly apolitical. Now international affairs began to steal into the kindly, banal expressions of fondness, and the correspondence took on a slightly awkward, euphemistic, official tone. The king's letters also became more frequent, perhaps four or five a year rather than the desultory one or two. 'I hope we shall always continue our old friendship to one another,' he wrote after Edward's funeral. 'You know I never change and I have always been very fond of you . . . you may be sure I shall show the same interest in Russia that He did . . . there may be difficulties with Germany, but I think they can be overcome, if only England, Russia and France stick together the peace in Europe is assured. God bless you, my dear old Nicky and remember, you can always count on me as your friend.' And in March 1911, 'I rather fear at the present moment that Germany is trying to isolate France, I may be wrong but that is what I think. No doubt Germany rather resents the friendly understanding which exists between England, Russia and France.'

George did have an ambition, however. A few months after his accession he told Lord Esher he wanted 'to do for the Empire what King Edward did for the peace of Europe'. Arthur Balfour had argued in 1901 that the British monarch was the one symbol with which the whole disparate, rambling empire identified. George fancied himself as the glue that bound it together – glue much needed, given new demands for self-government in Ireland and India. In the autumn of 1905 he had visited India and had loved it: the grand ceremonial gatherings; the opulence of the maharajahs who paid court with jewel-encrusted swords; the tiger- and elephant-hunting; the vast, bobbing, endlessly cheering crowds; and the sense that India, with its education system, universities and bureaucrats, was proof that the empire civilized and improved the lives of its subject peoples. The place moved him to uncharacteristic superlatives: he told Nicholas it was a 'wonderful country'. In fact, at the time of George's visit, the country had been in the aftermath of the disastrous partition of Bengal. He had taken against its author, the imperious outgoing viceroy, Lord Curzon. The Raj's officials assured him that the anger over partition, and the desire for self-government incarnated in the new Congress Party, had been terribly overstated. He very much wanted to believe them. 'I understand the look in the eyes of the Indians,' George had told Gokhale, the head of the Indian Congress Party, with breathtaking presumption. 'Would the peoples of India be happier if you ran the country?' Gokhale answered, 'I do not say they would be happier, but they would have more self-respect.' George had returned home convinced that a closer union between 'the Mother Country and her Indian Empire' would heal everything. Being Emperor of India excited George as little else about his new role did. It was so different from the limited, hemmed-in role he played in Britain. It conjured a less complicated and circumscribed idea of kingship, where subjects were simply and smilingly loyal.

Shortly after his accession George expressed his desire to return to India, to crown himself emperor at a durbar, the old mughal celebration adopted by the British. The cabinet was sceptical, wondering where the money to pay for a coronation extravaganza was going to come from. 'I think it a grand idea,' Nicholas wrote. '. . . I do not doubt that it will produce a tremendous impression in the whole world!' George was persistent, and no one had a better idea about how to counter the Indian independence movement. A gesture of confidence from the mother country in the shape of a visit from its monarch, combined with some reforms, might help. It was planned that the king would have his durbar and announce the end of the partition of Bengal and the moving of the capital from Calcutta to Delhi. George was, however, discouraged from his Napoleonic self-coronation – the idea was tactfully scuttled by the Archbishop of Canterbury, who suggested it might be out of place in a non-Christian country.

One hundred thousand people came to the durbar. It was, George told Nicholas, 'a magnificent sight and practically every Maharajah in India was present'. He and Mary sat under a golden dome on silver thrones in glittering coronation robes, while bejewelled Indian maharajahs came to offer homage. George wore a new crown made for the event, covered in 6,170 cut diamonds, sapphires, emeralds and rubies and costing £60,000. Forty thousand tents were pitched on the hills around to accommodate the throng who came to see the new emperor. Afterwards he went to Nepal for two weeks, where, with the local maharajah, 600 elephants and 1,400 beaters, he personally shot twenty-one tigers, eight rhinos and one bear. He was convinced his presence in India had made a difference. But the effects of such spectacles were never long-lived, and as an effective and unifying symbol of empire George was at least a decade too late. A year later a member of the Indian independence movement dressed as a woman threw a bomb at Sir Charles Hardinge, who was now Viceroy of India, as he entered Delhi on an elephant, killing his servant and wounding him seriously. The cabinet would not be persuaded to repeat the exercise – royal trips to the far-flung empire were expensive and took months. When George began talking about a trip to South Africa, one minister remarked, 'We decided he had much better stay at home and not teach people how easily the machine worked without a king.'

Edward's death would have been traumatic for George at any time. Coming as it did in May 1910, it plunged him into the middle of the most serious constitutional crisis in British politics for decades, one that had parallels with the constitutional struggles in Germany and Russia. The House of Commons was attempting to abolish the House of Lords' veto, the weapon the Conservative aristocracy – who sat in the Lords by virtue of its hereditary titles – had been using to block Liberal legislation and reforms already passed in the Commons. The matter had reached crisis point in late 1909 when the Lords threw out David Lloyd George's Budget, which, because it extended death duties and land taxes, they saw as an attack on them. The Conservative aristocracy did itself no favours with public opinion by reacting with almost comic hysteria – even though, as both sides suspected, the actual amounts raised would be pretty modest. The Duke of Buccleuch, who owned among other things a large collection of Poussins, claimed he couldn't afford the guinea for the subscription to Dumfries Football Club. The Earl of Onslow put large parts of Surrey up for sale, and the Duke of Rutland, who like many Tories seemed to think that radical Liberals and Labour Party members were the same thing, said that all Labour MPs should be gagged. As Prince of Wales, George's sympathies had been with the Lords. The much-loathed Lloyd George had drafted his Budget and launched it with speeches which cheerily and baldly pointed out the gap between rich and poor in a way that no British statesman ever had, and with great panache and humour. 'A fully equipped Duke costs as much to keep as two Dreadnoughts and is more difficult to scrap,' he said. The House of Lords was 'five hundred ordinary men chosen at random from among the unemployed'. In the Conservative press he was portrayed as a bomb-throwing anarchist or a highwayman – which he loved.

The House of Lords' rejection of Lloyd George's Budget had forced a general election in early 1910. The Liberals, who won only a couple more seats than the Conservatives, kept power in a coalition with the Irish nationalists and the Labour Party, giving them a 113-seat majority. For different reasons each party was raring to destroy the Lords' veto, and the Commons put forward a bill to do just that. Everyone knew the Lords would reject it. Prime Minister Asquith's solution was to threaten to flood the Lords with new Liberal peers, created by the king. Edward had hated being placed in such a position. An attack on the Lords, he and his advisers felt, was perilously close to an attack on the monarchy. He'd died furious with both Asquith and the Conservative Lords for having refused to compromise. Some of the more extreme Tories went so far as to claim that the prime minister's threats had killed the king.

George's unease and lack of experience were so palpable that Asquith promised him six months' grace, in which he tried and failed to reach a compromise with the Lords. But in December 1910 he was obliged to call another election, and came to see the king to ask him for a guarantee that he would create the peers if the Liberals won. Their interaction was a comedy of errors which painfully demonstrated how little George understood politics. Asquith, aware that the king hated the idea, asked for his guarantee in such overly delicate, allusive language that George thought he'd been let off the hook, realizing the truth only three days later. When Asquith returned to ask for the guarantee in plainer terms, he brought with him another minister, Lord Crewe. Just as George had misunderstood Asquith's previous attempts at delicacy and tact, so he now thought Crewe was there because Asquith didn't trust his word – whereas Asquith meant it as a courtesy to George. Then when the prime minister suggested that the guarantee be kept secret until it was actually needed, George assumed he was being asked to do something underhand. 'I have never in my life done anything I was ashamed to confess, and I have been accustomed to conceal nothing.' He failed to understand that the prime minister was trying to keep him out of the controversy unless it was entirely necessary. George later claimed Asquith had bullied the assurance out of him by threatening to resign and call a new election on the issue of the king and the peers against the people. He obsessed over it for years, imagining there might have been an alternative. When he found out in 1913 that Arthur Balfour, leader of the Lords' opposition, had offered at that moment to form a Conservative government and he hadn't been told, he fumed that he could have invited Balfour to form an administration and saved the Lords' veto. But this would have been potentially far more partisan and interventionist than what Asquith asked him to do.

Balfour would automatically have lost his first Commons vote, which would have triggered yet another election on a subject the country was sick of. That election would have been a vote of confidence on the king's decision to back the Conservatives – dragging the crown into politics as it had not been for over a century.

The abolition of the veto – and the power of the Lords – was eventually, and with much bitterness, passed in July 1911, and without George having to create the extra peers, but he worried about the process all the way through, relieving his feelings by bombarding Asquith with memos, and daily summoning ministers and Lords to air his worries.

One of Nicholas's biographers has written that 'In England where a sovereign needed only to be a good man in order to be a good king, Nicholas II would have made an admirable monarch.' Perhaps it was truer to say that in Russia George might well have been just as disastrous as Nicholas and that in Britain it didn't matter what the sovereign was like as long as he was sober and followed the rules. The Lords débâcle was an inauspicious beginning to George's reign; but he would be, as it turned out, a good king. The system would make him effective almost despite himself, compelling him to do things he would never have chosen to do, for example meeting and being polite to the man he loathed, Lloyd George (and forcing the radical chancellor to do likewise). Eventually, Lloyd George would become his prime minister. It wasn't quite as if Nicholas had been forced to meet, say, Lenin, or Wilhelm had socialized with the German Marxist Rosa Luxemburg, but, in George's head at least, it wasn't far off. In September 1911 Lloyd George went to stay at Balmoral for several days. Both sides were obliged to be on their best behaviour. Lloyd George went on picnics with the royal family, and George presented him with one of his father's walking sticks. After a few days Lloyd George had had enough. 'I am not cut out for Court life,' he wrote to his wife, 'I detest it. The whole atmosphere reeks with Toryism. I can breathe it and it depresses and sickens me. Everybody is very civil to me as they would be to a dangerous wild animal whom they fear and perhaps just a little admire for its suppleness and strength.' He was far from the only one to find the royal way of life – not just the opinions, but the arbitrary rules and rituals, the obligatory changes of clothes (at least four a day) and the hours of shooting – anachronistic and irritating. The next leader of the Conservative Party, Andrew Bonar-Law, an austere Scottish businessman with nothing in common with the old aristocratic grandees, would find his obligatory weekends with the royal family at Balmoral 'unendurable'.

It took the country a while to get the hang of George. With his melancholy direct stare and unflinchingly upright deportment, a fresh white gardenia eternally in his buttonhole, a hat (a homburg or a top hat – he would sooner have left his home naked than without one) and his immaculate old-fashioned tailoring, his deliberate, elegant figure communicated respectability, decency, steadiness and old-fashioned values. In a world that seemed to be getting faster, more confusing and more dangerous, there was something very reassuring about that. As king he would be a layer of foundation stones, a visitor of schools, mining towns, railway works and occasionally workers' cottages, though his diaries reveal nothing of what he made of these places. His was an unflashy, domestic kind of monarchy – one that seemed concerned to operate with the support of its subjects and to want to be in touch with them. Under George the British monarchy really would become, as Walter Bagehot had described it in his book *The English Constitution*, 'dignified' and 'symbolic'.

15. Celebrations and warnings (1911–14)

The reality of European politics was that Anglo-German relations were as stalemated as they'd ever been – as were Russo-German relations. Nevertheless, each country, each emperor, continued to paper over the cracks with cousinly gestures, each increasingly irrelevant. In May 1911 George invited the kaiser to the unveiling of the marble memorial to Queen Victoria outside Buckingham Palace. 'You are perfectly right in alluding to my devotion and reverence for my beloved grandmother, with whom I was on such excellent terms,' Wilhelm wrote to George. '. . . Never in my life shall I forget the solemn hours in Osborne near her deathbed when she breathed her last in my arms! Those sacred hours have riveted my heart firmly to your house and family.' It would be Wilhelm's final visit to England, and in his memoirs his account – pages on guards and Highland regiments, military colours, the family gathered round the monument, the welcome he received – was almost tender and saturated with longing. At the Theatre Royal Drury Lane, where George and Wilhelm saw the play of the day, *Money*, the audience gave them a standing ovation, and a specially designed curtain depicted the two emperors on horseback riding towards each other and saluting. The war minister and German-ophile Sir Richard Haldane gave a lunch for the kaiser and filled it with the most eminent and famous men in England: Lord Kitchener, Lord Curzon, J. A. Spender, the editor of the *Manchester Guardian*, the Labour MP Ramsay MacDonald, the writer Edmund Gosse, the senior general Sir Henry Wilson, the painter John Singer Sargent and Baden Powell, the hero of Mafeking and author of the recent runaway bestseller *Scouting for Boys*. Wilhelm was on fizzing form. 'I don't think I ever met a man so full of the zest of life, and so eager to show it and share it with other people,' said Sir John Morley.

It should have meant something, but actually it meant nothing. No British politician sought to buttonhole Wilhelm or tackle him on the naval race. 'His visit of course will be an absolutely private one and it has no political significance whatever,' George wrote to Nicholas. '. . . I wanted to tell you this in case the newspapers should print a lot of rubbish.' On his last day, the kaiser worked himself up into a fury on the subject of Britain's agreements with France and Russia in a conversation with Louis of Battenburg: 'You must be brought to understand in England that Germany is the sole arbiter of peace or war on the Continent. If we wish to fight we will do so without your leave.' He seemed particularly miffed by Britain's closeness to Russia.

It was as if each country's position had become so entrenched that there was no way to fill those deepening cracks of mistrust and tension. Germany clung to its unsatisfied need for recognition, its navy and its commitment to Austria; Britain was determined to maintain its world position and stay tied to France; Russia remained torn between knowing it couldn't afford conflict, but desperate to restore its Great Power status through some form of imperial expansion. By contrast, it took only one small aggressive gesture on the international stage to create a full-blown European crisis. No one wanted it to be like this (except possibly the German army) – not least because by 1911 each country was facing economic depression and considerable social unrest – but no one was willing to give way. The German chancellor, Bethmann-Hollweg, had started talks with Britain when he'd taken office in 1909, but quickly found his room for manoeuvre limited: the German Right – highly critical of the government – liked the navy, and the kaiser made it clear that if he pushed too hard for cuts he might be sacked. To placate his critics the chancellor insisted that, in return for a reduction in German ships, Britain must pledge neutrality in a European war, which the British regarded as evidence that the Germans wanted them out of the way to attack France. Asquith and Grey could see no point in further talks, though they paid lip-service to the idea of *rapprochement* as a sop to their critics on the Liberal and Labour backbenches. Even David Lloyd George, a consistent opposer of naval expansion and critic of Grey, was beginning to question German intentions.★ The German Foreign Office, meanwhile, was on the look-out for some diplomatic coup which would bring the government some much missed applause at home.

Then, just two months after Wilhelm returned from England, on 1 July 1911, Germany sent a gunboat, the *Panther*, to the port of Agadir, in Morocco, where the French had recently and illegally sent troops claiming they were needed to quell a local rebellion. By the terms of the Algeciras conference, Germany was entitled to compensation if the French changed the nature of their presence in Morocco. With the *Panther* (which, somewhat ironically, was not a beautiful shiny new warship but a squat, dirty old cruiser well overdue for the scrapyard) positioned threateningly on the coast, the German Foreign Office demanded the French hand over the whole of the French Congo, adding that if they did not respond positively Germany might be forced to extreme measures.

That the German Foreign Office was using a warship as leverage seemed to the British Foreign Office and Asquith a dangerous precedent: not merely another swipe at France, but a direct challenge to British naval supremacy and therefore its Great Power status – gunboat diplomacy had always been a particular British speciality. Their response was bluntly aggressive. On 21 July, in a speech at the Mansion House in the City of London, David Lloyd George announced that Britain was determined to keep her 'place and prestige' among the Great Powers of the world, even if it led to war. 'If a situation were to be forced upon us in which peace could only be preserved by the surrender of the great and

---

★ Lloyd George's views had begun to shift after a private visit to Germany in the summer of 1908. He'd gone ostensibly to examine Germany's social insurance system, but actually to see if he might bypass the Foreign Office and find what the German government's real attitude to Britain and arms reduction was. He had been taken aback by the pervasiveness of army culture and admiration for the army, and discouraged by the German government's refusal to engage with him. The only minister who would meet him, a then-unpromoted Bethmann-Hollweg, wouldn't discuss arms at all, and after a couple of beers started accusing Britain of hating Germany.

35. Wilhelm on board the *Hohenzollern*, early 1900s, wearing his 'fierce' look. After becoming kaiser, he was virtually never photographed in repose again

36. Edward, now king, with George's children, once again in Scottish gear, 1903

37. Edward and Wilhelm. Note neither looks at the other, *c.* 1901

38. One of a series of informal 'joke' photographs taken at Hesse-Darmstadt, home of Alix's brother Ernie, one of the few places where Alix (*sitting*) and Nicky (*behind left*) felt genuinely off-duty. Ernie's wife Victoria Melita, known as 'Ducky' (*sitting*), would run off with Nicky's cousin Grand Duke Kirill (*just right of him*) several years later

39. Nicky sitting in Alix's mauve boudoir, *c.* 1900–1904

40. Nicky and Alix and their children, Olga, Maria, Tatiana,
Anastasia and Alexis, *c.* 1910. He would have been forty-two,
she thirty-eight

41. German cartoon of the Entente Cordiale, 1906. John Bull walks
off with a French trollop, while Germany (complete with kaiser
moustache) tries to look as if he doesn't care

42. Nicholas, with court in full Russian regalia, opens the Duma, Russia's first elected assembly, 1906. One courtier said of the new Duma: 'They gave one the impression of a gang of criminals . . . waiting for the signal to throw themselves upon the Ministers and cut their throats'

43. Nicholas and Alix receiving Wilhelm at Peterhof, *c.* 1912. Peterhof was famously windy

44. Wilhelm and Nicholas walk along the Russian imperial yacht *Standart*, Swinemünde, 1907

45. British warship *en route* to Kronstadt, June 1914

46. Germans armoured cruisers, 1907

47. Wilhelm and Nicholas on a German shooting expedition

8. Nicholas examining the camera lens at Neskuchnoe Park, Moscow, May 1896

49. Sergei Witte, Nicholas's
chief minister

50. Lloyd George, the British Liberal
politician whom George loathed

51. Bethmann-Hollweg, Wilhelm's
wartime chancellor

52. Grigori Rasputin

53. Nicky (*left*) and George (*right*) in British naval dress at Barton Manor on the Isle of Wight in July 1909

54. Family picture taken on the Isle of Wight in 1909. *From left, standing*: future Edward VIII, Alexandra, George's daughter Mary, George's sister Toria, Olga, Tatiana; *seated, from left*: May, Nicky, Edward, Alix, George, Marie; *on the ground*: Alexis and Anastasia

55. Nine monarchs at Edward VII's funeral. *From top left*: Haakon VII of Norway; Ferdinand of Bulgaria; Manuel of Portugal; Wilhelm; George I of Greece; Albert of the Belgians; *sitting*: Alfonso XIII of Spain; George; Frederick XII of Denmark

56. George and Mary, as she now was, in full regalia

57. Nicholas and Wilhelm at the wedding of the kaiser's daughter Victoria, June 1913. The last time the three men met

58. George and Wilhelm with Prussian dragoons, 1913

59. Nicholas and George at Victoria's wedding, 1913

60. First World War: Wilhelm with Hindenburg and Ludendorff, the two generals who would eventually supersede him

61. George with (*left to right*) Marshal Joffre, French president Raymond Poincaré, Marshal Foch and General Haig, whom he supported against Lloyd George

62. British and US propaganda turned Wilhelm into a sinister monster egging his troops on to ever greater atrocities

63. Nicholas after his abdication.
He spent much of his time
chopping firewood

64. The Romanovs
aking the sun in Tobolsk,
their first stop-off in
Siberia, before their final
estination, Ekaterinburg,
vhere they were killed in
July 1918

65. George in 1923, on his way to open parliament. The war left its scars on him

66. Ever carefully striking a pose, Wilhelm in 1938, in exile in Holland

beneficent position Britain has won by centuries of heroism and achievement, by allowing Britain to be treated . . . as if she were of no account in the Cabinet of Nations, then I say emphatically that peace at that price would be a humiliation intolerable for a great country like ours to endure.'

The German government was astounded by the speech – that it was so direct and that Lloyd George had delivered it – but refused to back down. Within a few days both fleets were placed on alert; a colonial quarrel was transformed into an international crisis. The German press expressed outrage that Britain was dictating to Germany. In London *The Times* claimed that the German navy had vanished from the North Sea and might be about to attack. (In fact it was on its way to Norway to take part in friendly manoeuvres with the British Atlantic fleet.) Escalation with Britain was not what the Germans had intended at all. Behind the scenes the two sides negotiated a climb-down, and plans were made for Franco-German talks. But the French, emboldened by the English threats, refused the Germans demands for compensation. Talks and constant rumours of war dragged on through August and September. By October the German Foreign Office had run out of steam and finally agreed to take 100,000 square miles of all-but-useless equatorial jungle in the French Congo. An agreement was signed on 4 November.

Once again a German provocation had ended in defeat. 'Out of this mountain of a German-made crisis came a mouse of colonial territory,' wrote Grey. The German nationalist press and the nationalist German leagues, whose hopes of colonies had been raised so high and had been so constantly dashed, howled with disappointment and anger. Wilhelm was accused of cowardice: one German paper called him '*Guillaume le timide, le valeureux poltron!*' The German Centre and Left parties poured scorn on the government's ineptitude and pointless aggression. Senior German army officers sighed that the All Highest was so pusillanimous about taking extreme measures – Moltke had privately hoped for a 'reckoning with the English'. The German colonial minister resigned.

The kaiser himself had been extremely reluctant to send the *Panther* and anxious about the British reaction. Predictably, when it had initially proved popular, he had rushed to identify himself as its author. Throughout the subsequent months, however, he had seesawed queasily between anxiety and martial posturing. One moment the German foreign minister, Alfred von Kiderlen-Wächter, had to threaten resignation to keep him on-side, the next Wilhelm was publicly announcing he was prepared to use his sword if the French didn't acquiesce to German demands.

He also claimed that during his May visit to London he had told George of his intention to send a warship to France and that George had agreed – and thus that the British government's response was pure hypocrisy. This was familiar territory for Wilhelm – claiming an arrangement had been agreed with another monarch, then accusing them of betrayal. But it was new to George, who scrutinized his memory carefully. He said that Wilhelm had raised the subject of Morocco as he was leaving London; he might even have said something about a ship – but George had no recollection of it. 'I absolutely did not express to him my own, or my Government's consent.' For his own part he thought Wilhelm was 'a man of peace', under pressure from 'his own militarists'. 'No man likes to be called a coward.'

It was a depressing sign of the deadlock between the two countries that it was two international business magnates, not politicians, who initiated a final attempt to reach agreement. Albert Ballin was the director of the biggest shipping company in the world, the Hamburg-America Line, and one of Wilhelm's few Jewish friends; Ernest Cassel was one of Edward's coterie of Jewish financiers; his dealings and loans had kept several countries afloat, and he was a friend of Churchill and Asquith. Both felt that the German naval programme had gone too far and created pointless hostility. In January 1912 Ballin persuaded Wilhelm to invite a member of the British cabinet to Berlin to discuss the naval race, while Cassel encouraged the British to respond. Grey and Asquith sent Sir Richard Haldane to Berlin in the second week of February, but gave him no authority to make a deal. Everyone fell over themselves to express their hopes that agreement might be reached, but unsurprisingly the talks failed amidst recrimination and arguments over who had offered what. Once again Bethmann-Hollweg insisted on British neutrality before he would even discuss ships, and he couldn't promise any defence cuts, just a temporary slowdown.

Haldane was astonished by the apparent chaos in the upper echelons of the German government. The kaiser, the chancellor and Tirpitz disagreed on almost everything about foreign policy, naval expansion and what they wanted from the talks. He reckoned Bethmann-Hollweg wished to negotiate, but Tirpitz was opposed to any compromise. He was far from the first British visitor to remark on such confusion. As for Wilhelm, he seemed one minute utterly enthused, and the next cowed by Tirpitz. Haldane didn't know that on the day of his arrival, Wilhelm had published the new navy bill, and had told Metternich that he would mobilize the German navy if the British carried out their plan of concentrating their fleet in the North Sea (where they'd be on Germany's doorstep). Haldane left after three days with a bust of the kaiser, from the kaiser, tucked under his arm and a copy of the new German navy bill. The next day Wilhelm told the German industrialist Walter Rathenau that in the summer he would go to Cowes, 'and then he would settle everything. The King trusted him. His plan was: the United States of Europe against America. The English are not unsympathetic to this.'

When Haldane got back to London the British cabinet looked at the navy bill and discovered it made Bethmann-Hollweg's slowdown instantly irrelevant. Quite apart from asking for new battleships, the bill announced a 20 per cent increase in the number of fighting men on every ship and a huge increase in submarines and smaller warships. Picking his moment during the failing negotiations with France the summer before, when the kaiser had been stung by accusations of cowardice, Tirpitz had persuaded him that a new naval bill might win back the support of the German Right, that keeping up the pressure on the Royal Navy would frighten the British into judicious neutrality in the event of a European war – a demonstrably false argument – and that any cutbacks would mean an international loss of face. As it turned out, in the January 1912 elections, the German Social Democrat Party – the Socialists – who opposed higher defence spending, received their biggest ever vote and became the largest party in the Reichstag with one third of the seats.

The talks finally died on 19 March when Grey stated categorically that Britain could not promise to remain neutral in a European war. Their failure catapulted Wilhelm into depression. Dona told Tirpitz that he was on the verge of a nervous breakdown. 'At heart,' she said, 'he is enthusiastic about England and everything which is England, it is in his blood.' It was as if the two opposite pulls in his character had directly caused the collapse. He denounced the British cabinet as 'scoundrels', and said Grey was a 'Shylock'. He sacked Metternich, whose unvarnished explanations of why the British were hostile he could no longer bear to hear. When Grey praised Bethmann-Hollweg, whom the British had come to see as a sober and positive force in the German government, Wilhelm growled, 'I have never in my life heard of an agreement being concluded with reference to one definite statesman and independently of the reigning sovereign. It is clear that Grey has no idea who is master here, namely myself. He dictates to me in advance who is to be my minister if I am to conclude an agreement with England.' Tirpitz's full naval bill was put before the Reichstag days later.

Despite left-wing opposition, it was passed in April 1912, though in a slightly slimmer form. Paradoxically, in the long term it would prove a big setback for the German navy and Tirpitz. It prompted the British to withdraw ships from the Mediterranean and concentrate their fleet in the North Sea and the Channel, making it immediately apparent that Tirpitz's fleet was no match for the British navy, and wouldn't be for decades. And it irritated the German army, who felt that the navy had taken too much of the military budget for too long with little to show for it. It now demanded that it must get the lion's share of future defence-spending; Moltke, observing that the Russian army was dramatically increasing, had plans to enlarge the army by 25 per cent, 136,000 men. More worryingly, the British also agreed to defend the French Channel coast in return for the French navy policing the Mediterranean – an arrangement that made British involvement in a European war that bit more likely.

★

The Russians were just as imprisoned by their own sense of priorities. Since 1905 it had been government orthodoxy that Russia must be on good terms with all the Great Powers, and that foreign wars inevitably led to revolution and must be avoided at all costs. By 1911 Nicholas's chief minister, Peter Stolypin, and the new Russian foreign minister, Sergei Sazonov – who was uncoincidentally Stolypin's brother-in-law – and even Nicholas, wanted Britain to commit to a defensive alliance. With Britain behind them they believed Germany and Austria would be reluctant to bully or threaten them. Not that Russia could afford to be on bad terms with Germany either. When Sazonov had become foreign minister in the autumn of 1910, he had taken an initially reluctant Nicholas to Potsdam ('I cannot understand how he is so blind to the consequences of what he is doing,' the British ambassador had complained gloomily) and returned with an agreement. 'I was extremely pleased with my visit to William, who was in excellent spirits, calm and comfortable,' Nicholas wrote to George. The deal allowed the Germans and their railway into northern Persia, in return for an undertaking not to support Austrian ambitions in the Balkans. A week or so later Wilhelm, in a gust of enthusiasm, passed through Hesse where Alix was staying with the children, bringing 'heaps of presents'. 'To them he is "the German Uncle",' Nicholas wrote, 'and he loves playing with them. He looks well, but has grown older and is more sedate.' Alix could hardly bear Wilhelm to touch her children but she knew that getting on with Germany was necessary. Communications between Berlin and St Petersburg were as cordial as they'd been in years and Russia was noticeably silent during the international condemnation of Agadir.

It was also still orthodoxy in Russia, however, that the country's wounded Great Power status must be restored, and the only way to do that was by extending the empire and by asserting Russia's claims to imperial influence in the Balkans. Not surprisingly, the latter imperative constantly threatened to derail the need for peace. In 1912 the Russian minister to Serbia, a militant Pan-Slavist called Nicholas Hartwig, brokered a secret pact between the Balkan states of Serbia, Greece, Bulgaria and Montenegro. Hartwig was a rogue operator whose aim was to bring the Slav nations together so they could start a war to wrest back the Ottoman empire's last European territories, and in so doing allow Russia to take control of the Bosphorus and open the Turkish Straits. His efforts to bring together the Balkan states – no small feat as they were all extremely quarrelsome and competitive with each other – were half-hidden from the Russian government, and what they could see, Nicholas and his ministers treated with a kind of wilful blindness because they couldn't help feeling pleased that Russian influence had been re-established in the Balkans. Everyone knew that a war in the region would be exceptionally dangerous because Austria and Russia, both acutely aware of the vulnerability of their Great Power status, would feel compelled to intervene, and that Germany would almost certainly come in with Austria if it came to military conflict.

In June 1912 the Russian and German emperors and their chief ministers met on their yachts at Swinemünde in the Baltic on a blazing hot day. Wilhelm lavished gifts on Nicky's children and claimed to be vastly amused when the Russian officers got through sixty bottles of his champagne. 'Everything went off very well and quite informally,' Nicholas told his mother. 'He was very gay and affable and would have his joke with Anastasia.' But perhaps the most significant conversation that day took place between Nicholas's new chief minister, Vladimir Kokovtsov, and Bethmann-Hollweg, which Kokovtsov later recounted in his memoirs. Both men expressed a feeling of being trapped by an arms race they had no power to halt. Kokovtsov complained that Germany seemed to be 'arming herself at a feverish pace'. He explained it would be impossible for him to oppose demands for equivalent increases in the Russian army. Bethmann-Hollweg answered equally frankly that 'his own position was far from being as influential and independent as it might seem . . . He, too, had to consider the personal views of the Emperor . . . and especially the peculiar organization of the War Ministry, whose attitude was a very troublesome one.' The Duma would indeed vote vast sums for the Russian army in 1913, raising the number of troops from 1.3 million to 1.75 million. And this in turn would prompt the

Reichstag to vote even more money to the German army in 1913.

After Wilhelm left, Nicholas told his chief minister, 'Thank heaven! Now one does not have to watch one's every word lest it be construed in a way one had not even dreamed.' Like Edward he had learned to avoid talking politics too directly with Wilhelm, but he also told Kokovtsov several times, betraying considerable anxiety about the Balkans, 'that the Emperor William had assured him positively that he would not permit the Balkan complications to become a world conflagration'.

Three months later, in September, Sergei Sazonov came to Balmoral to try to persuade Sir Edward Grey to agree to military and naval 'discussions' – as the euphemism went – just like the ones Britain had with France. Stolypin thought Britain's backing would persuade Germany and Austria to stay out of the war that was now brewing in the Balkans. He neglected to mention that it was the Russians who had secretly helped to set up the conditions for war. 'He [Sazonov] is a straightforward and honest man and I appreciate him highly,' Nicholas wrote to George, adding, 'I always read the 'Daily Graphic' and therefore follow closely all your movements and all you have to do. It astonishes me often how enduring . . . you and May are both!' This was a courtesy to George because he took no role in the negotiations.

Sazonov evidently felt optimistic. British attitudes to Russia had shifted. By 1912 the country had become fascinated by its would-be ally. In January 1912 *The Times* published a 'Russian number', and a group of Liberal MPs visited Russia, a trip which Sir Charles Hardinge described as 'the pilgrimage of love'. Russian literature was everywhere – not just Tolstoy but Dostoevsky, Chekhov and Turgenev had all been recently translated into English. Beef Stroganov had insinuated itself on to fashionable British menus. The Ballets Russes had brought a fantasy of Russian exoticism, wildness and modernity to London; George went to see them on the eve of his coronation in 1911. But cultural fascination was not matched by political sympathy. British journalists reported the same old ugly Russian repressions and, most provocatively, Russian troops had moved into Persia's neutral sphere, where the shah, an old Russian client, was fighting a civil war against the

British-sponsored democratic parliament, the Majlis. This was bad enough, but the British Foreign Office, which despite this would have liked to pull closer to Russia, suspected that an annexation attempt wouldn't be far off. British public opinion simply wouldn't countenance a closer relationship, and the Persian business made it worse. But no matter what the new British ambassador, Sir George Buchanan, said, both Nicholas and Sazonov refused to acknowledge that their policy in Persia might have an effect in Britain.

Buchanan was Britain's new secret weapon in Russia. An old-school diplomat who had previously been minister to Alix's brother Ernst in Hesse-Darmstadt, he had a reputation for charm and old-world courtesy, and calmly smoothed over the conflicts and misunderstandings which regularly punctuated British dealings with Russia. In many respects St Petersburg was the last place he wanted to be – he hated the climate and found the Russian court a strain – but he had entirely fallen under Nicholas's quiet, smiling spell. 'I personally became wonderfully devoted to him. His Majesty had such a wonderful charm of manner that when he received me in audience he almost made me feel that it was as a friend, and not the Emperor, with whom I was talking. There was, if I may say so without presumption, what amounted to a feeling of mutual sympathy between us.' Buchanan was particularly amused by the tsar's keenness to talk about anything but politics.

Not surprisingly, Grey refused the military discussions Sazonov asked for. He wanted to talk about Persia. Public opinion on the subject was so strong, and there was so much concern that the Foreign Office might act unilaterally and contract a secret agreement without consulting parliament, that the Russian foreign minister's arrival had sparked demonstrations in London and such an angry response from Liberal backbenchers that Grey had to promise he wouldn't even *use* the phrase 'triple entente' to indicate the loose combination of Britain, Russia and France. Sazonov made vague promises about troops leaving, but Grey didn't really believe them.

The war in the Balkans broke out only a few weeks later. In Russia, the press demanded that the country come to the aid of its 'little brothers' – the Balkan states. But the 'little brothers' didn't need their big brother's help because within a month they had captured all Turkey's European territories. Serbia in particular had been extremely successful; it had virtually doubled in size and was threatening to annex part of the Adriatic coastline, all of which alarmed Austria. By mid-November Austria began to mass an army near the Russian border. Once again a local conflict suddenly took on much wider and frightening connotations. Kokovtsov and Sazonov were summoned to an audience at Tsarskoe selo one morning to discover that the tsar was cheerfully on the point of mobilizing the army against Austria. With him was the war minister, Vladimir Sukhomlinov, whom they loathed because he pandered to the tsar by keeping his reports short and simple and full of jokes. The two men managed to dissuade Nicholas by pointing out that this would bring on the European war he so feared, and that France would be unable to help as it would be quite unprepared.

Sir Edward Grey, meanwhile, tried to get the Great Powers to force the Balkan states to the negotiating table, and prevent Austria and Russia from trying to gain advantage – which would only prolong the conflict. Nicholas – seeing the prospect of a Russian-controlled Turkish Straits recede – grumbled at the British 'interference', which was 'hampering us more than anybody else'. He wrote to Wilhelm, 'I am sure you are also taking a keen interest in the Balkan war. I admire the splendid fighting qualities of the Bulgarians, Servians, etc but the Turks have sunk completely in my opinion. God grant we all may not have difficulties at the end!'

Rather to Europe's surprise Grey found an ally in Bethmann-Hollweg. The two worked together to bring everyone to the table. An armistice was signed on 3 December 1912 and a conference convened in London two weeks later to resolve the competing claims. Its eventual success – despite a second brief conflict breaking out in the Balkans in July 1913 and months of subsequent wrangling – appeared to demonstrate that together Britain and Germany could work to keep the peace of Europe after all.

It seemed as if the forces of peace had won out in the German government. But behind the scenes that was by no means evident. The day the armistice was arranged, Bethmann-Hollweg announced in the Reichstag that, if Austria was unexpectedly attacked by Russia, Germany would fight on its side. It was an odd gesture since peace terms were on the table, and the next day Sir Edward Grey and Sir Richard Haldane felt obliged to counter Bethmann-Hollweg's words with a statement to the German ambassador that, if Germany and Austria-Hungary should end up in a war against France and Russia, Britain would fight with France. For the British the matter ended there.

Wilhelm's brother Heinrich was in England and went to visit George at York Cottage. Heinrich had long hoped for a resolution between his homeland and Britain. He couldn't help feeling that if only Britain would shift its position just a little, their problems might be resolved. He asked George whether, if Germany and Austria went to war with Russia and France, England would help Russia and France. 'I answered,' George told Sir Edward Grey later, 'undoubtedly, yes – under certain circumstances. He [Heinrich] professed surprise and regret, but did not ask what the certain circumstances were. He said he would tell the Emperor what I had told him. Of course, Germany must know that we would not allow either of our friends to be crippled. I think it is only right that you should know what passed between me and the Emperor's brother on this point.'

Like many people who knew Wilhelm, Heinrich found it hard to tell his brother what he didn't want to hear. What he told Wilhelm was almost the opposite of what George had said. He reported that the British didn't want to go to war, and that if there was a war, Germany would have to reckon 'perhaps on English neutrality, certainly not on her taking the part of Germany, and probably on her throwing her weight on the weaker side'. The kaiser decided George had given an assurance that Britain would stay neutral – which the king certainly didn't have the authority to do. He scribbled on the letter, 'that settles it . . . we can now go ahead with France'. This was probably posturing as by now everyone including the Germans had agreed to send their ambassadors to the peace conference in London.

A couple of days later Wilhelm received word of Haldane's

statement that Britain would fight. He was horribly disappointed. The British regarded their warning as a way of dampening appetite for war in Europe. He saw it differently – as aggressive grandstanding which would egg both Russia and France on to involve themselves in a private argument between Austria and Serbia. He said it was a 'moral declaration of war'. He was so angry that he immediately summoned his senior army and naval staff. The meeting that resulted – the 'war council' of 8 December 1912, to which the chancellor was not invited – has sometimes been described as the moment when the German leadership began the countdown to war. In fact, it seems to have been mainly a chance for Wilhelm to let off steam, but it also allowed the military to reiterate their desire for a preventive war, though they couldn't agree with whom. Moltke told the meeting, 'I believe war is unavoidable and the sooner the better.' For him, it was obvious it should be a land war against Russia, not Britain. He had become convinced that Russia's military and economy were developing so fast that, by 1917, Russia would be too strong for Germany to beat. Tirpitz, on the other hand, wanted to delay; the navy wouldn't be ready to challenge Britain at least until 1917. Nothing specific was planned, but the meeting agreed that the German people should be 'prepared' for the possibility of war in the future. Guilty about his less than useful intervention, Heinrich wrote to George explaining that he had carried out 'your instructions to the letter', but might have omitted 'the one sore point . . . to the effect that I thought, if Germany were drawn into war with Russia and maybe, as a result of this, with France, England <u>might</u> be neutral, but that I feared she <u>might</u> also, <u>under circumstances</u>, side with our foes . . . We always were,' he continued, '– and I am still – in hopes that England and Germany might go together, for the sake of the world's peace!' He pleaded with George to 'Please consider the situation once more, before it is too late! If England and Germany were united, even mutually, who on earth would dare stir?' It sounded like a request from the 1890s. Once such a plea would have at least prompted a serious conversation between Queen Victoria and Lord Salisbury. But not any more.

Publicly the British and Germans were getting on better than

they had in years. Over the next eighteen months Bethmann-
Hollweg kept a guiding hand on foreign affairs, and the new
German ambassador in London, Prince Karl Max Lichnowsky,
turned out – to everyone's surprise – to be a gregarious Anglophile
with a passion for British society. He got on well with Edward
Grey and was soon robustly telling the German Foreign Office,
just like his predecessor, that the British would never agree to
neutrality in a European war. In early 1913 the latest German
foreign minister, Gottlieb von Jagow, told the Reichstag that he
was delighted by the 'tender plants' of cooperation with England.
The two countries had begun to negotiate on who might buy
Portugal's African colonies and how the long-planned Baghdad
railway might come through British-controlled Persia. But in the
circles around Wilhelm the subject of war with Russia never
seemed far below the surface.

The disconnect between the ceremonial public life of the monarchs
and the realities of politics and economics was more than ever
demonstrated by the plethora of dynastic celebrations that took
place in 1913. In Germany Wilhelm celebrated twenty-five years
as kaiser and King of Prussia, the hundredth anniversary of the
Prussian victory over Napoleon at Leipzig, and the wedding of his
only daughter, Victoria Louise. In St Petersburg Nicholas celebrated the 300th anniversary of the Romanov dynasty. Crowds
turned out to cheer them both. The official German press ran
dutiful eulogies describing the kaiser as the cornerstone of the
German nation. In Russia the imperial family embarked on a
tour from St Petersburg to Moscow. 'Wherever we went,' Olga
recalled, 'we met with manifestations of loyalty bordering on
wildness.' Nicky and Alix were convinced that the celebrations
had established a new rapport between the imperial family and the
people. 'We need only show ourselves once, and at once their
hearts are ours,' Alix told one of her ladies. 'The Tsar's closest
friends at Court,' remembered his chief minister, Vladimir
Kokovtsov, 'became persuaded that the Sovereign could do anything by relying on the unbounded love and utter loyalty of the
people.' There was talk in right-wing circles of re-establishing the

direct communion between the Russian people and the tsar against the depraved modernity of the Left and the trade unions, of closing down the Duma for good, and even of getting rid of the Council of Ministers. There were other reasons to be cheerful. The country had had astonishing industrial growth and manufacturing had hugely increased too. It was chasing Germany and America in production of steel and coal. So successful did it look, that the British worried that Russia might feel it no longer needed the Convention. And in Germany Bethmann-Hollweg and the army chief, Moltke, were both haunted by the thought that the future belonged to Russia, and that by the late teens of the century it would be so powerful Germany would be at its mercy.

On closer scrutiny, however, both sets of dynastic festivities offered a different lesson: that nations were divided, regimes were discredited, and citizenries were disappointed and angry. Although, as the *Berliner Tageblatt* observed, large numbers of the German people were still 'monarchically inclined', in Germany the celebrations pointed up stark divisions, and a jadedness with the kaiser. 'Never in the history of the German people, the most monarchical people in its conviction and character, its customs and habit,' the solidly establishment *Kreuzzeitung* wrote during the celebrations in June 1913, 'has the monarchical thought been so attacked, has the monarchy faced such a strong front of open and hidden opponents.' On the far Right and in the army Wilhelm was viewed with intense disappointment for failing to provide the strong leadership he had promised. In 1912, under a pseudonym, the head of the Pan-German League, Heinrich Class, had published *Wenn Ich Kaiser Wäre* ('If I were Kaiser') in which he had longingly described a 'strong, able leader', unafraid to shrink the franchise, pass anti-Jewish and anti-socialist legislation, and impose press censorship. A blizzard of books from the German Right was demanding wars, expansion and German hegemony in Europe. The South Germans, meanwhile, complained about the suffocating influence 'of Prussia and its Junker class' and their sense of exclusion from the Reich. Even the *Bürgertum*, the stalwart Prussian middle classes, could see the kaiser's public inadequacies, and the *Berlin Tageblatt* complained on their behalf of having 'been treated as a *quantité negligeable* for twenty-five years'; now, the paper said, the *Bürgertum* 'screams for reforms'. The Left had fought the 1912 election on demands for a republic and had won 35 per cent of the vote, 110 seats, making it the largest faction in the Reichstag. The Catholic Centre Party, with which Wilhelm and his government had refused to deal, came second with ninety-one seats. The vote looked very much like a referendum on Wilhelm's rule, its extravagant spending, its inequitable tax system, its sanctioning of high food prices, and inability to tackle rising unemployment. As a result, Bethmann-Hollweg no longer had control of the Reichstag, and had been forced to run the country without it by decree, financing govern-ment with foreign loans. The Left's triumph caused hysteria among the German political and industrial elite, and led to talk at court and in the army of coups to get rid of universal suffrage – discussions quashed by Bethmann-Hollweg. But it visited upon the chancellor, as well as the army, a sense of gloom and pessimism about the divisions in and the future of Germany, assailed as it seemed to be from both within and without.

In Russia the crowds had cheered the Romanov celebrations because a royal process was entertainment and a rare sight. But, as Chief Minister Kokovtsov wrote, 'There was nothing in the feeling of the crowd but shallow curiosity.' It was not hard to see why. There had been hopes of amnesties, new initiatives to restore public confidence, even a sense that the occasion wasn't simply about the Romanovs, but about the people too – but none was forthcoming. There were only the conventional manifes-tations of royal ritual: processions, gala dinners, religious services. The institutions around the tsar had treated the occasion with humourless stiffness. When commemorative cups and plates and stamps went on sale with the tsar and his family illustrated on them, the Ministry of the Imperial Court complained that it was not permitted for the tsar's head to appear on 'utilitarian objects', and the Holy Synod protested that it was improper for the sovereign's face to be stamped with a postmark. Even the aristocracy of St Petersburg society seemed half-hearted about the occasion. When it gave a ball for the imperial couple, the atmosphere, Nicholas's sisters observed, was 'hollow' and 'forced'.

The reality was that Russia's administration was more grid-locked than ever; its governance more brutal, its leadership more lost. Even its industrial gains had been made at enormous social cost. In the rest of Europe, working conditions had gradually been improving. Not in Russia. Nicholas was still locked away at Tsarskoe, worrying about his sick son, watching anxiously over his invalid wife, ever more estranged and alienated from everything around him save the tiny court, fretting about the state of his nation, but paralysed by indecision. He would toy with the idea of overturning the new political order, but instead just complained from the sidelines. He loathed the impudence of the Duma, which, no matter how the government manipulated the franchise, came back irrepressibly critical and determined to support representative government. He was no keener on his ministers. Having hailed Peter Stolypin as Russia's saviour in 1906, by 1911 he had become profoundly suspicious of him. Stolypin, a pragmatic conservative, had realized he had to work with the zemstvos – the local councils Nicholas's father had abhorred – and talk to the Duma. Just as he had with Witte, Nicholas gradually came to distrust and dislike him. It was widely rumoured the tsar was about to dismiss Stolypin when he was assassinated at the Kiev Opera House – in front of Nicholas and his two eldest daughters – in September 1911. There were whispers that he had been murdered by the Right, as the shooter turned out to be both a left-wing radical and a police informer, and had made no attempt to get at the tsar.

'I am sure Stolypin died to make room for you,' Alix told Stolypin's successor Vladimir Kokovtsov, rather chillingly, 'and this is all for the good of Russia.' But Kokovtsov also found the tsar quietly encouraging ministerial factions against him. Each time Nicholas did this, it disrupted and undermined government stability and effectiveness a little bit more. After sacking Kokovtsov in early 1914, he lectured his Council of Ministers on the need for unity. His need to feel in control overrode everything – even the effective governance of the country. 'The Emperor is by no means stupid, talks well and to the point, and is fully aware of what he is doing,' one particularly clear-eyed British diplomat reported in 1916, '. . . he is obstinate and vindictive, and quite obsessed with the idea that the autocracy is his and his children's by divine right.'

The stories that came out of Russia made the regime look increasingly nasty and indefensible. In 1912 tsarist soldiers shot dead 500 striking miners, and wounded hundreds of others at the Lena goldfields in Siberia. Conditions at the mine were horrendous: the men worked fifteen to sixteen-hour days, with an accident rate of 700 per 1,000 workers. Food, brought in from outside, was often rotten or insufficient. The strikers had been demanding an eight-hour day, a 30 per cent wage rise and the improvement of food supplies. Within days St Petersburg was engulfed in a huge general strike. The recently elected fourth Duma demanded explanations. They were not impressed by the latest minister of the interior's answer, 'Thus it has been so it always will be.' Relations deteriorated so badly that by the summer of 1912 ministers and Duma were barely in communication. Then there was the ugliness of the Beiliss affair in 1913, in which a completely innocent Jewish clerk was put on trial for ritual child murder. The almost comically hopeless case against him had been trumped up with the government's, and the tsar's, full knowledge – in the expectation that grass roots anti-Semitism would rally loyal Russians to the government. Nicholas himself sent the judge a gold watch on the eve of the trial, in anticipation of a guilty verdict. All the time the strikes continued: between 1912 and 1914 there would be 9,000 of them, many organized by the militant Bolsheviks, until between January and July 1914 there were a million and a half workers on strike.

Then there was Rasputin, whose exploits were becoming the stuff of grand guignol. Alix had come gradually to trust and rely on him for advice beyond Alexis's illness. She believed he'd been sent by God. She had drawn him into the heart of the family, allowing him to watch her daughters getting ready for bed – something which deeply shocked her mother and sisters-in law – and referred to him in letters to Nicholas as 'Our Friend'. In 1911 she had begun to ask for his advice about ministers she didn't like, and told Nicholas he should comb his hair with Rasputin's comb before makng difficult decisions. Secure in the imperial couple's favour, Rasputin exploited his position. The head of the imperial

Chancellery, Mossolov, found himself besieged by Rasputin's clients armed with notes from the *starets* demanding positions. Stolypin and Kokovtsov both fell foul of him. Kokovstov was said to have been sacked by Nicholas at least partly for failing to prevent stories about Rasputin from getting into the press – stories which circumvented the censorship laws because they didn't mention the imperial family by name. Perhaps inevitably, from 1911 stories about him had begun to circulate beyond Tsarskoe selo. By 1912 he was the subject of denunciatory speeches in the Duma, and by 1914 newspaper articles were spreading his fame across Russia. The stories demonstrated painfully how the previously closed world of the Russian court could no longer shut out the world, and at the same time paradoxically how isolated from and ignorant of the outside world the imperial family had become. Press coverage of Rasputin transformed him from a court favourite muttered over by the elite, into a national, and then international, symbol of the ills and poisons of the system. Scandalous rumours began to proliferate about his appetite for sex, booze and creating chaos.

The most notorious incident would come in 1915, when he turned up drunk at the Yar, a famous Moscow restaurant once frequented by Pushkin, accompanied by two women, and started a brawl. He called a newspaper editor to witness the scene, and as his *pièce de résistance*, took out his penis, laid it on the table, and said he could do what he liked with the 'Old Girl' – meaning the tsarina. No one dared remove him until the Ministry of the Interior was called for permission to arrest him. In the absence of other explanations about his influence within the imperial family, it was almost too easy to attribute it to their alarming credulity, or to some sinister sexual enthralment. The gossip in St Petersburg had it that Rasputin slept with the tsarina and her friend Anna Vyrubova, and had raped all the tsar's daughters – their defilement a kind of metaphor for the degradation of the regime itself. Nicholas and Alexandra were repeatedly warned about Rasputin by servants, officials, the police, Church figures and finally even by their family. They refused to listen. They had become practised at ignoring those who told them things they didn't want to hear.

Even stable Britain seemed to be succumbing to a new level

of public disaffection and violent disorder. Miners and railway workers' strikes threatened to bring the country to a standstill over 1912 and 1913, and the suffragettes' campaign to get the vote for women reached new levels of violence. Windows at Windsor Castle were broken in 1912, and then in 1913 Emily Davidson martyred herself at the Derby by throwing herself under George's horse. George, who had no sympathy with either strikers or suffragettes, was repelled and shocked. He told Asquith he should pass a law against picketing. 'The King is hostile to the bone to all who are working to lift the workmen out of the mire,' wrote Lloyd George, who talked the strikers back to work. 'So is the Queen. They talk exactly as the late King and Kaiser talked to me . . . about the old railway strike. "What do they want striking? They are very well paid." '

Just as in Russia and Germany, in Britain there was talk on the Right of taking radical action against the Left. When the Liberal government's bill to grant Home Rule to Ireland came up in the Commons in May 1912, Andrew Bonar Law, the new leader of the Conservative Party (whose full name, the Conservative Unionists, denoted their commitment to maintaining the union with Ireland by all means) told George that with the power of the Lords gone, the king should use his veto to stop the bill, dismiss his Liberal ministers and choose new ones – Conservative ones. By British standards this was strong stuff: the monarch was supposed to be above politics, no monarch had dismissed a minister since 1830 and no monarch had used the royal veto since 1708. It had the whiff of a palace coup, and was wholly at odds with the spirit of parliamentary democracy. George refused to do it, but the request instantly released a torrent of self-pity. 'Whatever I do I shall offend half the population . . . No Sovereign has ever been in such a position,' and the idea of the veto exercised an enduring fascination over him. In August 1913 he sent a 1,500-word letter to Asquith, quoting Bagehot and claiming the right to dismiss advisers and dissolve parliament on his own – which the prime minister ignored. The king also hated the thought of Home Rule. It was actually no more than the self-government that Australia and Canada already enjoyed, but to the king and the Conservative Party it seemed the first step in the dissolution of the British empire, and so – not least because the British government resisted so long – it would prove. As the Home Rule bill worked its way through parliament, George took to sending Asquith 'neurotic' letters, and summoning him for interviews in which he would complain about 'his own position, and the terrible cross-fire to wh. he conceives himself to be exposed'.

In May 1913, at the wedding of Wilhelm's youngest child and only daughter, Victoria, the three emperors came together for only the second time in their lives since 1889. The wedding was the last of the big royal gatherings that had been supposed to create such harmony in Europe. It was billed as a happy resolution to the old dispute over Prussia's swallowing up of the kingdom of Hanover in 1866: Victoria was marrying Prince Ernest August of Cumberland, son of Alexandra and Minny's sister Thyra, and grandson of Queen Victoria's cousin the King of Hanover. It was the last time all three would be together, the last time any of them met.

There were the familiar receptions and reviews, a gala dinner for 1,200. Fritz Ponsonby, as ever in attendance, noted that Wilhelm was in 'great spirits', that the Germans were harder than usual to talk to, and everyone had to stand for even longer than they'd expected.

Even so, the occasion raised in the protagonists a whisper of the old hopes that royal meetings made a difference. The kaiser, as usual, fancied the event as a moment of personal diplomacy. Afterwards he reported to Archduke Franz Ferdinand, 'It went off extremely pleasantly and favourably. King George V, the Emperor and I were agreed on an absolutely complete conformity regarding the affairs of the Balkan states . . . The King of England as well as the Tsar are in complete agreement with me and are firmly resolved to keep the unbridled Bulgarian desire for aggrandizement at the expense of Turkey and of other states strictly within bounds.' He decided that he and George had got on so well that he would arrange a return visit to Britain. He might even have a genuine shot at weakening the Entente.

In truth, during the wedding Wilhelm had been torn between delight at the turnout and jealousy of his cousins. He made it clear that George would not be welcome at the station when he went to meet Nicholas off the St Petersburg train, because he didn't want to be upstaged. And he was determined, George later recalled, not to allow his two cousins to be alone together, for fear that they would whisper behind his back. When the two did manage a few moments together, George was convinced that 'William's ear was glued to the keyhole'. A year later, as Europe lurched towards conflict, Wilhelm insisted his cousins – two men who never talked politics if they could help it – had been plotting against him at the wedding.

In fact, George had come to the wedding with a tiny flame of expectation. The previous December Heinrich had told him that he still nursed 'hopes that England and Germany might go together, for the sake of the world's peace!' and begged him to make a state visit to Germany. 'Please think about it seriously – it might do a world of good!' The king's ambitions, however, were quickly extinguished by the proximity of Wilhelm. George, one German courtier observed, was most at ease discussing horseflesh with the kaiser's Master of the Horse. He was genuinely pleased, though, to see Nicholas, who arrived by train with a hundred policemen. 'I had a long and satisfactory talk with dear Nicky, he was just the same as always,' he wrote in his diary. The same, of course, was good. George later wrote that Nicholas and he had 'entirely agreed upon the great importance of maintaining the most friendly relations between our two countries', in order to secure 'the peace of Europe'. Given the banality of their letters, it is hard to imagine that Wilhelm had anything to feel anxious about. In any case, all three men had long since withdrawn into their own national orthodoxies. Nicholas was resentful that the British and German moves to resolve the Balkan Wars had destroyed Russia's latest hope of taking the Straits, and at the Russian court Pan-Slavist, anti-German attitudes were very much in the ascendant. The German government was committed to supporting Austria in the Balkans, and Wilhelm liked to tell visiting Austrian envoys that they should get on and deal once and for all with the Serbs.

As if to confirm the irrelevance of the event, barely six months afterwards Russia and Germany found themselves once again trading threats as once again one small act took on frightening significance. A German lieutenant general called Liman von Sanders was appointed as instructor to the Turkish army and commander of the 1st Ottoman Army Corps, the garrison that guarded Constantinople. The Russians instantly saw the appointment as a deliberate move to put the Straits under German control. Nicholas asked Kokovtsov, who was in Berlin, to demand an explanation from the German government. In a scene played out many times before, Wilhelm assured the Russian minister that the whole matter had been thoroughly discussed during Nicholas's attendance at the wedding in May. Nicholas 'had then offered no objections ... his interference now that all details had been arranged was, to say the least, inconsistent'. Should he, the kaiser mused, consider these complaints 'an ultimatum'? Kokovtsov, unused to Wilhelm's manner, didn't know what to say; he could hardly challenge the word of an emperor. At lunch he shuddered as Wilhelm veered between joviality and indignation – listing the good deeds he had performed for Russia and complaining about her 'ingratitude'– and warnings: 'In spite of all this the outbursts of your press . . . have become insufferable; they will lead inevitably to a catastrophe which I shall be powerless to avert.'

Nicholas, outraged, 'flatly denied that any agreement had been reached'. The Russian government demanded that Liman von Sanders be removed, while the Russian press made angry denunciations. The Germans refused to stand down, protesting that the appointment was simply an exchange of personnel. There was a long tradition of European military staff giving training to the Turkish army; British naval officers had recently been seconded to its navy. Neither the British nor the French, indeed, could see why the Russians were so exercised.

At an emergency meeting of the tsar's Council of Ministers it was agreed that, if the Germans refused to back down, Russia would consider military action, including the seizing of Turkish ports, and seek military aid from France and Britain, in order to force Germany to capitulate. Behind the precipitousness of the reaction was a fear that Germany meant to be a player in the Near East. The appointment of Sanders, like the Baghdad railway, seemed evidence of German intentions.⋆ Kokovtsov reminded the meeting that war was the greatest misfortune that could befall Russia, but his words were ignored. It was a seismic, if not altogether unexpected, turnaround in the Russian government's thinking. The fundamental axiom of policy had been that war meant disaster. Now it seemed that humiliation and the potential loss of Russia's Great Power status were a greater priority. Thankfully, the Germans backed down in January 1914 and the Turks promoted Liman von Sanders to field marshal, which made him too senior to command a Turkish corps. 'Now I have only friendly smiles for Germany,' Nicholas told Count Pourtalès, the German ambassador, after the Germans backed down.

Actually the Sanders affair seemed to break the last shreds of Nicholas's belief in German goodwill. He was convinced it had proved the reality of the German threat. At the end of January 1914 he gave an audience to the former French foreign minister, Théophile Delcassé, and told him that he foresaw 'a perhaps inevitable and imminent collision between German ambitions and Russian interest', and said Russia would not allow itself to be trampled on. In March he told the British ambassador, Buchanan, that 'he had reason to believe that Germany was aiming at acquiring such a position at Constantinople as would enable her to shut in Russia altogether in the Black Sea. Should she attempt to carry out this policy He would have to resist with all His power, even should war be the only alternative.' He was not alone. As one of his courtiers observed, the belief 'that war is inevitable has grown and grown in all classes'. The extent of anti-German feeling among Russians prompted a former minister, Durnovo, to write a memo to the tsar outlining in horribly prescient detail the disasters a war

⋆ In fact Wilhelm did harbour fantasies of taking over the Turkish army. Seeing off von Sanders's mission he had told them their task was the 'Germanisation of the Turkish army through leadership and direct control of the organisational activity of the Turkish ministry of war', and said he hoped 'the German flag will soon fly over the fortifications of the Bosphorus' – but this, as so often, expressed an aspiration rather than a plan.

with Germany would bring, arguing that ties with Britain – ties which had brought Russia no real benefits – were simply accelerating the likelihood of that clash. But for Nicholas Germany had finally and indubitably taken Britain's place as Russia's main enemy. With the British, however, the conflicts had been fought out at a distance in Asia. Germany was on the doorstep.

Russian attempts to lure Britain into alliance, however, continued to fail. In May 1914 Nicholas summoned Buchanan and said he wanted to see France, Britain and Russia working much more closely together. But Russia was behaving so badly in Persia that the Convention was on the point of collapse. The British Foreign Office, moreover, suspected Russia now had its eye on Turkish Armenia. When Buchanan put the British position to Nicholas – as carefully as he could – the tsar refused to accept it: 'I can only tell you, as I have so often told you before, that my one desire is to remain firm friends with England and, if I can prevent it, nothing shall stand in the way of the closest possible understanding between our two countries.' Finally, in June, George was conscripted by Grey to bring the subject to the tsar's attention – or rather the Foreign Office drafted a letter and George copied it. He said he was now 'so anxious upon this subject, that I write this private letter to explain what is causing me this anxiety. It is the present unsatisfactory state of affairs in Persia. It is my great desire to see a friendly feeling towards Russia preserved in British public opinion and in both political parties . . . that makes me most anxious that our two Governments should have a frank and friendly exchange of views on the whole situation in Persia.' He knew, he added, that he could count on Nicky's friendship to remove any misunderstandings.

In Germany, meanwhile, talk of 'inevitable struggles' and 'preventive wars' just wouldn't go away. The idea of imminent war had acquired a momentum of its own. In November 1913 Bethmann-Hollweg had delivered a Reichstag speech warning against a preventive war. The Pan-German League announced in April 1914 that 'France and Russia are preparing for the decisive struggle with Germany and Austria-Hungary and they intend to strike at the first opportunity.' Moltke, the Chief of Staff, held talks that spring with the foreign minister, Jagow, and told him that, while now Germany was still a match for its enemies, in a couple of years they would be too strong. 'The Chief of Staff therefore proposed that I should conduct a policy with the aim of provoking a war in the near future.' The kaiser himself told the Hamburg banker Max Warburg that the Russians were preparing for a war in 1916, and mused that it might be better to attack first. On 27 June the American special envoy Colonel Edward House, who had come to Europe to try to broker a compact between the US, Germany and Britain to prevent a major war, came from Germany to meet Sir Edward Grey in London. He described to Grey 'the militant war spirit in Germany and the high tension of the people. I thought that Germany would strike quickly when she moved . . . I thought the Kaiser himself and most of his immediate advisors did not want war . . . but the army was military and aggressive and ready for war at any time.'

The next day Archduke Franz Ferdinand, heir to the empire of Austria-Hungary, and his wife, Sophy, were assassinated at Sarajevo.

16. July 1914

The month between the assassination of Archduke Franz Ferdinand and the outbreak of the First World War demonstrated perhaps more than anything how events had slipped away from Wilhelm, Nicholas and George. The kaiser was at the Kiel regatta racing yachts when he heard the news. He had been entertaining a squadron of visiting British battlecruisers, and the town was full of fraternizing British and German officers. He was clearly upset by the news. 'This cowardly, detestable crime has shaken me to the depths of my soul,' he cabled Bethmann-Hollweg. In recent years Franz Ferdinand had become one of his closest friends – they had been hunting the week before – even though, as with so many of Wilhelm's relationships, he regarded the friendship as instrumental: he liked to claim he had the Hapsburg heir in his pocket.

The tsar was on his annual Baltic summer cruise. Nine-year-old Alexis had fallen jumping from a ladder and twisted his ankle. He was haemorrhaging and crying with pain; Alix was white with worry. Then news came that Rasputin had been stabbed by a madwoman. Everyone on the boat apart from the imperial family hoped he was dead. Franz Ferdinand's assassination was barely registered.

George, too, was preoccupied. The latest chapter in Irish Home Rule had been dominated by bitter arguments over the fate of the predominantly Protestant six northern counties of Ireland, which had threatened to fight if they were separated from Britain. Large numbers of guns had been smuggled into the North. George was obsessed with what might happen if the British army – *his* army – had to fire on British citizens, and had complained repeatedly to Asquith about ' "the terrible cross-fire" to wh. he conceives himself to be exposed'. 'Terrible shock for the dear old Emperor', he wrote in his diary. As it happened, Franz Joseph was remarkably sanguine. He hadn't much liked his nephew and didn't even go to the funeral.

No one expected the shooting would result in war. Initially, there was collective outrage at the deed and sympathy for Austria. Even if the murder could be traced back to Serbia – the nineteen-year-old assassin, Gavril Princip, had said he'd killed 'an enemy of the Southern Slavs' to 'avenge the Serbian people' – everyone expected it to blow over. 'Kaiser Wilhelm will show his teeth,' the former Russian foreign minister, Alexander Izvolsky, told Nicholas's cousin Sandro. 'And everything will be forgotten by the fifteenth of the next month!' Wilhelm did show his teeth, in his characteristic way. On a memo from the German ambassador in Vienna, he wrote that the Serbs must be dealt with 'now or never . . . the Serbs must be disposed of, and that right soon'.

The Austrian government, however, saw the assassination as an opportunity. More than ever it regarded Serbia, which had doubled in size after the Balkan Wars and constantly proclaimed itself leader of the southern Slavs, as a threat to the Hapsburg empire. It had asked Germany for support to crush Serbia three times since mid-1913; Wilhelm had refused each time. The Austrian military was quite as enthusiastic about the idea of war as the most gung-ho of German officers. The Austrian chief of staff, Conrad von Hötzendorf, like Moltke, was a convinced Social Darwinist who believed that struggle was a fundamental principle of life, and had been itching to fight Serbia for years. In 1913 alone he'd demanded war twenty-five times.

A week after the murder, on 5 July, the Austrian ambassador came to Wilhelm with a confidential letter from Emperor Franz Joseph stating that the assassination had been traced to a plot organized by the Serbian government and Serbia must be 'eliminated'. It asked for German support. The implication was that Austria would launch a quick war to punish Serbia, while Europe was on its summer holiday. It would all be over before anyone could complain. Germany's role would be to make sure no other Powers would feel tempted to get involved. Wilhelm hesitated. Pointing out that acting against Serbia might 'bring about a serious European complication', he ate his lunch. Then he told the

Austrian ambassador that Austria could rely on Germany's full support against Serbia, even if the war threatened to spread, but Austria must act fast. Bethmann-Hollweg was summoned and entirely agreed.

Why did they agree? Wilhelm was upset by his friend's death; he saw Austria as the wronged party and believed Serbia was a poison in the Balkans. But before, when it had come to the crunch, he had always shied away from confrontation. He had often seen this as a weakness in himself. 'This time I shall not give in,' he told the armaments manufacturer Krupp. As for Bethmann-Hollweg, he had spent four years countering the military's calls for war. His decision seems to have emerged from a deeply depressed sense that Germany was trapped and had almost nowhere else to go: his attempts to ease its foreign relations had failed, while the country's internal divisions made it increasingly ungovernable. And like the army, he had begun to obsess about Russia as a future threat. 'Russia grows and grows and weighs on us like a nightmare,' he said. As Germany's only consistent ally, Austria, meanwhile, needed to be supported. A small war would allow it to recover its dignity and eliminate the threat of Serbia. What seems to have convinced them both was the perception that any war would be quick and localized – it was almost as if after all the talk of European conflagrations, it was easy to agree to a small war in which Germany would not actually take part. But there was always a risk. Crucially both men were certain that Russia was not, as Wilhelm said, 'ready for war and would think twice before it appealed to arms'. It wasn't an unreasonable assumption. For months the German ambassador in St Petersburg had been sending reports about the problems in Russia: the millions of striking workers, the barricades on the Moscow streets. Wilhelm was sure, moreover, that Nicholas wouldn't put himself on the side of regicides. He told his political and military chiefs that he didn't want war preparations made, so convinced was he that only the threat would be needed. The next day he set off for his annual yachting trip along the Norwegian coast.

Two weeks later the Austrians had accomplished precisely nothing. They had failed to find any evidence incriminating Serbia in the assassination. They had failed to draft an ultimatum. And it transpired they wouldn't be able to gather together an army until after the harvest in mid-August. So much for a quick war. Finally, on 19 July, the German Foreign Office cabled the kaiser that an Austrian ultimatum would be delivered to the Serbians on 23 July, and that he must be reachable, in case important decisions needed to be made. As the possibility of European war suddenly became real to him, Wilhelm was seized with anxiety. He wanted to return to Berlin, but Bethmann-Hollweg – dreading the thought of the kaiser sweeping back to Berlin in a flurry of inflammatory pro-nouncements – insisted he stayed put, telling him that cutting short his trip might alarm the British navy.

At midnight on 23 July the Austrians delivered their ultimatum to Serbia. They'd deliberately delayed it because the French presi-dent, Raymond Poincaré, had been visiting the tsar in St Petersburg and they wanted to wait until he was out of port so France and Russia could not coordinate a response. The ultimatum demanded that Austrian officers be allowed to enter Serbia to conduct their own investigation, that all Serb nationalist propaganda be sup-pressed, that all Serb nationalist societies be disbanded and that Serbian military officers regarded as 'anti-Austrian' be dismissed. It gave the Serbs forty-eight hours to reply. The ultimatum's ferocity stunned European diplomats. Sir Edward Grey felt that no sover-eign state could possibly agree to it.

The day after the Austrians issued their ultimatum, Sergei Sazonov convened a meeting of the Russian Council of Ministers. He told his colleagues that he was sure Austria had been encouraged by Germany, which wanted to dominate the continent, and that the two states thought they could win a war against Russia. He desperately wanted to avoid war, but at the same time he was convinced that if it came to it and Russia did not stand up for Serbia and failed 'to fulfil her historic mission she would be considered a decadent State and would henceforth have to take second place among the powers'. Another 'humiliation' was simply too much to bear. Moreover, 'public opinion' – or what passed for it – demanded action. The Russian press was near-hysterically insisting that this couldn't be another Bosnia. Knowing that if Russia went to war it might end in revolution, the ministers convinced themselves that if it didn't, the country might rise against them in patriotic disgust.

Even so, Sazonov tried to head off a conflict. He asked the Austrians to extend the deadline to Serbia and asked Grey to do the same. He advised the Serbs to accept as many of the Austrian demands as they could and suggested everything else be adjudicated at The Hague. He appealed to the German Foreign Office to mediate, unaware that they were Austria's secret backers. The German ambassador insisted Germany knew nothing about the ultimatum and the matter was between Austria and Serbia. He told Sazonov that Austria simply wanted to teach Serbia a lesson and he should try negotiating with Austria direct. The Austrians turned down all Sazonov's requests.

Nicholas dreaded the thought of a conflict and was sure Wilhelm did too. He told the French ambassador in St Petersburg, Maurice Paléologue, 'I can't believe the Emperor wants war . . . If you knew him as I do! If you knew how much theatricality there is in his posing!' One of his ministers recalled later:

He told me that he thought Sazonov was exaggerating the gravity of the situation and had lost his nerve . . . War would be disastrous for the world and once it had broken out it would be difficult to stop. The Emperor did not think it likely that the Note had been sent after consultation with Berlin. The German Emperor had frequently assured him of his sincere desire to safeguard the peace of Europe and it had always been possible to come to an agreement with him, even in serious cases. His Majesty spoke of the German Emperor's loyal attitude during the Russo-Japanese war and during the internal troubles that Russia had experienced afterwards. It would have been easy for Germany to level a decisive blow at Russia in those circumstances.

The tsar tried to continue life as before: playing tennis, canoeing with his daughters, having tea with his relatives, meeting the Master of the Horse of the court of Mecklenburg-Strelitz. But he was sick with worry and struggled to remain cheerful. 'We had only to see him during that terrible last week of July,' his son's tutor wrote later, 'to realise what mental torture he had passed through.'

When Wilhelm returned to Potsdam on 27 July, he was shaken to discover Austria had ordered a partial mobilization of its army, before Serbia had replied to the ultimatum. He also found the German army chiefs very much in the ascendant in arguments over what Germany should do next. In contrast to German civilian government, which had become chaotic and divided, making opposition to the war very much harder to coordinate, the army chiefs were well organized and spoke with one voice. They had been allowed, indeed encouraged, to remain entirely beyond the control or scrutiny of civilian authority, they were disdainful of civilian culture and convinced that war was a good in itself, while civilian culture was saturated with admiration for them.

Though Austria had been a grave disappointment, the army chiefs were convinced that it was time to fight and were determined that the kaiser's pusillanimity would not be allowed to prevent a war. Moltke had an even larger agenda. Since the beginning of the crisis he had argued that the assassination provided the perfect opportunity for a different war, the great war of reckoning with Russia. He'd been secretly encouraging his Austrian opposite number, Conrad von Hötzendorf, for weeks. The idea half-horrified him and he veered between pushing for it and then arguing against it. The war minister Falkenhayn, and the head of Wilhelm's military cabinet, Lyncker, also agreed the moment was right, and they thought a war would silence, if not flush out, degenerate socialist elements in Germany. Crucial to Moltke's plan – what has come to be known as the Schlieffen Plan –* was the fact that Austria was willing to fight with Germany. The plan was predicated on the idea that in a war Germany would have to deal with two aggressors – France and Russia – simultaneously. The

---

* The German war plan known as the Schlieffen Plan was once thought to have been formulated in 1905–6, and was therefore named after the then-incumbent chief of staff, Schlieffen. It is now known that the plan was adopted as the sole German war plan only in 1913, during Moltke's time as chief of staff.

strategy was that the army would knock out France quickly before its forces could mobilize, then wheel round to attack Russia, which was known to be slow to mobilize its huge army. Wilhelm was said to have called the idea, which had been first suggested around 1905, 'Paris for lunch, dinner at St Petersburg'. Austria was needed to keep the Russians at bay until Germany was ready.

The plan had fairly devastating implications: firstly, regardless of whether France had been in any way involved, it would be invaded. The same went for the neutral states of Belgium and Luxembourg, which were on the route into France. An Eastern European conflict would instantly become a Europe-wide war. Secondly, the plan obliged Germany to mobilize and make the decision for war before anyone else, and rush into hostilities in order to eliminate France in time. As a consequence Moltke was in a hurry. The plan was typical of the way the German officer corps had come to see strategic problems in a vacuum, entirely from their narrow viewpoint, and without recourse to the nuances of diplomacy or the needs of politics. It was also the result of Moltke's conviction that the war which would decide the fate of Europe was coming anyway, and France would have to be dealt with, just like Russia. Most significantly of all, perhaps, it had been kept secret from the civilian government.

Bethmann-Hollweg, both disappointed and relieved by the Austrians' failure to act, had questioned the need for a war, but by the time Wilhelm returned he was in the process of being talked round, though he still wanted hostilities to be limited. German army values had so percolated into government that diplomacy had come to seem almost a cowardly way to resolve international problems. Perhaps solutions to difficult problems did require extreme, risky measures. Half-appalled, half-resigned to the situation, he offered to quit. Wilhelm refused: 'You have cooked up this broth, now you are going to eat it.'

The Serbs' reply to the ultimatum came on 28 July. It was breathtakingly humble and acquiescent; it acceded to everything the Austrians could reasonably have asked and swung international opinion back Serbia's way. Wilhelm was enormously relieved. He wrote to his foreign minister, Jagow, 'A great moral success for Vienna; but with it every reason for war drops away.' Instead he thought Austria might perhaps occupy a part of Serbia, until the Serbs had undertaken what they had promised. 'I am ready to mediate for peace,' he said, and he told Jagow to notify the Austrians that they must not go to war. His orders were ignored. Bethmann-Hollweg cabled Vienna but did not tell the Austrians to stop their war preparations. The day before, indeed, Jagow had encouraged them to declare war on Serbia at once. When Wilhelm told his ministers that he wanted to avoid war, his war minister, Falkenhayn, informed him that he 'no longer had control of the affair in his own hands'. It was an expression of the general disdain with which the senior ranks of the army now regarded the kaiser. We don't know what Wilhelm said to this, but he didn't challenge it.

The Austrian government rejected the Serb reply, refused Sazonov's request for talks with Russia and declared war on Serbia. In St Petersburg, the German ambassador, Pourtalès, had lunch with the British ambassador, Buchanan, and explained to him that the Germans assumed the Russians wouldn't get involved because he'd assured them that Russia wasn't capable of fighting a war over Serbia. Buchanan couldn't believe how his German colleague had misread the political atmosphere.

That day Nicholas ordered the partial mobilization of Russian troops. The idea was to move Russian soldiers on to the frontier with Austria, while carefully keeping them away from the borders of Germany so as not to give offence. But he worried about it and thought about rescinding the order.

It was only on 27 July that George seemed to register the Balkan crisis. 'It looks as if we were on the verge of general European war, caused by the sending of Ultimatum to Serbia by Austria, very serious state of affairs,' he wrote in his diary. The British government had been so preoccupied with the prospect of civil war in Ireland that the Austrian ultimatum had taken it by surprise. Indeed, the German Foreign Office was counting on Ireland keeping Britain out of the Serbian crisis altogether. Asquith had told the king it was 'the gravest event for many years in European politics'. He also reassured George that there was little reason why 'we should be anything more than spectators'. Barely anyone in Britain had ever heard of Serbia, and the government did not feel at all inclined to fight a war on Russia's behalf. It wasn't perhaps surprising that when Heinrich came to see George on 26 July, on his way home after his latest visit to England, the king reassured him – at least in Heinrich's recollection – that 'We shall try all we can to keep out of this and remain neutral.'

Initially sympathetic to Austria's desire to make Serbia account-able for its role in the assassination (which had encouraged the Germans), Sir Edward Grey was now determined to prevent the war. He had concluded, against the advice of several of his most senior officials, that Berlin's intentions were honourable and it had no intention of supporting a war. He endorsed Sazonov's request that the matter go to The Hague, and when the Austrians turned it down, suggested a conference, like the one that had resolved the Balkan Wars, of England, Germany, France and Italy. Lichnowsky, the ambassador, who knew nothing of the German government's decisions, passed the idea to the German Foreign Office with an enthusiastic endorsement. Bethmann-Hollweg realized that Grey's proposal might actually stop the war. He felt obliged to forward it to Austria so as to avoid laying Germany open to accusations that it wanted war, but he told the Austrian Foreign Office to ignore it. On 27 July he rejected the proposal himself, claiming that it would unfairly force a decision on Austria – but salving this with a suggestion that Austria and Russia were about to enter negotiations. The next day the Austrians declared war.

Even now, the British still felt that they had little reason to get involved. Three-quarters of the cabinet were against the idea and Asquith noted that it was 'still not a British war'. But Grey told parliament that the minute the conflict spread beyond Austria and Serbia it would become 'the greatest catastrophe that has ever befallen the Continent of Europe'. He did not, however, tell parliament about all the military and naval talks with France of the previous eight years, which he now believed had created an obligation to come to France's aid.

George complained to his younger son that he'd had to cancel his annual trip to Goodwood races, and was regretting the loss of his weekend sailing at Cowes.

Late on the 28th, after the Austrians had declared war, and as the roll towards European war seemed inexorable, Wilhelm and Nicholas exchanged telegrams, each appealing to the other to stop the conflict. Nicholas still hoped that, if Germany could pull Austria back from attacking Belgrade, war could be stopped: 'I appeal to you to help me . . . I foresee that very soon I shall be overwhelmed by pressure brought upon me, and forced to take extreme measures which will lead to war.'

Wilhelm for the last time, appealed to monarchical solidarity: '. . . You will doubtless agree with me that we both, you and me, have a common interest as well as all Sovereigns to insist that all the persons morally responsible for the dastardly murder should receive their deserved punishment. In this case politics plays no part at all.' He reassured Nicholas that Germany was doing its best to try to bring about an agreement between Vienna and St Petersburg – though he would not promise that he would stop the attack on Serbia.

> I fully understand how difficult it is for you and your Government to face the drift of your public opinion. Therefore, with regard to the hearty and tender friendship which binds us both from long ago with firm ties, I am exerting my utmost influence to induce the Austrians to deal straightly to arrive to a satisfactory understanding with you. I confidently hope that you will help me in my efforts to smooth over difficulties that may still arise.
>
> Your very sincere and devoted friend and cousin Willy

Wilhelm didn't know that his own Foreign Office had advised the Austrians to go to war, and that Bethmann-Hollweg had accompanied his demand to the Austrians to stop in Belgrade with a note that it wasn't to be taken seriously and was simply for propaganda purposes.

Nicholas wrote to George too, asking for support from Britain if Russia did find itself at war, and assuring him that he was doing all he could to avoid it.

Austria has gone off upon a reckless war, which can easily end in a general conflagration. It is awful! My country is confident of its strength and of the right cause it has taken up . . . Now we are compelled to take strong measures in case of emergency – for our own defence . . . If a general war broke out I know that we shall have France's and England's full support. As a last resort I have written to William to ask him to bear a strong pressure upon Austria so as to enable us to discuss matters with her.

'Where will it end?' George wrote plaintively. '. . . Winston Churchill came to see me, the Navy is all ready for War, but please God it will not come. These are very anxious days for me to live in.'

On 29 July Wilhelm summoned his military leaders. Most of the army chiefs were keen to go to the next level of preparedness for mobilization – *Kriegsgefahr*, the 'state of impending war', the stage before mobilization – but Bethmann-Hollweg and Moltke, visited by one of his moments of anxiety, argued against it and Wilhelm eventually sided with them. He also announced he had received a message from Heinrich telling him of George's words of a few days before – that Britain would try to keep out of the conflict. He seized on this as an official assurance of British neutrality. When Tirpitz suggested he might have misinterpreted it, Wilhelm said grandly, 'I have the word of a King, and that is enough for me.' But in the afternoon Lichnowsky sent the German Foreign Office a telegram describing a meeting with Sir Edward Grey, who, after suggesting that the Austrians should stop in Belgrade, added that, if Germany and France became involved in a war, Britain wouldn't be able to remain aloof.

Grey's message was far from being an explicit threat – he couldn't know that the German response to a Balkan conflict would include attacking France – but it shocked Bethmann-Hollweg, who still hoped the war might be localized. News that the Russians were starting to mobilize, and a dressing down from

Wilhelm when he suggested that Germany should sacrifice the fleet in order to keep Britain neutral, convinced him the conflict was escalating too fast and too far. Contradicting his previous messages, he sent three increasingly desperate telegrams to Vienna asking that the Austrian army stop when they got to Belgrade. But a few hours before, Moltke had cabled Conrad von Hötzendorf, the Austrian chief of staff, and told him to go to full mobilization. The Austrians shelled Belgrade; Bethmann-Hollweg was too late. It was a horrible instance of the German government's confusion. Even Moltke was far from delighted by what he had done. He wrote a memo to the government that day in which he described a war 'which will annihilate the civilization of almost the whole of Europe for decades to come'.

In a final effort to head off British involvement, Bethmann-Hollweg summoned the British ambassador, Edward Goschen, and suggested that, if the British agreed to stay neutral, the Germans would not invade Holland and that, while perhaps invading France, the Germans wouldn't try to take any of its territories. The British were amazed that the chancellor had all but admitted that Germany was going to attack France. Grey called it 'a disgrace'.

Meanwhile, still under the illusion that he could mediate between Russia and Austria, that the Austrians had heeded his message to stop at Belgrade, and certain that Russia could be deterred from getting involved, Wilhelm replied to Nicholas's telegram. He told the tsar that Russia could easily 'remain a spectator without involving Europe in the most horrible war she has ever witnessed . . . Of course military measures on the part of Russia would be looked upon by Austria as a calamity we both wish to avoid.'

In St Petersburg, the German ambassador, Pourtalès, had twice visited Sazonov to tell him that any partial mobilization by Russia would mean war between their two countries. His words seemed to contradict Wilhelm's 'conciliatory and friendly message', and Nicholas cabled to ask for clarification and suggested that the dispute be taken to The Hague. He signed it, 'Trust in your wisdom and friendship, Your loving Nicky.' No answer came back. The Russian General Staff was pressuring him to mass

Russian troops on the Austrian border in retaliation for the shelling of Belgrade. Nicholas sent Wilhelm another telegram explaining that he had allowed partial mobilization to go ahead – an order that originally dated from several days before. He promised that Russian troops would not take the offensive, as long as talks with Austria continued. 'I hope from all my heart that these measures won't interfere with your part as mediator which I greatly value. We need your strong pressure on Austria to come to an understanding.'

When he got the telegram Wilhelm decided that Nicholas had taken a deliberately provocative step. He thought the Russians were now ahead in mobilization, or maybe he was just looking for a reason to be angry. He scribbled on it, 'And these measures are for defence against Austria which is in no way attacking him!! I cannot agree to any more mediation since the Tsar who requested it has at the same time secretly mobilized behind my back.' Next to Nicky's last sentences about his mediation, he wrote, 'No, there is no thought of anything of that sort!!!' On the morning of 30 July Wilhelm wrote back to Nicholas:

> Austria has only mobilised against Servia [*sic*] & only a part of her army. If, as it is now the case, according to the communication by you & your Government, Russia mobilises against Austria, my rôle as mediator you kindly intrusted me with, & which I accepted at you[r] express prayer, will be endangered if not ruined. The whole weight of the decision lies solely on you[r] shoulders now, who have to bear the responsibility for Peace or War
>   Willy.

In Tsarskoe selo, Sazonov and the Russian generals spent hours trying to persuade Nicholas to allow the Russian army to proceed to a general mobilization. If he did it, they told him, he would reconnect with his people; if he failed, the state would be damaged abroad and at home. He would look weak, and the Russian people would never forgive him. Nicholas seemed on the verge of tears. Eventually he gave in. He sent Wilhelm another telegram:

It is technically impossible to stop our military preparations which were obligatory owing to Austria's mobilisation. We are far from wishing war. As long as the negotiations with Austria on Servia's [*sic*] account are taking place my troops shall not make any provocative action. I give you my solemn word for this. I put all my trust in Gods mercy and hope in your successful mediation in Vienna for the welfare of our countries and for the peace of Europe.

Your affectionate, Nicky.

Wilhelm fell into a furious tantrum and shouted that Nicholas had shown himself to be a partisan of bandits and regicides. The truth was, however, that Russian mobilization was not the same as German mobilization – as the Russians explained and as everyone knew. The Russians, like the Austrians, took weeks to get ready to fight; mobilization was a posture, a warning. They could march up and down behind their border almost indefinitely, whereas for the German army, trained and organized down to the minute, mobilization meant imminent war. The Russian mobilization was a gift to the German government. 'In my endeavours to maintain the peace of the world I have gone to the utmost limit possible,' Wilhelm told Nicholas. 'The responsibility for the disaster which is now threatening the whole civilized world will not be laid at my door. In this moment it still lies in your power to avert it.' Bethmann-Hollweg was able to argue that Russia had made the first move. The argument brought the German press on board and even the German Left.★

In the evening Wilhelm was finally shown Lichnowsky's telegram about Grey's warning that if France became involved Britain wouldn't be able to stand by, two days after it had arrived. He exploded with rage, accusing George of reneging on his 'promise'

★ The German Socialist Party had gradually become infected by the fear and antipathy towards Britain and Russia that had taken hold of almost every class in Germany. In 1907, at an International Socialist Congress at Stuttgart, their delegation had voted against the idea of using a general strike to try to prevent a European war. In subsequent years senior members, such as August Bebel, had begun to say that patriotism was not incompatible with Socialism: that if war came, they would pick up a gun and fight for the fatherland.

of neutrality. On both sides of the document Wilhelm denounced the English as 'a mean crew of shopkeepers revealed in their "true colours" . . . Grey proves the King a liar, and his words to Lichnowsky are the outcome of a guilty conscience, because he feels that he has deceived us. At that, it is a matter of fact a threat combined with a bluff, in order to separate us from Austria and to prevent us from mobilising, and to shift the responsibility for the war.' Now there was someone else to blame if the war widened: Grey. If he 'were to say one single, serious sharp and warning word at Paris and St Petersburg, and were to warn them to remain neutral, that [*sic*] both would become quiet at once. But he takes care not to speak the word, and threatens us instead! Common cur! England alone bears the responsibility for peace and war, not we any longer!'

The notion that the British could have stopped the Russians from going to war was a fantasy, and also a characteristic exaggeration of Britain's influence in Europe. The Russians were determined that their very future was in the balance if they let Austria beat the Serbs; British neutrality wasn't going to stop them. It was true, however, that for eight years Grey had made Britain the fulcrum in Europe, hinting at crucial moments that if it came to war, Britain would side with the victim of aggression. But he had always shied away from committing himself entirely, to avoid the risk that the promise of British support might actually encourage France or Russia to start a conflict. His position encouraged both sides to ask for commitments, one for help, the other for neutrality. It has sometimes been suggested that if Grey had announced on 28 or 29 July that Britain would definitely fight with France and Russia if it came to a war, Germany might have been sufficiently chastened to withdraw. He himself, after all, believed that Britain had built up an obligation to defend France if it were attacked. The problem was he couldn't make the announcement because the majority of the British cabinet were against the idea of fighting. Moreover, like the rest of the cabinet, he had no desire to support Russia on its own. It's also worth noting that though Bethmann-Hollweg and Wilhelm worried about British involvement, the German military no longer seemed to care one way or the other.

They knew the war would be a land war, they calculated that British ships would be irrelevant, and the British army numbered barely 70,000 men.

For Wilhelm, Grey's warning together with Russian mobiliz-ation, brought back all the old anxieties. He saw Europe, led by England, ganging up on him, and the hand of his dead uncle:

So the celebrated encirclement of Germany has finally become an estab-lished fact, and the purely anti-German policy which England has been pursuing all over the world has won the most spectacular victory. England stands derisive, brilliantly successful; her long-mediated purely anti-German policy, stirring to admiration even him who it will utterly destroy! The dead Edward is stronger than I who am still alive . . . Our agents and all such must inflame the whole Mahommedan world to frantic rebellion against this detestable, treacherous, conscience-less nation of shopkeepers; for if we are to bleed to death, England shall at all costs lose India.

In Britain most people, including the cabinet and George, still be-lieved that Britain wouldn't come into any war. The Liberal Party was still vigorously against it, the Conservatives were still undecided.

Even now, however, Wilhelm hesitated. It was Bethmann-Hollweg who insisted that war must be declared even if Russia agreed to negotiations. It was Falkenhayn, the war minister, who pressed the kaiser to authorize *Kriegsgefahr* and order that a German ultimatum be delivered to Russia to halt her mobilization within twelve hours or Germany would declare war. When Pourtalès, the German ambassador, came to deliver the ultimatum, the head of the tsar's court Chancellery, Mossolov, told him it would be impossible. 'You can't stop a car that is going at 60 miles an hour. It would inevitably capsize.'

The next day, 1 August, Nicholas sent a last telegram pleading with Wilhelm to continue negotiating: 'Understand you are obliged to mobilize but wish to have the same guarantee from you as I gave you, that these measures do not mean war . . . Our long proved friendship must succeed, with God's help, in avoiding bloodshed. Anxiously, full of confidence await your answer.'

German mobilization, however, *was* different. Their war mobilization led to immediate action – so this was not a guarantee the
kaiser could give. But he did draft a telegram suggesting that talks
might take place if Russia halted its mobilization. It was not,
however, sent until late in the evening, well after Pourtalès had
tearfully delivered the German declaration of war to Sazonov.

Nicholas was 'praying with all the fervour of his nature that
God would avert the war which he felt was imminent'. His son's
tutor, Pierre Gilliard, was struck by 'the air of weary exhaustion
he wore . . . The pouches which always appeared under his eyes
when he was tired seemed to be markedly larger.' After he got the
news from Sazonov, 'The Czar appeared, looking very pale, and
told them that war was declared, in a voice which betrayed his
agitation, notwithstanding all his efforts.' When she heard, Alix
began to weep, and all the daughters seeing her cry began to cry
too. Wilhelm's delayed telegram arrived late that night. Nicholas
saw it as proof of his duplicity, though it was more a sign of his
powerlessness:

He was never sincere; not a moment,' he said bitterly. 'In the end he
was hopelessly entangled in the net of his perfidy and lies . . . it was half
past one in the morning of August 2 . . . There was no doubt that the
object of this strange and farcical telegram was to shake my resolution,
disconcert me and inspire me to some absurd and dishonourable act. It
produced the opposite effect. As I left the Empress's room, I felt that all
was over forever between me and William. I slept extremely well.

In the early hours of 1 August the British Foreign Office made a
last attempt to close down the war. They received a telegram
from Berlin, informing them that despite Wilhelm's readiness to
mediate, Russia had mobilized against Austria: 'We are unable to
remain inactive . . . We have therefore informed Russia that, unless
she were prepared to suspend within twelve hours the warlike
measures against Germany and Austria, we should be obliged to
mobilise, and this would mean war.' Asquith and Grey decided to
use George to get to the tsar. 'The poor King was hauled out of
his bed,' Asquith wrote, 'and one of my strangest experiences . . .

was sitting with him – he in a brown dressing gown over his nightshirt with copious signs of having been aroused from his first "beauty sleep" – while I read the message and the "proposed" answer.' George described the telegram as 'a last resort to try to prevent war'. George's contribution, according to Asquith, was to add 'my dear Nicky', and sign it.

George's message forwarded the German telegram and added:

> I cannot help thinking that some misunderstanding has produced this deadlock. I am most anxious not to miss any possibility of avoiding the terrible calamity which at present threatens the whole world. I therefore make a personal appeal to you, my dear Nicky, to remove the misapprehension which I feel must have occurred, and to leave still open grounds for negotiation and possible peace. If you think I can in any way contribute to that all-important purpose, I will do everything in my power to assist in reopening the interrupted conversations between the Powers concerned.

The message was entrusted to Buchanan and a shorter telegram was sent to Tsarskoe selo asking the tsar to see the British ambassador as soon as possible. But the tsar was a hard man to get at. By the time Buchanan managed to see him it was late in the evening and Germany had already declared war on Russia. 'Whether we shall be dragged into it God only knows,' George wrote, 'but we shall not send an Expeditionary Force of the Army now. France is begging us to come to their assistance. At this moment public opinion here is dead against our joining in the War but I think it will be impossible to keep out of it as we cannot allow France to be smashed.'

Nicholas's reply to George's telegram arrived the next day. 'I would gladly have accepted your proposals, had not the German Ambassador this afternoon presented a Note to my Government declaring war,' he wrote. He had done 'all in my power to avert war', while Germany and Austria had rejected 'every proposal'. He had moved to general mobilization only, 'owing to quickness with which Germany can mobilise in comparison with Russia . . . That I was justified in doing so is proved by Germany's sudden declaration of war, which was quite unexpected by me as I had given most categorical assurances to the Emperor William that my troops would not move so long as mediation negotiations continued.' He hoped, he added, that Britain would support them.

The Russian government's justification for going to war was that the people demanded it – an extraordinary claim from an autocratic state that barely ten years before hadn't even recognized the existence of public opinion. At some level Nicholas believed it, but of course 'public opinion' was not the hundreds of thousands of strikers or the people on the barricades in Moscow. It was true, however, that with only one exception – the tiny pro-German court faction – the entire government, bureaucracy, the educated classes, the buyers of papers, demanded intervention in Austria's war with Serbia, which gave Germany an excuse to attack. If there had been no Nicholas, Russia would still have gone to war. Though he had his doubts, Nicholas was not strong enough to counter such feeling. On the other hand, in his twenty years in power, Nicholas had done so much to weaken and stunt the emergence of a properly functioning modern government, so much to ensure that it was about as chaotic as it could be, that it is possible to speculate that a more professional government might have managed to hold on to the obvious fact that war was a threat to its very existence, and that this reality ought to trump everything else.

Nicholas felt he had been forced to do it, and he blamed Germany. 'The German Emperor knew perfectly well that Russia wanted peace,' he told Buchanan bitterly, 'and that her mobilisation could not be completed for another fortnight at least but he had declared war with such haste as to render all further discussion impossible.'

Even at this late stage, Wilhelm, Bethmann-Hollweg and Lichnowsky, the ambassador in London, still hoped that Britain would stay out, and the war wouldn't need to spread beyond the East.

On 1 August Ambassador Lichnowsky reported excitedly that Grey had asked whether, if France remained neutral, Germany would leave it alone. Lichnowsky answered yes, deciding that this was an offer to stay out if Germany stayed out of France. Wilhelm received the message just after he'd reluctantly handed Moltke the signed order for general mobilization – which meant armies would soon be pouring into France. The kaiser and the chancellor jumped at the offer. Wilhelm sent a telegram to George telling him he had just received 'the communication from your Government, offering French neutrality under the guarantee of Great Britain'. He assured George that he would not attack France if it offered neutrality and if that was guaranteed by the British army and fleet. 'I hope that France will not become nervous, the troops on my frontiers are in the act of being stopped by telegraph and telephone from crossing into France.' The kaiser told Moltke that the soldiers could all be sent off to Russia. Moltke practically burst into tears. He insisted mobilization couldn't be halted, that it would be mad to leave Germany exposed to France. Wilhelm replied sullenly, 'Your uncle would have given me a different answer.' He had the order to stop at the Luxembourg border phoned through to the troops. 'I felt as if my heart was going to break,' Moltke the warmonger sniffed, as he set off miserably for general headquarters, devastated that the Kaiser 'still hoped for peace'.*

George's reply, when it came, was not what Wilhelm had hoped. 'I think there must be some misunderstanding of a suggestion that passed in friendly conversation between Prince Lichnowsky and Sir Edward Grey this afternoon, when they were discussing how actual fighting between German and British armies might be avoided.' The French had refused to be neutral. Wearing a military greatcoat over his nightshirt, Wilhelm recalled Moltke. 'Now you can do what you like,' he growled. At 7 p.m., the German army were in Luxembourg. France was in the war by the next afternoon. The French ambassador in Berlin, Paul Cambon, told Edward Goschen that there were three people in Berlin who regretted the war had started. 'You, me and Kaiser Wilhelm.'

The next day Lichnowsky came to see Prime Minister Asquith in tears. The kaiser was no longer answering his telegrams. The

---

* Moltke later wrote, 'Something in me broke and I was never the same again.' Unable to take the strain of running the war, he had a breakdown almost immediately after it started and resigned his commission.

Germans were now threatening to enter Belgium. The Belgian king had appealed to the British government, through George, to safeguard his country's neutrality. The German occupation created an extraordinary volte-face in British public opinion. It also provided the cabinet, which had gradually come round to Grey's argument that Britain was not only obligated to defend France, but that strategically it couldn't allow France to be invaded by Germany, with a justification for action: the defence of 'plucky little Belgium'. The decision to go to war was extraordinarily united. Only two cabinet members resigned, and only one MP, the Labour member Ramsay MacDonald, spoke against Grey, who told parliament that Britain must go to war to defend Belgium out of 'honour'. MacDonald observed that 'There has been no crime committed by statesmen of this character without those statesmen appealing to their nation's honour' – both the Crimean and Boer Wars had been justified for the sake of 'honour'.

On 2 August George wrote in his diary: 'At 10.30 a crowd of about 6,000 people collected outside the Palace, cheering and singing. May and I went out onto the balcony, they gave us a great ovation.'

The next day he added almost enthusiastically: 'Public opinion since Grey made his statement in the House today that we should not allow Germany to pass through the English Channel or into the North Sea to attack France and that we should not allow her troops to pass through Belgium, has entirely changed . . . and now everyone is for war and our helping our friends.' On 4 August he continued: 'Fairly warm, showers and windy . . . I held a Council at 10.45 to declare war with Germany, it is a terrible catastrophe but it is not our fault . . . Please God it may be soon over.' The declaration of war included the empire; with one signature 450 million subjects were bound into the conflict.

Wilhelm would spend the rest of his life apportioning blame for the First World War. He wrote to Woodrow Wilson, the US president, ten days after the outbreak, claiming that George had promised neutrality and then reneged on it. Deeply stung by the accusation that he might have given assurances that weren't his to give, George always maintained that he had never made any such promise. To his last breath Wilhelm would insist that Nicholas had wanted war all along, that Russia had been secretly preparing for war for months before, that the Entente had been hoarding gold since April 1913.

Neither George, nor Nicholas, nor even Alix believed that Wilhelm was personally responsible for the war. 'I don't believe Wilhelm wanted war,' George told the departing Austrian ambassador. Alix told her son's tutor, Pierre Gilliard, that though she had never liked Wilhelm – 'if only because he is not sincere' – she was 'sure he has been won over to the war against his will'.

And it was true. When it came to it, Wilhelm had not wanted war. But he couldn't stop it. In the week before it broke out he was traduced and ignored repeatedly by his civilian and military staff. Forces beyond his power had begun to dictate the direction the country was going in. But in many respects he had brought the situation on himself. Twenty-six years of haphazard intervention had left a dangerous legacy. He had encouraged a powerful army, conscious of its own strength and convinced of the benefits and inevitability of a European war, and he had kept it beyond government control. He had initiated a shipbuilding programme which had created bitter hostility with Britain where before there had been none, and refused to temper it in any way. His insistence that his government deal only with the Right had made it a hostage to nationalist interest groups and alienated the rest of the country. His embracing and encouragement of a public rhetoric which bristled with violence, racial stereotyping and threats had helped to bolster an image abroad of a nation hungering for conflict. And finally, he had allowed chains of command and decision-making in civilian government to become chaotic and confused because it suited him for them to remain so. Virtually all his positions were the result of weakness and immaturity, the pursuit of appetites and wishes with no thought to the consequences: over-excitement at the idea of the might of the army and his notional control of it; a craving to look powerful and strong, and to identify himself with the aggressive masculine stereotypes of the German army; and above all a desire to be popular.

PART IV

Armageddon

17. A war (1914–18)

In London, Berlin and St Petersburg, the three monarchs were cheered uproariously by the people; at that moment all three seemed the epitome of nationhood and unity. 'May and I went for a short drive in the Russian carriage down the Mall to Trafalgar Square through the Park and back by Constitution Hill,' George wrote on 3 August 1914. 'Large crowds all the way who cheered tremendously . . . We were forced to show ourselves on the balcony three different times.' When Nicholas appeared on the balcony of the Winter Palace on 2 August the vast crowd fell on their knees. 'Russia seemed to have been completely transformed,' the British ambassador marvelled. The Duma proclaimed its undying support and passed a massive war budget. The barricades disappeared and the revolutionaries melted away. The country, everyone agreed, had not felt so vibrantly alive, nor been so united, since Napoleon's invasion of 1812. And in Germany the Berlin crowds cheered Wilhelm at the Brandenburg Gate. In a gush of enthusiasm the Reichstag voted to devolve its power to the Bundesrat, the council of German princes, effectively giving Wilhelm and the army the power to do whatever they liked, including levy taxes. Even the Socialists voted for it. The Russian revolutionary Bukharin called the 'betrayal of the Germans . . . the greatest tragedy of our lives'. The war promised, one German paper wrote, 'a resurrection, a rebirth of a nation. Suddenly shocked out of the troubles and pleasures of everyday life, Germany stands united in the strength of moral duty.'

In Moscow Nicholas told an audience at the Kremlin, 'A magnificent impulse has gripped all Russia, without distinction for tribe or nationality.' *Utro Rossii*, the newspaper of the Russian Centre-Left, wrote 'There are now neither Rights not Lefts, neither government nor society, but only one United Russian Nation.' Wilhelm used almost the same words when he told the

Reichstag on 4 August, 'In the struggle that lies before us I recognize no more parties among my people. There are only Germans.'
He called on all the party leaders to come and take his hand, and
as they walked away he raised a clenched fist and brought it down,
as if swiping with a sword. The kaiser, one paper breathed, was
'today truly a People's Kaiser'. As for George, though he wasn't
required to say anything, he put on a military uniform, gave his
civilian clothes away and presented himself to his people as the
incarnation of the values for which they were fighting: 'a good
sportsman, a hard worker, and a thoroughly good man'.

The great extended royal family of Europe, however, was anything but united – national divisions had broken it. In Russia Alix
was cut off from her sister Irene and her beloved brother Ernst.
George and Nicky's cousin Ernest of Cumberland, now Duke of
Brunswick, who had married Willy's daughter Victoria, took the
German side. So did Charles Edward, the British cousin who had
inherited the dukedom of Saxe-Coburg-Gotha after Affie's death
in 1900, and had taken a commission in the German army. The
German-born Louis of Battenburg, a naturalized Englishman since
the age of fourteen, with a German wife (Alix's sister Victoria),
was forced to resign as the most senior admiral in the British navy
by a xenophobic campaign by the right-wing press. (He would
also change his name to Mountbatten.) The British government
would force George to withdraw British peerages and titles from
all his German relations. When he met a couple of Greek cousins
there was outrage – though Greece was neutral, cousin Constantine's 25-year marriage to Wilhelm's sister Sophy raised British
hackles.

Within a short space of time each emperor had become almost
completely irrelevant.

George and Mary threw themselves into the war effort, but
their endeavours only emphasized George's inability to distinguish
between the trivial and the important and in the main the results
were negligible. The king forswore the theatre, closed Balmoral,
put the gardens at Frogmore to potatoes, turned the lights and
heating off at Buckingham Palace, used the napkins more than

once to save on washing, insisted on boiling fowl and mutton instead of poussin and lamb, and at Lloyd George's request took a pledge in April 1915 to forswear alcohol for the duration of the war, in order to provide an example to the working classes. Prime Minister Asquith privately complained of having to listen to 'those infinitesimal problems which perplex and perturb the Court mind – whether he should drive to Westminster in the old gingerbread coach . . . or . . . ride on his charger with the streets lined with Khaki-men. Isn't it marvellous that such things should be read as worth 5 minutes discussion? I am to go to him [the King] early tomorrow to settle this and other equally momentous issues.' When a visitor to York Cottage came to breakfast late and asked for a boiled egg, the king 'accused him of being a slave to his inside, of unpatriotic behaviour and even went so far as to hint that we should lose the war on account of his gluttony'. The country at large wasn't experiencing rationing – and wouldn't until the last year of the war. As for Lloyd George's initiative, it was a total failure; virtually no other public figures agreed to take the pledge and the working classes remained unimpressed.

There were admirable gestures – the austerity drive allowed George to hand back £100,000 in savings to the Treasury; convalescing officers and their families were invited to use the grounds of Buckingham Palace – but the palace was oddly reluctant to publicize them, taking its cue from the king who called the press 'filthy rags'. The king was left alcohol-less – though the Duke of Windsor claimed that after dinner his father would retire to his study 'to attend to a small matter of business', which everyone assumed was a glass of port.

George's war work quickly came down to a carefully logged relentless trudge: 7 inspections of naval bases, 5 visits to the French front, 450 military inspections, 300 hospital visits, and 50,000 decorations and medals personally pinned on, along with an uncounted number of trips to munitions factories and bombed areas. It was a job he performed with great and gloomy diligence. 'The King came to see us this morning,' the prime minister's son, Raymond Asquith, wrote from France, 'looking as glum and dyspeptic as ever.'

In December 1916 George's secretary, Stamfordham, asked the cabinet secretary if the king 'ought to take a more active share in the government of the country'. The answer was a resounding no. George, however, longed to be more than a figurehead. 'I am quite ready to sacrifice myself if necessary, as long as we win this war,' he told his mother in 1917. Quite apart from his constitutional position, the king, while sincere, decent and honest, was well known to be almost obsessively resistant to all change and ruled by his own prejudices. He opposed the reappointment of Admiral Fisher in 1915 because he disliked and mistrusted him. He stayed loyal to Asquith long after everyone else in government had lost faith in the prime minister's casual, hands-off style, because he had become used to him and couldn't bear to see him go. Unable to see Lloyd George's qualities and offended by his cheerfully ruthless methods, he criticized him publicly. (Lloyd George was no less quietly dismissive: describing a memo from George in 1915 as 'about as futile a document as I have seen . . . everything that comes from the Court is like that. But then, as Balfour said to me once, "Whatever would you do if you had a ruler with brains?"') He fought Lloyd George's efforts to dislodge Asquith and take control of the war effort in December 1916, regarding them as an iniquitous betrayal. He ended up in a blazing row with Andrew Bonar-Law, the Conservative leader, when he insisted that Lloyd George was the only man for the moment. 'The King expressed his entire disagreement with these views,' Stamfordham minuted euphemistically. But there was nothing he could do. Lloyd George ousted Asquith in what was essentially a coup; Asquith helped himself into the wilderness by refusing to serve under another prime minister. Lloyd George's new government – a new six-man war cabinet – effectively amounted to what Beatrice Webb called 'a dictatorship by one, or possibly three, men'. He can't have been unaware of the irony that as prime minister he had more power than any British monarch had wielded for 250 years.

Where the king was able to exercise some influence, it was to potentially tragic effect. He consistently supported General Haig, chief of the General Staff, against Lloyd George. Haig and his colleague General Robertson's commitment to trench warfare – in the belief that conscripted soldiers were too untrained to do anything other than stand in a line and walk forward – had a devastating effect on the casualty lists. Lloyd George believed there must be another way to use the men Haig seemed almost blithely to pour on to the stalemated battlefields. The king, in an echo of his cousins' deference to the military, believed the professionals knew best. He liked Haig, whose wife had been lady-in-waiting to Mary. Haig energetically exploited the connection – he had used it to dislodge his predecessor, General French. When Lloyd George tried to get rid of Haig, the king explicitly told the general not to resign, and asked him to write secretly to him whenever he liked. In other circumstances George's support would have had little force, but the Conservative press and Party also supported Haig, and Lloyd George – now in a coalition of largely Conservative ministers – needed their support. George's intervention added ballast to Haig's position. Through 1916 and 1917 in the Somme and at Passchendaele, Haig sent hundreds of thousands of men into the trenches and over the top. At Passchendaele there were between 240,000 and 260,000 British casualties and barely a foot of territory was won to justify them. Haig complained he hadn't succeeded because he hadn't had enough men. The king, who believed one did not question military men, wrote to Nicholas, 'The French and ourselves have made good progress on the Somme and we hope to continue to do so.' Lloyd George never got rid of Haig and it took him several years to sideline him.

In Russia and Germany, however, the aristocratic officer class showed even less concern for their cannon fodder. The German crown prince, Little Willy, expended a million men trying to take the fortress at Verdun. After the terrible Russian defeats of Tannenburg and the Masurian Lakes in 1914, which cost 250,000 lives, Grand Duke Nicholas told the French, 'We are happy to make such sacrifices for our allies.'

Where George didn't follow his people was in his repulsion at the surge of xenophobia expressed in Britain – due not least to the extraordinarily effective anti-German propaganda purveyed in posters and the mass-market press. The invasion of Belgium produced monstrous stories in newspapers such as the *Daily Mail* of women raped, children's hands cut off, priests murdered, libraries burned, and even a Canadian soldier crucified by German troops. None of the accounts were verified. Wilhelm, who had so longed for the British to love him, was turned into a hate figure, portrayed as the incarnation of the evils of German militarism and widely regarded as responsible for the war. Propaganda posters showed him blood-soaked and hunched over the corpses of Belgian women, or goose-stepping in front of burning libraries. In 1900 he'd made an over-excited, ill-advised speech as he saw off a squadron of German soldiers going to quell the Boxer rebellion in China, telling them to put the rebels to the sword, 'like the Huns under their King Attila a thousand years ago . . . pardon will not be given, prisoners will not be taken. Whoever falls into your hands will fall to your sword.' The speech was disinterred by British war propagandists who characterized the Germans as 'dirty Huns', the barbaric enemies of civilization – a historic nonsense; it was the Germanic tribes who had beaten back the Huns.

George tried to resist when the War Office – responding to a campaign by the *Daily Mail* – asked him to deprive Wilhelm and the German relatives of their honorary military commands, and remove their banners from St George's Chapel at Windsor Castle. When Sir Richard Haldane, former war minister, founder of the London School of Economics and well-known Germanophile, was hounded out of office by a hysterical campaign in the right-wing press, George awarded him the Order of Merit. He was offended by the mistreatment of German prisoners of war and the internment of alleged enemy 'aliens'. And when, on a visit to the front, Ponsonby regretted the sympathy he'd shown for a gassed soldier who turned out to be German, the king rebuked him, 'after all he was only a poor dying human being'. As the war went on, however, George found it hard not to hate the Germans. 'These zeppelin raids,' he wrote to Nicholas, '. . . murder women and children and have done no harm to any workshop or military establishment; they show that they are simply brutes and barbarians.'

★

Wilhelm's eclipse was more dramatic. Within days of the war's beginning, he joined the army at military headquarters, as his grandfather had in the Franco-Prussian War of 1870, then promptly collapsed and took to his bed. For years he had let rip teeth-baring rhetoric, and claimed that in a war he would be his own chief of staff. He had talked of leading his troops into battle as if it were a genuine possibility. A week after the war started the Supreme Warlord, the *Oberster Kriegsherr*, told the German General Staff that the war was their responsibility not his, and handed over to Moltke permission to issue orders in his name, while promising not to interfere in operations. He seemed entirely unable to cope. What must it look like, wondered Admiral Muller, who ran his naval cabinet, 'inside the head of this man to whom war is, at base, repulsive'. From German army HQ, the Prince of Pless wrote to his English wife, Daisy, in October 1914, 'He is extremely nervous and it gets worse, the longer the war drags on. It is difficult to find another topic of conversation, because he seldom listens to anything else. If we could only persuade him to play Bridge . . .'

He veered between euphoria, fury and dramatic lows. One moment he would demand that his soldiers take no prisoners; the next he would declaim with his old grandiosity that if one German family starved as a result of the British naval blockade, he would 'send a Zeppelin over Windsor castle and blow up the whole royal family of England'. Then he would be plunged into depression and knocking back sleeping pills. The entourage and Dona, committed to protecting the kaiser and the senior generals, determined to stop him interfering, colluded to shield him from bad news and keep his *faux pas* to a minimum. Generals briefed him each day but, as the war minister, Falkenhayn, observed only weeks after the war started, 'Now he is no longer told about anything that is at the planning stage, all he hears about is what had already happened, and only the favourable events.' By 1916 the war was barely mentioned at government meetings when he was present: 'the Conference . . . was confined to stories of the harvesting at Pless, the birth of a zebra calf at Cadinen and the instructions he had given to Hindenburg,' Muller observed. His entourage shuffled him between the fronts and army headquarters to assuage his endless restlessness, and let him stride before the troops in his splendid uniforms and make encouraging speeches. He pinned on medals and shook hands. He was found pointless projects to occupy him – the building of an extravagant fountain at Homburg for which a war contractor gave the money – and was scolded for fraternizing too warmly with British prisoners of war. In moments of self-pitying clarity, Wilhelm grumbled about his position. 'The General Staff tells me nothing and never asks my advice. If people in Germany think that I am Supreme Commander, then they are grossly mistaken,' he said in November 1914. 'I drink tea and cut wood and go for walks, which pleases the gentlemen.' In 1916 he complained he'd found out about the latest Verdun attack only from the newspapers. It was vitally important to him, however, that he appear to be in charge: 'I put my oar in as little as possible, but for the outside world Falkenhayn must maintain the fiction that I personally order everything.'

He was needed to sign orders and issue decrees, so the generals kept him close and isolated from his civilian staff in order to get what they wanted from him, which they almost invariably did, even if he initially disagreed. Seeing him at army headquarters, the Austrian foreign minister thought he was 'living an illusion' and described him as 'the prisoner of his generals'. As the war progressed, he was deprived gradually of a war minister he liked, Falkenhayn, a chancellor he wanted to keep, Bethmann-Hollweg – who he felt had been loyal and whom he supported for months – and kept away from peace plans he might have favoured. He was eventually talked into agreeing to a policy of submarine warfare against neutral shipping of which he personally profoundly disapproved, a policy which directly brought America into the war. 'No gentleman would kill so many women and children,' he told the American ambassador embarrassedly, after a German submarine sank the *Lusitania* in 1915, killing over 1,000 civilians.

The irony was that there was a huge role for the kaiser, had he been able to fill it. The state and the military needed a coordinating figure to hold the balance between the two, someone who could make major political decisions. In the constitution the government had no authority over the armed forces, only the kaiser did – a situation Wilhelm had encouraged throughout his reign. But totally out of his depth and in thrall to the glamour of the army, he was incapable. His failure would have a devastating effect on the war effort and Germany's future. The army and the government slid further and further apart, utterly disagreeing on the war's basic goals, whether the territories invaded should be annexed, what the criteria for peace should be. It would not be the civilian authorities who would fill the vacuum Wilhelm left, but the army, the most focused, single-minded institution in Germany, which Wilhelm himself had deliberately kept beyond parliamentary control.

As for the German navy, the war exposed it as the vanity project it had always been. After all the bitterness and expense it was immediately clear that naval power would not win the war. The navy was deployed only once, at the Battle of Jutland in May 1916, and then never came out of port again. It was trapped by the British naval blockade, which gradually starved the civilian population of Germany, and Wilhelm was reluctant to sacrifice even one of his beautiful shiny ships to try to break it. The ships rusted and the sailors became disaffected. When at the end of the war, in November 1918, the naval chiefs tried to organize a last 'death ride', the sailors mutinied. 'The Navy has deserted me,' Wilhelm sniffed as he boarded his train out of Germany. 'I no longer have a Navy.'

Like George and Wilhelm, Nicholas became a reviewer of troops, a pinner-on of medals, a visitor of munitions factories and hospitals – sometimes he saw as many as 3,000 wounded a day. Like Wilhelm he had fantasized about leading his armies, a less unrealistic prospect in Russia where the supreme army command had gone to his largely decorative, popular, six-foot-six cousin, Grand Duke Nicholas Nicholaevich. Just like Wilhelm, he installed himself in the peculiar unreal atmosphere of Russian army headquarters, a grand officers' mess under spreading pines and birches in Baranovichi in Poland, packed with the aristocratic officer elite of the cavalry regiments, with whom Nicholas had always loved to mix. There he persuaded himself he was in the thick of it, surrounded by officers who mostly owed their promotions to court connections. He took long walks, ate hearty lunches, lingered over cigars and conversation, organized boat races and charmed foreign visitors. Stavka, as it was called, bore as much relation to the front commands where the men were dying in droves, as Mount Olympus to a pile of stones, and it was almost functionless, proving quite unable either to supply the various fronts properly or to coordinate them.

Nicholas's flight was perhaps understandable. The Russian war effort went disastrously wrong within three months. Vast sums had been poured into the army, but it was still run by courtiers. War-planning had been minimal. No one had expected a prolonged conflict and the state's creaking mechanisms simply weren't up to running a long war. Several devastating defeats – the result both of German effectiveness and the hopelessly archaic ideas of the Russian top brass – were followed by the call-up of barely trained reserves, and a supply crisis. The Ministry of War had made no provision for winter uniforms and boots; ammunition began to run out. By early 1915 soldiers were told to limit themselves to ten bullets a day. Losses were huge and pointless. One British observer saw 1,800 new recruits arrive at the front without a single rifle. They waited until casualties made guns available. He then watched as 1,600 of them died. Nicholas's sister Olga, working as a nurse on the Austrian front, was told that Russian soldiers were going to meet German machine guns 'with sticks in their hands'. Surgeons came to her begging her to intervene with the tsar for medical supplies, and generals came pleading for reinforcements. As with Wilhelm, the worst news was kept from Nicholas. One soldier recalled the tsar's visit to his unit. The most presentable bits of uniform were scavenged piecemeal from all the other regiments to dress one company, while the rest of the men shivered in trenches without trousers, boots or anything much else. At Warsaw train station the president of the Duma, Mikhail Rodzianko, was horrified to find 17,000 wounded soldiers left lying in the rain. There was nowhere for them to go.

As the losses mounted and morale collapsed, the army was, as one historian has vividly put it, 'gradually turned into one vast revolutionary mob'. Nine million men were called up in the war's first year. Officer casualties were enormously high – not least because of their habit of leading charges dressed in their brightest uniforms. The soldiers who survived found themselves divested of their traditional aristocratic leaders, alienated and very angry at the vast, pointless losses, and began to ask themselves why they were fighting at all. The new Russian officer corps of 1915 – those below the rank of captain who actually fought with the men – were soon the biggest meritocracy Russia had ever seen: young men from peasant backgrounds with a talent for survival and leadership, all too aware of the army elite's lack of interest in the men's conditions and their losses.

In Russia, as in Germany, there would have been a role for Nicholas as civilian leader, coordinating the government, ensuring the army was supplied, the wounded cared for, the refugees provided for, and that the country worked. But Nicholas, like Wilhelm, was in thrall to the romance of the army, looked down on the civilian administration and was too overwhelmed by government failures to know even where to start. Instead the Zemstvo Union sorted out supplies and relief, turning itself in the process into a formidable machine, and the Duma, working quietly with a number of government ministers, got industry mobilized again. Unable to get beyond the old autocratic orthodoxies, Nicholas refused to see these initiatives as anything other than challenges to his own increasingly compromised authority. When in mid-1915 the Duma demanded a coalition between the government and itself to restore the nation's confidence and run the war, Nicholas closed it down.

His solution to the crisis was to assume supreme command of the army in September 1915. In a piece of desperate wishful thinking, he had convinced himself that it would be the cure-all for Russia's ills: if he took charge God would save Russia, and the devoted peasants would fight all the harder. He loved the thought of fighting alongside his soldiers, and escaping the intrigues and cabals and 'low personal interests' of St Petersburg – now renamed Petrograd in order to denude it of its German connotations. 'At the front,' he told his son's tutor, Pierre Gilliard, confidently, 'there is only one thought – the determination to conquer.' Alix had been urging him to do it for months, telling him he was Russia's saviour and God would protect him. It was so clearly a bad idea that when Nicholas announced it his entire Council of Ministers fell silent. 'This is so terrible,' Sazonov wrote in his diary, 'that my mind is in chaos.' It was a decision, another minister noted drily, 'fully in tune with his spiritual frame of mind and his mystical understanding of his imperial calling'. The Council of Ministers, after years of endemic infighting, took the unprecedented action of writing a collective letter begging him not to do it. Even Goremykin, the ultimate yes-man, signed it. Even Nicholas's mother, even his sister Olga, thought it was a 'catastrophe'. He went ahead anyway. Entirely inexperienced in strategy or battle, at headquarters Nicholas was quickly regarded as an irrelevance. The decision had the predicted effect of making him look more than ever directly responsible for Russia's deepening military disaster.

Nicholas's departure from Petrograd and civilian government left a hole which Alix felt herself obliged to fill. Raising herself from her sickbed, she decided to give Russia what she clearly believed would be a masterclass in autocracy. Within four days of Nicholas's departure she began dismissing ministers with bewildering speed. As even her own household could see, she 'made politics a matter of sentiment and personalities'. The entire government war effort was transformed into a personal struggle between those she regarded as for and those she regarded as against her. The ministers who had asked the tsar not to make himself head of the army were systematically weeded out and sacked. Anyone who suggested that it might actually be sensible to work with the Duma was dismissed. Anyone she disliked or felt had opposed her or criticized Rasputin – whose advice on politics she now actively canvassed, and who, as Pierre Gilliard observed, simply confirmed her 'secret wishes' – was sacked. Even old Goremykin fell out of favour. Her letters to Nicholas – still written in English – were saturated with references to 'Our Friend' and demands that ministers should be removed. 'How I wish one cld. hang Rodzianko [the Duma's president],' she wrote, 'awful man, & such an insolent fellow.' She urged him to be assertive and autocratic. She ran through ministers with almost comic speed, getting through four chief ministers – each more right-wing and less effective than the one before – in sixteen months, desperate to find that one 'loyal' minister, the man who would show sufficient hatred of the Duma and sufficient respect for Rasputin. Her favourite minister was Alexander Protopopov, a former Duma representative who had attached himself to Rasputin's coat tails, who was widely regarded as mentally unstable, if not actually mad. The empress promoted him, even though she acknowledged that he was 'extremely nervous and often loses the thread', because he 'listened' to Rasputin and was, as she put it, 'so devoted to us!' Protopopov appears to have been in the last stages of tertiary syphilis.

Pierre Gilliard, who entirely sympathized with Alix's agony over her son's illness, thought she might have gone slightly mad: 'She often had periods of mystic ecstasy in which she lost all sense of reality.' Meanwhile, her obsessively polarized view of the world caused her to publicly favour Rasputin and turn a blind eye to his increasingly open exploitation of his privileged position. Long-serving court figures such as Mossolov, head of the imperial Chancellery, watched helplessly while the government descended into chaos. Appointments and sinecures were suddenly filled by Rasputin's toadies and clients, and there seemed nothing to be done but accept it. The government, already in seizure, became even more ineffectual, ridiculous and corrupt. Beside it the Duma and the zemstvo movement appeared effective and appealing. Combined with Nicholas's assumption of army command, the effect on the imperial couple's reputation was devastating. Alexandra, long disliked by the Russian upper classes, was soon actively hated. Nicholas looked a weak failure. Resentment at the strains and disasters of the war began to combine with stories about corruption and chaos and even treachery at the top. Given the disasters at the front and the government's apparent indifference and inability to solve the most basic problems, it was perhaps unsurprising that wild rumours about Alix's alleged German sympathies and her bizarre relationship with Rasputin began to spread ever more widely beyond the elite into the country and the disaffected army. By 1916 it was widely believed that Rasputin and his cronies were German agents, planning to deliver Russia into

German hands, and that the German-born empress was working with them.

Rumour and suspicion blighted Russia's relationships with Britain and France. From early in the campaign the Russians complained that their huge sacrifices were not appreciated by their allies. They accused the British of using them to take the brunt of the German attack. Lloyd George wrote worriedly, the Russians said 'We are not doing enough, and are "on the make".' (It was a centuries-old complaint in continental wars that island Britain sat back safe while in Europe they slugged it out.) The Russian government accused the British of holding back much-needed supplies, and on the streets of western Russia it was said that Britain had dragged Russia into the war – from which it had nothing to gain. The British in turn were exasperated by the Russian collapse in the East, Russia's incapacity to coordinate with the Entente, and the incessant grumbling and demands for money and supplies; by 1915 Britain had effectively become Russia's banker and main supplier of munitions. It lent £40 million over 1914 and 1915, backed a further loan of £100 million, and sent millions of pounds of supplies. When in 1916 Alix took the reins, the British watched the government move ever further to the Right, and every liberal-minded minister purged. They heard the stories about Rasputin, and wondered disgruntledly whether their money was going to hold up a regime that stood for everything they claimed to be fighting against.

Relations between the two royal families were one of the few bright spots – that and the warm relationship Nicholas seemed to enjoy with the British ambassador, Sir George Buchanan. Several grand duchesses had taken up residence in England for the duration, and telegrams bounced between the families, for all the world giving the war an air of a family outing: 'Aunt Alix wires to say they know for certain that the Germans intend to attack Warsaw this week and she hopes we are aware of it . . . Does Nikolasha [Grand Duke Nicholas] know?'; 'I have just had a telegram from aunt Alix who wires in despair that they have lost six battleships. But I do hope the German losses are even heavier.'

'It is such a good thing to keep in touch with one another now that the communication between our two countries is so difficult,' Nicholas wrote to George in early 1916. 'We all highly admire the wonderful manner in which the allied troops left Gallipoly [*sic*].' (The whole Gallipolli campaign had been a disaster – though one conceived in part to take the strain off the Eastern Front.) After the naval battle of Jutland, George wrote to Nicholas, 'William's speech at Kiel about the great navy victory of the German fleet made me laugh. I am quite convinced that they lost more ships and more men than we did and we drove them back to their ports.'

Their relationship, however, became gradually infused with the wider politics and suspicions of the war. Their letters were thick with unsaid things and unasked-for explanations. 'I was very busy about some changements [*sic*] among the ministers, which you have probably heard of,' Nicholas wrote after the disastrous Russian retreats of mid-1915. '. . . That retreat in Galicia . . . had to be effectuated to save our army – solely on account of the lack of ammunition and of rifles. And this reason is a most painful one. But my country has well understood it and everywhere the people are setting to work for the needs of the army with redoubled energy . . . it will soon be a year that this terrible war is raging and goodness knows how long it may last – but we shall fight to the end!' George's answer picked up on another implied criticism: 'I can assure you that in England, we are now straining every nerve to produce the required ammunition and guns and also rifles and are sending the troops of our new armies to the front as fast as we possible can.' Meanwhile, Minny, whose relationship with Alix had degenerated badly since the tsarina had started sacking ministers – 'she is ruining both the dynasty and herself', she told Kokovtsov – passed stories of her excesses on to her sister. 'I am sure she thinks herself like their Empress Catherine,' Alexandra told George. Attitudes to Alix started perceptibly to harden in the British family.

Succumbing to old Foreign Office fears, Sir George Buchanan began to take the gossip about Alix and her German sympathies seriously. He was convinced that she was rooting out pro-English moderates such as Sazonov, whom she sacked in 1915, in order to replace them with right-wing pro-Germans who would detach Russia from the Entente. He wondered if she was a conspirator, but decided she was more likely Rasputin's dupe. His anxieties found their way into the heart of the British government. 'The pro-Germans in the Russian government have succeeded in turning out General Alexaeff [*sic*], the one hope of the Russian Army,' Lloyd George told his secretary towards the end of 1916. 'They are one by one getting rid of all the good men in Russia and putting in rotters or Pro-Germans.' Buchanan was utterly wrong. The imperial couple were completely committed to the war. It was the nation which was turning violently against it. Nicholas couldn't bear the thought of another defeat. Alexandra had abjured the country of her birth. Germany, she told her son's tutor, had become 'a country I did not know and had never known'. She now presented herself, the French ambassador remarked, as an Englishwoman 'in her outward appearance, her deportment, a certain inflexibility and Puritanism'. No one followed the British armies' fortunes more devotedly. When her brother Ernst tried to contact her through an old servant living in Austria, she rebuffed him.

The British, however, continued to worry that Russia would leave them in the lurch. In August 1916, almost certainly encouraged by the government, George wrote to warn and express his anxiety to Nicholas. 'German agents in Russia have recently been making great efforts to sow division between your country and mine by exciting distrust and spreading false reports . . . I hear it is repeated and in some quarters believed in Russia that England means to oppose the possession or retention of Constantinople by Russia [which Grey had promised in 1915]. No suspicion of this sort can be entertained by your government.' He begged Nicholas if he had the slightest concerns that 'you will at any time instruct your ministers to enter into the frankest explanations with my Government or will yourself communicate direct with me. You know, my dear Nicky, how devoted I am to you and I can assure you that my Government regards your Country with equally strong feelings of friendship.' In October he wrote again asking for reassurance: the Germans believed they could ' "detach Russia and are working hard to this end." What nonsense, they little know you and your people.'

By the end of 1916 the war had had a devastating effect on all three men. For Wilhelm the pressures had been too much from the start. By 1916 he was frequently described by senior soldiers and political advisers as a 'broken man'. Depression made him lethargic and his entourage worried about complete breakdown and how worn and ill he looked. 'Violent and unpredictable,' one of his entourage wrote, 'dominated by a single thought, "Leave me in peace." ' Bad news and hard decisions inevitably insinuated themselves into army headquarters. The generals wanted him to back submarine warfare, to sack Bethmann-Hollweg. His attempts to hold out made him anxious and bad-tempered. Unlike his cousins he rarely referred to the casualties and sufferings of his subjects – in the German army it was understood that one was not pessimistic about the effects of war, but Wilhelm had always had difficulty in empathizing with others' difficulties. As the industrialist and writer Walther Rathenau wrote of him, 'The Emperor had no consciousness of tragedy, even the unconscious feeling of the problem.'

George looked at least ten years older than he was: his beard had almost turned white, his face was lined and bagged, he looked, someone remarked, like an old, worn penny. His dogged, melancholic, unsmiling stare became ubiquitous. 'He feels it profoundly,' Lord Esher wrote of the king, 'every pang that war can inflict.' Each year he made an increasingly gruelling visit to the Western Front. The more he saw, the more depressed he became. 'Very often I feel in despair,' he wrote to Mary in 1918. In October 1915 he had a serious accident there when the horse he was riding got frightened, reared up and fell on him. With the typical concern of the British royal family he anxiously enquired after the horse; his own fractured pelvis and ribs weren't diagnosed for several days. It was an injury from which George never quite recovered; the pain made him more grumpy, but he was at least now permitted a small occasional tipple for medicinal purposes. 'I still have to walk with a stick,' he told Nicholas in early 1916. 'A horse is a very heavy thing to fall on you and I suffered a great deal of pain, as I was badly crushed and bruised.' In July 1917 the queen and her old friend Mabell, Countess of Airlie, accompanied George on his fourth visit to the Western Front. The royal couple seemed to feel it was their duty not to acknowledge too vividly how awful it was: a gruelling parade of ammo depots, railway depots, hospitals and walks – to the sound of far-off artillery shells – through a no-man's land blasted by enormous craters. The Countess of Airlie felt no such compunction. 'The most harrowing sight . . .' she wrote,

a vast stretch of land that had once been fertile and smiling with crops, but was now only a tumbled mass of blackened earth fringed by sparse and splintered trees . . . We climbed over a mound composed of German dead . . . all that was left of a whole regiment who had died in wresting a strip of land from Our troops, only to lose it again . . . We stood there speechless. It was impossible to find words. The Queen's face was ashen and her lips were tightly compressed. I felt that like me she was afraid of breaking down.

At the hospitals the countess was struck by the 'terrible sameness of young faces and broken bodies'. Even the reticent George wrote of driving through 'ruined villages and towns, utterly destroyed by shell fire'. He described the deaths in a night raid, during the visit, of twenty-five patients and three staff at a nearby hospital. And he recorded a story he'd heard about the Premier of New South Wales standing next to an Australian general, who was killed by a shell only yards away from him. The carnage he saw in France over-whelmed him; xenophobia depressed him, republicanism alarmed him. 'You can't conceive what I suffered going round those hospitals in the war,' he said years later.

By the end of 1916 Nicholas was stick thin and looked somehow hollowed out. When his former chief minister, Kokovtsov, saw him for the first time in a year in January 1917, he was genuinely disturbed. It wasn't just the ageing. The tsar's famously 'kind eyes' were faded, yellowed and 'lifeless'. He wore a constant, awful, vacant, almost 'sickly', smile, he glanced about nervously. In the middle of the conversation he completely lost the thread. There was an awkward silence. A simple question reduced him 'to a perfectly incomprehensible state of helplessness'. Almost in tears, Kokovtsov told Nicholas's doctor, Botkin, that he was convinced the tsar must be on the verge of a breakdown. Botkin smiled and said he was merely tired. But the French ambassador had reached similar conclusions. 'Despondency, apathy and resignation can be seen in his actions, appearance, attitude and all the manifestations of the inner man,' he wrote in the autumn of 1916.

Through the last months of 1916 and into 1917, person after person tried to alert Nicholas to the bomb under his throne – how angry the country was and how the malign influence of Rasputin and the disastrous meddling of the empress were making it so much worse. He remained deaf to all warnings. Contradiction now constituted betrayal. Vladimir Orlov, one of his few friends, was exiled to his estates for criticizing Rasputin. The tsar's devoted court chancellor, Fredericks, breaking the habit of a lifetime, spoke out and was warned, 'Let us remain friends and never, mind you, never, touch on the subject again.' Sandro's brother Grand Duke Nicholas Mikhailovich, well known for his liberal constitutional beliefs, returned from England in November 1916 with news that George was genuinely worried because 'well-informed agents of the British Secret Service predicted a revolution in the very near future'. The grand duke wrote Nicholas a letter urging him to get rid of Rasputin and to make the reforms the Duma wanted before it was too late. Nicholas passed the letter to Alix, who professed herself disgusted and told him to send Mikhailovich to Siberia. At the end of 1916 Alix's sister Ella left the convent where she had lived since 1905, to plead with her to send Rasputin away. 'She dismissed me like a dog,' Ella reported. Alix wrote to Nicholas interspersing descriptions of their new kitten climbing into the hearth with hysterical denunciations of Duma members and demands that ministers be sacked. 'Be the Master, & all will bow down to you.' He signed himself, 'your very own poor little huzy with a tiny will'.

Three days later, on 17 December 1916, Rasputin was murdered.

The assassins were Prince Felix Yusupov, a 29-year-old bisexual cross-dresser and Oxford graduate, who was the son of the richest woman in Russia and married to Nicholas's niece Irene; Grand Duke Dmitry Pavlovich, a first cousin of Nicholas's; and Vladimir Purishkevich, an extreme right-wing anti-Semitic monarchist. The idea was to save the monarchy and the nation by killing Rasputin and consigning Alix to a mental institution. They lured Rasputin to a small 'party', with the promise that he would meet the Grand Duchess Irene, and tried to poison him. When several pieces of cyanide-filled cake and a glass or two of poisoned Madeira failed to do the trick, they shot him in the back. When he staggered up again, they panicked, fired an entire gun barrel into him, loaded his body with chains, and threw it into the Neva. In England, Alexandra – informed by Minny – told George, 'the wretched Russian monk caused a tremendous sensation in the world! but [is] only regretted by poor dear Alix who might have ruined the whole future of Russia through his Influence'. The murder had entirely the opposite effect to that intended. It merely reinforced the imperial couple's sense that the world was against them, and drew them closer together. 'I believe in no one but my wife,' Nicholas told his cousin Sandro (Yusupov's father-in-law) 'icily' in the aftermath.

By mid-January several Romanov family plots to get rid of Alix and depose Nicholas were being so widely discussed in the salons of Petrograd that General Henry Wilson, a member of the British delegation which had come to Russia in a last-ditch attempt to try to coordinate strategy, noted wonderingly that 'Everyone – officers, merchants, ladies – talks openly of the absolute necessity of doing away with them.' Even Minny and Nicholas's sister Xenia discussed the plan to send Alix and her much-hated best friend, Anna Vyrubova, to a convent. 'If things don't change it will be the end of everything,' Xenia wrote to her mother. The president of the Duma, Rodzianko, requested an audience with the tsar and told Nicholas tactfully that the country wanted a new government and that the empress was universally hated and must be stripped of all authority. Rodzianko claimed the tsar put his face in his hands and asked him, 'Is it possible that for twenty-two years I tried to

act for the best and that for twenty-two years it was all a mistake?'
To which Rodzianko answered 'Yes.'

One of the people who, as he described it, made 'one last
effort to save the Emperor, in spite of himself', was the British
ambassador, Sir George Buchanan. Like many others he had been
charmed by Nicholas and had come to feel almost protective of
him. In his last audience with the tsar, fully aware he was over-
stepping his position, he told Nicholas that he felt 'like a man
trying to save a friend whom he sees falling over a precipice'. He
said that Protopopov was 'bringing Russia to the verge of ruin', that
the empress was 'discredited and accused of working in German
interests', warned him about the gossip in Petrograd, and asked him
to give the Duma what they wanted – a representative government.
Buchanan knew he was treading a fine line, but thought on balance
the interview had gone well – Nicholas pressed his hand as he left.
In fact, the tsar, so characteristically veiling his true feelings, was
outraged by Buchanan's presumption. According to two of Alix's
ladies-in-waiting, he had turned against the ambassador months
before, after he discovered he had been talking with several senior
Duma members and had therefore, as Nicholas saw it, joined the
other side. In her memoirs, Anna Vyrubova accused Buchanan of
being 'personally' involved in the grand ducal plot to overthrow
Nicholas, in order to 'weaken' Russia when peace negotiations
came. Nicholas had apparently considered asking George to recall
him, but decided he didn't want to make public his distrust of his
British allies.

The level of denial seems astonishing. A couple of weeks before
the end Nicholas crossly upbraided the courtier Mossolov when
he made a stray comment that betrayed anxiety about the future:
'What! You Mossolov, are you too going to tell me of the peril
that menaces the dynasty? People are continually harping on this
supposed peril. Why, you have been with me and have seen how
I was received by the troops and the people! Are you too, even
you, panicking?' Mossolov answered, 'I have seen all that Sire, but
I also see them when they are not in Your Majesty's presence.
Forgive my freedom of speech.' Nicholas collected himself and
reverted to his usual 'smile' to denote he was not put out.

Why was Nicholas so insistently resistant to the warnings? Because they attacked his wife. Because he had become practised at dismissing the rest of the world as wrong. Because he had come to believe that the October manifesto, which he regarded as his greatest failure, had been unnecessary and extracted from him by deceit, and that if he'd held his nerve he would never have had to agree to it. Because, encouraged by Protopopov, he'd convinced himself that the alarming reports of growing disaffection were simply a ploy to frighten him into more reforms he didn't want to make. And perhaps because, at some level, he wanted a crisis, something so awful, a national catastrophe so great, that he would be forced to abdicate, to give away the burden of ruling which depressed, overwhelmed and crushed him, and be able to tell himself he hadn't done so willingly. That's not to say that the tsar brought on the revolution, but that he did nothing to stop it. Several observers half-suspected something of this nature. A few weeks before the end, his cousin Sandro felt he'd given up, taking refuge in his infuriating fatalism. 'God's wishes shall be fulfilled,' Nicky told him. 'I was born on May sixth, the day of Job the Sufferer, I am ready to accept my doom.' The French ambassador, Paléologue, seeing the tsar for the last time, wrote that he 'feels himself overwhelmed and dominated by events, that he has lost faith in his mission'; he had '. . . abdicated inwardly and is now resigned to disaster'.

By February 1917 Petrograd was a seething hub of anger and desperation. It was the third year of the war, and the whole of Europe was thick with 'war weariness'. Millions had died on battlefields across Europe; the civilian populations of Russia and Germany were suffering from terrible shortages. In Petrograd neither food nor fuel was arriving in sufficient quantities to supply the population, which had swollen by a third since 1914. Lack of fuel had brought industry to a standstill in December 1916. In January 1917 150,000 people hunger-marched through the capital, frightened by rumours that the city would be left to starve. The railway network was sagging under the demands from the front. It couldn't deal with supplying the civilian population too. In his last letter to George, Nicholas wrote about 'the weak state' of the railways. 'The question of transport of stores and food becomes acute.' The cold reached minus thirty-five. 'Children are starving in the most literal sense of the word,' ran one secret police report. Some food prices had more than quadrupled since 1914 – eggs, for example – while wages had decreased in real terms by 20 per cent.

On 8 March 1917 by the Western calendar, an angry group of women textile workers marched up Nevsky Prospekt demanding bread. Crowds poured on to the streets to join them. Within a few days there was full-scale anarchy. By 10 March, most of working Petrograd was on strike, trams had stopped running and newspapers had not been printed. Locked up in her palace, like the rest of aristocratic Petrograd, Xenia could hear shooting and shouting. The crowds chanted slogans against 'the German Woman', Protopopov and the war. The Council of Ministers cabled the tsar begging him to return to Petrograd. With the exception of Protopopov, they offered their resignations and asked him to appoint a ministry acceptable to the Duma.

Back at army headquarters, Nicholas insisted that the disturbances were minor. His children had come down with measles and all he could think about was missing them and worrying about Alexis. He sent a telegram to Petrograd's military governor ordering him to 'make these disorders stop immediately'. The next day, 11 March, soldiers shot dead 200 people across the capital, but they failed to disperse the crowds, and some regiments began to refuse to fire on civilians and retired to their barracks. In an attempt to communicate the seriousness of the situation, the Duma president, Rodzianko, sent a final cable to Nicholas, telling him the troops were joining the revolution, begging him to appoint someone trusted by the country to run a government. Nicholas told his senior commander Alekseev, 'Fat Rodzianko has sent me some nonsense which I shall not even bother to answer,' and suspended the Duma.

On 12 March the Petrograd garrisons mutinied and joined the revolution. In the church at army headquarters that morning, Nicholas was stricken with 'an excruciating pain in the middle of my chest', that left him almost unable to stand for fifteen minutes. That night the Council of Ministers, despairing of the tsar, adjourned and handed itself over to the Duma – even Protopopov, who initially muttered that he was going off to shoot himself. The Duma, by no means confident that it could control the mobs and soldiers, announced it would form a government, and that workers and soldiers would be represented by a Soviet, their own council. The celebrations on the streets of Petrograd were frighteningly intense. Several units shot their commanding officers. The last soldiers abandoned the defence of the Winter Palace. At Stavka, Nicholas wrote in his diary that his officers were uneasy, and decided to take the imperial train to Tsarskoe selo the next morning. En route to Tsarskoe selo, Nicholas's generals effectively kidnapped him, took him up a branch line and told him to abdicate. General Alekseev had been in touch with Rodzianko and the new provisional government, whose hold on power was fragile. The crowds in Petrograd were baying for the imperial couple's blood, the new workers' Soviet looked disconcertingly powerful, and the provisional government had agreed that the tsar must go. A voluntary abdication might help to stabilize the situation. Alekseev knew Nicholas would need pushing. So he canvassed the generals at the fronts. Their replies were unanimous: the tsar must go to save the war effort.

Even Grand Duke Nicholas 'begged on his knees' for Nicholas to abdicate. Nicholas looked vacant. He went for his afternoon walk. He returned for tea. He agreed. 'My abdication is necessary,' he wrote in his diary, '. . . to save Russia and bring order back to the armies on the front.' Throughout the whole process he seemed, the officers all agreed, unnervingly calm, even when he signed the document of abdication on the evening of 15 March. But in his diary he wrote, 'All about me is treachery, cowardice and deceit.' Unable to bear the thought of separation from Alexis, and the pressure on his health, Nicholas had decided to abdicate on his son's behalf too. This left his younger brother Misha as heir and he, confronted by the scary crowds on the Petrograd streets demanding a republic, quickly stepped down too.

'Bad news from Russia,' George had written in his diary on 13 March, 'practically a revolution has broken out in Petrograd, and some of the Guards Regiments have mutinied and killed their officers. This rising,' he added, 'is against the Govt. not against the war.' By 15 March there was more information. 'I fear Alicky is the cause of it all and Nicky has been weak . . . I am in despair.'

He was almost the only one. Across the streets of the Russian empire, from Moscow to Tiflis, the end of autocracy was greeted with bells, songs, cheering and flags. The symbols of imperial power, the insignias and statues, were ripped off buildings and plinths. In France and Britain the fall of the tsar was greeted with relief. The regime's excesses had become an embarrassment, and it was hoped a democratic Russia would be much less likely to make a deal with Germany. The USA, which had just entered the war, enthusiastically recognized the new government a week after the abdication. Lloyd George, who was struggling to combat war-weariness with the idea that the Entente's sacrifices were in the great cause of Liberty and Democracy, sent a telegram congratulating the revolution, 'the greatest service that the Russian people have yet made to the cause for which the Allies are fighting'. It demonstrated 'the fundamental truth that this war is at bottom a struggle for popular government as well as for liberty. It shows that, through the war, the principle of liberty, which is the only sure safeguard of peace in the world, has already won a new resounding victory.'

George hated the telegram, unable to see that it had been written as much for domestic consumption as for the new Russian government (which, as it happened, contained a significant number of new members who were far more enthusiastic about British political traditions than anyone in the tsarist regime). Stamfordham was instructed to complain that it was 'a little strong', especially coming from a monarchical government. Lloyd George reminded the king's secretary that the British constitution itself had been founded on a revolution – the bloodless revolution of 1688.

George decided to send his own message of support to Nicholas: 'Events of last week have deeply distressed me. My thoughts are constantly with you and I shall always remain your true and devoted friend, as you know I have been in the past.' The provisional government's foreign minister, Pavel Miliukov, a former Duma member who revered Sir Edward Grey and admired Britain's liberal traditions, told Buchanan that it couldn't be delivered. The new Soviet was showing worrying signs of wanting to execute the tsar. Petrograd's political climate was so uncertain that George's telegram would make things worse. Miliukov's solution was to get the emperor out of Russia as soon as possible. When, on 21 March Buchanan delivered a warning that 'any violence done to the Emperor or his family would have a most deplorable effect and would deeply shock public opinion in this country', Miliukov asked him if Britain would offer the Romanovs asylum. In reporting the foreign minister's request, Buchanan added his own opinion that it ought to be heeded.

That same day the ex-imperial family was placed under house arrest. Soldiers had arrived at Tsarskoe selo a week before, surrounded the palace, and cut off the water supply. Alix heard nothing about Nicholas for three days. Alexis had contracted measles and was in terrible pain. The tsarina almost fainted when she heard about the abdication, then reacted with all-too-characteristic fatalism: 'It's for the best. It's the will of God. God will make sure that Russia is saved. It's the only thing that matters.' The provisional government told their captives that arrest was only a precaution to keep them safe. The plan, they were told, was to get them to the Finnish border and coast, only a few hours away, and to put them on a British cruiser to England. Nicholas, who was permitted to take his leave of Stavka before returning to Tsarskoe selo, told the British military attaché there that he hoped to retire to the Crimea but 'if not, he would sooner go to England than anywhere else'.

Lloyd George didn't love the idea of giving sanctuary to the discredited autocrat of all the Russias, but in consultation with Edward's old adviser Sir Charles Hardinge and Stamfordham, he agreed 'that the proposal . . . could not be refused'. Stamfordham added that Buchanan should 'throw out a hint' that the Russian government should provide money for the ex-tsar to live on. When

Lloyd George suggested (no doubt deliberately provocatively) that the king might hand over 'one of his houses', he said very sharply that the king 'had got no houses except Balmoral', which was entirely unsuitable.

Nicholas arrived back at Tsarskoe selo that day, running the gauntlet through rooms of curious soldiers who now had no reason to stand to attention or salute. When he reached the family's private apartments he broke down and sobbed. He looked, another courtier wrote, 'like an old man'. When he tried to go for a walk, six soldiers surrounded him and prodded him with their rifles. 'You can't go there, Gospodin Polkovnik,'* they said. 'Stand back when you are commanded, Gospodin Polkovnik.' Nicholas stood, small, quiet and expressionless. Later that evening, three armoured cars of over-excited soldiers from Petrograd arrived and announced they were taking the ex-tsar to the St Peter and Paul fortress – another sign of how tenuous the provisional government's hold on the army was. They were eventually persuaded to leave after they were allowed to see him. Sometime after midnight, another group of soldiers broke into Rasputin's tomb in the imperial park, exhumed the body and burned it.

Miliukov assured Buchanan that the Russian government would fund the tsar's asylum, but asked him not to reveal that the request for sanctuary had come from them, for fear of inflaming public opinion and the Petrograd Soviet. It was clear that smuggling the imperial family into Finland wasn't going to be straightforward. A week passed. England and George were clearly on the family's mind. Nicholas wrote in his diary that he was planning to start packing the things he would take to England, Alix began to talk constantly about her memories of Osborne, and the children asked their tutors what life would be like there.

In London, George started to harbour serious doubts about the wisdom of bringing his cousin to England. On 30 March Stamfordham wrote to the former prime minister, Arthur Balfour, whom Lloyd George had brought in as foreign secretary:

---

* 'Gospodin': Mr, the new semi-honorific that had replaced the old imperial titles; 'Polkovnik': Colonel.

The King has been thinking much about the Government's proposal that the Emperor Nicholas and his family should come to England. As you are doubtless aware, the King has a strong personal friendship for the Emperor and therefore would be glad to do anything to help him in this crisis. But His Majesty cannot help doubting not only on account of the dangers of the voyage, but on general grounds of expediency, whether it is advisable that the Imperial Family should take up residence in this country.

Balfour sent an uncompromising reply. Miliukov had just sent another telegram asking that the tsar leave Russia at once, and while 'His Majesty's Ministers quite realize the difficulties to which you refer in your letter . . . they do not think, unless the position changes, that it is now possible to withdraw the invitation which has been sent, and they therefore trust that the King will consent to adhere to the original invitation, which was sent on the advice of His Majesty's Ministers.'

On 3 April two of Alix's ladies-in-waiting, Lili Dehn and the much-hated Vyrubova, were arrested and taken to Petrograd for questioning, and the couple were ordered to live apart while the question of Alix's treason was investigated.

On 6 April Stamfordham wrote to Balfour insisting the invitation be withdrawn. 'Every day,' he wrote,

the King is becoming more concerned about the question of the Emperor and Empress coming to this country. His Majesty receives letters from people in all classes of life, known or unknown to him, saying how much the matter is being discussed, not only in clubs but by working men, and that Labour Members in the House of Commons are expressing adverse opinions to the proposal . . . I feel sure that you appreciate how awkward it will be for our Royal Family who are closely connected with both the Emperor and Empress . . . The King desires me to ask you whether after consulting the Prime Minister, Sir George Buchanan should not be communicated with, with a view to approaching the Russian Government to make some other place for the future residence of their Imperial Majesties?

Several hours later he sent another letter:

He must beg you to represent to the Prime Minister that from all he hears and reads in the press, the residence in this country of the ex-Emperor and Empress would be strongly resented by the public, and would undoubtedly compromise the position of the King and Queen from whom it is already generally supposed the invitation has emanated . . . Buchanan ought to be instructed to tell Miliukoff that the opposition to the Emperor and Empress coming here is so strong that we must be allowed to withdraw from the consent previously given to the Russian Government's proposal.

On 10 April Stamfordham bearded Lloyd George in Downing Street, 'to impress upon him the King's strong opinion that the Emperor and Empress of Russia should not come to this country, and that . . . It would,' he added, 'be most unfair upon the King . . . if TIM's [Their Imperial Majesties] came here when popular feeling against their doing so is so pronounced.' Then he went to complain to Balfour, saying that he had seen a telegram from Buchanan, who 'evidently took it for granted that the Emperor and Empress were coming to England and it was only a question of delay'. The king felt that Buchanan should already have been told to withdraw the invitation.

Stamfordham's harangues touched a nerve in the government. Lloyd George knew harbouring the Romanovs was not going to be popular in Britain, and he didn't want to do anything to alienate the increasingly unstable Russian government – he dreaded the thought that it might suddenly bow out of the war leaving the Western Front to take the full German assault. Balfour reflected that the king had been 'placed in an awkward position'. No one would believe that the invitation hadn't come from the court. Perhaps the Romanovs should go to the South of France instead? The Foreign Office issued a statement: 'His Majesty's Government does not insist on its former offer of hospitality to the Imperial family.' Balfour cabled Buchanan and told him to say nothing further about the invitation. The ambassador obediently agreed, Miliukov hadn't referred to it for a few days, the subject had clearly become a hot potato within the Russian government, and obviously if there was 'any danger of an anti-monarchist movement', England was not the right place for the tsar. He suggested that the foreign minister might sound out the French. But at home, his daughter later wrote, it was clear that he was deeply upset.

At Tsarskoe selo 'The days passed and our departure was always being postponed.' Talk of England gradually ceased.

Would Nicholas's presence in Britain have put George's throne in danger? It seems, in hindsight, highly unlikely. It was true that Britain had not been immune to the strikes and riots that had broken out across Europe since the Russian Revolution. Small issues caused sudden strikes. In 1918 12,000 aircraft factory workers in Coventry walked out because of false rumours that they were to be conscripted. Moreover, England, like the rest of Europe, had seen a surge in left-wing rhetoric calling for change, revolution and even a republic. A week after the Foreign Office took back its invitation to the tsar, H. G. Wells wrote to *The Times* declaring that Britain should rid itself of 'the ancient trappings of throne and sceptre', and proposed the formation of republican societies across the country. (Wells had famously described George's circle as an 'alien and uninspiring court', to which George made his only ever recorded witty riposte: 'I may be uninspiring, but I be damned if I'm an alien.') There was, however, no answering surge of revolutionary republicanism – nothing, for example, on the scale of the hundreds of republican clubs that sprang up in the 1870s. Of all the civilian populations of Europe engaged in the war, the British suffered the least in terms of want and number of deaths – German civilian deaths were far greater than British ones* – and were furthest away from the fighting. Lloyd George dealt with the unrest he did encounter more successfully than any other leading statesman in Europe. Though his ministry was dominated by Conservatives, his own enormous popularity and his record of social

---

* There is great variation in estimates of civilian deaths during the First World War, but all figures agree that German civilian deaths were at least twice and perhaps even four times the British ones. See, for example, the website 20th century Atlas – death tolls.

amelioration gave him credibility with the strikers, and his political instincts led him to meet them halfway, while other European governments responded with heavy-handed repression. All the while he told the country it was fighting to defend Liberty – as manifested by the British system – and to destroy the German military caste and its oppression of the German people.

If Lloyd George and his fellow politicians had really thought that bringing the ex-tsar to England posed a threat to the crown and the constitutional structure of England – something none of them wanted – they would never have agreed to taking him in the first place. It was another great irony entirely lost on George that Lloyd George, the man whose politics were anathema to him, was the man who kept his throne secure. He would also be the man who would cover up George's involvement in the rejection of the Romanovs, omitting his role entirely from his *War Memoirs* and taking the weight of what opprobrium there was – though he also falsely claimed that Britain never withdrew the invitation, and stated more truthfully, that it wasn't clear the provisional government would have been able to extricate the tsar out of Russia. Buchanan would also bear the weight of blame for the British failure to do so: he would spend the rest of his life unhappily trying to exonerate himself – he too assumed the source of the decision to revoke the invitation was Lloyd George.

The truth was George had become immensely sensitive to criticism of himself or the monarchy – in that respect he was now far more attuned and attentive to public opinion than either of his cousins. Any whisper of it 'rankled unduly' and made him deeply depressed. Just how hair-triggerishly anxious George was would be well illustrated a few months later, in July 1917, when he became so upset about insinuations that the royal family might not be entirely loyal because of their German names and antecedents, that he changed the family name from Saxe-Coburg-Gotha to the entirely made-up 'Windsor'. George wasn't wrong to imagine that giving sanctuary to his cousin would have been a very unpopular move in a country whose government was now justifying the war as a fight for freedom against autocracy. But it is extremely unlikely that it would have cost him his throne. He panicked and placed his worries ahead of the family relationship which he had always said counted for so much, and the cousin he had professed to care so deeply for. It was a final blow to the cult of family which his queen empress grandmother had so heartily embraced. It was also a decision that revealed a monarchy aware of the need to sell itself to its subjects if it was to survive.

Over the next fourteen months the tide of scepticism about George would turn: the grim-faced visits to the front, to hospitals, to factories, the stories of royal belt-tightening that gradually leaked out, began to be seen as a testament to his commitment to duty, hard work and to sharing the burden of the long years of struggle. George's frayed but stoic ordinariness seemed like a counter or even a rebuke to the overblown Wagnerian swagger, the mystical claims to perfection, of the European absolutist monarchies the country felt it was fighting against. By the end of the war *The Times* would write of 'the wonderful popularity with Londoners – as we are convinced, with the whole country – of THEIR MAJESTIES the KING and QUEEN . . . this signal outburst of loyal feeling is born of the conviction that the CROWN, well-worn, is the symbol and safeguard of unity, not only here in England, but in the free dominions overseas, and in India'.

In July 1917, the month George changed his name, there was a surge of angry unrest in Petrograd – 'the July days'. Alexander Kerensky, recently made head of the provisional government, decided he must try again to get the imperial family out of the country. He went to Buchanan, who replied – according to Kerensky with tears in his eyes – that the British government had withdrawn its offer of asylum. A month later, in August, the family were sent to Tobolsk, a small backwater in western Siberia.

The former tsar had proved consistently patient, gracious and polite to his captors. Amazingly, he did not seem bitter, accepting his 'restraints with extraordinary serenity and moral grandeur. No word of reproach ever passed his lips.' Kerensky, charged with the investigation and safety of the former tsar and his family, found him 'an extremely reserved, reticent man, with much distrust and infinite contempt for others', and was struck by 'his utter indifference to the world around him, as though he loved and valued no one, and was not surprised by anything that happened'. The household found Kerensky unbearably high-handed, but Nicholas decided to trust him. Passive fatalistic acceptance was very much in keeping with the strain of mystic Russian Orthodoxy which had inspired Alix and him, but one might have concluded that the ex-tsar was almost relieved that the terrible weight of responsibility had been taken from his shoulders. Kerensky certainly thought so. Apart from certain constraints on his movement – he wasn't allowed to go for long walks – the fabric of life wasn't so remarkably different. The provisional government had taken on the upkeep of the emperor's household (a sum so vast it was decided it should be kept secret), but now there were no decisions, no meetings, no need to take umbrage at others' infringements of his prerogatives. He spent time with his family, played with the children, read aloud, smoked and slept well. When spring came, he gardened and played tennis. Alexandra, however, remained unresigned. Volubly bitter, she spent most days in bed or on her *chaise longue*.

July 1917 was the month Wilhelm found himself eclipsed by the imperial General Staff. After three years at war, the divisions in German society were creating their own chaos; the country was riven with strikes and protests against falling wages and food shortages. In the Reichstag the Left was demanding an end to the war, on the streets protesters clamoured for political reform, while the Right and the army were insisting Germany fight on and annex Poland and the Baltic states.

As the war had progressed the German High Command had gradually taken control of the state. In August 1916, with the war at stalemate, shortages at home and the government and the country increasingly divided, Wilhelm had been pressured against his wishes to sack Falkenhayn (who had become chief of staff after Moltke's health had failed in September 1914) and install the two heroes of Germany's Eastern Front, Generals Hindenburg and Ludendorff, instead. It was a move that compounded Wilhelm's irrelevance and signalled the start of his total eclipse. The most successful generals in the war had their own agenda. They were incipient Napoleons, convinced that the war must be won on the Eastern Front against Russia, impatient that the civilian government wasn't sufficiently acquiescent to their needs, and not afraid to interfere in politics. Wilhelm admired them and resented them equally: they were enormously popular and he feared their influence.

By early 1917 Ludendorff and Hindenburg had their sights on removing Bethmann-Hollweg, whom they saw as too unbiddable and alarmingly sympathetic to demands for political reform. The Left, which now dominated the Reichstag, wanted peace without annexations or indemnities. A month after Nicholas's abdication, in April 1917, Bethmann-Hollweg, believing it was the only solution, persuaded a deeply reluctant Wilhelm to commit to political reform of the deeply inequitable franchise in Prussia after the war. In July Ludendorff and Hindenburg made their move, threatening to resign unless the chancellor was sacked. In a panic Wilhelm refused, but Bethmann-Hollweg had also lost all support in the Reichstag, and resigned himself. The new chancellor, selected with almost comical arbitrariness, was an administrator called Michaelis whom Wilhelm had met once and described as 'an insignificant little man'. 'Now I may as well abdicate,' Wilhelm told his former chancellor. He spent his time going for walks, playing card games, arguing with Dona. In September 1917 Hindenburg took Wilhelm's title of Supreme Warlord, and the army's press agency sent out his portrait throughout the country. In the nation's mind, Hindenburg gradually replaced Wilhelm as the strong-man, the absolute leader, the surrogate kaiser – for whom the country apparently longed. In January 1918, when Wilhelm tried to challenge the generals' plans to annex Poland, they punished him by forcing the dismissal of his most trusted officials, the chiefs of his civil and military cabinets, Valentine and Lyncker, and installing their own candidate, Friedrich von Berg zu Markienen, who never let Wilhelm out of his sight. Germany had become essentially a military dictatorship; Wilhelm was the flimsy fig-leaf.

In Tobolsk the Romanovs lived in the governor's mansion, perhaps not in imperial levels of comfort, but with a household which nevertheless included six chambermaids, ten footmen, three chefs and a wine steward. There was space to exercise, and the local people were respectful, removing their caps and crossing themselves when they saw the former tsar. The Bolshevik victory in early November 1917 hardly registered – it took a week for the news to arrive. What upset Nicholas most was that Lenin had immediately begun peace talks with Germany, an outcome the British government, whose contacts within the Bolsheviks were minimal, had dreaded. Thankfully for them, the Americans had now joined the war. Though Lenin regarded the war as a bourgeois fight foisted on the peasants and workers, the peace deal was a bitter pill even for the Bolsheviks: German military successes and the Russian army's collapse meant that Germany got Poland, Finland, the Baltic states, the Ukraine, the Crimea – where Nicholas's sisters and mother were holed up – and most of the Caucasus, a million miles of Russian territory which contained virtually all its coal and oil, half its industry and a third of its population. For Nicholas, it nullified the whole justification for his abdication – a meaningful sacrifice so long as others would win the war and save Russia. 'It now gave him pain to see that his renunciation had been in vain,' Pierre Gilliard, who had followed the family to Siberia, wrote. When the Peace of Brest-Litovsk was signed in March 1918, Nicholas was deeply depressed by it: 'It is such a disgrace for Russia and amounts to suicide . . . I should never have thought the Emperor William and the German Government could stoop to shake hands with these miserable traitors.'

Captivity turned harsher that month. The soldiers became markedly less friendly, luxuries disappeared from the table. Servants and members of the suite were gradually dismissed. Two days before the Brest-Litovsk Treaty was signed, the tutor Gilliard wrote in his diary, 'Their Majesties still cherish hope that among their loyal friends some may be found to attempt their release.' After arguments over whether Nicholas should stand trial in Moscow – Trotsky fancied himself as principal prosecutor – the family were moved to Ekaterinburg, the centre of Bolshevik militancy in the Urals, in April 1918. They were met by an angry crowd, and imprisoned in a large house which was swiftly enclosed with a high wooden fence. The windows were painted over; the family were confined to their rooms for most of the day, and Alix and the girls were accompanied to the lavatory by guards who graffitied drawings of her and Rasputin having sex on the lavatory walls. The former empress was now barely able to walk and spent days on her bed. The daughters did the housework, and Nicholas read *War and Peace* for the first time in his life, and daydreamed about a nice hot bath. The top brass in Ekaterinburg wanted an execution, but the order for their murder came from Lenin in Moscow, who decided – as the counter-revolutionary White troops, representing an uneasy coalition of anti-Bolshevik groups, and a Czech regiment closed in on Ekaterinburg in July 1918 – that they could not afford the tsar to be a 'live banner'.

On 3 July in the old-style calendar (16 July by the Western one), at 1.30 in the morning, the prisoners – the tsar, his family and all that remained of his servants, his doctor, valet, cook and Alix's maid – were woken and led down to the basement. They were told there had been shooting in the town and they would be safer there. Nicholas carried his sleepy son. At his request chairs were brought for Alix and Alexis. Anastasia brought her dog. After several minutes the local secret police chief, Yakov Yurovsky, came into the room with an eleven-man squad, one to shoot each victim. The room was too small, however, and the executioners found themselves facing the wrong people. Yurovsky read out the order to shoot the Romanovs. As Nicholas spoke an incredulous 'What?' Yurovsky shot him point blank. His men started firing. Most of the adults died quickly, but Alexis, protected by his father's arms, survived the first volley, as did the daughters, who were protected by the jewels they had sewn into the bodices of their dresses for safe-keeping. They were bayoneted. The bodies were taken fourteen miles from Ekaterinburg and burned, the remains thrown down a mine shaft, their faces deliberately disfigured to prevent identification if they were found. Eight days later the town fell to the Whites.

We have such a horribly vivid account of the Romanovs' murder because one of the executioners, Medvedev, was later captured by the White Russian army and described every detail to Nikolai

Sokolov, an investigator appointed by the Whites to uncover the fate of the ex-tsar. Its hideous graphicness gave the Romanovs' deaths a terribly poignant immediacy. In death – as never in life – they stood in for the millions of victims of undescribed, anonymous murders and massacres that would be perpetrated by the Soviet regime and other totalitarian regimes of the twentieth century, regimes that would prove so good at killing, but little else. In death also, Nicholas would become the martyr-tsar, a useful figurehead for the Whites, who had had no use for him alive.

Over previous months there had been several tragically in-effectual attempts to plan a rescue. With Alix's permission, the Romanovs' English tutor, George Gibbes, who followed them to Siberia, wrote a letter meant for George, addressed to the former tsarina's English governess, with a full plan of the family's house in Tobolsk and details of their routine. There's no indication it ever reached him. Several monarchist groups managed to raise funds but failed to come up with anything approaching a plan; money was sent to Tobolsk, but it never arrived. There were rumours that the German terms of the Treaty of Brest-Litovsk included a demand that the imperial family must be handed over to Germany unharmed. Nicholas had not been able to bear the thought: 'This is either a manoeuvre to discredit me or an insult.' The rumours were not, as it turned out, true. In Moscow, Nicholas's old court chancellor, Benckendorff, brother of the former British ambassador, tried to get the German ambassador Mirbach, to support a rescue mission. In Kiev, now occupied by the Germans, Mossolov attempted to persuade the German commanders to back a plan to travel up the Volga to Ekaterinburg. He wrote personally to the kaiser about it. He never received a reply. A former German ambassador to Petrograd told him with much embarrassment that the kaiser couldn't reply without con-sulting his government, and the local German commanders refused to help.

After the war Wilhelm swore that he had tried to get the tsar out. 'I did all that was humanly possible for the unhappy Tsar and his family, and was seconded heartily by my Chancellor,' he told General H.-H. Waters, whom he'd known as a British military attaché in Berlin, in the 1930s. He said that Bethmann-Hollweg had come to him with a Danish plan for rescuing the tsar. 'How can I do that? There are two fighting lines of German and Russian troops facing each other between him and me!' Wilhelm quoted himself. 'Nevertheless I ordered my Chancellor to try and get in touch with the Kerensky government by neutral channels, informing him that if a hair of the Russian Imperial family's head should be injured, I would hold him personally responsible if I should have the possibility of doing so.' In Wilhelm's version, Kerensky answered that he was only too happy to provide a train. Wilhelm said he had informed Bethmann-Hollweg he would order the High Commander on the Eastern Front to arrange safe conduct for the tsar's train, and told his brother Heinrich to escort the ship holding the tsar through the minefields. 'The blood of the unhappy Tsar is not at <u>my door</u>; not on <u>my hands</u>,' he told Waters, though why this foolproof plan had failed he was unable to say.

What Wilhelm certainly did do was give his permission on 24 March 1917 to allow Vladimir Lenin – a man more radical than any German Social Democrat – to travel via Germany to Russia, with the explicit intention of creating as much chaos and destabilization in Russia as possible.* The German authorities had already spent hundreds of thousands of marks on funding *agents provocateurs* to encourage strikes and unrest in Russia, and on Lenin's own circle of Bolsheviks. Lenin was taken from the Swiss border through Germany in a 'sealed' train – no passport or luggage inspections – 'like a plague bacillus' in Winston Churchill's famous phrase.

On 16 July, the day of Nicholas's murder, George went to Roehampton to watch the balloon-training wing of the RAF. The news of the former tsar's death was officially announced three days later. The Bolsheviks claimed the rest of the family were still alive. On 25 July George decreed a month of court mourning and wrote that he and May had attended 'a service at the Russian church in Welbeck street in memory of dear Nicky, who I fear was shot last month by the Bolshevists [*sic*]. I was devoted to Nicky,

---

* Lenin, not expecting help from the German government, had at one stage planned to get through Germany disguised as a deaf, dumb and blind Swede.

who was the kindest of men, a thorough gentleman: loved his country and people.' Three days after that he noted that the former British vice-consul in Moscow, Robert Bruce Lockhart, had reported that 'dear Nicky' had been shot by the local Soviet at Ekaterinburg. 'It was nothing more than a brutal murder.' At the end of August he wrote, 'I hear from Russia that there is every probability that Alicky and four daughters and little boy were murdered at the same time as Nicky. It is too horrible and shows what fiends those Bolshevists are. For poor Alicky, perhaps it was best so. But those poor innocent children!'

George and Stamfordham seem to have tacitly agreed on a kind of wilful amnesia. They were also quick to blame the government for the failure to act. The day of the memorial service for Nicholas, Stamfordham wrote in an outraged tone to Lord Esher:

Was there ever a crueller murder and has this country ever before displayed such callous indifference to a tragedy of this magnitude: What does it all mean? I am so thankful that the King and Queen attended the memorial service. I have not yet discovered that the PM . . . [was] even represented. Where is our national sympathy, gratitude, common decency . . . Why didn't the German Emperor make the release of the Czar and family a condition of the Brest-Litovsk peace?

This was somewhat disingenuous, as only three days before Stamfordham had told Balfour that George shouldn't attend the service for fear of irritating public opinion.

George's son, the Duke of Windsor, said that the murder shook his father's 'confidence in the innate decency of mankind. There was a very real bond between him and his first cousin Nicky.' He claimed that his father 'had personally planned to rescue him with a British cruiser, but in some way the plan was blocked. In any case, it hurt my father that Britain had not raised a hand to save his Cousin Nicky. "Those politicians," he used to say. "If it had been one of their kind they would have acted fast enough."'

Wilhelm's time came three months after Nicholas's death. In August 1918 Ludendorff overstretched the German army on the

Western Front and the Entente – or the Allies, as it now called itself – began to break through. Wilhelm spent most of his time at German military headquarters at Spa, in Belgium, in a Marie-Antoinette-esque villa that looked as if it had been built from spun sugar. He entertained himself by digging little trenches and diverting a dam. The industrialist Albert Ballin met him for the last time at the end of September when even the German High Command had admitted it was all but over. He was accompanied by a military minder.

I found the Emperor very misdirected and in the elated mood that he affected when a third party was present. Things had been so twisted that even the fearful failure of the offensive, that had caused a severe depression in him at first, had been turned into a success . . . the offensive had achieved no more than the loss of the lives of round 100,000 valuable people. The whole thing was served up to the poor monarch in such a way that he had not noticed the catastrophe at all.

In early October, with Wilhelm back in Berlin, a new chancellor, Max von Baden, a cousin of Wilhelm's, formed a government which claimed to represent the liberal left-wing Reichstag majority for the first time, and asked the Allies for an armistice. They demanded stiff terms. The American president, Woodrow Wilson, issued a series of 'notes' insisting that Germany must become a full parliamentary democracy and divest itself of its emperor. 'It aims directly at the fall of my house, and above all at the abolition of the monarch!' Wilhelm sputtered of Wilson's note of 14 October. The fact that his abdication was being debated across Germany was kept from him.

On 29 October, encouraged by Dona and the entourage, Wilhelm left Berlin for army headquarters at Spa. It was a bad move; it looked as if the kaiser was running away to the army. Austria made terms that week, and the whole of Germany – with almost the sole exception of Wilhelm's entourage, his family and a few of the High Command – came to believe the kaiser must go. But once in Spa Wilhelm delayed and delayed, chopping wood to calm himself down, saying that if the 'Bolsheviks' tried to make him abdicate he would put himself at the head of his army, march to Berlin and hang the traitors, or at very least, 'shoot up the town'. The army and navy chiefs were full of mad plans: a march to Berlin; a suicide cavalry charge led by Wilhelm to save the honour of the monarchy; a last-ditch 'death ride' by Wilhelm's beloved navy.

With almost exquisite irony, it was that 'death ride' plan that sparked the German revolution. On 4 November, at Kiel, the sailors on Wilhelm's precious ships mutinied. They demanded political reform and the removal of the royal family. Workers' risings spread across Germany. By early November there was a general strike in Berlin. The revolutionaries threatened to put up barricades if Wilhelm didn't go. The Reichstag was terrified that the workers' councils might take over as they had in Russia. Still Wilhelm held out. On the 9th the latest war minister told the kaiser that the army would not fight for him if there was a civil war, and he must abdicate. Wilhelm stared vacantly through lunch and bit his lip. He said he would abdicate as emperor but remain King of Prussia, and sent someone off to draft the papers. Half an hour later he was wondering whether he really had to abdicate at all. The news came that Chancellor Max von Baden had lost patience. With Berlin on the verge of uproar and both the kaiser's phones engaged, he announced that Wilhelm and his eldest son were renouncing the throne, then resigned himself, handing over power to the leader of the Reichstag Socialists, Friedrich Ebert. When he heard the news Wilhelm shouted, 'Treachery, treachery, shameless, outrageous, treachery!'

In London George wrote in his diary:

We got the news that the German Emperor had abdicated, also the Crown Prince. "How are the mighty fallen". He has been Emperor just over 30 years, he did great things for his country, but his ambition was so great that he wished to dominate the world and created his military machine for that object. No one man can dominate the world, it has been tried before, and now he has utterly ruined his Country and himself and I look upon him as the greatest criminal known for having plunged the world into this ghastly war with all it's [*sic*] misery.

While his generals tried to persuade him to make for neutral Holland, only thirty miles away, Wilhelm sat and smoked, refused to move, insisted that he would return to Berlin or stay with the troops, and grumbled about his former subjects. 'The German people are a bunch of pigs,' he said, and 'There is no other instance in History of a universal act of treachery by a nation against its ruler.' In Berlin the revolutionaries broke into the Berlin Schloss and somewhat appropriately stole the emperor's clothes.

Eventually Wilhelm was persuaded to leave Spa in the small hours of 10 November. Foreign troops were said to be only a few miles away. He was quietly driven to the Dutch border in a car from which all imperial insignias had been scratched off. He reached Holland early in the morning of 11 November. He seemed completely crushed and was desperate not to be left alone, telling his entourage that he was a broken man. The message came finally that the Dutch would offer him asylum, at least temporarily. It was decided that Wilhelm should be moved by train to a small seventeenth-century manor house called Amerongen in Utrecht.

His first words at Amerongen were, 'How about a cup of good, hot, real English tea?' As he sat down to contemplate his new life, the armistice was signed in Marshal Foch's train in the forest of Compiègne.

'William arrived in Holland yesterday,' George wrote in his diary. 'Today has indeed been a wonderful day, the greatest in the history of this Country.' Elsewhere in Europe, it was not a good moment for monarchies. Within Germany, the kings of Bavaria and Wurttemburg had been deposed; the ruling grand dukes of Coburg, Hesse and Mecklenburg-Strelitz had all abdicated; the latter had then shot himself. Emperor Karl of Austria-Hungary, who had inherited after the death of his great-uncle Franz Joseph in 1916, had abdicated on Armistice Day. Ferdinand, self-styled 'tsar' of Bulgaria, who had cast his lot in with Germany at the height of its successes, also went that month. George's cousin 'Tino', King of Greece, had abdicated in 1917 in favour of his younger son, who would be little more than a puppet and would die of a monkey bite in 1920. In Turkey, Sultan Mehmed V had died in May; his brother and successor, Mehmed VI, would be deposed in 1922.

As the Armistice Day crowds came to Buckingham Palace to cheer, George was the only emperor still standing on his balcony.

Epilogue

Eight and a half million soldiers were dead (an estimated 750,000 British, 2 million German, 1.8 million Russian – though the figures vary), and at least another million or so civilians – up to 700,000 in Germany alone. A further 21 million soldiers had been wounded. The post-war world was a very different place from the pre-war world, one not amenable to the old hierarchies and the whims of kings; in many respects, an ugly world. Europe was not 'cleansed' and the worst was by no means over. The violent tearing out of the monarchy in Russia and Germany had left gaping holes which would be filled by extremism and more violence. Russia was already in the grip of a new five-year civil war on a scale even more hideous than the one that had preceded it. It would leave an estimated 8–10 million victims of massacres, pogroms, disease and starvation, in circumstances and numbers which seemed only to demonstrate the absolute nadir of human cruelty and destructiveness. Germany was in the midst of a bitter short-lived Communist revolution. Its brutal quelling was the awkward cradle in which German democracy, under the Weimar Republic, was born in January 1919, in circumstances which only worsened the horrible fractures in German society. The radical Left felt betrayed by the new governing Social Democrats. The extreme Right, nationalists and the army continued to dream of an authoritarian past, coining a powerful but false myth that it was not they who were responsible for Germany's downfall, but the revolutionaries and mutineers who had stabbed Germany in the back just at the point when it was winning. It was a myth that would help to lead Germany into another world war.

Soon after the Armistice there were calls for the ex-kaiser to be punished for his part in the war. Someone, it was felt, should be called to account for the carnage. On 7 December David Lloyd George, fighting a general election in London, said that the ex-kaiser should hang and that he planned to try him in Westminster Hall. Immediately the British press was full of headlines: 'Hang the Kaiser!', 'Make Germany Pay!' In February 1919 the Allies tried to pressure the Dutch into handing him over. The Treaty of Versailles demanded the extradition of over 1,000 German war criminals for trial, including Wilhelm.

Wilhelm was convinced he'd be executed if he stood trial abroad. He worried about being kidnapped and taken to The Hague, and wondered about getting himself a police guard. He knew that his presence was not popular in Holland. There had been a number of half-hearted attempts to get at him – none of them very serious. With typical operetta-style ineffectuality, his entourage discussed disguising him and sending him into hiding. Wilhelm refused to shave off his moustache, though he said he could turn the ends down, and pointed out people would recognize his withered arm – one of the few occasions when he directly mentioned it. Instead he grew his beard and took to his bed for six weeks, wearing a bandage around his head, hoping it would make the Dutch feel sorry for him. It was Dona, however, who was genuinely ill. She had heart disease, a condition she had consistently minimized so as not to burden her husband; after her arrival at Amerongen, she spent most of her time in bed.

The ex-kaiser's entourage considered asking George to protest about Wilhelm's extradition. The king utterly disapproved of his cousin being treated as a war criminal – he subjected Lloyd George to a 'violent tirade' on the subject. He would not, however, intervene on Wilhelm's behalf. In the war's four years he'd lost all sympathy for his cousin. When his son Bertie encountered Wilhelm's daughter Victoria a few weeks after the Armistice, she said she hoped that 'we should be friends again'. Bertie told her that he didn't think it would be possible. George agreed: 'The sooner she knows the real feeling of bitterness which exists here against her country the better.' To the end of his life, he refused to have any contact with Wilhelm.

The Dutch government rejected every attempt to extradite the former kaiser; there were laws in Holland protecting aliens who had sought sanctuary there on political grounds. After Versailles, moreover, the demands for Wilhelm's punishment were never pursued, at least on Lloyd George's part, with much real energy. He regarded them as crowd-pleasing rhetoric for an angry domestic market, and hoped they would divert criticism from the new German government.

When the US president, Woodrow Wilson, came to London in December 1918, George took an instant dislike to him. Wilson, who was even more awkward and shy than George, had become, with his talk of free states, the flag-bearer of republicanism and independence. The king also felt the president was high-handed, gave America too much credit for winning the war and failed to acknowledge the sacrifices that British troops had made. Perhaps he could feel the initiative in world affairs shifting quietly and permanently from Britain to America as they spoke. When he suggested that Wilson march his troops to Russia to 'protect the country from Bolshevism', Wilson told him the American army had come to Europe for one purpose only. 'After that I never thought much of the man . . . I could not bear him, an entirely cold academical professor – an odious man.'

By Russian and German standards, Britain was calm and stable. The monarchy was intact. The war actually increased the size of the British empire. Because its armies were in control of the Middle East, it found itself the dominant power there. At the Versailles Conference it scooped up the old German colonies in Africa. And since the war had been fought with imperial troops – Canadian, antipodean, South African and Indian soldiers had all contributed – it looked like an imperial victory, a triumph binding the empire more closely than ever.

The feeling of elation at the war's end quickly gave way to a sense of disappointment and frustration: a generation of young men was dead, and there was no sign of the promised Elysium. There was anger at low war pensions, a housing shortage, high inflation. Shortly after the war, George went to Hyde Park with his son and heir, David, Prince of Wales, to inspect a parade of 15,000 ex-servicemen disabled by the war. There was, David gradually realized as he watched his father ride down the lines, something wrong, 'a sullen unresponsiveness' in the men. Suddenly, banners appeared. Someone shouted, 'Where is this land fit for heroes?' A group of soldiers broke rank and ran towards George. He was cut off from his entourage and seemed about to be pulled to the ground. As it turned out the men just wanted to touch his hand. But it was a frightening moment. The king had no vocabulary for what he'd witnessed. ' "Those men were in a funny temper," he said. And shaking his head, as if to rid himself of any unpleasant memory, he strode indoors.'

The war marked the high point of British territorial acquisition, and also the beginning of the empire's unravelling. In Ireland, the British government fought a war from January 1919 to 1921, acquiescing with bad grace to Irish independence in 1922. The Versailles Conference confirmed the right of the Dominions (the white colonies) to be autonomous nations within the Commonwealth – a right they believed they'd earned by fighting. Never again would a British king be able to declare war on their behalf. The 800,000 Indian troops (of whom 60,000 died) who had fought in the war encouraged the Indian independence movement to argue that India too had earned its right to self-government, and to begin a campaign of disobedience. The reaction of the British colonial government – the imposition of a dictatorial regime in 1918 worthy of tsarist Russia, complete with press censorship, arrest without warrant, detention without trial, martial law and an ugly and wholly avoidable massacre of 379 civilians at Amritsar in April 1919 – only strengthened that conviction, and caused so much shame in Britain that it set India, slowly, on the road to independence.

When Nicholas's sister Xenia and his mother, Marie, escaped from the Crimea with a boatload of Romanov relations in 1919, George offered the women asylum – the men were told 'their presence would be blamed on the King's influence'.* Marie retired to Denmark, where she infuriated her nephew the Danish king with her extravagance. George settled a pension on her (which several

---

* They mostly went to France and America.

of his in-laws complained about having to contribute towards) but wouldn't let her have a cheque book in case she spent it all at once. To Xenia, who was also disastrous with money (she mainly kept giving it away to down-at-heel Romanov relations), George gave a pension and a grace-and-favour house at Windsor and later at Hampton Court. After Marie died in 1928 her famous jewellery collection, which had been valued at one time, according to Fritz Ponsonby, at between £350,000 and half a million pounds, was sold off to provide money for her two daughters. It brought in just over £100,000 and Mary bought a lot of it. The difference in value could be accounted for by the slump and the fact that the market was awash with Russian heirlooms, but the sisters found it hard to shake the feeling that there was something a little discomfiting about their cousin-in-law, on whom the family now so depended, acquiring the family jewels at a cut-price rate.

Separated by a small channel of water and a war on a scale that no one had seen before, George, fifty-three, and Wilhelm, sixty, in early 1919, contemplated the future. Nicholas lay in an anonymous grave in Eastern Siberia.

Wilhelm spent the rest of his life in Holland. He moved in 1920 to Haus Doorn, a modest seventeenth-century manor house, bought with the proceeds of the sale of a couple of yachts. There he lived with a small court of forty-six, including twenty-six servants, for the next twenty-three years. The house was stuffed with the contents of the twenty-three railway wagons, twenty-five furniture wagons, twenty-seven wagons of packages (including a car and a boat) which the Weimar government had sent him from Germany. The German government also agreed to acknowledge $2 million of land Wilhelm owned in Berlin, and in 1926 arranged for the transfer of millions of marks in cash and some 10–12 million marks of stocks and bonds. Wilhelm, nevertheless, always complained he'd been shoddily treated by the German government; to requests for financial assistance he always replied that he barely had enough to live on himself. He died worth an estimated 14 million marks. An equivalent figure in today's money would be around $62.5 million. Perhaps if one had been Emperor of Germany it wouldn't have seemed that much.

As a symbol of what he'd lost, he abandoned the military uniforms he'd worn since he was eighteen and adopted civilian dress – blue serge suits, loden capes, a little hunting hat and a tie pin with a miniature of Queen Victoria on it. He gave up hunting and riding – and made his entourage do so too – and took to walking round his estate and feeding the ducks in the moat, taking very occasional car rides round the nearby countryside in his Mercedes cabriolet. It must have been deeply oppressive for a man who had become accustomed to escaping from himself – and awkward feelings – with incessant and compulsive travel. Instead he let off steam by cutting down trees (with the help of a couple of servants), a habit that became an addiction. He chopped down his 20,000th tree on his seventieth birthday in 1929. The logs were distributed to the poor or turned into matchsticks and handed out like decorations to the curious and the faithful who came to visit.

In September 1920 Dona and Wilhelm's youngest son, and her favourite, Joachim, shot himself in the depths of depression. He was addicted to gambling and his wife had left him. A devastated Dona died seven months later, in April 1921. Wilhelm received 10,000 messages of condolence – a mark perhaps more of the respect with which Dona had been regarded in Germany than real enthusiasm for himself. There was no message from George, which particularly stung Wilhelm. The only member of the British family who did write was his aunt Beatrice, two years his senior, whom he'd always disliked. The kaiser, his young aide Sigurd von Ilsemann noted, was miserable for two weeks. After that, he complained about being lonely. He remarried eighteen months later in 1923. The bride, Princess Hermine von Schönaich-Carolath, was thirty years his junior, a determined widow with five children who had set out to bag the ex-kaiser and liked to be addressed as 'Empress'. The entourage and Wilhelm's children regarded her as an egregious gold-digger with a nasty face. Some felt they deserved each other, but she did at least make life with the ex-kaiser a little easier.

Never learning, never changing, cooped up in Haus Doorn

unable to escape himself, Wilhelm was very difficult to live with. He raged at the injustice of fate and the 'lies of Versailles', engaged in permanent self-justification, rewriting the past, blaming everyone else for the fall of Germany, the end of the Hohenzollerns and the failures of his reign, and hoping that the German people – for whom he expressed only contempt – would come to their senses and 'beg me to come and save them'. In 1922 his valet of twenty years, unable to bear it any more, ran off in tears. None of his children chose to share exile with him, all but one returned to Germany, where Willy, Eitel Frederick and August-Wilhelm 'Auwi' became mixed up in monarchist and far-right circles, hoping to see the monarchy returned, and later flirted with Nazism. Adalbert, the third son, disassociated himself from his relations and was considered to be strongly anti-Nazi. He moved quietly to Switzerland. It was hard to avoid the feeling that the family was broken. A rump of the entourage, habituated to a lifetime of deference and obedience, unable to imagine a German republic, stayed, continuing to stand for hours after dinner, exasperated but uncomplaining, while Wilhelm monologued over and over about how Edward VII had conspired against him; how Tirpitz and Ludendorff and Hindenburg and Max von Baden had betrayed him; how George had gone to war to further Edward's encirclement plans; and how the Freemasons and the Catholics, the French, the British, the Bolsheviks and, increasingly and more darkly as the years passed, the Jews especially, had plotted to destroy him. Reading Bernhard von Bülow's memoirs in the late 1920s, Sigurd von Ilsemann, the endlessly patient young aide who had followed Wilhelm into exile after only a few weeks of service in 1918, was 'struck over and over again by how little the Kaiser has changed since those times. Almost everything that occurred then still happens now, the only difference being that his actions, which then had grave significance and practical consequences, now do no damage.'

Safe from the threat of a trial, the ex-kaiser set about writing – or having ghostwritten – his version of the events that had led to the war. *Ereignisse und Gestalten*, 'Events and Figures', came out in 1922; *Aus Meinem Leben*, published in Britain as 'My Early Life', in

1927. The books were, predictably, litanies of injustices perpetrated against him – from his mother's pushing and his tutor's bullying, through his chancellors', ministers' and relations' betrayals, to the criminal fickleness of British ministers and the German people – drenched in self-pity and, occasionally and unintentionally, very comic. Never did Wilhelm accept that he was in any sense responsible for the end of the Hohenzollern dynasty. He'd convinced himself he was a martyr to his people – winning the war until Hindenburg forced him to abandon his troops and flee to Holland. In all the years of exile, no one ever recorded Wilhelm expressing any remorse or sadness or empathy for the way his people had suffered, starved and died during the war.

The war permanently changed George. He never lost his worn, baggy-eyed look. 'That horrible and unnecessary war' haunted him and he found the post-war world a foreign, chilly place, one where the codes by which he had been brought up had less purchase. He hated the thought of losing Ireland, but hated the brutal methods the British were using to quell the resistance. More than ever he took refuge in the past and the familiar. He continued to wear the fashions of 1900; at court he insisted on the correct coats, jackets and hats that had been *de rigueur* in his father's time. As Lord Esher wrote towards the end of the war, with a trace of exasperation: 'Either the world has stopped or Buckingham palace remains unchanged. The same routine. A life made up of nothings – yet a busy scene. Constant telephone messages about trivialities.' Resistance to change seemed tied up with the rejection of 'gaiety' or liveliness, style or curiosity. 'The element of fun was notably absent,' Mary's biographer wrote. To the country, however, the fact that George was stuck in the past made him popular – that and his ordinariness. He seemed an anchor of stability, reliability and old-fashioned values. He was firmly identified with the 'spirit of hard work and personal sacrifice which had won us the war', as the young socialist thinker Harold Laski wrote in 1919, adding, 'The Monarchy, to put it bluntly, has been sold to the democracy as the symbol of itself.'

Even so, George never lost his sense of the fragility of his position, and after the war he and his advisers made a conscious decision to re-pitch the crown to the country. Stamfordham wrote that the monarchy must justify itself,

as a living power for good, with receptive faculties welcoming information affecting the interests and social well-being of all classes, and ready, not only to sympathize with those questions, but anxious to further their solution . . . if opportunities are seized, during His Majesty's visits to industrial centres, in conversation with the workmen, to show his interest in such problems as employers and employed will have to solve, these men will recognize in the Crown those characteristics – may I say "virtues"? – which I have ventured to enumerate above. In other words, as disinterested but engaged with the people, especially the working classes.

It was George who established the British monarchy as the domestic, decorative, ceremonial, slightly stolid creation it is today. He threw himself into the project, steeled himself to become more visible to his people, visited the poor industrial regions of South Wales, the Potteries and the North East, and cooperated with the press that he so disliked. Charities were set up, philanthropic projects adopted. As the children came of age they too were coopted into the family project – the smoothly handsome David was sent to meet the unemployed and tour the Commonwealth; the second son, Albert, went to visit factories and shipyards and lent his name to a camp where public-school and working-class boys could mix. Eventually, George put up a map at Buckingham Palace with flags marking family members' visits, and at the end of each year he would draw up a chart showing who had done the most. When the children got married, Labour MPs were invited to their weddings. In 1932 George made his first radio broadcast from a script written by Rudyard Kipling. He loathed doing it and the paper still shook as he read it out, but to his immense surprise his slow, deliberate delivery was a huge success.

His now habitual caution dictated that he no longer pushed or challenged the limits of his constitutional role, and he trained himself to steer away from partisan politics. Combined with the gradual political changes of the previous twenty years, it made him a far more marginal figure than his father or grandmother had been, and he found himself presiding over social and political changes of which he utterly disapproved. Women over thirty got the vote in 1918. In December 1923, after the Conservative Party lost its majority in the House of Commons, leaving the Labour Party as the next largest party, George didn't hesitate before asking its leader, Ramsay MacDonald, to form a government. His promptness arguably helped to make this political shift less seismic than it might have been, and anchored the Labour Party into Britain's political traditions. He decided to be graceful about the situation. 'I must say they all seem to be very intelligent and they take things very seriously,' he wrote in his diary. '. . . they ought to be given a chance.' Between themselves, however, he and Mary continued to refer to Keir Hardie as 'that beast', and he wondered in his diary what Victoria would have thought. As many of the surviving kings in Europe – in Italy, Serbia, Spain and Romania – fought social and constitutional reform, and even personally ushered in fascist dictatorships, George showed no interest whatsoever in the small English neo-fascist organizations of the 1920s which claimed they wanted to restore the monarchy.

There were some things he wouldn't do. The Labour Party wanted to re-establish links with the Soviet Union. George said he wouldn't shake hands with 'the murderers of his relatives'. 'The King was rather excited over Russia, and talked a lot of man-in-the-bus nonsense about Bolsheviks [*sic*], etc,' Ramsay MacDonald wrote. When a Russian delegation arrived to discuss trade and compensation for confiscated British property in 1924, George did not receive it. He pleaded illness when the new Russian ambassador came to present his credentials to Buckingham Palace in 1929, and was furious when he was forced to shake hands with the Soviet commissar for foreign affairs, Litvinov, in 1933.

As the 1930s darkened, George dreaded the thought of another war. He had no doubt that Hitler was a bad thing. Less than a year before his death, in 1935, the king met Lloyd George. The subject of Mussolini, who had just sent an Italian army into Ethiopia, was raised. 'HM fired up and broke out vehemently, "And I will not have another war, I will not. The last war was none of my doing, and if there is another one and we are threatened with being brought into it, I will go to Trafalgar Square and wave a red flag myself sooner than allow this country to be brought in."'

Wilhelm, meanwhile, flirted with the Nazis. Some of the party's senior figures hoped they might glean a useful blessing from the ex-kaiser, and Hermann Goering came to visit Wilhelm at Doorn twice in 1931, talking vaguely and flatteringly of restoration. Wilhelm fancied the Nazis might sponsor his return, and four of his sons became mixed up with the party in the early 1930s. Willy, the former crown prince, wrote articles supporting Hitler in the British press, and Friedrich Eitel and Oskar both appear to have briefly joined the Brownshirts in the 1930s. They drifted away, as it became obvious that the Nazis didn't plan on restoring the Hohenzollerns. Auwi, however, moved up the Nazi hierarchy until he fell out of favour with Hitler in 1942. Neither side had any respect for the other. Privately, Goering considered Wilhelm an 'incorrigible fool'; Hitler, who had no intention of restoring the monarchy, said he was 'pro-Jew'. Wilhelm seemed alternately jealous of and horrified by Hitler's success – and, of course, considered him common. He was chilled by the 'night of the long knives' – he'd talked about suspending the rule of law but had never actually done it.

In 1935 George's Silver Jubilee confirmed the success of the royal post-war project. He and Mary were obliged to appear on the balcony at Buckingham Palace every night for a week; they were cheered in streets in the East End of London which Lord Salisbury had once told Victoria were full only of socialists and the lowest Irish, and the Jubilee Trust set up by the crown to raise money for charity made a million pounds in a few weeks. George was seventy. He smoked too much and his heart was weak, and by the end of 1935 his health was seriously failing. Late on 20 January 1936, as he drifted in and out of consciousness, the court doctor administered a lethal injection of cocaine and morphine, the timing dictated, he later admitted, by 'the importance of the death receiving its first announcement in the morning papers rather than the less appropriate field of the evening journals'. It was a mark of just how attuned the British monarchy had become to the requirements of 'the people'.

Wilhelm took the opportunity to make contact with the English family once more. He wrote to Mary and sent his grandson Fritzi to the funeral.* Despite everything, he had been unable to rid himself of his attraction to all things English. He continued to read the English papers, drank English tea, guffawed over PG Wodehouse, and sprinkled his conversation with 'ripping', 'topping' and 'damned good fellow'. In his memoirs he wrote wistfully about his former popularity in England. Mary still had what one of her courtiers called 'a soft spot' for Wilhelm and felt sorry for him. She gave Fritzi a gold box from George's writing desk as a memento for Wilhelm. 'Deeply moved by the kind thought that prompted you to send me this gift as a souvenir,' he wrote to her, and signed himself her 'devoted cousin'.

After Munich, in 1938, he wrote again. 'I have not the slightest doubt that Mr N Chamberlain was inspired by Heaven and guided by God.' Then when Germany marched into Czechoslovakia twelve days later, he wrote, demonstrating the peculiar mix of understanding and complete misunderstanding that had dogged him his whole life: 'I am absolutely horrified at the late events at home! Pure bolshevism!' In November he denounced the Kristallnacht pogrom, even though he had become increasingly anti-Semitic himself. He told visitors that it would all go wrong for Hitler, just as it had for him. When war broke out in September 1939, he wrote to Mary of the 'political lunacy . . . May heaven preserve us from the worst!' But as the Germans ploughed across Europe, it began to seem to Wilhelm as if old scores were finally, gratifyingly, being settled. When they marched into Paris he cabled congratulations to Hitler – an act that would result in the confiscation of Haus Doorn after the war. He died of a heart attack on 4 June 1941 at eighty-one, the same age as his grandmother, proud that 'his' generals had conquered half of Europe. At the same time,

---

* Fritzi, Crown Prince Willy's third son, married into the Guinness family, and became a British citizen in 1947.

determined to deny Hitler a propaganda opportunity, he had left instructions that his body was not to be returned to Berlin. He was buried at Doorn, with no swastikas. Of his children, only two, Victoria and Oskar, both quietly living on their estates, would outlive him by more than ten years; the crown prince, Eitel Friedrich and Auwi, all of whom had become mixed up with German politics, would die broken, to some extent, by their experiences of the war.

In the early 1990s, Nicholas's remains and those of his family were disinterred in a copse outside Ekaterinburg and their identities confirmed by DNA testing. In 1998 their bodies were reinterred in the Peter and Paul Church in St Petersburg. Where they died in Ekaterinburg there is now a large white and gold onion-domed church 'on the blood' (on the site of their actual deaths). In 2000 the Russian Orthodox Church, buoyed by a great surge in Russian patriotism and a desire to wipe away seventy-two years of Soviet rule, declared the last tsar and his family saints.

Notes

Titles of most books quoted from in the text have been abbreviated in the Notes. Where the full title is not cited, it can be found in the Bibliography. The following abbreviations are used:

People

V – Vicky, Empress Frederick of Germany
QV – Queen Victoria
W – Wilhelm, Kaiser of Germany
G – George V
N – Nicholas, Tsar of Russia
A – Alix, Alexandra of Russia
E – Edward VII

Books

GP + number volume (e.g. *GP*, 24) – Johannes Lepsius, Albrecht Mendelssohn Bartholdy, Friedrich Thimme (eds.), *Die Grosse Politik der Europäischen Kabinette, 1871–1914: Sammlungen der Diplomatischen Akten des Auswartigen Amtes*, 40 vols., 1922–7 (German diplomatic papers)

LQV + series and volume numbers (e.g. *LQV*, 3.3) – *Letters of Queen Victoria*, ed. various (see Bibliography)

DDF + series and volume numbers (e.g. *DDF*, 2.9) – *Documents Diplomatiques Français*, 3 series (1871–1901, 16 vols.; 1901–11, 14 vols., 1911–14, 11 vols.) Paris, Imprimerie Nationale, 1929–59 (French diplomatic papers relating to First World War)

Introduction

xix **started and grew**: Nicolson, *King George*, p. 309

xx **declining popularity . . . bunch of idlers**: 13–21 July 1917, Gorlitz, *The Kaiser*, pp. 285–9

xi **what suffering our**: Radzinsky, p. 188

1: Wilhelm: an experiment in perfection (1859)

3 **horrible . . . electric shock**: Röhl, *Young William*, pp. 8–10

3 **legion of Fritzes**: Cecil, *Wilhelm*, 1, p. 13

4 **a fine fat child**: 25 Sept. 1860, RA VIC/MAIN/ QVJ

4 **Our mutual grandson**: QV to Augusta of Prussia, 30 Jan. 1859, Bolitho, p. 104

7 **The German stands**: Pakula, *An Uncommon*, pp. 72–3

9 **The "English"**: A. Ponsonby, p. 10

10 **It is very hard**: note, Princess Mary Louise, p. 56

10 **She loved England**: Walpurga, Lady Paget, p. 61

10 **the Dragon**: Pakula, *An Uncommon*, p. 103

11 **You cannot think**: V to QV, 23 July 1863, Fulford, *Dearest Mama*, p. 241

11 **That wretch**: V to QV, 19 July 1862, ibid., p. 96

11 **I enjoy**: E. F. Benson, p. 18

12 **porphyria**: for more on this controversial subject, see J. Röhl, M. Warren and D. Hunt, *Purple Secret: Genes, 'Madness' and the Royal Houses of Europe*, London, Bantam, 1998

12 **You do not know**: Vicky to QV, 14 May 1859, RA MAIN/Z/ 7/130

12 **The welfare**: St Aubyn, *Edward VII*, p. 22

12 **Still I dote**: V to QV, 19 Aug. 1868, Fulford, *Your Dear Letter*, p. 206

13 **his poor ugly**: V to QV, 7 Aug. 1872, Fulford, *Darling Child*, p. 57

13 **awfully backward**: V to QV, 23 May 1874, ibid., p. 139

13 **defective**: Cecil, *Wilhelm*, 1, p. 13

13 **I cannot tell you**: V to QV, 16 July 1859, RA VIC/MAIN/Z/ 2/28

13 **He gets so**: V to QV, 23 Jan. 1861, RA VIC/MAIN/Z/10/47

14 **He has been**: V to QV, 28 April 1863, RA VIC/MAIN/Z/15/15

14 **nervously tense**: Röhl, *Young William*, p. 43

14 **intolerable pain**: MacDonogh, p. 23

14 **Nice little**: V to QV, 8 Dec. 1861, RA VIC/MAIN/ Z/12/44

14 **Willy is a dear**: V to QV, 10 Dec. 1866, Fulford, *Your Dear Letter*, p. 112

14 **thumping his**: Röhl, *Young William*, p. 77

14 **We have a gt**: V to QV, 18 August, 1860, RA VIC/MAIN/Z/3/35

14 **a furious tantrum**: Louisa, Countess of Antrim, p. 12

15 **Of all the**: Balfour, *The Kaiser*, p. 75

15 **None of your**: Poultenay Bigelow in MacDonogh, p. 34

15 **that terrible**: V to QV, 27 Jan. 1865, Fulford, *Your Dear Letter*, p. 16

15 **There were lately**: W to QV, 20 May 1869, RA VIC/MAIN/Z/78/3

15 **organ grinder's**: V to QV, 16 Jan. 1869, Fulford, *Your Dear Letter*, p. 218

15 **she dressed him up**: V to QV, 25 May 1861, RA VIC/MAIN/Z/11/15

15 **He is so fond**: V to QV, 6 July 1864, RA VIC/MAIN/Z/16/60

15 **extolling England's**: Röhl, *Young William*, p. 267

16 **How entirely . . . earliest recollections**: Wilhelm II, *My Early Life*, pp. 66, 2

16 **Albert loved that**: QV to V, 27 Jan. 1862, Fulford, *Dearest Mama*, p. 45

16 **a cause of . . . interest either**: QV to V, 8 May 1872, Fulford, *Darling Child*, p. 40

16 **a duck . . . with it all**: RA QV Journal, 28 Feb. 1863

16 **She was a proper**: Wilhelm II, *Aus Meinem Leben*, p. 72

18 **To his eternal**: Wilhelm II, *My Early Life*, p. 46

18 **a certain receptiveness . . . it was patrotic**: Feb. 1871, Röhl, *Young William*, p. 178

18 **grow up in ignorance**: V to QV, 30 Jan. 1871, Fulford, *Darling Child*, p. 316

19 **perpetual renunciation**: see Röhl, *Young William*, p. 170

19 **the grim poetry**: Wilhelm II, *My Early Life*, p. 20

19 **He is very . . . his being**: V to Fritz, 22 Dec. 1870, Röhl, *Young William*, pp. 171–3, 199–200

20 **It is impossible**: F. Ponsonby, *Empress Frederick*, p. 168

20 **grasp hold . . . humiliation**: Kohut, *Wilhelm II*, p. 41

20 **false estimation**: Röhl, *Young William*, p. 199

20 **When nobody looked**: Wilhelm II, *Aus Meinem Leben*, p. 30

21 **The impossible was**: Wilhelm II, *My Early Life*, p. 18

21 **button her own boots**: see Marie, Grand Duchess, *Things*, p. 5

21 **poor boy's**: Röhl, *Young William*, p. 195

21 **what we will do**: Pakula, *An Uncommon*, p. 363

22 **He was the acknowledged**: Anonymous, *Recollections*, p. 79

22 **el dorado**: Röhl, *Young William*, p. 367

22 **Like all**: Balfour, p. 80

22 **complete failure**: Röhl, *Young William*, p. 227

22 **coldness**: Cecil, *Wilhelm*, 1, p. 35

22 **Before I entered**: Cecil in Röhl and Sombart (eds.), p. 98

23 **bitter disappointment**: Viereck, p. 38

23 **His military adjutant**: Cecil, *Wilhelm*, 1, p. 60

23 **A high spirited**: Pless, p. 93

24 **nothing short of**: Röhl, *The Kaiser*, p. 83

25 **I have known**: Röhl and Bellaigue, p. 188

25 **Liebchen**: Hull, p. 199

25 **Prince Wilhelm is**: Röhl, in Sombart and Röhl (eds.), p. 33

25 **The Prince is**: Waldersee 1, 26 Dec. 1884, p. 247

26 **self-willed**: 6 Jan. 1884, Holstein, 2, p. 46

26 **Willy and Henry**: V to QV, 18 Jan. 1882, RA VIC/MAIN/Z/36/5

26 **The visit was**: for Wilhelm's account see Wihelm II, *My Early Life*, pp. 245–7, 322

27 **a blunt soldier . . . a series of notes**: W to Tsar Alexander, 13 March 1885, Lee, 1, pp. 485–6; see also Röhl, *Young Wilhelm*, p. 441 (for the original French of these letters, quoted both in Sir S. Lee and J. Röhl, see Polovtsova, *Krasny Arkhiv*, 2, pp. 120–26)

27 **It would be such a**: 3 May 1885, Röhl, ibid., p. 446

27 **as interesting**: Tsar Alexander III to W, 7 [OS]/19 May 1885, Geheimes Staatsarchiv, HA Rep 53 J Lit R Nr 6

28 **obsequious**: Witte, pp. 401–3

28 **The tsar told him**: Röhl, *Young Wilhelm*, p. 582

29 **That very foolish**: QV to V, 13 Feb. 1885, Fulford, *Beloved Mama*, p. 183

29 **club the Battenburger**: Röhl, *Young William*, p. 517

29 **The dream of my**: 23 April 1887, F. Ponsonby, *Letters of*, p. 215

29 **He is a <u>card</u>**: V to QV, 26 March 1887, RA VIC/MAIN/Z/39/13

29 **He hates her**: Radolinsky to Holstein, 4 July 1887, Holstein, 3, p. 214

30 **to prove to**: Herbert von Bismarck 1891, quoted in Röhl, *Young William*, p. 688

30 **It was high time**: 1 June 1887, Eulenburg, 1, p. 225

30 **in deep grief**: Radolinsky to Holstein, 10 Nov. 1887, Holstein, 3, p. 227

31 **the slightest possible**: Kennan, p. 366

31 **HM did not . . . the opposite**: Röhl, *Young William*, p. 744

2: George: coming second (1865)

33 **Its empire of 9.5 million**: see Ferguson, *Empire*, p. 240; also source of other figures

34 **retired widow . . . insinuated itself**: Bagehot, *English Constitution*, OUP, 2001, pp. 38, 48

36 **the most unmilitary and richest**: for more on this see Lieven, *Aristocracy*

37 **the comfortable products**: Nabokov, p. 79

38 **I had no childhood . . . duties**: Plumptre, p. 24

38 **His intellect**: Weintraub, p. 274

39 **Oh! that boy**: Fulford, *Dearest Mama*, p. 152

39 **an air of**: Zola, *Nana*, ch. 5

39 **The special joke . . . admire this**: Bradford, pp. 21, 11

40 **Are you aware**: Weintraub, *Victoria*, p. 321

40 **The melancholy**: Battiscombe, p. 216

41 **He had**: Lord Greville quoted in Plumptre, pp. 17–18

41 **Very small**: Hibbert, p. 138

41 **I cannot admire**: Rose, p. 1

42 **Oh! If Bertie's**: QV to V, 13 Feb. 1864, Fulford, *Dearest Mama*, p. 45

42 **How I hate**: A to Dagmar, 10 Feb. 1864, Klausen, *Alexandra*, p. 88

43 **the rough, off-hand**: Marie, Queen of Romania, pp. 226–7

44 **He even wrote regular**: the letters are now in the Russian archives at GARF

45 **trash**: F. Ponsonby, *My Recollections*, p. 134

45 **They are dear**: QV to V, 2 June 1874, Fulford, *Darling Child*, p. 140

45 **The Princess said . . . them at all**: Gore, pp. 14, 17 n. 1

46 **most wretched**: QV to V, 27 Jan. 1869, Fulford, *Your Dear Letter*, p. 222

46 **as a small boy**: Newnes, p. 8

46 **a jolly . . . the cleverest**: Gore, p. 14

46 **fairy-like**: QV to V, 10 Feb. 1869, Fulford, *Your Dear Letter*, p. 223

46 **The house of**: Owen Morshead in Lees-Milne, p. 230

46 **But I thought**: quoted in Bradford, p. 12

46 **Alexandra's deafness**: Alexander Mikhailovich, p. 113

47 **to maturity and**: Gore, p. 9

47 **I shall . . . little face**: Battiscombe, p. 143

47 **My own Darling**: Gore, p. 26

47 **bullied the whole**: Lees-Milne, p. 224

47 **just a glorified**: Vorres, p. 53

47 **Mama**: Battiscombe, p. 242

48 **constantly he**: Gore, p. 74

48 **with a softening**: Rose, p. 53

48 **be his slave**: Bradford, p. 18

48 **stilted and**: Gore, p. 177

48 **lovable**: F. Ponsonby, *My Recollections*, p. 275

48 **rather afraid of**: Cook, *Prince Eddy*, p. 109

48 **if children**: Battiscombe, p. 121

49 **a letter from**: see Magnus, p. 172

49 **abnormally dormant**: Rose, p 8

49 **some affliction of**: Lees-Milne, p. 231

49 **fretfulness**: Rose, p. 6

49 **I am so sorry**: W to QV, 20 May 1869, RA VIC/MAIN/Z/78/3

49 **admitting me into**: W to QV, 28 Jan. 1877 RA VIC/MAIN/Z/64/104

50 **Be very punctual**: QV to G, 1 June 1873, Nicolson, *George V*, p. 10

50 **Good boys**: Nicolson, *George V*, p. 14

50 **Prince Albert Victor requires**: ibid., pp. 12–13

50 **a very rough**: Gore, p.12

51 **I could never**: St Aubyn, p. 243

51 **Is there not**: Lord Derby to Disraeli, quoted in Weintraub, p. 411

51 **It never did**: Nicolson, *George V*, p. 15

52 **Victoria says**: Rose, p. 8

52 **evil associations**: Nicolson, *George V*, p. 17

53 **As we sang**: G to Alexandra, 19 Sept., 1880, Gore, p. 41

53 **he tentatively voiced**: see Magnus, p. 197

53 **I miss you**: G to Alexandra, Oct. 1886, Nicolson, *George V*, p. 38

53 **the king had**: Nicolson, *Diaries*, p. 167

53 **What a fearless**: 16 Feb. 1877, *LQV*, 2.2, p. 521

54 **withering**: Marie of Romania 2, p. 30

54 **deficient in even**: Rose, p. 15

54 **had not been his**: Marie of Romania, 2, p. 30

54 **one of the dullest**: Edward, Duke of Windsor, *A King's Story*, p. 37

54 **so laborious**: Lees-Milne, p. 229

54 **wrinkled brow**: Marie of Romania 2, p. 30

55 **My word**: Lees-Milne, p. 237

55 **Our greatest**: E to QV, 2 May 1880, Nicolson, *George V*, p. 23

55 **strictly in accord**: Marie, Grand Duchess of Russia, *Things*, p. 3

56 **How much I miss . . . in the dirt**: Nicolson, *George V*, p. 35

56 **it is the greatest**: Battiscombe, p. 173

56 **a ripper**: Lees-Milne, p. 230

57 **The success**: J. Morris, 2, p. 426

57 **Sailors didn't**: Gore, p. 148

57 **was a most**: 21 June 1887, RA GV/PRIV/GVD

57 **She was an**: 7 May 1884, Holstein, 2, p. 1391

58 **celebrated anniversary**: Nicholas's diary, 9 [OS]/21 June 1887, GARF 601/1/221(1)

58 **a large family**: 22 June 1887, *LQV*, 3.1, p. 330

58 **Uncle Fritz . . . Mossy**: 20–26 June 1887, RA GV/GVD/PRIV

3: Nicholas: a diamond-studded ivory tower (1868)

59 **Less than 20 per cent**: see Charques, p. 5

61 **Anton Chekhov remembered**: Bartlett, p. 27

62 **built like a**: Lincoln, p. 447

62 **He tried to be**: Mossolov, p. 4

63 **to read books**: Vorres, p. 39

63 **who came out**: Klausen, *Dagmar*

63 **What joy it was**: Bokhanov, p. 18

64 **Servants, pets**: Vorres, p. 56

65 **girlish . . . simple man**: Lieven, *Nicholas*, pp. 30–32

65 **gave the impression**: quoted in Massie, *Nicholas*, p. 10

65 **You are**: Lieven, *Nicholas*, p. 30

65 **of dissimulation**: Mossolov, p. 6

65 **I hope my**: M to N, 23 April 1891, Bing, pp. 57–8

65 **My mother just**: Vorres, p. 59

66 **at 15,000**: see ibid., p. 25

66 **Dickens in a**: Duke of Windsor, *A King's*, p. 52

67 **exactly 50 minutes**: Mossolov, pp. 288–9

67 **immorally good**: Vorres, p. 37

68 **That old dotard**: Mossolov, p. 6

68 **simple-minded . . . data required**: Alexander Mikhailovich, pp. 165–6

69 **Aristocrats are born**: Lieven, *Nicholas*, p. 35

69 **I had rarely**: Witte, p. 179

69 **Friendly, generous and humble . . . petty officialdom**: Vorres, pp. 38, 62

70 **they kept me purposely**: Marie, Grand Duchess of Russia, *Things*, p. 3

71 **His face was**: quoted in M. Buchanan, p. 5

71 **We shall preside**: Maylunas, p. 7

71 **Christ-killers**: Lincoln, p. 591
72 **new proud, imperial**: Alexander Mikhailovich, p. 71
72 **noble outstanding**: Witte, p. 37
72 **We have just two**: Alexander Mikhailovich, p. 67
74 **and the monstrous**: ibid., p. 71
74 **the Teutons and the Slavs**: see Laqueur, p. 46
74 **Prussian barbarians**: Klausen, *Dagmar*, pp. 29–30
75 **Cold, disgusting**: Van der Kiste and Hall, p. 11
75 **naturalists**: Vorres, p. 32
75 **an explosion in**: Alexander Mikhailovich, p. 57
75 **prison**: Van der Kiste and Hall, p. 15
75 **at glorious . . . an education**: Vorres, pp. 53, 52
75 **I fear that your**: A to Minny, 7 July 1876, quoted in Van der Kiste and Hall, p. 3
76 **whom we all disliked**: Vorres, p. 52
76 **dear old Fatty**: G to Alexander III, Christmas 1891, GARF 677/ 1/753
76 **close friends . . . Ottoman**: Vorres, p. 54
76 **Motherdear**: for examples for Nicholas see Maylunas, p. 77
76 **I am in love**: Bokhanov, p. 28
78 **It is an axiom**: Donald Mackenzie Wallace, memo on Russia foreign policy, 1903, RA VIC/MAIN/W/44/15c
80 **Yes, thought I**: Chekhov to Suvorin, 9 Dec. 1890, A. Chekhov, *Letters*, ed. Yarmolinsky, Cape, 1997, p. 169
80 **The Whispering Gallery**: Vorres, p. 50
80 **Those detestable**: Weintraub, *Victoria*, p. 425
80 **wicked, villainous**: St Aubyn, p. 293
80 **horrible, deceitful . . . towards war**: Weintraub, *Victoria*, pp. 425, 428
80 **He said she was . . . interfering**: Vorres, pp. 54, 49
80 **Visiting German**: see H. von Bismarck, 25 July 1888, GP 6, p. 328
80 **I have formed**: Weintraub, *Victoria*, p. 291
81 **he respected . . . well-polished leather**: Vorres, pp. 237, 52
81 **I can hardly . . . value whatsoever**: E to Gladstone, 10 April 1885, Magnus, p. 191
82 **Bismarck's son Herbert**: Röhl, *Young William*, p. 742
82 **It's possible that**: see Lee, 1, p. 682

82 **I could only**: Nicholas, p. 12

83 **whom he venerated**: Mossolov, p. 10

83 **dominating personality**: Duff, p. 250

83 **deprived of**: Gilliard, pp. 86–7

84 **I miss you terribly**: Minny to N, 21 July 1887, Bing, p. 32

84 **One has to be**: N to Minny, 25 June 1887, ibid., p. 34

4: Wilhelm emperor (1888–90)

87 **People in**: V to QV, 16 March 1888, RA VIC/MAIN/Z/41/27

87 **hated him more**: Röhl, *Young Wilhelm*, p. 804

87 **Good heavens**: Caprivi quoted 28 June 1887, Holstein, 2, p. 346

87 **aspiring toadies . . . knew everything**: Röhl, *Young Wilhelm*, p. 764

88 **afraid that, if**: Salisbury to QV, 21 April 1888, *LQV*, 3.1, pp. 397–8

88 **delighted**: Malet to Salisbury, 28 April 1888, RA VIC/MAIN/I/56/45

88 **extraordinarily gracious**: Holstein, 2, p. 373

88 **If you throw him**: V, 25 April 1888, RA VIC/MAIN/Z/500/2

88 **bonbon**: F. Ponsonby, *Letters*, p. 304

89 **Poor dear Uncle**: 15 June 1888, RA GV/PRIV/GVD

89 **as though**: E. Ludwig, p. 54

89 **follow the same**: F. Ponsonby, *Letters*, p. 322

90 **Hail to the**: Cecil, *Wilhelm*, 1, p. 133

90 **cried and sobbed**: St Aubyn, p. 273

90 **instead of**: Nicolson, p. 40

90 **unfit to**: F. Ponsonby, *Letters*, p. 317

90 **that in fact**: Malet to Salisbury, 24 June 1888, RA VIC/Z/MAIN/68/131

90 **more . . . than was**: H. Ponsonby, quoted in Balfour, *The Kaiser*, p. 110

90 **Edward sent a written**: see E to Christian of Schleswig-Holstein, 3 April 1889, *LQV* 3.1, p. 488

91 **The Queen is**: QV to Ponsonby, 28 June 1888, *LQV*, 3.1, p. 421

91 **I do not like**: Roberts, p. 484

91 **leaning towards**: QV, Journal, 27 June 1888, *LQV*, 3.1, p. 421

92 **insane passion**: Salisbury, *DNB*

92 **Until my own mind**: Roberts, p. 511

92 **Whatever happens**: Balfour, *Britain and*, p. 239

92 **believed they**: Frances, Countess of Warwick, *Afterthoughts*, p. 24

93 **the national will**: Roberts, p. 316

93 **very unmanageable**: Cecil, *Wilhelm*, 1, p. 120

93 **Let me also**: QV to W, 3 July 1888, *LQV*, 3.1, p. 423

93 **I am doing**: W to QV, 6 July 1888, RA VIC/MAIN/I/56/84

93 **that fat, dumpy**: Pakula, *An Uncommon*, p. 500

93 **which will**: W to QV, 6 July 1888, RA VIC/MAIN/I/56/84

94 **gave way to . . . best imaginable**: Wilhelm II, *My Memoirs*, p. 26

94 **How sickening**: QV to E, 24 July 1888, *LQV*, 3.1, p. 433

94 **Trust that we shall**: QV to Salisbury, 7 July 1888, ibid., p. 429

94 **those people . . . single stone**: Benson, p. 73

95 **the Emperor . . . unfounded**: Malet to Salisbury, 14 July 1888, RA VIC/MAIN/I/56/86

97 **magic tie uniting**: Viereck, p. 74

97 **friendly, neighbourly**: Herbert von Bismarck to W, 3 July 1888, *GP*, 6, p. 314

97 **frank, guileless**: Pourtalès to Holstein, 25 July 1888, Holstein, 3, p. 293

97 **enchantingly natural**: Schweinitz to Bismarck, 25 July 1888, *GP*, 6, p. 334

98 **some pointedly**: H. von Bismarck, 25 July 1888, *GP*, 6, p. 328

98 **Rarely before**: Schweinitz to Bismarck, 25 July 1888, *GP*, 6, p. 334

98 **The Russians were**: Pourtalès to Holstein, 25 July 1888, Holstein 3, p. 290

98 **still not very close**: ibid., p. 335

98 **no other royals**: Cowles, *Edward VII*, p. 89

98 **Nothing could have been**: E to Christian of Schleswig-Holstein, 3 April 1889, *LQV*, 3.1, p. 488; see also Walpurga Paget, *Embassies*, 1, p. 460

99 **to his company**: E to QV, *LQV*, 3.1, p. 488

99 **that he had claimed**: Salisbury to QV, 13 Oct. 1888, *LQV*, 3.1, pp. 438–40

100 **The Germans all say**: Paget, *Embassies*, 1, p. 461

100 **As regarding**: QV to Salisbury, 15 Oct. 1888, *LQV*, 3.1, pp. 440–41

100 **discussions of this kind**: *LQV*, 3.1, pp. 440–41

100 **From the hints**: Salisbury to QV, 15 Oct. 1888, *LQV*, 3.1, p. 442

101 **It would be**: QV to Salisbury, 24 Oct. 1888, RA VIC/MAIN/I/56/95

101 **extreme untrustworthiness . . . brutal**: Salisbury to QV, 25 Dec. 1888, Roberts, p. 524

102 **false and intriguing**: W to Tsar Alexander, 13 March 1885, Lee, 1, pp. 485–6

102 **round fat King Edward**: Kohut, *Wilhelm II*, p. 203

103 **knew about his letters**: see Lee, 1, p. 682

103 **My illustrious . . . 19th century**: St Aubyn, pp. 278–9

103 **Oh he is a**: A to G, 17 Oct. 1888, Rose, p. 164

103 **great affection and**: Malet to QV, 29 March 1889, *LQV*, 3.1, p. 484

104 **as friendly**: Roberts, p. 486

104 **everything English**: H. von Bismarck, 1891, quoted in Röhl, *Young Wilhelm*, p. 688

104 **William must not**: QV to E, 7 Feb. 1889, *LQV*, 3.1, p. 467

104 **That good**: Malet to QV, 30 March 1889, RA VIC/MAIN/I/57/20

104 **The assertion**: Christian of Schleswig-Holstein to E, 8 April 1889, *LQV*, 3.1, p. 491

104 **he could not do**: Christian of Schleswig-Holstein to E, 13 April 1889, *LQV*, 3.1, p. 493, n. 1

105 **Fancy wearing**: W to Malet, 14 June 1889, *LQV*, 3.1, p. 504

105 **Her Majesty wrote**: Corti, p. 323

105 **sacrificed**: Knollys to Christian of Schleswig-Holstein, 8 June 1889, *LQV*, 3.1, p. 501

106 **He must have been**: G to Alexandra, 2 Oct. 1888, RA GV/PRIV/AA/36/21

106 **she had assured**: QV to V., 17 July 1889, Ramm, p. 91

106 **kissed me affectionately . . . their legs**: QV, Journal, 2 Aug. 1889, *LQV*, 3.1, pp. 521–2

107 **no Sovereign**: V to QV, 27 Sept. 1889, F. Ponsonby, *Letters*, pp. 389–90

107 **It was not in the least**: QV to V, 14 Aug. 1889, Ramm, p. 90

107 **like a child . . . he said**: Röhl and de Bellaigue, pp. 102–3

107 **It really gave**: W to QV, 17 Aug. 1889, RA VIC/MAIN/I/57/53

107 **a great treat**: W to QV, 30 Oct. 1889, RA VIC/MAIN/I/57/67

108 **The French look**: W to QV, 22 Dec. 1889, RA VIC/MAIN/I/57/75

108 **humble suggestions**: W to QV, 6 Feb. 1891, RA VIC/MAIN/E/56/40

108 **would not be**: Henry Ponsonby to QV, 25 Feb. 1891, RA VIC/MAIN/E/56/41

109 **The Emperor's attitude**: Salisbury to QV, 24 Oct. 1889, RA VIC/I/MAIN/57/66

109 **detestable . . . the worst**: Tuchman, p. 288

110 **the tsar had shown no**: see Pourtalès to Holstein, 22 Feb. 1890, Holstein, 3, p. 327

110 **pipsqueak . . . worship him**: Kennan, p. 398

111 **If Bismarck won't**: Holstein, 1, p. 250

111 **another short . . . the visit**: Waldersee, 2, pp. 71–2

112 **I certainly have**: Cecil, *Wilhelm*, 1, p. 132

112 **A good heart**: Pakula, *An Uncommon*, p. 519

112 **spent the time talking**: N to Minny, 20 Oct. 1889, Bing, p. 39

112 **brought 67**: 26 Oct. 1889, RA GV/PRN/GVD

112 **Another fine**: Mallet, p. 52

113 **Everyone laid**: Waldersee, 2, p. 73

113 **mad, an untrustworthy . . . I am mad**: ibid., pp. 115–16

113 **like a sovereign . . . this country**: Lee, 1, p. 622

114 **So my Georgie boy**: Alexandra to G, 11 April 1890, Nicolson, *King George*, p. 42

114 **That's a brave**: Airlie, p. 119

114 **infallibly have died**: W to QV, 27 March 1890, RA VIC/MAIN/I/58/32

114 **We talked**: 23 March 1890, RA GV/PRIV/GVD

114 **a guarantee**: Malet to Salisbury, 12 Feb. 1890, *LQV*, 3.1, pp. 565–6

114 **the most conspicuous**: *Daily Chronicle*, 4 July 1891

115 **absolute confidence**: Rich, 1, p. 307

115 **It is a curious**: Salisbury to QV, 7 April 1890, *LQV*, 3.1, p. 591

115 **the circumstances were so**: Sir Schomberg Mcdonnell to G, 26 Oct. 1914, RA PS/PSO/GV/M/688a/1

5: Young men in love (1891–4)

116 **a jolly crowd**: Alexander Mikhailovich, p. 16

116 **late-morning lie-ins**: see 1890 entries, Nicholas II

116 **cures for VD**: see De Jonge, p. 101

117 **obsessed**: Zedlitz-Trützschler, p. 95

117 **differentiate a**: King, p. 246

117 **Uniforms, no**: Bedford, p. 24

118 **It is very interesting**: St Aubyn, p. 104

118 **The absence of public**: Charques, p. 18

119 **the unbearableness**: Nicholas II, p. 36

120 **I am simply**: Nicholas II, 15 Dec. 1891, GARF 601/1/227

120 **He would not even have**: Vorres, p. 67

120 **He's nothing more**: Nicholas II, p. 45

120 **A great financial**: W to QV, 8 Dec. 1891, RA VIC/MAIN/I 59/53

121 **an almost fanatical . . . was British**: Edward, Duke of Windsor, *A King's*, p. 27

122 **were often fearfully**: J. Morris, 2, p. 425

122 **broken all the Ten**: St Aubyn, p. 170

123 **The only one**: W to QV, 18 Jan. 1892, RA VIC/MAIN/Z/ 93/91

123 **The poor boy**: Nicholas II, 2 Jan. 1892, p. 39

123 **No two brothers . . . with him**: Nicolson, *King George*, p. 46

124 **Hate the whole**: 27 July 1892, RA GV/PRIV/GVD

124 **George had fallen**: see Pakula, *The Last*, pp. 53–8

124 **Have you seen**: QV to G, 6 April 1892, quoted in Rose, p. 25

125 **mésalliance!!!**: V to QV, 26 Nov. 1891, RA VIC/MAIN/Z/ 51/49

125 **made it unlikely**: Pope-Hennessy, *Queen Mary*, p. 186

125 **ugly, unhealthy**: Balfour to Salisbury, quote in Cook, *Prince Eddy*, pp. 226–7

125 **Beloved Chum**: see Pakula, *The Last*, pp. 53–8

126 **George is such . . . delight**: Pope-Hennessy, *Queen Mary*, p. 247

126 **Copenhagen**: see *Royal Family in Denmark* albums, Royal Collection, Windsor

126 **It certainly is**: G to Oliver Montagu, 28 Sept. 1892, Gore, p. 106

126 **William was most kind**: G to QV, 2 Nov. 1892, RA VIC/MAIN/476/21

126 **abundantly satisfied**: Rose, p. 27

126 **Quite pleased**: Journal, 4 May 1893, *LQV*, 3.2, p. 253

126 **He is a nice**: 21 June 1893, Wilfred Scawen Blunt, *Secret Memoirs XVI*, Fitzwilliam Museum, Cambridge

127 **It is sad to**: Nicolson, p. 50

127 **I am very . . . shy and cold**: Pope-Hennessy, *Queen Mary*, pp. 262–3

128 **romps**: Nicholas's diary, 1 June [OS]/13 1884, GARF 601/1

128 **My dream**: ibid., 21 Dec. 1891 [OS]/2 Jan. 1892, ibid.

128 **the best part . . . Santa Claus**: Buxhoeveden, pp. 12, 8

128 **the handsomest**: Fulford, *Beloved Mama*, p. 24

129 **completely from the rest . . . of her life**: Buxhoeveden, p. 15

129 **There was a curious . . . at times**: Lutyens, pp. 66–8

129 **bent on securing**: March 1888, quoted in Cook, *Prince Eddy*, p. 142

129 **doesn't look**: Epton, p. 196

130 **My father thought**: Vorres, p. 54

130 **nothing came of it**: see Röhl and de Bellaigue, pp. 495–6

130 **Niki made an**: W to QV, 28 Jan. 1893, *LQV*, 3.2, p. 215

131 **I am still under**: 25 Jan. 1893, GARF 601/1/229

131 **I should so**: G to QV, 4 June 1893, RA VIC/MAIN/Z/476/113

131 **barbaric habits**: N to G, March 1907, RA W51 59/29

132 **Uncle Bertie is in**: N to Minny, 24 June [OS]/6 July 1893, Bing, p. 71

132 **looks like a jail**: Nicholas's diary, 21 June [OS]/3 July 1893, GARF 601/1/230

132 **Our hostess**: Nicholas's diary, 25 June [OS]/7 July 1893, ibid.

132 **what a pity**: Nicholas's diary, 26 June [OS]/8 July 1893, ibid.

132 **I am delighted**: Bing, p. 71

132 **Everyone finds**: Nicholas's diary, 20 June [OS]/2 July 1893, GARF 601/1/230

132 **to no end of**: 5 July 1893, *LQV*, 3.2, p. 273

133 **the top of the**: 1 July 1893, RA VIC/MAIN/QVJ

133 **undiplomatic bellowing**: Weintraub, *Victoria*, p. 181

133 **Nicky as he is . . . unaffected**: 1 July 1893, RA VIC/MAIN/QVJ

133 **a big round ball**: Nicholas's diary, 19 June [OS]/1 July 1893, GARF 601/1 230

133 **radiant . . . sisters also**: Bing, p. 72

133 **the last time alone**: 2 July 1893, RA/GV/PRIV/GVD

134 **Fancy me**: Pope-Hennessy, *Queen Mary*, p. 286

134 **as I would**: Alix to Xenia, Maylunas, p. 45

134 **Even my dear Mama**: 19 April 1894, Lutyens, p. 65

134 **I was in a state . . . with Alix**: N to Minny, 10 April 1894, Bing, p. 75

135 **the part of cupid . . . for Alix**: Viereck, p. 184

135 **We were left alone**: Bing, p. 76

135 **quite thunderstruck . . . end of June**: Journal, *LQV*, 3.2, p. 395

135 **Granny**: Nicholas II, p. 54

135 **As she has**: QV to N, 10 [OS]/22 April 1894, Maylunas, p. 59

136 **Please do not**: A to QV, ibid., p. 57

136 **I am quite**: G to N, 21 April 1894, GARF 601/1/1219

136 **My dearest old**: N to G, 14 [OS]/26 April 1894, RA GV/PRIV/AA 43/35

136 **paradisiacal happiness**: Nicholas II, p. 81

136 **in a certain place**: Nicholas's diary, 14 [OS]/26 June 1894, GARF 601/1/232

137 **walked in bare . . . ever say**: 7 July 1894, Nicholas II, pp. 77–8

137 **is most affectionate**: 11 July 1894, *LQV*, 3.2, p. 413

137 **She is very**: A to N, 10 [OS]/22 April 1894, Maylunas, p. 60

137 **good Granny's . . . how ghastly!**: Nicholas II, pp. 81, 78

137 **delicate-looking**: Morrow, p. 49

137 **very bashful . . . than otherwise**: Eckhardstein, p. 76

137 **gaping more at us**: N to A, 16 June 1894, Maylunas, p. 76

138 **Most of them**: N to Minny, 27 June 1894, Bing, p. 84

139 **Because a man**: Lee, 1, p. 399

139 **Either the brute**: Cowles, p. 159

139 **mortally ill**: W to QV, 24 Aug. 1894, *LQV*, 3.2, p. 423

139 **Lord, Lord**: 20 Oct. [OS]/2 Nov. 1894, Nicholas II, p. 107

140 **harassed**: Vorres, p. 68

140 **What am I to do?**: Alexander Mikhailovich, p. 168

140 **He was in despair . . . Prince of Wales**: Vorres, p. 67

140 **I cannot tell you**: N to QV, 30 Oct. 1894, Maylunas, p. 102

140 **I wonder what**: Vorres, p. 68

141 **It would interest me**: Lee, 1, pp. 268–9

141 **Popular opinion in**: 21 June 1894, RA VIC/MAIN/H/46/68

142 **That old, tiresome**: St Aubyn, p. 299

142 **dear Papa**: 22 Oct. [OS]/4 Nov. 1894, Nicholas II, p. 110

142 **barbarous and**: Ellis to QV, 23 Nov. 1894, RA VIC/Z/MAIN/ 499/145

142 **opportunity to see**: Magnus, p. 246

142 **most fatiguing for**: Lascelles to QV, 14 Nov. 1894, RA VIC/ MAIN/Z/499/120

142 **the crowd was so**: Lascelles to QV, 19 Nov. 1894, RA VIC/ MAIN/Z/499/134

142 **the smell was**: Magnus, p. 248

142 **Tomorrow morning**: QV to V, 25 Nov. 1894, Ramm, p. 173

142 **He had come by**: 1 Nov. 1894, RA/GV/PRIV/GVD

143 **Dear Alicky**: G to QV, 28 Nov. 1894, RA VIC/MAIN/Z/ 274/52

143 **dreadfully pale**: Charlotte Knollys, quoted in St Aubyn, p. 298

143 **somebody else's**: King, p. 345

143 **Our marriage**: Massie, *Nicholas*, p. 44

143 **Even at this supreme**: Marie, Queen of Romania, p. 68

143 **Everything had the appearance**: Ellis to QV, 26 Nov. 1894, RA VIC/Z/MAIN/274/43

143 **As they drove**: Vorres, p. 76

144 **This is the first**: G to QV, 28 Nov. 1894, RA VIC/MAIN/ 274/52

144 **greatly embarrassed**: Gore, p. 121

144 **The Duke of York**: Ellis to Knollys, St Aubyn, p. 298

144 **It is impossible**: Ellis to Bigge, 1 Nov. 1894, RA VIC/MAIN/ Z/499/68

144 **a liberality**: *Daily Telegraph*, 26 Nov. 1894

144 **another young Emperor**: Ellis to QV, RA VIC/MAIN/Z/ 499/145
144 **The character and personality**: Lee, 1, p. 692
145 **Our relations with**: Neilson, p. 147
145 **unsurpassed tact**: *The Times*, 6 Dec. 1894
145 **It is scarcely**: *The Standard*, 3 Dec. 1894
145 **I can't tell you**: G to N, 25 Dec. 1894, GARF 601/1/1219

6: Wilhelm Anglophile (1891–5)

146 **his own Minister ... out the orders**: Paget, *Embassies*, 1, p. 496
147 **an instrument of**: quoted in Röhl and de Bellaigue, p. 276
147 **I believe I**: Clark, *Wilhelm II*, p. 62
148 **at least ... a man**: *Contemporary Review*, April 1892, p. 458
148 **succeeded from childhood**: MacDonagh, p. 261
149 **that her sons**: Epkenhans, p. 27
149 **The importance**: *Standard*, 16 July 1891
149 **He will be able**: *The Times*, 2 July 1891
149 **the old jackboot**: *Justice*, 30 June 1888
149 **I have always felt**: *Daily Telegraph*, 10 July 1891
150 **He is rather short**: Morley, 1, p. 272
150 **extraordinary energy**: Arthur Balfour to Lady Elcho, quoted in K. Young, p. 121
150 **They are all**: 21 April 1891, Mallet, p. 52
151 **that dreadful tyrant**: Marie to Charlotte, *c.* July 1890, quoted in Röhl and de Bellaigue, p. 641
151 **How I love**: Kohut, *Wilhelm II*, p. 202
151 **She was, she wrote**: Journal, 4 July 1891, *LQV*, 3.2, p. 49
152 **stereotyped graciousness**: Marie of Romania, p. 227
152 **stiffness, rudeness**: Ernst zu Hohenlohe-Langenburg, quoted in Röhl and de Bellaigue, p. 362
152 **she was not brought up**: Bülow, 1
152 **I shall count**: W to QV, 28 Jan. 1893, *LQV*, 3.2, p. 215
152 **Even as a child**: Duke of Windsor, *A King's*, p. 15
152 **it was a great ... bushes**: F. Ponsonby, *My Recollections*, p. 13

153 **unrestrained conversation**: Admiral Hollman, quoted in Hull, p. 204

153 **The old and strong**: W to QV, 20 July 1891, RA VIC/MAIN/ T/59/42

154 **brutal colonists**: see Roberts, p. 486

154 **revered by all**: W to QV, 22 May 1892, RA VIC/MAIN/I/ 59/80

154 **to visit you quite**: W to QV, 15 March 1892, *LQV*, 3.2, p. 106

154 **nervous breakdown**: Malet to H. Ponsonby, 4 April 1892, *LQV*, 3.2, p. 110

154 **be mad**: 22 Dec. 1891, Waldersee, 2, p. 228

154 **too much overworked**: W to QV, 15 March 1892, *LQV*, 3.2, p. 10

155 **Distractions**: 4 Oct. 1890, Waldersee, 2, p. 153

155 **continually talking**: Hohenlohe, *Denkwürdigkeiten*, 2, p. 430

155 **It is unendurable**: MacDonagh, p. 220

156 **never thinks of doing**: 17 July 1892, Röhl, *Germany Without*, p. 102

156 **in a state of**: Topham, pp. 125–6

157 **Wilhelm II wants**: quoted in Bülow, 1, p. 3

158 **The hope of a**: Pan-German League newspaper advert, 24 June 1890

158 **shoot down . . . crush**: Balfour, *The Kaiser*, p. 159

158 **appointed by an authority**: Röhl and de Bellaigue, p. 275

159 **The World**: Waldersee, 2, 16 March 1892, p. 235

159 **Altogether beg**: QV to V, 22 Sept. 1891, ed. Ramm, p. 132

160 **almost always was**: Kohut, *Wilhelm II*, p. 234

160 **it would be**: Salisbury to QV, 14 April 1892, *LQV*, 3.2, p. 110

160 **No no I really**: A. Ponsonby, p. 297

160 **The Queen never**: QV to H. Ponsonby, 15 June 1892, RA VIC/ MAIN/I/59/86

160 **hint that these**: H. Ponsonby to Malet, 24 June 1892, *LQV*, 3.2, p. 125

160 **Not in the least**: E to G, 5 Aug. 1892, Magnus, p. 240

160 **immensely**: St Aubyn, p. 284

162 **one quarter of the world's**: see Ferguson, *Empire*, p. 240

162 **We assist England**: Kennedy, *The Rise*, p. 213

164 **expressed satisfaction**: Grey, *25 Years*, p. 15

164 **If one is not . . . soothe him**: Haller, 1, pp. 142–3

164 **continuously fighting**: Hull, p. 17

165 **the fat unwieldy**: Haller, 1, pp. 144–6

165 **rubber Mackintoshes**: MacDonagh, p. 180

165 **a capable . . . some damage**: Haller, 1, pp. 144–6

165 **Much startled and**: 2 Aug. 1893, RA VIC/MAIN/QVJ

166 **as Wilhelm apologized**: Eckhardstein, p. 55

166 **new about-turn**: Röhl and de Bellaigue, p. 486

166 **almost incomprehensible**: Rich, p. 365

167 **demonstrate the disadvantages**: ibid., p. 370

167 **turtle doves**: Eckhardstein, *Lebeserinnerungen und Politische Denk-würdigkeiten II*, Leipzig 1919–20, p. 161

167 **Splendid, corresponds**: Wilhelm on Hatzfeldt to Caprivi, *GP*, 8, p. 439

167 **We must have**: Athlone, p. 147

167 **Never you mind**: Heinrich to G, 17 May 1900, RA GV/PRIV/AA/43/95

168 **shameless**: Röhl and de Bellaigue, p. 492

168 **This fishing**: Benson, p. 109

168 **thoroughly insufferable**: Kennedy, *The Rise*, p. 215

168 **overwhelmed**: W to QV, 24 April 1894, *LQV*, 3.2, p. 396

168 **He told the British**: Malet to QV, June 1894, RA VIC/MAIN/I 60/77

168 **graciously acknowledged**: *Daily Telegraph*, 7 Aug. 1894

169 **angry complaints**: see Gosselin to FO, 5 Nov. 1894, RA VIC/MAIN/I/60/100

169 **The next time England**: Nov. 1894, Kimberley, RA VIC/I/MAIN/60/102

169 **The abrupt**: Grey, p. 10

169 **It is difficult**: Craig, p. 245

170 **England would only be**: 12 Oct. 1896, Holstein to Radolin, Holstein, 3, p. 548

170 **I cannot deny**: 3 May 1895, Eulenburg to Holstein, ibid., pp. 511–12

170 **The rudeness of**: 4 Dec. 1895, Lascelles, PRO FO 800/17 F

171 **the sudden impulse**: Monson to FO, 8 Nov. 1894, RA VIC/MAIN/I/60/101

171 **In view of the**: Röhl, *Germany Without*, p. 73

171 **Hobbesian war**: Steinberg, 'The Kaiser', p. 7

171 **The army**: Cecil, *Wilhelm*, 1, p. 124

172 **lead three**: Afflerbach, p. 202

173 **Boss of**: St Aubyn, p. 284

174 **taken this as a slight**: 10 June 1895, Hohenlohe, p. 76

174 **Fat old Wales**: Kiderlen Wächter to Holstein, 7 Aug. 1895, Holstein, 3, p. 537

174 **the Old Peacock**: Eckhardstein, p. 56

174 **very unkind**: W to QV, 8 Jan. 1896, RA VIC/MAIN/Z/500/5

174 **like a jealous**: Roberts, p. 612

174 **especially the Kaiser**: QV to Salisbury, 8 Aug. 1895, *LQV*, 3.3, pp. 547–8

175 **the prime minister**: see 7 Aug. 1895, Holstein, 3, p. 538

175 **I very much**: Undersecretary von Rotenhan to Holstein, Kohut, 'Kaiser Wilhelm II and his parents', pp. 84–5

7: Perfidious Muscovy (1895–7)

176 **The first acts**: Ellis to QV, 26 Nov. 1894, RA VIC/MAIN/Z/274/43

176 **How not to**: Konstantin Romanov's diary, 9 Nov. 1894, Maylunas, p. 106

176 **couched in the most**: Lascelles to Kimberley, 12 Feb. 1895, RA VIC/MAIN/H/46/110

177 **I shall maintain . . . impression**: Charques, p. 54

177 **the most distressing**: Radzinsky, p. 42

177 **cordial relations with England**: Lascelles, 26 Feb. 1895, RA VIC/MAIN/H/46/112

177 **I find them such nice**: N to E, 3 [OS]/15 Feb. 1895, RA VIC/MAIN/T/10/41

177 **would be received**: *Daily Telegraph*, 16 Nov. 1895

178 **They saw no reason . . . a pinch came**: Neilson, pp. 155–6

178 **how deeply I and my**: QV to N, 15 May 1895, RA VIC/MAIN/H/46/121

179 **I must say**: N to QV, 10 [OS]/22 May 1895, GARF 601/1/1111

179 **discouraging . . . in Russia**: Lascelles report, 9 Oct. 1895, RA VIC/MAIN/H/46/132

180 **at heart unfriendly**: Neilson, p. 64

180 **almost a diseased mistrust**: O'Conor, 7 Sept. 1896, ibid.

180 **encouraging France**: Journal, 8 April 1896, *LQV*, 3.3, p. 39

180 **very unhappy**: Journal, 6 April 1896, ibid.

181 **a government**: E. Morris, p. 245

181 **No impossible**: W note on Radolin to Holstein, 28 Dec. 1897, Holstein, 4, pp. 60–61

181 **the Tsar drinks**: Radolin to Holstein, 19 Nov. 1895, Holstein, 3, p. 565

181 **exasperatingly polite**: Witte, p. 179

181 **possessed in a**: Rosen, 1, p. 101

182 **nervous strain . . . worried**: Vorres, p. 108

182 **Nothing remains secret**: Neilson, p. 82

183 **charming, agreeable**: W to QV, RA VIC/MAIN/I/59/98

183 **I can only**: W to N, 27 Oct. [OS]/8 Nov. 1894, Maylunas, pp. 100–101

183 **Our relations with**: Eulenburg to Holstein, 11 Jan. 1895, Holstein, 3, p. 489

183 **opening the doors . . . itself strong**: W to N, 7 Feb. 1895, Grant, pp. 7–8

184 **I have great . . . but evil**: Munster to Holstein, 11 June 1895, Holstein, 3, p. 517

184 **the great task . . . race**: W to N, 26 April 1895, ibid., p. 10

184 **to tie Russia down**: *GP*, 9, no. 2318

184 **do all in my power . . . nice**: W to N, 26 April 1895, Grant, p. 10

184 **His Majesty has thus**: quoted in Röhl and de Bellaigue, p. 755

185 **every German**: see Hohenlohe, *GP*, 9, 12 Sept. 1895, no. 2319, pp. 360–61, also McLean, pp. 29–30

185 **damned rascals . . . an allegorical drawing**: W to N, 26 Sept. 1895, Grant, pp. 20–21

185 **the danger which**: W to N, 25 Oct. 1895, ibid., p. 23

185 **Queen Victoria felt**: F. Ponsonby, *My Recollections*, p. 54

186 **HM is beginning**: Holstein to Radolin, 30 Oct. 1895, Holstein, 3, p. 556

186 **I received Moltke**: 18 Sept. 1895, Nicholas II, p. 134

186 **a quiet man**: Jefferson, p. 220

186 **boorish and bossy**: see Duff, p. 192

187 **traitor to her faith**: Röhl and de Bellaigue, p. 650

187 **I quite agree**: W to N, 19 April 1896, Grant, p. 37

187 **the last stronghold**: Mossolov, p. 108

187 **uninterested in politics**: see Holstein to Radolin, 6 July 1895, Holstein, 3, p. 530

188 **the intriguing of**: 24 June 1895, ibid., p. 137

188 **strong humanitarian**: Mackenzie Wallace, 1903, RA VIC/ MAIN/W/44/15c

188 **dark spot ... serious consequences**: Kennedy, *The Rise*, pp. 218–19

189 **even so undiplomatic**: W to N, 25 Oct. 1895, Grant, p. 27

189 **entirely normal**: Röhl and Bellaigue, p. 784

189 **astonishing accusations ... and affected**: W to Marschall, 25 Oct. 1895, *GP*, 11, pp. 8–11

190 **The conduct of**: F. Lascelles, 4 Dec. 1895, PRO FO 800/17

191 **I declare quite**: Röhl and de Bellaigue, p. 764

191 **the same thing to the hapless**: W to Hohenlohe, *GP*, 10, pp. 251–5

191 **What happens now**: Holstein to Eulenburg, 21 Dec. 1895, Holstein, 3, pp. 576–7

191 **rabid**: Chirol quoted in Röhl and de Bellaigue, p. 784

191 **The Transvaal republic**: W to N, 2 Jan. 1896, Grant, p. 29

192 **encouragement of Chamberlain**: Balfour, *Britain and Joseph*, p. 229

192 **a threatening formal note**: Röhl and de Bellaigue, p. 787

192 **I express my**: W to President Kruger of Transvaal, 3 Jan. 1896, *GP*, 11, pp. 31–2

192 **The Nation will**: St Aubyn, p. 285

193 **outrageous and**: Journal, 2 Jan. 1896, *LQV*, 3.3, p. 6

193 **a most gratuitous**: Knollys to Bigge, 4 Jan. 1996, ibid., p. 7

193 **true feelings**: Bülow, 4, p. 665

193 **spoke loud**: 22 Feb. 1896, Lady Lytton, p. 60

193 **As your grandmother**: QV to W, 5 Jan. 1896, *LQV*, 3.3, p. 8

194 **I was so incensed**: W to QV, 8 Jan. 1896, RA VIC/MAIN/Z/ 500/5

194 **fully to accept**: Salisbury to QV, 12 Jan. 1896, *LQV*, 3.3, pp. 20–21

194 **the old woman**: Roberts, p. 626

194 **so concerned by the ... destroy England**: Röhl and de Bellaigue, pp. 789, 796–7

194 **the Russians had been**: see Holstein to Radolin, 21 May 1896, Holstein, 3, p. 615

194 **had been sanctioned by**: *GP*, 11, no. 2771

194 **literally horrified**: Hatzfeldt quoted in Röhl and de Bellaigue, p. 798

195 **seemed more excitable**: G to N, 26 April 1896, GARF 601/1/1219

195 **certainly be booed**: see Hatzfeldt to Holstein, 28 April 1896, Holstein. 3, p. 608

195 **he invited ... for compensation**: Röhl and de Bellaigue, p. 968

195 **should be so unworthy ... teapot**: Wickham-Steed, p. 67

195 **tippling grandmother**: Mons to Bülow, April 1896, Bülow, 1, p. 32

195 **to treat him badly**: Waldersee, 2, pp. 356–7

196 **I must say**: G to N, 17 April 1896, GARF 601/1/1219

196 **at Windsor it was said**: Lady Lytton, p. 68

196 **describing in detail**: see for example, O'Conor to QV, 31 May 1896, RA VIC/MAIN/H/47/17

196 **How outrageous can**: Maylunas, p. 151

196 **may be blamed**: QV to O'Conor, 3 June 1896, RA VIC/H/MAIN/47/19

196 **violence to their**: O'Conor to QV, 2 June 1896, RA VIC/MAIN/H/47/17

197 **a Scottish accent**: Lady Lytton, p. 36

197 **Lord Rosebery said**: F. Ponsonby, *My Recollections*, p. 15

197 **Siberia**: Roberts, p. 406

198 **She is marvellously**: N to Minny, 13 [OS]/25 Sept. 1896, Bing, p. 118

198 **Dear Nicky and Alicky**: QV to V, 25 Sept. 1896, Ramm, p. 195

198 **unmistakably lovely ... jolly**: Lutyens, pp. 74, 80

198 **From the very first ... and rain**: N to Minny, 2 [OS]/14 Oct. 1896, Bing, pp. 119–20

198 **I'm glad**: N to Minny, 13 [OS]/25 Sept. 1896, ibid., p. 118
198 **Had a talk**: 22 Sept. 1896, RA GV/PRIV/GVD
199 **I remarked that**: Journal, 24 Sept. 1896, *LQV*, 3.3, p. 83
199 **The Emperor is**: QV to Salisbury, 24 Sept. 1896, ibid., p. 81
199 **I had two**: N to Minny, 2 [OS]/14 Oct. 1896, Bing, p. 120
200 **the absurdity of . . . of Germany**: Jefferson, pp. 217–18, 128
200 **I am extremely**: W to the Foreign Ministry, 9 Sept. 1896, *GP*,
    11, no. 2861, p. 360
201 **this was a rather**: Jefferson, p. 220
201 **much struck by**: Journal, 28 Sept. 1896, *LQV*, 3.3, p. 84; see also
    Jefferson, p. 216
201 **very different from**: 27 Sept. 1896, Lutyens, p. 80
201 **distinctly averse . . . an imprudence**: Salisbury to QV, 29 Sept.
    1896, *LQV*, 3.3, pp. 85–102
201 **he thought it . . . at peace**: QV account of talk with N, 2 Oct.
    1896, RA VIC/MAIN/H/48/4
201 **a breathtaking tip**: Mallet, p. 94, n. 2
202 **kindly use**: QV to N, 5 Oct. 1896, RA VIC/H/MAIN/48/10
202 **As to Egypt . . . His deeds**: N to QV, 10 Oct. 1896, GARF
    601/1/1111
203 **would unquestionably have**: Rosen, 1, p. 128
203 **met his mother**: Radolin to Hohenlohe, 17 Jan. 1897, Hohenlohe,
    pp. 292–4
203 **black, dark and**: N to Minny, 2 [OS]/14 Oct. 1896, Bing, p. 125
203 **In his presence**: W to Hohenlohe, 20 Oct. 1896, *GP*, 11, no.
    2868
204 **swine**: Kiderlen-Wächter to Holstein, 15 Jan. 1907, Holstein, 4,
    p. 3
204 **a friend of France . . . after him**: Holstein to Radolin, 10 Jan.
    1897, ibid., 4, p. 1
204 **conceited and vain**: Neilson, p. 65
204 **Russia doesn't**: O'Conor to FO, 24 Jan. 1897, RA VIC/ MAIN/
    H/48/32, see also Buchanan, 1, p. 169
204 **Special Branch**: Cook, *M*, pp. 135–6
204 **Have you any**: W to QV, 2 Jan. 1897, RA VIC/MAIN/I/61/1
205 **And I am**: Röhl and de Bellaigue, p. 967
205 **I feel like**: W to QV, 10 April 1897, RA VIC/MAIN/Z/500/7

205 **personal hatred**: Journal, 29 Aug. 1897, *LQV*, 3.3, p. 197

205 **The German Emperor**: 31 May 1897, Mallet, p. 21

206 **completely unassailable**: J. Morris, 2, p. 28

206 **It now occupied**: Ferguson, *Empire*, p. 240

206 **the most wonderful**: 22 June 1897, RA GV/PRIV/GVD

206 **a loose aggregate**: J. Morris, 2, p. 422

206 **The most dangerous**: *The Times*, 17 July 1897

207 **which does not**: Roberts, p. 627

207 **very much depressed**: 5 Nov. 1896, Mallet, p. 95

207 **the uglier side of empire**: see Mike Davis, *Late Victorian Holocausts*, p. 141

207 **Emperor Nicholas**: Bülow to the Foreign Ministry, 10 Aug. 1897, *GP*, 13, p. 76

207 **Nicholas said**: see 20 Aug. 1897, *GP*, 13

208 **Thank God . . . *a vomir***: N to Minny, 23 July 1897, Bing, p. 128

208 **We have . . . to**: W to FO, 6 Nov. 1897, *GP*, 14, p. 67

209 **he wasn't opposed**: Bülow to FO, 11 Aug. 1897, *GP*, 14, p. 58

209 **agreement with the Emperor**: Röhl and de Bellaigue, p. 960

209 **Thank God we**: N to George, 29 March 1898, Maylunas, p. 171

209 **a scramble for China**: see Neilson, pp. 184–95

210 **We follow in**: W to N, 1 Jan. 1898, Grant, p. 44

210 **cold and**: Bülow, 1, p. 205

210 **I never say**: von Derenthall to Hohenlohe, 21 June 1899, *GP*, 13, p. 213

210 **ninny . . . grow turnips**: Cecil, 'Wilhelm II and', p. 123–4

8: Behind the wall (1893–1904)

211 **kind eyes**: Buxhoeveden, p. 245

211 **charming, sympathetic**: Tuchman, p. 230, 2nd quote: W. T. Stead account of meeting Nicky, Nov. 1898, RA VIC/H 48/62

211 **After tea**: 24 Oct. 1894, Nicholas II, p. 134

211 **Never did I**: ibid., p. 125

211 **My sweet old**: 10 June 1895, ibid., p. 130

212 **I only hear**: Radolin to Holstein, 19 Nov. 1895, Holstein, 3, p. 565

213 **loved a homely . . . English house**: Buxhoeveden, p. 52

214 **She longed to**: ibid., p. 58

215 **over sensitive and**: Marie, Grand Duchess of Russia, *A Romanov*, p. 82

215 **If Alicky smiled**: Vorres, p. 73

215 **stinging answers**: Mossolov, p. 54

215 **publicly reprimanding**: King, p. 250

215 **It was contrary**: Buxhoeveden, p. 77

215 **showed jealousy**: Mossolov, p. 30

215 **Why? So as to hear**: Buxhoeveden

215 **Neither the Tsar**: Mossolov, p. 239

216 **so reserved and closed-off**: Radolin to Hohenlohe, 18 Aug. 1897, *GP*, 13, p. 79

216 **The sovereigns themselves**: Botkin, p. 31

216 **on their magisterial**: Lytton, p. 81

216 **Neither touched us**: Dehn, ch. 2

217 **royally bored**: Mossolov, p. 197

218 **It almost seemed**: Ethel Howard, p. 177

218 **Wilhelm liked to say**: F. Ponsonby, *My Recollections*, p. 257

218 **Anything stiffer**: Count Gleichen to E, 10 March 1905, RA VIC/ W 45/126

218 **The elderly generals**: Topham, pp. 125–6

219 **Gustav von Neumann**: Gorlitz, *Der Kaiser*, p. 206

219 **one day at table . . . dictionary**: Witte, p. 101

219 **The poor workmen**: Buxhoeveden, p. 109

220 **I felt green**: N to Minny, 7 [OS]/19 Aug. 1896, Bing, pp. 116–17

220 **unable to change**: Vyrubova, pp. 57–8

221 **The enchanted little**: Botkin, p. 61

221 **Our young monarch**: Lamsdorff, *Dnevnik*, p. 401

221 **He remains**: Konstantin Romanov's Journal, 27 Dec. 1897, May-lunas, p. 167

221 **The Emperor is**: Neilson, p. 54

221 **The reputation of**: Tschirrsky to Hohenlohe, 16 June 1898, Auswartiges Amtes, Russland No. 82/1/Bd 4, R10691

221 **Today one thing**: MacDonogh, p. 220

222 **lie low . . . body**: Mossolov, pp. 127, 13

223 **The bureaucracy is**: ibid., p. 129

223 **to keep him on track**: see Mackenzie-Wallace, 10 Nov. 1902, RA VIC/W 43/149

224 **The very idea**: Mossolov, p. 10

224 **He only grasps**: Polovtsova, *Krasny Arkhiv*, 3, p. 131

224 **Iron, steel and coal**: US Library of Congress Country Studies, 1996

225 **like a butler**: Pares, p. 157

225 **He has nobody**: Buxhoeveden, pp. 108–9

225 **We talked for**: Witte, p. 179

225 **It is a complete**: Minny to N, 1[OS]/12 Oct. 1902, Bing, pp. 162–3

226 **a strong and steady . . . grief**: N to Minny, 20 Oct. [OS]/2 Nov. 1902, ibid., p. 167

226 **glum little villa**: Nicolson, p. 51

226 **a poky and inconvenient**: Athlone, p. 123

226 **a leaden pelican . . . saddened**: Nicolson, p. 51

227 **His engagements**: see Gore, p. 126

227 **For seventeen years**: Nicolson, *Diaries*, p. 174

228 **667 dead**: 3 Dec. 1893, Nicholas II, p. 43

228 **33,967 animals . . . beasts**: MacDonogh, p. 231

228 **it is a misfortune**: Cannadine, *Decline*, p. 369

228 **bear London**: 21 May 1894, in St Aubyn, *Royal George*, p. 300

228 **not for their**: Gore, p. 126

228 **reactionary . . . deference**: A. Ponsonby, *The Decline of the Aristocracy*, pp. 142–4

229 **Every time I**: Journal, Sept. 1897, *LQV*, 3.3, p. 202

229 **You know by this**: Pope-Hennessy, *Queen Mary*, p. 280

229 **I know that you . . . success**: ibid., p. 368

230 **Do try to**: ibid., p. 279

230 **her jealousy**: Airlie, p. 107

230 **which certainly gives**: Pope-Hennessy, *Queen Mary*, p. 282

230 **So my poor**: Battiscombe, p. 258

230 **dreadful Russian**: Pope-Hennessy, *Queen Mary*, p. 52

230 **Sometimes**: Gore, p. 129

231 **a life of**: Brown, p. 29

231 **sacrificed everything**: Pope-Hennessy, *Queen Mary*, pp. 423–4

231 **King George V**: F. Ponsonby, *My Recollections*, p. 279

231 **No one ever**: Pope-Hennessy, *Queen Mary*, p. 292

232 **Just a little bit**: Rose, p. 64

232 **Off the record**: Pope-Hennessy, *Lonely Business*, p. 214

232 **I did not think**: G to N, 21 Dec. 1901, GARF 601/1/1219

232 **Princess May will**: 14 Dec. 1897, Mallet, p. 121

232 **Princess May is very**: 3 Aug. 1898, ibid., p. 137

233 **hard crust of**: Airlie, p. 102

233 **She was a different**: Pope-Hennessy, *Lonely Business*, p. 215

233 **He retained a . . . the spirit**: Windsor, *A King's*, p. 8

233 **Get it out**: Bradford, p. 38

233 **revolting . . . cry over it**: Nicolson, p. 39

234 **The tragedy was**: Airlie, pp. 112–13

234 **bathed in perpetual**: Windsor, *A King's*, p. 47

234 **He was more of**: 'Prince John: The Windsors' Tragic Secret', Channel 4, 17 Nov. 2008

235 **was reliable, but**: Metternich to Bülow, 23 Feb. 1900, Auswartiges Amtes, Russland No. 82/1/Bd 42, R10661

235 **remarkable success . . . districts**: Nicolson, *King George*, p. 57

236 **I wish that the newspapers**: 6 Jan. 1896, RA VIC/MAIN/Z/500/6

236 **we are so actively**: 5 Nov. 1896, Mallet, p. 95

236 **swine . . . half-wits**: Lincoln, p. 590

237 **made him angry**: Nicholas II, p. 141

237 **how they are made**: Röhl and de Bellaigue, p. 758

237 **he doubted if**: O'Conor to FO, 24 Jan. 1897, RA VIC/MAIN/H/48/32

237 **never set the Russian**: Röhl and de Bellaigue, p. 758

237 **that in Germany**: Bülow, 1, p. 314

238 **British papers had circulations**: see Lucy Brown, pp. 48–53, see also Alan J. Lee

238 **for those who could**: Roberts, pp. 667–8

239 **I am the sole**: W to E, 30 Dec. 1901, RA VIC/MAIN/X 37/51

239 **public opinion**: Bülow, 1, p. 314

239 **Probably in no other**: Lerman, p. 120

239 **All parties were**: Rosen, 1, pp. 190–91

9: Imperial imperatives (1898–1901)

240 **The bad feeling**: QV to Vicky, 18 Aug. 1897, Ramm, p. 206

240 **Sir Thomas Sanderson**: Steiner and Neilson, pp. 68–9

241 **read more Machiavelli**: Balfour, *The Kaiser*, p. 202

241 **He is so**: Craig, pp. 273–4

242 **not live**: Röhl and de Bellaigue, p. 1027

242 **Balfour's mannerism**: Tuchman, p. 227

242 **the most wisely**: Bülow, 4, p. 625

242 **really honest**: Kennedy, *The Rise*, p. 227

242 **with indifference**: Bülow, 4, p. 159

243 **we would definitely**: Cecil, *Wilhelm*, 2, p. 75

243 **For Germany**: 15 June 1897, ibid., p. 224

244 **international consequences**: see Bigge to QV, 14 March 1898, RA VIC/MAIN/I/61/31

244 **silly boy**: Lee, 1, p. 735

245 **he would eat**: Warwick, p. 47

245 **to go to war**: Balfour, *Britain and*, p. 239

246 **the one that**: ibid., p. 243

246 **world-saving idea**: Vicky to W, 31 May 1898, Röhl and de Bellaigue, p. 976

246 **I for the last three**: W to Vicky, 1 June 1898, Holstein, 4, p. 82

246 **We must hold**: Kennedy, *The Rise*, p. 235

247 **Shameless scoundrel!**: Röhl and de Bellaigue, p. 981

247 **Princess Beatrice**: 20 July 1898, Eulenburg, 3, no. 1381

247 **something between a**: W to Vicky, 2 Aug. 1898, *LQV*, 3.3, pp. 262–3

247 **He told the queen**: Salisbury to QV, 1 Aug. 1898, RA VIC/MAIN/I/61/57

247 **He noted that**: Lascelles to Knollys, 24 March 1905, RA VIC/MAIN/W/45/146

247 **he told Philipp zu Eulenburg**: Zedlitz-Trützschler, 10 Oct. 1905, pp. 150–51

248 **about Grand Mamma and**: Cecil Spring-Rice, quoted in Steinberg, 'The Kaiser and the British', p. 124

248 **scant consideration ... instructions**: Röhl and de Bellaigue, p. 983

248 **The moment**: W to V, 20 Nov. 1898, ibid., p. 985

249 **I attempted . . . Half an hour**: Lascelles to Salisbury, 21 Dec. 1898, Gooch and Temperley, vol. 1, pp. 102–4

249 **You cannot have . . . his side**: Bülow quoted, 3 Nov. 1904, Zedlitz-Trützschler, pp. 93, 27

250 **Grandmama refused to**: Grierson to Bigge, 1 April 1899, RA VIC/MAIN/I/62/9a

250 **universal peace . . . to avert**: Tuchman, pp. 212 -13

250 **the greatest living**: Stead, Aug. 1898, RA VIC/MAIN/H/48/ 62, see also Tuchman, p. 230

251 **Nicky is quite**: Vicky to QV, 31 Aug. 1898, Ramm, p. 218

251 **dodge . . . nor we**: Warwick, *Afterthoughts*, p. 138

251 **Imagine!**: Tuchman, p. 224

252 **exchanging views**: Neilson, p. 118

252 **would undermine**: Mackenzie Wallace to E, 1903, RA VIC/ MAIN/W/44/15

253 **No triumph**: Fromkin, p. 41

253 **honest collision**: A. J. Mahan, 'The Conference and the Moral Aspect of War', *North American Review*, Oct. 1899

253 **every opportunity**: QV to N, 1 March 1899, GARF 601/1/1194

254 **to set [Russia]**: Journal, 17 Feb. 1899, *LQV*, 3.3, p. 340

254 **I am so happy**: N to QV, 13 March 1899, GARF 601/1/1111

254 **offered to help**: see Journal, 28 Oct. 1898, *LQV*, 3.3, p. 300; see also Scott to Salisbury, 17 Nov. 1898, RA VIC/H 48/63

254 **All that Russia**: N to QV, 13 March 1899, GARF 601/1/1111

254 **Mouravieff is a terrible**: Neilson, p. 202

255 **his consistent**: Grierson to Lascelles, 5 May 1899, *LQV*, 3.3, pp. 357–9

256 **slightly mad**: Grierson to Bigge, 4 May 1899, RA VIC/MAIN/ I62/10a

256 **I cannot help**: P. Kennedy, *The Samoan Tangle*, Dublin, Irish University Press, 1984

256 **This way of treating . . . of civility**: W to QV, 18 May 1899, RA VIC/MAIN/I/62/14

257 **I doubt**: QV to W, 12 June 1899, RA VIC/MAIN/I/62/18

257 **disenchanting effect**: see Cecil, *Wilhelm*, 1, p. 326

257 **Old Victoria's**: Röhl and de Bellaigue, p. 998

257 **Psychologically speaking**: 21 July 1898, Haller, 2, pp. 61–2

258 **to <u>run after</u>**: Röhl and de Bellaigue, p. 1049

258 **I am an utter . . . one's back**: Roberts, p. 666

259 **incessant storm**: RA VIC/MAIN/W/42/16

260 **unequal and unjust**: N. to Minny, 9 [OS]/21 Nov. 1899, Bing, p. 142

260 **My dear**: J. Morris, *Pax Britannica*, 3, p. 91

260 **declaring the**: 19 Feb. 1900, Mallet, p. 187

260 **downtrodden serfs**: Fraser, p. 177

260 **idle young men**: Mallet, p. 184

260 **Please understand**: Weintraub, *Victoria*, p. 611

260 **brave and godly . . . politeness**: Bülow, 1, pp. 301, 310

261 **His tenacity**: *Daily News*, 20 Nov. 1899

261 **A man whose**: *The Times*, 20 Nov. 1899

262 **In England**: Bülow, 1, p. 305

262 **mushroom . . . spiteful utterances**: ibid., pp. 319, 305–6, 320

263 **comprehensive understanding . . . small things**: ibid., p. 315

263 **do everything that**: Eckhardstein to Hatzfeldt, 31 July 1899, Holstein, 4, p. 146

263 **humbug**: Bertie to Bigge, 28 Nov. 1899, RA VIC/I 62/71

263 **a fat malicious**: Bülow, 1, p. 339

263 **shot remarkably**: 27 Nov. 1899, RA GV/PRIV/GVD

263 **far-seeing English**: Lee, 1, p. 748

264 **Instead of the**: W to E, 21 Dec. 1899. RA VIC/MAIN/W/60/26

264 **to thank the kaiser**: E to W, 8 Feb. 1900, Lee, 1, pp. 758–9

264 **he pushed me**: Townley, pp. 66–77

264 **This clearly shows**: W to E, 23 Feb. 1900, RA VIC/MAIN/ W/60/89

265 **Muraviev suggested**: Geyer, p. 201

265 **attack Northern India**: see Lee, 1, pp. 563–5

265 **Muraviev suggested . . . Wilhelm now said**: ibid., 1, pp. 766–7

266 **Sundry Peoples**: W to E, 23 Feb. 1900, RA VIC/MAIN/W/ 60/89

266 **My warnings**: W to E, 3 March 1900, RA VIC/MAIN/W 60/105

266 **he would keep**: Lascelles to Salisbury, 9 March 1900, RA VIC/ MAIN/I/62/83

266 **from a most dangerous**: W to QV, 31 March 1900, Lee, 1, p. 773

266 **There lingers**: Salisbury to QV, 10 April 1900, *LQV*, 3.3, p. 525
266 **shown papers which**: Weintraub, *The Importance*, p. 379
266 **humiliate England**: *Daily Telegraph*, 27 Oct. 1908
267 **lachrymose about the**: F. Ponsonby, *My Recollections*, p. 73
267 **I think of all**: Bülow, 1, p. 500
268 **the petticoats . . . the world**: Rennell, p. 96
268 **ordinary man . . . and quickly**: Wilhelm II, *My Memoirs*, p. 99
268 **He behaved in**: F. Ponsonby, *My Recollections*, p. 82
268 **Willim was**: E to V, 1 Feb. 1901, St Aubyn, p. 314
268 **She looked just . . . distressing**: 20–22 Jan. 1900, RA GV/
PRIV/GVD
268 **softly passed away**: Wilhelm II, *Ereignisse und Gestalten*, p. 87
269 **The Queen was everything**: 9 Jan. 1901, Maylunas, p. 204
269 **She was so remarkably**: N to E, 16 [OS]/29 Jan. 1901, GARF
601/1/1131
269 **The lying is unprecedented**: Hamilton, March 1901, in Neilson,
p. 217
269 **We may be**: *Daily Telegraph*, 5 Feb. 1901
269 **This presumptuous**: *Justice*, 2 Feb. 1901
270 **We seem to have**: 3 Feb. 1901, Henry James, *Letters*, ed. Edel,
Belnap Press, Cambridge, MA, 1987, pp. 328–9
270 **The old English**: W to Bülow, 29 Jan. 1901, *GP*, 17, no. 4987,
pp. 24–9
270 **a slap in the**: Bülow, 1, p. 502
270 **Oh! If only the**: Kohut, 'Kaiser Wilhelm II and his parents', p. 85
271 **the two Teutonic . . . our permission**: Kennedy, *The Rise*, p. 224
271 **safe and mothered**: Weintraub, *Victoria*, p. 390
271 **Her death in**: Edel, 3, p. 87
271 **the dead queen**: Waters, p. 63

10: The fourth emperor (1901–4)

275 **a world where . . . feudal**: Sackville-West, p. 15
275 **insinuendoes**: Ettie Desborough to Arthur Balfour, late Feb. 1906,
Derv. C1085/10, Desborough papers, Hertford archives and county
record office

276 **as your Royal**: Antrim, p. 47

276 **for some intimate**: Warwick, *Afterthoughts*, p. 16

278 **What will they**: J. Vincent (ed.), *The Crawford Papers*, 1984, p. 39

278 **He had the most . . . inconvenience**: F. Ponsonby, *My Recollections*, pp. 274, 124

279 **You don't**: Fisher, p. 5

279 **life expectancy** (and subsequent figures): 'Edwardian Winners and Losers', BBC4, 16 May 2007

279 **some of the vilest**: Wilson, p. 582

280 **the speeches were written**: see F. Ponsonby, *My Recollections*, p. 275

281 **I fear sometimes**: G to Bigge, 25 Dec. 1907, Nicolson, *King George*, p. 65

281 **The King is no longer . . . rules it**: Balfour to E, 6 Feb. 1901, ibid., pp. 67–8

282 **tiresome functions**: G to N, 3 Jan. 1902, GARF 601/1/1219

282 **a strong feeling of**: Nicolson, *King George*, p. 70

283 **barbaric . . . The vulgar**: J. Wilson, p. 349

283 **I fear that**: E to Lansdowne, 31 Dec. 1902, Lee, 2, p. 280

283 **He has got nothing . . . attitudes**: Bülow to FO, 4 Nov. 1901, *GP*, 18(i), pp. 34–5

283 **weak as water**: Tuchman, p. 230

283 **The Russians have**: Lee, 2, p. 279

284 **smooth matters down**: McLean, p. 98

285 **be wrapped in the Union Jack**: Bülow, 1, p. 528 and Pakula, *An Uncommon Woman*, pp. 597–8

285 **King Edward**: F. Ponsonby, *My Recollections*, p. 122

285 **Uncle Bertie**: Athlone, p. 148

285 **Ferdinand of Bulgaria . . . the dwarf**: see Cecil, 'Wilhelm II and his Russian colleagues', p. 99

286 **to all the obstacles**: Kennedy, *The Rise*, p. 246

286 **a pack of**: see Waters, p. 37

286 **already had to**: Eckhardstein, p. 217

287 **and walk hand in hand**: E to Lascelles, 25 Dec. 1901, RA VIC/MAIN/X/37/49

287 **The press is awful**: W to E, 30 Dec. 1901, RA VIC/MAIN/X 37/51

288 **no one can be**: Cecil, *William*, 2, p. 84

288 **conglomeration**: W to E, 6 Jan. 1902, RA VIC/MAIN/X 37/52

288 **quantité negligeable**: Lascelles to Knollys, 17 Jan. 1902, FO 800/10

288 **I think that under**: E to W, 15 Jan. 1902, RA VIC/MAIN/W/ 42/58

288 **This is most**: G to Bigge, 9 Jan. 1902, Gore, p. 176

288 **he'd never received**: see Knollys to Lansdowne, 22 Jan. 1902, RA VIC/W 42/65

289 **most civil . . . kindness itself**: G to May, 27 Jan. 1902, RA QM/ PRIV/CC3/13

289 **frank talk . . . the future**: Bülow, 1, pp. 548–50

289 **The amount one . . . another uniform**: G to M, 27 Jan. 1902, RA QM/PRIV/CC3/13

289 **hurt abominably**: 26 Jan. 1902, RA GV/PRIV/GVD

289 **admired and . . . was past**: Topham, p. 197

289 **nothing but an . . . Exactly**: Eckhardstein to Bülow, 17 Sept. 1902, Auswartiges Amtes, England 78/Bd 6

290 **none of his parents' heat**: see Bülow, 1, p. 333

290 **royalty ridiculous**: Pope-Hennessy, p. 289

290 **all safe and**: W to E, 28 Jan. 1902, RA VIC/MAIN/W/42/70

290 **Yellow Peril . . . white race**: Bülow, 2, p. 61

290 **civilized**: Balfour, *DNB*

291 **a guarantee of**: W to E, 26 Feb. 1902, RA VIC/MAIN/X 37/55

291 **Thank God**: 1 June 1902, RA GV/PRIV/GVD

291 **an estimated 75,000 dead**: estimates for casualties for the Boer War (and other wars of the time) vary enormously; my figures are from Hobsbawm, p. 306, Ferguson, *Empire*, p. 280 and T. Pakenham, *The Boer War*, London, Weidenfeld, 1979

292 **a new, crude**: *History of The Times*, 3, pp. 366–8

292 **settled dislike**: Neilson, p. 67

293 **as hearty . . . the devil**: 1 June 1902, Lee, 2, pp. 145, 153

293 **2201 pheasants**: 12 Nov. 1902, RA GV/PRIV/GVD

293 **He made himself**: G to N, 30 Dec. 1902, GARF 601/1/1219

293 **Thank God he's**: Eckhardstein, p. 245

294 **with such brutal frankness**: 3 Feb. 1903, RA VIC/MAIN/W/ 43/49

294 **We should remember**: Lascelles to Knollys, 20 March 1903, RA VIC/MAIN/W 43/63

294 **There is a**: Kennedy, *The Rise*, p. 230

294 **in good spirits**: N to Minny, 2 [OS]/15 Sept. 1901, Bing, p. 151

294 **always fight**: Bülow to FO, 14 Sept. 1901, *GP*, 18, pp. 24–9

295 **the politest man**: Hardinge, p. 108

295 **Witte's man**: Izvolsky, p. 29

295 **between peoples with**: 19 July [OS]/1 Aug. 1901, Geyer, p. 166

296 **a thorough . . . a complete wreck**: Mossolov, p. 204

296 **though he apparently**: Bülow, 1, p. 541

296 **Be friendly and**: Alix to N, 22 July 1902, Maylunas, p. 216

296 **the Admiral of**: Bülow, 1, p. 573

296 **He's raving**: Mossolov, p. 203

297 **I will arrange everything**: Bülow to W, 11 July 1902, *GP*, 18(i), p. 55

297 **It is one of**: Mossolov, p. 246

298 **I am so sorry**: G to N, 3 Jan. 1902, GARF 601/1/1219

298 **more and more**: Mackenzie Wallace, 10 Nov. 1903, RA VIC/ W 43/149

298 **Russia ought not . . . change**: Mackenzie Wallace to Knollys, 1 Sept. 1903, RA VIC/MAIN/W/43/121

299 **an unbecoming**: Hardinge, *DNB*

299 **made all the**: F. Ponsonby, *My Recollections*, p. 159

300 **The King, however**: see Cambon, 22 Dec. 1920, *The Times*

300 **Most of the . . . history**: F. Ponsonby, *My Recollections*, pp. 154, 170

300 **Your presence in**: Heffer, p. 188

301 **I can still**: Vorres, p. 88

302 **he had to**: Bülow, 7 Nov. 1903, *GP*, 18(i), no. 5422, p. 71

302 **democratic countries**: W to N, 19 Nov. 1903, Grant, p. 99

303 **regarded with**: Osten-Sacken, 15 [OS)/28 April 1904, GARF 601/1/703

303 **the foreign secretary resented**: F. Ponsonby, *My Recollections*, p. 128

304 **So far as I**: Young, p. 202

304 **long sustained discussion**: Grey, p. 206

11: Unintended consequences (1904–5)

305 **China, Tibet, Afghanistan**: Geyer, p. 190

305 **from a French brothel**: Figes, *A People's*, p. 169

305 **According to Edward VII**: Bülow, 2, p. 28

306 **little short-tailed**: Lincoln, p. 640

306 **absolutely indifferent**: Hardinge to Knollys, 25 May 1906, RA VIC/MAIN/W/44/103

307 **zhids**: Witte, p. 189

307 **British-built**: Alexander Mikhailovich, p. 217

307 **the Japanese**: W to N, 9 Jan. 1904, Grant, p. 106

307 **To us . . .**: W to N, 3 Jan. 1904, ibid., p. 105

307 **nothing could be**: Balfour, Neilson, p. 239

307 **a personal message**: Lansdowne to Edward, 18 Feb. 1904, RA VIC/MAIN/W/44/34

307 **The Entente Cordiale**: see Cecil, *Wilhelm*, 2, p. 389, n. 7

308 **German tariffs**: Geyer, p. 168

308 **The king expressed . . . his Majesty**: Lee, 2, p. 285

308 **a man of . . . earnest desire**: E to N, 12 May 1904, RA VIC/MAIN/W/44/95

309 **I am looked upon**: Hardinge to Knollys, 25 May 1904, RA VIC/MAIN/W/44/103

309 **an intruder hiding**: Hardinge to Knollys, 19 Sept. 1904, RA VIC/MAIN/W/45/88

309 **I approve**: Patrick French, *Younghusband*, 1994, p. 253

309 **Edward's overtures**: see Alvensleben to Bülow, 11 May 1904, *GP*, 19(i); see also W note on Bernstorff to Bülow, 5 May 1904, England, Nr 81 Nr 1, Bd 12, Geheimes Staatsarchiv

310 **it couldn't**: Bülow to W, *GP*, 20(i), p. 24, no. 6379

310 **The importance**: Zedlitz-Trützschler, 21 July 1904, p. 80

310 **a whole troop of**: Bülow, 2, p. 23

310 **hardly able . . . overestimated**: Zedlitz-Trützschler, pp. 80–81

311 **a universal necessity . . . Great Powers**: Bülow, 2, p. 27

311 **He is very lively**: 28 June 1904, Lee, 2, p. 295

311 **Everyone is**: Zedlitz-Trützschler, 21 June 1904, p. 80

311 **a brave, chivalrous . . . smallest boat**: Bülow, 2, pp. 25–8, 23

312 **been greeted by**: Marder, p. 477

312 **There awoke in me . . . an invasion**: Bülow, 2, pp. 30, 26

313 **Mere apologies . . . painful impression**: Lee, 2, p. 302

313 **These suspicions**: Kokovtsov, p. 46

313 **luring**: N to E, 24 Oct. 1904, Lee, 2, p. 301

313 **English perfidy . . . to me**: Hardinge, p. 108

313 **If they imagined**: G to E, 24 Oct. 1904, Nicolson, *King George*, p. 83

313 **The English are**: N to Minny, 13 [OS]/26 Oct. 1904, Bing, p. 178

313 **Strongly deprecate**: Lee, 2, pp. 303–4

314 **I have no words**: N to W, 16 [OS]/28 Oct. 1904, GARF, 601/1/1200

314 **private source . . . incendiaries**: W to N, 30 Oct. 1904, Grant, p. 139

314 **not being**: W to N, 21 Dec. 1904, Grant, p. 151

314 **direct provocation**: 17 Nov. 1904, ibid., p. 142

314 **urgent assurances**: see N to W, 28 Nov. [OS]/11 Dec. 1904, GARF 601/1/1200

315 **convinced that it is**: 21 Nov. 1904, Zedlitz-Trützschler, p. 106

315 **absolutely apprised**: Bülow, 2, p. 83

315 **The Emperor has often**: Zedlitz-Trützschler, p. 161

315 **Edward told**: see Cambon, 17 Nov. 1904, *DDF*, 2.5, p. 535

315 **the Russian Baltic fleet**: 7 Dec. 1904, Zedlitz-Trützschler, p. 109

315 **that is beginning**: 29 June 1905, Maylunas, p. 278

315 **A terrible and**: 21 Dec. 1904, Nicholas II, p. 197

316 **A terrible day**: 9 Jan. 1905, ibid., p. 207

316 **indisputable . . . lower classes**: Hardinge, pp. 113–14

316 **I am glad**: W to N, 6 Feb. 1905, Grant, p. 160

316 **such an appearance**: W to N, 21 Feb. 1905, Grant, p. 171

316 **the traitors and**: Nicholas II, p. 204

316 **the Tsar viewed**: Kokovtsov, p. 50

317 **He lets everything**: Figes, *A People's*, p. 171

317 **I feel very . . . with happiness**: Hardinge to Knollys, Feb. 1905, RA VIC/W45/109

317 **her fierce stare**: E. Morris, *Theodor Rex*, p. 385

317 **illiterate Russian**: Waters to Davidson, 7 May 1905, RA VIC/MAIN/X/19/32

317 **It makes me**: N to Minny, 19 Oct. [OS]/1 Nov. 1905, Bing, p. 187

318 **All reports seem**: Hardinge to Knollys, 6 June 1905, RA VIC/ MAIN/W/46/36

319 **the agitation and disturbance**: Hardinge to Knollys, 5 July 1905, RA VIC/MAIN/W 46/64

319 **Such nonsense is**: Hardinge to Knollys, 22 Aug. 1905, RA VIC/ MAIN/W 46/144

320 **jumpy . . . clumsy**: Cecil, *Wilhelm*, 2, p. 95

320 **The most mischievous**: Lee, 2, p. 340

321 **A gratuitous**: E to Louis of Battenburg, 15 April 1905, Hough, p. 188

321 **to President Roosevelt**: see Magnus, p. 345, and Lascelles to Knollys, 24 March 1905, RA VIC/MAIN/W/45/146

321 **It is a wild**: Roosevelt to Spring-Rice, 16 June 1905, quoted in Fiebig von Hase, p. 153

322 **divide father . . . her slipper**: St Aubyn, p. 334

322 **off-colour remarks**: Bülow, 2, p. 182

323 **Although I like**: G to Knollys, 26 March 1905, RA VIC/MAIN/ W/45/147

323 **might create**: Seckendorff to E, 15 Aug. 1905, RA VIC/MAIN/ W/46/231

323 **run after [him]**: Knollys to Seckendorff, 23 Aug. 1905, RA VIC/ MAIN/W/46/285

323 **he talks and**: Newton, p. 330

323 **unrepeatable**: Bülow, 2, pp. 146–7

323 **At home nobody**: N to W, 7 [OS]/20 July 1904, GARF 601/1/ 1200

324 **the greatest mischief-maker**: GP, 19(ii), no. 6220, p. 460

324 **the British were using**: Cecil, *Wilhelm*, 2, p. 389, n. 7

324 **absolute passion for**: GP, 19(ii), no. 6220, p. 460

324 **a ray of sunlight**: Bülow, 2, p. 13

324 **must remember . . . of the world**: W to N, 27 July 1905, Grant, pp. 192–4

325 **from the hideous pincers**: GP, 19(ii), no. 6220

325 **even Japan may . . . firm friend**: W to N, 27 July 1905, Grant, pp. 192–4

325 **he seemed very**: Izvolsky, p. 49; see also Macdonald, p. 80

326 **boundless vanity**: Lerman, p. 90

326 **To be treated . . . children**: see Bülow, 2, pp. 138–47; *GP*, 19(ii), no. 6237, pp. 499–500

326 **We joined hands**: W to N, *GP*, 19(ii), pp. 513–14

326 **In England, of course**: N to Minny, 27 Oct. [OS]/9 Nov. 1905, Bing, p. 191

327 **Either you sign it**: Witte, p. 247, Mossolov, p. 90

327 **There were only . . . a year**: N to Minny, 19 Oct. [OS]/1 Nov. 1905, Bing, pp. 186–7

12: Continental shifts (1906–8)

328 **Germany's conduct**: E. Morris, p. 441

329 **a sign of weakness**: Hull, '*The Entourage*', p. 129

329 **a question of honour**: Oppel, p. 324

330 **the whole of Europe . . . machinations**: 13 March 1906, Zedlitz-Trützschler, pp. 169, 160–62

330 **We are – my**: Lee, 2, p. 525

330 **The whole letter**: W to E, 1 Feb. 1906, RA VIC/MAIN/X/37/62

331 **All the wretched**: *GP*, 21(i), 9 March 1906, pp. 267–8

331 **carrying on against**: 19 March 1907, Zedlitz-Trützschler, pp. 177–8

331 **a clear, practical**: 13 March 1906, ibid., p. 162

332 **In his heart of**: 13 March 1906, ibid., pp. 169–70

333 **I'm sure not . . . envious**: Lee, 2, pp. 352, 528

333 **not the slightest . . . in the air**: F. Ponsonby, *My Recollections*, p. 182

333 **Who can fail**: 15 April 1907, Lee, 2, pp. 541–2

334 **l'Allemagne c'est l'Ennemie**: Esher, 2, pp. 182–3

334 **Germany, he wrote . . . in the World**: Steiner, p. 43

335 **With more experience**: Grey, p. 85

335 **the most violent**: Spring-Rice to Knollys, 1 March 1906, RA VIC/MAIN/W/46/75

335 **patriotic . . . 690 pogroms**: Figes, *A People's*, p. 197

335 **a whole mass**: N to Minny, 27 Oct. [OS]/9 Nov. 1905, Bing, pp. 190–91

336 **virtual prisoners**: N to Minny, 30 Aug. [OS]/12 Sept. 1906, ibid., p. 217

336 **The Emperor is**: Spring-Rice to Grey, 18 April 1906, FO 800/72

336 **Personal contact with**: Nicolson, 2 Jan. 1907, RA VIC/MAIN/W/50/152

336 **I have never seen such**: N to Minny, 12 [OS]/25 Jan. 1907, Bing, p. 212

337 **progressive hysteria**: Massie, *Nicholas*, p. 153

337 **Minny complained . . . to ache**: Maylunas, p. 291

338 **It is more**: Battiscombe, p. 254

339 **They gave one**: Mossolov, p. 139

339 **repulsive faces**: Maylunas, p. 293

339 **They looked at us**: Kokovtsov, p. 131

339 **I felt so**: Alexander Mikhailovich, pp. 228–9

339 **Nabokov's great-uncle**: Nabokov, p. 60

340 **because the working**: Tuchman, p. 344

340 **the massacres in**: Dugdale, 1, p. 335

341 **The old idea**: Steiner, p. 139

341 **The great Unionist**: Arthur Balfour, *DNB*

341 **whether the country was**: St Aubyn, p. 402

341 **All down history**: Bentley Brinkerhoff, p. 17

342 **good taste and propriety**: Plumptre, p. 189

342 **almost more**: E to G, 19 March 1906, Jenkins, p. 91

342 **deplorably common**: St Aubyn, p. 409

342 **not quite**: Rose, p. 71

342 **These people**: Hibbert, p. 210

342 **an overgrown**: A. C. Benson, 10 Nov. 1908, Rose, p. 119

342 **how you can**: 15 May 1910, Hobhouse diaries, ed. David, p. 91

343 **One must let**: N to Minny, 29 March [OS]/11 April 1907, Bing, pp. 228–9

344 **Vive la Douma!**: Grey, p. 145

344 **A grotesque deputation**: Nicholas II, p. 219

344 **been prevented from**: Lascelles to Grey, Nov. 1906, RA VIC/W 50/39

344 **a triumph of**: Witte, p. 432

344 **Russian despotism**: Grey, p. 154

345 **It will complete**: Grey to Knollys, 28 March 1906, Trevelyan, p. 183

345 **little Edward icons**: Pless, p. 159

345 **the German army . . . as a whole**: von Miquel to Bülow, 27 Sept. 1907, *GP*, 25(i), no. 8537, pp. 45–7

345 **Hardinge gang**: see Steinberg, 'The Kaiser and the British', p. 130

345 **What a long time**: G to N, 28 Dec. 1907, GARF 601/1/1219

346 **made everything look different . . . greatness**: Alexander Mikhailovich, p. 233

346 **Everything is so**: Minny to N, 28 Feb. [OS]/13 March 1907, Bing, p. 222

347 **despairing, horrified**: Wilhelm, Crown Prince of Germany, p. 15

347 **He [Wilhelm] sat**: Witte, p. 457

347 **the repression of**: Sombart, in Röhl and Sombart, p. 304
Homosexualität: first used in Britain in translations and glosses of Krafft-Ebing's work, see *OED*

348 **disgusting orgies**: *The Times*, 25 Oct. 1907

348 **Am suffering**: W to E, 31 Oct. 1907, RA VIC/MAIN/W/52/47

348 **in very good**: Bülow, 2, p. 296

349 **Your telegram**: E to W, 31 Oct. 1907, RA VIC/MAIN/W/52/48

349 **There were great**: 13 Nov. 1907, RA GV/PRIV/GVD

349 **coming home**: Steinberg, 'The Kaiser and the British', p. 137

349 **Even those**: Morley, 2, p. 237

349 **Be a member**: Haldane, p. 221

349 **Our King makes a**: Esher, 2, p. 285

349 **He is always anxious**: Zedlitz-Trützschler, p. 38

350 **It transpired that the kaiser**: Steinberg, 'The Kaiser and the British', p. 134

350 **except perhaps . . . air of fraud**: 14 Dec. 1907, Holstein, 4, p. 509

350 **You may laugh**: 20 Dec. 1907, Morley, 2, p. 238

350 **unmitigated balderdash . . . the sea**: Lee, 2, p. 605

351 **Only now!**: W on Metternich to Bülow, *GP*, 24, no. 8193, p. 46

351 **An Insult to our Country**: MacDonald, *The Labour Leader*, May 1908

352 **couldn't be destroyed**: Plumptre, p. 208

352 **should have known**: Heffer, p. 253

352 **deplorably unsophisticated . . . business**: Cecil, 'William II and his Russian', pp. 132–3

352 **A constitutional monarch**: Felix Semon, *Autobiography*, 1926, p. 267

353 **marked difference . . . at him**: Hardinge, p. 157

353 **a *déclassé* accent**: Trewin, p. 10

353 **Except when on duty . . . their company!**: Mossolov, pp. 211, 210

353 **sobbing alone**: Hardinge, p. 156

353 **sing weird Russian**: F. Ponsonby, *My Recollections*, p. 196

354 **feast of peace**: Gibbes, p. 8

354 **confess his impotence**: Grey, p. 212

355 **very searchingly**: Brook-Shepherd, p. 330

355 **conniving to encircle**: St Aubyn, p. 363

355 **the blackest and most nauseous**: 12 Aug. 1908, C. Howard, p. 176

355 **German Bill**: ibid., p. 11

355 **I cannot resist . . . catastrophe**: Wickham-Steed, p. 282

356 **That's complete . . . an idea**: Bülow, 2, p. 313

356 **a lot of nonsense**: Hardinge, p. 162

356 **frank conversation**: Bülow, 2, p. 313

356 **The only result**: Zedlitz-Trützschler, 19 April 1907, p. 183

357 **Albert Ballin**: Bülow to W, 15 July 1908, *GP*, 24, no. 8216, pp. 96–9

357 **a mere bagatelle**: Steinberg, 'The Kaiser and the British', p. 134

357 **mechanical toy**: Epkenhans, p. 15

358 **impulsive sovereign**: Clemenceau to Pichon, 29 Aug. 1908, *DDF*, 2.11, pp. 749–52

358 **impossible . . . the King!**: 26 Sept. 1908, Esher, 2, p. 343

358 **Stop the King!**: W on Stumm to Bülow, 8 Sept. 1908, Auswartiges Amtes, England Nr 78, Bd 6

13: A Balkan crisis (1908–9)

360 **Unless some hope is**: E to Asquith, 13 Oct. 1908, RA VIC/ MAIN/R/29/53

361 **a rare audience**: Nicolson to Grey, 4 Nov. 1908, Neilson, p. 58, Grey papers, FO 800/222

361 **very straightforward**: Neilson, p. 302

361 **denied all knowledge . . . aggressor**: Kokovtsov, p. 216

362 **sincere and impulsive**: *Nation*, 31 Oct. 1908

362 **well meant**: *Westminster Gazette*, 31 Oct. 1908

362 **amazing**: Esher, 2, 28 Oct. 1908, p. 352

362 **dynamite bomb**: Bülow, 2, p. 376

362 **Of all the**: Magnus, p. 400

362 **The Emperor is**: Haller, 2, p. 72

362 **Poor Phili**: Hull, 'PKW and the Liebenburg Circle', p. 145

363 **Bülow had read it**: Cecil, *Wilhelm*, 2, p. 13

363 **more muddle**: C. Howard, p. 28

363 **He seemed ostensibly . . . with restraint**: T. Cole, 'The Daily Telegraph Affair', p. 256

364 **all-out betrayal**: Cecil, *Wilhelm*, 2, p. 137

364 **not for the . . . energetic pirouettes**: Zedlitz-Trützschler, 8 Feb. 1909, pp. 252–3

364 **rigor mortis was so far**: Tuchman, p. 310

364 **rotten and marching**: 11 Nov. 1908, Hardinge papers 1, Cambridge University Library, see also Hardinge, p. 170

365 **I know the E**: E to Knollys, 25 Nov. 1908, RA VIC/MAIN/ W/53/37

365 **announced that he could**: see Zedlitz-Trützschler, 26 Nov. 1908, p. 224

365 **a kind of . . . was terrifying**: Topham, pp. 200–201

365 **He was the**: F. Ponsonby, *My Recollections*, p. 259

365 **I am not . . . marvellous times**: Hardinge, p. 171

366 **The German Emperor**: Trevelyan, pp. 154–5

366 **a piece of brigandage**: Mansergh, p. 127

366 **European conflagration**: Bülow to W, 11 Jan. 1909, Geheimes Staatsarchiv, Rep 53, Lit B 16a, Bd Iv

366 **Helmuth von Moltke . . . provoked a war**: Fromkin, pp. 74–5

366 **were 'propitious' . . . difficulties**: Berghahn, pp. 91, 93

367 **to resolve the crisis**: N to W, 15 [OS]/28 Dec. 1908, *GP*, 26(i), no. 9187, pp. 387–8

367 **a genuine surprise . . . more and more**: W to N, 5 Jan. 1909, *GP*, 26(i), pp. 388–91; W to N, 8 Jan. 1909, Grant, pp. 243–4

367 **informal relations . . . put up with**: E to Knollys, 25 Nov. 1908, RA VIC/MAIN/W/53/37

367 **The King of England**: Zedlitz-Trützschler, 10 Feb. 1909, p. 258

367 **horror**: F. Ponsonby, *My Recollections*, p. 253

367 **terribly upset**: Redesdale, 1, p. 78

368 **the closest cooperation**: Hardinge, pp. 163–4

368 **the dearest**: Hardinge to Knollys, Lee, 2, p. 262

368 **useful results**: W to N, 8 Jan. 1908, Grant, p. 242

368 **forced jokes**: F. Ponsonby, *My Recollections*, p. 258

369 **openly expressed her . . . big stores**: W to Franz Ferdinand, 12 Feb. 1908, Kann, p 332

369 **in every respect**: McLean, p. 134

369 **had a very**: Kann, p. 332

369 **The effect of this**: F. Ponsonby, *My Recollections*, p. 258

370 **We expect a**: Pourtalès to Izvolsky, *GP*, 26, p. 693

370 **Shame! Shame!**: Lieven, *Origins*, pp. 22, 21

370 **the enemies**: ibid., p. 132

370 **It was considered**: Nicolson to Grey, 29 March 1909, in Grey, *25 Years*, p. 189

371 **The form and the method**: N to Minny, 19 March [OS]/2 April 1909, Bing, p. 241

371 **a token of undiminished**: W to N, 3 April 1909, Grant, pp. 246–7

371 **be turned into a military**: Hardinge to E, 7 April 1909, RA VIC/MAIN/W/55/16

371 **considered worthless**: McLean, p. 60

371 **lacked all appetite for it**: Zedlitz-Trützschler, 26 March 1909, p. 265

371 **great diplomatic triumph**: 9 April 1909, ibid., p. 267

371 **I hate the Slavs**: Cecil, *Wilhelm*, 2, p. 176

371 **When Germany made**: Roosevelt to Sir G. O. Trevelyan, 1 Oct. 1911, *Letters of T. Roosevelt VII*, ed. Morrison, p. 397

372 **incredible as it might**: K. Young, p. 248

372 **he had Edward informed**: see RA VIC/MAIN/X/22/64

372 **conviction or principle**: Massie, *Dreadnought*, p. 621

372 **told him to stonewall**: ibid. and n.

372 **Nonsense!**: Woodward, p. 238, n. 4

373 **that England**: F. Ponsonby, *My Recollections*, pp. 264–5

374 **If I am supported**: T. Cole, 'The Daily Telegraph Affair', p. 261

375 **civil liberties record**: Neilson, p. 308

375 **October 1908**: 10 March 1909, ibid., p. 304

375 **Dear Nicky looking**: 2 Aug. 1909, RA GV/PRIV/GVD

375 **elaborate police guard**: Duke of Windsor, *A King's*, p. 69

376 **Britain would never**: Mossolov, p. 109

14: Edward's mantle (1910–11)

377 **Witch of the Air**: 6 May 1910, RA GV/PRIV/GVD

377 **moulded the destinies ... antagonist**: Brook Shepherd, pp. 536–7

377 **He might have been**: Scawen Blunt, *My Diaries*, London, 1919, pp. 721–2

378 **honour and interest**: Wickham Steed, p. 289

378 **The scheming and ... much calmer**: W to Bethmann-Hollweg, 7 May 1910, Abteilung 1A, England Nr 78, Secretissima, Ban 25 (R 5791)

378 **An English country**: Görlitz, *Der Kaiser*, p. 78

378 **I have lost**: 6 May 1910, RA GV/PRIV/GVD

378 **How deeply I**: N to G, 28 April [OS]/8 May 1910, RA GV/PRIV/AA 43/129

379 **around £325,000**: Google The Victorian Web: wages, the cost of living and contemporary equivalents

379 **beautifully arranged**: Minny to N, 7 [OS]/20 May 1910, Bing, p. 254

379 **the great arbiter**: *Daily Telegraph*, 24 May 1910

380 **international affairs**: ibid., 20 May 1910

380 **where we put**: 19 May 1910, RA GV/PRIV/GVD

380 **a symbol**: *Daily Chronicle*, 20 May 1910

380 **None who saw**: *Daily Mail*, 20 May 1910

380 **being at Windsor**: W to Bethmann-Hollweg, *GP*, 28, p. 326

380 **Willie dear**: Battiscombe, p. 274

381 **Let him get**: Epkenhans, p. 33

381 **at five in the**: 16 May 1910, Esher, 3, p. 3

381 **the most trying**: 7 May 1910, RA GV/PRIV/GVD

381 **The little King**: David Cecil, *Max*, London, Bodley Head, 1964, p. 331

382 **Her devotion**: Airlie, p. 128

382 **George sulked . . . such rot**: F. Ponsonby to Ria Ponsonby, 4 April 1913, quoted in Rose, p. 147

383 **everything complex**: Pope-Hennessy, *Queen Mary*, p. 421

383 **We are back**: 18 April 1911, Esher, 3, pp. 48–9

383 **We have seen**: Rose, p. 96

383 **that curious**: 21 Aug. 1910, Esher, 3, p. 15

383 **Is it not hard**: Rose, p. 77

383 **I want sympathy**: G to Godfrey-Faussett, 28 July 1914, ibid., p. 158

384 **idlers and wastrels . . . uncalled for**: Rose, p. 173

384 **mangold-wurzels**: Blake, *Bonar Law*, p. 167

384 **the extraordinary**: 21 Jan. 1914, Esher, 3, p. 54

384 **The King is**: 8 Sept. 1910, Lloyd George, *Letters*, p. 152

384 **I understand that**: Rose, p. 110

384 **He is a nice**: Asquith to Venetia Stanley, Sept. 1912, Asquith, p. 42

385 **Really it is**: 12 May 1912, Rose, p. 160

385 **splendid isolation**: see Metternich to Bethmann-Hollweg, 25 Sept. 1911, *GP*, 29, pp. 244–6

385 **I hope we shall**: G to N, 27 May 1910, GARF 601/1/1219

385 **I rather fear**: G to N, 15 March 1911, ibid.

385 **to do for the Empire**: 25 Aug. 1910, Esher, 3, p. 17; G to N, 14 Feb. 1912, GARF 601/1/1219

386 **I understand the . . . and her Indian Empire**: Gore, p. 197

386 **I think it a**: N to G, 15[OS]/26 Jan. 1911, RA GV/PRIV/AA 43/151

387 **a magnificent**: G to N, 14 Feb. 1912, GARF 601/1/1219

387 **We decided he**: Oct. 1912, Hobhouse, *Diaries of Charles Hobhouse*, ed. E. David, London, Murray, 1977, p. 123

388 **The Duke of Buccleuch**: see Tuchman, p. 362

388 **A fully equipped**: Plumptre, p. 243

389 **I have never in my life**: 14 Oct. 1911, Esher, 3, p. 65
390 **In England where a sovereign**: Massie, *Nicholas*, p. xiii
390 **I am not cut**: 16 Sept. 1910, Lloyd George, *Letters*, p. 158
391 **unendurable**: Adonis, *Bonar Law*, p. 114

15: Celebrations and warnings (1911–14)

392 **You are perfectly right**: W to G, 15 Feb. 1911, RA GV/PRIV/ AA 43/152
392 **saturated with longing**: Wilhelm II, *My Memoirs*, pp. 139–41
392 **I don't think**: 19 May 1910, Morley, 2, p. 344
393 **His visit**: G to N, 15 March 1911, GARF 601/1/1219
393 **You must be**: Hough, p. 242
394 **place and . . . ours to endure**: Strachan, p. 40
395 **Out of this**: Grey, p. 233
395 **reckoning with the**: Mombauer, *Helmuth von Moltke*, p. 122
396 **prepared to use his sword**: Massie, *Dreadnought*, p. 740
396 **I absolutely . . . called a coward**: Nicolson, p. 186
397 **and then he would**: H. Pogge von Strandemann (ed.), *Rathenau, Notes and Diaries*, Oxford, OUP, 1985, p. 147
397 **irrelevant**: Asquith, cabinet meeting notes, 15 Feb. 1912, RA PS/ PSO/GV/C/R/157
398 **At heart**: Epkenhans, p. 27
398 **scoundrels . . . Shylock**: Cecil, *Wilhelm*, 2, p. 172
398 **I have never**: W to Metternich, *GP*, 31, p. 183
399 **I cannot understand**: Neilson, p. 69
399 **an agreement**: Sazonov, *Fateful Years*, pp. 27–34
399 **I was extremely**: N to G, 15 [OS]/28 Nov. 1910, RA GV/ PRIV/AA 43/146
399 **heaps of . . . more sedate**: N to Minny, 31 Oct. [OS]/13 Nov. 1910, Bing, p. 260
400 **Everything went off**: N to Minny, 20 June 1912, Bing, p. 270
400 **arming herself at . . . world conflagration**: Kokovtsov, pp. 320–23
401 **He is a straightforward**: N to G, 1 [OS]/14 Sept. 1912, RA GV/ PRIV/AA 43/187

401 **the pilgrimage of**: Neilson, p. 323

402 **I personally became**: Buchanan, 1, p. 170

403 **interference . . . anybody else**: N to Minny, 12 [OS]/25 Oct. 1912, Bing, p. 279

403 **I am sure you are**: N to W, 23 Oct. [OS]/5 Nov. 1912, Geheimes Staatsarchiv, BPH 53/247

404 **I answered**: G to Grey, 8 Dec. 1912, RA PS/PSO/GV/C/M/ 520A/1A

404 **perhaps on . . . with France**: Heinrich to W, *GP*, 39, p. 119

405 **moral declaration**: Cecil, *Wilhelm*, 2, p. 186

405 **I believe war**: Strachan, p. 42

405 **your instructions . . . dare stir?**: Heinrich to G, 14 Dec. 1912, RA PS/PSO/GV/C/M/520A/2A

406 **tender plants**: Woodward, p. 405

406 **Wherever we went**: Vorres, p. 130

406 **We need only**: King, p. 401

406 **The Tsar's**: Kokovtsov, p. 360

407 **Never in the history**: quoted in Sösemann, p. 53

407 **strong able leader**: Kershaw, *Hitler*, 1, p. 80

407 **of Prussia and its**: *Frankische Tagespost*, 1913, quoted in Sösemann, p. 54

407 **been treated as**: *Berlin Tageblatt*, 1913, ibid., p. 58

408 **There was nothing**: Kokovstov, p. 360

408 **utilitarian objects**: King, p. 410

408 **hollow**: van der Kiste, p. 79

408 **forced**: Vorres, p. 130

409 **I am sure**: Kokovtsov, p. 283

409 **The Emperor is by**: Bruce-Lockhart to Grey, 22 Jan. 1916, Neilson, p. 83

410 **Thus it has been**: Kokovtsov, p. 308

411 **Old Girl**: Paléologue, 1, p. 331

412 **The King is hostile**: Lloyd George, 16 Sept. 1911, p. 158

412 **Whatever I do**: Undated memo, RA PS/PSO/GV/C/K/2553/ 1/70

413 **his own position**: Asquith to Venetia Stanley, 26 March 1914, Asquith, p. 61

413 **great spirits**: F. Ponsonby, *My Recollections*, p. 299

413 **It went off**: W to Franz Ferdinand, 27 May 1913, Kann, p. 348

414 **William's ear was**: quoted in Rose, p. 166

414 **hopes that England**: Heinrich to G, 14 Dec. 1912, RA PS/PSO/
GV/C/M/520A/2A

414 **discussing horseflesh**: Maclean, p. 243

414 **a hundred policemen**: F. Ponsonby, *My Recollections*, p. 293

414 **I had a long**: 23 May 1913, RA GV/PRIV/GVD

414 **entirely agreed upon**: G to N, 16 June 1914, RA PS/PSO/GV/
C/M 624/3

415 **had then offered**: Kokovtsov, p. 389

415 **In spite of . . . been reached**: ibid., pp. 391, 398

416 **Now I have only**: Oldenburg, p. 133; see Kokovtsov, pp. 402–3,
Macdonald, pp. 193–5

416 **a perhaps inevitable**: McLean, p. 67

416 **he had reason to**: ibid., p. 197, PRO FO 371 2.092, 15,312,
3 April 1914, pp. 292–6

416 **that war is inevitable**: Paul Benckendorff quote in Lieven,
Nicholas II, p. 197

416 **Germanisation of the**: Fischer, pp. 334–6

417 **I can only tell**: Buchanan, 1, p. 117

417 **so anxious upon**: G to N, 16 June 1914, RA PS/PSO/GV/C/
M 624/3

417 **France and Russia**: Pan-German League declaration, 19 April
1914

418 **The Chief of Staff . . . at any time**: Fromkin, p. 110

16: July 1914

419 **the terrible cross-fire**: G to Asquith, 26 March 1914, Asquith,
p. 61

419 **Terrible shock for**: 28 June 1914, RA GV/PRIV/GVD

420 **Kaiser Wilhelm will**: Alexander Mikhailovich, p. 257

420 **now or never**: Geiss, pp. 64–5

420 **he'd demanded war**: Strachan, p. 11

420 **eliminated . . . complication**: Cecil, *Wilhelm*, 2, p. 200

421 **This time I**: Fromkin, p. 164

421 **ready for war**: Geiss, p. 77

422 **fulfil her historic**: Macdonald, p. 204

423 **I can't believe**: Paléologue, 1, pp. 12–13

423 **He told me**: quoted in Lieven, *Nicholas II*, p. 200

423 **We had only to see**: Gilliard, p. 100

425 **You have cooked**: Bülow, 3, p. 184

426 **A great moral**: Geiss, p. 222

426 **no longer had**: Fromkin, p. 219

426 **Buchanan couldn't believe**: Buchanan, 1, p. 198

426 **It looks**: 25 July 1914, RA GV/PRIV/GVD

427 **the gravest event**: Asquith to G, 25 July 1914, RA PS/PSO/
   GV/C/R/157

427 **We shall try all**: Nicolson, *King George*, p. 246

427 **Lichnowsky, the ambassador**: Geiss, p. 206

427 **still not a**: Jenkins, p. 325

428 **he'd had to cancel**: Bradford, p. 76

428 **I appeal to you**: N to W, 29 July 1914, 1 a.m.

428 **You will doubtless . . . cousin Willy**: W to N, 29 July 1914,
   1.45 a.m.

429 **Austria has gone**: N to G, 16 [OS]/29 July 1914, RA PS/PSO/
   GV/C/Q 1549/1

429 **Where will it**: 29 July 1914, RA GV/PRIV/GVD

429 **I have the word**: Nicolson, *George V*, p. 245

430 **which will annihilate**: Fromkin, p. 224

430 **a disgrace**: Grey, p. 317

430 **remain a spectator**: W to N, 29 July 1914, 6.30 p.m.

430 **Trust in your**: N to W, 29 July 1914, 8.20 p.m.

431 **I hope from all**: N to W, 30 July 1914, 1.20 a.m.

431 **And these measures**: Massie, *Nicholas*, p. 257

431 **Austria has only**: W to N, 30 July 1914, 1.20 a.m.

432 **It is technically**: N to W, 31 July 1914

432 **In my endeavours**: W to N, 31 July 1914

433 **a mean crew**: Geiss, p. 290

433 **were to say one**: Geiss, pp. 288–90

434 **So the celebrated**: W. on Pourtalès to Jagow, 30 July 1914, Geiss,
   p. 295

434 **You can't stop**: Mossolov, p. 256

434 **Understand you are**: N to W, 1 Aug. 1914

435 **praying with all . . . his efforts**: Gilliard, p. 105

435 **He was never sincere**: Paléologue, 1, pp. 196–7

435 **We are unable to remain**: FO telegram, quoting telegram from German government, 1 Aug. 1914, RA PS/PSO/GV/C/Q/1549/11

435 **The poor King**: Asquith to Venetia Stanley, Asquith, p. 140

436 **a last resort**: 31 July 1914, RA GV/PRIV/GVD

436 **my dear Nicky**: Asquith to Venetia Stanley, Asquith, p. 140

436 **I cannot help**: G to N, 1 Aug. 1914, RA PS/PSO/GV/C/Q/1549/11; also in archives at GARF, 601/1/1219

436 **Whether we shall**: 1 Aug. 1914, RA GV/PRIV/GVD

436 **I would gladly**: N quoted by Buchanan to G, 2 Aug. 1914, RA PS/PSO/GV/C/Q/1549/15

437 **The German Emperor**: ibid.

438 **the communication from**: W to G, 1 Aug. 1914, RA PS/PSO/GV/C/Q/1549/12

438 **Your uncle would have**: Tuchman, *Guns of August*, pp. 80–81

438 **still hoped for peace**: Clark, *Wilhelm II*, p. 213

438 **I think there must**: G to W, 1 Aug. 1914, RA PS/PSO/GV/C/Q/1549/1

438 **Now you can**: Tuchman, *Guns of August*, p. 81

438 **You, me and**: Balfour, *The Kaiser*, p. 385

438 **Something in me**: Tuchman, *Guns of August*, pp. 80–81

439 **There has been**: *The Times*, 4 Aug. 1914

439 **At 10.30 . . . soon over**: 2–4 Aug. 1914, RA GV/PRIV/GVD

440 **I don't believe**: Röhl, 'Delusion or Design', p. 87

440 **if only because . . . his will**: Gilliard, p. 107

17: A war (1914–18)

443 **May and I**: 3 Aug. 1914, RA GV/PRIV/GVD

443 **the vast crowd**: Gilliard, p. 107

443 **Russia seemed to have**: Buchanan, 1, p. 213

443 **betrayal of the**: Figes, *A People's*, p. 292

443 **a resurrection**: Kershaw, *Hitler*, 1, p. 89

443 **A magnificent**: Radzinsky, p. 1, n.

443 **There are now**: Figes, *A People's*, p. 252

444 **In the struggle**: MacDonogh, p. 364

444 **a good sportsman**: Somervell, p. 495

445 **those infinitesimal**: 14 Oct. 1914, Asquith, p. 278

445 **accused him**: F. Ponsonby, *My Recollections*, p. 329

445 **filthy rags**: Rose, p. 225

445 **to attend to**: Windsor, *Family Album*, p. 54

445 **7 inspections**: Nicolson, *King George*, p. 252

445 **The King came**: Rose, p. 169

446 **ought to take**: ibid., p. 201

446 **I am quite ready**: G to Alexandra, 18 Nov. 1917, RA GV/ PRIV/AA37/73

446 **about as futile**: 25 Jan. 1915, Stevenson, p. 25

446 **The King expressed**: Nicolson, *King George*, p. 288

446 **a dictatorship by**: Grigg, p. 499

447 **The French and**: G to N, 1 Oct. 1916, RA PS/PSO/GV/C/ Q/1550/314

447 **We are happy**: Figes, *A People's*, p. 256

448 **like the Huns**: Balfour, *The Kaiser*, pp. 226–7

448 **after all he was**: F. Ponsonby, *My Recollections*, p. 317

448 **These zeppelin raids**: G to N, 15 Jan. 1916, RA PS/PSO/GV/ C/Q 1550/302

449 **inside the head**: Hull, p. 267

449 **He is extremely nervous**: Oct. 1914, Pless, p. 295

449 **send a Zeppelin**: Gerard, p. 237

449 **Now he is no**: Afflerbach, p. 202

449 **the Conference**: Görlitz, *The Kaiser*, p. 190

450 **The General Staff . . . gentlemen**: 6 Nov. 1914, ibid., p. 42

450 **I put my**: Afflerbach, p. 209

450 **living an . . . his generals**: Clark, *Kaiser Wilhelm*, p. 227

450 **No gentleman**: Gerard, p. 179

451 **The Navy has**: Epkenhans, p. 35

452 **ten bullets a day**: Figes, *A People's*, p. 262

452 **One British observer**: Knox, 1, p. 319

452 **with sticks in**: Vorres, p. 147

452 **the tsar's visit**: Figes, *A People's*, p. 263

452 **17,000 wounded soldiers**: Rodzianko, *Rasputin*, pp. 115–17

452 **gradually turned into**: Figes, *A People's*, p. 263

453 **low personal interests . . . to conquer**: Gilliard, p. 137

454 **This is so**: Lincoln, p. 692

454 **fully in tune**: Krivoshein, quoted in ibid.

454 **catastrophe**: Vorres, p. 148

454 **made politics a . . . secret wishes**: Gilliard, pp. 205, 142

454 **How I wish**: 30 Aug. 1916, Fuhrman, p. 558

455 **extremely nervous**: Mossolov, p. 174

455 **She often had**: Gilliard, p. 143

456 **We are not**: 17 Jan. 1915, Stevenson, p. 26

456 **It lent £40 million**: see Neilson, p. 351

456 **Aunt Alix wires**: Minny to N, 1 [OS]/14 Feb. 1915, Bing, p. 292

456 **I have just**: Minny to N, 22 May [OS]/4 June 1916, ibid., p. 297

457 **It is such**: N to G, 11 [OS]/24 Jan. 1916, RA PS/PSO/GV/C/ Q 2551/5

457 **William's speech at**: G to N, 13 July 1916, GARF 601/1/1219

457 **I was very busy**: N to G, 25 June [OS]/8 July 1915, RA PS/ PSO/GV/C/Q 2551/3

457 **I can assure you**: G to N, 8 Aug. 1915, GARF 601/1/1219

457 **she is ruining**: Kokovtsov, p. 296

457 **I am sure she**: Alexandra to G, RA GV/PRIV/AA35/6

458 **The pro-Germans in**: 22 Nov. 1916, Stevenson, p. 127

458 **a country I did not**: Gilliard, p. 110

458 **in her outward**: Maylunas, p. 412

458 **German agents . . . friendship**: G to N, 23 Aug. 1916, RA PS/ PSO/GV/C/Q/1500/313

459 **detach Russia and**: G to N, 1 Oct. 1916, RA PS/PSO/GV/C/ Q/1550/314

459 **Violent and . . . in peace**: 8 Aug. 1916, Görlitz, *The Kaiser*, p. 191

459 **The Emperor had no**: Strandemann (ed.), *Rathenau*, p. 126

459 **He feels it**: Esher, 3, p. 207

459 **Very often I**: Pope-Hennessy, *Queen Mary*, p. 505

459 **I still have to**: G to N, 7 Jan. 1916, GARF 601/1/1219

460 **The most harrowing**: Airlie, p. 138

460 **ruined villages . . . New South Wales**: 4–11 July 1917, RA/ PRIV/GVD

460 **You can't conceive**: Gore, p. 293

460 **hollowed out**: Buxhoeveden, p. 245; see also Vorres, p. 150

460 **lifeless . . . helplessness**: Kokovtsov, p. 478

461 **Despondency, apathy**: Maylunas, p. 475

461 **Let us remain**: Mossolov, p. 162

461 **well-informed agents of**: Alexander Mikhailovich, p. 185

461 **She dismissed me**: Yusupov, p. 157

461 **Be the Master . . . tiny will**: 14 Dec. 1916, Alexandra Fedorovna, p. 456

462 **the wretched Russian monk**: Alexandra to G, RA GV/PRIV/AA35/6

462 **I believe in no**: Alexander Mikailovich, p. 275

462 **Everyone – officers**: Massie, *Nicholas*, p. 368; see also Alexander Mikhailovich, pp. 283–4

462 **If things don't**: Xenia to Minny, 21 Jan. 1917, van der Kiste, p. 97

462 **Is it possible**: Rodzianko, p. 252

463 **one last effort**: Buchanan, 2, p. 41

463 **like a man trying to**: Buxhoeveden, p. 240

463 **bringing Russia**: Buchanan, 2, p. 47

463 **According to two**: Buxhoeveden, p. 240

463 **in the grand ducal**: Maylunas, p. 513

463 **What! You Mossolov**: Mossolov, p. 131

464 **God's wishes shall**: Alexander Mikhailovich, p. 186

464 **feels himself overwhelmed**: Paléologue, 3, pp. 151–2

465 **the weak state**: N to G, 4 [OS]/17 Feb. 1917, RA PS/PSO/GV/C/Q 2551/8

465 **come down with measles**: N to Alix, Nicholas II, *Letters*, p. 313

465 **make these disorders**: Nicholas II, p. 278

465 **Fat Rodzianko**: Pares, p. 443

465 **an excruciating**: N to Alexandra, 26 Feb. [OS]/11 March 1917, Fuhrman, p. 696

466 **his officers were uneasy**: Nicholas II, p. 279

466 **begged on his knees**: Mossolov, p. 27

466 **My abdication . . . deceit**: Nicholas II, 2 [OS]/15 March 1917, p. 278

467 **Bad news from Russia . . . in despair**: 13–15 March 1917, RA GV/PRIV/GVD

467 **the greatest service**: Grigg, *Lloyd George, War Leader*, p. 58

467 **a little strong**: Stamfordham, memo on discussion with Lloyd George, 22 March 1917, RA PS/PSO/GV/C/M

467 **Events of last**: G to N, 19 March 1917, RA PS/PSO/GV/C/Q1550/318

468 **to get the emperor out of Russia**: Buchanan, 2, p. 104

468 **any violence done**: Nicolson, *King George*, p. 300

468 **It's for the best**: Buxhoeveden, p. 262

468 **put them on**: see Gilliard, p. 217, Benckendorff, pp. 30–35, Hanbury Williams, p. 170

468 **if not, he**: Hanbury Williams, p. 170

468 **that the proposal . . . except Balmoral**: Stamfordham memo, 22 March 1917, RA PS/PSO/GV/C/M/M/1067/29

469 **and sobbed**: Vyrubova, p. 212

469 **like an old**: Dehn, p. 189

469 **You can't go**: Vyrubova, p. 213

469 **Nicholas wrote**: Nicholas's diary, 5 April 1917, GARF 601/1/221

470 **The King has**: Stamfordham to Balfour, 30 March 1917, quoted in Nicolson, *King George*, p. 301

470 **His Majesty's Ministers**: Balfour to Stamfordham, 2 April 1917, ibid.

470 **Every day**: Stamfordham to Balfour, 6 April 1917, LG/F/3/2/19, Parliamentary Archives

471 **He must beg**: Stamfordham to Balfour, 6 April 1917, RA PS/PSO/GV/C/M/1067/52

471 **to impress upon him . . . of delay**: Stamfordham memo, 10 April 1917, RA PS/PSO/M/1067/61

471 **placed in an**: Balfour to Lloyd George, 6 April 1917, LG/F/3/2/19, Parliamentary Archives

471 **His Majesty's**: Balfour to Buchanan, 13 April 1917, FO 800/205 PRO

472 **any danger**: Buchanan to FO, 15 April 1917, FO 800/206 PRO

472 **deeply upset**: Meriel Buchanan, p. 196

472 **The days passed**: Gilliard, p. 217

472 **the ancient trappings**: *The Times*, 21 April 1917

472 **alien and . . . an alien**: Nicolson, *King George*, p. 308

473 **though he also falsely**: Lloyd George, *War Memoirs*, 3, p. 1644

473 **rankled unduly**: Nicolson, p. 309

474 **the wonderful popularity**: *The Times*, 13 Nov. 1918

474 **restraints with extraordinary**: Gilliard, p. 216

474 **an extremely reserved**: Kerensky, p. 125

475 **Nicholas decided to**: Benckendorff, p. 77

476 **an insignificant little**: Görlitz, *The Kaiser*, p. 285

476 **Now I may as**: Clark, *Wilhelm II*, p. 238

477 **It now gave him . . . traitors**: Gilliard, pp. 244, 257

477 **Their Majesties**: ibid., p. 256

478 **live banner**: Figes, *A People's*, p. 638

478 **What?**: Kerensky, p. 237

479 **I did all that was**: Waters, pp. 254–5

480 **on Lenin's own**: see Michael Pearson, *The Sealed Train*, London, Macmillan, 1975

480 **a deaf, dumb and blind**: Figes, *A People's*, p. 385

480 **a service at . . . brutal murder**: 25, 28 July 1917, RA GV/PRIV/GVD

481 **I hear from**: 31 Aug. 1918, RA GV/PRIV/GVD

481 **Was there ever**: 25 July 1918, Stamfordham to Esher, quoted in Rose, p. 217

481 **George shouldn't**: Stamfordham to Balfour, 22 July 1917, ibid., p. 216

481 **confidence in the innate**: Windsor, *A King's*, pp. 131–2

482 **I found the Emperor**: B. Hulderman, *Albert Ballin*, London, Cassel, 1922, p. 375

482 **It aims directly**: MacDonogh, p. 402

483 **shoot up the town**: ibid., p. 406

483 **Treachery, treachery**: ibid., p. 412

483 **We got the news**: 9 Nov. 1918, RA GV/PRIV/GVD

484 **The German people . . . its ruler**: MacDonogh, p. 414

484 **How about a**: Lady N. Bentinck, *The Ex-Kaiser in Exile*, London, Hodder, 1922, p. 23

484 **William arrived**: 11 Nov. 1918, RA GV/PRIV/GVD

Epilogue

486 **the figures vary**: for a digest of casualty figures for the First World War see for example the website 20th century Atlas – death tolls

487 **violent tirade . . . the better**: Rose, pp. 231, 229

488 **protect the country . . . odious man**: Airlie, p. 142

489 **a sullen . . . strode indoors**: Windsor, *A King's*, p. 131

489 **their presence would be**: van der Kiste, p. 166

490 **in today's money**: I am indebted to Jasper Heinzen for his calculations using Samuel H. Williamson, *Six Ways to Compute the Relative Value of a U.S. Dollar Amount, 1790 to Present*, MeasuringWorth, 2008; see measuringworth.com/uscompare/

492 **lies of . . . .and save them**: Cecil, *Wilhelm*, 2, p. 306

492 **struck over and over**: Röhl, 'The Emperor's New Clothes', p. 29

493 **That horrible and**: Rose, p. 388

493 **Either the world**: 16 Feb. 1918, Esher, 4, p. 181

493 **The element of**: Pope-Hennessy, *Queen Mary*, p. 522

493 **spirit of hard work**: Harold Laski, *Authority in the Modern State*, 1919

494 **as a living**: Stamfordham to Bishop of Chelmsford, 25 Nov. 1918, RA PS/PSO/GV/O/1106/65

495 **I must say they**: G to Alexandra, 17 Feb. 1924, RA GV/PRIV/AA/38/65

495 **the murderers . . . about Bolsheviks, etc**: Rose, pp. 333–4

496 **HM fired up**: 10 May 1935, Stevenson, p. 309

496 **incorrigible . . . pro-Jew**: Cecil, *Wilhelm*, 2, p. 352

496 **the lowest Irish**: Weintraub, *Victoria*, p. 12

497 **the importance of the death**: Rose, p. 408

497 **a soft spot**: Lees-Milne, 2, p. 237

497 **Deeply moved by**: W to Mary, 2 Feb. 1936, RA PS/PSO/GV/C/O 2572/19

497 **I have not the**: W to Mary, 1 Oct. 1938, RA PS/PSO/GV/C/C 46/270

497 **I am absolutely**: W to Mary, 13 Oct. 1938, RA PS/PSO/GV/C/C 46/272,3

497 **political lunacy**: W to Mary, 30 Aug. 1939, RA PS/PSO/GV/C/C 45/1199

Bibliography

Afflerbach, Holger, 'Wilhelm II as Supreme Warlord in the First World War', in Mombauer and Deist, eds.

Airlie, Mabell Countess of, *Thatched with Gold*, ed. Ellis, Jennifer, London, Hutchinson, 1962

Alexander Mikhailovich, Grand Duke, *Once a Grand Duke*, London, Cassell, 1932

Alexandra Feodorovna, *Letters of the Tsaritsa to the Tsar 1914–1916*, London, Duckworth, 1923

Allrey, Anthony, *Edward VII and His Jewish Court*, London, Weidenfeld & Nicolson, 1981

Almedingen, E. M., *An Unbroken Unity: A Memoir of Grand Duchess Serge of Russia*, London, Bodley Head, 1964

Anon, *Recollections of Three Kaisers*, London, Herbert Jenkins, 1929

Antrim, Louisa, Countess of, *Louisa Lady in Waiting*, ed. E. Longford, London, Cape, 1979

Asquith, Herbert, *Letters to Venetia Stanley*, ed. M. and E. Brock, Oxford, OUP, 1982

Athlone, Alice, Countess of, *For My Grandchildren*, London, Evans Brothers, 1966

Balfour, Michael, *The Kaiser and His Times*, London, The Cresset Press, 1964

—, *Britain and Joseph Chamberlain*, London, Allen and Unwin, 1985

Bartlett, R., *Chekhov: Scenes from a Life*, Illinois, The Free Press, 2004

Battiscombe, Georgina, *Queen Alexandra*, London, Constable, 1969

Bedford, Sybil, *A Legacy*, London, Penguin, 1999 (Weidenfeld, 1956)

Benckendorff, Constantine, *Half a Life*, London, Richards Press, 1954

Benckendorff, Count Paul, *Last Days at Tsarskoe Selo*, London, Heineman, 1927

Benson, E. F., *The Kaiser and the English Relations*, London, Longmans, Green and Company, 1936

Bentley Brinkerhoff, Gilbert, *David Lloyd George, A Political Life*, London, Batsford, 1987

Berghahn, Volker, *Germany and the Approach of War in 1914*, London, Palgrave Macmillan, 1993

Bigelow, Poultenay, *Prussian Memories 1864–1914*, London, G.P. Putnam's Sons, 1916

Bing, Edward J., ed., *The Letters of Tsar Nicholas and Empress Marie*, London, Ivor Nicholson and Watson, 1937

Bokhanov, A. N., Knodt, M., Oustimenko, V., Peregudova, Z. and Tyutyunnik, L., *The Romanovs: Love, Power and Tragedy*, Leppi Publications, 1993

Bolitho, Hector, ed., *Further Letters of Queen Victoria, From the Archives of the House of Brandenburg-Prussia*, London, Thorton Butterwood Ltd, 1938

Botkin, Gleb, *The Real Romanovs*, New York, Fleming H. Revell, 1931

Bradford, Sarah, *George VI*, London, Penguin, 2002 (Weidenfeld, 1898)

Brook-Shepherd, Gordon, *Uncle of Europe*, London, Collins, 1975

Brown, Lucy, *Victorian News and Newspapers*, Oxford, Clarendon Press, 1985

Brown, Tina, *The Diana Chronicles*, London, Century, 2007

Buchan, John, *The King's Grace*, London, Hodder, 1935

Buchanan, Sir George, *My Mission to Russia*, 2 vols., London, Cassell, 1923

Buchanan, Meriel, *The Dissolution of an Empire*, London, John Murray, 1932

Bülow, Prince Bernhard von, *Memoirs*, 4 vols., London, Putnam, 1931

Buruma, Ian, *Voltaire's Coconuts, Anglomania in Europe*, London, Weidenfeld, 1999

Buxhoeveden, Sophy, *The Life and Tragedy of Alexandra Feodorovna, Empress of Russia*, London, Longman, 1928

Byrnes, R. F., *Pobedonostsev, His Life and Thought*, Bloomington, Indiana University Press, 1968

Cannadine, David, 'The Concept, Performance and Meaning of Ritual: The British Monarchy and the "Invention of Tradition" c. 1820–1977', in *The Invention of Tradition*, ed. E. Hobsbawm and T. Ranger, Cambridge, CUP, 1983

—, *The Decline and Fall of the British Aristocracy*, New Haven, Yale University Press, 1990

—, 'Kaiser Wilhelm II and the British Monarchy', in *History and Biography. Essays in Honour of Derek Beales*, ed. T. C. W. Blanning and D. Cannadine, Cambridge, CUP, 1996

Cecil, Lamar, *Wilhelm II*, 2 vols., Chapel Hill, University of North Carolina Press, 1989

—, 'History as Family Chronicle: Kaiser Wilhelm II and the Dynastic Roots of the Anglo-German Antagonism', in Röhl and Sombart, eds., *Kaiser Wilhelm, New Interpretations* . . .

—, 'Wilhelm II and His Russian "Colleagues"', in C. Fink, I. Hull and M. Knox, eds., *German Nationalism and the European Response*, Oklahoma, University of Oklahoma Press, 1985

Charques, Richard, *The Twilight of Imperial Russia*, London, Phoenix House, 1958

Chekhov, Anton, *Letters of*, ed. Yarmolinsky, London, Cape, 1997

Clark, Alan, ed., *A Good Innings: The Private Papers of Lord Lee of Fareham*, London, John Murray, 1974

Clark, Christopher, *Wilhelm II*, Harlow, Longman, 2000

—, *Iron Kingdom. The Rise and Downfall of Prussia, 1600–1947*, London, Allen Lane, 2006

Cole, Terence, 'The Daily Telegraph Affair and its Aftermath,' in Röhl and Sombart, eds.

—, 'Kaiser versus Chancellor', in R. J. Evans, ed.

Cook, Andrew, *Prince Eddy, the King Britain Never Had*, Stroud, Tempus, 2006

Corti, Egon, *The English Empress, a Study in the Relations between Queen Victoria and her Eldest Daughter*, London, Cassell, 1957

Cowles, Virginia, *Edward VII and His Circle*, London, Hamish Hamilton, 1956

Craig, Gordon, *Politics of the Prussian Army*, Oxford, OUP, 1955

—, *Germany 1866–1945*, Oxford, OUP, 1981

Dehn, Lili, *The Real Tsaritza*, London, Thornton Butterworth, 1922

Deist, Wilhelm, 'Kaiser Wilhelm II in the Context of His Military and Naval Entourage', Boston, Little Brown, in Röhl and Sombart, eds.

Duff, David, *Hessian Tapestry*, Newton Abbot, David and Charles, 1979

Dugdale, Blanche, *Arthur James Balfour*, 2 vols., London, Hutchinson, 1936

Dunlop, Ian, *Edward VII and the Entente Cordiale*, London, Constable and Robinson, 2004

Eckhardstein, Hermann von, *Ten Years at the Court of St James*, London, Thornton Butterworth, 1921

Edel, Leon, *Henry James, 1901–1916*, London, Rupert Hart Davis, 1972

Edward, Duke of Windsor, *A King's Story*, New York, Putnam, 1951

Eley, Geoff, *Society, Culture and the State in Germany 1870–1930*, Ann Arbor, University of Michigan Press, 1996

Epkenhans, Michael, 'Wilhelm II and "His" Navy, 1888–1918', in Mombauer and Deist, eds.

Epton, Nina, *Victoria and Her Daughters*, London, Weidenfeld, 1972

Esher, Reginald, Viscount, *The Journals and Letters of Reginald, Viscount Esher*, 4 vols., London, Ivor Nicholson and Watson, 1934

Eulenburg, Philipp, *Philipp Eulenburg's Politische Korrespondenz*, 3 vols., ed. Röhl, John, Boppard am Rhein, 1976–83

Evans, Richard J. ed., *Society and Politics in Wilhelmine Germany*, London, Croom Helm, 1978

Fehrenbach, Elizabeth, 'Images of Kaiserdom, German Attitudes to Kaiser Wilhelm II', in Röhl and Sombart, eds.

Ferguson, Niall, *Empire, How Britain Made the Modern World*, London, Allen Lane, 2003

—, *The War of the World*, London, Allen Lane, 2006

Fiebig von Hase, Ragnild, 'The Uses of Friendship, the "Personal Regime" of Wilhelm II and Theodore Roosevelt, 1901–1909', in Mombauer and Deist, eds.

Figes, Orlando, *A People's Tragedy, the Russian Revolution, 1891–1924*, London, Pimlico, 1997

—, *Natasha's Dance, A Cultural History of Russia*, London, Penguin, 2003

Fischer, *War of Illusions, German Policies from 1911 to 1914*, London, Chatto, 1975

Fisher, Baron John Arbuthnot, *Memories*, London, Hodder, 1919

Fraser, Peter, *Joseph Chamberlain: Radicalism and Empire, 1868–1914*, London, Cassell, 1966

Friedman, Dennis, *Darling Georgie; the enigma of George V*, London, Peter Owen, 1998

Fromkin, David, *Europe's Last Summer*, London, Heinemann, 2004

Fuhrman, Joseph T., *The Complete Wartime Correspondence of Tsar Nicholas II and Empress Alexandra*, Westport, Connecticut, Greenwood Press, 1999

Fulford, Roger, ed., *Dearest Child, the Private Correspondence of Queen Victoria and the Crown Princess of Prussia, 1858–1861*, London, Evans Brothers, 1964

—, *Dearest Mama*, 1861–1864, London, Evans Brothers, 1968

—, *Your Dear Letter*, 1865–1871, London, Evans Brothers, 1971

—, *Darling Child*, 1871–1878, London, Evans Brothers, 1976

—, *Beloved Mama*, 1879–1885, London, Evans Brothers, 1981

Geiss, Immanuel, ed., *July 1914 – The Oubreak of the First World War: Selected Documents*, London, Batsford, 1967

Gerard, James, *My First 83 Years*, New York, Doubleday, 1951

Gerois, B. V., *Souvenirs de Ma Vie*, Paris, Académie, 1969

Geyer, Dietrich, *Russian Imperialism, the Interaction of Domestic and Foreign Policy, 1860–1914*, London and New Haven, Yale University Press, 1987

Gilliard, Pierre, *Thirteen Years at the Russian Court*, London, Hutchinson, 1921

Gooch, C. P. and Temperley, H., *British Documents and the Origins of the War*, 11 vols., London, Stationery Office, 1926–32

Gore, John, *King George V: A Personal Memoir*, London, John Murray, 1941

Görlitz, ed. *The Kaiser and His Court*, London, Macdonald, 1961

—, ed. *Der Kaiser . . . Aufzeichnungen des Chefs des Marinekabinetts Admiral Georg Alexander v. Müller über die Ära Wilhelms II*, Göttingen, Musterschmidt Verlag, 1965

Grant, N. F., ed., *The Kaiser's Letters to the Tsar Copied from the Government Archives in Petrograd and Brought from Russia by Isaac Don Levine*, London, Hodder, 1920

Grenville, J. A. S., *Lord Salisbury and Foreign Policy*, London, Athlone, 1964

Grey of Fallodon, Sir Edward, *25 Years*, London, Hodder, 1925

Grigg, John, *Lloyd George, From Peace to War*, London, Methuen, 1985

—, *Lloyd George, War Leader*, London, Allen Lane, 2002

Hall, Coryne, *Imperial Dancer*, Stroud, Sutton, 2005

Haller, Johannes, *Philipp Eulenburg, the Kaiser's Friend*, 2 vols., London, Secker, 1930

Hannaford, Ivan, *Race, the History of an Idea in the West*, Baltimore, Johns Hopkins University Press, 1996

Harcave, Sidney, *Count Sergei Witte and the Twilight of Imperial Russia*, London, M. E. Sharpe, 2004

Hardie, Frank, *The Political Influence of the British Monarchy, 1868–1952*, London, Batsford, 1970

Hardinge, Sir Charles, *Old Diplomacy*, London, John Murray, 1947

Heffer, Simon, *Power and Place: the political consequences of Edward VII*, London, Weidenfeld, 1998

Hibbert, Christopher, *Edward VIII: A Portrait*, London, Allen Lane, 1979

Hobsbawm, Eric, *The Age of Empire 1875–1914*, London, Weidenfeld, 1987 (this edition Cardinal, 1989)

Hohenlohe-Schillingfürst, *Denkwürdigkeiten*, 2 vols., Stuttgart, Deutsche Verlags-Anstalt, 1907

Holstein, Friedrich von, *The Holstein Papers, The Memoirs, Diaries and Correspondence of Friedrich von Holstein*, 4 vols., ed. N. Rich and M. H. Fisher, Cambridge, CUP, 1953–63

Hough, Richard, *Louis and Victoria*, London, Weidenfeld & Nicolson, 1974

House, E. M., *Intimate Papers*, 4 vols., ed. C. Seymour, New York, Kessinger Publishing, 2005

Howard, C., ed., *The Diaries of Sir Edward Goschen, 1900–1914*, London, Royal Historical Society, 1980

Howard, Ethel, *Potsdam Princes*, New York, Dutton, 1915

Hull, Isabel V., *The Entourage of Wilhelm II*, Cambridge, CUP, 1982

—, 'Military Culture, Wilhelm II, and the End of the Monarchy in the First World War', in Mombauer and Deist, eds.

Izvolsky, Count Alexander, *The Memories of Alexander Izvolsky*, ed. C. L. Seeger, London, Hutchinson, 1920

Jefferson, Margaret, 'Lord Salisbury's Conversations with the Tsar at Balmoral 27–29 September 1896', *The Slavonic Review*, vol. 39, no. 2, December 1960

Jelavich, Barbara, *Russian's Balkan Entanglements 1806–1914*, Cambridge, CUP, 1991

Jenkins, Roy, *Asquith*, London, Collins, 1964

Joll, James, *The Origins of the First World War*, Harlow, Longman, 1992 (2nd edition)

Jonge, Alex de, *The Life and Times of Grigorii Rasputin*, London, Collins, 1982

Judd, Denis, *George V*, London, Weidenfeld, 1973

Kann, Robert A., 'The Emperor William II and Archduke Franz Ferdinand in Their Correspondence', *American Historical Review*, no. 57, p. 323

Kennan, George, *The Decline of Bismarck's European Order: Franco-Russian Relations 1875–1890*, Princeton, Princeton University Press, 1979

Kennedy, Paul M., *The Rise of Anglo-German Antagonism*, London, Allen and Unwin, 1980

—, 'The Kaiser and German Weltpolitik: Reflections on Wilhelm II's Place in the Making of German Foreign Policy', in Röhl and Sombart, eds.

—, *The Rise and Fall of the Great Powers*, London, Unwin Hyman, 1988

Kerensky, Alexander, and Bulygin, Paul, *The Murder of the Romanovs*, London, Hutchinson, 1935

Kershaw, Ian, *Hitler*, vol. 1, London, Allen Lane, 1998

King, Greg, *The Court of the Last Tsar*, New Jersey, John Wiley, 2006

Klausen, Inge-Lise, *Alexandra of Wales, Princesse fra Danmark*, Copenhagen, Lindhardt-og Ringhof, 2001

—, *Dagmar, Zarina fra Danmark*, Copenhagen, 1997

— *Tak for dansen Louise*, Copenhagen, Aschehoug, 2003

Knox, *With the Russian Army, 1914–1917*, 2 vols., London, Hutchinson, 1921

Kohut, Thomas A., *Wilhelm II and the Germans*, Oxford, OUP, 1991

— 'Kaiser Wilhelm II and his parents', in Röhl and Sombart, eds.

Kokovtsov, Count Vladimir, *Out of My Past*, ed. H. H. Hisher, Stanford, Stanford University Press, 1935

Koss, Stephen E, *Lord Haldane, Scapegoat for Liberalism*, New York, Columbia University Press, 1969

Kschessinska, Matilde, *Dancing in Petersburg*, London, Dance Books, 2005 (Gollancz, 1960)

Lamsdorff, N., *Dnevnik*, Moscow, 1926

Laqueur, Walter, *Russia and Germany, a Century of Conflict*, London, Weidenfeld, 1965

Lee, Alan J., *The Origins of the Popular Press in England 1855–1914*, London, Croom Helm, 1976

Lee, Sir Sidney, *Edward VII: A Biography*, 2 vols., London, Macmillan, 1927

Lees-Milne, James, *Harold Nicolson, vol. 2 1929–1968*, London, Chatto, 1981

Lepsius, Johannes, Bartholdy, Albrecht Mendelssohn, Thimme, Friedrich, eds., *Die Grosse Politik der Europäischen Kabinette, 1871–1914: Sammlungen der Diplomatischen Akten des Auswartigen Amtes* (rendered in text as GP + no. of volume)

Lerman, Katherine, *The Chancellor as Courtier, Bernhard von Bülow and the Governance of Germany*, Cambridge, CUP, 1990

Lieven, Dominic, *Nicholas II, Emperor of All the Russias*, London, John Murray, 1993

—, *Russia and the Origins of the First World War*, New York, St Martin's Press, 1983

—, *The Aristocracy in Europe, 1815–1914*, New York, Columbia University Press, 1993

—, 'Pro-Germans and Russian Foreign Policy 1890–1914', in *International History Review*, 2, no. 1, January 1980

Lincoln, William Bruce, *The Romanovs Autocrats of All the Russias*, London, Weidenfeld, 1981

Lloyd George, David, *Letters to Family 1885–1936*, ed. A. J. P. Taylor, Oxford, OUP, 1973

—, *War Memoirs*, 3 vols., London, Odhams Press, 1938

Longford, Elizabeth, *Victoria RI*, London, Weidenfeld, 1964

Ludwig, Emil, *Wilhelm der Zweite*, Berlin, Ernst Rowhlt Verlags, 1926

Lutyens, Mary, ed., *Lady Lytton's Court Diary*, London, Rupert Hart Davis, 1961

McDonald, David, *United Government and Foreign Policy in Russia 1900–1914*, Cambridge, MA, Harvard University Press, 1992

Macdonald, Peter, *United Government and Foreign Policy in Russia 1900–1914*, Cambridge, MA, 1992

MacDonogh, Giles, *The Last Kaiser*, London. Weidenfeld, 2000

MacKenzie, David, *Imperial Dreams, Harsh Realities: Tsarist Russian Foreign Policy, 1815–1917*, Fort Worth, Harcourt Brace, 1994

McLean, Roderick, *Royalty and Diplomacy in Europe 1890–1914*, Cambridge, CUP, 2001

Magnus, Sir Philip, *Edward VII*, London, John Murray, 1964

Mallet, Marie, *Life with Queen Victoria*, London, John Murray, 1968

Mansergh, Nicholas, *The Coming of the First World War*, London, Longman, 1949

Marder, Arthur, *The Anatomy of British Sea Power*, New York, Knopf, 1940

—, *From Dreadnought to Scapa Flow; The Royal Navy in the Fisher Era*, vol. 1 (of 5), Oxford, OUP, 1978 (2nd edn)

Marie, Grand Duchess of Russia, *Things I Remember*, London, Cassell, 1930

Marie, Grand Duchess of Russia [apparently a different one], *A Romanov Diary*, New York, Atlantic, 1988

Marie, Queen of Roumania, *The Story of My Life*, London, Cassell, 1934

Mary Louise, Princess, *My Memories of Six Reigns*, London, Evans Brothers, 1956

Massie, Robert K., *Nicholas and Alexandra*, London, Gollancz, 1967 (reissued, Indigo, 2000)

—, *Dreadnought*, New York, Ballantine Books, 1992

Maylunas, Andrei, and Mirolenko, Sergei, *A Lifelong Passion, Nicholas and Alexandra Their Own Story*, London, Weidenfeld, 1996

Mombauer, Annika, *Helmuth von Moltke and the Origins of the First World War*, Cambridge, CUP, 2001

—, *The Origins of the First World War: Controversies and Consensus*, Harlow, Longman, 2002

Mombauer, A. and Deist, W., eds., *The Kaiser, New Research on Wilhelm II's Role in Imperial Germany*, Cambridge, CUP, 2003

Morley, John, *Recollections*, 2 vols., London, Macmillan, 1918

Morris, Edmund, *Theodore Rex*, London, HarperCollins, 2002

Morris, James (Jan), *Pax Britannica*, 3 vols., London, Faber, 1978 (reissued, 1998)

Morrow, Anne, *Cousins Divided, George V and Nicholas II*, Stroud, Sutton, 2006

Mossolov, A. A., *At the Court of the Last Tsar*, trans. E. W. Dickes, London, Methuen, 1935

Nabokov, Vladimir, *Speak, Memory*, London, Vintage, 1989

Neilson, Keith, *Britain and the Last Tsar*, Oxford, Clarendon Press, 1995

Newnes, George, *HRH, the Prince and Princess of Wales*, London, William Clowes and Sons Ltd, 1902

Newton, *Lord Lansdowne: A Biography*, London, Macmillan, 1929

Nicholas II, *Journal Intime de Nicholas II*, trans. A. Pierre Agrege, Paris, Payot, 1925

—, *The Letters of the Tsar to the Tsaritsa, 1914–1917*, trans. A. L. Hynes, London, Bodley Head, 1929

Nicolson, Harold, *Diaries and Letters 1945–1962*, ed. Nigel Nicolson, London, Collins, 1968

—, *George V, His Life and Reign*, London, Constable, 1952

Nish, Ian, *The Origins of the Russo-Japanese War*, London, Longman, 1985

Oppel, Bernhard F., 'The Waning to a Traditional Alliance, Russia and Germany during the Portsmouth Peace Conference', *Central European History* 5, December 1972

Paget, Walpurga, Lady, *Scenes and Memories*, London, New York, Scribner's Sons, 1912

—, *Embassies of Other Days*, 2 vols., London, Hutchinson, 1923

Pakula, Hannah J., *An Uncommon Woman, The Empress Frederick*, London, Weidenfeld, 1996

—, *The Last Romantic: Marie, Queen of Roumania*, London, Weidenfeld, 1986

Paléologue, Maurice, *An Ambassador's Memoirs*, 3 vols., New York, George H. Doran, 1923–5

Pares, Bernhard, *The Fall of the Russian Monarchy*, London, Jonathan Cape, 1939

Penner, C. B., 'The Buelow-Chamberlain Recriminations of 1901–1902', in *The Historian*, 1907, vol. 5, issue 2, pp. 97–109

Pipes, Richard, *Russia under the Old Regime*, London, Penguin, 1982

—, *The Russian Revolution, 1899–1924*, London, Penguin, 1994

Pless, Daisy, Princess of, *From My Private Diary*, London, John Murray, 1931

Plumptre, George, *Edward VII*, London, Pavilion, 1995

Ponsonby, Arthur, *Henry Ponsonby*, London, Macmillan, 1943

Ponsonby, Frederick, ed., *Letters of the Empress Frederick*, London, Macmillan, 1928

—, *My Recollections of Three Reigns*, London, Odhams Press, 1935

Pope-Hennessy, James, *Queen Mary*, London, Allen and Unwin, 1959

—, *A Lonely Business*, ed. P. Quennell, London, Orion, 1981

Pugh, Martin, *We Danced All Night*, London, Bodley Head, 2008

Radzinsky, Edvard, *The Last Tsar, The Life and Death of Nicholas II*, London, Hodder, 1992

Radziwill, Princess Catherine, *The Intimate Life of the Last Tsarina*, London, Cassell, 1927

Ramm, Agatha, ed., *Beloved and Darling Child, Last Letters between Queen Victoria and Her Eldest Daughter, 1886–1901*, Stroud, Sutton, 1990

Redesdale, Lord, *Memories*, 2 vols., London, Hutchinson, 1916

Reinermann, Lothar, *Der Kaiser in England*, Paderborn, Schöningh, 1999

Ribblesdale, Lord, *Impressions and Memories*, London, Cassell, 1927

Rich, Norman, *Friedrich von Holstein*, 2 vols., Cambridge, CUP, 1965

Roberts, Andrew, *Salisbury, Victorian Titan*, London, Weidenfeld, 1999

Rodzianko, M., *The Reign of Rasputin: An Empire's Collapse*, London, Philpot, 1927

Röhl, John, 'The Emperor's New Clothes,' in Röhl and Sombart, eds.

—, *Philipp Eulenburgs Korrespondenz*, 2 vols., Boppard, 1976

—, *Young Wilhelm, The Kaiser's Early Life, 1859–1888*, vol. 1 (of three), trans. Gaines and Wallach, Cambridge, CUP, 1998

—, *The Kaiser and His Court*, Cambridge, CUP, 1994

—, *Germany without Bismarck*, London, Batsford, 1967

Röhl, John, and de Bellaigue, Sheila, *Wilhelm II, the Kaiser's Personal Monarchy 1888–1900*, Cambridge, CUP, 2004

Röhl, John, and Sombart, Nicolaus, eds., *Kaiser Wilhelm II – New Interpretations*, Cambridge, CUP, 1983

Rose, Kenneth, *George V*, London, Weidenfeld, 1983 (new edn, Phoenix Press, 2000)

Rosen, R. R., *40 Years of Diplomacy*, 2 vols., London, Allen and Unwin, 1922

Sackville-West, Vita, *The Edwardians*, London, Hogarth Press, 1930

Sarolea, Charles, *The Anglo-German Problem*, London, Nelson, 1912

Sazonov, Sergei, *Fateful Years*, New York, Stokes, 1928

Snyder, Timothy, *The Red Prince*, London, Bodley Head, 2008

Somervell, D. C., *King George the Fifth*, London, Faber, 1935

Sösemann, Bernd, 'Hollow-sounding Jubilees: Forms and Effects of Public Self-display in Wilhelmine Germany', in Mombauer and Deist, eds.

St Aubyn, Giles, *Edward VII, Prince and King*, London, Collins, 1979

Steinberg, Jonathan, 'The Kaiser and the British: The State Visit to Windsor, November 1907', in Röhl and Sombart, eds.

—, *Yesterday's Deterrent, Tirpitz and the Birth of the German Battlefleet*, London, Macdonald, 1965

Steiner, Zara, *The Foreign Office and Foreign Policy, 1898–1914*, Cambridge, CUP, 1969

Steiner and Neilson, *Britain and the Origins of the First World War*, Basingstoke, Palgrave Macmillan, 2003

Stone, Norman, *Europe Tranformed*, London, Fontana, 1983

Strachan, Huw, *The First World War*, London, Simon and Schuster, 2003

Taylor, A. J. P., *The Struggle for Mastery in Europe, 1848–1918*, Oxford, OUP, 1971

The Times, *The History of The Times*, vol. 3, 1884–1902, The Times, 1947

Topham, Anne, *Chronicles of the Prussian Court*, London, Hutchinson, 1926

Townley, Lady Susan, *'Indiscretions' of Lady Susan*, New York, Appleton, 1922

Trevelyan, G. M., *Grey of Fallodon*, London, Longman, 1940

Tuchman, Barbara, *The Proud Tower*, London, Hamish Hamilton, 1966

van der Kiste, John, and Hall, Coryne, *Once a Grand Duchess: Xenia, Sister of Nicholas II*, Stroud, Sutton, 2002

Verner, Andrew M., *The Crisis of Russian Autocracy*, Princeton, Princeton University Press, 1990

Victoria, Queen, *The Letters of Queen Victoria*, first series, 1837–1861, 3 vols., ed. Benson, A. C. and Viscount Esher, London, John Murray, 1908 (rendered in text as LQV 1.1 etc.)

—, *The Letters of Queen Victoria*, second series, 1862–1885, 3 vols., ed. Buckle, G. E., London, John Murray, 1926

—, *The Letters of Queen Victoria*, third series, 1886–1901, 3 vols. (vol. 1, 1886–90; vol. 2, 1891–5; vol. 3, 1896–1901), ed. Buckle, G. E., London, John Murray, 1931

Viereck, Sylvester, *The Kaiser on Trial*, London, Duckworth, 1938

Vierhaus, Rudolf, ed., *Das Tagebuch der Baronin Spitzemberg*, Göttingen, Vandenhoek und Ruprecht, 1961

Vorres, Ian, *The Last Grand Duchess*, London, Hutchinson, 1964

Vyrubova, Anna, *Memories of the Russian Court*, London, Macmillan, 1923

Waldersee, Graf Alfred, *Denkwürdigkeiten*, 2 vols., Stuttgart, Deutsche Verlags-Anstalt, 1922

Warwick, Frances, Countess of, *Afterthoughts*, London, Cassell, 1931

Waters, Gen. Brigadier, W. H. -H., *Potsdam and Doorn*, London, John Murray, 1935

Weintraub, Stanley, *Victoria*, London, John Murray, 1897

—, *The Importance of Being Edward, King in Waiting, 1841–1901*, London, John Murray, 2001

Wickham Steed, *Through 30 Years*, 2 vols., London, Heinemann, 1924

Wilhelm, Crown Prince of Germany, *Memoirs*, London, Thornton Butterworth, 1922

Wilhelm II of Germany, *My Early Life*, London, 1927 (English edn of *Aus Meinem Leben 1859–1888*)

—, *My Memoirs, 1878–1918*, London, Cassell, 1922

—, *Aus Meinem Leben, 1859–1888*, Berlin, Verlag von K. F. Koehler, 1927

Wilson, A. N., *The Victorians*, London, Arrow, 2003

Wilson, John, *CB, A Life of Campbell-Bannerman*, London, Constable, 1973

Winder, Robert, *Bloody Foreigners: The Story of Immigration to Britain*, London, Abacus, 2005

Windsor, Duke of, *A King's Story*, London, Putnam, 1951

—, *A Family Album*, London, Cassell, 1960

Witte, Count Sergei, *The Memoirs of Count Witte*, trans. A. Yarmolinsky, London, Heinemann, 1921

Woodward, et al., *Great Britain and the German Navy*, Oxford, OUP, 1935

Young, Kenneth, *Balfour*, London, Bell and Sons, 1963

Yusupov, Prince Felix, *Lost Spendour*, London, Cape, 1953

Zedlitz-Trützschler, Count Robert zu, *Twelve Years at the Imperial Court*, London, Nisbet, 1924

Zola, Emile, *Nana*, trans., London, Penguin, 1973

Archives

RA – Royal Archives, Windsor Castle

Auswartiges Amtes and Geheimes Staatsarchiv, Berlin

GARF State Archive of the Russian Republic

Acknowledgements

I'd like to thank Lyuba Vinogradova, surely the doyenne of Russian researchers, for helping me out in Moscow and doing it so perfectly. And Philip Oltermann for his work on the German documents and archives, for being so nice to work with and for not laughing at my lamentable German. Thanks also to Jasper Heinzen, Charlotte Riley and Julie Elkner for reading the manuscript and making some much-needed corrections. I must also thank David Cannadine. I owe a great debt to my agent and friend Bill Hamilton and my brilliant editors Juliet Annan and Carol Janeway, whose comments and suggestions helped immeasurably in making this a better book, and who have been extremely patient with me. I am also immensely grateful to my exemplary copy-editor, Bela Cunha, who turned a potentially terrifying task into (almost) a pleasure, and was herself a pleasure to work with. Needless to say, any mistakes that have slipped back into the text are entirely mine.

Papers from the Royal Archives at Windsor are quoted by gracious permission of Her Majesty The Queen. Extracts from the letters between Queen Victoria and the Empress Frederick in the four volumes edited by Roger Fulford and Agatha Ramm are quoted by kind permission of the Queen and Landgraf Moritz von Hessen. Extracts from Kenneth Rose's biography of George V are reprinted by permission of Phoenix House (publishers).

I'd like to thank the Geheimes Staatsarchiv and the archive of the Auswartiges Amtes in Berlin, and the State Archive of the Russian Federation, GARF, in Moscow, for generously allowing me to quote from their documents. I'd like to thank the State Archive of Film and Photographic documents at Krasnogorsk for digging out some great, previously unseen, pictures. At the Royal Archives at Windsor, Jill Kelsey was extremely helpful and forbearing, and at the Royal Photographic Collection, Lisa Heighway brought out album after album of wonderful pictures; I owe her great thanks.

This book is written very much on the shoulders of other writers' research. I must acknowledge in particular Sir John Röhl's body of work on the Kaiser and Wilhelmine Germany, especially his remarkable three-part biography of Wilhelm, which has turned up page after page of new and fascinating biographical documents, and Kenneth Rose's *George V*.

Finally, I'd like to thank my husband, John Lanchester, for the hot meals, the advice and the unwavering support through some very hard times, and to ask him to forgive me for all the shouting and grumpiness.

Index

Russia and Asia from west to eastern borders, *c.* 1870–1914

FINLAND

RUSSIA

St Petersburg

Tobolsk

Perm

Tver

Ekaterinburg

Moscow · Nizhniy Novgorod

Om

Kiev

Volga Ural

Lake

Aral Sea

Sebastopol · Yalta

Caspian Sea

Black Sea

Constantinople

Euphrates Tigris

Tehran

AFGHANISTAN

Mediterranean Sea

PERSIA

Indus

ARABIA

EGYPT

Arabian Sea